Report Writing
for Management
Decisions

Report Writing for Management Decisions

PETER J. HAGER

JAMES MADISON UNIVERSITY

H. J. SCHEIBER

FLORIDA INSTITUTE OF TECHNOLOGY

MACMILLAN PUBLISHING COMPANY

NEW YORK

MAXWELL MACMILLAN CANADA

TORONTO

Editor: Barbara A. Heinssen
Production Supervisors: Marcia Craig and Ann-Marie WongSam
Production Manager: Nicholas Sklitsis
Text and Cover Designer: Robert Freese
Illustrations: Publication Services, Inc.

This book was set in Zapf Book Type by Publication Services, Inc.
and was printed and bound by R. R. Donnelly & Sons.
The cover was printed by Lehigh Press.

Macmillan Publishing Company
866 Third Avenue, New York, New York 10022

Macmillan Publishing Company is
part of the Maxwell Communication
Group of Companies.

LIBRARY OF CONGRESS CATALOGING-IN-PUBLICATION DATA
Hager, Peter J.
    Report writing for management decisions / Peter J.
Hager, H.J. Scheiber.
        p.   cm.
    Includes index.
    ISBN 0-02-406711-3
    1. Communication in management. 2. Business report writing.
3. Industrial management—Decision making. I. Scheiber, Howard Jeffrey
II. Title.
HD30.3.H33   1992
658.4'53—dc20   91-27572
                                                    CIP

Printing: 1 2 3 4 5 6 7   Year: 2 3 4 5 6 7 8

DEDICATION

To Maria Asuncion Ortega Garcia de Hager, Dalia and Noam Scheiber,
and the memory of Natalie and Karl Scheiber

Preface

Because effective managerial communication is the central means by which organizations achieve their desired goals and objectives, the focus of this book is on planning, researching, writing, revising, and presenting effective written and oral management-based reports. Additionally, our focus concerns ways that both written and oral reports provide professionals with data and information that are essential for formulating and implementing sound, intelligent management decisions.

Orientation of the Text

Report Writing for Management Decisions presents an in-depth examination of the functions of managerial reports in contemporary business, industrial, and governmental organizations. Because the manager is generally considered "the connecting point"—the decision center—in the communication segment of the decision-making process, our orientation in this book has been to emphasize management report writing in the context of organizational decision making. We wanted that salient organizational fact, or "theme," to underlie and inform every aspect of our book.

In short, *Report Writing for Management Decisions* revolves around the notion that all important organizational messages—from brief informational memo-reports to complex, data-based analytical reports—will be communicated to, through, or from the manager, functioning as the decision center of virtually any organization. The forms and purposes of managerial, professional, and technical reports are presented in various management and decisional contexts.

The book contains numerous examples of business-oriented, managerial, and professional–technical reports from a wide variety of sources and reflecting an equally wide variety of forms, lengths, and styles. We have included documents from a broad cross section of business, technical, and industrial contexts because we believe that groups of students and working professionals—reflecting a wide range of backgrounds and experiences—will benefit not only from an examination of documents that seem familiar to them but also from those that seem, in some sense, foreign. More importantly, though, we believe that the variety of documents we present promotes an ease of application to the diversity of real-world professional settings, organizational "cases," and management communication problems.

Specifically, we have emphasized the following: organizational perspectives on the management report writer; the management decision maker and the decision-making process; individual readers and organizational audiences; the classification of managerial reports; the management report writing process; aspects of report style(s), language, and paragraph arrangement; methods of research and documentation for management reports; the use of, and need for, both short and long managerial documents; and the preparation and delivery of oral presentations for management decisions.

While we have strongly emphasized the theme of management report writing in the context of organizational decision making throughout our book, we have equally emphasized the notion of *process* in report writing. We believe that managers must approach the task of report writing as a process or, really, as a series of interrelated processes. Report writers in today's complex organizations must view the construction of their documents as open, recursive, and collaborative processes that consist of a variety of subprocesses (e.g., planning, drafting, revising, editing, and publishing). And these subprocesses—what we call "steps to effective report writing"—must directly involve (a) individual co-workers on a regular basis and (b) *teams* of colleagues, supervisors, senior-level executives, technical experts, and, frequently, layout, design, and production staff.

Organization of the Text

To emphasize the management report writing process, the book is divided into five parts which should be read in sequence. The content in each part and its constituent chapters build upon the writing strategies, discussion, and sample documents provided in previous parts and chapters. Part I, for example, examines the function of reports in the management decision-making process, the role and responsibilities of report writers, individual readers and organizational audiences for management reports, and the classification of managerial reports.

In these initial chapters we stress the key rhetorical variables and organizational relationships inherent in the managerial report writing process. That is, we focus particularly on issues surrounding

(a) managerial report writers and their *aims*,
(b) organizational documents and their *purposes*,

(c) individual *readers* and organizational *audiences* and their *needs*, and
(d) the *uses* to which a wide variety of organizational documents are put.

In Part II we present an overview of the management report writing process, emphasizing our six steps toward effective report writing and introducing our collaborative report writing model. In this part of the text, we compare and contrast *revising* and *editing* practice and we review key issues in the document production process. We also discuss prose style(s), language, clear report writing, and composing issues frequently faced by management report writers.

Part III explores the major "development" phases in the management report writing process: conducting both *primary* and *secondary* research; assembling and analyzing data and information; and organizing and documenting the evolving product. In addition, we devote a full chapter to designing report graphics (e.g., tables, charts, graphs, computer-generated graphics) and integrating graphic aids successfully into management reports. Finally, Part IV provides finished products of the report writing process—exhibiting short and long report samples along with relevant discussion and annotation.

In the last section of the book, Part V, we devote two chapters to an in-depth examination of the central processes involved in preparing and delivering oral presentations intrinsic to, and always necessary for, effective management decision making.

The book contains an Appendix section as well. Appendix A offers useful information for management report writers on conducting the kinds of statistical analyses managers must understand, and frequently employ, in order to embark on and complete research-writing projects undertaken in a wide variety of business, technical, and industrial contexts. Appendix B contains an additional sample (long) report concerning technical subject matter, exemplifying the types of reports some managers—working, for example, in research capacities in industry or government—often generate.

Real-World Examples

Organizational situations, rhetorical occasions, and sample documents referred to, discussed, or displayed within the text have been garnered from our own consulting experiences or have been made available to us by business organizations throughout the United States for use in this book. Consequently, university students and professional managers using our text will be regularly confronting and analyzing real-world business documents taken from a variety of managerial contexts and representing numerous business, industrial, and governmental organizations.

We see our book as useful primarily to those advanced students and practicing managers whose current or future professional lives dictate a need to learn how to produce effective, real-world managerial reports—both brief, routine reports, as well as longer, more complex documents.

A Text for the Practicing Professional

While the content, pedagogical approach, and applications of this book will prove most appropriate for university use, we believe that working managers in business, industry, and government environments will benefit significantly from the text if integrated into professional development and management training programs within their organizations. We have provided (and suggested) cases in the *Instructor's Manual* which should prove relevant to both student and working professional. Cases included reflect subject areas such as the following: corporate (long-range) strategic planning; investment (mutual fund) analysis; audience analysis (and design) for advertising campaign-related reports; corporate ethics policy statements (revision and research strategies); and organizational relocation issues and concerns.

Case-based writing tasks will involve the creation of brief, straightforward documents as well as those that are relatively long and multifaceted. Depending on how an instructor chooses to approach the managerial report writing course, students might generate both individual and collaborative (team-oriented) documents, such as these: letter- and memo-reports of various lengths; standard progress reports; "ancillaries" and attachments to full-length decisional reports; and full-length analytical reports incorporating graphic aids.

Acknowledgments

We would like to express our deep gratitude to all the Macmillan professionals who assisted us in designing, writing, and producing a book whose content and form are both current and truly work-world in its application. We especially wish to thank Barbara Heinssen, our editor, whose foresight, guidance, and patience allowed us to construct the kind of management report writing text we feel students and professionals alike have needed for some time. Moreover, we want to extend our sincerest appreciation to the following people whose work proved invaluable to us throughout the long process of constructing this first edition: Marcia Craig and Ann-Marie WongSam, our production supervisors; Cindy Branthoover, our manuscript editor; and Rachel Wolf, editorial assistant.

We also want to note and underscore our large debt to the diligent reviewers of this book during the manuscript development and revision process: Lecia Archer, University of Colorado; Carol M. Barnum, Southern College of Technology; Robert D. Gieselman, University of Illinois; Jennie Hunter, Western Carolina University; Fred Reynolds, Old Dominion University; Carolyn Spillers Roberts, Pembroke State University; Baron Wells, The University of Southwestern Louisiana; Jack Yuen, San Francisco State University. Their valuable comments, numerous suggestions, and scrupulous attention to detail can only have enhanced the breadth of our coverage and the clarity of our presentation.

We would like to acknowledge the following individuals and organizations for supplying us with production quality graphic materials or allowing us to include corporate reports and portions of corporate documents in our book: R. E. Norris, Manager of Marketing Communications, Applied Magnetics Corporation; Mark H. Thomashow, Advertising Liaison, NIKE, Inc.; Vince White, Director of Investor Relations, Arch Petroleum Inc.; Angelo Savino, Project Coordinator of Mexico Operations, Rochester Products Division of General Motors Corporation; Terry McGarrity, Data Processing Manager, El Paso Electric Company; and William B. Shapbell, Jr., NASA/Kennedy Space Center (Florida).

We are particularly grateful to, and wish to publicly acknowledge, the help we received from these individuals and organizations: the United States Department of the Interior for the use of brief governmental documents; the American Management Association for permitting us to include in our book one of their excellent surveys, an accompanying cover letter, and assorted managerial reports; Ms. Gloria Reece, a graduate student in Florida Institute of Technology's Technical and Professional Communication Program for designing high-quality figures (and assorted graphics) that concretize ideas or processes we discuss in key spots throughout the book; Professor Carol Shehadeh, a colleague at Florida Institute of Technology, whose editorial suggestions have made information in this book clearer and more accessible to readers; and Professor Jane Patrick, Head, Department of Humanities at Florida Institute of Technology, and Professor David Jeffrey, Head, Department of English at James Madison University for their overall support of this project.

We wish to express our appreciation for the assistance given to us by colleagues and support staff at James Madison University, The Johns Hopkins University, and Florida Institute of Technology (notably Sue Downing and Peggy Machado).

Contents

CHAPTER **4** _____

The Nature and Classification of Managerial Reports 43

PART **II** _____

Effective Report Writing: Process, Style, and Composing Issues

CHAPTER **5** _____

The Management Report-Writing Process 101

PART**III**

Researching, Organizing, and Documenting the Management Report

CHAPTER**8** _____

Conducting Primary Research for Management Reports   207

PART **IV**

Presenting Short and Long Managerial Reports

CHAPTER **13**

The Short Report: A Useful Form for Communicating in the Managerial Arena   383

CHAPTER **14**

Assembling the Long Formal Report   405

CHAPTER **15**

Designing the Formal Report   437

PART **V**

Preparing and Delivering Oral Presentations for Management Decisions

CHAPTER **16**

Preparing Oral Presentations   479

CHAPTER **17**

Delivering Oral Presentations 517

APPENDIX **A**

Conducting Statistical Analysis 533

APPENDIX **B**

PART I

Management Report Writers and Their Audiences

CHAPTER 1

The Management Report Writer: An Organizational Perspective

Books on the "art" of report writing traditionally devote considerable amounts of space to the principles of report construction and to the product itself, the report. Ours will, too. Recent books in the allied fields of business, technical, and managerial writing tend to focus on the *process* of writers writing. We think that the process(es) involved in report writing must play a significant role in any book on report construction. Our book will reflect that emphasis on process as well. But first things first. Perhaps even more fundamental in the scheme of report-writing concerns are the report writers themselves. Therefore, we first want to

  identify management report writers as a group within the business organization.

  define their organizational roles.

  explore how report writers communicate ideas in an organizational environment.

  locate and describe readers of, and audiences for, managerial reports.

The Manager's Job in Contemporary Organizations: A Brief Overview ⎯⎯⎯⎯⎯⎯⎯⎯⎯⎯

Before answering, even before posing, the twofold question "Who are management report writers and what do they do?" we need to identify what managers generally do in a variety of organizational settings. "Someone, only half in jest," according to Henry Mintzberg (professor of management at McGill University) "once described the manager as that person who sees visitors so that everyone else can get his work done" (1975, p. 51). Yes, Mintzberg concluded in his now classic study on how executives spend their time, managers do have "certain ceremonial duties" to perform.

But obviously the contemporary manager's job is considerably more complex than that. Managers perform a large number of duties and wear an equally large number of hats in any organization. Just a few of the manager's duties include planning, organizing, directing, decision making, leading, motivating, and controlling. It might be helpful, though, to narrow the manager's duties just a bit and delimit managerial duties and behaviors into several broad areas or roles. In fact, Mintzberg (1975, pp. 54–59) identifies three broad roles, or "organized sets of behaviors," associated with the position of manager in any organization:

1. Interpersonal roles
2. Informational roles
3. Decisional roles

Since all managers, Mintzberg postulates, "are vested with formal authority over an organizational unit," and since a certain "status" level derives from this "formal authority," then involvement in interpersonal relations naturally follows from the manager's position of *status*:

> From formal authority comes status, which leads to various interpersonal relations [role number one], and from these comes access to information [role number two]. Information, in turn, enables the manager to make decisions and [plan] strategies for his unit [role number three]. (Mintzberg, 1975, p. 54)[1]

In the overall context of managerial report writing and in a text on that dimension of managerial work, our concerns will be chiefly with the manager as he or she transacts business on a daily basis and acts out Mintzberg's latter two roles—"informational" and "decisional." While we are well aware that managers do write extensively in their interpersonal roles in order to perform their daily jobs, it is the manager acting in the *information-processing* and *decision-making* roles with which we are primarily concerned throughout this report-writing text.

[1]Mintzberg actually isolates 10 "observable" roles that, when grouped together, "form a *gestalt*—an integrated whole" and define a manager's job and the nature of managerial activity. We refer the reader to Mintzberg's book *The Nature of Managerial Work* (1973, pp. 54–99) for a complete examination of these 10 roles: Interpersonal ([1] figurehead, [2] leader, [3] liaison); Informational ([4] monitor, [5] disseminator, [6] spokesperson); Decisional ([7] entrepreneur, [8] disturbance handler, [9] resource allocator, and [10] negotiator).

Management Report Writers—
What Do They Do? Whom Do They Address?

A major portion of any manager's work week consists of constructing and disseminating a wide variety of written documents—brief letters and memos, proposals, formal meeting agendas, memo-reports, analytical reports—for an equally wide variety of readers. Managerial documents regularly influence decision making inside the organization; these documents

> deliver information and data.
>
> clarify information and data.
>
> move individuals to action through analysis and key recommendations.
>
> record decisions reached.

Managers perform a welter of writing-related activities: they **prewrite**—brainstorming, speculating, planning, and generating ideas on paper; they **write**—drafting, revising, rewriting, and organizing memo-reports, analytical reports, progress reports, and resource allocation reports; and they **publish**—formatting recommendations, "packaging" decisions, "marketing" appeals for action, disseminating information. All of the documents constructed by managers acting primarily in informational and decisional roles—the concrete results of the decison-making process—constitute the cornerstone of managerial work.

The readers of, or **audience** for, a manager's written communications—whether they are brief action memos or lengthy analytical reports—might, of course, be members of the manager's own work group, area, or department. That is, a data-processing (DP) manager may regularly generate **action**, **informational**, or **clarification** memos for the consumption of individuals in a group of systems programmers working under that manager's supervision.

On the other hand, that same DP manager might frequently (weekly, monthly, semiannually) generate status reports, problem-solving reports, or corporate planning reports for individual readers or audiences of multiple readers at some organizational distance from the DP department. A single DP planning report could, for example, be written for an individual, such as a senior vice president for corporate affairs. At the same time, the DP manager could be called on to communicate via a written report simultaneously with a group of marketing researchers, an inventory specialist, a systems analyst, and an executive vice president for finance. Readers with markedly divergent backgrounds, educations, professional skills, interests, and needs must be able to find, digest, and make decisions based on the information and recommendations found in these "hierarchical" reports.

In addition, to paraphrase Joe Batten, the author of *Tough-Minded Leadership* (1989), when even one of the recipients (one "communicat**ee**") of such a hierarchical report does not comprehend what the "communicat**or**" intended, the responsibility remains that of the communicat**or**, in this case our DP manager. Well-done managerial report writing is a difficult but rewarding job, a job involving, as one textbook writer asserted some 20 years ago, high-order skills of thinking, writing, and language use—from isolating and defining the problem to gathering, analyzing, and interpreting data and information (Robinson, 1969).

Along with Peter Drucker, the founding father of modern management science, we, too, have reached the conclusion that while managing requires "making effective decisions" and while the decision-making process requires communication within and outside of the organization, communication is not a means of organization, a means to a specific end. Rather, communication—especially written communication—invariably proves to be the mode of organization, that which actually defines the contemporary business organization and dictates the way things are done (Drucker, 1974, pp. 464, 493). In other words, written communication is so integral to the overall success of the contemporary organization that without effective communication, business organizations would be stymied, would continually lose large sums of money, and would ultimately cease to function. Indeed, during the past decade, *The Wall Street Journal* has regularly emphasized the centrality of successful business communication in its pages; witness, for example, the following item in its "Labor Letter" on October 19, 1982: "*Shortcomings* in business writing prompt *remedial* steps by some firms" (italics added).

Management Reports: Writers and Readers

Virtually every manager at every level of the organizational hierarchy, from senior executive to middle manager to line or staff supervisor, in every kind of business organization is, at one time or another, a report writer. At times, a manager might construct a report individually from beginning to end—conducting research, drafting, revising text, and disseminating the written product; at other times, the same manager might work on or with a team of managers or specialists (for example, a mixed group of specialists in finance, quality control, marketing, or sales), constructing long or complex reports together. The more dominant (and more efficient) report-writing approach used in contemporary business and governmental organizations, the team or **collaborative approach**, involves a number of professionals working together on the construction of a single report, each team member having carefully delineated research, writing, editing, or "publishing" responsibilities. In business and throughout the professional world, according to one expert on collaborative writing, "a single author is almost *never* entrusted with sole responsibility either for researching or preparing a written or oral report. Writing and collaboration are, in practice, the same thing" (Spear, 1988, p. 14).

Writing Collaboratively

Whenever management report writers work collaboratively, individuals might draft sections independently and submit their subsections to a team "editor" for refining, organizing, and polishing. Another individual member of our report writing team might generate conclusions derived from the research and data analysis performed by other area managers and specialists (say, in DP, marketing, or personnel). Still other team members might be involved in finalizing the same report—articulating concrete, action-oriented recommendations for management decision making; refining, formatting, and publishing the report for internal use; and submitting the finished product to key senior managers within the organization (to VPs, for example, in corporate planning, finance, or manufacturing).

Whether the manager is employed in the area of accounting, training, finance, or DP, communicating clearly in written reports generated collaboratively to a wide variety of readers with an equally wide variety of professional expertise, knowledge, and needs is essential managerial work conducted on a daily basis in business, industry, and government.

Management Report Readers— Where Are They Found in the Organization?

Readers of managerial reports are a varied group. They may be found in just about every section or department of your organization, from human resources to DP and from research and development (R&D) to corporate legal staff. Readers are equally varied in their professional roles, job titles, training, education, and experience. Your readers might have technical expertise in accounting, finance, engineering, law, statistics; or they could have managerial experience as support staff supervisors, department heads, DP managers, or VPs for corporate relations. Your readers might be located in close proximity to you and your department or they might be far from your department, either at some vertical distance up the organizational chart or horizontally removed from your own position in the organization. Your readers may be close colleagues, systems analysts within your own group, or fellow accountants within the financial accounting department. On the other hand, your readers could be marketing, manufacturing, or finance department managers awaiting data from a report generated by you and your associates in data processing.

In essence, your readers might differ significantly in the following areas:

1. Their interest in, need for, and use of data, results, and recommendations.
2. Their knowledge of your general topic and their knowledge of specific subtopics or issues you deal with.
3. Their practical experience, level of formal education, and time available to read and digest your report.

As we have indicated earlier in this chapter, more often than not, your readers—the audience(s) for your report—will be hierarchical, many, and varied. You may be generating your reports—the same reports—for at least three levels of readers simultaneously:

- **Primary audiences** of organizational decision makers (managers, senior managers, VPs). These readers will make organizational decisions based on the data and information you supply them with, the analysis you perform, and the recommendations you submit.
- **Secondary audiences** of managers, senior managers, and VPs who will be affected directly or indirectly by your report. These readers will be influenced by, or will put to some specific or technical use, the data and information you present, the analysis you perform, the discussion and results you articulate, and the recommendations you submit.
- **Proximal audiences** of midlevel managers. This reader, usually your immediate boss and directly "attached" to you and your report-writing peer group, will transmit your report to upper management for review, approval, and decision making. Generally this proximal audience or reader is an individual but might occasionally be two or three.

Management report writers should always attempt to define their audiences for a given report-writing project and anticipate the professional and technical needs of the readers and general audiences to whom they are communicating. Report writers should always attempt to assess the nature of the audience(s) for whom they are currently writing by posing the following kinds of questions to themselves and their report-writing peers:

- Is the report only for peers in my (our) own field? For fellow systems analysts? Accountants? Manufacturing or marketing specialists?
- Is this report addressed to an audience of midlevel managers only?
- Is the report intended for a mixture of individuals in our organization—peers, technical personnel, managers, senior-level managers, VPs?
- Is the report intended for a variety of individuals with differing job functions, levels of formal education, interests, needs—for those both close to our department and those elsewhere in the organization?
- Will the report be read and acted on by managerial decision makers?
- Will the report be read and acted on by senior-level managers and/or VPs?
- Will the report recommendations be read and implemented by technical and/or support personnel? By manufacturing and marketing specialists? By R&D specialists?

In short, any report you write will be appreciably more successful and will more likely be read by your intended readers if you carefully delimit the audience(s) you want to reach and initially anticipate the needs of those readers.

Writing for Organizational Authority

For better or worse, report writers regularly write upward—for a boss, for someone more senior in the organizational hierarchy, or for someone with considerably more authority and responsibility than they. As Drucker has noted,

"One cannot communicate downward anything connected with understanding, let alone with motivation. This requires communication *upward* [italics added], from those who perceive to those who want to reach their perception" (1974, p. 490). An **upward** process, then, constitutes the only real direction in which communication takes place in contemporary business organizations. For Drucker, a **downward** communication process simply doesn't exist. "All one can *communicate* [italics added] downward," he argues, "are commands," what he calls "prearranged signals" (1974, p. 490).

While some communication experts agree with Drucker on this point, many do not. Advocates of genuine **two-way** communication—upward as well as downward—argue that **feedback** from subordinates is essential to effective managerial decision making. Feedback from subordinates, for example, enables management to assess behaviors and adjust policies that one-way (downward only) communication does not permit. Yes, management will continually send messages ("signals") downward to subordinate staff; however, to ensure that those messages are received, management needs employee feedback through upward communication (Driver, 1980, pp. 24–29).

Writing Under the Signature of Your Boss

Managers and teams of managerial specialists writing reports individually and collaboratively in every organization frequently write "under the *signature* of" more senior members of the organizational hierarchy. Report writers often draft documents for individuals having considerably more authority and responsibility than the writers themselves. In these very common instances, report writers draft documents as if they were the senior manager, the vice president, or the director of information systems. Of course, writing reports for other individuals more senior in the organization than the writer, no matter who those more senior individuals are, presents all sorts of problems to writers.

Basic Stylistic Problems

Report writers frequently face problems of a stylistic nature. Just how, for example, does a writer, a subordinate in the organization, imitate or emulate the style of her or his boss? Because style is to a great extent a reflection of a writer's personality and position, and the blending of a host of idiosyncratic emotional and cognitive character traits, just how can a writer virtually become another person for a brief period of report-writing time? And how can that same writer possibly pretend to be different people, say, hourly or daily whenever she or he is called on to draft memos and reports for a variety of more senior members of an organization? How does a report writer convey in writing the personality, presence, and position of a "Mr. X"? How does a managerial report writer reflect in a memo or report the authority and responsibility of a more senior "Ms. Y"? Surely, such a state of affairs has prompted some of the most common complaints uttered throughout the contemporary business organization. How often, John Fielden muses in a recently anthologized *Harvard Business Review* article, have we heard statements like the following:

> I find it difficult, almost impossible, to write letters [memos, reports] for my boss's signature. The boss's style is different from mine.

Or the reverse, from the more senior individual's point of view:

> It takes new assistants about a year to learn my style. Until they do, I have no choice but to bounce letters back for revision. I won't sign a letter if it doesn't sound like me. (1988, p. 135)

Report Writers—
Authority and Responsibility

Stylistic concerns don't tell the whole story, however. Such report writers' concerns probably mask even deeper organizational and operational concerns about the problematic nature of managerial **authority** and **responsibility.** Questions relating to authority and responsibility—and their indelible connections to the report-writing process—emerge too often from the lips of management report writers as they conduct research, synthesize data and information, and generate lists of recommendations on a daily basis. Questions much like those in the following group, posed by David M. Robinson back in 1969, still echo in the offices, halls, and meeting rooms of middle managers in just about every present-day business organization:

- What is the purpose of this report? To advise, recommend? Or, to persuade or direct or dictate (ideas, solutions, recommendations) to report readers?
- Do I have the *authority* to direct readers of this report? To dictate conclusions and recommendations to them?
- Will I actually bear the ultimate *responsibility* for the content of this report? Or, is the content the responsibility of my supervisor?
- Will I have the responsibility for the necessary "follow-up" that will surely result from the recommendations articulated in this report? Or, will follow-up be undertaken by my supervisor? By a VP? (1969, pp. 8–11)

Writers who frequently write under the signature of more senior members of their organizations agonize a great deal during the report-writing process, and rightly so. They complain, too, about their report-writing tasks and responsibilities to top-level managers, to colleagues, and, more than occasionally, to themselves. Robinson has synthesized these complaints into the following three broad categories:

1. Those that reflect problems the writer finds in obtaining cooperation from individuals from whom information or data are being sought.
2. Those that reflect the writer's own lack of clarity—or sense of ambiguity—in identifying her or his authority and responsibility during the course of a given project.
3. Those that reflect the report writer's period (i.e., time frame) of responsibility for any document produced and distributed. (1969, p. 10)

Many of the concerns expressed by report writers—and the problems associated with managerial report writing per se—simply cannot be eliminated. As long as managers do not construct entire reports themselves, under their own authority and under their own signatures, these issues and even deeper concerns will continue to surface. What might be done by the report writer with a vague or confused sense of responsibility and authority about her or his project? The report writer we're speaking of could represent just about all of us—at one time or another—who draft and disseminate managerial reports of every conceivable sort.

Report Writers— Delimiting Your Project Role

In order to prevent later misunderstandings with your colleagues, your supervisor, and her or his boss, simply work very closely with those who have ultimate control—responsibility and authority—over the outcome of the project. Whether that individual is (a) your direct supervisor, (b) a senior manager, or (c) an organizational VP, negotiate your own organizational role for the duration of the project. That is, negotiate your responsibilities and the nature and scope of your authority. Also, be sure to maintain constant contact with all three levels of management if communication between and among those individuals (or those levels) is not that frequent, open, or effective.

Negotiate carefully, and up front, all aspects of the report-writing process from beginning to end. Be certain, too, that you, your supervisor, and a senior-level manager associated organizationally with the report's content and the overall thrust of the project agree on the report-writing task; the time frame of the project; and all important research, writing, editing, and production deadlines.

Determine exactly what your role as the report writer will be during the research, data analysis, drafting, and editing stages of the document construction process. Above all, attempt to get your project role and short- or long-term authority spelled out. Have your boss or a senior-level manager issue an **authorization** memo defining the scope of the project. A memo such as that exhibited in Figure 1.1, for example, rarely covers all anticipated questions and contingencies but does minimize future misunderstanding.

In addition, be sure to determine exactly what your role will be during the period following the internal distribution of the document. Following initial negotiations with your supervisor (and, possibly, with a senior-level supervisor), be sure that you have outlined the time frame that has been allotted for the entire report-writing period as well as the schedule for the completion of report writing and related (editing, polishing, word-processing) tasks:

- According to your estimate, how long should the project take from initial brainstorming, data-gathering, and drafting of the report through word-processing, production, and publishing (desk-top or external)?
- When should an initial draft be finished so that all project-related supervisors, senior managers, and VPs will have sufficient time for input and document review?

Granges Financial Services Group, Inc.

MEMORANDUM

January 3, 1991

TO: Carol Vargas, Manager
Corporate Communications

FROM: Roland M. Goode, Vice President
Corporate Relations

SUBJECT: Report on Revision of Corporate Ethics Policy
Statement

Please reactivate your five-member ethics policy development team to review our corporate "Policy Statement on Ethics and Ethical Behaviors" in preparation for an updated document to be distributed in-house and externally.

By July 1 please submit to me a report of your team's findings, including the following: (a) an executive summary noting major emphases of your report; (b) a synopsis of findings drawn from your data analysis and research; and (c) a discussion of your recommendations for our revised ethics policy document to be finalized and printed during the Fourth Quarter, 1991.

Your group must first determine whether our current ethics policy statement has been a practical guide to managers and staff within the organization on matters of ethical behaviors and values. You should also determine whether managers and staff believe our document has been effective as a clear statement of corporate ethics policy for external consumption.

To help us ascertain how effective, useful, and clear our ethics policy has been, during the First Quarter of 1991 (by March 31) your group should:

(a)   interview a sample of 25 professional employees selected randomly from all corporate units;

(b)   survey 100 representative professional and support staff from each corporate unit via a questionnaire; and

(c)   analyze the text of the current ethics policy statement according to the criteria previously developed on clarity and utility of the document.

During the Second Quarter of 1991, your group will examine data collected from personal interviews, surveys, and your group's critiques of the document. You should try to meet regularly to discuss all possible additions to the document, as well as deletions and proposed recommendations.

If I can offer your team assistance at any stage of this project, please contact me or any member of my staff. I am confident that your team will produce a thorough report reflecting corporate opinion on our ethics policy statement.

RMG:pm

FIGURE 1.1
Sample memo of authorization.

- At what point should the final draft of the document be reviewed, edited, and proofed so that the report production schedule can be met?
- What kinds of postproduction and postdistribution responsibilities will you, the report writer, retain? Will you retain some level of responsibility for management decisions based on your conclusions and recommendations? Will you have the authority for follow-up, implementation of recommendations, and postproduction queries from senior-level management? If not, who will? What role will you, the report writer, play in the resultant decision-making process?

Summary

In this chapter we have reviewed the manager's job and role in the contemporary business organization and have presented an overview of the management report writer's place in that organization. We have shown what management report writers do when they write reports, and we have explored the writing process. Management report writers generate a wide variety of documents—from brief letters and memos to proposals, formal meeting agendas, memoreports, and analytical reports—that are disseminated among a diversity of readers within their organizations.

In addition, we have noted that managers construct reports while operating in both informational and decisional roles. Managerial documents regularly shape and influence decisions inside corporate and governmental organizations in four central ways: They (1) deliver information and data to readers (e.g., decision makers), (2) clarify information and data for readers, (3) move individuals to action through analysis and recommendations, and (4) record decisions reached. In constructing reports, managers perform a welter of writing-related tasks subsumed under the larger, more general tasks of prewriting, writing, and publishing.

At one time or another, virtually every manager operating at every level in the organizational hierarchy and in every conceivable area of work must write (and read) reports. Indeed, writing a broad range of informational and decisional reports simply goes with managerial turf. Although at times management report writers might write as individuals, they more frequently write in **collaborative** teams.

In this chapter, we have also discussed management report readers—who they are and where they are located in contemporary organizations. Report readers differ significantly depending on their need for and use of data and information; professional knowledge base; and experience, education, and time commitments. Three audience levels to whom writers will simultaneously address their reports are **primary** audiences, **secondary** audiences, and **proximal** audiences.

Finally, in this chapter we have identified the concerns that management report writers have articulated over issues of **authority** and **responsibility** that seem to surface throughout the report-writing process. We also have identified a variety of problems, including those of a stylistic nature, that report writers must overcome, or at least face, when writing under the signature of bosses such as immediate supervisors, senior-level managers, or even organizational VPs.

In attempting to overcome such organizational (and individual) problems and concerns, we have reviewed the strategies report writers might engage in when receiving a writing task from a supervisor. We have recommended, for example, that in order to avoid or minimize future misunderstandings, a report writer should immediately clarify or "negotiate" a newly received assignment with the supervisor (whether mid- or senior-level manager or VP).

Related Reading

BARNES, LOUIS B., and MARK P. KRIGER. "The Hidden Side of Organizational Leadership." *Sloan Management Review* 27 (Fall 1986): 15–25.

BATTEN, JOE D. *Tough-Minded Leadership.* New York: AMACOM, American Mgmt. Assn., 1989.

BENNIS, WARREN, and BURT NANUS. *Leaders: The Strategies for Taking Charge.* New York: Harper, 1985.

BENREY, RONALD M. "Top-Down Management Communication: The View from Mid-Channel." *IEEE Transactions on Professional Communication* PC-28 (1985): 17–20.

BRIGHTMAN, HARVEY J. *Group Problem Solving: An Improved Managerial Approach.* Atlanta: Business Publishing Division, College of Business Administration, Georgia State U, 1988.

D'APRIX, ROGER. *Communicating for Productivity.* New York: Harper, 1982.

DRIVER, RUSSELL. "Opening the Channels of Upward Communication." *Supervisory Management* 25 (1980): 24–29.

DRUCKER, PETER F. *Management: Tasks, Responsibilities, Practices.* New York: Harper, 1974.

EWING, DAVID W. *Writing for Results: In Business, Government, the Sciences and the Professions.* 2nd ed. New York: Wiley, 1979.

FIELDEN, JOHN. "What Do You Mean You Don't Like My Style?" *People: Managing Your Most Important Asset*, a compilation of articles from *Harvard Business Review.* Boston: Harvard Business Rev., 1988, 135–145.

HANDY, CHARLES B. *Understanding Organizations.* 3rd ed. New York: Viking-Penguin, 1986.

"Labor Letter." *Wall Street Journal.* 19 Oct. 1982: A1.

MINTZBERG, HENRY. "The Manager's Job: Folklore and Fact." *Harvard Business Review* 53 (July–Aug. 1975): 49–61.

———. *The Nature of Managerial Work.* New York: Harper, 1973.

PATTON, BOBBY R., KIM GRIFFIN, and ELEANOR NYQUIST PATTON. *Decision-Making Group Interaction.* 3rd ed. New York: Harper, 1989.

ROBINSON, DAVID M. *Writing Reports for Management Decisions.* Columbus, OH: Merrill, 1969.

SAGEEV, PNEENA. *Helping Researchers Write . . . So Managers Can Understand.* Columbus, OH: Battelle P, 1986.

SPEAR, KAREN. *Sharing Writing: Peer Response Groups in English Classes.* Portsmouth, NH: Boynton/Cook-Heinemann, 1988.

CHAPTER 2

The Management Decision Maker: The Decision-Making Process and Organizational Barriers

As discussed in Chapter 1, managers perform a wide variety of organizational functions. One of those functions is, of course, communication—within and outside of the organization. Another major managerial function is making what Peter Drucker calls "effective decisions." As we have seen, managers, and management report writers, perform many kinds of jobs in addition to making decisions (see Mintzberg, 1973). But, according to Drucker, only "executives," or managers, make decisions. Moreover, the making of "effective" decisions, Drucker argues, is the premier managerial skill (1974, p. 465). Drucker goes on to explain his point:

> Decision-making is only one of the tasks of an executive. It usually takes but a small fraction of his time. But to make decisions is the *specific* executive task.... Indeed, to be expected—by virtue of position and knowledge—to make decisions that have significant impact on the entire organization, its performance, and results defines the executive.... Effective executives, therefore, make effective decisions ... as a systematic *process* [italics added] with clearly defined elements and in a distinct sequence of steps. (Drucker, 1967, p. 113)

Though contemporary management theorists regularly disagree over what constitutes the "decision-making process," most seem to agree that (a) decision making is a *process* and (b) effective decision-making is necessarily *participatory*.

The Management Decision-Making Process and the Function of Report Writing

The participatory aspect of decision making recently has evolved into what Louis B. Barnes and Mark P. Kriger call "the decision *drama*," that is, the interaction in large organizations of "everyone from executives to workers as though they were producers, directors, actors, and audience at different times in a complex decision drama" (Barnes & Kriger, 1986, p. 16). Naturally, there are a variety of views on exactly what the decision-making process entails, but the basics of the process seem to consist of the following three elements first identified by Herbert A. Simon some 30 years ago:

1. Finding occasions for making a decision;
2. Finding possible courses of action; and
3. Choosing from among courses of action. (1970, p. 1)

A somewhat more complex, nonlinear, and recursive evocation of the decision-making process evolves from Milan Zeleny's 1981 article, "Descriptive Decision-Making and Its Applications":

> Decision making is a dynamic process: complex, redolent with feedback and sideways, full of detours, information gathering, and information ignoring, fueled by fluctuating uncertainty, fuzziness, and conflict; it is an organic unity of both predecision and postdecision stages. (Harrison, 1987, p. 37)[1]

Zeleny's definition of the decision-making process is of particular interest to the management report writer for two essential reasons: (1) much like the report-writing process itself, the decision-making process à la Zeleny is far from clear, straightforward, and direct; and (2) within his definition of the process, Zeleny specifically mentions the "gathering" and "ignoring" of *information* as an integral part of the process. Indeed, management report writing could be seen fundamentally as the gathering and presenting of information (descriptive information and data of various sorts) for the sole purpose of affecting the decision-making process—the actual decisions themselves, follow-up activities, and ultimate implementation. That notion of report writing underscores our

---

[1]For other, increasingly elaborate views on the nature of the decision-making process, see Harrison, 1987, pages 33–66.

approach to report writing in this text: Report writing results in, or, at the very least, influences positively or negatively the management decision-making process and all major management decisions themselves.

The Manager's Role as the "Decision Center" in the Decision-Making Process

E. Frank Harrison, in the most recent edition of his popular text, *The Managerial Decision-Making Process*, echoes Drucker in arguing that the single most significant work a manager performs—the "current and lasting impact of managerial performance" (1975, p. 5)—centers on the effectiveness of managerial *choices* or decisions. What's more, because the decision making of professional managers so often results in organizational change, those decisions will necessarily affect key areas and policy issues such as the following:

1. The allocation of financial resources
2. The timetable(s) for hiring personnel and the distribution of human resources
3. Short- and long-term corporate planning

As Harrison emphasizes, the impact of managerial decisions will be visible throughout an organization because such decisions provide the foundation for virtually every aspect of the organization's operation, from corporate strategy formation to daily administration:

> Decisions made by top management are often vital to the long-term strategy of the organization, so that clearly such *choices* [italics added] are highly significant. Decisions made by middle managers are usually concentrated in the major administrative responsibility centers of the organization. The success of these *choices* [italics added] undergirds the strategic decisions made by top management. And…the day-to-day commitments of resources made by operating management in the technical areas of the organization provide a foundation for the commitments and changes initiated by decisions made at the higher levels of management. (1987, pp. 5–6)

But on what, exactly, are these strategic decisions and operational choices based? Of course, the answer to that question very much depends on the kind of organization the manager (or senior-level executive) is employed by (e.g., retail, manufacturing, information services) and the function of the manager's division within that organization (e.g., research and development [R&D], marketing, data processing [DP]). However, regardless of the organization or the manager's departmental or divisional affiliation, the variety of choices and decisions of which Harrison and the other managerial decision-making specialists have spoken must be based on the analysis and interpretation of data and descriptive information. That is, managerial decisions must be based primarily on a wide range of written documents: memos, brief reports, analytical reports, data-based reports, audit reports, feasibility studies, and corporate annual reports.

As we see it, the managerial decision-making process must involve, on a regular and consistent basis, presenting, reading, scrutinizing, analyzing, and interpreting all sorts of written documents, short and long, data-based and informational, divisional and corporate. Therefore, written communications themselves—documents of all sorts, from memos to lengthy analytical reports—form the very foundation of the strategic decision-making process that corporate managers engage in and so, in Harrison's terms, undergird all of the significant choices managers make and generate for other corporate managers and for top-level management.

Responsible for initiating and monitoring the decision-making process, the manager is generally acknowledged as the **decision center**. The manager is the connecting point—the **nexus**—in the decision-making structure, advising, counseling, and communicating with those below (marketing researchers, salespeople, accountants, computer programmers/analysts) and above (senior managers, divisional directors, VPs) in the organizational hierarchy. From the communication standpoint in the decision-making process, managers are regular and active participants. Managers:

1. Receive data and information in written form via memos and reports and first-hand observation from subordinates, both line and staff personnel (from clerical employees, machine operators, purchasing staff, marketing researchers, financial analysts, accountants).

2. Read through (or observe), examine, analyze, evaluate, and respond to data and information received (or observed) from those below them in the organizational hierarchy.

3. Generate analyses, syntheses and summaries, and recommendations—very often additional data and descriptive information—in written form (via more memos, memo-reports, analytical reports) either (a) informing senior-level executives of decisions they have made, or (b) providing senior-level executives with the data and/or descriptive or statistical information necessary to make strategic decisions affecting the manager's own department, several corporate divisions, or even the entire organization.

Figure 2.1 depicts the manager as decision center in the communication segment of the organizational decision-making process.

At this point in our discussion of the decision-making process, we want to emphasize the fact that all important organizational messages—whether decisional, informational, or observational—must be communicated to, through, and from the manager, functioning in a nexus capacity as the decision center of the organization.

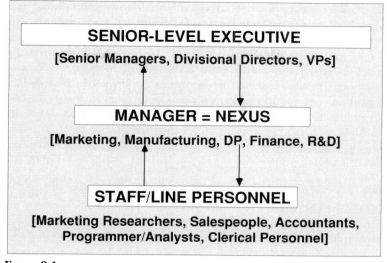

FIGURE 2.1
Manager as nexus in communication segment of organizational decision-making process.

Managers as Business Decision Makers

Because managers (a) receive messages *from* those above and below them in the organizational hierarchy, (b) generate messages and send them *to* those above and below in the organization, and (c) store messages in the form of written (or observed) data and information that have been sent to them, managerial communication experts have likened their function to that of the digital computer which also receives input, stores data, and generates output. Herbert Simon, in his classic text, *The New Science of Management Decision*, even uses the phrase "human information *processor*" (italics added) to describe contemporary managers and other communicators inside organizations who are paid to generate information and solve problems (1970, pp. 106–107).

Of course, computers cannot actually make decisions; computers cannot reason, infer, intuit. Nor can computers, except within extremely limited and well-defined technical environments, apply data and information to problems of a different, or even analogical, nature. Managers think: They process information through analytical and synthetic reasoning; they examine multiple sides of any given question; they intuit, guess, "play" hunches, and speculate; and they learn from previous experiences (including their own mistakes).

In short, the manager as business decision maker is a complex professional performing an equally complex job on a daily basis, a job that is especially complex because, as one management communication expert has put it, "the accuracy, reliability, appropriateness, and completeness of the information on which...decisions are based" are her or his individual responsibility (Robinson, 1969, p. 371). Digital computers do not now, nor might they ever, generate carefully constructed messages such as those in memos and reports for specific, narrowly defined audiences. Nor are computers capable of (a) presenting well-constructed arguments, (b) deriving carefully reasoned conclusions, and (c) proposing finely etched recommendations for the purpose of arriving at important organizational decisions. Managers, however, regularly do. In addition, managers must continually evaluate those same aspects—accuracy, reliability, completeness, appropriateness, and overall worth—of the messages they receive from above and below them in the organization's hierarchy.

The Dynamic Nature of the Management Decision Process

As we noted earlier in this chapter, the manager constitutes the center, or nexus, of the organizational decision process. Managers, though, should not, in any sense, be considered in static terms. Rather, because decision making is an organizational process, and because managers routinely communicate with, and interact with, those above and below them in the organizational hierarchy, the manager's position is an especially dynamic one. According to one classical management theorist, decision making "is shaped as much by the *pattern of interaction* [italics added] of managers as it is shaped by the contemplation and cognitive processes of the individual" (Sayles, 1964, p. 207).

Through written communication (documents of various kinds) and oral interaction with those above and below them in the organization, managers find, shape, or receive information with which to make appropriate organizational choices and to solve organizational problems. The manager's role, then, is dynamic and central to the decision-making process chiefly because a number of the organization's

> special-interest groups *converge or intersect at the point at which the decision must be made, namely, the manager* [italics added]. Most of the external groups to which the manager is exposed provide him [or her] with the intensely specialized point of view of the expert. But since many, if not most, questions to which he [or she] must find solutions are composite generalist problems (e.g., production *and* personnel, product reliability *and* cost, etc.), he [or she] cannot rely on only one view, nor does top management want this parochialism to exist. (Sayles, 1964, p. 207)

Because interaction with, and communication between, manager and specialists (e.g., production supervisor, systems analyst) and manager and top-level management (e.g., senior vice president for finance) is so essential to the smooth operation of the organization as a whole, we see the manager's communication activities as inextricably bound to the managerial job function. We cannot emphasize enough that a manager's communication skills are as important to the job function as her or his observational skills and as inseparable a part of that job as, say, planning or decision making itself. Managers are, simply, communicators: They must be effective communicators to be effective decision makers; they must routinely communicate and interact with a wide variety of experts, specialists, and senior-level organizational leaders.

How Are Management Decisions Communicated in Organizations?

Management theorists claim that managers accomplish their objectives— they solve problems, they make decisions—by persuading people with special knowledge and points of view in the organization to agree with them against those (other managers, other specialists) who seek alternative objectives. Exactly how, though, do managers *persuade* or even *inform* others in their organizations? How do they communicate their solutions, choices, decisions, and points of view? Additionally, what organizational barriers in the communication process might negate or short-circuit the results of decisions articulated in written reports and, thus, lessen the impact of those reports?

Our view of management decision making centers on the notion that effective decision making must regularly involve and heavily rely on written (and oral) communication. Without the use of written documents carefully articulating problems, solutions, decisions, and recommendations at either beginning or final stages of development, those above or below the manager simply will not participate in the decision-making process. That is, without the necessary reliance on, and dissemination of, managerial communications in the form of memos and reports in many directions to and from the manager, organizational decision making can never really take place.

Ultimately, decisions must be communicated in written form for review and examination by staff and specialists below the manager in the organizational hierarchy and for acceptance and rejection by relevant senior-level executives above the manager. Written documents are essential, not because they are necessary for any movement toward consensus strictly speaking, although for that reason alone they are necessary. Rather, depending on the problem or issue at hand, all relevant individuals at various levels of the organizational hierarchy must be completely informed about that particular organizational problem. Otherwise subsequent decisions, choices, or solutions will not be supported, identified with, or "owned." And if decisions are not *owned*—that is, received, accepted, and internalized—by the manager and those above and below in the hierarchy, then organizational direction(s) will be at best either knowingly or inadvertently ignored and at worst rendered useless through group or individual sabotage.

Organizational Barriers in the Communication Process

Clearly, if organizations are going to run smoothly and if decisions are going to be made on a reasonably well-paced schedule, then information received and generated by managers must be carefully communicated in a timely fashion. Poor communication—for whatever reason—is, according to one specialist in organizational studies, "a reliable symptom of some underlying disorder in the organization" or in the relationships between and among the people or groups involved (Handy, 1986, p. 357). But poor communication or, at least, inadequate or ineffective communication pretty much goes with the territory of bureaucratic organizations. What's more, few of us communicate, especially in written form, as carefully and effectively as we believe we do. So it is no wonder that large, multilevel organizations present many types of barriers to effective communication on a regular basis. In fact, managerial psychologists and organizational development specialists have identified a wide variety of organizational barriers and blocks to successful communication that consistently surface in large business enterprises and tend to disrupt or stymie the decision-making process.

Indeed, there are probably thousands of strategies managers and other individuals can employ to obstruct decision-making activities as they are played out in complex business organizations. Nevertheless, we'd like to isolate and briefly describe what we believe are the central barriers or blocks to successful communication within the managerial decision-making process. We rely heavily here on the work of managerial psychologists, organizational development specialists, and organizational communication theorists and refer you to our Related Reading list at the end of this chapter for additional details. These, then, are the eight **barriers** to successful organizational communication that we consider of central importance in disrupting, retarding, short-circuiting, or terminating the managerial decision-making process:

1. Organizational distance
2. Immediacy
3. Relative status of the communicator
4. Lack of clarity
5. Receiver bias
6. Sender distortion
7. Information load
8. Tactic of conflict

Organizational Distance

The farther away a particular manager is from top management and supervisory staff, the less frequently she or he tends to communicate with senior-level management (e.g., a VP) and with lower-level supervisors and staff members. Distance as a communication barrier can be subdivided into physical distance and hierarchical distance, two separate (but often linked) issues.

Physical Distance

According to Charles Handy (1986), studies have shown that "an inverse relationship has been found between physical distance separating persons and the likelihood of communication between them" (pp. 357–358). That is, communication is less likely to take place between a manager and a VP who are a floor apart or two or three floors apart than it is when both work on the same floor in close proximity to each other. Similarly, staff supervisors working physically close to managers will communicate more frequently with their managers than they would if the physical distance between them were greater (e.g., two or three floors separating them) (Handy, 1986, pp. 357–358).

Hierarchical Distance

Much as the physical distance between members of an organization might impede the communication process, so the hierarchical distance between individuals might also prove a barrier to communication. Data and information in written form must proceed through channels up or down the organizational hierarchy, stopping at various intermediary levels for approval in the complex structure of most large business organizations.

In this process, naturally, even a report rich in valuable data and information and vital to decision-making efforts might be inordinately delayed or permanently side-tracked. For example, a midlevel manager, regardless of physical nearness to a senior manager or VP, might be less likely to communicate with those more senior executives precisely because of the bureaucratic and often unwieldy chain of command involved. At the same time, that same midlevel manager could end up communicating rather frequently with another middle manager—a hierarchical peer who might be physically distant—simply because the complex organizational hierarchy could be avoided in the communication process.

Immediacy

Generally speaking, within complex organizations the more immediate communication—and the more immediate *form* of communication—drives out, shunts aside, or holds up the less immediate. For example, a telephone call might interrupt a discussion, which in turn might displace the reading of a written communication (Handy, 1986, p. 359). Because written reports containing important information and data central to the decision-making process *appear* to be less pressing and to have a lower level of immediacy, they may be read and acted on later than communications via the telephone, at a meeting, or during a one-on-one discussion that seem to have a greater urgency and so pre-empt the manager's attention to written forms of communication.

Relative Status of the Communicator

Specialists in organizational communication consistently remind us that the status of the communicator in the organizational hierarchy determines which documents will be read first, later, or not at all, or which will not be read by a particular reader but passed on to other readers at other levels in the organization. Unfortunately, in the managerial decision-making process, the *content* of an organizational document, whatever its merits, will often prove less significant than the name or title of the individual from whom the communication originates, that is, the source of the communication.

The name and title of the memo writer as well as the name and professional level of the report writer will determine whether a document is read immediately, later, or even at all. Data and information originating with certain low-level sources, for example, might be thought of as suspect or simply not credible. Data and information originating from high-level sources or *perceived* high-status sources (e.g., certain senior managers or VPs or even organizational leaders of informal groups within larger departments) might be regarded as credible and therefore read immediately.

Another issue of communicator status or power revolves around the use of one's managerial position to "garner and secrete [data and] information instead of sharing it" (Handy, 1986, p. 357; also see Ch. 5). Individuals in positions of organizational power often choose to disseminate data and information—the "news"—to a small and very limited number of associates. This method of selective communication, or "information secretion," enables individuals to withhold information from those above or below them in the organizational hierarchy who may need the information to perform their own managerial work. Such an approach to communication aids certain individuals in retaining their own positions of power and status in the communication network of the organization.

Lack of Clarity

Unfortunately, communications generated by managers, reviewed by managers, and directed toward managers from above and below are not always clear communications. Frequently written documents—memos and reports of every variety—are imprecise, long-winded, overloaded with details, ambiguous, abstract, misleading, jargon-freighted, and burdened with stilted phraseology. All of those "sins" in diction, syntax, logic, and professional usage result in written communications that are either not read at all or not read completely. Too many decisional documents are utterly confusing and unclear to any reader who takes the time to read through them.

Two communication barriers working against document clarity that deserve further comment are **ambiguity** and **abstracting**.

Ambiguity

The use of ambiguous discourse can, of course, become a barrier to successful managerial communication in many ways. Placing words or phrases that have two or even multiple meanings in a given memo or report will almost always result in confusion: miscommunication, reader misunderstanding, or even the creation of misinformation. For example, if words are chosen poorly (to impress readers rather than to accurately describe ideas), if sentences are routinely too long (say, beyond 25 or 30 words), and if paragraphs are long-winded and full of complex information, then readers are likely to misunderstand the content of a document. This kind of writer-centered (even ego-centered) prose usually results in partial or complete communication failure or miscommunication.

Often, readers tend to get lost in this kind of imprecise prose, or they give up trying to make meaning out of the chaos of ambiguous words, phrases, sentences, and paragraphs amassed into long and confusing decisional documents. In addition to imprecise word choice, needlessly long sentences plagued by awkward ("vicious") syntax, and opaque paragraphs that function in documents like "black holes" in the universe, managers frequently generate ambiguous decisional documents that prove to be confusing to readers for other reasons as well. For example, managerial decision-oriented documents may be:

- Aimed at the wrong reader(s) or the wrong *level* of readers in the organizational hierarchy.
- Published or disseminated at an inappropriate time.
- Researched and written according to faulty logical principles or careless reasoning.
- Based on an incorrect understanding of the initial writing task or a misinterpretation of the original organizational problem.

Abstracting

In the broad arena of managerial decision-oriented documents, the concept of abstracting is associated with the following questions: How specific or general should the management decisional document actually be? Or, how much or how little data or information should the management report writer present to an organizational decision maker?

Generally speaking, and for clarity's sake, our operating principle must be "Less is more." But, as we argued in our first chapter, management report writers must take into account their readers' needs and the organizational levels of their intended audiences. Certain report readers—those at middle or lower levels in the organizational hierarchy—need greater detail and specificity than those at higher levels. Midlevel managers, for example, need specific kinds of information and a wide range of data at their disposal because they must regularly make decisions with very specific corporate objectives in mind. On the other hand, senior managers or VPs have less of a need for concrete detail and a greater need for broader, more concept-based information that tends to illuminate organizational trends and directions. [2]

---

[2]See Robinson (1969, pp. 386–387) for a discussion of the role of abstracting in organizational communication. He presents what he calls an "information hierarchy" and examines this hierarchy in relation to aspects of traditional management hierarchy.

Receiver Bias

Readers of organizational documents frequently exercise their own biases when reading through and responding to decisional memos and reports. Many organizational development and communication experts have noted that recipients of both oral and written communications hear or perceive only what they *want* to hear or receive or what they *are ready* to hear or receive.

Data, information, or simply news that readers consider unwelcome, too negative, or potentially harmful (to themselves and their careers) frequently is "filtered out" of any response they generate based on that initial communication. In other instances, the bad news is retained but is passed on in some future communication in a distorted form noticeably different from that of the original. This kind of **filtering** process might occur when a managerial communicator (writing a memo or report) wants to look good in the eyes of a superior such as a senior-level manager or a VP. Management report writers can filter out or change information transmitted through them virtually at will.

Organizational writers who do engage in that sort of unethical practice produce communications that are dominated by self-satisfaction rather than professional integrity. They consciously choose to change or eliminate data, information, and news and so influence more senior-level organizational decision makers. Decision makers at every level of the organizational hierarchy should be on their guards against bias, distortion, and the practice of filtering on the part of those with whom communications originate. Indeed, organizational decision makers must continually evaluate the sources of the data and information on which their decisions are based.

Sender Distortion

Linked directly to receiver bias, the practice of sender distortion should alert all managerial readers and routinely enlist them in the counterpractice of carefully evaluating all sources and source data and information. In addition to distorting documents, organizational writers might frequently withhold personally injurious items or key decisional data from a given message or "pollute" the message in order to promote themselves and their careers and to rid their written communications of items potentially threatening to them. The sender of a decisional communication may also distort the reception of the overall message by using highly emotive language to describe the data and information contained in, say, a memo or report. Thus, the emotional tone of a seemingly objective communication can distort the way a reader reads, and responds to, the data and information presented (Handy, 1986, p. 357 and Ch. 3).

One final type of sender distortion that we consider a barrier to organizational communication and to effective managerial decision making is that of lack of trust. Organizational communication specialists are quick to point out that if we don't trust someone—a colleague, supervisor, manager, or VP—we carefully screen (even censor) the data and information we send to that individual by way of memos and reports. Mellinger's study of 330 scientists, for example, found that "when an individual lacks trust in the recipient, he tends to conceal his own attitude, the result being evasive, compliant or aggressive communications" (Handy, p. 357).[3]

Information Load: Over- and Undercommunication

We've briefly discussed the question of information load in organizational communication and the managerial decision-making process (see Lack of Clarity). Many organizational communication experts agree that too much data and information results in "communication confusion" (Handy, 1986, p. 357).[4] But just how much data and information is enough? When, exactly, does the amount of data and information provided to a decision maker become too great, too cumbersome, and too confusing? And when does data and information overload disrupt the decision-making process and even managerial productivity?

The question of how much information is enough (or too much) is, indeed, a complex question. The key, however, for the managerial report writer in addressing that question is to determine (a) *what* a decision maker needs to receive in writing on a given occasion and (b) *when* more or less is better for a particular purpose. For example, report writers communicating with their managers must determine whether their reports will be decision-oriented or merely informational and "consultative."

Will a manager reach a decision based on reading a particular report or will the report only transmit data and information to the manager who will, in turn, transmit the contents of the communication to a more senior-level decision maker? On the other hand, if report writers themselves are the decision makers, they must assess the amount of data and information they regularly receive from their subordinates.

The managerial decision maker needs *brief* reports—summaries of data and information—when, for example, she or he requires considerable amounts of data and information from a wide variety of sources, all of which must be assessed at roughly the same time interval. On other occasions, the report writer must provide considerably more detailed reports because the managerial decision maker will receive the necessary data and information—and support materials—from only one source.

Thus, we can only conclude that the managerial report writer must solve the "information-load" puzzle according to the particular professional situation, or occasion, and the decision maker's needs at any given time. Managerial report writers must assess their own informational needs if they are decision makers; they must assess the needs of management if they are generating reports for senior-level decision makers. Whatever the occasion, though, report writers need to determine (a) who their readers are, (b) what their readers need to know and receive (e.g., more or less data and information), and (c) what their own aims or purposes are in writing the report in the first place.

---

[3]For a brief discussion of trust and honesty in the context of interpersonal organizational communication, see Gary L. Kreps, *Organizational Communication*, 2nd ed. (White Plains, NY: Longman, 1990), pages 162–165.

[4]See also Robinson, 1969, pages 387–388.

Tactic of Conflict

In many large organizations (in some much more routinely than others), management report writers and senior-level managers might choose to withhold data from or distort key information for decision makers at any organizational level. While this practice sometimes is performed orally, managers often choose deliberately to distort or withhold important data and information in their written communications. Such a strategic maneuver on the part of a manager or senior-level decision maker generally results in organizational conflict. This tactic of conflict, instigated by a manager (whether a report writer or senior-level executive), often leads to a literal breakdown in organizational communications (Handy, 1986, p. 359).[5] When used orally or in written documents, such a miscommunication tactic might prove extremely destructive both to the organization and to the individuals involved in what Charles Conrad has called "escalating cycles" of "*destructive* conflict":

> Escalating cycles of threat, coercion, expansion of issues, and personalization lock parties into competitive, zero-sum patterns of interaction. Sometimes—perhaps often—more powerful employees [e.g., senior-level decision makers] accidentally initiate destructive cycles. They misperceive less powerful people as jealous, resentful, or hostile and overreact, adopting confrontative, competitive strategies when other approaches would have been more appropriate (1990, p. 308).

Final Note on
Organizational Communication Barriers _____

Naturally, when managers, report writers, or senior-level decision makers intentionally create contexts of organizational *mis*communication—when they erect barriers to consistent and clear communication—movement toward action will be obstructed. Because the most important aim or purpose of any managerial document is to move others (managers, senior-level executives, corporate VPs) to action, communication barriers will short-circuit or retard the entire organizational decision-making process and result in some kind of organizational conflict.

Therefore, smart organizational leaders must intervene, according to Leonard Sayles, to either prevent or minimize conflict whenever a work-oriented situation appears to be moving toward a state of inaction. A manager functioning as "a leader," says Sayles, "must lead actively and must not wait for others to take the initiative" (1964, p. 149). In communication situations—daily occurrences involving a broad array of documents in the decision-making process—

---

[5] For a broader discussion of organizational conflict and the management of conflict, see Charles Conrad, *Strategic Organizational Communication: An Integrated Perspective*, 2nd ed. (Fort Worth, TX: Holt, Rinehart and Winston, 1990), pages 306–314.

active managerial leadership, or intervention, should result in providing organizational direction that will eliminate conflict and result in the *movement toward action*.

Summary

In Chapter 2 we have examined the role of the management communicator in organizational decision making. Decision making is, in fact, a *process*, and the most effective decision making is *participatory*. The management decision-making process is a "drama" involving the interplay of three variables: (a) occasions for decision making, (b) possible courses of action, and (c) choices between or among specific types of actions.

We have argued that the managerial report writer's role of gathering and presenting data and information is an essential element in the organizational decision-making process. The report writer's role is essential to the actual decisions themselves, to follow-up activities in the organization, and, ultimately, to senior management's implementation of courses of action. In addition, we have demonstrated that the manager, especially in the role of report writer, is the **nexus** or decision center in the organization.

In this highly important and visible organizational role, managers advise, counsel, and communicate with those below and above them in the organizational hierarchy. The data and information managers communicate in written documents (e.g., long analytical reports or brief memo-reports) become the source of strategic organizational decisions and the basis of operational choices.

In this chapter we have isolated and explored eight **barriers** or blocks to successful communication, each of which individual managers at any level of the organization's hierarchy might employ to disrupt or stymie decision-making activities. These eight central barriers to organizational communication are the following: organizational distance, immediacy, relative status of communicator, lack of clarity, receiver bias, sender distortion, information load, and tactic of conflict.

As we have emphasized, managers are communicators. They must be effective communicators to be effective decision makers. They must regularly communicate and interact with a variety of experts, specialists, and organizational leaders to perform their jobs successfully and overcome communication barriers—*to move others toward action*.

Related Reading

Appley, Lawrence A. *Management In Action: The Art of Getting Things Done through People.* New York: American Mgmt. Assn., 1956.

Barnes, Louis B., and Mark P. Kriger. "The Hidden Side of Organizational Leadership." *Sloan School of Management Review* 28 (Fall 1986): 15–25.

BERLO, DAVID K. *The Process of Communication: An Introduction to Theory and Practice.* New York: Holt, 1960.

CONRAD, CHARLES. *Strategic Organizational Communication: An Integrated Perspective.* 2nd ed. Fort Worth, TX: Holt, 1990.

DRUCKER, PETER F. *The Effective Executive.* New York: Harper, 1967.

———. *Management: Tasks, Responsibilities, Practices.* New York: Harper, 1974 (especially pp. 481–493).

HANDY, CHARLES B. *Understanding Organizations.* 3rd ed. New York: Viking-Penguin, 1986.

HARRISON, E. FRANK. *The Managerial Decision-Making Process.* 3rd ed. Boston: Houghton, 1987.

KREPS, GARY L. *Organizational Communication.* 2nd ed. New York: Longman, 1990.

LEWIS, PAMELA S., and PATRICIA M. FANDT. "Organizational Design: Implications for Managerial Decision-Making." *Sam Advanced Management Journal* 54 (Autumn 1989): 13–16.

MINTZBERG, HENRY. *The Nature of Managerial Work.* New York: Harper, 1973.

ROBINSON, DAVID M. *Writing Reports for Management Decisions.* Columbus, OH: Merrill, 1969.

SAYLES, LEONARD. *Managerial Behavior: Administration in Complex Organizations.* New York: McGraw, 1964.

SHELBY, ANNETTE N. "A Macro Theory of Management Communication." *The Journal of Business Communication* 25 (Spring 1988): 13–27.

SIMON, HERBERT A. *The New Science of Management Decision.* Rev. ed. Englewood Cliffs, NJ: Prentice, 1970.

TARGOWSKI, ANDREW S., and JOEL P. BOWMAN. "The Layer-Based, Pragmatic Model of the Communication Process." *The Journal of Business Communication* 25 (Winter 1988): 5–24.

TEAD, ORDWAY. *The Art of Leadership.* New York: McGraw, 1935.

CHAPTER 3

Managerial Reports: Individual Readers and Organizational Audiences

Managerial reports, as we have seen in our first two chapters, are essential to organizational decision making. True, decision makers in contemporary organizations often complain about the almost boundless cycle of generating, reading, reviewing, and responding to managerial reports. Nevertheless, managers and senior-level executives throughout the organizational hierarchy know almost instinctively that written reports are rarely the "corporate time wasters" that, say, meetings frequently seem to be. (For a brief and incisive discussion of managers' perceptions of meetings and steps toward improving the effectiveness of meetings, see Gary English, "How About a Good Word for Meetings?" in *Management Review* (June 1990), pp. 58–60.)

Report writing is perceived by many to be the oil that lubricates the organizational engine; the modern organization simply can't run effectively without the written report. Management reports and the resultant communication(s) that they produce between and among various organizational audiences—in meetings, individual conferences, and in other documents—provide the basis and contain the substance for the entire managerial decision-making process. In short, the manager's daily job, like it or not, is dominated by written communication with supervisors, subordinates, and senior-level executives: The manager must present, examine, review, and accept (or reject) data and information collected and published in reports.

Management Report Readers—Organizational Audiences

If report writers, as we emphasized in our introductory chapter, are executives, managers, supervisors, and professional-technical employees found just about everywhere in contemporary organizations, then report audiences—real readers in need of data, information, and analysis—will also be found just about anywhere in an organization. For example, report readers comprise technical experts, staff specialists, line and staff supervisors, managers, and VPs in areas such as human resources, finance, accounting, legal services, data processing (DP), systems design, engineering, quality assurance, research and development (R&D), product sales, marketing, technical documentation, communications, inventory, manufacturing, contracts, and customer service.

Individual Readers versus Multiple Audiences

Managerial reports might be directed toward **individual readers** or groups of readers, or **audiences**, from just about every professional niche and level of an organization. Some report readers or audiences might reside within the writer's own work group; a systems analyst, say, might produce a document for other systems analysts or for the DP director. Other report readers or audiences might work at some organizational distance from the writer; our systems analyst, on another occasion, might research and write a report directed toward an individual inventory specialist or for submission to the director of manufacturing.

Still other managerial report writers might generate a single report for groups of readers, or **multiple** audiences, working in a wide variety of departments and at several different levels within the organization. Readers working in a variety of organizational settings or contexts might have very different educational backgrounds with which to process a management-oriented report as well as different professional needs that must be satisfied by a given document.

Readers of a single managerial report, then, might physically and/or hierarchically reside

within the writer's own work group.
in close proximity to the writer's work group or the writer's own division/ department.
at some distance from the writer's work group or department or just about anywhere within the organization.
outside of the writer's organization completely (e.g., an external auditor or consultant).

For a discussion of **physical** and **hierarchical** distance within contemporary business organizations, see Chapter 2.

A DP manager might generate an action-oriented and informative report both for an individual reader such as a systems analyst working in her/his own department and for multiple audiences working in a variety of capacities throughout the organization. One technical communications manager with whom we are acquainted has been drafting a series of reports on a project involving documenting "expert systems." Her audiences, as she has explained,

> can range from business professionals with little programming experience or exposure to expert system technology to experienced knowledge engineers who specialize in developing expert system applications. Naturally, users need to know how a product works, but they also have to understand abstract concepts, such as artificial intelligence and object-oriented programming. (Moore, 1990, pp. 6–7)

The Delta Organization: A Report and Its Audiences

At this point our discussion of report readers and organizational audiences might prove more useful if we look at a specific case, a management report entitled "Is Ergonomics Worth the Investment?" and the distribution of that report in- and outside of The Delta Organization. (Both the report and the organization referred to here are fictitious, but the following article has proved useful in providing us with appropriate technical terms (including job categories) and relevant data: Michelle M. Robertson and Mansour Rahimi, "A Systems Analysis for Implementing Video Display Terminals," *IEEE Transactions On Engineering Management* (February 1990), pages 55–61.) The report was written chiefly by the manager of Delta's human resources department with the aid of an industrial psychologist and the senior manager of the human factors department. The report presented and examined a large number of issues (and "factors") related to purchasing and "implementing" stress-reducing, ergonomically sound computer workstations throughout the organization. Some of the issues and factors examined in the report were the following:

1. Job stress
2. Employee morale
3. Safety
4. Operator performance
5. Absenteeism
6. Litigation cases
7. Compensation cases
8. Facility operations (e.g., lighting)
9. Funding and material resources
10. Ergonomic redesign
11. Training

As can readily be seen from the above mixture of issues and factors, a formal report of this nature—central to the management decision-making process of The Delta Organization—must be circulated to a wide range of readers at many organizational levels: from senior-level executives, midlevel managers, and technical managers to project leaders, technical experts, and staff/employees based in different departments. Readers of reports like the one under discussion will invariably be members of one (or more) of the following three organizational audience levels:

- A **primary** audience, who will make organizational decisions based on the data and information supplied in the report, the analysis performed, and the recommendations submitted. In the case of Delta's report, for example, the primary audience will be composed of industrial psychologists, human resources staff, project leaders, senior managers, and VPs.
- A **secondary** audience, who will be affected by the report and its recommendations, will provide some kind of input, but will not directly participate in the decision-making effort. In Delta's case, the secondary audience will involve project leaders, engineers, other technical experts, senior managers, and other VPs.
- A **proximal** audience of mid- or senior-level managers (usually the immediate boss of the report writer), who will transmit the report and all findings and recommendations to upper management for action. In Delta's case, such a direct audience will be the VP for human resources and training, as well as senior managers in human factors, safety engineering, accounting, and finance.

Indeed, a considerable number of individuals and organizational audiences will have been approached for input on issues stemming from the two central questions considered in the report:

1. Does ergonomics "pay," generally?
2. Should we at Delta adopt an ergonomics policy and implement an ergonomically sound workstation environment?

Readers from a variety of departments close to and far away from the chief writer's own organizational work group will need to read the document, review portions of it, and possibly respond to it with recommendations for senior management at Delta. (See Figure 3.1 for a display of readers and organizational audiences for this management report, their proximity to the report writer, and their job titles.)[1]

Senior executives, professional managers, technical managers, and technical experts from the departments of human resources, human factors/safety engineering, DP, legal services, finance, and manufacturing will be among those who have received copies of the report and from whom senior management will expect input. In addition, external consultants, a labor law attorney, and an Occupational Safety and Health Administration (OSHA)/Department of Labor administrator will have received copies of the report and provided input into Delta's decision-making process.

---

[1]An "egocentric organization chart" depicting audiences for an engineering report (within/outside of a large corporation) appears in Mathes and Stevenson, *Designing Technical Reports: Writing for Audiences in Organizations* (New York: Macmillan, 1987), page 17.

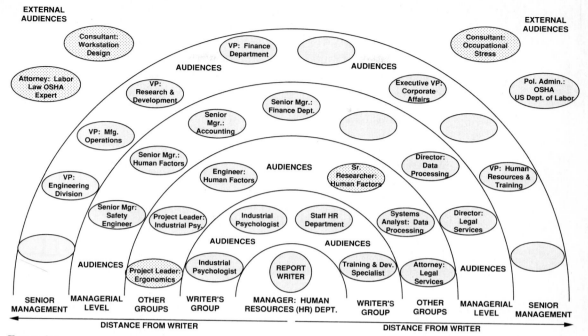

FIGURE 3.1

Report readers and organizational audiences for the Delta Organization's report, "Is Ergonomics Worth the Investment?" (*Note:* Modeled on materials developed by Dwight Stevenson and J. C. Mathes for the University of Michigan's College of Engineering summer institute in professional-technical communication.)

Hierarchical Documents

Management documents like Delta's report "Is Ergonomics Worth the Investment?"—documents written for multiple audiences throughout an organization, up or down the organizational ladder—are known as **hierarchical** documents. Managerial reports often take the form of relatively complex hierarchical documents because they must at once

- address a wide variety of readers and audience levels clearly and completely.
- satisfy the professional needs of many kinds of readers, with different job responsibilities and levels of expertise.
- reflect the wide range of professional uses to which their readers will put them.

Hierarchical documents, therefore, must be written so that all readers and audience members can easily access, process, and frequently respond to what they have discovered of real professional value in a given report, whether they have focused on data, information, method(s) of analysis, concrete recommendations, or simply an executive summary. We will have more to say about the hierarchical nature of management reports later on in this chapter and throughout this book.

How Varied Are Organizational Readers?

As we have shown, readers of management decisional reports vary according to their job titles and job functions; they might reside close to management report writers or at some physical or hierarchical distance from them in organizations. But organizational audiences and individual readers can be different in many respects beyond job title, function, and location. Organizational audiences may differ, too, with regard to the following 10 variables:

1. Interest in and need for recommendations
2. Interest in and need for results
3. Interest in and need for data and information
4. Interest in and need for method(s) or approach
5. Knowledge of the general report topic
6. Knowledge of the specific report subject matter
7. Motivation to read (self-interest in) the report's subject matter
8. Time available (time to devote) to read a report
9. Formal education/technical training
10. Practical experience (on the job, in the field, with the organization)[2]

Therefore, management report writers must carefully analyze, or characterize, their intended audiences (primary, secondary, and proximal) so that they will not misinterpret the professional needs (and interests) of individual readers or audience groups. Through a process of audience analysis, report writers must ask themselves specific questions about their intended readers and organizational audiences. For example:

- What kinds of data and information will my intended readers need?
- Are my readers interested in (in need of) details, broad patterns or trends, concrete recommendations?
- Will my readers take action(s) or make organizational decisions based on the results discussed or the recommendations I make?
- Will readers devote the time to read the entire document or will they read only a specific section or subsections of the report (e.g., summary, results, conclusions/recommendations)? If readers will read only specific report sections, are those sections complete, self-contained units, designed to be read independently of the whole?
- What sorts of technical or educational backgrounds or job experiences will my readers need to read through and comprehend (a) the whole report, (b) specific sections of the report, (c) my recommendations, or (d) an abstract or executive summary of the report?

[2]The authors wish to acknowledge the consulting firm Communication Strategies for Advanced Technologies, Inc., of Albuquerque, New Mexico, for initially bringing some of these audience variables to our attention several years ago.

• Will readers of my report prefer material organized in a **direct** (deductive) or **indirect** (inductive) presentational mode? Are readers of my report likely to be hostile to the content or conclusions/recommendations I present? If so, should I adopt an indirect approach? If my readers are likely to be neutral or positive, would a direct, deductive approach prove more appropriate?

Management report writers frequently present solutions to complex organizational problems for individual readers and audience groups via their reports. Likewise, middle managers and senior executives use reports produced by other managers to identify and solve complex organizational problems. Because management reports (a) identify organizational priorities, (b) analyze data and information, (c) enhance the decision-making process, and (d) ultimately move readers to action, they must present ideas in an efficient, complete, and, above all, *reader*-centered manner.

In order to produce reader-centered informational and decisional documents, we believe it is imperative that report writers first characterize their readers, analyzing their informational needs (e.g., the need for data vs. the need for results), educational backgrounds, and levels of professional/technical knowledge. Furthermore, report writers must predict the varied uses to which their documents might be put and acknowledge the routine time constraints under which their readers might operate.

The more scrupulously report writers analyze their intended readers and organizational audiences before a report is drafted, the more likely readers will read, process, and respond to their reports efficiently. Indeed, the informational needs of readers and audience groups—wherever they reside in the organizational hierarchy—will, in effect, determine what a management report should contain, how long a given report should be, what emphasis will be placed where, what organizational structure should be followed, and which sections of a report should come first.

Informational Needs of Organizational Readers _____

Individual readers and audience groups close to and distant from managerial report writers have, as we suggested above (see Figure 3.1), varied informational **needs** that must be (a) initially identified by report writers during preliminary stages of the report writing process, and (b) continually reviewed and evaluated by report writers as they draft and revise their entire reports. The four areas concerning organizational audiences—and the ways they differ—that might be considered first by report writers when they identify the professional needs (interests or central concerns) of their readers are as follows:

1. Need for recommendations
2. Need for results
3. Need for data and information
4. Need for method (or approach)

These four broad areas begin, at least, to identify the professional needs of individual readers or the corporate needs of audience groups at some specific level(s) in an organization's hierarchy.

By virtue of its subject matter, then, and the variety of audiences at many levels throughout the organization targeted to read, review, and possibly respond to The Delta Organization's report "Is Ergonomics Worth the Investment?" the report will, you may recall, be classified as a complex hierarchical document. Therefore, the report writer, the manager of Delta's human resources department, must (a) address all members of the report's target audience—employees exhibiting a wide variety of professional needs and corporate interests—and (b) structure the document in such a way that all report readers will succeed in reading through and comprehending all or portions of the document. Certain Delta readers and audience groups will need to review, for example, **recommendations** on ergonomic policy and, possibly, **results** related to the study of ergonomics in the workplace and in workstation environments specifically. Other readers and audience groups will need **data** and **information** concerning, say, cost analyses of ergonomically sound workstations. Still other readers will need to become fully acquainted with the **method(s)** of analysis and/or approach used in the research-based portion of the study for use in future (related) research projects conducted by Delta.

Industrial psychologists, for example, working in the report writer's own group, will need to read, comprehend in full, and internalize the method(s) of analysis and/or approach to the research used in the ergonomics study in order to replicate (or validate) possible future research. Senior managers in accounting and finance will need to review cost analyses and budgetary constraints and might need to approve of budgetary items for the research project and for future purchases of ergonomically sound office and workstation equipment. Senior-level Delta executives—for example, the VPs for finance and corporate affairs—will need to examine the results of the ergonomics research report and the concrete, action-oriented recommendations presented to and for decision makers in the organization.

Other Differences Among Organizational Readers _____

Beyond readers' immediate interest in and organizational need for the content presented in managerial reports like Delta's, their ability to read and comprehend all or only portions of such documents will depend on

> their knowledge of or expertise in the topic or subject matter under study— in this case, the field of ergonomics in general and on ergonomics policy as applied to corporate environments, computer workstations, and employees who use such workstations daily.
>
> their motivation to read, toleration for, or self-interest in a given subject matter—in this case, the field of ergonomics and related issues in occupational stress, human factors, safety, workstation design, and law.
>
> the time they have or wish to devote to the particular document—for example, a report entitled "Is Ergonomics Worth the Investment?"

their technical and educational backgrounds and practical, on-the-job experiences related to (or suited for) the broad subject area of ergonomics and the various other relevant topics and issues (budgetary, accounting, R&D, legal, psychological, training).

The final six areas, then, differentiating individual readers and organizational audiences that report writers must address for themselves prior to planning and drafting reports can be summarized as follows:

1. Knowledge or level of expertise in general report topic
2. Knowledge or level of expertise in specific report topic
3. Motivation to read (self-interest in) report subject matter
4. Time available to read the report
5. Technical and educational background
6. Practical (job) experience in a specific field(s)

Readers' Uses of Organizational Documents

The needs of individual readers and audience groups will also be based on the **use(s)** to which they put organizational documents. That is, in addition to analyzing readers' needs according to the variables presented in the previous section, one major complementary concern of report writers must involve focusing carefully on the intended use(s) of the data and information presented in reports.

As we indicated in our first chapter, a manager's duties include planning, organizing, directing, decision making, leading, motivating, and controlling. Perhaps we might add advising, auditing, serving, and stabilizing to make our list of managerial duties more complete.[3] Because the manager's job involves making "things happen which would not have come about but for his [or her] leadership" (Appley, 1956, p. 182),[4] any one of the duties listed here might result in a report. Because managerial documents involve making the writer's ideas—and sometimes feelings—known to subordinates, midlevel supervisors, and senior corporate staff, reports routinely influence the behaviors (decisions and actions) of others up and down the hierarchy of the organization.

Senior corporate staff, supervisors, and subordinates, in turn, put managerial reports like Delta's "Is Ergonomics Worth the Investment?" to a wide variety of uses, reflecting, of course, their location in the organizational hierarchy. Some readers—Delta's VP for corporate affairs, for instance—might use a managerial report to *act* or to *move other people to action*. Other readers, such as Delta's project leader in industrial psychology or an engineer in human factors, might use a report to analyze data or to record prior or current accomplishments. Still other readers—say, Delta's director of data processing—might use a managerial report to identify corporate or divisional priorities or to enhance the decision-making process.

---

[3]See Sayles, 1964, pages 112–127, for a discussion of the range of "administrative patterns" managers must fulfill in the contemporary business organization.

[4]See Appley, 1956, pages 181–184, for a brief discussion of management and communication.

Thus, a single hierarchical report, like the one constructed and disseminated by Delta's human resources manager, will be put to a wide variety of uses by an equally wide variety of professional readers within and beyond the organization. The uses to which a hierarchical report like Delta's might be put by individual readers (e.g., a systems analyst, an engineer, an industrial psychologist) and audience groups (e.g., industrial psychologists, senior managers, VPs) include the following broad areas:

1. To act or to move people to action
2. To enhance the decision-making process
3. To identify organizational (corporate, divisional) priorities
4. To plan corporate strategy
5. To analyze data and review information
6. To clarify and document information
7. To advise and motivate organizational staff
8. To record prior or current accomplishments

Naturally, report readers and audience groups at all levels of an organization use managerial documents to perform a myriad of individual and corporate functions. The eight functions delineated here represent only the major functional areas to which corporate readers and audiences put managerial documents.

Final Comment on Managerial Report Readers

Because report readers and audience groups differ widely in (a) the kinds of data and information they need to perform their jobs and (b) the uses to which the data and information they receive will be put, management report writers must ensure that all readers get what they want, what they need, and, above all, what they have requested. If a management report is to meet with success it must address all members of the report's audience and all of that audience's needs. The report must also reflect the uses to which readers will put the report's data and information, taking into account the whole range of possible report functions, from moving people to action to planning corporate strategy. If readers don't get—or can't readily find—what they need, they cannot act, make decisions, plan successfully, analyze data, or advise and motivate others.

Remember: Provide all individual readers and audience groups you are addressing with the data and information they need in a well-organized report that promotes readability. It's *your* job to satisfy your readers' needs. Why, for example, would your intended readers care about your report? *What's in it for them?* How will individual readers *use* your report? Or, as one of our colleagues has put it, what do you have that they *need*?

Also, remember that your report will not necessarily be read by all readers in full, from beginning to end. Certain readers—most of them—will read only portions of your report because they need only certain portions of the presented material. Because most readers will not often read the reports you generate from beginning to end, you can make their search for the data and information they need a relatively easy one. Structure your reports with a clear and logical organizational pattern; use appropriate and helpful headings and subheadings throughout your document. Make your reports visually appealing so that they permit readers to glance over the whole of a document before attending to any part of it.

We will have much more to say about report structure, organizational patterns, the use of headings and subheadings, and visual appeals later on. For now, we simply urge you to benefit from the audience analysis ideas, questions, and methods we have discussed in this chapter. Keep in mind that the most successful reports in any managerial, decision-making environment are those that have benefited most completely from an analysis of readers and audience groups addressed by the document.

Summary

In Chapter 3 we have focused on management report readers and audience groups. Management report readers in need of data, information, and analysis can be found just about anywhere in contemporary business organizations. Readers of management reports and audience groups at which reports are aimed reflect a diverse cross-section of professional employees within and outside of an organization.

In this chapter we have emphasized that managerial reports might be directed toward **individual readers** and groups of readers, or **audiences**. Readers and audience groups might reside in just about any corner of an organization, from the report writer's own group to individuals and groups at some physical or hierarchical distance from the report writer.

Management report writers often produce documents for **multiple** audiences working at a wide variety of job functions, in various departments, and at many organizational levels. Readers of reports aimed at multiple audiences might have different corporate roles, educational/technical backgrounds, and professional needs.

In order to demonstrate the variety of individual readers and audience groups affected by management reports, we have highlighted a report produced by the manager of human resources at The Delta Organization. This complex hierarchical report focuses on issues related to implementing an ergonomically sound workstation environment throughout the company. The Delta report involves various individual employees and audience groups who might receive, read, and respond to a managerial report. The report (a) addresses a wide variety of readers and audiences, (b) satisfies the professional needs of many readers, and (c) reflects a range of professional uses to which readers put similar documents.

Next, we have reviewed differences between and among individual readers and audience groups within The Delta Organization in light of 10 audience variables affecting employees and their needs. We have recommended that management report writers analyze their audiences prior to planning and drafting documents. To produce reader-centered documents, report writers should characterize their intended readers by analyzing readers' informational needs, educational backgrounds, and levels of technical knowledge.

Finally, we have discussed the **uses** to which individual readers and audience groups might put organizational documents. We have suggested that Delta's staff—at various levels—will read managerial reports differently because they put them to different uses: a VP might use a report to act or to move others to action; a manager might use a report to analyze data or record accomplishments; a senior manager might use a report to identify corporate priorities or to enhance decision making.

Because report readers and audience groups differ widely, management report writers must ensure that all readers get what they want, what they need, and what they have requested. Managerial reports are rarely read from beginning to end; therefore, report writers must structure their reports so readers will find the data and information they need with ease and efficiency.

Related Reading

APPLEY, LAWRENCE A. *Management in Action: The Art of Getting Things Done through People.* New York: American Mgmt. Assn., 1956.

ENGLISH, GARY. "How About a Good Word for Meetings?" *Management Review* 79 (June 1990): 58–60.

ESTRIN, HERMAN A., and NORBERT ELLIOT. *Technical Writing in the Corporate World.* Los Altos, CA: Crisp, 1990.

GIBSON, JANE W., and RICHARD M. HODGETTS. *Business Communication: Skills and Strategies.* New York: Harper, 1990.

MARROW, ALFRED J. *Making Management Human.* New York: McGraw, 1957.

MATHES, J. C., and DWIGHT W. STEVENSON. *Designing Technical Reports: Writing for Audiences in Organizations.* 2nd ed. New York: Macmillan, 1991.

MOORE, JENNIFER. "Making Artificial Intelligence a Reality." *TechLines* (May 1990): 6–7.

MUNTER, MARY. *Guide to Managerial Communication.* 2nd ed. Englewood Cliffs, NJ: Prentice, 1987.

MURRAY, MELBA W. (JERRY). *Engineered Report Writing.* Rev. ed. Tulsa, OK: PennWell, 1969.

NADZIEJKA, DAVID E. "Make Your Writing Stand Out." *Chemical Engineering* 96 (August 1989): 147–152.

SAYLES, LEONARD. *Managerial Behavior: Administration in Complex Organizations.* New York: McGraw, 1964.

SCHEIBER, H. J. "From Prose Paladin to Peer Editor: Teaching Engineers (and Others) to Write and Communicate." *Journal of Technical Writing and Communication* 17 (1985): 385–395.

SOUTHER, JAMES W., and MYRON L. WHITE. *Technical Report Writing.* 2nd ed. New York: Wiley, 1977.

SUCHAN, JAMES, and RON DULEK. "Toward a Better Understanding of Reader Analysis." *The Journal of Business Communication* 25 (Spring 1988): 29–45.

TEBEAUX, ELIZABETH. "The Trouble with Employees' Writing May Be Freshman Composition." *Teaching English in the Two-Year College* 15 (Feb. 1988): 9–19.

WELLS, BARRON, and NELDA SPINKS. *Organizational Communication: A Strategic Approach.* 2nd ed. Houston: Dame, 1989.

CHAPTER 4

The Nature and Classification of Managerial Reports

Throughout the first three chapters of this text, we have been discussing managerial reports as if there were only one type of written report produced by a wide variety of report writers. Although the reports to which we have been referring reflect some generic properties common to a number of written documents produced by a broad range of managers, executives, and corporate decision makers, managerial reports actually vary significantly in content, structure, and format, depending on their aims, their purposes, and the uses to which they will be put by their readers.

Variety of Managerial Reports

Managerial reports can take the form of brief memos and letters concerning quick actions to be taken by individual employees or groups. Reports might simply (and briefly) *inform* readers about

> upcoming and important division deadlines.
>
> issues discussed during a weekly meeting of supervisory staff and decisions reached.
>
> routine weekly or monthly inventory data.

Reports can also take the form of rather lengthy documents stating and explaining corporate policies and procedures. More specifically, reports might list, define, and discuss corporate situational ethics policy. Managerial reports might discuss, explore, and recommend concrete, time-oriented elements of strategy necessary for corporate long-range planning. Or reports might examine various options for information storage and on-line retrieval methods and present the best, most cost-effective systems with which to accomplish those tasks.

In any event, a wide variety of managerial reports are constructed and distributed each day by an equally wide variety of report writers. Managerial reports can be classified in a number of ways determined by what they contain, why they have been written, who they have been written for, and which elements they have in common. Reports might be classified according to the following interrelated and overlapping variables:

1. Internal versus external readers or audience groups
2. Formats (one- to five-page memo or letter to multipage report)
3. Degree of formality (informal to formal)
4. Time frame or interval (routine or nonroutine, special or regular, periodic or progress)
5. Subject matter, content, or activity
6. Function (present information, examine, analyze)

In this chapter we will discuss the various types of managerial reports commonly written, read, and circulated in contemporary business organizations. We will examine managerial reports according to the variables just outlined and explore the purposes and uses of reports in each category within the framework of the business organization.

Internal versus External Readers _____

Perhaps the largest volume of written communications generated by managers and circulated within the ranks of middle managers, executives, and professional/technical employees consists of brief reports in letter and memo form. Letter and memo reports are constantly disseminated between and among all levels of managerial, supervisory, and professional/technical employees working in business organizations today. Memo-reports are sent to **internal** readers and audience groups working within the organization. Often used in more formal situations than memo-reports, letter-reports are sent to **external** readers and audience groups working outside of the organization.

Reports sent to readers outside of the writer's own organization and those submitted to readers within the writer's organization might in other respects prove to be quite similar—in content, structure, even purpose. For example, both a letter-report and a memo-report generated by a manager at Periwinkle Petroleum, Inc., might include the following information: a corporate profile, an operating profile, financial data, a market profile, and a series of recommended management actions. However, the *uses* to which a letter-report and a memo-report containing data and information of that sort might be put will very likely differ. An external reader or audience group might use this information to determine whether to invest in Periwinkle Petroleum. An internal reader or audience group might use the data and information to plan corporate strategy at Periwinkle or to enhance Periwinkle's decision-making process regarding property acquisitions or future drilling activities.

Documents to be used for external consumption might differ significantly in layout and structure from those that will be distributed internally. Organizational memos and memo-reports usually follow a specific **format**, often specific to, and developed by, individual organizations (see Figures 4.1a, 4.1b, and 4.1c). Letters and letter-reports, on the other hand, gener-

Pro Comm®

BETZ PROCESS CHEMICALS INC.

DATE: August 5, 19--

NUMBER: 29-29

FROM: J. J. Perugini

RECOMMENDED FILING: 1990 ProChem Product Guide E. B. Section

New Demands on Desalter Operations

Bill Witzig presented the attached paper at the NPRA Annual Meeting in San Antonio this year.

This paper is an excellent primer discussing the cause and effect relationships of key desalter variables. The methodology for managing the data to allow desalting operation optimization and defining performance targets and limitations is discussed.

Of significance is the fact that the emulsion breaking process in an electric desalter vessel is two distinct separation processes. These are crude oil dehydration and effluent water deoiling.

FIGURE 4.1A

Example of organizational memo format—Betz Process Chemicals, Inc.

United States Department of the Interior
BUREAU OF RECLAMATION
RIO GRANDE PROJECT
109 N. OREGON STREET P.O. DRAWER P
EL PASO, TEXAS 79952-0002

IN REPLY
REFER TO: 450

MEMORANDUM

TO: Regional Director, Amarillo, Texas
            Attn: SW-400 and SW-800

FROM: Project Superintendent

SUBJECT: Report of Excess Real Property—Rio Grande Project
            (Del Rio Drain)

This office has determined that the Del Rio Drain parcel of land containing
approximately 1.57 acres is excess to the needs of the Rio Grande project.

We, therefore, recommend that this parcel of Del Rio Drain right-of-way,
as described by the attached documents, be declared *excess real
property* and turned over to the General Services Administration (GSA)
for disposal.

FIGURE 4.1B
Example of organizational memo-report format—U.S. Department of the Interior.

ally reflect traditional business-letter format (see Figure 4.2). Many contemporary organizations—multisite, large, or international—use hybrid formats such as the **interorganization letter** (see Figure 4.3) or **interoffice letter** (see Figure 4.4).

Report Formats and Degree of Formality

As we have shown, the format of a managerial report is, at least in part, dictated by the location of report readers who will use the report. Report readers and audiences within an organization will receive memo-reports; external readers will receive letter-reports. Report format, though, is also dictated by the level of **formality** inherent in the communication situation.

LOCKHEED SPACE OPERATIONS

TO: Manager, Logistics Engineering

FROM: Supervisor, Research and Identification

DATE: 06/11/90   CONTROL NUMBER: FIT-1

SUBJECT: RECOMMENDED CHANGES TO PROCESSING
                    SHELF-LIFE CODED MATERIAL

REFERENCE: SPI LG-345 (7) KV, Management of Shelf-life Stock
                    Material, Revision E

1. *Action Statement:* The current standard for reviewing and accepting newly received shelf-life coded stock material should be changed from "age on delivery" to "shelf-life remaining." The new standard based on the use of the manufacturer's expiration date will improve the acceptance criteria and enhance procurement and receiving activities while continuing to provide reliable shelf-life inventory control.

2. *Problem Statement:* The current procedure used to review and accept shelf-life material is creating an unnecessary administrative burden on and an unusually high rejection rate during the inspection and procurement process. Both problems are caused by the overly restricted and unforgiving nature of the SPI-directed receiving guidelines.

3. *Discussion:*
a. As shown below, the receiving criteria for newly arriving shelf-life controlled material is highly restrictive and in the higher shelf-life periods it requires the material to be virtually new.

FIGURE 4.1c
Example of organizational memo-report format—Lockheed Space Operations.

Long and Short Reports

Long reports are generally formal in nature. Long, formal reports are most often

> multipage documents (bound or with cover sheets and/or title pages).
>
> sent up the organizational hierarchy to groups of (or individual) managers, senior executives, and VPs.
>
> in-depth informational, examinational, and analytical and usually contain the traditional report sections (from letter or memo of transmittal and table of contents to summaries and conclusions/recommendations).

We'll have considerably more to say about long, formal reports later in this chapter as well as in Chapter 14.

June 29, 19--

Mr. J. R. Lopez, Chief
Branch Office Texaco, Inc.
P. O. Box 2005
El Paso, TX 79968

Subject: Soil and Foundation Study CRU—Texaco

Dear Mr. Lopez:

Submitted here is a report of our study of soil and foundation conditions at the site proposed for an addition to existing facilities to be located in the El Paso Plant.

Presented in this report are our conclusions and recommendations pertaining to the type and depth of foundations and the allowable bearing pressure for the structure contemplated. An oral progress report has been provided to you during the conduct of this analysis.

This engineering report has been prepared for the use of Texaco, Inc., for the design purposes in accordance with generally accepted Geotechnical Engineering practices. This report may not contain sufficient information for purposes of other parties or other uses.

We appreciate the opportunity to be of service to you on this project. Please call us if we can be of additional assistance during the materials testing—quality control phase of construction.

Very truly yours,

Newt Soren

Newt Soren, Project Superintendent
Rocke—Ryland Engineering Consultants

NS:gt

Enclosures

FIGURE 4.2
Traditional letter-report format.

ROCHESTER PRODUCTS DIVISION

GENERAL MOTORS CORPORATION

ROCHESTER, NEW YORK   14603

INTER-ORGANIZATION LETTERS ONLY

DATE February 1, 19--

SUBJECT: MPFI UPDATE ASSEMBLY & TEST

FROM: A. Savino

TO: T. P. Gilligan   cc: F. Knapp

1. <u>ASSEMBLY V-6 THROTTLE BODY</u>

   All workplace development has been completed with a line balance of 93%. All jobs have been simulated and videotaped for future training need. Estimated labor savings $232,000.

2. <u>ASSEMBLY—V-6 FUEL RAIL</u>

   All workplace completed with line balance of 93%. All jobs have been simulated and videotaped. Estimated labor savings of $148,317. See attached detail #1 and 2.

3. Process for flow test of throttle body and fuel rail has been defined and working on developing procedures and workplace.

FIGURE 4.3
Interorganization letter-report format.

Short reports, on the other hand, are usually informal, appreciably less comprehensive in content and scope, and less rigid in structure. Short reports are generally

- within the one- to five-page range (sometimes even a single handwritten paragraph or less in length).
- aimed at an immediate supervisor or a regular client, customer, or other external reader.
- written in memo-report or letter-report format, with a limited number of attachments.

Memo- and Letter-Reports

Memo-reports and letter-reports, as we have indicated, serve precisely the same purposes. While the uses to which these documents are put might prove

---

INTEROFFICE LETTER

TO	"Labor and Production Reporting"	WRITTEN FROM
All Concerned	S.P.I. No. 02-31-03	Business Systems
FROM		**DATE**
C. V. Lange		November 23, 19--

Attached is a copy of Standard Practice Instruction No. 02-31-03 entitled "Labor and Production Reporting." This instruction applies to the Fuel Systems Works of the Tapco Group and will be effective December 1, 1991.

The purpose of this instruction is to outline the methods used in preparing the labor tickets, applying current and inventory standards to the labor tickets and updating the inventory standard hours when a manufacturing operation is deleted or combined into another operation.

Additonal copies of this S.P.I. may be obtained by calling the Business Systems Department on extension 8225.

C. V. Lange

C. V. Lange
Business Systems Manager

FIGURE 4.4
Interoffice letter-report format.

to be different, both types of short reports function in several similar ways for their readers. Both **memo-** and **letter-reports**, for example, might

> suggest action(s) to take.
> identify goals or priorities.
> examine data (numerical, descriptive).
> analyze data (generate recommendations).
> present or review information.
> clarify or document information.
> advise (on policy).
> record (procedures).

A sample memo-report from the El Paso Electric Company is displayed in Figure 4.5. In a brief space (less than a full page of text), this carefully organized

MEMORANDUM

TO: Mr. Dean Jacobson   February 22, 1990

FROM: Mr. Terry McGarrity

Data Base Administrator

I believe that El Paso Electric needs a Data Base Administrator (DBA).

- The Company spends $8,000,000 to store its data
- The Company's $450,000,000 in revenues depends on that data
- The Company does not currently have a Data Base Administrator to manage these resources
- The most critical tasks in data base administration are being divided among the other Technical Support Staff; there is no specialist giving full-time attention to this function
- The Technical Support action plan for 1990 requires more than 100% of the existing staff's time if we do not have a DBA

The Company is considering adding another data base system (DB2) at a cost of approximately $150,000 to support a General Ledger package. If we assign someone to work with this as required to support it properly, then we will take away from the support on our VM operating system or our terminal network.

I have attached a list of tasks which a Data Base Administrator normally would do. I have also attached a copy of the 1990 work plan for Technical Support, which shows the work for each person as well as for a DBA. There is more than enough work to occupy a DBA full-time.

cc: Ms. Neva Uphoff

SAFETY IS NO ACCIDENT

Figure 4.5

Sample memo-report—the El Paso Electric Company.

memo-report (a) suggests specific action to take (i.e., recommends hiring a data base administrator), (b) examines corporate data, (c) presents new data and information, (d) clarifies information, and (e) advises.

A sample memo-report from the U.S. Department of the Interior appears in Figure 4.6. In this brief memo-report, a project superintendent (a) suggests specific actions to take (i.e., recommends that a land parcel "be declared excess real property and turned over to the General Services Administration . . . for disposal"), (b) documents data and information, and (c) reviews and clarifies information.

Finally, a sample interoffice letter-report from Thompson Ramo Wooldridge, Inc., on "Labor and Production Reporting" is shown in Figure 4.7. This interoffice letter-report, signed by the business systems manager, (a) presents information; (b) reviews, clarifies, and presents methods or procedures; and (c) advises (e.g., "Additional copies of this S.P.I. may be obtained . . . "). Included within the report package are the following materials:

1. A five-page document outlining the purpose and scope of the "Standard Practice Instructions" mentioned in the letter-report
2. A detailed discussion of the "responsibilities of the departments involved"
3. A complete set of instructional attachments describing methods to be used in reporting data and information regarding labor
4. Copies of the forms to be used

Reports Based on Time Frames or Business Intervals

Just as we can classify or categorize managerial reports according to the location of their readers (internal vs. external audiences), formats writers use (memo- vs. letter-reports), and degree of formality writers employ (short or handwritten vs. long and word-processed), we can also classify reports according to **time frames** and **business intervals** over which or during which they are written, required, or due. Managerial reports, then, might be classified as (a) routine or nonroutine, (b) regular or special, (c) periodic or progress.

Just about all of the report categories discussed in this chapter thus far overlap. That is, a brief memo-report—generally informal—might, on certain occasions, be rather formal; the same might be true of a brief letter-report. Letter-reports—directed at chiefly external audiences—might, on certain occasions, be less or more formal and shorter or longer, depending on other variables inherent in the communication situation (e.g., the content or subject of the report, the frequency of the report, or the readers addressed by the report).

United States Department of the Interior
BUREAU OF RECLAMATION
RIO GRANDE PROJECT
109 N. OREGON STREET P.O. DRAWER P
EL PASO, TEXAS 79952-0002

MEMORANDUM

TO: Regional Director, Amarillo, Texas
            Attn: SW-400 and SW-800

FROM: Project Superintendent

SUBJECT: Report of Excess Real Property—Rio Grande
            Project (Del Rio Drain)

This office has determined that the Del Rio Drain parcel of land
containing approximately 1.57 acres is excess to the needs of the Rio
Grande Project.

We, therefore, recommend that this parcel of Del Rio Drain right-of-
way, as described by the attached documents, be declared *excess real
property* and turned over to the General Services Administration (GSA)
for disposal.

Attached are the following documents pertaining to the Del Rio Drain
excess land parcel:

  (1) Standard form 118 and 118b
  (2) Description of excess land parcel
  (3) Plat of excess land parcel
  (4) Status of ownership and appraised value
  (5) Land appraisal report
  (6) Certificate of inspection and statement of land
       use and records
  (7) Right-of-way acquisition file
  (8) Categorical exclusion file

The Del Rio Drain parcel was acquired by quit claim deed May 18,
1937, from Dionicio Banegas and Eva Chamberlain Banegas for use
as Del Rio Drain Right-of-way. This reach of the Del Rio Drain has
been abandoned and the ditch has been filled in.

Attachments

FIGURE 4.6
Sample memo-report—U.S. Department of the Interior.

```
┌─────────────────────────────────────────────────────────────────────┐
│                                                                     │
│                   INTEROFFICE LETTER                                │
│                                                                     │
├──────────────────────┬─────────────────────────┬───────────────────┤
│ TO                   │                         │ WRITTEN FROM      │
│    All Concerned     │ "Labor and Production   │ Business Systems  │
│                      │   Reporting"            │                   │
├──────────────────────┤ S.P.I. No. 02-31-03     ├───────────────────┤
│ FROM                 │                         │ DATE              │
│    C. V. Lange       │                         │ November 23, 19-- │
└──────────────────────┴─────────────────────────┴───────────────────┘
```

Attached is a copy of Standard Practice Instruction No. 02-31-03
entitled "Labor and Production Reporting." This instruction applies to the
Fuel Systems Works of the Tapco Group and will be effective December
1, 1991.

The purpose of this instruction is to outline the methods used in
preparing the labor tickets, applying current and inventory standards to
the labor tickets and updating the inventory standard hours when a
manufacturing operation is deleted or combined into another operation.

Additonal copies of this S.P.I. may be obtained by calling the Business
Systems Department on extension 8225.

C. V. Lange

C. V. Lange
Business Systems Manager

FIGURE 4.7
Sample letter-report—Thompson Ramo Wooldridge, Inc.

Routine, Regular, and Special Reports

Routine, regular, and special report types fulfill universal business needs and
are widely used. Generated and submitted at regular and specified times during
the year (e.g., the first of each month, every Monday morning) or during key
business intervals (e.g., quarterly), these reports might be formal or informal,
brief or lengthy, and in either memo or letter format. **Routine** and **regular**
reports will be written, and are expected, at regular business intervals that
vary, depending on the organization and the purpose of the report. Examples
of routine or regular reports include the following:

1. *Sales reports*—noting units sold, identified pricing, inventory data
2. *Travel or activity reports*—noting miles driven, contacts made, summaries
of meetings, recommendations

SUPERSEDES:	SPI No.	PAGE No.	DATED	EFFECTIVE DATE	PAGE 2
SUBJECT Labor and Production Reporting				OTHER DIVISIONS AFFECTED	

1.0 PURPOSE

To establish the methods and define the responsibilities for reporting actual and standard labor to Fuel Systems Accounting.

2.0 SCOPE

This instruction encompasses the responsibilities of the departments involved; the methods used in reporting actual and standard labor; and the forms used.

3.0 RESPONSIBILITIES

3.1 PRODUCTION CONTROL—DISPATCHER

(a) When preparing a direct labor ticket for a standard cost F.R., duplicate the proper lot release card into the labor ticket, provided the following conditions are satisfied:

    (1) The current department charged is in accordance with the latest routing or R.C.A.

    (2) The current standard hours per 100 pieces is in accordance with the latest routing or R.C.A.

    (3) The words "DO NOT USE FOR LABOR" do *not* appear on the lot release card.

(b) When preparing an indirect 113 account set-up labor ticket for a standard cost F.R., duplicate the proper lot release card into the labor ticket, provided the current department charged is in accordance with the latest routing or R.C.A.

(c) Prepare manually all labor tickets not covered in 3.1(a) and (b) above.

(d) At the end of each shift, deliver all labor tickets to timekeeping after obtaining proper approvals from manufacturing supervision.

(e) Receive from the central lot control section the lot release change notice attached to the pink copy of the R.C.A. denoting deleted or combined operations. This form letter identifies those operations for the F.R.s indicated whose labor tickets are not to be duplicated from the lot release cards.

R. J. Janoch		*W. P. Bente*
R. J. Janoch		W. P. Bente
Accounting Manager		Works Manager

FIGURE 4.7

Continued

40M-14 10/83

Rockwell
MANUFACTURING COMPANY

QUALITY HISTORY SHEET

PLANT ____________________

PART NAME ____________________

PART NUMBER __________ CHG. ________

CUSTOMER ____________________

DATE ISSUED ____________________

PAGE __________ OF __________

DISTRIBUTION:
1. DIECAST
2. ENGINEERING
3. FINAL INSPECTION
4. TOOL ROOM
5. QUALITY CONTROL
6. PLANT MANAGER
7. CLEANING OR PRINTING
8. LAYOUT
9. MFG. DEPT.
10. MANUFACTURE DEPT.
11. PURCHASING
12. PROCESS INSPECTION
13. RECEIVING INSPECTION

DATE	REASON FOR REJECTION	REJECTION NUMBER	QUANTITY REJECTED	QUANTITY ACCEPT	CASTING DATE

Figure 4.8a
Example of preprinted company form—Rockwell Manufacturing Company.

3. *Expenditure reports*—noting out-of-pocket expenses, carfare, travel advances, meal monies

Many routine business reports are submitted to management on **preprinted company forms.** Sales, activity, expenditure, labor, and certain accounting or statistical reports might be generated weekly, monthly, or quarterly by (or for) supervisors, managers, or program directors. To record routine data and information for any of these routine business reports, preprinted company forms like those found in Figures 4.8a and 4.8b might be used.

Special reports are not written or required on a routine or regular basis. Rather, special reports are written in response to an organizational need or a specific request. Special reports are generated to (a) identify (new) problems or issues; (b) explore major problems or issues that have surfaced; (c) solve particular problems or, at least, recommend possible solutions to them; and (d) evaluate, review, survey, or audit personnel, systems, programs, and departments. For example, special reports might

RECAP OF INDIRECT LABOR

4400 POWER, HEAT, & LIGHT DEPT.

PAY No.   47

WEEK OF:

RECAP OF INDIRECT LABOR		NAPERVILLE	BINGHAMTON	KANKAKEE	DALLAS	INGLEWOOD	CLEVELAND	CHARLOTTE	PITTSBURG
SUPERVISORY	04		89.50	55.42					
	05								
	06								
P.H. & L. OPR. & HELPER	07			133.16					
	08								
JANITORS	09								
	10								
	11								
	12								
	13								
	14								
	15								
FIREMEN	16	79.54	354.08	110.81	80.33	50.81	184.80		
NITE SHIFT PREM. DIRECT LABOR	17								
NITE SHIFT PREM. INDIRECT LABOR	18		14.36	4.86					
XTRA OPERATIONS	19								
INSTRUCTION (4900 WHSE. DRIVER)	20								
APPRENTICE (4200 CAFE)	21								
DISPATCH DIFFERENTIAL	22								
DIFFERENTIAL—DIRECT LABOR	23								
OVERTIME—DIR. LABOR	24								
OVERTIME—IND. LABOR	25	9.05	48.52	40.27	8.66	4.52			
UTILITY	26								
MAT. HAND. (4500 DRIVER)	27								
MAINT. MACH'Y.	28	18.82	74.45	.73	3.58				
MAINT. BLDG. & GROUNDS	29								
SMALL SCHEDULE ALLOWANCE	30								
STOCKK'R & HELPER	31								
INSPECT (6400 CUSH. CHECK)	32								
ELEVATOR OPERATOR	33								
WATCHMEN	34								
REPAIR	35								
MOVING DEPT. AND EQUIP.	36								
DISPATCHER AND LINE SUPPLIER	37								
DISPATCH HELPER, JOB HANDLER	38								
ACCUMULATOR, CHECKER	39								
CLEAN AND PATCH	40								
LOAD AND UNLOAD	41								
INTERPLT. DISPATCHER	42								
(6700 TRUCK LOADING)	43								
INVENTORY (6700 SCHEDULER)	44								
SALVAGING STOCK	45								
	46								
	47								
FIRST RUN ALLOW.	48								
WAITING TIME (4200 FIRST AID)	49								
MISCELLANEOUS									
TOTAL									
DIRECT LABOR									
% INDIRECT LABOR TO DIRECT									

FIGURE 4.8B

Example of preprinted company form—"Recap of Indirect Labor."

call for the formation of a steering committee to explore a request from users to automate the manual processes of a plant's accounting system.

provide an overview of experimental work currently being conducted in the study of "leakage potential in light water reactor (LWR) containments" for the Nuclear Regulatory Commission.

audit the industrial-relations policies and practices of a manufacturing company to survey what is actually occurring, determine levels of employee satisfaction with ongoing practices, and evaluate the relationship between articulated company policies and ongoing practices.

articulate a handwashing policy to prevent the cross-contamination of newborns for all hospital personnel who come into direct contact with newborns.

outline a contingency plan for drilling operations of a mining company for dissemination to all site managers throughout the organization.

review information on antifouling techniques, treatment philosophy, service, and applications for a major presentation to a client company.

Special reports might address internal or external audiences in a formal or informal manner; they might also vary from brief memo- and letter-reports to multipage comprehensive or research reports.

Periodic and Progress Reports

Within the broad category of reports based on time frames and business intervals are two additional kinds of reports that we should briefly explore. Periodic and progress reports are actually variations of routine, regular, and special reports. **Periodic** reports are generated at regular business intervals and, much like routine and regular reports, will be submitted weekly, biweekly, monthly, semimonthly, quarterly, or annually. Sales reports, travel or activity reports, and expenditure reports might be classified as periodic reports in certain organizations but as regular or routine reports in others. Employee evaluation reports, for example, might be classified exclusively as periodic reports; reports generated at specific intervals for federally funded projects might also be classified as periodic.

Progress reports generally provide management with some combination of data and information—sometimes coupled with analysis and recommendations—concerning long-range corporate projects. Figure 4.9 shows a progress report (in memo-report format) written by a systems analyst for a project involving the data base of an organization's leverage employee stock option plan (LESOP).

MEMORANDUM

October 8, 1991

TO: Terry McGarrity
FROM: Dalia Sofer
SUBJECT: Changes That Will Occur Due to the Introduction of LESOP

The introduction of LESOP will affect the existing STOCK system in four areas.

1. The STOCK data base will have to be expanded to include new accounts for eligible employees (87 accounts), a HOLDING account (99999999_??), and perhaps another account to retain the shares left behind by nonvested terminated employees (a SUSPENSE account).

2. A new shares program will have to be added to other yearly run programs in order to process the annual LESOP allocation of shares.

3. The existing quarterly closing programs—STK201 through STK214—will have to be modified in order to process LESOP quarterly dividend calculation and distribution.

4. Another new program will have to be created to allow for all needed notifications (quarterly statements, annual allocation report, and yearly valuation information) to be printed at the user's convenience.

1. Stock Data Base Expansion

The current STOCK system allows the user to enter an ESOP account and assign it a number starting with 0088, while the rest of the account types (except for the 81 accounts) start with 01 and are numbered sequentially by the system. The crucial factor for the entering of ESOP accounts is the ESOP_CODE field that must have E in it. Failing to provide the ESOP code will cause the ESOP account number to be rejected.

In order to apply the option available for ESOP to LESOP accounts, the user will have to enter an L for the ESOP_CODE when entering an 87 account, and the on-line program STK402 will have to be modified.

As for the on-time entering of a HOLDING account and the SUSPENSE account when specific account numbers need to be assigned, further considerations will be required.

FIGURE **4.9**

Sample progress report—"Changes that will occur due to the introduction of LESOP."

Page 2
October 8, 1991

STK402

This program allows the user to enter new STOCK accounts and correct existing ones. It also enables the user to enter certificate information from the transfer sheets (certificate issue and surrender). The total number of the real certificate shares and/or the reinvestment shares is accumulated and displayed on the screen.

STK402 needs to be changed so it can accept an L as a valid value for the ESOP_CODE.

2. Annual Allocation of LESOP Shares

At present, program STK623 handles the ESOP annual allocation of money by implementing the following objectives:

- checking for employee LESOP eligibility (the necessary code is entered by PAYROLL);
- calculating the percent and actual amount of money for each eligible employee based on the total amount allocated by the company (provided by CORPORATE);
- printing a listing of all eligible employees and their ESOP allocation in percent and in money.

If the program is run in the READ ONLY mode, it executes only the above steps. However, if an UPDATE is requested, the program updates the STOCK data base by inserting a CASH segment for each ESOP participant.

The task of converting each individual cash amount into shares is carried out by program STK102, which also updates the data base by inserting REINVESTMENT segments containing ESOP shares and generates the annual ESOP letters.

The new program for LESOP will be designed to accomplish objectives that are quite similar to those delineated above (currently executed by programs STK623 and STK102). . . .

FIGURE 4.9
Continued

At times, progress and periodic reports might, of necessity, prove to be one and the same. Figure 4.10 exhibits a memo-report written jointly by the Director of Operations and the Chief Engineer of a manufacturing facility, the Rochester Products Division of General Motors, to GM senior-level management.

ROCHESTER PRODUCTS DIVISION
General Motors Corporation
Mexico Operations

October 23, 19--

TO: Charles Robinson

FROM: A. Savino and L. Strassner

SUBJECT: Mexico Operations—Accomplishment Report

In its first year of production, which is historically plagued with high costs, quality problems, and delivery obstacles, the Mexico Operation has been successful in achieving the three major objectives of (1) First Time Quality, (2) Cost, and (3) Deliverability.

Since January 1, 1989 (start of production) to date, 175 units were rejected in-house and only two (2) at B.O.C. Over $8,000. was saved in the budget and, as of this writing, we enjoy the enviable schedule position of being one week ahead of B.O.C. A total of 28,672 units have been shipped to date. As of November this year, two (2) more models will be added to the existing schedule and more equipment will have been installed.

In-House Resources:

(1) One technico (tradesman) partially trained to assist with PM and routine maintenance
(2) One student rotating every three (3) months
(3) Delco-Remy assistance limited to minor tool room and maintenance of facilities
(4) One (1) computer with modem for PSIC transactions to and from Rochester, NY.

Considering the present workload and looking ahead to consistently maintaining the Mexico Operation, it is evident that more Engineering and Manufacturing support is needed. The following proposals are for your review:

Immediate Support:

Rotate an engineer at this site for three (3) months at a time. This program change would be more effective and would not add to existing cost. Currently we are using an apartment and transportation for students all year round.

FIGURE 4.10
Sample progress/periodic report—Rochester Products Division of General Motors.

Page 2
October 23, 19--

Long-Term Support:

Add two (2) more heads to existing budget: one (1)
engineer and one (1) quality analyst. We can also discuss
the possibility of filling two positions with qualified
Mexican nationals.

As you know, only two of us currently operate the Mexico facility;
therefore, the additional personnel should be prepared to serve in
other needed support capacities in addition to their original key
assignments.

cc: D. Mead
    K. Langston

FIGURE 4.10
Continued

The memo-report shown in Figure 4.10 provides both data and information concerning GM's Mexico operation; the document focuses on the following: (a) success in meeting the three major objectives of the Mexico plant; (b) the production schedule, unit output, and overall product quality; (c) in-house resources; and (d) a projection of site needs (both immediate and long term). Thus, a single, relatively brief report reviews production objectives and evaluates progress toward meeting those objectives and periodically (monthly) informs senior-level management of successes, resources, and on-site needs.

Reports Classified by Subject Matter, Content, or Activity

Managerial reports can also be classified according to their subject matter or content and by the activity the writer has reviewed, presented, or described in the document. Naturally, every business organization regularly produces and disseminates both brief and lengthy reports aimed at, or organized around, broad **subjects** or themes such as the following:

1. Labor
2. Accounting
3. Property
4. Marketing
5. Productivity
6. Sales projections
7. Procedures
8. Staff training and development
9. Strategic planning

Figure 4.11 exhibits a sample (brief) **procedures** report aimed at the broad area of "allowable" and "prohibited" petty cash expenditures.

Equally common in contemporary business organizations of every variety are those reports—brief or long, internal or external, regular or special—focusing on specific **content** areas, such as these:

1. Labor and production reporting
2. Petty cash—allowable expenditures
3. Digital magnetic tape review
4. Value/cost analysis
5. Evaluation of defective units
6. Advantages and benefits of robotic arc welding
7. Five-year strategic plan—manufacturing, marketing, sales
8. Investment merits and analysis

Reports are also commonly classified according to the major **activity** on which a particular report or series of reports focuses. Activity reports might be generated by managers according to a well-defined periodic schedule (monthly, quarterly) and might regularly reflect individual, departmental, or organizational progress. Activity reports, for example, might focus on such areas as the following:

1. On-site building evaluation
2. Computer systems maintenance
3. Review of in-house publications
4. Inventory control visitations
5. Soil analysis and testing results
6. Zero-defect units produced/shipped
7. Vendor contacts
8. Quarterly sales—staff activities
9. Professional/technical conference attendance
10. Results of in-house planning interviews

COMMUNITY ACTION FOR LEGAL SERVICES, INC.
PROCEDURES

SUBJECT		PROCEDURE NO.	
	Petty Cash		1.01

CATEGORY		PAGE
	Allowable Expenditures	

EFFECTIVE DATE	SUPERSEDES

ALLOWABLE

Petty cash may be used to reimburse employees when they have expended their own funds in the normal course of performing assigned duties. Expenses which will be reimbursed from petty cash are:

A.   Carfare—subways, buses, and other public transportation. Taxicabs may only be used when public transportation is not available or practicable. The reason for using a taxicab rather than other public transportation must be provided on the petty cash voucher by the employee. When a taxicab is used, a signed receipt must be obtained by the employee and submitted with the petty cash voucher.

B.   Out-of-pocket telephone expenditures.

C.   Postage and local delivery charges.

D.   Supper money—$15.50. Actual time worked must be indicated on the petty cash voucher by the employee. Supper money is due an employee working at least two hours of previously authorized overtime.

E.   Urgent expenditures under $50.00 which cannot be feasibly channeled through normal purchasing procedures. However, all such expenditures must be approved in advance by the Attorney-in-Charge.

PROHIBITED

Petty cash may not be used for the following:

A.   Cashing checks of any type.

B.   Travel advances, or any other advances not specifically allowed herein.

C.   Any expenditures which are prohibited by O.E.O., funding sources or contractual regulations.
    The following are examples of prohibited expenditures:

   1.   Expenses of a personal nature such as the cost of transportation between the Corporation and a staff member's home.

   2.   Food or refreshments for staff except in connection with out-of-town travel.

   3.   Entertainment costs of any type.

   4.   Taxes from which an exemption is available, such as local and state sales tax.

   5.   Fines or penalties such as tickets for illegal parking or moving violations.

   6.   Real estate brokerage fee.

   7.   Uniform guard service.

The rules governing allowability of expenditures are necessarily complex so that questionable items should be reviewed with the CALS Comptroller.

FIGURE 4.11

Sample procedures report—Community Action for Legal Services, Inc.

Management Hybrids — Announcements and Bulletin Reports _____

Corporate announcements and **bulletin reports** serve managers and their organizations in precisely the same way. Both of these report types are used to announce recent decisions, new plans, schedule changes, updated corporate enterprises or purposes, and the like. Announcements and bulletin reports are not directed toward specific readers but rather at general audiences such as the following: employees, staff, new support personnel, senior managers, investors, training coordinators, inventory control administrators, field supervisors, emergency room nursing staff, customers.

Because these sorts of reports are not written for specific, individual readers, they are considerably less personal than, for example, more typical memo- and letter-reports. On the other hand, they serve to communicate timely, important information to larger audiences within organizations or external to them. The audience segments to which organizational announcements and bulletin reports are directed sometimes share job functions, work schedules, or professional needs. Often, though, the audiences for announcements and bulletin reports might be general and heterogeneous, with few qualities, traits, or assets in common—for example, new personnel, investors, employees, and customers.

Figures 4.12 through 4.14 display the initial portions of corporate announcements or bulletin reports, each document directed at quite different audiences: general accounting supervisors (Figure 4.12), investors (Figure 4.13), and employees (Figure 4.14).

Reports Classified by Function _____

Reports classified by their **function** and use within business, industrial, research and development (R&D), and governmental organizations are often the longest and most comprehensive reports with which we are concerned in this text. The most important to organizations as a whole, the most widely written, and the most frequently used report types within this classification are the following:

1. Informational
2. Examinational
3. Analytical
4. Operational

TO: General Accounting Supervisors   March 24, 19--

FROM: Mr. Gordon Heggem

REVISED DATA PREPARATION PROCEDURES

Below are the revised procedures for General Accounting Department (supersedes procedures contained in memo dated December 8, 19--):

1. *Definition of terms:*

   (a) Prepared By—originator or preparer of the data.

   (b) Math Check By—a mathematics check of all data presented. This function should be documented by the use of symbols such as $\wedge$ or S or other appropriate symbols to show that the footing, cross-footing, extension of the numbers presented, etc., have been done. Additional documentation will be completed by signing and dating in the space provided (see number 3 below).

   (c) Detail Review By—detailed checking of the data to include tracing to source documents, presentation, format, and theory. All items presented should be dotted or marked in some manner by the person doing this review to make it clear that the data are completely detail-reviewed. The math check and detail review can be performed by one person, but that person will be required to sign and date for having completed both procedures (see number 3 below) as well as the other required documentation.

   (d) Approved By—a review which will satisfy the approver as to the correctness of the data. Responsibility is taken for correctness, theory, presentation, etc.

2. *Color coding:*

Function	Pencil Color
Prepared by	Black
Math check by	Red, non-photo blue
Detail review by	Red, non-photo blue
Approved by	Green, non-photo blue

3. *Signatures:*

   Documentation of the cycle of prepare — check — review — approve. The signature will be first initial and last name followed by the date in a form, such as 12/1/91.

FIGURE 4.12

Sample corporate announcement—general accounting department, El Paso Electric Company.

Arch *Petroleum Inc.*

Investor Focus - March '90

Corporate Profile

Arch Petroleum Inc. is an independent oil and gas company headquartered in Fort Worth, Texas. Its principal business activities are exploration for and development and operation of domestic oil and gas properties. The primary objective of management is to increase the value of the company by building high quality oil and gas reserves through planned programs of exploration, development and acquisition.

Operating Profile

Arch Petroleum Inc. currently operates approximately 400 wells and owns an interest in over 800 wells located primarily in Texas and New Mexico. As of November 1, 1989, Arch owns estimated proved reserves of approximately 29 billion cubic feet of natural gas and 4.2 million barrels of oil.

FINANCIAL HIGHLIGHTS

(In thousands)	1989	1988	1987*
Operating Data:			
Operating revenues	$5,493	$2,770	$1,247
Income (loss) before extraordinary items	1,500	203	(331)
Net income (loss)	1,500	330	303
Balance Sheet Data:			
Cash	$1,759	$2,393	$146
Total assets	15,076	11,383	3,372
Long-term debt	1,890	42	894
Convertible redeemable preferred stock	7,000	7,000	
Common shareholders' equity	3,875	3,089	1,626

*1987 consists of 10 months activity due to change in year-end

Market Profile

NASDAQ Symbol	ARCH
Common Shares Outstanding	6,676,002
Common Stock Options Outstanding	1,195,548
Float in Shares	4,455,536
Shares Held by Management	1,920,466
Per Share Price (April 1990 Closing Bid)	2 3/4
Investor Contact	Vince White
Market Makers	Oppenheimer & Co., Inc.
	Bateman Eichler, Hill Richards Inc.
	Southwest Securities Inc.
	Troster Singer
	Fahnestock & Company Inc.
	Herzog, Heine, Geduld, Inc.
	Wien Securities Corporation
	Sherwood Securities Corporation
	Mayer & Schweitzer, Inc.
	Mascera & Company Inc.
	Nash, Weiss & Co.

Oil and Gas Properties

Number of Wells Operated:	Approx. 400
Proved reserves at October 31, 1989:[1]	
Oil (Bbls)	4,181,000
Gas (MCF)	29,151,000
Estimated Future Net Cash Flows from Proved Reserves [1]	$123,432,000
Present Value of Future Net Cash Flows from Proved Reserves [1] (Discounted at 10% per annum)	$66,126,000

(1) Proved reserves and future net cash flows were computed using escalated prices and costs. The escalated pricing scenario resulted in average prices over the life of the reserves of $25.78 and $2.13 for oil and gas, respectively.

Suite II•777 Taylor Street•Fort Worth, Texas 76102
Phone: 800-772-8558

FIGURE 4.13

Sample bulletin report—"Investor Focus," Arch Petroleum Inc.

Southern Pacific
Transportation Company

Southern Pacific Building • One Market Plaza • San Francisco, California 94105

September 17, 19--

Dear Employee:

It has been a while since we have written you directly to update you on the merger and divestiture process.

Our purpose in writing is to keep you informed of the facts about our joint purchase of the company, to dispel any false rumors or misleading information, and to remind you of the process to be taken by our parent, SFSP, and the ICC.

SFSP has identified three principal approaches that might be pursued to accomplish the divestiture of SPT. These include:

(1) The sale of SPT's rail operations in its entirety to a railroad, a non-carrier, or an employee group.

(2) The spin-off of SPT's shares to SFSP stockholders, in which case SPT would become an independent, publicly held corporation with stock traded on the open market.

(3) The sale of SPT on a segmented basis, which would mean that several major route segments would be sold to different railroad companies. SFSP has held preliminary discussions with potential purchasers. The parent company has also made public its desire to access St. Louis, Memphis, and New Orleans, presumably over lines currently operated by SPT and/or SSW.

As you will recall from some of our letters to you prior to the Commission's denial of the SPT–SFe merger, we urged your support in seeing the merger approved. We also told you that, should the merger be denied, we would have to return to you for substantial labor agreement restructuring to permit us to compete as an independent carrier. We regret that the Commission has denied the merger, but dwelling on that history serves no useful purpose. Our task now is to focus on what we can do to run an independent and profitable company and to take the opportunity that the divestiture process presents to achieve that goal . . . .

FIGURE 4.14

Sample announcement/bulletin report to employees, Southern Pacific Transportation Company.

5. Formal proposal

6. Feasibility study

7. Annual (quarterly, interim)

Informational Reports

Informational reports, as the category denotes, include all nonanalytical reports whose primary function is to present or convey information. Naturally, just about all management-based business reports convey some amount of information; nevertheless, reports whose central or singular function is to convey information without the analysis, discussion, or interpretation of data can be classified separately as informational. With regard to informational reports, management (and other) report writers do not have the authority, nor have they been given the responsibility, to analyze, explain, or interpret data. They simply present raw data and descriptive information to selected organizational readers who will explore this material and determine its significance.

Readers of informational reports must themselves interpret facts, data, and information. They must for example, (a) draw inferences from the presented data; (b) derive conclusions from the data; (c) evaluate the data's significance; and (d) make appropriate recommendations based on their reading of the data and information presented. Often informational reports contain raw numerical or statistical data, like those on the data page shown in Figure 4.15 extracted from an operations report. A senior-level manager or, more immediately, the director of plant operations will scrutinize the data presented in an informational report of this kind, determine their significance, and make decisions based on her or his own careful reading of the report.

Informational reports may be very brief (a single page or less). They may also be long and comprehensive, ranging from multipage clipped or stapled to bound volumes of, say, statistical abstracts or financial data. As with all reports classified functionally, informational reports reflect a wide variety of lengths and degrees of comprehensiveness and an equally broad base of organizational subject matter and purposes.

Examinational Reports

Examinational reports are a variant of informational reports. Examinational reports do not present full-blown analyses of data and information to readers; neither do they include conclusions derived nor recommendations made by the report writer based on the data and information presented. Rather, examinational reports structure and interpret data and information in such a way as to aid readers in developing their own conclusions from the information presented. The data and information in an examinational report focus on the

	MONTH	JANUARY	FEBRUARY	MARCH
	ACCTG. DAYS	20		

CAPITAL ADDITION AND DISMANTLING (Expended This Month)

		JANUARY		
21.	TOTAL COST	299,382		
	21A. Capital Additions—Plant Force	98,044		
	21B. Capital Additions—Contract (Vouchers)	186,168		
	21C. Dismantling—Plant Force	11,464		
	21D. Dismantling—Contract (Vouchers)	3,706		
22.	CAPITAL ADDITIONS PER MAINTENANCE ACCOUNTING DAY (CONTRACT VOUCHERS EXCLUDED)	9,902		

CAPITAL ADDITIONS AND REPLACEMENT (Approved This Month)

23.	TOTAL APPROVAL	97,261		
	23A. Capital Addition (New)	80,001		
	23B. Capital Addition (Replacement)	17,260		

STRUCTURE OF REPAIRS (% by Work Classification)

24.	EQUIPMENT	35		
25.	PIPING	26		
26.	BUILDINGS	6		
27.	PAINTING	2		
28.	ASSIST OPERATIONS	15		
29.	ALL OTHERS	16		

MINOR REPAIR WORK ORDERS

30.	TOTAL NUMBER OF MRO'S COMPLETED THIS MONTH	5,434		
	30A. Number of Overrun (See Footnote.)	131		
31.	TOTAL NUMBER OF MRO'S (BACKLOG END OF MONTH)	1,521		
	31A. Number of Over Two Months Old	269		
32.	DIRECT LABOR $—TOTAL EXPENDED THIS MONTH	108,978		
33.	DIRECT LABOR $—AVERAGE PER MRO THIS MONTH	20		

MANPOWER

34.	NUMBER OF SALARIED EMPLOYEES (END OF MONTH)	65		
35.	NUMBER OF HOURLY EMPLOYEES (END OF MONTH)	485		
	35A. Total Effective Manpower (See Footnote.)	474		
	35B. Number of Men Loss Due to Absence, Vacation, etc.	24		
	35C. Number of Men Gain Due to Overtime Worked	13		
36.	NO. MEN USED ON REPAIRS—OVER/UNDER BUDGET AVG. ALLOWED	2		

OVERHEAD

37.	TOTAL OVERHEAD EXPENSE	114,670		
	37A. Shop Expense (Dept. 811)	21,524		
	37B. Mech. Supervision (Dept. 812)	23,146		
38.	APPARENT OVERHEAD (AS % OF TOTAL DIRECT LABOR)	58		

MATERIAL ACCOUNTS

39.	PURCHASE THIS MONTH	226,404		
40.	DISBURSEMENT THIS MONTH	194,570		
41.	STOCK BALANCE END OF MONTH	801,221		
42.	(S-25 SURPLUS) DISBURSEMENTS THIS MONTH	1,884		
43.	(S-25 SURPLUS) STOCK BALANCE END OF MONTH	21,628		
44.	TOTAL STOCK BALANCE END OF MONTH	822,849		

DOWN TIME INDEX

45.	% MECHANICAL AVAILABILITY	95		
46.	% WORK TO ASSIST OPERATIONS	97		

FOOTNOTES:

30A. Max. MRO allowance $350—Max. permissible overrun is 2% of item 30 (Total MRO's completed this month).

35A. Total effective manpower—Number of men after adjusting absence, vacation, and overtime.

FIGURE 4.15

Section from "Summary of Operations Report—Maintenance Department," John F. Queeny Plant.

presentation of a management-based problem, issue, idea, or topic for *future* consideration, discussion, and decision making.

The writer of examinational reports, then, does not generate solutions or decisions, nor does the writer present conclusions or recommendations. Other specialists in the organization—for example, in finance, R&D, marketing, data processing (DP), and human resources—will review and interpret the data and information in examinational reports. Various specialists within organizations will, often routinely, derive and generate conclusions and make recommendations to senior-level decision makers based on their review of data and information in examinational reports. Likewise, senior-level executives frequently review examinational reports received from their subordinate (midlevel) managers, drawing conclusions and making recommendations for use in solidifying decisions.

Figure 4.16 shows a portion of an examinational report from a DP manager to a senior-level decision maker. In this memo-report, the DP manager of the organization has provided a senior-level executive with all requisite data and information with which to make a thoughtful decision. The decision maker, on the other hand, must then review the data and information before her to determine whether to "renew the old terminals or to replace them with new terminals."

As can be seen in Figure 4.16, examinational reports have a direct impact on the decision-making process because they (a) present data to organizational decision makers and (b) mediate or shape those data for their audiences. Although the DP manager in this case—or, for that matter, any other midlevel manager—might not interpret the data or formulate specific recommendations, the report writer's examinational document will have had a direct effect on the organizational decision-making process.

Analytical Reports

The **analytical** report is considerably more complex, comprehensive, and sophisticated than either informational or examinational reports. Of all the reports constructed in and distributed within business, industrial, research, and governmental organizations, analytical reports most closely model traditional academic research studies in structure and function. These reports fully document a management writer's problem-solving activities during the course of any problem-solution investigation.

Whereas informational and examinational reports do not present a manager's analysis and interpretation of the collected and reviewed data and information, analytical reports document all aspects of the report writer's research and inquiry process: from the initial problem or question through data interpretation, analysis, and discussion of results to the conclusions and recommendations. The structure of typical full-length analytical reports prepared by managerial report writers within most contemporary organizations looks much like the following:

MEMORANDUM

TO: Ms. Deana Jacobs   March 2, 19--

FROM: Mr. Timothy McNamee

RE: VPA for Terminals

During the next twelve months we have over 150 terminals whose leases will expire. We have the option either to renew the old terminals or to replace them with new terminals.

The new models are the 3471 and 3472 terminals. The 3471 is the basic model and will replace terminals in Customer Service and other areas where special features are *not* required. The 3472 terminals will have additional capabilities such as 132-character display (which is very important for programmers and for spreadsheet users) and also 10-key pad option at no extra charge.

In some instances we will also replace 3192 color graphics with 3472 color (but no graphics). DCIS is one major area for this. The 3472 with color costs much less than our 3192s.

In the chart below I show the cost per month for renewal for 12-, or, 24-month periods and for the lease of new terminals for a 36-month period. We have already had the old terminals for 36 months; so, if we extend them, then they will be five years old when we replace them. I have shown only the current 3191s and a mix of 80 3472s and 70 3471s.

The rates are given as best estimates based on quotes from leasing companies and past experience. The old terminals include maintenance for 1990 and also a 10% increase in maintenance for 1991. The new terminals are covered for three years of maintenance. The rate for the new terminals is based on a 2.7% lease rate. (That is, the monthly charge is 2.7% of the original purchase price.) All prices include tax.

Device Type	3191	3191	3472	3471
Lease Period	12-month	24-month	36-month	36-month
Monthly Rate (1 terminal)	39.31	33.41	37.56	29.51
One Year Cost (150 terminals)	70, 758	60,138	60,846 (80/3472–70/3471)	

FIGURE 4.16

Beginning section from examinational report—DP manager to decision maker.

72

ANCILLARY MATERIALS	Memo (or letter) of transmittal
	Title page
	Executive summary
	Table of contents
	List of exhibits (or figures)—tables, graphs, charts, lists, photographs, maps
REPORT BODY—SECTIONS I THROUGH IV	Section I: Introduction—purpose statement (or problem statement), aim and scope of project, design or method, limitations
	Section II: Review of related literature (previous studies, library research)—a review and brief examination of related research and relevant studies previously conducted
	Section III: Analysis and discussion—an analysis and discussion of collected data and information; use of descriptive, statistical, and graphic techniques to present data and amplify content under discussion
	Section IV: Summary, conclusions, and recommendations—action-oriented items
REFERENCES, APPENDIXES	References—sources, bibliography, works cited
	Appendixes—data, materials, graphic exhibits (e.g., tables, lists, maps, photos) of supplementary value but not essential to include in any of the major report sections

Some writers of full-length analytical reports include additional ancillary materials just before the table of contents, such as a

copyright notice
memo (or letter) of authorization
memo (or letter) of acceptance
memo (or letter) of approval

Depending on the topic or research question under examination, some report writers will want to include additional sections and subsections within the bodies of their reports, focusing at length, for example, on methodology or results. (We discuss the organization and structure of analytical reports in considerable detail in Chapters 14 and 15, which focus on assembling and presenting long formal reports.)

Figure 4.17 shows a brief portion of a strategic planning report written by long-range planners at the DBM Mining & Technology Corporation. DBM's strategic planning report is a full-length analytical report whose structure conforms to the outline in this section. The portion shown here is an extract from Section IV, "Summary, Conclusions, and Recommendations." Notice how the

(FROM: Section IV: SUMMARY, CONCLUSIONS, AND RECOMMENDATIONS)

SUMMARY

In summary, the Strategic Planning Team believes that even though DBM Mining & Technology is currently experiencing losses, with continued acquisitions, we should realize profits within the next three years.

CONCLUSIONS

While DBM Mining & Technology may be realizing negative income now, we are at the normal level for an emerging mining company. Sonora, one of our key mining operations, should soon bring in revenue that will boost DBM's financial position.

Ratios related to assets are below industry average levels, but this situation appears to be appropriate for our current stage of development. Low ratios are occurring because the company is financing its expenses through stock sales. Also, there are no accounts receivables or inventory, as is typical in the gold mining industry.

Investment of DBM's equity into its subsidiaries is beginning to pay off. DBM is now receiving 15% net profit from Sonora's Jamestown mine. Also, as more stocks are sold, more funds will be channeled toward exploration. Expenses in this area should be at least 20% higher than the 5% spent in 1987.

. . . The economic situation looks favorable for DBM. Inflation is expected to remain stable, which should not affect the price of gold. While demand for gold is the best way to forecast the price, the declining dollar on the world market is presently increasing the price. However, if the abundant supply of gold continues as we suspect, the price may decline . . . .

RECOMMENDATIONS

To continue to grow and earn profits, DBM should pursue the following recommendations:

- Purchase, with existing equity, the remaining 30% of Sonora's Jamestown mine in the fourth quarter of 19--.

- Conclude the development process of Goldenbell's Pine Tree site in the first quarter of 19--. Construction should be completed so that Goldenbell can begin to contribute revenue. Stock sales should be used to finance the project.

- Complete the feasibility studies for United and Inca in the fourth quarter of 19--. If reserves found are of a poor grade, DBM should discontinue further development of these mines.

- Allocate 25% of operating expenses to exploration in 19-- to help the company locate other potentially profitable mining sites.

- Implement the use of flotation mining in the first quarter of 19-- to reduce present open-pit mining costs.

FIGURE 4.17

Portion of DBM Mining & Technology Corporation's 19-- strategic planning report.

items in the recommendations subsection have evolved from the conclusions, which, in turn, were derived from the research by the members of the strategic planning team. In contrast to informational and examinational reports, this report presents concrete, action-oriented items to senior-level management for review, ratification, and corporate decision making.

Operational Reports

Operational reports focus primarily on the daily, weekly, or monthly operation of the business, industrial, or governmental enterprise. These reports are concerned with the nuts-and-bolts, routine, and administrative aspects of the organization's operation—or, as one writer has put it, the "pulse" of the enterprise. Within the broad category of operational reports are many differing report types: formal and informal; brief and full-length; special (one time only), periodic, and progress; and procedures and performance. We illustrated many of these report types within other categories discussed earlier in this chapter. For example, we reviewed the purposes and aims of periodic and progress reports in our section of that title (see Figures 4.9 and 4.10, as well as our discussion of those report types). We also reviewed procedures reports, their aims and purposes, in the section Reports Classified by Subject Matter, Content, or Activity (see Figure 4.11 and our discussion of the procedures report).

Operational reports address various subjects and areas of organizational concern; this kind of report frequently addresses—that is, discusses, delineates, and formalizes—organizational practices, policies, procedures, performance (individual, unit or departmental, divisional), conditions, and codes. Operational reports, therefore, aid in fulfilling various managerial duties and responsibilities, including, according to one management specialist, those that might surface in the following broad areas: (a) organizing, (b) designing, (c) controlling, and (d) planning.[1] The major aims or purposes of operational reports can be subdivided as follows:

1. To convey data and/or information only
2. To present, examine, and interpret data and information without drawing conclusions or making specific recommendations
3. To identify problems and/or solutions via an extensive analysis and interpretation of data and information accompanied by conclusions and action-oriented recommendations

Specifically, report writers might generate operational reports that address the following subjects or areas of organizational need:

1. Establishing product standards
2. Planning phases of production

[1]See Ricky W. Griffin, *Management*, 2nd ed. (Boston: Houghton Mifflin, 1987), pages 611–637. His discussion (in Chapter 20) of the operations management function—the managerial processes involved in planning, organizing, and controlling operations—might prove particularly instructive for new managers to review while reading our discussion of the aims and functions of operational reports.

3. Determining inspection practices and procedures
4. Sequencing production-control procedures
5. Constructing purchasing policies
6. Identifying performance appraisal standards
7. Assigning staff members to decisional teams or quality circles
8. Delineating sales (manufacturing, personnel, R&D) budgets
9. Designing methods of expense distribution
10. Designing methods of resource allocation
11. Organizing advertising and sales promotions
12. Classifying costs
13. Preparing divisional operating budgets
14. Designing inventory-recording procedures
15. Constructing codes of ethics
16. Developing in-house communication policies

A portion of a typical operational report is exhibited in Figure 4.18. The report, provided by the American Management Association, concerns procedures and policies for the "Disposition of Tangible Capital Assets" of a large U.S. multifacility manufacturing company and was generated by managers within the purchasing department.

Formal Proposals and Feasibility Studies

Formal proposals and feasibility studies are managerial documents closely related in structure and purpose to analytical reports, discussed earlier in this section. In fact, as problem-solution documents, both the formal proposal and the feasibility study might best be considered first cousins of the analytical report. Like the analytical report, the purpose of these documents is to *persuade* readers, based on research support and data analysis, of a recommended policy, program, organizational strategy, solution, method, new direction, or product line. Often, though, these problem-solution documents offer a set of recommendations that can be implemented only after additional research has been conducted. One writer has labeled formal proposals and feasibility studies as "advocacy documents."[2] Perhaps a more apt, no-frills name for these sorts of problem-solving reports would be *sales* documents because selling—ideas, solutions, methods, directions, or products—is their explicit aim.

According to James VanOosting, a **formal proposal** sometimes "represents an unsolicited recommendation" for some kind of change (1983, p. 250). Of course, at other times, a formal proposal is generated in response to an advertised call or request for proposals (RFP) from either private (corporate) or public (governmental) sources.

---

[2]See James VanOosting, *The Business Report: Writer, Reader, and Text* (Englewood Cliffs, NJ: Prentice-Hall, 1983), pages 250–252. VanOosting argues that proposals and other kinds of problem-solving reports "are linked by their common aim: to *advocate* [italics added] an idea. They manifest themselves by similar structures of logical intercourse..." (p. 250).

GENERAL PROCEDURE	COVERAGE **Company-wide**	NO: **FIN-9**

	DATE:	PAGE: **1 of 5**
DISPOSITION OF TANGIBLE CAPITAL ASSETS (SURPLUS AND OBSOLETE EQUIPMENT)	APPROVED:	REPLACES
	ORIGINATING AREA: **Purchasing**	

I. PURPOSE AND SCOPE

General Policy FIN-9 assigns approval authority for the Disposition of Tangible Capital Assets. When the disposition of equipment has been authorized, it is the responsibility of the Vice President, Purchasing, to direct the actual disposition. This procedure has been prepared to inform all concerned of their responsibilities and the actions to be taken to effect equipment dispositions.

II. JOB TITLES

Since this is a corporate-wide procedure, the job titles used will not necessarily be appropriate for all locations. Therefore, to implement this procedure, each organziational element is reponsible for modifying the titles used as may be necesssary to reflect local assignment of responsibilities.

III. RESPONSIBILITIES

A. The department head in charge of the equipment is responsible for informing the Plant Engineer that he/she has surplus equipment within his/her department.

B. The Plant Engineer is responsible for determining whether or not the equipment can be used by another department within the plant.

C. The Purchasing Agent is reponsible for disposing of the equipment in the best interest of the Company; advising all other manufacturing locations within the Company of the surplus equipment as it becomes available; reviewing the items with the Plant Manager to seek his/her recommendations and to furnish Corporate Purchasing Headquarters with two copies of the items on an "as available basis"; checking current lists of surplus and obsolete equipment prior to ordering new equipment to ensure that purchases of new equipment are not made when another plant may have the same equipment as surplus.

FIGURE 4.18
Portion of operational report—policies and procedures for "Distribution of Tangible Capital Assets."

IV. PROCEDURE

A. Declaring Surplus Equipment

1. Using department head:

   a. Notifies the Plant Engineer, who determines if the equipment can be used within the plant by any other department.

   (1) If it can be used internally, the requesting department head is responsible for advising the present using department head of the need, and is responsible for having it transferred.

   (2) If it can be used internally, the Plant Engineer advises the using department head who proceeds as follows in 1.b through 1.d. inclusive.

   b. Tags the item with a surplus equipment tag. (This can be made from plain tags but should have the words "SURPLUS EQUIPMENT" written in bold letters. It should state: "Do not move or use without approval of _____.")

   c. Inspects the equipment to obtain:

       (1) Name plate data
       (2) Manufacturer and description of equipment
       (3) Lists of accessories
       (4) Design changes from standard
       (5) List of missing parts
       (6) Operating condition
       (7) Estimate of repair cost
       (8) Estimate of weight
       (9) Estimate of cost to load for shipment
       (10) Estimate of current scrap value
       (11) Location
       (12) Asset and/or equipment or fleet numbers
       (13) Motor data

   d. Notifies the Purchasing Agent by submitting the above information on *Form FC-1225, Disposition Request - Tangible Capital Assets,* that the equipment is surplus, is of no use to any department within the plant, and is available for disposition . . . .

FIGURE 4.18
Continued

As with other kinds of reports we have discussed, the audience(s) for formal proposals—composed of potentially neutral, interested, or even hostile readers—will dictate the structure of the individual document. We discuss the organization and arrangement of long, formal reports in full in Chapter 14.

Reports, it should be stressed here, can be arranged either deductively or inductively. A report writer's decision to use either of these organizational patterns must always be based on an analysis of the following variables:

1. The aim(s) or purpose(s) of the document
2. The subject matter under discussion
3. The organizational audience or individual readers and their needs
4. The occasion for the production (and dissemination) of the report (e.g., a response to an RFP)

A **deductively** arranged report first identifies the report's purpose or the problem studied and then, anticipating an interested readership or favorable response from readers to ideas and solutions, offers conclusions/ recommendations up front, immediately following introductory material.

Business, managerial, and governmental report writers routinely structure their proposals **inductively**. The proposal writer's "case," or argument, is built from the general to the specific; the writer introduces the problem or purpose and gradually presents information and the analysis of data *before* presenting conclusions and/or recommendations. Typically, formal proposals mirror the format of inductively arranged analytical reports and are composed of the following broad sections:

- **Transmittal memo** or **letter**—introducing, summarizing, and/or abstracting the project proposal
- **Formal introduction**—involving
     a statement of the problem to be solved or proposal purpose statement
     a statement of project needs and proposed project scope
- **Body** or **text**—presenting
     information, facts, method
     data analysis and discussion
     proposed solution(s) and implementation
- **Conclusions/recommendations**—summarizing
     reemphasis of project's needs
     future research, future direction(s)
     findings, advantages, recommendations
- **References** and **appendixes**

Figure 4.19 presents a portion of the introductory section of a formal proposal for conducting research on the use of psychoactive drugs by medical students and physicians.

In industries where consultant organizations regularly generate proposals for submission to clients, proposals might be produced as form documents on which factual details, information, and data are simply filled in according to the specifications of the proposed project. A portion of a standard proposal generated by an engineering consulting firm for geotechnical engineering services is shown in Figure 4.20.

INTRODUCTION

Subject and Purpose

In order to arrive at a clear picture of the extent of drug dependency among future physicians and those currently practicing in the profession, a comprehensive statistical analysis of drug abuse among medical students and physicians is considered essential. The Committee on Physician Impairment, in conjunction with the Harvard School of Public Health, proposes to undertake a survey of drug use in a cross-section of physicians and medical students in Massachusetts.

Need

With the recent concern over misuse of psychoactive drugs among medical professionals, all 50 states have developed impaired-physicians programs. In addition, the American Medical Association sponsors conferences addressing this problem. Without a statistical analysis of physicians' and medical students' drug use, the success of such programs will be difficult, if not impossible, to evaluate. Data on drug-use will serve as a basis for measuring the progress of these programs.

Scope

The proposed research will focus on four general areas: (1) the frequency of drug use among medical students and physicians; (2) the recency of drug use by these groups; (3) the kinds of drugs used; and (4) the purpose of use. The purpose of use includes instrumental (to perform better or longer in sports, work, or study), recreational, and self-treating. The survey will cover the following drug categories: marijuana, cocaine, hallucinogens, stimulants, sedatives, analgesics, tranquilizers, and opiates. As a means of comparison, drug use among pharmacists and pharmacy students also will be investigated.

In addition to drug use, general information, such as the practice, specialty, the availability of drugs, and the extent of drug education, will be surveyed.

Data Sources

A questionnaire will be sent to 500 physicians, 504 medical students, 510 pharmacists, and 470 pharmacy students randomly chosen from professional societies and professional schools in Massachusetts. The sample sizes are based on the percentage of each group in the state, relative to the number of physicians surveyed.

Qualifications of Personnel

The University of Texas Health Science Center at Houston Committee on Physician Impairment was one of the first programs of its kind in the country. The Committee comprises 8 members who have spent most of their careers studying the causes and effects of drug abuse. Three are physicians with specialties in psychiatry. . . .

FIGURE 4.19

Portion of introductory section—proposal for epidemiologic research on the use of psychoactive drugs by medical students and physicians.

PROPOSAL NO. _____

TO: _____
_____
_____

Attn: _____   **Date:** _____

Dear _____ :

In response to your recent request, we are pleased to submit this proposal to provide Geotechnical Engineering Services to you in connection with the above captioned project. A description of the Basic Geotechnical Engineering Services is presented on an attachment. The new facilities to be considered in this investigation will be constructed on a tract of land located _____ _____. Facilities proposed include _____ _____. The new structure will create _____ _____ loads to be carried by the foundation system and preliminary plans provide for the floor system to be designed as slabs-on-fill or at grade.

The broad objectives of our investigation will be to determine soil conditions at the site and to develop information to guide design and construction of safe and economical foundations for the building. To investigate soil conditions at the site, we propose a minimum of _____ borings to be drilled _____. On the basis of geologic evidence, the structure configuration and the performance of existing buildings in the locale, we anticipate that the borings will extend to maximum depths of about _____. Samples will be taken using conventional Shelby tube, split-spoon sampling, and rock coring techniques. Representative portions of all samples obtained will be sealed and packaged for transportation to our laboratory.

Upon completion of the field phase of the investigation, a testing program will be designed to define the strength and volume change characteristics of the foundation soils. Supplementary tests, such as water content and plasticity tests, will be performed to extend the usefulness of the primary test data. The cost estimate given subsequently includes an appropriate allowance for this testing program.

The results of the field and laboratory phases of the investigation will be analyzed by our staff of engineers and geologists. The results of these analyses, together with the supporting field and laboratory data, will be presented in an engineering report of the investigation. Included therein will be specific recommendations to guide foundation design and

Figure 4.20

Portion of standard form/fill-in proposal—Raba-Kistner Consultants, Inc.

Proposal No.
Page 2

construction together with an evaluation of the swell potential of the near surface soils. . . .

Our fee for the study outlined herein will be determined on the basis of the unit charges given on the enclosed fee schedule. With a boring and testing program, as outlined above, we estimate that the total cost of the investigation will be in the order of $ _____. This estimate is not applicable after _____ and does not include costs incurred to provide access to sites which are inaccessible to our truck-mounted drill rigs and support vehicles. . . .

We appreciate the opportunity of submitting this proposal and look forward to working with you in the development of this project. Please return one signed copy of this proposal to provide authorization for our firm to commence work on the services outlined herein. . . .

Very truly yours,

RABA-KISTNER CONSULTANTS, INC.

Herbert F. Emmett, Jr., P.E.
Vice-President/Managing Engineer

HFE:amt
Copies submitted: Above (2)
Attachments: Fee Schedule
                       Basic Foundation Engineering Services
                       Data Sheet

Approved By: _____;

Date: _____.

FIGURE 4.20
Continued

A **feasibility study** is a document developed and written either from within or external to an organization in response to a perceived organizational need or problem. Generally, organizational needs or problems resulting in feasibility studies are identified by senior-level managers (e.g., a VP for finance or manufacturing) or by in-house technical experts (e.g., a senior systems analyst or a chief corporate economist). The feasibility study itself might be written in either of the following ways: (a) in-house by an individual manager, a team of management-level researchers and writers, or an internal consultant or team of such consultants or (b) externally by a paid consultant or consultant group.

While feasibility studies generally resemble analytical reports in structure, featuring the same or similar divisions and subdivisions, many of these reports display industry-specific formats and, in large measure, reflect the nature of the individual organizations (engineering, R&D, manufacturing) that produce them. Feasibility studies vary considerably, then, in structure and format, length and complexity, use of visuals, numbers of references, and depth of data (or design) analysis. In some industries, companies generate feasibility studies structured as brief memo-reports; in other industries, companies produce feasibility studies akin to long, formal analytical reports replete with the following divisions and subdivisions:

- Cover memo (or letter) of transmittal
- Abstract or executive summary
- Table of contents
- List of exhibits (figures, illustrations)
- Introduction (project overview)
      problem or purpose statement
      broad goals, objectives of study
      scope of project, scope of services
      limitations
- Body or text
      background information or relevant research
      conditions (regarding the investigation)
      data (statistical) analysis, design analysis, field and/or laboratory results
      summary, conclusions/recommendations
- References and appendixes (graphs, illustrations, lists, forms, correspondence)

Figure 4.21 shows the first page of the text portion (body) of a feasibility study conducted by an engineering firm, Raba-Kistner Consultants, Inc. The full-length Raba-Kistner, Inc., feasibility report includes the following: (a) cover letter of transmittal, (b) introduction, (c) scope of services, (d) limitations, (e) results of both field and laboratory investigations, (f) engineering design analyses, (g) recommendations, (h) construction guidelines, and (i) appendixes (consisting of project-related illustrations).

INTRODUCTION

Raba-Kistner Consultants, Inc., has completed the authorized sub-surface exploration for the proposed plant expansion to be constructed at the Texaco Houston Plant. This report briefly describes the procedures used during this study and presents the findings along with our evaluation of the data and recommendations for site preparation and foundation design.

SCOPE OF OUR SERVICES

The broad objectives of this feasibility study were the following:

1. To evaluate the engineering characteristics of the soil stratigraphy present at the site by an adequate number of soil borings and laboratory tests.

2. To formulate recommendations for the design of foundations to support the proposed structures and construction guidelines.

LIMITATIONS

The analyses and recommendations submitted in this report are based on the data obtained from six (6) soil borings drilled at this site. This report may not reflect the exact variations of the soil conditions across this site. The nature and extent of variations across the site may not become evident until construction commences. If variations then appear evident, it will be necessary to reevaluate our recommendations after performing on-site tests and observations to establish the engineering significance of any variations.

FIELD INVESTIGATION

Soil Borings

Soil conditions at the site were explored by six (6) borings at the locations shown on the Plan of Borings, Plate 1, in the Illustrations Section of this report. The boring locations were determined by tape and right angle measurements from existing street intersections, buildings, other structures, or property corners. The locations of the borings should be considered accurate only to the degree implied by the method used. The borings were drilled to depths of 40-ft. below existing grade. The field . . .

FIGURE 4.21
First page of text portion—feasibility study, Raba-Kistner Consultants, Inc.

Annual, Quarterly, and Interim Reports

A few years ago, John A. Byrne, a financial journalist writing in *Business Week*, characterized annual reports as "Corporate America's spring missive to share-holders . . . [revealing] a mix of self-promotion, mind-numbing statistics, and an occasional management confession" (1986, p. 40). To a large extent, we agree with Byrne's assessment of the contents of corporate annual reports. Annual reports are often excessively long-winded, unabashed public relations (PR) documents filled with what we call "rhetorical smoke" and "statistical mirrors" (Hager & Scheiber, 1990, pp. 113–130). They are sometimes less than honest, sometimes confusing, but always informative because of their covert as well as their actual content.

Annual reports are the formal financial statements produced and issued by publicly owned corporations throughout the world. These documents attempt to project a positive corporate image, financial well-being, and the overall "position" of the corporation at the close of business for a given year. Annual reports are team efforts, researched, written, and constructed collaboratively; they are based on data and information collected from other corporate reports (e.g., informational, analytical, progress, periodic). Rich in financial data and related information, annual reports include such items as sales projections, new product lines, expansion trends, and personnel profiles.

Annual reports contain corporate news, often presented via colorful photos of management, board members, and employees, as well as charts, graphs, tables, and lists displaying data on sales, earnings, capital expenditures, and solvency-related ratios.[3] Targeted at a variety of professional and lay audiences—stockholders, potential investors, financial analysts, mutual fund managers, journalists—these corporate documents are read with varying degrees of sophistication, comprehension, and care.

While the organization and general content of annual reports are fairly uniform. Certain sections included in annual reports are mandated by the Securities and Exchange Commission (SEC). All reports must include at least the following components:

1. Consolidated financial statements
2. An independent accountant's report
3. A "notes" component, specifying accounting procedures used and offering additional financial disclosures.

While the SEC does not specifically require a management's discussion and analysis component, it does closely monitor that report component for management's views on three areas of the corporation's business: results of operations, capital resources, and liquidity. The SEC does, however, require that

---

[3]For a glossary of business, investing, and related terms useful to inexperienced readers of annual reports, see Venita VanCaspel, *Money Dynamics for the 1990s* (Simon & Schuster, 1988), pages 515–532.

corporations address all data and information—favorable or unfavorable—that have affected, and may continue to influence, those three areas to prevent possible abuse by management of stockholder investments.

Although some corporations have issued shorter versions of the traditional annual report, the short summary report—which discloses some SEC-mandated and basic financial data—has not caught on. Most reports, though, adhere to some minor alteration of the following organization:

- Financial highlights
- Letter to shareholders
- Review of operations
- Financial statements
    - Report of independent accountants (auditors)
    - Consolidated financial statements
    - Statement of changes in financial condition
    - Notes to financial statements
    - Supplementary tables
    - Management's discussion and analysis
- Investor's information
- Directors and officers of corporation

While the organization of different annual reports might be similar to that modeled here, the treatment of the data and information contained in these corporate reports—the style and tone in which they are written and the format and visuals through which information is conveyed—varies greatly from one report to another.[4]

Sections from the Applied Magnetics Corporation 1987 Annual Report appear in Figure 4.22. Included are the following report components: letter to shareholders, management's discussion and analysis, consolidated balance sheets (assets and liabilities), portion of notes to consolidated financial statements, and auditors' report.

In addition to annual reports, corporations produce and distribute **quarterly** or **interim** reports. Quarterly and interim reports are considerably less glossy, less rich in the breadth of corporate news, and less expansive in the coverage of financial data and information reported than their big corporate siblings. Yet, these brief corporate reports have a very specific function; they alert readers to quarterly and interim changes in and/or results of decisions,

---

[4]*FW/Financial World* magazine honors annual reports every year with awards for financial writing and reporting, graphics, design and typography, and photography. *FW's* Gold Award goes to the one report (nearly 1,000, for example, were submitted in the 1991 competition) "that best combines informative financial statements with clear writing, careful organization, compelling graphics and effective design." *FW's* Gold Award winner for 1991 was ARCO. The Equitable received *FW's* Louis Guenther Award for best financial writing and reporting. For additional information and 1991 winners in other categories, see "The 51st Annual Report Competition Winners," *FW/Financial World* (November 12, 1991), pages 62–72.

Applied Magnetics Corporation and Subsidiaries
Comparative Highlights

(in thousands, except employment and per share amounts)	1987	1986	1985	1984	1983
Operations:					
Net sales	$211,940	$128,119	$120,751	$145,938	$101,591
Income from continuing operations before extraordinary item	$ 14,219	$ 4,103	$ 1,037	$ 779	$ 6,710
Net income	$ 15,544	$ 5,487	$ 3,087	$ 1,091	$ 6,907
Income per common and common equivalent share (Note A):					
Income from continuing operations before extraordinary item	$ .98	$ .31	$ .08	$ .06	$ .54
Net income	$ 1.07	$ .41	$ .24	$ .08	$ .55
Weighted average common and common equivalent shares outstanding (Note A)	14,495	13,498	12,991	13,372	12,508
Order backlog	$ 88,264	$ 43,311	$ 36,843	$ 59,075	$ 77,615
Year-end employment	6,940	4,067	3,898	4,487	3,936
Balance Sheet:					
Current assets	$110,243	$ 66,477	$ 66,825	$ 70,773	$ 80,095
Current liabilities	$ 29,024	$ 20,394	$ 21,509	$ 26,243	$ 22,505
Working capital	$ 81,219	$ 46,083	$ 45,316	$ 44,530	$ 57,590
Current ratio	3.8:1	3.3:1	3.1:1	2.7:1	3.6:1
Total assets	$195,578	$127,186	$125,400	$125,916	$119,988
Total debt	$ 4,959	$ 1,515	$ 11,593	$ 14,112	$ 3,475
Shareholders' investment	$150,413	$ 99,874	$ 92,714	$ 89,021	$ 91,388
Shareholders' investment, per share (Note A)	$10.31	$ 7.89	$ 7.35	$ 7.06	$ 7.36

Note A: All share and per share data have been adjusted to reflect the two-for-one stock split distributed on December 3, 1987.

Company Profile

Applied Magnetics was founded in Goleta, California, in 1957. The Company designs, manufactures, and markets magnetic heads used in disk and tape drives. Its products are sold primarily to original equipment manufacturers (OEM's) in the peripheral data storage segment of the computer industry. Applied Magnetics currently has 15 facilities in 7 countries and employs over 6500 persons worldwide. Company sales offices are strategically located throughout the world. The Company has been publicly owned since 1967 and its shares were listed on the New York Stock Exchange in 1971 (symbol APM).

Applied Magnetics is recognized and respected for the excellent quality of its products and its leadership in magnetic head technology. It is the world's largest independent manufacturer of magnetic heads for the computer industry.

30th
Anniversary 1957-1987
Applied Magnetics

1

FIGURE 4.22

Sections from Applied Magnetics Corporation 1987 annual report.

1987 Product Mix

Revenue From Continuing Operations
$ in millions

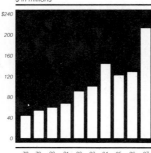

Fiscal 1987 was our thirtieth anniversary year, and it was the best year ever in Company history. Record sales of $211,940,000 were 65% higher than last year and net income of $15,544,000, or $1.07 per share, reflected an increase of 183% over 1986. These record results did not occur easily. Many employees around the world worked long hours during the year.

This substantial increase in sales was due to three major factors: first, the demand for magnetic disk and tape heads increased; second, sales reflected the acquisitions of Brumko and Nortronics; and, third, we gained an additional share of the market. Backlog of open orders at year end totaled $88,264,000, more than double last year's figure of $43,311,000.

In our *rigid-disk head business,* customer requirements increased at a faster rate for head/carriage

Our thirtieth anniversary year was the best year ever in Company history.

subassemblies, sometimes referred to as E-blocks, as compared to basic slider/flexure assemblies. These subassemblies require higher levels of engineering and production expertise for which Applied Magnetics is respected throughout the industry.

Demand continued strong for *monolithic technology disk heads,* with sales this year totaling over $100 million. New developments, such as metal-in-gap construction, hold promise to extend the performance of monolithic heads and assure their market life for several more years.

In *composite technology disk heads,* demand exceeded production capacity. Capacity is being increased, and next year we expect to more than double this year's sales. Applied Magnetics became fully integrated in 1987 in the manufacture of composite heads.

During the year, we developed and produced a wide variety of *thin-film technology disk heads* for use in 3.5-inch to 14-inch diameter drives. Production rates are now at an annualized total of 1.3 million heads with plans to increase this to over 4 million by mid-1988.

In the *tape head segment* of our business, heads for cartridge tape drives dominated the product mix with shipment levels exceeding 10,000 heads per week during the year. The acquisition of Nortronics allowed us to provide dual source support to a number of key customers, and, in addition, has given Nortronics access to the worldwide marketplace.

Pilot production of 3480-compatible, 18-track thin-film tape heads continued at increasing rates through the year. Full production status is planned for the second quarter of fiscal 1988.

After many years of heavy investment in *thin-film technology,* a very important goal was reached during the year. Net operating losses, resulting from research, development, and engineering, coupled with high production costs peaked in the fourth quarter of fiscal 1986 and have decreased each successive quarter as sales of thin-film heads increased dramatically and costs per unit were reduced. This is an extremely important fact for the

An important goal was reached this year. Net operating losses on thin-film heads decreased each quarter as sales increased dramatically.

Company inasmuch as operating losses on this program have been significant over the past few years.

I anticipate that sales of thin-film heads will increase three- to four-fold next year, and that net operating losses will be reduced by three to five million dollars, reaching a break-even point during 1988. I feel that after this period of heavy investment we now have the technology, production know-how, and facilities to be a major supplier of thin-film disk and tape heads.

Our *repair and refurbishment of rigid-disk and cartridge tape drives*

2

FIGURE 4.22
Continued

is continuing to grow. We have now established separate wholly-owned subsidiaries under a parent company, *Applied Peripherals Technology*, in Belgium, the United States, Singapore, and the United Kingdom. I believe that this portion of our business will be one of the fastest growing segments over the next few years.

Because of the recent significant overall devaluation in the stock market, the coming year is more difficult to forecast than usual. Before this worldwide devaluation, we had forecasted Company growth of approximately 20% to 25%. I believe that even if we should not achieve

Our financial position is extremely sound.

this increase in sales, we could continue to show profit improvement as increased sales of thin-film heads dramatically reduce net operating losses and as we reach that program's break-even point. Regardless, we are well equipped to move quickly in any direction to accommodate our customers' changing requirements.

In addition, our financial position is extremely sound with current assets of $110,243,000, including cash of $32,331,000, and long-term debt amounting to $3,605,000. Current ratio is 3.8:1, and inventory turns are at an exceptionally good rate of 6.9.

Thanks so very much to our employees and vendors who worked long and hard to make this outstanding year happen. Also, thanks to our customers who on occasion suffered when it was impossible to meet all delivery requirements; and to our shareholders who certainly have been on a roller coaster ride with stock prices going from one extreme to another.

A special thanks goes to Harold R. Frank, Chairman and Founder of the Company, to whom we dedicate this thirtieth year annual report.

Ben J. Newitt

Ben J. Newitt
Vice Chairman and Chief Executive Officer

Left to right: O.M. Fundingsland, Executive Vice President, Sales and Marketing;
G.P. Sprague, Jr., Executive Vice President and Treasurer; Ben J. Newitt, Vice Chairman and
Chief Executive Officer; and William R. Anderson, President.

On the occasion of our thirtieth anniversary, it is appropriate to share with you our Company goals. It is important to remind ourselves of these goals as we are continually running very fast to meet our day-to-day commitments.

FIGURE 4.22

Continued

Management's Discussion and Analysis
of Financial Condition and Results of Operations

The Company's operations consist primarily of Applied Magnetics Corporation and its subsidiaries which design, manufacture and market magnetic recording heads.

Results of Operations

1987 COMPARED TO 1986:
Net sales increased 65.4% from 1986 to 1987. The increase was primarily due to increased disk head sales (monolithic, composite and thin film product lines) and sales by Nortronics Company, Inc. (Nortronics), acquired in December 1986. The increase in net sales resulted in the gross profit percentage increasing from 27.8% to 29.5% in 1987. This improvement would have been greater except for the impact on gross profit caused by costs incurred in the production ramp up of the thin film and composite product lines.

Income from operations increased $14.5 million over 1986 to $17.4 million. The increase was primarily due to higher net sales and gross profit and a reduction in operating expenses as a percent of sales from 25.5% to 21.3%. Engineering, research and development expenses increased $2.5 million in 1987 over 1986 reflecting additional engineering expenditures required to support production volume increases. Selling, general and administrative expenses increased from 1986 primarily as a result of operating costs associated with the increased sales volume. Other expense of $454,000 in 1987 compares with other income of $1.1 million in 1986, primarily reflecting the effect between years of translating yen denominated net assets into dollars. Interest expense increased in 1987 due to funding a portion of the production ramp up with short-term debt and interest associated with mortgage debt assumed in the Nortronics acquisition. The increase in interest income in 1987 over 1986 reflects the investment of the proceeds from the sale of 850,000 shares of common stock in May, 1987.

The effective tax rate in 1987 was 21.6% compared to 15.6% in 1986. The increase between years reflects the tax effect of profitable domestic operations in 1987 being only partially offset by income generated in tax beneficial jurisdictions. Extraordinary items were recorded in 1987 and 1986 relating to the utilization of domestic net operating loss carryforwards in 1987 and the carryback of domestic net operating losses and tax credits in 1986. The Company does not expect that the Tax Reform Act of 1986 will have a significant impact on its results of operations.

1986 COMPARED TO 1985:
Net sales in 1986 increased 6.1% from 1985 primarily due to the acquisition of Brumko Magnetics Corporation in January, 1986 and increased disk head sales. The gross profit percentage increased from 26.8% to 27.8% in 1986 due to continuing operating efficiencies and cost reduction efforts. Engineering, research and development expenses increased $909,000 reflecting the continued investment in thin film recording technology. Selling, general and administrative expenses as a percent of net sales were 12.3% for both 1986 and 1985. Interest expense decreased significantly in 1986 due to the payment of substantially all outstanding debt in December, 1985. Interest income decreased slightly in 1986 from 1985 due to a decline in interest rates earned on cash investments. The decrease in the effective tax rate in 1986 was due to income generated in tax beneficial jurisdictions. The extraordinary items recognized in 1985 and 1986 related to the carryback of domestic net operating losses and tax credits to prior years.

Liquidity and Capital Resources

In May 1987, the Company sold 850,000 shares of common stock in a public offering generating net proceeds of $31.3 million. A portion of the proceeds from the stock sale were used to repay short-term debt, with the balance available to fund capital expenditures and working capital requirements. Excluding the proceeds from the stock sale, working capital increased $3.8

million from 1986 to 1987. The increase is primarily attributable to funds provided from operations of $34.0 million and proceeds from stock options exercised of $3.0 million which were partially offset by funds utilized in the acquisition of the net long-term assets of Nortronics of $8.0 million and the acquisition of plant and equipment of $25.7 million. The components of working capital reflect, in general, the effects of funding increased sales and production levels and the acquisition of Nortronics.

At September 30, 1987, total debt amounted to $5.0 million, substantially all of which was attributable to the Nortronics acquisition. In addition, the Company had a $6.5 million line of credit and a $15.0 million revolving credit agreement available, neither of which were utilized at year end.

Capital expenditures in 1987 amounted to $25.7 million. The expenditures related primarily to plant, machinery and equipment required to meet increasing production levels. Major 1987 additions included the acquisition and construction of new facilities in Singapore and Korea and expansion of existing facilities and manufacturing capacities in Korea and Goleta, California. Capital expenditures in 1988 are estimated to be similar to those incurred in 1987.

It is anticipated that cash on hand and internally generated cash flow should be adequate to meet the Company's operating cash requirements in 1988.

4

FIGURE 4.22
Continued

90

Applied Magnetics Corporation and Subsidiaries
Consolidated Balance Sheets
September 30,

ASSETS	1987	1986
Current Assets:		
Cash and equivalents ($30,198,000 in 1987 and $12,124,000 in 1986)	$ 32,331,000	$ 13,946,000
Accounts receivable, less allowances of $1,200,000 in 1987 and $818,000 in 1986	42,865,000	24,946,000
Inventories, at lower of cost (first-in, first-out) or market	27,531,000	19,687,000
Prepaid expenses and other	5,197,000	5,846,000
Deferred income taxes (Notes 1 and 3)	2,319,000	2,052,000
	110,243,000	66,477,000
Property, Plant and Equipment, at cost (Notes 1, 3, 5 and 7):		
Land	4,914,000	4,107,000
Buildings	35,236,000	28,911,000
Manufacturing equipment	59,694,000	43,502,000
Other equipment and leasehold improvements	12,779,000	9,191,000
Construction in process	9,672,000	3,623,000
	122,295,000	89,334,000
Less—Accumulated depreciation and amortization	(40,133,000)	(31,360,000)
	82,162,000	57,974,000
Other Assets	3,173,000	2,735,000
	$ 195,578,000	$ 127,186,000

LIABILITIES AND SHAREHOLDERS' INVESTMENT	1987	1986
Current Liabilities:		
Current portion of long-term debt	$ 1,354,000	$ 775,000
Accounts payable	11,965,000	8,438,000
Accrued payroll and related liabilities	8,981,000	5,497,000
Income taxes (Notes 1 and 3)	2,812,000	3,216,000
Other current liabilities	3,912,000	2,468,000
	29,024,000	20,394,000
Long-term Debt, less current portion (Note 5)	3,605,000	740,000
Other Liabilities (Note 1)	12,536,000	6,178,000
Commitments (Note 2)		
Shareholders' Investment (Notes 1, 3, 4 and 8):		
Common stock, $.10 par value, authorized 20,000,000 shares, issued 14,594,800 shares in 1987 and 6,326,906 shares in 1986	1,459,000	633,000
Paid-in surplus	92,818,000	59,347,000
Retained earnings	55,117,000	39,573,000
	149,394,000	99,553,000
Cumulative translation adjustment	1,019,000	321,000
	150,413,000	99,874,000
	$ 195,578,000	$ 127,186,000

The accompanying Notes to Consolidated Financial Statements are an integral part of these balance sheets.

6

FIGURE 4.22
Continued

Applied Magnetics Corporation and Subsidiaries
Notes to Consolidated Financial Statements

1. Summary of Significant Accounting Policies

Principles of Consolidation: The consolidated financial statements include the accounts of Applied Magnetics Corporation and its subsidiaries (the "Company"). All significant intercompany accounts and transactions have been eliminated. Certain 1986 and 1985 accounts have been reclassified to conform with 1987 presentation.

Translation of Foreign Currencies: Financial statements and transactions of subsidiaries operating in foreign countries are translated into U.S. dollars in accordance with Statement of Financial Accounting Standards No. 52. The effects of exchange rate fluctuations on translating assets and liabilities stated in foreign currency into U.S. dollars for foreign subsidiaries whose functional currency is the local currency are included as part of the "Cumulative Translation Adjustment" component of Shareholders' Investment. For foreign subsidiaries whose functional currency is the U.S. dollar, the effect of translating assets and liabilities stated in foreign currency is included as a component of Other Income (Expense) in the Consolidated Statements of Income. Translation and transaction losses of $616,000 were charged to income in 1987, and translation and transaction gains of $1,052,000 and $603,000 were credited to income in 1986 and 1985, respectively.

Depreciation and Amortization Policies: Plant, equipment and intangible assets are depreciated or amortized over their estimated useful lives primarily using the straight-line method, except for certain production assets with a net book value of $5,288,000 at September 30, 1987, which are being depreciated on a modified units of production method to more closely match depreciation with estimated consumption. Estimated useful lives are as follows:

Buildings	15-40 Years
Manufacturing equipment	3-10 Years
Other equipment	2-10 Years
Leasehold improvements	Term of Lease
Manufacturing processes, included in other assets	10 Years

Depreciation and amortization expense amounted to $11,829,000, $8,723,000 and $6,022,000 in 1987, 1986 and 1985, respectively.

The Company follows the policy of capitalizing expenditures that materially increase asset lives. Maintenance and minor replacements are charged to income when incurred. Maintenance and repair expenses charged to operations were $2,640,000, $2,208,000 and $1,801,000 in 1987, 1986 and 1985, respectively. When assets are sold or otherwise disposed of, the cost and related accumulated depreciation or amortization are removed from the accounts, and any resulting gain or loss is included in income.

The cost of buildings and equipment includes interest expense incurred prior to the time such assets are placed in service. Interest expense of $133,000 was capitalized in 1985. No interest was capitalized in 1987 or 1986.

Income per Common and Common Equivalent Share: Income per common and common equivalent share is calculated using the treasury stock method. See Note 8.

Stock Dividends and Repurchases: The Company charges retained earnings for the market value at the declaration date of stock issued, and cash paid in lieu of fractional shares, in connection with stock dividends. Retained earnings are also charged for the amount paid in excess of par value on stock repurchases. Cumulative charges to retained earnings for stock dividends and repurchases amounted to $29,003,000 at September 30, 1987.

Engineering, Research and Development Costs: The Company is actively engaged in basic technology and applied research and development programs which are designed to develop new products and product applications. The costs of these programs are charged to operations as incurred. Substantial ongoing product and process improvement engineering and support programs relating to existing products are conducted within production engineering departments. These latter costs are also classified as engineering, research and development expenses.

Other Liabilities: Other liabilities are primarily composed of the noncurrent portion of accrued expenses related to various employee compensation plans.

Income Taxes: The provision for income taxes includes deferred income taxes which result from timing differences in the recognition of revenues and expenses between financial accounting and income tax reporting. Investment tax credits are recorded on the flow-through method. See Note 3.

Stock Options: Proceeds from the sale of common stock issued upon the exercise of stock options are credited to common stock and paid-in surplus accounts at the time the option is exercised. Income tax benefits attributable to stock options exercised are credited to paid-in surplus. See Note 4.

2. Lease Commitments

A portion of the Company's facilities and equipment are leased. These non-cancellable operating leases provide for aggregate future rentals, net of minimum rentals on non-cancellable subleases, of $6,733,000 payable as follows: 1988—$1,898,000, 1989—$1,962,000, 1990—$1,400,000, 1991—$1,085,000, 1992—$86,000 and thereafter—$302,000.

Total rental expense, net of sublease rental income, for the years ended September 30, 1987, 1986 and 1985, including items on a month-to-month basis, was approximately $1,724,000, $1,214,000 and $1,078,000, respectively. Rentals were principally for facilities and data processing equipment.

9

Figure 4.22

Continued

Applied Magnetics Corporation and Subsidiaries
Notes to Consolidated Financial Statements

7. Acquisitions

On December 22, 1986, the Company acquired all of the outstanding stock of Nortronics Company, Inc. ("Nortronics") for $6,800,000 in cash and notes. Concurrent with the acquisition, the Company repaid approximately $2.4 million of Nortronics' outstanding debt. Nortronics is engaged primarily in the manufacture and sale of magnetic tape heads used in computer tape drives, card and check readers, money changers, aircraft recorders and industrial analog audio devices. The transaction was accounted for as a purchase, and the results of operations have been consolidated with those of the Company from the date of acquisition. The purchase price has been assigned to the net assets acquired based on the fair value of such assets and liabilities at the date of acquisition.

The following unaudited pro forma combined results of operations for the years ended September 30, 1987 and 1986 give approximate effect to the acquisiton of Nortronics as if it had occurred at October 1, 1985:

	Pro Forma (Unaudited) For the Years Ended September 30,	
	1987	1986
Net sales	$ 215,338,000	$ 142,380,000
Income before extraordinary item	$ 13,651,000	$ 3,514,000
Net income	$ 14,976,000	$ 4,898,000
Income per common and common equivalent share	$ 1.03	$ .36

In January, 1986, the Company acquired all of the outstanding stock of Brumko Magnetics Corporation ("Brumko") for $2,600,000. Brumko is engaged primarily in the business of refurbishing and repairing magnetic recording disk heads for the computer industry. The transaction was accounted for as a purchase, and the results of operations have been consolidated with those of the Company from the date of acquisition.

8. Subsequent Event

On October 12, 1987, the Company's Board of Directors authorized a two-for-one split of the common stock effected in the form of a 100% percent stock dividend distributed on December 3, 1987, to holders of record on November 2, 1987. Accordingly, retroactive effect has been given to the stock split in the Shareholders' Investment accounts as of September 30, 1987, and in all share and per share data included in the accompanying financial statements.

Auditors' Report

To the Board of Directors and Shareholders of
Applied Magnetics Corporation:

We have examined the consolidated balance sheets of Applied Magnetics Corporation (a Delaware corporation) and subsidiaries as of September 30, 1987 and 1986 and the related consolidated statements of income, shareholders' investment and changes in financial position for each of the three years in the period ended September 30, 1987. Our examinations were made in accordance with generally accepted auditing standards and, accordingly, included such tests of the accounting records and such other auditing procedures as we considered necessary in the circumstances.

In our opinion, the financial statements referred to above present fairly the financial position of Applied Magnetics Corporation and subsidiaries as of September 30, 1987 and 1986 and the results of their operations and the changes in their financial position for each of the three years in the period ended September 30, 1987, in conformity with generally accepted accounting principles applied on a consistent basis.

Arthur Andersen & Co.

Los Angeles, California,
November 9, 1987.

12

FIGURE 4.22

Continued

accomplishments, projections, new products, quarterly earnings, and interim goals. They might justify, for example, short-term stock and bond price fluctuations for a corporation's shareholders or for other market watchers. Figure 4.23 shows Nike, Inc.'s Interim Report of February 28, 1989. As can easily be seen, the document is brief, easy to follow, straightforward, and clear; the state of the entire company for the identified period can be absorbed at a glance by an educated reader.

Summary

A broad spectrum of managerial reports are written, circulated, and read in contemporary business, industrial, and governmental organizations. These managerial reports can take the form of brief memos and letters that provide information to readers or result in action. Reports can also take the form of rather long documents detailing corporate policies or procedures or analyzing data and information. In any case, report size, structure, and content depend on the purposes of the document, the situation out of which it grew, and the uses to which it will be put by readers.

Managerial reports can be divided into many broad categories and classified in a number of ways based on what they contain, why they were written, whom they have been written for, and which key elements they share. While report categories overlap and interrelate, reports can be classified according to these variables: internal versus external readers; formats (e.g., brief memo-reports versus multipage reports); degree of formality; time frame or business interval; subject matter, content, or activity; and function.

Letter-reports (for external consumption) and **memo-reports** (for internal use) might prove quite similar in content, structure, or purpose—that is, in all respects other than audience. Letter- and memo-reports might both, for example, call for action, identify priorities, or clarify procedures. Report format, though, is also dictated by degree of **formality** inherent in the communication situation. Long (multipage) reports are generally formal, highly structured, comprehensive documents. Short reports (within the one- to five-page range) are often less formal, less comprehensive in scope and content, and less rigid in structure.

We can also classify reports according to the **time frame** or **business interval** during which they were written or are due. According to this classification, managerial reports might be **routine** or **nonroutine**, **regular** or **special**, **periodic** or **progress**. Depending on their purpose, routine and regular reports will appear at expected business intervals or on specific calendar dates. Special reports, on the other hand, respond to specific organizational needs and are written on request. Periodic and progress reports might be written with weekly, monthly, quarterly, or annual deadlines in mind.

NIKE, INC. CONSOLIDATED STATEMENT OF INCOME

	Three months ended		Nine months ended	
	Feb. 28, 1989	Feb. 29, 1988	Feb. 28, 1989	Feb. 29, 1988
	(In thousands; except per share data)			
Revenues	$464,663	$331,787	$1,297,382	$ 849,023
Costs and expenses:				
Cost of sales	292,924	225,390	823,185	576,281
Selling and administrative	87,946	60,801	250,438	168,301
Interest	3,970	2,017	10,834	6,051
Other income	(5)	(1,420)	(1,964)	(21,237)
	384,835	286,788	1,082,493	729,396
Income before income taxes	79,828	44,999	214,889	119,627
Income taxes	31,000	17,400	84,300	48,400
Net income	$ 48,828	$ 27,599	$ 130,589	$ 71,227
Net income per common share	$ 1.30	$ .74	$ 3.48	$ 1.89
Average number of common and common equivalent shares	37,580	37,152	37,546	37,751

CONSOLIDATED BALANCE SHEET

Assets

	Feb. 28, 1989	Feb. 29, 1988
	(In thousands)	
Current Assets:		
Cash and equivalents	$ 77,228	$ 67,617
Accounts receivable	370,669	284,013
Inventories	206,301	151,455
Deferred income taxes	10,033	13,292
Prepaid expenses	16,003	11,162
Total current assets	680,234	527,539
Property, plant and equipment	135,874	104,949
Less accumulated depreciation	62,465	54,652
	73,409	50,297
Goodwill	82,575	2,875
Other assets	14,218	14,061
	$850,436	$594,772

Liabilities and Shareholders' Equity

	Feb. 28, 1989	Feb. 29, 1988
	(In thousands)	
Current Liabilities:		
Current portion of long-term debt	$ 1,844	$ 1,543
Notes payable	122,284	61,570
Accounts payable	56,023	38,337
Accrued liabilities	66,001	47,551
Income taxes payable	26,849	18,980
Total current liabilities	273,001	167,981
Long-term debt	34,504	34,057
Non-current deferred income taxes and purchased tax benefits	14,614	13,841
Redeemable Preferred Stock	300	300
Shareholders' equity	528,017	378,593
	$850,436	$594,772

TO OUR SHAREHOLDERS:

I am very pleased to report NIKE's third quarter earnings of $1.30 per share—NIKE's strongest third quarter ever and the second best quarter in our history.

It has been two years since we delivered the first group of NIKE-AIR® footwear products to the market. Those products and the products that followed have allowed NIKE to be the first brand in the industry to regain the number one U.S. market share position after losing it to a competitor. Now the real work begins.

I am quite pleased with our futures orders scheduled for delivery from March through July. One year ago we experienced our largest bookings ever for that time period. This year we have improved on that by 13 percent in dollars and have an opportunity to increase the gross margin earned on those sales. In addition, futures orders do not include bookings for domestic apparel or international products and we believe both of these areas could grow faster than domestic footwear over the next six to twelve months.

Future earnings growth will not come as rapidly or dramatically as it has over the past two years. Competiton within this industry is very intense, and yet NIKE has never been in a better position to capitalize on the many growth opportunities ahead. From the "collections" strategy in our sport categories to Cole Haan and our new brands for women, "i.e." and "SIDE 1," our focus remains firmly on improving profitability through continued product innovation, sound inventory management, creative marketing and superior customer service.

Philip H. Knight
Chairman

MANAGEMENT DISCUSSION AND ANALYSIS:

Net income for the three and nine months ended February 28, 1989 was $48.8 and $130.6 million, compared to $27.6 and $71.2 million in the prior year periods. Revenues increased 40% and 53% over the prior year periods. Domestic footwear revenues increased 45% for the quarter with growth coming in all major product categories. Domestic apparel revenues grew 50% during the quarter and foreign revenues increased 17%.

Consolidated gross margin improved to 37.0% for the quarter compared to 32.1% in last year's third quarter. The increase is a result of effective inventory management, strong demand for products in all categories and a greater proportion of higher margin products in the sales mix.

For the quarter, selling and administrative expenses were 18.9% of revenues compared to 18.3% a year ago. Through nine months, selling and administrative expenses were 19.3% of revenues compared to 19.8% last year.

FIGURE 4.23

Nike, Inc. interim report, February 28, 1989.

Managerial reports can also be classified by the **subject matter, content**, or **activity** with which the writer has dealt in the document. Every business organization regularly produces and distributes reports aimed at broad subject areas such as labor, accounting, productivity, or sales. Equally common are reports involving more specific content—value/cost analysis, evaluation of defective unit output, or the five-year strategic plan for manufacturing. Activity reports might focus on such areas as vendor contacts, sales activities, or inventory control visitations.

Management report writers also produce reports of a hybrid nature such as **bulletins** and **announcements**. These documents are used by organizations to acquaint broad, general audiences with recent decisions, schedule changes, new plans, or new directions. Often these hybrid documents communicate timely and important information to large audiences within (and sometimes outside of) an organization.

Finally, reports can be classified by their **function** within organizations. Reports in this group are often among the longest and most comprehensive with which we are concerned. The most important, most widely written, and most frequently used report types within this category are **informational, examinational, analytical**, and **operational** reports; the **formal proposal**; the **feasibility study**; and the **corporate annual (quarterly, interim)** report. The function of these reports, and the uses to which they are put, are varied. Teams of report writers might, for example: (a) present information to senior-level management for review; (b) analyze data and information and make recommendations; (c) present and discuss aspects of corporate operations; (d) propose a new method, strategy, or product; (e) solve an organizational or client-based problem through a formal study; or (f) construct a complete financial package depicting a corporation's yearly "health" for a wide variety of readers.

Related Reading

Bethel, Lawrence L., Franklin S. Atwater, George H. E. Smith, and Harvey A. Stackman, Jr. *Industrial Organization and Management.* New York: McGraw, 1945.

Blumberg. Rhoda Lois. *Organizations in Contemporary Society.* Englewood Cliffs, NJ: Prentice, 1987.

Byrne, John A. "Annual Reports: The Good, the Bad, and the Ridiculous." *Business Week* 7 April 1986: 40.

"The 51st Annual Report Competition Winners." *FW/Financial World* 12 November 1991: 62–72.

Forman, Janis, and Patricia Katsky. "The Group Report: A Problem in Small Group or Writing Processes?" *Journal of Business Communication* 23 (1986): 23–35.

Gallagher, William J. *Report Writing for Management.* Reading, MA: Addison, 1987.

Griffin, Ricky W. *Management.* 2nd ed. Boston: Houghton, 1987.

HAGER, PETER, and H. J. SCHEIBER. "Reading Smoke and Mirrors: The Rhetoric of Corporate Annual Reports." *Journal of Technical Writing and Communication* 20 (1990): 113–130.

LILLICO, MICHAEL. *Managerial Communication.* Oxford, UK: Pergamon, 1972.

MERRILL LYNCH, PIERCE, FENNER & SMITH, INC. *How to Read a Financial Report.* 6th ed. N.p.: Merrill Lynch, 1990.

THOMSETT, MICHAEL C. *The Little Black Book of Business Reports.* AMACOM/American Mgmt. Assn., 1988.

VANCASPEL, VENITA. *Money Dynamics for the 1990s.* New York: Simon, 1988.

VANOOSTING, JAMES. *The Business Report: Writing, Reader, and Text.* Englewood Cliffs, NJ: Prentice, 1983.

VARDAMAN, GEORGE T., and PATRICIA BLACK VARDAMAN. *Communication in Modern Organizations.* Malabar, FL: Krieger, 1982.

WEISS, W. H. *Decision Making for First-Time Managers.* New York: AMACOM/American Mgmt. Assn., 1985.

PART II

Effective Report Writing: Process, Style, and Composing Issues

CHAPTER 5

The Management Report-Writing Process

Having examined the functions and objectives of management report writers, their readers, and their organizational audiences, and having classified a wide range of managerial reports, we now want to focus on the **process** of report writing. We believe that managers should approach the task of report writing as a process or, more accurately, as a series of interrelated processes.

A Note on Process Theory

According to James Britton, a noted researcher and theorist on composing, and his co-workers, the basic processes that comprise writing of any kind are the following:

- **Conception**—the events that lead up to the writer's decision to write (whether the decision is the writer's own or that of a supervisor or senior-level executive). Conception, for Britton, is actually a prewriting stage of the larger process. At this stage, prior to production, writers crystallize their ideas, activate long-term memory, and mentally prepare for the report-writing task.

- **Incubation**—the period of planning a document that involves the writer's concentration on additional prewriting strategies, such as how to (a) package important data, (b) arrange and organize information logically, and (c) clarify the writing task further.

- **Production**—the point at which writers put pen to paper or fingers to computer keys and begin drafting a document. Britton and his associates consider production the "point of utterance," that part of the process during which we begin to shape our ideas on paper (or computer screen). Here, report writers continue to organize data and information and refine the writing task. During the production stage, writers proceed to discover what they want and need to say through writing (Britton et al., 1978, pp. 19–32).

While Britton's conception of the writing process might seem somewhat abstract and idealized, his thinking has been central in identifying writing as a nonlinear, recursive process. According to this process-oriented model, stages in the process will be repeated over and over again by writers as they move between prewriting, drafting, revising, and editing activities. Conception and incubation processes, Britton and his co-workers argue, will take place simultaneously; they do not end when the writer begins writing because "the redefining, the planning and sorting are still going on" (1978, p. 26).

For example, during the production stage of the process, report writers might return to a preliminary stage to further clarify or even redefine their basic task. Report writers might interrupt the production of a current draft of their document—consciously or not—to do more planning, organizing, or data arranging. During the production stage of the process, report writers will continue to clarify, incubate, and package their ideas. Even during later—second or third—drafts of a document, report writers might continue to redefine the report-writing task and reevaluate their approach to completing it. In fact, we have found the description by Britton and his associates of the writing process to be extremely useful in developing our own process model, which we now offer to managerial report writers.

Six Steps to Effective Report Writing

Report writers in today's organizations should think of the construction of their documents as an open, recursive, and collaborative process. The report-writing process will involve movement forward and backward between and among (a) a variety of subprocesses such as planning, drafting, revising, and editing and (b) people such as peers, supervisors, and senior-level executives. Naturally, the report-writing process will result in a draft or succession of drafts; the draft(s) will be revised further; and an end product, the report, will emerge after numerous drafts and revisions of a management writer's original text.

Because writing is a process of discovery and learning, management report writers often learn a great deal (more) about the ideas and subjects of their reports through planning, drafting, revising, and editing their original rough texts. Indeed, the process of report writing, according to Roger Garrison, is the "act of pulling together, of making pieces of information coherent, of presenting examples that illuminate the information" (1985, p. 122). Writing—the act of composing, constructing, revising—will be the manager's chief method of finding what Garrison calls the "relatedness" of apparently unrelated data and information. Ultimately, the process of writing reveals—frequently to a large organizational audience—to what extent managers truly know their subjects and how much they still might need to learn or comprehend.

The management report writer's central task, though, is to produce well-organized, well-paragraphed, logically ordered, and carefully structured documents that best facilitate organizational decision making. The report writer's immediate task is to shape and mold successive drafts of documents in order "to come as close to your [the writer's] intentions as possible" (Garrison, 1985, p. 15).[1] The report writer's long-range goal, however, must be to provide others—for example, senior-level managers, VPs, technical personnel, internal and external consultants—with the data and information, analysis, and input necessary to arrive at effective individual, group, departmental, or organizational decisions that can be implemented successfully.

Although the writing process, as we have seen it in Britton and his co-workers' description, is actually complex, cyclical, and idiosyncratic, we believe that management report writers will profit if the various elements of the process can be broken down into do-able steps. As the central mission of their writing process, management report writers must learn to restructure their initial *writer*-centered drafts—often poorly organized, poorly paragraphed, and unclear—into solid, finely tuned *reader*-centered communications. Moreover, because report writers, as we suggested in Chapter 3, must communicate with both individual readers and a mixture of business audiences at various organizational levels, they must regularly produce reader-centered documents that can be read ("processed") quickly and efficiently.

We believe that the managerial report-writing process can most effectively be broken down into the following six major units or steps (summarized in Figure 5.1):

1. Forecasting the document and seeing it whole
>   Identifying your purpose and desired results
>   Identifying and delimiting your audience
>   Identifying reader needs and priorities
>   Forecasting or predicting the document's format and overall design

2. Incubating, planning, speculating, and list making
>   Clarifying your writing task for yourself and your co-writers, partners, and collaborators
>   Brainstorming, activating long- and short-term memory
>   Speculating and jotting down preliminary ideas
>   Making lists of essential information "bits"
>   Planning data collection and planning the document's organization

3. Assembling and pulling together data and information
>   Identifying facts and information you will need
>   Conducting a library search for secondary research materials
>   Collecting data (through surveys and interviews) and reviewing primary data
>   Analyzing and synthesizing data and information

---

[1] See Garrison, 1985, Chapter 4—"Revision: 'Seeing Again' "—for Garrison's very practical examination of *rewriting* as "the key to good writing."

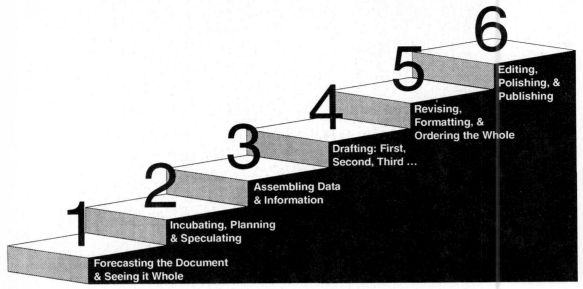

FIGURE 5.1
Six steps to effective report writing—the process.

4. Drafting the document—first, second, third, and additional drafts

Plunging in, writing at a point that attracts (not necessarily at the beginning)

Generating multiple drafts

Suspending criticism and standards of "correctness" during initial draft(s)

Sharing drafts with colleagues; **peer review** during various drafting stages of the process

5. Revising, formatting, and ordering the whole document

Sharing drafts during additional peer review(s) of structure, format, design of document

Arranging and moving portions of your text during late drafting stages

Rewriting drafts for multiple (hierarchical) or different audiences

Reordering and reformatting your document

Waiting for objectivity, taking a break, eliciting a final critique from a peer

6. Editing, polishing, and publishing the document

Checking your document for conciseness, clarity, readability, and appropriate emphases and structure

Redrafting where necessary

Proofreading with a peer

Printing, word-processing, or publishing (via desktop software programs) your report

Operationalizing the Process _____

Much of what we present in these six steps to effective report writing is elaborated in chapters throughout this book, each one devoted specifically to a major aspect of the report-writing process. Our main emphasis here, though, is introducing the overall process and its elements—that is, the six major steps and the subordinate or functional steps in the larger process. Equally important, we want to operationalize the report-writing process; we want to acquaint management report writers with what they must do on a daily basis to improve their report-writing skills and to internalize our six-step process. Management report writers must

- Practice the steps in this recursive process—that is, drafting, revising, arranging, redrafting—as they write for
    individual readers and organizational audiences.
    various informational, analytical, and decisional purposes.
- Demonstrate their knowledge of the writing process by writing (i.e., planning, drafting, revising, arranging, editing documents) on a daily basis as most managers must.
- Review regularly the documents of others (subordinates, peers, superiors) and intervene whenever possible in the report construction process of others—as editors and peer reviewers—in a **collaborative** effort aimed at
    strengthening research, writing, revising, and editing skills.
    becoming more authoritative as professional/technical report readers and peer reviewers.
    evaluating document effectiveness (based, for example, on attention to audience needs and report purposes).
    increasing the number and frequency of successful managerial reports in their departments; hence, increasing productivity in the organization.

The Collaborative Report-Writing Model _____

In present-day business, industry, and government, very few report writers work in isolation. Just about all managerial writing tasks and activities, especially those central to the organizational decision-making process, are group-oriented and collaborative in nature. That is, although the manager of a human resources (HR) department might have the chief responsibility for producing a report, other professionals working closely with the HR manager might share responsibilities for planning, brainstorming, researching, analyzing data, drafting, and revising the document or for polishing and preparing the document for dissemination within (or outside of) the organization.

In Chapter 3, we noted that management reports (e.g., The Delta Organization's report, entitled "Is Ergonomics Worth the Investment?") are frequently circulated to and read by a wide variety of readers at many organizational levels. Those readers include senior-level executives (VPs), midlevel managers, technical managers, project leaders, technical experts, corporate attorneys, and other members of the organization's professional or supervisory community. Similarly, during the report construction period, a number of individuals are frequently involved.

To produce Delta's report on ergonomics, for example, the HR manager might (a) supervise the project; (b) guide the development of the document and move it toward completion; and, possibly, (c) publish the finished report and disseminate it to various organizational audiences. Nevertheless, numerous additional professional and technical staff members within (or outside of) the HR manager's own department might play major roles in the construction of the document, functioning as members of a temporary, formal, or ad hoc report-writing team throughout the major stages of the writing process. The HR staff and other professionals outside the manager's home department—for example, technical writers, researchers, data analysts, statisticians, industrial psychologists, human factors engineers, financial analysts, and corporate attorneys—all might make important contributions at different stages of the process, providing

- Input, information, ideas
- Preliminary or speculative comments
- Methods of data collection
- Data interpretation
- Drafts of report sections
- Major revisions
- Editorial feedback
- Graphics preparation

Collaborative, team-oriented activity is common and particularly useful during the preparation period for constructing long, complex, multidimensional informational or analytical reports, quarterly or interim reports, proposals, or feasibility studies. Collaborative activities might include: devising work plans, schedules, or time lines; meeting to assign (or reassign) staff or team responsibilities; meeting to clarify tasks and brainstorm; collecting and interpreting data; conducting interviews or library-based research; drafting, revising, peer editing, and reformatting; finalizing and polishing reports for publication and dissemination; and orally presenting report findings (conclusions and recommendations) to senior-level management.

Evaluating the Product Along the Way

During the various stages of the report-writing process, members of formal collaborative writing teams or informal writing groups would do well to read through, and share responses to, questions like those that follow:

1. *Who will be using our report?* To what degree will an individual reader or organizational audience rely on the data and information presented to make a decision?

2. *What types of managerial decisions will be made* from the data and information presented and analyzed in our report?

3. *What degree of detail should we present?* Should our report simply review or summarize key ideas, data, or information items? Or should key ideas, appropriate background material, and analysis be presented? What amount of background material would be appropriate and useful for individual readers and organizational audiences? Which readers or audiences might need greater detail? Which might need less?

4. *What might be the best way to display our data?* Which graphic aids or comparative visuals might enhance or complement our textual material? What relationships between or among sets of data might prove useful to exhibit?

5. *How much time should a reader (e.g., a manager, a VP) spend reading our report?* Should key ideas and major recommendations be readily grasped in just a matter of minutes? Or will readers take (and be willing to devote) a considerable amount of time to read through the report in full?

6. *Should report data and information be presented in order of importance?* Should the most important data and information be presented up front? Should less important information be presented throughout the report in descending order of importance?

7. *If our report will be a decisional document, should we present our recommendations concisely on a separate cover page or attachment such as an executive summary?* Should all supporting report material follow the cover page and be attached? If so, exactly how? In a bound format? In a binder? Clipped or stapled together? On a diskette?

8. *Is our report designed specifically to meet the needs of organizational decision makers as well as the needs of the business occasion?* How can we tell? What changes might we make to ensure that the report meets the needs of decision makers?

9. *As far as we can tell, is the report clear? Accurate? Readable? Useful? Timely?* Can the report, by itself, be relied on for organizational decision making, support, analysis? How can we be sure?

During revising and editing stages of the writing process, we recommend that report writers, that is, members of report-writing teams, share drafts of report sections (or drafts of entire reports) with peer editors to elicit suggestions and input on a wide range of content and stylistic issues. During the report construction period, corporate peer editors, wherever they might be located, can aid managers in further shaping their documents. Corporate peer editors might help managers revise, restyle, restructure, reformat, even rethink their documents in draft form.

Such writer/editor collaboration might involve professionals from very different fields or corporate enterprises. A human resources manager, for example, functioning as chief report writer for a given project, might elicit editorial feedback from a systems analyst or a human factors engineer. Senior managers (or even VPs) in finance, corporate affairs, data processing, operations, research and development (R&D)—all might, at times, give (or receive) editorial feedback to (or from) members of collaborative report-writing teams just about anywhere in the organization.

Using Report Worksheets with Corporate Peer Editors

Corporate peer editors who receive preliminary drafts—working copy—of a managerial writer's or team's report might want to systematize the editorial process. Through the use of **report worksheets**, editors can focus on specific aspects (say, organization or readability) or issues (for example, readers/audiences or style) surrounding a document. Packages of editorial materials for use in corporate peer review and evaluation might contain (a) a draft(s) of the report itself or a section of the report (first draft, second, or third) and (b) an editorial report worksheet (see Figures 5.2 and 5.3).

Members of report-writing teams might use **self-evaluation** report worksheets before final editing, polishing, and preparing the report for production to determine for themselves how effective their document seems to be. A sample self-evaluation worksheet appears in Figure 5.4.

REPORT WORKSHEET—EARLY DRAFT

(Space allotment for peer editor's written response has been eliminated here.)

1. On the document itself, put a question mark in the margin next to anything that confuses you—along with a brief note about what is confusing.

2. Comment on the **organization** of this document. Does the report draft follow basic principles of organization and arrangement, such as most important information first? Is information presented in accessible chunks? If not, what changes would you suggest?

3. Comment on the **coherence** and **unity** of this document. Does it hold together well? Do any sections seem out of place? Are **transitions** from section to section successfully accomplished? Are **headings** and **subheadings** now included? If yes, are they effectively used and helpful to potential readers? What changes would you suggest?

4. Identify this document's major **strength** at this point in the report writing process.

5. What **recommendation(s)** would you make to improve this document for future drafts?

FIGURE 5.2
Sample peer editorial worksheet for early report drafts.

REPORT WORKSHEET—LATER DRAFT

1. Comment on the **readability** of this document at this point in the report writing process. Refer to style, word choice, sentence structure, sentence length. Suggest any changes that might improve clarity and conciseness.

2. Identify the **purpose(s)** and overall **message** of this report. Has the report's message been appropriately presented and adequately supported with relevant data and information? If not, what changes can you suggest to the writer(s) to make the document more effective?

3. Has the report been designed for a specific audience, following the most appropriate plan for that **audience**—direct or indirect? If not, explain what, in your opinion, seems to have gone wrong.

4. Does the report seem to be **functional** for the designated audience(s) and the writer's purpose(s)? If not, explain to the writer how to revise the report draft so that it becomes much more functional and audience–centered.

5. Does the writer represent her/himself as a credible professional, using an appropriate format, standard business English, an appropriate tone ("voice"), and (if pertinent) by creating goodwill for her/his organization?

FIGURE 5.3

Sample peer editorial worksheet for later report drafts.

Of course, corporate peer editorial worksheets might contain a wide variety of emphases on many aspects of writing and the report construction process. These materials might focus, for example, on

questions of writer/reader relationships and organizational audiences—for example, multiple readers, hierarchical audiences.

report organization—arrangement, logical order of presentation.

Is the information presented in order of importance to the primary reader(s) of the document?
Will secondary readers easily find what they need?

clarity of language, paragraph unity, and overall report coherence.

style—sentence length and variety, diction, appropriateness of words for the business situation, rhetorical context, and organizational audience(s).

clarity and complexity of technical diagrams, charts, tables, and figures.

Gradually, as the drafting/editing portion of the report-writing process becomes more natural and more important to individual writers and writing

---

SELF-EVALUATION WORKSHEET

1.   Identify the **primary** reader(s) or organizational audience for this report. How does the report draft fulfill her/his or their needs specifically?

2.   Identify the **secondary** reader(s) or organizational audience for this report. How does the report draft fulfill her/his or their needs specifically?

3.   List the different sections (and sub-sections) of this report draft. Have you clearly identified each **section** in your report text so that data and information will be **accessible?** How might you arrange your next report draft to ensure that data and information will be easily accessible to all readers?

4.   Comment on the **style** of your report. Are words and sentences appropriate for your reader(s), organizational audience(s), and purpose(s)? How, specifically?

5.   Identify what you (and members of your writing team) like **best** about this report draft.

6.   What possible **weakness** might your report draft still suffer from? How might you correct or improve this in subsequent drafts?

FIGURE 5.4
Sample self-evaluation worksheet for report drafts.

teams, and as the texts of managerial documents become increasingly specialized, management report writers will want to develop their own peer editing materials for use with colleagues. These more personalized peer editorial worksheets will enable managers to elicit, and editors to focus on, the kind and depth of editorial feedback desired for any particular report or report section.

In addition, as members of management report-writing teams continually draft, revise, restructure, and reformat their documents, they will refine their own editorial skills until they can effectively—to their own satisfaction—assess, critique, and edit the documents they generate. Managers will develop important rhetorical skills by using peer review materials tailored to (a) their own (their group's, division's, organization's) needs or felt weaknesses and (b) the specific business occasions and purposes of the documents themselves.

Through the continued use of collaborative techniques, management report writers should gain confidence in both writing and editing spheres. As managers from all organizational areas take on more report-writing and editing responsibilities, constructing documents for diverse individual and multiple audiences and for different business occasions and purposes, their report-writing skills will develop significantly. Resulting organizational documents should become better organized, more carefully arranged, appropriately styled, clearer and more coherent, and, most important, reader-centered.

Revising versus Editing

During the drafting portion of the report-writing process, individual report writers and writing team members will participate in two subprocesses: revising and editing. **Revising** generally takes place during the initial drafting stages of the report-writing process—for example, after first, second, or, perhaps, third drafts of a document. Revising should be thought of as a developmental strategy or, according to Roger Garrison, an "exploratory" process (1985, p. 26). Revising occurs when a document remains tentative in organization, structure, and format and is still being planned and ordered. During revision, report writers will be rewriting and moving blocks of text (e.g., sentences, paragraphs, sections, "chunks" of prose); reorganizing portions of text; restructuring or rearranging an entire report or significant portions of report text; and rethinking or "revisioning" reader needs and priorities, data analysis and presentation, and overall report design.

Editing, on the other hand, is a more technical-mechanical process that usually occurs during the final stages of the drafting portion of the report-writing process. Editing involves "tinkering" with sentence lengths, variety, and rhythms. Editing can simply be regarded as the subprocess of polishing a document—eliminating surface errors (misspellings, typographical errors, basic punctuation problems); considering and evaluating aspects of language and style ("weighing one word choice against another"); and correcting mistakes of every variety.

During initial drafting or large-scale revision, report writers should make every effort to suspend criticism, judgment, and standards of correctness; report writers should simply plunge in and write. Because editing is actually a process of correcting, editorial work should be engaged in only *after* the first few drafts of a report have been generated. Editing for clarity, conciseness, and proper emphases should always follow initial report construction. As Garrison has pointed out: "The habit of compulsive premature editing doesn't just make writing hard, it also makes writing dead" (1985, p. 26).

The Direct Writing Process

Once management report writers have negotiated a deadline for generating (and disseminating) a document, or whenever a deadline has been imposed from above by a corporate VP or senior-level manager, report writers would do well to follow what Peter Elbow has called the "**direct writing process**" (1981, pp. 26–31). Elbow suggests that the direct writing process can be very effective when the report writer doesn't have lots of time to produce a report but has a considerable amount of data and information to present.

The direct writing process is "a kind of let's-get-this-thing-over-with writing process" (Elbow, 1981, p. 26). The following is a summary of Peter Elbow's direct writing process as it might be used by management report writers working under a strict deadline:

1. Once you have negotiated your deadline, simply divide in half the total time available to you (and the members of your team).

   Allocate one-half of your time for drafting ("raw" writing).

   Use the other one-half of your time for revising, editing, and polishing your document.

2. Write down and include everything relevant to the completion of your document—and keep writing.

3. Consider your intended readers, the organizational audience, and the purpose of your document, but temporarily ignore those variables if consideration of them constrains your raw writing.

4. Try to keep yourself goal-oriented and on task; prevent yourself from digressing, repeating material, or getting lost; however, temporarily suspend judgment and self-criticism. Wherever possible, simply ignore

   the order and arrangement of what you have written.

   your style, language, and sentence structure (wording).

   your impulse to edit and proofread as you continue to draft your document.

5. Be certain to end the *drafting* (raw writing) portion of your process when you've used up one-half your allocated time. Switch to revising, even if your document remains unfinished.[2]

Remember: The direct writing process is most useful whenever you have a considerable amount of data and information to present, you can easily generate material, and you have negotiated a tight deadline for your document. We believe that management report writers will best profit from Elbow's direct writing process when they are writing in a hurry, know what they want to say, and aren't striving for "creativity or brilliance." In addition, Elbow notes that the direct writing process can "work well for very important pieces of writing" as well as those "where you haven't yet worked out your thinking at all" (1981, p. 30).

Publishing Your Document

Managers and members of collaborative writing teams must guide their documents through the final step in our six-step report writing process: production

---

[2]We have adapted these elements of the direct writing process from Peter Elbow's "Main Steps in the Direct Writing Process" (Elbow, 1981, pp. 30–31).

or **publication**. Generally, a management report writer or leader of a report-writing team will be responsible for report production. During this final step in the report-writing process, managers will supervise last-minute editing, polishing, and production details.

In some cases, of course—in small organizations or in rushed situations—managers or teams of report writers will actually construct an entire document themselves. Report writers then will conduct all background research, draft initial and final versions of the text, copyedit the document, produce all relevant graphic aids or visuals, and word-process or publish (via desktop software) the finished product.

Word-processing, printing, or publishing responsibilities for important managerial documents are typically delegated to technical departments or specialists. Annual reports, strategic plans, or substantial decision-oriented reports are frequently delegated to corporate "technical" communicators, copyeditors, public relations staff, graphic artists or designers, computer graphics experts, illustrators, typographers, or proofreaders.

When the production portion of the process involves technical specialists from other departments, the management report writer or lead team member will still possess complete responsibility for the finished document. Rightly or not, says James VanOosting, a management report writer may very well "be held *accountable* [italics added] for all production elements and, thus, must oversee their execution with the same attention to detail exercised during composition" (1983, p. 40). Individual managers and members of report-writing teams are routinely responsible for polishing and reviewing final versions of their documents and for ensuring that graphic aids or visuals (figures, tables, charts) are appropriately integrated within the text of the printed or word-processed document.

Remember that an effective management report communicates because of the total impact it has on readers. The quality of paper, suitability of print size and typeface, appropriateness of graphic aids, writing style, and precision in language all contribute to your report's overall presentation. Successful managerial report writers must consider a report's "total communication impact" (VanOosting, 1983, p. 40).

Summary

In Chapter 5 we presented an overview of the management report-writing process. We first offered a brief introduction to process theory based on a review of James Britton and his colleagues' conception of the writing process. They organize the writing process into three interrelated, nonlinear segments: **conception, incubation,** and **production**.

Following a brief overview of process theory, we then presented our six steps to effective report writing. Report writing should be an open, recursive, and collaborative process involving both forward and backward movement between and among (a) a variety of subprocesses (e.g., planning, drafting, revising, editing) and (b) people (such as peers, other managers, and senior executives). The six report-writing steps were identified in order to aid managers and members of report-writing teams to revise—reorganize, rethink, restructure—initial *writer*-centered drafts into polished, finely tuned *reader*-centered communications.

Our discussion of basic elements in the writing process turned next to our model of **collaborative** report writing. We reviewed how managers and report writers might function successfully within a group-oriented, collaborative writing environment. We also offered suggestions of ways that managers and other organizational specialists might function effectively as members of team writing projects.

The remainder of that section focused on specific team-oriented activities such as devising work plans and editing report text and on the effective editing of report drafts by corporate **peer editors** reviewing successive document drafts for organization, readability, or style. Indeed, collaborative report-writing activities are central to the organizational decision-making process.

Our next section emphasized key aspects of **revising** and **editing**. Although these two subprocesses are interrelated, they must be attended to separately during different steps in the report-writing process. Both revising and editing can best be done collaboratively, within the context of writing teams and by using corporate "editors" from a variety of departments and organizational areas.

Report writers who have negotiated (or imposed) strict deadlines would do well to consider using the **direct writing process**. Developed by Peter Elbow, this process can be extremely effective whenever the report writer does not have a large amount of time to produce a report but does have considerable data and information to include and present.

Finally, we discussed the **production** portion of the managerial report-writing process, reviewing word-processing, printing, and publishing responsibilities of individual managers and writing team members. Important, corporatewide documents (such as annual reports) are often produced with the help of various specialists housed in technical departments. However, managers and leaders of report-writing teams generally retain total responsibility for meeting deadlines and for finished corporate documents.

Related Reading

BELL, ARTHUR, and ROGER WYSE. *The One-Minute Business Writer.* Homewood, IL: Dow Jones-Irwin, 1987.

BRITTON, JAMES, et al. *The Development of Writing Abilities, 11–18.* London: Macmillan, 1978.

BRUFFEE, KENNETH A. *A Short Course in Writing: Practical Rhetoric for Teaching Composition through Collaborative Learning.* 3rd ed. Boston: Little, 1985.

Chicago Guide to Preparing Electronic Manuscripts: For Authors and Publishers. Chicago: U of Chicago P, 1987.

DIXIT, AVINASH, and BARRY NALEBUFF. *Thinking Strategically: The Competitive Edge in Business, Politics, and Everyday Life.* New York: Norton, 1991.

ELBOW, PETER. *Writing with Power: Techniques for Mastering the Writing Process.* New York: Oxford UP, 1981.

GARRISON, ROGER. *How a Writer Works.* Rev. ed. New York: Harper, 1985.

KAYE, SANFORD. *Writing under Pressure: The Quick Writing Process.* New York: Oxford UP, 1989.

KEYES, ELIZABETH. "Information Design: Maximizing the Power and Potential of Electronic Publishing Equipment." *IEEE Transactions on Professional Communication* PC-30 (1987): 32–37.

LANHAM, RICHARD A. *Revising Business Prose.* 3rd ed. New York: Macmillan, 1991.

LAUER, DAVID A. *Design Basics.* 3rd ed. New York: Holt, 1990.

PARKER, GLENN M. *Team Players and Teamwork: The New Competitive Business Strategy.* San Francisco: Jossey, 1990.

ROUNDY, NANCY. "A Program for Revision in Business and Technical Writing." *The Journal of Business Communication* 20 (1983): 55–66.

SCHEIBER, H. J. "From Prose Paladin to Peer Editor: Teaching Engineers (and Others) to Write and Communicate." *Journal of Technical Writing and Communication* 17 (1987): 385–395.

STRATTON, CHARLES R. "Collaborative Writing in the Workplace." *IEEE Transactions on Professional Communication* 32 (1989): 178–182.

TRIMBLE, JOHN R. *Writing with Style: Conversations on the Art of Writing.* Englewood Cliffs, NJ: Prentice, 1975.

VanOOSTING, JAMES. *The Business Report: Writing, Reader, and Text.* Englewood Cliffs, NJ: Prentice, 1983.

CHAPTER 6

Clear Report Writing: Language, Style, and Paragraph Management

Throughout this book, we've discussed the manager's position in the organizational hierarchy and in the decision-making process. We've emphasized the value of the manager's role as virtual center of the corporate report-writing and distribution function. We've also demonstrated that managerial reports (a) provide data, information, and recommendations to senior-level corporate managers and executives and (b) influence or result in decision-making activities that lead to corporatewide action.

Because the managerial report-writing function is so critical to the planning (short- and long-range) and operation (daily and overall) of contemporary organizations, managers must concern themselves, above all, with producing reports whose messages are delivered with clarity, conciseness, vivid language, and style. Morris Bogard, who has studied the middle manager's primary organizational purpose—to communicate needs and desires and to motivate activities in the service of efficient productivity—has summed up the need for effective managerial report-writing skills:

> Reports are the essence of most management communication systems because they furnish much of the information upon which decisions are made. Unfortunately, too many reports are poorly written, dull, and ponderous; some are unintelligible and confusing, and [more than a few] are vague and disordered to the point of being useless. (1979, p. 153)

Bogard goes on to say that good reports are difficult to write because report writers must have a deep-rooted knowledge of their subjects and readers, as well as "a strong sense of logical order, and a good command of the language used." Management report writers, he concludes, must write and revise their documents until they have defined their purposes and supported their arguments "with the most pertinent information arranged in the clearest, most logical form and directed to the idiosyncracies or particular demands of... [their] reader[s]" (1979, p. 153).

We agree completely with Morris Bogard's assessment of the contemporary manager's need for razor-sharp *micro* and *macro* report-writing skills. In this chapter, therefore, we will focus primarily on the sharpening of the manager's report-writing skills in three major domains:

1. *Language precision*—micro matters of clarity, simplicity, brevity, and conciseness
2. *Style*—micro matters of word choice (or diction), sentence variety and length, personal style
3. *Paragraph management*—macro matters of arrangement, development, organization.

Throughout the first three chapters of this book, we discussed the variables managerial report writers must consider in delimiting their relationship(s) with report readers. In Chapter 3, we focused on the needs and priorities of individual report readers and multiple audiences at varying levels and in various positions in the organizational hierarchy. We also examined the process of effective report writing in Chapter 5, placing primary emphasis on drafting and revising documents and presenting key steps toward effective managerial report writing.

Language Precision

Precision in the use of language must be a high priority for management and decision makers at all levels and at all times. Because a major portion of any manager's job is to communicate in writing with individual readers and wider audiences throughout and beyond the organization, managers must draft and distribute reports that are as clear and unambiguous as they can be—at all times. Indeed, for communication to occur at all, a writer's meaning(s) must be successfully conveyed. In business and elsewhere, successfully conveying one's meaning(s) is not always an easy matter; it is often hard work. In fact, successfully conveying one's meaning in writing often seems so difficult that, to paraphrase Rudolf Flesch, managers will frequently want to try anything else *but write* when they are faced with a job involving even relatively simple explanation (1962, p. 193).

As we have seen, though, managers must often generate documents that go far beyond simple explanation. Managers must communicate, often simultaneously, in different directions and to many readers: (a) upward to senior-level managers and corporate executives for the purposes of decision making and action; (b) horizontally to other managers and technical specialists for the purposes of informing, clarifying, collaborating, or responding; and (c) downward to staff and line supervisors and employees for the purposes of directing, documenting, or announcing. Management report writers must communicate their messages—composed of data, information, ideas, and recommendations—so effectively that the meanings they intend will be sewn into the fabric of their documents with such clarity, precision, and, where possible, simplicity that, as one specialist in this field has put it, they "cannot possibly be misunderstood" (Bates, 1985, p. xv).

An attitude toward precision in the language of managerial documents must be cultivated and refined to ensure and enhance successful communication. Matters of clarity, simplicity, brevity, and conciseness must not be taken lightly by managers who must regularly write and share reports. The management report writer, in fact, ought to personify Theodore M. Bernstein's concept of "the careful writer," a writer whose chief aim is the "clear expression" of logical thought in delivering his or her message to a reader (1980, p. vii).

Micro Matters of Clarity, Simplicity, Brevity, and Conciseness

Writing clearly and simply is not an easy matter. Producing successful managerial reports is always a matter of hard work, conscious effort, and desire. Some managers simply aren't willing to take the time or make the effort to communicate carefully in writing. Perhaps they don't recognize that carefully written, reader-centered documents pay off in the form of new accounts, favorable contracts, or individual raises. But most managers understand that they must communicate effectively to perform their jobs productively.

We've always thought that a good many managers could stand a serious dose of consciousness raising about the need for, and ingredients essential to, producing solid, purposeful professional documents. Before we introduce some of the essential ingredients for producing effective documents, however, we'd like to make it clear that, above all, managers must want to communicate. Managers must want to convey meaning(s) and successfully engage their readers; they must want to

share data and information with readers.

clarify or document their ideas for readers.

propose solutions to readers' problems.

present new strategies to readers.

explain a process, procedure, or method to readers.

persuade readers and sell a point of view.

move readers to action.

Without the desire to produce clear documents that others will actually want to read, a manager could not even begin to consider the essential ingredients, let alone absorb the process, with which to do so.

Clarity and Simplicity

Producing clear managerial documents means that report writers must make a conscious effort to use straightforward, unambiguous language. Words and phrases report writers use in their documents must not be cloudy, muddy, or vague; their meanings must be precise, easily understood, and not readily open to misinterpretation by confused readers. As one communication expert sums up this point, report writers should strive not to produce "crossword puzzles" and send needlessly complex, confusing documents on to their readers.

When a management report writer includes a sentence like the following in an important memo-report, most readers would respond in pretty much the same way—with a glazed look or blank stare:

EXAMPLE   To facilitate making determinations of priorities on our time for meeting technical assistance requests as well as having an orderly procedure for requesting technical assistance, usage of the attached form is being reinstituted.

Readers of sentences of this sort will justifiably be confused, put off, and, even more problematic, uncertain of what the writer wants them to *do*. The language used by this writer seems to be almost intentionally perplexing, repelling, and vague (although we know this writer wanted to be helpful).

Writers of this kind of prose simply do not concern themselves with what we call **micro** matters of document construction:

1. The words and phrases writers use at the sentence level—*within* sentences—to make meaning.
2. The way those words and phrases are chosen and arranged to promote or impede reader comprehension.

Matters of stylistic choice will be discussed later in our section on style. Here our focus will be on report writers' use of language at the sentence level to communicate their messages to readers.

To communicate their messages to individual readers and wider organizational audiences, managerial writers must be conscious of sentence-level, or micro, matters when they draft and revise their reports. Report writers must select words and phrases carefully so that the language promotes, rather than impedes or detracts from, their readers' ability to comprehend a document.

Unfortunately, many management report writers have taken Shepherd Mead's advice far too literally. In his classic satire, *How to Succeed in Business without Really Trying*, Mead warns potentially "successful" executives that

the memo, like the meeting, is concerned only incidentally with its apparent subject. The main object of the memo is to *impress the people who read it*. (1952, p. 60)

Nearly forty years later, management report writers continue to follow Mead's suspect imperative. They write to *impress* their readers—immediate supervisors, senior-level executives—when they should at all times write to *ex-*

INSTEAD OF	USE	INSTEAD OF	USE
1. gratify	please	26. encourage	urge
2. indicate	say	27. contribute	give
3. customary	usual	28. optimum	best
4. transmit	send	29. initial	first
5. preference	choice	30. modification	change
6. commence	begin	31. apparent	clear
7. superior	better	32. approximately	about
8. substantiate	support	33. detrimental	harmful
9. compensate	pay	34. explicit	clear
10. demonstrate	show	35. utilization	use
11. proficiency	skill	36. inflexible	rigid
12. function	job/duty	37. termination	end
13. document	record	38. inquire	ask
14. discontinue	stop	39. increase	grow
15. cognizant	know	40. capabilities	talents
16. apprehension	fear	41. opportunity	chance
17. jeopardize	risk	42. determine	decide
18. endeavor	try	43. subsequent	next
19. initiate	start	44. inaugurate	start
20. immediately	now	45. ultimate	final
21. anticipate	expect	46. selection	choice
22. facilitate	ease	47. influence	affect
23. assistance	help	48. habitual	usual
24. additional	extra	49. proceed	go
25. appropriate	take	50. contemplate	think

FIGURE 6.1

Big words to avoid.

press their thoughts and ideas as clearly as possible. In filling a document with incoherent sets of words and phrases such as

To facilitate making determinations of priorities on our time...

report writers are only trying to prove how much smarter, more current, in-the-know, or "educated" they are. Whenever a management report writer aims, consciously or otherwise, to impress a superior with a document, the document usually evolves into a set of awkward, confusing, or opaque sentences that, when strung together, result in communication failure.

Former editor-in-chief of the *Reader's Digest*, Edward T. Thompson, counsels writers to (a) use familiar, **first-degree words** and phrases and (b) avoid what he calls big, **second-** and **third-degree words**. Second- and third-degree words need to be "translated" before a reader can process or comprehend them. Whenever you have a choice, choose the more concrete word over the abstract one, the more precise word over the vague one. "First-degree words," according to Thompson, "are usually the most precise words" a writer can choose:

FIRST-DEGREE WORDS	SECOND- AND THIRD-DEGREE WORDS
face	visage, countenance
stay	abide, remain, reside
book	volume, tome, publication (1979, n.p.)

Figure 6.1 on p. 121 presents a much more extensive list of big words to avoid.

Naturally, report writers should not draft documents in insultingly low levels of language. Managers should not, for instance, routinely construct reports for audiences reading at eighth-grade levels or below simply to ensure ease of comprehension. That's not exactly what we mean. We believe, though, that business documents of all sorts will be read much more quickly, eagerly, and efficiently if complex messages are written in direct, simple, unambiguous language.

In the following examples we present two versions of the same memo-report. Example 1 contains a large number of second- and third-degree words (italicized) that inhibit efficient reader comprehension. Example 2, on the other hand, presents a briefer, clearer version of the same memo-report content. The revised latter version of the memorandum has been written in more direct, simpler language; many second- and third-degree words have been replaced with clearer, first-degree words (italicized) that ensure efficient comprehension and promote successful communication.

EXAMPLE 1   *Original Memo-Report with Second- and Third-Degree Words*

April 11, 1989

TO: Sara L. Mager, Human Resources
         Department Director

FROM: G. T. Guttierez, Manager, Section A

RE: Management Team Policies Update

Regarding the management policies listed here for discussion, it is my *initial* reaction that *modifications* should be made in this list. It is *apparent* that one of these policies, according to *approximately* five of the staff, is *detrimental* to the morale and motivation of our employees. I would like to explain more *explicitly* what I mean.

Our section feels that as the policy is *currently* written it does not *utilize* all levels of knowledge in our organization. It appears to be too *inflexible* in the use of authority to *terminate* projects that are not productive. I would like to *inquire* why this policy cannot be changed to allow for more individual control.

Our employees will not *increase* in their management *capabilities* if we do not give them the *opportunity* to *determine* which projects are profitable and which are not.

Therefore, my *subsequent* proposal would be to *inaugurate* profit centers to put the *ultimate* responsibility of the operation in their hands. Through their *selection* of services and expenditures, they will become directly responsible for their entire area. It is important to these people that they *influence* the outcome of their efforts.

Though it has been our *habitual* practice to *solicit* approval on projects and expenditures, I suggest we *proceed* to this plan. To do otherwise would be *injurious* to the growth and development of our employees.

EXAMPLE 2   *Revised Version with Precise, First-Degree Words*

April 11, 1989

TO: Sara L. Mager, Human Resources
         Department Director

FROM: G. T. Guttierez, Manager, Section A

RE: Management Team Policies Update

Regarding the management policies listed here for discussion, it is my *first* reaction that *changes* should be made in this list.

It is *clear* that one of these policies, according to *about* five of the staff, is *harmful* to the morale and motivation of our employees. I would like to explain more *clearly* what I mean.

Our section feels that as the policy is *now* written it does not *use* all levels of knowledge in our organization. It appears to be too *rigid* in the use of authority to *end* projects that are not productive. I would like to *ask* why this policy cannot be changed to allow for more individual control.

Our employees will not *grow* in their management *talents* if we do not give them the *chance* to *decide* which projects are profitable and which are not.

Therefore, my *next* proposal would be to *start* profit centers to put the *final* responsibility of the operation in their hands. Through their *choices* of services and expenditures, they will become directly responsible for their entire area. It is important to these people that they *affect* the outcome of their efforts.

Though it has been our *usual* practice to *seek* approval on projects and expenditures, I suggest we *go* with this plan. To do otherwise would be *harmful* to the growth and development of our employees.

As you can see in comparing these two examples, the use of more concrete, precise, first-degree words improves the overall clarity of managerial documents. Whenever a management report writer uses clearer, simpler language, reader comprehension tends to become much more efficient. Wherever possible, let's help readers process documents efficiently. Let's promote the efficient reading of complex, action- or decision-oriented management reports by using clear, simple language. In doing so, we can avoid misinterpretation and maximize writer–reader communication.

An important business lesson for Charles Wolf, Jr., Director of the RAND Corporation's research program in International Economics, consists in his continued ability "to avoid ambiguity" wherever "it may lurk" (Wolf, 1991, p. 48). Management report writers would do well to learn Wolf's lesson.

Brevity and Conciseness

In addition to producing management reports that use clear and simple, first-degree words and phrases, report writers should revise their documents for brevity and conciseness. Once again, avoid Shepherd Mead's pronouncements on memo and report writing at all costs. When Mead says,

NEVER COME STRAIGHT TO THE POINT

> A good... [writer] can expand the simplest subject into three or four closely written pages, during the course of which he [she] can inject sympathetic understanding, wit, and a few well-chosen anecdotes. (1952, p. 61)

shun him. If your immediate supervisor actually insists that sheer "quantity of output"—that is, number of report pages—makes a document important, explain that readers at all organizational levels benefit from brief and concise documents.

Managerial reports, as we've emphasized throughout this book, should be as brief and concise as possible. After all, most readers of action- and decision-oriented managerial documents are busy managers and executives themselves with precious little extra time to peruse lengthy reports from beginning to end for needed data and information. So, in counseling report writers not to send their readers needlessly complex and ambiguous documents cluttered with unclear, abstract language, we also counsel report writers not to be long-winded.

We agree with Edward Thompson when he insists that writers shorten—condense—whatever they write so that every management document is tight; straightforward; and easy to read, understand, and consult later on. To paraphrase Thompson, management report writers should not waste words telling readers what they already know (1979, n.p.). Report writers should cut unnecessary words and phrases from all documents they produce. That is, report writers must learn to recognize **filler**, **false starts**, and **fog**[1] in drafts of their written work and then make the effort to eliminate such wordy and imprecise language in the revised versions of their documents. Report writers should

---

[1]Here we are using the term *fog* to mean wordy, cluttered, and unclear language—the unreadable words and phrases that too often dominate the prose of business, government, and technical writers. Although Rudolf Flesch doesn't use the term, he defines the problem it represents in *The Art of Readable Writing* (1962) in his chapter titled "Rx for Readability," pages 141–151.

also guard against **redundancies** and the use of avoidable **legalisms** in their managerial documents. The following are some examples of the kinds of wordy expressions and imprecise constructions that thoughtful, reader-centered report writers should avoid:

		USE
FILLER	*at this time*	now
	at the present time	now
	at the moment	now, currently
	it sometimes happens that	occasionally
	in accordance with	by
	with respect to	about
	pertaining to	about
	to serve as a basis for	for
	in the area of	in
	based on the fact that	because/since

FALSE STARTS

Considering the fact that you are one of my most valued clients...

Revision

Since you are one of my most valued clients...
or
Because you are one of my most valued clients...

It is interesting to note that economic trends have caused a further reduction of...

Revision

Economic trends have caused a further reduction of...

It is significant to note that employees with B.S., B.B.A., or M.B.A. degrees comprise only 51% of the total work force in our finance department.

Revision

Employees with B.S., B.B.A., or M.B.A. degrees comprise only 51% of the total work force in our finance department.

It is imperative that we research alternative fuel sources...

Revision

We must research alternative fuel sources...
or
We should research alternative fuel sources...

In view of the fact that senior managers in this organization have taken responsibility for...

Revision

Because senior managers in this organization have taken responsibility for...

Inasmuch as organizational development consultants seem to be a luxury for management now . . .

Revision

Since organizational development consultants seem to be a luxury for management now . . .

It would be my objective that future meetings of our management team will review . . .

Revision

I'd like future meetings of our management team to review . . .
or
Future meetings of our management team should review . . .

REDUNDANCIES AND LEGALISMS

Pursuant to our earlier conversations *over recent months* . . .

Revision

Following our earlier conversations . . .

The *past history* of corporate hiring procedures and policies in the area of data processing . . .

Revision

The history of corporate hiring procedures and policies in the area of data processing . . .

The *total sum* of all office equipment and supplies budgeted for 1992 reflects a 17% increase over 1991.

Revision

The sum of all office equipment and supplies budgeted for 1992 reflects a 17% increase over 1991.

Senior-level division managers should *plan in advance [preplan?]* for reductions in software expenditures during the third quarter of the current fiscal year.

Revision

Senior-level division managers should plan for reductions in software expenditures during the third quarter of the current fiscal year.

U.S. Department of Labor attorneys have suggested that we *cease and desist* in our operation of . . .

Revision

U.S. Department of Labor attorneys have suggested that we cease our operation of . . .

The research and development contract we negotiated with three senior scientists is now *null and void*.

Revision

The research and development contract we negotiated with three senior scientists is now void.

FOG The plane crashed because it made an unstabilized approach that resulted in a descent below the published descent profile.

Revision

The plane crashed because it came in too low.

To facilitate making determinations of priorities on our time for meeting technical assistance requests as well as having an orderly procedure for requesting technical assistance, usage of the attached form is being reinstituted.

Revision

Please use the attached form to request technical assistance. We are using this form again so that you receive timely technical assistance on an orderly, first-come first-served basis.

In accordance with the normative assumption that favorable growth margins and significant profit potential underlie the computer accessory business, and that it is consonant with UtiliTech's current marketing and manufacturing capabilities, steps should be initiated in the pursuit of opportunities in this market niche.

Revision

We assume that solid growth margins and profits underlie the computer accessory business. Since UtiliTech is now capable of marketing and manufacturing these products, we should pursue this market.

A large amount of fog—just like that shown in the preceding examples—is produced by writers of what we call **Institutional English**. Institutional English is a kind of anonymous prose that seems to issue directly from institutions, bureaucracies, and organizations, and *not from human beings*. When writers produce such official-sounding, anonymous prose, they tend to alienate their readers. Institutional English is difficult to read and to make sense of; it does not communicate very well. To understand and absorb what writers of this kind of prose mean, readers must read, and carefully reread, each sentence. That's why most readers prefer reading memos, letters, and reports with what one editor calls a "human touch" (Grazian, 1988, p. 3). How might you respond to either of the two statements that follow if you had met them toward the beginning of a brief informational report?

EXAMPLE 1 *It* might appear desirable to offer clear-cut suggestions on how to avoid competitive blind spots...

EXAMPLE 2   *It* should be brought to your attention that Tilco, Inc., will be inaugurating the use of quality circles among *its* line personnel beginning the first quarter of 1992. Further instructions will be circulated to all line personnel by Friday of next week.

What might a reader think of writers who regularly produce statements like these for consumption within your company? What frame of mind might anonymous prose of this variety put *you* in?

Would you feel a little less like an automaton and, perhaps, a bit more human if personal pronouns like *I*, *you*, or *we* had been used in place of the vague, official-sounding *it* (or *its*)? If the writers of each of these statements had used personal pronouns, would you comprehend the message more readily? With greater ease? The following are revised versions of the two preceding examples, using personal pronouns that business readers can relate to as people. We think that these reader-centered revisions communicate the writer's message with greater concern and empathy for the people who read them.

EXAMPLE 1   *We* should offer clear-cut suggestions on how to avoid competitive blind spots...
or
Let's offer clear-cut suggestions on how to avoid competitive blind spots...

EXAMPLE 2   *I'd [We'd]* like you to know that Tilco, Inc., will begin the use of quality circles among *our* line personnel beginning the first quarter of 1992. *I'll [We'll]* circulate additional instructions to *you* by next Friday.

Managers should avoid resorting to official-sounding prose in their business and technical documents. Institutional English simply does not communicate in human terms that real readers can relate to.

Professional Jargon

In just about every professional field today, practicing members use and continue to create a set of words and phrases—a highly specific, often abstract language—to communicate primarily with each other. Attorneys, military officers, insurance agents, educators, psychologists, human resource trainers, computer programmers, and, of course, managers all use the **jargon** of their respective professions in their daily written communications.

Professionals working within a particular field seem to understand the documents they write and share with others who also work in that field. They have all learned to "speak" and comprehend a second, or "professional," language because growth and success within every professional field require that practitioners learn and regularly use its jargon. But what happens when practitioners attempt to communicate with people beyond their own immediate fields—when educators attempt to speak to attorneys, when attorneys attempt to speak to programmers or trainers? Yes, as you might have anticipated or experienced on more than one occasion, utter confusion rules.

Profession-based language, or jargon, simply does not transfer from one field to the next. When it does attempt to cross professional boundaries, communication failure usually results. Clear, two-way communication is blocked because jargon is impenetrable, opaque language; it is mere mumbo-jumbo for those not acquainted with the "official language" of a given profession. Legalese, educationese, financialese, and bureaucratese are all second languages composed of words and phrases made deliberately obscure in order to mystify or confuse uninitiated, "lay" readers when they confront such languages in daily and routine business situations.

But why dwell on jargon and professional second languages in a chapter on precision, clarity, and style in managerial report writing? Precisely because business, government, and managerial documents of all kinds regularly overwhelm their readers with a steady stream of jargon-freighted language—more fog resulting in comprehension difficulties and, ultimately, miscommunication. Even more alarming, though, is the fact that attempting to read documents filled with large and ever-increasing amounts of second-language jargon routinely wastes the time and money of executives and managers in businesses and governmental agencies throughout the country.

Of course, concern about poor writing in business, industry, government, and academe has not gone unnoticed by editors, sociocultural critics, the general public, or the press.[2] Witness, for example, the following portion of a front-page "Labor Letter" item appearing recently in *The Wall Street Journal*:

> Shortcomings in business writing prompt remedial steps by some firms.
>
> About 95% of 200 executives polled by Communispond, New York consultants, find business correspondence they get is "wordy" or "unclear." And 72% of those surveyed dislike writing letters and memos themselves. . . .
>
> An SCM tax official decided to try to write more clearly after one of his complex memos elicited *"cloudy stares or puzzlement"* [italics added]. Levi Strauss's president once kept a month's worth of memos to prove there were too many and most were too long. To correct poor English and boring memos, a U.S. Leasing vice president conducts writing sessions for . . . top managers. (1982, p. A1)

Second-Language Prose Samples

Jargon-filled prose that elicits "cloudy stares" and "puzzlement" shows up just about everywhere these days. In another brief example, *The Wall Street Journal* offers readers a sample of the latest in political "diplo-jargon": "scenario-dependent post-crisis strategy." Their translation: "We'll figure out what to do when the war's over" (1991, p. A1). Management reports, government studies, legal documents, and educational research results are all conspicuously mired by various forms of what the National Council of Teachers of English calls professional "**doublespeak**." Samples of jargon-filled, second-language prose, or doublespeak, are handily found; here are just a few:

EXAMPLE 1   Effective July 10, 1989, the Field Operations/Branch Services Division successfully completed the *reaffiliation* of all Branch Offices *affiliated* with Memphis Service

---

[2]See, for example, Richard Mitchell's *Less Than Words Can Say* (Boston: Little, Brown and Co., 1979) or *The Leaning Tower of Babel and Other Affronts by the Underground Grammarian* (Boston: Little, Brown and Co., 1984).

Center. Branch Offices previously *associated* with the Memphis Service Center are now *affiliated* with either the Atlanta Service Center or the Texas Service Center. New Accounts functions for these Branch Offices have been *reaffiliated* to the New Accounts Processing Center in Denver.

EXAMPLE 2 Additionally, *AP&L* has come to the conclusion that we need to develop an *EPRI* management program, in order to obtain the *benefit/cost ratios* and the successful technology transfer of *EPRI* research into *AP&L*. *AP&L* is interested in developing the same mutual relationship *EPRI* has with the participants of your *BAP*. Any future evaluation will necessarily incorporate this feature. Perhaps you can provide some guidance as that evaluation develops.

EXAMPLE 3 The style of discourse is the message carried by the *frequency-distributions* and *transitional probabilities* of its linguistic features, especially as they differ from those of the same features of the language as a whole.

EXAMPLE 4 The standardized flight types (or purposes) are *payload deployment*, *on-orbit servicing* of satellites, *payload retrieval*, and *on-orbit operations* with an attached payload. At times, more than one flight purpose may be combined in a single flight, depending on the combination of payloads. The user will be assigned a flight that fits his defined purpose.

The user's responsibilities in support of launch site operations are defined through *standard interfaces* and *documentation sequences* summarized here.... A *Launch Site Support Manager (LSSM)* will be assigned early in the planning program and will be the *primary interface* with the user.

EXAMPLE 5 Internal Revenue Code Section 2036 requires such accounts to be included in the *decedent's gross estate* if the *decedent* retained power to control, use, possess, [*sic*] right to income or other enjoyment of the funds during her lifetime or for a period not ascertainable without reference to the *decedent's* death....

Consequently and regretfully, it is my opinion that all three accounts, including principal and accrued interest to date of death, are includable in the *decedent's gross estate* for federal estate and state inheritance tax purposes. Attached hereto are copies of the appropriate Sections of the Internal Revenue Code and certain *precedent cases* applying same in accordance with this opinion.

EXAMPLE 6 The *punctuated equilibrium paradigm* offers a new lens through which theorists can make fresh discoveries about how managers, work groups, organizations, and industries both [*sic*] develop over time and react to changes in their environments. The *construct of a deep structure* that keeps systems basically stable during *equilibrium periods* offers a new way to understand systems' resistance to change.

EXAMPLE 7 *BKA** provides a *standard relational repository* for storing knowledge about work, rules, and information relationships. *BKA** is not an absolute requirement to support *BKA* techniques; however, computerized support greatly facilitates the creation, storage, updating, and access of information. *BKA** uses the Oracle Corporation's *RDBMS*, *SQL*, and personal computer hardware; however, any *RDBMS* could be used for this purpose. The *BKA** program is not complex and relies mainly on *standard name pattern matching*.

EXAMPLE 8　　Newcomers' levels of *cognitive complexity* also may affect their *information-seeking behavior*. In particular, individuals who are more *integratively complex* will sample more sources for information and usually will seek more information than individuals who are less *integratively complex*. Other *individual difference factors* that may affect newcomers' *information-seeking behavior* include their levels of *self-efficacy experience* in making *role transitions*, and familiarity with work environments similar to the new work environment.

Additionally, newcomers' *information-seeking behaviors* may be greatly affected by the manner in which the organization socializes their new hires. For instance, it is likely that newcomers who receive *individual socialization* will establish personal relationships with *incumbents* from whom they can directly seek information. In contrast, newcomers who experience *collective tactics* may try to reduce uncertainty by seeking out information from other recruits who are undergoing similar experiences. . . .

Frankly, we often wonder whether initiated readers—groups of professional readers for whom these documents are intended—can possibly comprehend all, or even most, of what they read in prose of this type. After all, second-language words and phrases—the use of jargon alone—should not retard communication among professionals within a given field. But each of these prose samples exhibits other varieties of language imprecision that, when mixed together in a single paragraph or passage, result in either comprehension difficulties or communication failure.

While we have already reviewed issues of clarity, simplicity, brevity, and conciseness, the linguistic categories that follow identify additional sentence-level concerns. When report writers rely on—or overuse—any of these linguistic forms and sentence constructions in their documents, the result is often a proportionate increase in fog, doublespeak, imprecision, or just plain reader confusion:

1. High density of abstract words and phrases
　　Nouns like *interfaces*
　　Phrases like *transitional probabilities, punctuated equilibrium paradigm,* or *standard relational repository*

2. Extensive use of nominalizations or nouns made from verbs
　　"Successfully completed the *reaffiliation of* all Branch Offices affiliated with . . ."
　　"*Determinations of* priorities on our time . . ."

3. Surplus of weak *to be* or linking verb forms
　　"Branch Offices previously associated with . . . *are* now . . ."
　　"AP&L *is* interested in developing . . ."
　　"It *is* my opinion that . . ."
　　"For instance, it *is* likely that newcomers who . . ."

4. Abuse of passive voice

"Newcomers' information-seeking behaviors may be greatly affected by the manner in which the organization socializes their new hires."

"Attached hereto are copies of the appropriate Sections of..."

5. Large percentage of acronyms

"*AP&L* is interested in developing the same mutual relationship *EPRI* has with the participants of your *BAP*."

"*BKA** uses the Oracle Corporation's *RDBMS*, *SQL*, and personal computer hardware; however, any *RDBMS* could be used for this purpose."

As Nasty as Professional Writers Can Get

The second-language passages we've just cited might confuse even their intended readers with their notable linguistic imprecision and opacity. Reading them, our own eyes sometimes become glassy with those same cloudy stares of puzzlement noted by *The Wall Street Journal*. But passages like the following, unearthed by "the underground grammarian," Professor Richard Mitchell, reach heretofore unknown levels of linguistic nastiness, imprecision, and miscommunication:

> Project WEY—Washington Environmental Yard...is a manifestation of the intercommunal, process-oriented, interage, interdisciplinary type of change vehicle toward an environmental ethic from the school-village level to a pan-perspective. The urban focus of the project as the medium has been inestimably vital since it is generally speaking the message. Situated near the central downtown area of the city of Berkeley and a mere block from civic center, Washington Elementary School courts the thousands of daily onlookers/passersby...traveling on a busy boulevard with easy access to the physical transformation and social interactions (at a distance to close-up)—a virtual open space laboratory. It has served evocatively as a catalyst for values confrontation, even through a soft mode of visual/physical data exchange system. Since 1971, the dramatic changes have represented a process tool for the development of environmental/educational value encounters on-site/off-site, indoors/outdoors and numerous other bipolar entities and dyads. (1979, p. 131)

Might a professional educator even begin to comprehend the crossword puzzle content of this passage? Might anyone—ever?

Although this passage ranks among the worst we've ever attempted to read and make sense of, we come across hundreds of samples of cloudy, second-language prose each year in a great many business contexts. The kind of language Professor Mitchell labels "**dysfunctional**" (just reread the WEY passage for a working definition of this term) often comprises the very language of managerial decision making. Report writers writing in all sorts of situations—from administrators working for governmental agencies in Washington, D.C., to midlevel managers at "Fortune 500" corporations—routinely generate memo-reports, proposals, feasibility studies, and analytical reports that hinder rather than enhance decision making. The widespread reliance on imprecise, unclear, and abstract language resulting in dysfunctional decision-oriented documents will surely continue if not checked now by senior-level managers, senior executives, and CEOs who understand the consequences in corporate dollars and lost time.

Sexism and Bias

Language that reflects sexist attitudes, biases, or behaviors remains common in business and managerial documents of all kinds. Much like sexist advertising or sexist remarks, the use of sexist language in managerial reports continues to foster sex stereotyping in the contemporary organization. Sometimes the use of sexist language appears to be unintentional, even mechanical; at other times, such language use is condescending and abusive. Although managers and senior-level executives are becoming increasingly sensitive to sexism and sexist issues in their organizations, many still produce reports and policy manuals filled with gender-specific terms and pronouns rather than their **gender-neutral** equivalents. The continued presence of masculine- or feminine-dominated language has, indeed, become an irritant to many technical and managerial professionals who both write and read reports on a consistent basis.[3]

In addition, managers should strive to avoid other instances of biased, discriminatory, or otherwise offensive language in their decisional and technical reports. The following are a few basic rules managers should follow in an effort to eliminate sexist, racist, and biased language from business communications and technical/professional reports:

Rule 1

Use gender-neutral equivalents instead of gender-specific terms, titles, or phrases. According to the staff of the Document Design Center at the American Institutes for Research, however, writers should avoid awkward new terms like *spokesperson* or *chairperson* (*Simply Stated*, 1982, p. 2).

DON'T USE	CONSIDER USING
foreman/forelady	supervisor
salesman/saleslady	salesperson, sales representative (or rep)
mailman	mail carrier
chairman/chairwoman	chair, head, moderator, leader
spokesman	speaker, representative
businessman/businesswoman	executive, manager, supervisor
hostess	host
female engineer	engineer
waiter/waitress	server
man-hours	hours, staff hours, working hours, production hours

---

[3]To ensure gender-neutral content, writers must frequently revise larger sections of text than just a sentence here or there. For suggestions about revising larger or more complex sections of text, see Mary Corbett, "Making State Laws Gender-Neutral," *Simply Stated* (No. 75, September–October, 1987), pages 1–2 and 4. For a broader discussion of nonsexist language issues and practices, see Casey Miller and Kate Swift, *The Handbook of Nonsexist Writing: For Writers, Editors, and Speakers*, 2nd ed. (New York: Harper & Row, 1988).

manpower	work force, personnel
stewardess	flight attendant
secretary	assistant, administrative assistant
journeyman	experienced worker
barman	barkeeper

Rule 2

Eliminate gender-specific pronouns wherever possible; use gender-neutral pronouns that won't cause readers comprehension problems.

REVISE YOUR TEXT

Initial Text

Every member of the Harris team should have in *his* possession a copy of the Code of Corporate Ethics and Staff Conduct.

Revised Text

Every member of the Harris team should possess a copy of the Code of Corporate Ethics and Staff Conduct.

Initial Text

A manager must depend on *his* intuition in determining if a job applicant is lying.

Revised Text

A manager must depend on intuition in determining if a job applicant is lying.

PLURALIZE YOUR TEXT

Singular

An interviewer should be aware of *his* own personality traits—those that might affect *his* judgments of people or *his* interpretations of their behaviors.

Plural

Interviewers should be aware of their own personality traits—those that might affect their judgments of people or their interpretations of human behaviors.

SUBSTITUTE OR SWITCH PRONOUNS

DON'T USE	CONSIDER USING
He analyzes	One analyzes
	You analyze
	He or she analyzes
His interviewing techniques	One's interviewing techniques
	Your interviewing techniques
	His or her interviewing techniques

ROTATE USE OF MASCULINE AND FEMININE PRONOUNS WHENEVER

your readers will not be confused.

such rotation will be clear given a specific context or subject matter.

such rotation will be done on a consistent basis.

Rule 3

Adopt nonsexist, gender-neutral salutations in all letter-reports and correspondence.

DON'T USE	*CONSIDER USING*
Dear Sir(s):	Dear Colleague:
Gentlemen:	Dear Reader:
Dear Madam:	Dear Customer:
Ladies:	Dear Computer User:
	Dear Investor:

Rule 4

Avoid all discriminatory or potentially offensive words and phrases, or terms that might reinforce racial or ethnic stereotypes.

DON'T WRITE	*CONSIDER WRITING*
A senior black manager in our Kansas City subsidiary	A senior manager in our Kansas City subsidiary
The Japanese forelady in Plant X	The supervisor in Plant X
	The manufacturing supervisor in Plant X
Our inventory system was evaluated by your handicapped analyst	Our inventory system was evaluated by your analyst
Marjory, the firm's aggressive new accounts officer	Marjory, the firm's new accounts officer
Han Hoon-mok, our industrious Korean marketing chief	Han Hoon-mok, our marketing chief

Style

Much of what we've spoken about in the preceding section on language precision relates directly to the examination of style. As we have shown, a report writer's attention to micro matters of clarity, simplicity, brevity, and conciseness will surely have an effect on a document's readers and, perhaps, make a managerial document appreciably more readable. The most successful professional documents, however, project a sense of style that captures the reader's interest and maintains the reader's attention.

reveals something about the writer's personality, individuality, or imagination.

enhances the writer's intended meaning in specific business situations.

While sentence-level precision is an important aid in the basic reading-comprehension process, carefully written presentations should exhibit a *sense of style* that also fosters reader involvement, maintains reader interest during the reading process, and heightens reader recall of key elements after the initial reading process has drawn to a close. But what exactly is prose style? And what language variables shape a writer's prose style?

What Is Prose Style?

Linguists, literary critics, rhetoricians, discourse analysts, and others have long argued over the "problem of style."[4] Few solutions to the problem have evolved over the centuries. In fact, little agreement has emerged concerning what the term *style* actually designates. About the only idea that interested parties seem to agree on is that there is such a phenomenon as style.

For some writers, style is a way of writing or even a matter of technique. For others, style is a quality or recognizable attribute of writing. Some linguists consider style a matter of formal language patterns or linguistic variables. One linguist has perceptively argued that style is a matter of "epistemic choice"— the choice of words and phrases writers make based on an accumulation of individual experiences and personal knowledge.[5]

If style is a matter of the *choices* writers make as they draft, revise, and consider why and for whom they are writing, then experiences, attitudes, and accumulated knowledge certainly shape the products that are created. If style is a combination of individual choices and past experiences, then style might also be considered a rough linguistic equivalent of personality—the result of putting our personal imprint on the language we use.

If we accept that view, then style becomes not a static linguistic construct apart from content, but a dynamic force that we can all marshall in a number of ways as we respond to diverse professional situations calling for our prose. Depending on what a particular business situation might call for, we can consciously choose or unconsciously apply—manipulate or adopt—an appropriate style for our own purposes. To speak of style, then, in this dynamic sense is to speak of both power and control; effective writers manipulate the language they use in powerful ways to control their readers' responses. To paraphrase George Orwell, powerful writers abandon the "dreary patterns" and "prefab-

---

[4]For an introduction to the field of stylistics and style study, see the following: Bennison Gray, *Style: The Problem and Its Solution* (The Hague: Mouton, 1969); Graham Hough, *Style and Stylistics* (London: Routledge & Kegan Paul, 1972); E. L. Epstein, *Language and Style* (London: Methuen, 1978); and Richard A. Lanham, *Analyzing Prose* (New York: Scribner's, 1983).

[5]For an elaboration of this view of style, see Richard M. Ohmann, "Literature as Sentences," in Seymour Chatman and Samuel R. Levin, eds., *Essays on the Language of Literature* (Boston: Houghton Mifflin, 1967), pages 231–238.

ricated phrases" that anesthetize a portion of their readers' brains; they use unique language in original ways.

In drafting reports for managerial decision makers, we might best define **style** in a functional manner: Style is a *way* of writing and, as such, is a matter of personal choice. Style is *situational*, context-based, and closely associated with a writer's intended meaning and a reader's perceived meaning. For managerial report writers, style is not simply a frill, an afterthought, or an element that can be separated from content. Style is a matter of having a *point of view*—a unique way of looking at and talking about the world—and applying that point of view wisely in different situations to make meaning and shape readers' responses.

The stylistic choices managerial report writers make—the words and phrases that are selected to inform, clarify, analyze, or call to action—become an integral part of content and a matter of meaning. In short, style, as a recent *Wall Street Journal* headline has asserted, is substance.

What, then, are the managerial report writer's stylistic options? How varied are a report writer's choices? To what degree does a particular stylistic decision reflect, or even mold, a writer's interpersonal relationships? How might a particular business situation or report-writing task affect a manager's choice of one style over another?

Style, Situation, Rhetorical Occasion

Managerial report writers have a variety of stylistic options from which to choose when drafting documents. Report writers, for example, might select a powerful or forceful style, a consultative style, a plain style, or even a chummy or intimate style. The stylistic options available to report writers are many, but the style that is ultimately chosen will depend on at least two basic situational variables:

1. The **organizational context** out of which the manager is writing and responding
2. The **rhetorical occasion** out of which the document—the written response—has evolved.

Organizational Context

Managerial report writers, as we have already demonstrated, do not construct documents in a vacuum; rather, they construct documents within very definite organizational contexts. They draft and distribute documents to individual readers up and down the organizational hierarchy and also to readers outside their organizations. Effective report writers must, therefore, choose a style appropriate for the specific business situation or organizational context out of which they are writing.

Throughout the drafting process writers must consider their initial and ongoing relationships with individual readers and wider organizational audiences. The nature of the relationship between the report writer and individual reader must be defined. Likewise, the nature of the relationship between the report writer and wider, more diverse organizational audiences must be determined. Whatever the character of the business relationship—whether distanced and formal, consultative, casual, chummy or intimate—the report writer must adopt a style consistent with that relationship. Of course, writers at all organizational levels have a variety of relationships and so must choose a style appropriate for each individual relationship and business situation. When necessary, writers should be able to effect any one of a number of useful styles:

1. Formal
2. Tough or forceful
3. Official (impersonal, legal, bureaucratic)
4. Consultative or professional
5. Plain
6. Vigorous
7. Personal or friendly
8. Casual
9. Chummy or intimate.

For example, report writers often choose to communicate in a formal or **official** style whenever

> hierarchical or physical distance separates writer and reader(s).
> the amount or level of authority wielded by writer and reader(s) differs.
> their relationship is characterized by formality.
> the shared data and information are of a technical nature.

Report writers tend to adopt or resort to an official style when they need to convey data or information to readers in an objective, pseudoscientific manner.

In the two passages (Examples A and B) that follow, notice how the use of a formal, official-sounding prose style conveys information in impersonal, passive, relatively long, and complicated sentences. Notice, too, how readers of this sort of prose are addressed only indirectly as members of generic groups—"the holder" or "employees"—and never as individual, flesh-and-blood members of an organization.

EXAMPLE A   Stock options granted under provisions of the Stock Option Plans permit the purchase of shares of the company's common stock at exercise price equivalent to the average market price of the stock on the date the options were granted. The options have a term of 10 years and normally become exercisable in increments of up to 25% on each anniversary date following the date of grant. Stock Appreciation Rights (SARs) may from time to time be affixed to the options. Options exercised in the form of SARs permit the holder to receive stock, or a combination of cash and stock, equivalent to the excess of the average market price on the exercise date over the exercise price.

(*Source:* Phillips Petroleum Company, from "Incentive Compensation Plans")

EXAMPLE B   Although movement of employees between these ancillary activities will occur infrequently and only as required to fill losses or to provide a depth of backup support to a specific area, all employees will continue to maintain their proficiency in the R/ID function. In fact, the actual cross training effort will be clearly identified for each employee and records will be maintained to reveal the type and extent of cross training to be accomplished.

(*Source:* Lockheed Space Operations Company, from "Cross Training—Research and Activities" report)

Report writers might consider adopting a **consultative** style when they are constructing documents for distribution to readers who

function at or near their own hierarchical levels.
hold similar amounts of organizational clout or authority.
reside within or outside of their own organizations.

Whether writer and reader are fully or only partially acquainted, a consultative style—full of personal pronouns such as *we, you,* and *our*—might be used to create a sense of commitment or involvement or a genuine, shared concern for an enterprise, as the following example demonstrates:

EXAMPLE C   *We* manage a growing enterprise with a simple philosophy—to concentrate on doing what *we* know how to do best—and do it to the best of *our* ability. That philosophy is due to *our* success as a company and the success of the people who make up that company.

(*Source:* Glenfed, Inc., *Annual Report,* from "Review of Operations," italics added)

Report writers might also adopt a consultative style to project a feeling of friendly professionalism, helpfulness, and mutual participation in a continuous business dialogue:

EXAMPLE D   *We* have concluded that the damage to the building was confined to the exterior window and wall, interior partitions, ceiling, and contents—and not to the structural elements. *Our* conclusions are based on *our* review of the drawings which show the structural system, and *our* visual review of the components of the building after certain repairs had been completed. *We* have not relied on the results of material testing or any other types of tests.

Therefore, although *we* have concluded that there was no structural damage caused by the roller, *we* cannot guarantee the condition of the building. If *you* need additional information or would like to review *our* report with *us, we* will be happy to meet *you* at *your* convenience.

(*Source:* Robert Navarro & Associates Engineering, Inc., from "Evaluation Report," italics added)

In addition, when adopting a consultative style, report writers should supply readers with sufficient background information and details in any given situation, because a reader's precise knowledge base might prove somewhat different from the writer's own.

At times, managerial writers might want (or need) to adopt a **casual** style such as the following for those readers who are perceived as friends, close acquaintances, or organizational "insiders":

EXAMPLE E   Just a follow-up note to let you know *we've* scheduled a quarterly Process Chemicals review for Wednesday, September 2, 1987 at 1:30. *I've* reserved the small conference room for the group. That format seemed to work well last time out. Again, *we'll* try to keep the meeting brief and informative.

Any conflicts with T and D? Please let *me* know before *you* leave Aurora.

(*Source:* Betz Process Chemicals, Inc., italics added)

A casual, chummy, or intimate style can often be identified by the (a) relative absence of background information and details, (b) use of words and phrases (jargon, or even slang) understood only by members of the in-group, and (c) coupling of personal pronouns with contractions. Indeed, some large organizations, like Betz, consistently use a **chummy** or **intimate** style—projecting their corporate culture—even in reports conveying technical information such as the following:

EXAMPLE F   I feel that *we're* pretty clear on the kind of information *we'll* need in the near future. . . .

As *we* discussed, the remaining antifoulant *business* at Conoco *could fall* in three different ways. The first is that Rusty Rios will call me into his office *one day out of the blue,* ask me how we plan *to handle* the sole supplier account, and *I'll walk out of there* with all the business 15 minutes later. Although doubtful, it is still a possibility.

Secondly, Conoco will gradually give *a piece of business here* and *a piece of business there* until we finally develop the account into a bigger base.

Finally, there is a chance that we may have one more meeting *with the folks* at the Denver refinery where *we'll* give our recommendations, service commitments, monitoring procedures, etc., in detail.

If the third option becomes a reality, *we'll* need a lot of information from the antifoulant group, including the following: (1) chemical recommendations and dosages; (2) feed locations and feed systems; (3) base case data and graphs of all competitively treated systems; (4) a detailed demonstration of our monitoring capabilities, including XDUTY, cleaning incentives, networking, INSITE device, and characterizations; and (5) a plan on how *we'll* present and update the data for Conoco on a regular basis.

Things are still looking pretty good at Conoco, Barry.

(*Source:* Betz Process Chemicals, Inc., from District Manager's letter-report, italics added)

A casual or chummy style adopted by business writers can prove to be a very powerful communication technique. Using such a style might, for example, make an insider of any reader simply by addressing that reader as an organizational or group insider.[6]

Rhetorical Occasion

In addition, the stylistic decisions report writers must make as they draft their documents will also be dictated by the rhetorical occasion out of which a particular document has arisen. That is, the purpose for the document—the written response—will determine, in part, the style adopted by the report writer. For example, which style might prove most effective if a midlevel manager, a colleague, requested an informational report that would be used in the quarterly budgeting process? Similarly, which style would be appropriate to adopt if a senior corporate executive who had more power and greater organizational clout than the writer requested the researching and construction of a portion of a long-range divisional plan, involving extensive analysis and the presentation of concrete, action-oriented recommendations?

In either of those organizational contexts, the writer must choose a style suitable for the writer–reader relationship, as well as for the particular occasion. A consultative or personal style might be just right for the former case, in which the writer is communicating with a colleague, another midlevel manager; a formal or more impersonal style might prove effective in the latter case, in which the audience involves at least one, and possibly more, senior-level corporate executives with greater decision-making authority than that of the report writer. Even the memo of transmittal accompanying each of these reports should reflect the writer–reader relationship, business context, and rhetorical occasion. A breezy, casual, or, more likely, consultative memo might be drafted to accompany an informational report aimed at a colleague; a formal, no-nonsense, persuasive memo may likely accompany the long-range planning report called for by a representative of top management.

Whichever stylistic option is adopted, however, report writers must ensure that the style

- communicates appropriately, effectively, and comfortably with individual readers or audiences at specific organizational levels.
- reflects established (or new) relationships between writer and reader(s).
- jibes with the interpersonal and organizational demands of the rhetorical occasion out of which the document has grown.
- matches or enhances the content of the report.
- projects the organization's corporate culture when and if desired.

Whenever an appropriate style has been adopted successfully in the construction of a given business document, a writer's *intended* meaning and the reader's *perceived* meaning of the same content are much more likely to be in accord.

---

[6]For a brief and insightful look at style in writing and speech, see Martin Joos, *The Five Clocks: A Linguistic Excursion Into the Five Styles of English Usage* (New York: Harcourt, Brace & World, 1967). Our discussion of stylistic options has been informed by Joos's usage scales, classifications, and examples.

Dimensions of Prose Style

In reviewing the concept of style, we noted that certain authorities have defined style as a quality or recognizable attribute of writing. Although this definition doesn't really solve the problem of style for us, it does help us begin to understand style operationally. That is, specific qualities or attributes of language actually do identify, result in, or build up a particular prose style. These **dimensions** of prose style account for the different impressions writers make—and readers feel—in the documents writers construct for various purposes and in varied organizational contexts.

Dimensions of prose style that are particularly useful to management report writers in identifying their stylistic options consist of the following:

Sentence Length

Report writers should vary lengths of sentences in their documents. Documents containing large numbers of short sentences can be made more effective if writers combine short, simple sentences into longer units.

EXAMPLE 1   *Original*

We have all had busy schedules. We were still able to get together. We all put in quality time.

Revision

Despite busy schedules, we were all able to get together and put in quality time.

On the other hand, large numbers of consistently long sentences—25 to 30 words or more—might be broken up into shorter units using (a) additional punctuation, (b) appropriate transition words and phrases, (c) in-text enumerated lists, or (d) bulleted items.

EXAMPLE 2   *Original*

As part of a comprehensive strategic plan, Glenfed is instituting major changes in the company's cost infrastructure, along with a freeze on management salaries, and liquidating or selling all noncore business lines to achieve a targeted annualized reduction in noninterest expense in excess of $160 million within the next 18 months.

Revision

As part of a comprehensive strategic plan, Glenfed is instituting major changes in the company's cost infrastructure. Within the next 18 months, Glenfed will (a) freeze management salaries and (b) liquidate or sell all noncore business lines to reduce targeted annual noninterest expense in excess of $160 million.

EXAMPLE 3   *Original*

In a period of economic slowdown, Kelly Services will be able to maintain a leadership role by capitalizing on the shifting marketplace in Florida, emphasizing changing workplace technologies and employing retiring professionals who are increasing the age of the population in Brevard County.

Revision

In a period of economic slowdown, Kelly Services will be able to maintain a leadership role by

- emphasizing changing workplace technologies.
- capitalizing on the shifting marketplace in Florida.
- employing the influx of retiring professionals who are increasing the age of Brevard County's population.

STYLISTIC RESULT

Strings of short, choppy sentences reveal a lack of stylistic maturity and may bore management report readers. On the whole, strings of long sentences might be less clear, less vivid, and less comprehensible. Varying sentence length should lend an added degree of interest to a business document and, as some argue, rescue your prose style from monotony.

Sentence Types

Report writers should vary sentence types and structures in their documents. Writers should mix **simple sentences** such as

Ramsay HMO operates managed health care centers in South Florida.

with **complex sentences** like

By implementing the recommendations we have provided [subordinate clause], Ramsay HMO should reach its goal of expanding into other geographic areas and increasing the number of Spanish-speaking physicians on staff [main clause].

to achieve appropriate variation.

STYLISTIC RESULT

Varying sentence types and structures throughout a document will make the document less repetitive, less monotonous, and generally more interesting for readers.

Diction

A report writer's choice of words, selection of phrases, and reliance on vague or abstract words will affect a document's style and reader comprehension.

EXAMPLE   *Vague, Abstract Original*

Two years ago Ramsay HMO had many problems, including debt, low earnings, and a lack of facilities.

Concrete, Specific Revision

Two years ago Ramsay HMO suffered from many problems, including massive debt, negative earnings, and a lack of up-to-date medical facilities.

STYLISTIC RESULT

Writers concerned with *how* they express the content of their reports—as much as they are concerned with the content itself—will want to minimize the use of vague and abstract words. Documents that contain concrete, specific words will communicate information to business readers much more effectively and far less impersonally. Precise and vivid words and phrases enhance reader attention, involvement, and comprehension, enabling writers to exploit the rich resources of the English language with appropriate linguistic diversity.

Nominalizations

Nominalizations can be defined as nouns (e.g., *recommenda**tion,** develop**ment,** avoid**ance,** or engage**ment***) constructed from verbs (*recommend, develop, avoid,* or *engage*). The use or overuse of nouns, noun phrases, and noun forms of verbs will result in documents that exhibit a nominal style. Professional appraisers of style suggest that a nominal style is inferior to a verbal style.

EXAMPLE 1   *Noun-Based or Nominalized Original*

Ametek management has proposed a *recommendation* calling for the *termination* of its electromagnetic division.

Verb-Based Revision

Ametek management *recommends terminating* its electromagnetic division.

EXAMPLE 2   *Noun-Based Original*

Two of the *options* Harsco has are the *development* of new products and the *revision* of products currently in *production*.

Verb-Based Revision

Harsco can *develop* new products and *revise* products it currently *produces*.

STYLISTIC RESULT

A noun-based or nominal style generally consists of longer sentences filled with longer, polysyllabic words. A nominal style is considered more static and more confusing for a reader to process and comprehend than a verbal style. Report writers should adopt a verb-based style whenever they want to produce dynamic, involving, forceful, and efficient documents.

Passive Voice

Whenever report writers use the passive voice, the subjects of their sentences do not act but are instead acted upon. In passive voice constructions, the agent of the action seems to have been withheld or hidden. Passive voice constructions often follow two basic structures, implying action rather than indicating action directly performed:

1. Form of verb *to be* + past participle + preposition ("Quality circles at Harris were organized by unit supervisors.")
2. Form of verb *to be* + past participle ("The study has been followed up as was requested.")

EXAMPLE 1   *Passive Voice Construction*

Flexible-hour shifts *were instituted by management* in the main semiconductor plant.

Active Voice Construction

Management instituted flexible-hour shifts in the main semiconductor plant.

EXAMPLE 2   *Passive Voice Construction*

If an employee's individual productivity file (IPF) *has been favorably reviewed,* then a raise *should be seriously taken into consideration.*

Active Voice Construction

Supervisors should seriously consider a raise if *they have favorably reviewed* an employee's individual productivity file (IPF).

EXAMPLE 3   *Passive Voice Construction*

A seminar on current training practices *will be given by the American Management Association* at the Orlando Omni in March.

Active Voice Construction

The American Management Association will give a seminar on current training practices at the Orlando Omni in March.

STYLISTIC RESULT

Often coupled with the use of nominalizations, the passive voice has become a hallmark of official-sounding prose—for example, bureaucratic, governmental documents—for which an impersonal, objective style is desired. A passive construction might be more appropriate in the following sentence from a formal budget report:

The results were compiled and the data were broken down into three major categories.

Here the emphasis is not on a staff member and what she or he has done, but on the fact that items were "compiled" and "broken down." The passive voice, therefore, might be used effectively in situations where the agent of action is less important than the action itself. Nevertheless, report writers should be cautioned that passive voice constructions frequently involve long, wordy sentences that have a decidedly static feel to them.

By contrast, the active voice relies on the use of active verbs and more straightforward noun-verb constructions. The active voice should be the preferred construction in situations where an emphasis has been placed on the individual involved and what she or he has done:

Our human factors specialist should look into the current lighting situation immediately.

The active voice is more suitable in situations where the report writer wants to effect a forceful, dynamic, or personal style—where people, and not just their actions, are the writer's major thrust.

Linking Verbs

The use of nonactive, linking verbs such as *be, have, seem, tend,* or *appear* often (a) results in a nominal or impersonal style and (b) relies on passive voice constructions.

EXAMPLE 1   *Original Linking Verb Form*

There is a relationship between the use of graphic aids in presentations and the level of audience response.

Revised Action Verb Form

A relationship *exists* between the use of graphic aids in presentations and the level of audience response.

EXAMPLE 2   *Original Linking Verb Form*

Active recruitment of MIS staff *seems to be continuing.*

Revised Action Verb Form

Active recruitment of MIS staff *continues.*

EXAMPLE 3   *Original Linking Verb Form*

It appears that all interested parties *have agreed* in principle to a plan that will enable Meritor Trust to emerge from bankruptcy proceedings.

Revised Action Verb Form

All interested parties *agreed* in principle to a plan that will enable Meritor Trust to emerge from bankruptcy proceedings.

EXAMPLE 4   *Original Linking Verb Form*

While allowing its operating units a wide degree of independence, Groupe SEB *tends to infuse* its companies with resources of many kinds.

Revised Action Verb Form

While allowing its operating units a wide degree of independence, Groupe SEB *infuses* its companies with resources of many kinds.

STYLISTIC RESULT

Whenever report writers overuse weak, linking verbs, their prose takes on a dead, lifeless character. Sentences become bland, wordy, and more difficult for readers to comprehend. False starts such as *it is, this is, there is,* and *there are,* dominate the reports of managers who use linking verb forms excessively. Wherever possible, report writers should replace weak, linking verbs with active verb forms to produce briefer, clearer, more forceful documents.

Negative Words and Phrases

Negative words such as

no	not	never
cannot	couldn't	shouldn't
won't	regret	problem
hardly	scarcely	unsound
unless	unreasonable	unfortunately
mistake	failed	inadequate
worthless	error	difficulty

and "not un-" (or "not in-") phrases such as

not unlike	not unprepared
not untoxic	not unhealthy
not unacceptable	not unwelcome
not unprofitable	not unstable
not insignificant	not insurmountable

create a tone of, well, negativity. Excessive use of negative words and phrases within a single document might impede a reader's attention to report content. Negative words, therefore, should be used with some restraint.

EXAMPLE 1

Negative Statement

Unfortunately, your *failure* to respond to our second and final request for payment has caused us to terminate your credit card account immediately.

Positive Statement

Since you seem to have overlooked our final request for payment, continued use of your credit card is suspended as of April 14.

EXAMPLE 2

Negative Statement

The *problem* with your computer's hard drive *cannot* possibly be attributed to anything other than your own *error* in loading *inordinately* large amounts of accounting software in your root directory.

Positive Statement

When users load large amounts of software in the root directory of a hard drive, they can experience what seems to be a computer malfunction but is actually just a matter of hard disk organization.

EXAMPLE 3

Negative Statement

Failure to properly install your unit will result in *degradation* of performance level.

Positive Statement

If you want to ensure a high performance level, install your unit properly.

EXAMPLE 4   *Negative Statement*

Do *not* store tape in (a) direct sunlight, (b) strong magnetic fields, or (c) high-humidity areas.

Positive Statement

Store tape away from (a) direct sunlight, (b) strong magnetic fields, or (c) high-humidity areas.

EXAMPLE 5   *Negative Statement*

Angelo's organizational development strategy is *not without* merit.

Positive Statement

Angelo's organizational development strategy has merit.

EXAMPLE 6   *Negative Statement*

Harsco's short-term manufacturing decisions were *not unsound*.

Positive Statement

Harsco's short-term manufacturing decisions were sound.

STYLISTIC RESULT

Because negative statements are more complex and generally longer than positive ones, they are easily misunderstood by report readers. When report writers consistently use negative words and phrases, they alienate well-intentioned readers and confuse otherwise interested ones.

On the other hand, readers find positive statements easier to process and recall. As one writer has recently suggested, readers instinctively seek out affirmative information, preferring it to the negative. Wherever possible, revise negative statements into positive forms.

In special circumstances the use of negative language might be considered the preferred mode of expression. In cases involving a need for extreme caution or in warnings of potential danger, writers might want to construct their messages in the negative:

Do *not* enter this building *without* protective clothing. Fissionable materials contained within.

But not necessarily. For example, the use of "Proceed with caution!" or "Danger—Keep out!" both seem to get the job done.

These dimensions of prose style account for the basic ways in which professional writing styles vary. Of course, some of these dimensions of style will invariably prove considerably more relevant and useful than others depending on the particular

Thrust,

Impact, or

Emphasis

individual writers want (or need) to achieve in drafting documents for business situations that confront them.

When report writers consider these basic dimensions of style and manipulate them for their own rhetorical purposes, they are actually selecting a particular set of linguistic options that molds and results in a style. For example, what kind of style might be achieved by report writers who construct documents with an abundance of (a) long, complex sentences; (b) abstract words; (c) nominalizations or noun strings; (d) passive voice constructions; and (e) *to be* verbs? Very likely these writers will end up with a static, formal, quasi-scientific, and unnecessarily complex prose style that will be difficult for their readers to comprehend. However, writers such as these may have consciously chosen—and for very specific purposes—to effect a style characteristic of an impersonal, objective, official-sounding bureaucrat.

On the other hand, what if writers choose a more moderate approach to constructing their documents, relying on (a) a mixture of short and long sentences; (b) many concrete words, vivid phrases, and colorful modifiers; (c) active voice constructions; and (d) active, forceful verbs? These writers will likely produce more personal, dynamic, and persuasive documents that readers will comprehend readily. Report writers adopting this moderate approach to "styling" their business documents may be on their way to developing effective casual, consultative, or forceful prose styles.

These two illustrations represent only a fraction of the stylistic possibilities managers have before them whenever they begin to draft business documents. We want to reemphasize here that the style a report writer decides to adopt should, simply, never be cast in stone. A manager should remain open and flexible when choosing a style for a specific business situation that demands a written response. Managerial report writers should cultivate a variety of writing styles—or stylistic options—that can be applied strategically to produce one effect or another, depending on

the results they wish to achieve.

the demands of a specific writer-reader relationship.

the particular organizational context(s) in which they are writing.

the rhetorical occasion out of which a given document has grown.

Style and Computer Software

Managers should apprise each other about the effectiveness of their report drafts and the suitability of the writing styles they adopt for specific business purposes. Often, though, business people simply don't have the time to meet and discuss drafts of even their most important documents. Now report writers have access to direct electronic feedback on their documents, feedback that is potentially useful when a writer can't obtain the human variety.

Though computer software can aid managerial report writers in styling more effective documents, software currently available has not yet eliminated the need for human editorial contact. That is, managerial report writers can certainly profit from substantive editorial comment provided by their colleagues and supervisors. After all, a report writer's document—the sum of many stylistic and rhetorical decisions that must be made by a writer—is a response to very real constraints evolving out of organizational contexts that a machine's "intelligence" cannot even begin to assess. In fact, speaking of a machine, or a "customizable" computer program, as actually *assessing* or *evaluating* anything is attributing to a machine or its software a wide range of human cognitive (and emotional) activities certainly light years beyond what computers are now capable of doing.

Nevertheless, computer software that can be helpful to report writers is available. Relatively simple, straightforward, inexpensive "style checkers" such as RightWriter® and Grammatik® can identify countable grammatical and stylistic features of a document. For example, these programs, which are compatible with most major word processors, can "flag"

> errors in spelling.
>
> instances of wordiness (e.g., wordy sentence structure).
>
> use of jargon, slang, or colloquialism.
>
> improperly used words.
>
> passive voice constructions.
>
> weak phrases (those with *to be* or other weak linking verbs).
>
> long sentences with multiple clauses.

However, these programs cannot tell you if or when the use of, say, the passive voice might prove rhetorically more effective given the particular context, occasion, or purpose out of which a document has grown.

Although programs like RightWriter claim to apply different rules to the analysis of a document, depending on the type of writing under consideration (e.g., business, technical, proposal, manual), they still cannot deliver the kinds of editorial insights a colleague can. Typically, style checkers identify only about 25 percent of the errors caught by human editors. The situational and rhetorical knowledge of a colleague working collaboratively with a report writer cannot be offset by the mechanical recommendations of even the best style checkers.

More sophisticated "text analyzers" like Bell Labs' Writer's Workbench® (a UNIX®-based set of programs) and IBM's Critique® can, among other things, help report writers to

> increase readability in a general sense.
>
> consider paragraph development and length.
>
> "cut the fog" by flagging passives, nominalizations, *to be* verbs, and long sentences.
>
> check for vague or abstract words.
>
> catch instances of multiple negation or *who's/whose* confusion.
>
> insert missing commas.
>
> eliminate incorrect pronoun errors and noun–verb agreement problems.
>
> isolate awkward sentences (a pretty remarkable achievement for a machine!)

A quick review of that brief list should suggest that programs like Writer's Workbench and Critique have much to offer managerial report writers interested in perfecting their documents. We believe these programs have the potential to improve business documents if they are used with utmost care by confident writers during drafting and revising stages of the writing process. While heeding the useful advice these programs can provide, report writers should recognize the limited range and depth, and mechanical nature, of the suggestions given to them.

Despite the number of grammatical, syntactic, and stylistic areas in which text analysis software can be of real help to report writers, major *rhetorical* decisions, and many other decisions involving matters of style and language, must still be made by writers themselves and their colleagues. Although computer programs can aid writers in a number of concrete ways, they simply cannot dissect or respond to the key situational variables—purpose, writer–reader relationship, organizational context, occasion—affecting the construction and ultimate success of any managerial report.

Logic in Paragraphing

Well-crafted, coherent paragraphs strengthen reports at what we call the **macro** level of a document's structure—the level of organization beyond the sentence. As essential to producing useful reports as a writer's choice of words and style(s), carefully arranged paragraphs having a logical internal development foster reader comprehension of the larger units of prose that make up the whole.

Because paragraphing is fundamentally a visual device, good paragraphing encourages readers to see textual material before attempting to read through it at length. Readers expect well-organized, carefully constructed paragraphs that permit them to

- preview the overall design of a printed page—*before* the reading process begins—at the point of initial eye contact.
- predict the relative importance of information that appears on the page in various chunks and subsections.

Don't disappoint them. Well-organized, highly focused paragraphs help readers process and comprehend report content rapidly.

Coherent, carefully structured paragraphs should present major points— key ideas, issues, topics—to readers in some kind of logical order. Generally, readers proceed from one point to the next within paragraphs according to either a deductive or inductive arrangement. Paragraphs organized deductively articulate major points up front followed by minor points of support, detail, and exemplification. Whenever paragraphs are arranged inductively, minor points lead to the major point, which appears in the final sentence of the paragraph.

Structuring paragraphs deductively, with key ideas presented in topic sentences up front, ensures that interested readers can scan paragraphs quickly to gain some sense of the sequence of ideas presented in the whole document. In well-focused, deductively arranged business reports, the first sentence of each paragraph can stand alone as a "lead-in" to the ideas presented in the rest of the paragraph. Conversely, the final sentence in any paragraph often, though by no means always, serves as a "wrap-up" or conclusion to the paragraph.

In order to enhance clarity and promote ease of reader comprehension, we suggest that report writers carefully weigh the advantages of constructing paragraphs that

> focus on a single idea, major issue, or key point.
>
> display an internal logic or coherence based on a deductive arrangement.
>
> place the topic, lead-in, or main sentence up front.

Whenever paragraphs that form your document are carefully focused and cohesively related to one another, efficient readers can acquire a document's central message simply by reading the first and last sentences of each paragraph. Effective documents contain paragraphs that promote skimming and scanning by busy managers who need data and information fast.

Paragraph Length

Just as long sentences impede rather than promote reader comprehension, long paragraphs function just about the same way. Just as long sentences should be broken up into smaller, more manageable units, particularly long paragraphs should be divided into more compact, more unified chunks of prose. Most readers have a difficult, if not impossible, time isolating key points and focusing on major ideas that appear within long, amorphous paragraphs. All but the most diligent readers end up getting lost.

Writers must style their paragraphs to promote comprehension. Readers simply cannot afford to spend valuable time deciphering or untangling the meanings of heaps of sentences found in long shapeless paragraphs. Moreover, readers cannot readily determine the relative importance of ideas occurring in overlong chunks of prose. Figure 6.2 shows a sample overlong paragraph, a unit of prose found in a systems analyst's report that would easily lose even the most motivated reader.

Alternatively, report pages composed largely of very brief paragraphs of a sentence or two usually end up confusing readers as well. When writers consistently deploy short paragraphs on a single page of text or throughout an entire document, the content appears fragmentary and underdeveloped to readers. Reading through bunches of "headline"-like paragraphs suggests to readers that the writer cannot fully develop an idea with sufficient support and exemplification. If used strategically, however, single-sentence paragraphs can effectively call attention to, and encapsulate, a central idea, major issue, or key point.

Remember, the primary job of report writers is to make the job of report readers easy. Constructing well-formed paragraphs must be considered a major part of that job. Exactly how long, though, should a well-developed, reader-centered paragraph be? And how long is too long? One rule of thumb

This approach demands the creation of duplicate functional environments in both data center locations. Gradually over an extended period of time users are migrated from the old data center to the new. There are many difficulties involved in this approach. One of the greatest difficulties that will be encountered in this approach will be identifying, segregating, and moving individual users' data. This applies to data stored on all types of media supported by the data center. The tasks related to data stored on real discs could be handled with less difficulty than those related to the other types of storage media. The tasks related to data stored in the tape library and the mass storage facility could demand more manpower resources than are available. One of the difficulties that is more obvious is that of moving data that is shared by multiple users. Now the task becomes one of identifying which users must be moved as a group. The situation could possibly exist that some data would have to be maintained in duplicate in both data centers for some period of time. This possibility creates some operational problems related to scheduling of some of the users' work. The likelihood of error also increases in the case of recovery situations. Examples of some duplication possibilities are the control data sets that are required by the Tape Management System, the Hierarchical Storage Manager, and the mass storage facility. An additional problem of clean-up will exist at the time the duplication will be eliminated. Aside from the problems of identifying and segregating the individual users, this approach could require considerable time to accomplish. The longer it takes to complete the move, the greater the possibility for a higher exposure of impact on our user community. Impact caused by an increase of the time required for the move can manifest itself in a number of ways regardless of the choice of the technique selected to accomplish the move. The most noticeable would be the impact caused by the loss of certain hardware redundancy for some period of time. The inability to provide switching capabilities to multiple CPU's and 3705's certainly will impair our backdrop capabilities.

[Supplied by Communication Strategies, Inc., of Albuquerque, NM]

FIGURE 6.2
Example of overlong, shapeless paragraph.

regarding paragraph length is this: If a report writer suspects that a paragraph might prove too long for a reader to read and process quickly, then that paragraph should be cut down during the process of revising the document in a second or later draft. Report writers can often divide extremely long sections of prose—when logically arranged—into two, three, or more moderate-size paragraphs (as demonstrated in Figure 6.3). As was the case at the sentence level, variation in paragraph length serves to keep readers attentive and interested, enabling them to digest report content at a reasonably rapid pace.

ORIGINAL

During the past year we have made significant progress toward expanding our product line and developing new market opportunities. First, Version 66 of MSC/NASTRAN offers users new capabilities in several key areas, especially in "design optimization." We believe this new feature has the potential of playing a major role in improving our clients' design procedures. Second, our adaptation of MSC/NASTRAN to new computer hardware now makes our product's powerful computational features available on platforms ranging from the personal computer to the world's most powerful supercomputers. Third, we have recently released our new interactive pre- and postprocessor, MSC/XL. MSC/XL's outstanding user interface will greatly simplify the tasks of preparing input for MSC/NASTRAN and digesting its output. Fourth, we are now developing an advanced electromagnetics analysis product called MSC/EMAS for release in the latter part of 1989. MSC/EMAS combines the power and sophistication of MSC/NASTRAN's numerical procedures with the engineering content of the electromagnetics packages MSC/MAGNUM, MSC/MAGNETIC, and MSC/MAGGIE that we acquired from A. O. Smith and continue to market. Fifth, we have recently released our new crash-dynamics analysis package, MSC/DYNA, which we adapted from a public domain program and upgraded to meet MSC's rigorous standards of engineering quality and support.

REVISION

During the past year we have made significant progress toward expanding our product line and developing new market opportunities. First, Version 66 of MSC/NASTRAN offers users new capabilities in several key areas, especially in "design optimization." We believe this new feature has the potential of playing a major role in improving our clients' design procedures.

Second, our adaptation of MSC/NASTRAN to new computer hardware now makes our product's powerful computational features available on platforms ranging from the personal computer to the world's most powerful supercomputers.

Third, we have recently released our new interactive pre- and postprocessor, MSC/XL. MSC/XL's outstanding user interface will greatly simplify the tasks of preparing input for MSC/NASTRAN and digesting its output.

Fourth, we are now developing an advanced electromagnetics analysis product called MSC/EMAS for release in the later part of 19 – –. MSC/EMAS combines the power and sophistication of MSC/NASTRAN's numerical procedures with the engineering content of the electromagnetics packages MSC/MAGNUM, MSC/MAGNETIC, and MSC/MAGGIE that we acquired from A. O. Smith and continue to market.

Fifth, we have recently released our new crash-dynamics analysis package, MSC/DYNA, which we adapted from a public domain program and upgraded to meet MSC's rigorous standards of engineering quality and support.

FIGURE **6.3**

Example of long paragraph—original plus revision.

> *During the 1980s, Baldor completely restructured manufacturing operations* [TS]. *In the early 1980s, major capital investments were made* [TP] in state-of-the art equipment, tooling and hardware. *In the late 1980s, Baldor installed* [TP] Flexible Flow manufacturing *and retrained* [TP] all employees in the latest quality concepts. *Baldor also developed* [TP] sophisticated yet easy to use information systems to support the computer hardware and the restructured manufacturing plants. *These improvements have resulted in* [TP] improved quality, improved deliveries, shorter cycle times, and lower inventory levels.

FIGURE 6.4

Example of well-focused, moderate-size paragraph.

Note: Italicized portions of text identify intitial topic sentence (TS), which indicates paragraph's main idea, and key transition points (TP) within the paragraph.

Unified, well-focused paragraphs found in the best, reader-centered managerial reports usually contain four to six sentences on average. Figure 6.4 exhibits a well-focused, relatively brief paragraph culled from a recent corporate annual report.

Paragraphing as a Stage in Revision

Report writers need not be concerned with the elements of effective paragraphing until they have gotten beyond at least the first draft of a document. Arranging, developing, and organizing paragraphs should occur during the revision stage of the report-writing process rather than during initial drafting. Writers might ask themselves the following questions as they begin to shape paragraphs during the revision stage of the report-writing process:

- Does each of my paragraphs seem unified and focused, emphasizing a single idea, major issue, or key point?
- Do my paragraphs display internal coherence based on a deductive arrangement? An inductive arrangement?
- Does each paragraph in my report contain a topic or lead-in sentence? Placed up front, at the beginning of the paragraph? Placed at the end, summing up an idea?
- Are my paragraphs too long? Will excessive paragraph length impede clear communication? If so, how can long paragraphs best be broken up into smaller, more comprehensible units?
- Are my paragraphs sufficiently elaborate, with proper support, details, and examples? If not, which short paragraphs might be combined to eliminate fragmentation of ideas and improve development?
- Are my paragraphs arranged so that a reader can comprehend the message of the whole document using a logical, step-by-step process?

Final Note on Language and Managerial Decision Making

All too often, managerial decision making is deprived of important ideas, valuable data, and essential solutions because the information report writers present—and managers must read—is buried in unclear, wordy, poorly styled, and badly organized documents. The ability of executives, managers, government administrators, and other professionals to design, construct, and present data and information successfully in written form can mean the difference between an organization's meeting its goals and objectives or losing its competitive edge.

The ability of managers and other professionals in business, industry, and government to communicate useful information efficiently and effectively has become one of the most important resources available to the leadership in just about any contemporary organization. In fact, in an overwhelming number of today's business, industrial, military, and governmental contexts, information has surpassed the status of mere resource and has become, according to one communication expert, the most valuable commodity an organization can produce, manage, and market.

Summary

Because report writing is critical to planning for and operating contemporary organizations, managers must be concerned with producing reports that are, above all, clear, concise, and written with style in precise, vivid language. In this chapter, therefore, we have concentrated on three major domains essential to constructing effective reports: (1) language precision (**micro** matters of clarity, simplicity, brevity, and conciseness); (2) style (micro matters of word choice and sentence variety and length); and (3) paragraph management (**macro** matters of organization, arrangement, and development).

Throughout this chapter we have presented and reviewed numerous prose samples, both strong and weak, taken from a wide range of managerial reports. We hope our examination of prose samples has helped to raise the awareness level of report writers about the need for and ingredients essential to producing effective professional documents. Managerial writers should write to express ideas rather than to impress others. They should use clear, concise, vivid, straightforward language in their reports. And, in order to ensure the successful communication of their messages up and down the corporate ladder, writers should use precise **first-degree** words, avoiding longer, more abstract words and phrases whenever possible.

In addition, we have discussed what we call "professional second languages," or **jargon,** and have demonstrated how the use of jargon can create major comprehension difficulties for many readers. Frequently, the use of jargon, coupled with, say, an abundance of acronyms, redundancies, or the passive voice, results in complete communication failure for groups of readers whose expertise or profession falls outside a report's field of inquiry.

Next, we have discussed **style.** We have defined style as a matter of personal choice closely associated with a writer's intended meaning and the reader's perceived meaning of report content. Style is, above all, a way of writing and a situational matter. Managers should consider adopting writing styles tailored to (a) specific organizational contexts, (b) rhetorical occasions eliciting documents, (c) established writer–reader relationships, and (d) desired results.

To illustrate our discussion of style, we have reviewed a variety of report-writing styles that managers might choose, depending on their needs in particular business situations. Among the more common report-writing styles we have considered are the following: **official, consultative, casual,** and **chummy.** We also have reviewed a number of stylistic **dimensions** that report writers can manipulate for their own rhetorical purposes. Among those dimensions of prose style are abstract words, passive versus active voice constructions, nominalizations, weak linking verbs (e.g., *to be*), and negative words and phrases.

Although writers now have access to computer software such as RightWriter and Writer's Workbench that aids managers in styling their reports, software currently available has not yet eliminated the need for human editorial contact.

Finally, we have examined **paragraph management.** Well-crafted, coherent paragraphs strengthen reports at the macro level of a document's structure. A paragraph is basically a visual element, and good paragraphing enables a reader to preview text in advance of reading a given page at length. Writers should construct documents with carefully arranged paragraphs that have logical internal development. Highly focused paragraphs, arranged logically, foster rapid reading and comprehension of a whole document's central message.

Related Reading

BATES, JEFFERSON D. *Writing with Precision: How to Write So That You Cannot Possibly Be Misunderstood.* Washington, DC: Acropolis, 1985.

BERNSTEIN, THEODORE. *The Careful Writer: A Modern Guide to English Usage.* New York: Atheneum, 1980.

BOGARD, MORRIS R. *The Manager's Style Book: Communication Skills to Improve Your Performance.* Englewood Cliffs, NJ: Prentice, 1979.

CORBETT, MARY T. "Making State Laws Gender-Neutral." *Simply Stated* 75 (Sept.–Oct. 1987): 1–2 and 4.

CROW, PETER. "Plain English: What Counts Besides Readability?" *The Journal of Business Communication* 25 (1988): 87-95.

DOCUMENT DESIGN CENTER. "Eliminating Gender Bias in Language." *Simply Stated* 28 (1982): 2.

EPSTEIN, E. L. *Language and Style.* London: Methuen, 1978.

FIELDEN, JOHN S. " 'What Do You Mean You Don't Like My Style?' " *Harvard Business Review* 60 (May–June 1982): 128–138.

FLESCH, RUDOLF. *The Art of Readable Writing.* New York: Macmillan, 1962.

GRAY, BENNISON. *Style: The Problem and Its Solution.* The Hague: Mouton, 1969.

GRAZIAN, FRANK. "Can Plain English Survive?" *Communication Briefings* 7.8 (1988): 3.

HARBAUGH, FREDERICK W. "Accentuate the Positive." *Technical Communication* 38 (1991): 73–74.

HOLCOMBE, MARYA W., and JUDITH K. STEIN. *Writing for Decision Makers: Memos and Reports with a Competitive Edge.* 2nd ed. New York: Van Nostrand, 1987.

HOUGH, GRAHAM. *Style and Stylistics.* London: Routledge, 1972.

JOOS, MARTIN. *The Five Clocks: A Linguistic Excursion into the Five Styles of English Usage.* New York: Harcourt, 1967.

"Labor Letter." *Wall Street Journal* 19 Oct. 1982: A1.

LINTON, CALVIN D. *Effective Revenue Writing 2.* Washington, DC: Dept of Treas./IRS, U.S. GPO, 1962 (Training No. 129).

MEAD, SHEPHERD. *How to Succeed in Business without Really Trying: The Dastard's Guide to Fame and Fortune.* New York: Simon, 1952.

MELLINKOFF, DAVID. *Legal Writing: Sense and Nonsense.* St. Paul, MN: West, 1982.

MENDELSON, MICHAEL. "Business Prose and the Nature of the Plain Style." *The Journal of Business Communication* 24 (1987): 3–18.

MILLER, CASEY, and KATE SWIFT. *The Handbook of Nonsexist Writing: For Writers, Editors, and Speakers.* 2nd ed. New York: Harper, 1988.

"Minor Memos." *Wall Street Journal* 15 Feb. 1991: A1.

MITCHELL, RICHARD. *The Leaning Tower of Babel and Other Affronts by the Underground Grammarian.* Boston: Little, 1984.

———. *Less than Words Can Say.* Boston: Little, 1979.

MUNTER, MARY. *Guide to Managerial Communication.* 2nd ed. Englewood Cliffs, NJ: Prentice, 1987.

OHMANN, RICHARD M. "Literature as Sentences." *Essays on the Language of Literature.* Eds. Seymour Chatman and Samuel R. Levin. Boston: Houghton, 1967.

ORWELL, GEORGE. "Politics and the English Language." *The Orwell Reader.* Intro. Richard H. Rovere. New York: Harvest-Harcourt, 1956.

PORTER, KENT. "Usage of the Passive Voice." *Technical Communication* 38 (1991): 87–88.

STEWART, ROY. "Writers Overuse the Passive Voice." *Technical Communication* 31 (1984): 14–16.

SUCHAN, JAMES, and RONALD DULEK. "An Empirical Assessment of Style: Trained and Untrained Students' Responses." *The Journal of Business Communication* 23 (1986): 57–65.

THOMPSON, EDWARD T. "How to Write Clearly." *Power of the Printed Word Reprint Series.* Elmsford, NY: International Paper, 1979.

TICHY, H. J. *Effective Writing for Engineers, Managers, Scientists.* 2nd ed. New York: Wiley, 1988.

WILLIAMS, JOSEPH M. *Style: Ten Lessons in Clarity and Grace.* 3rd ed. Glenview, IL: Scott, 1989.

WOLF, CHARLES, JR. "Decision Makers—Profile." *Management Review* Feb. 1991: 48.

WYDICK, RICHARD C. *Plain English for Lawyers.* 2nd ed. Durham, NC: Carolina AP, 1985.

PART III

Researching, Organizing, and Documenting the Management Report

CHAPTER 7

Conducting Secondary Research for Management Reports

Research is the systematic process of collecting, synthesizing, organizing, and evaluating data and information, and it is central to the successful planning and execution of all business activities. Organizations regularly face new questions, problems, and challenges, and they increasingly look to research for answers. The types of research required by today's organizations are as diverse as the kinds of management decisions for which the research is intended.

Businesses, for example, depend heavily on financial research to make wise capital investments with their profits. To improve the sales and distribution of their products, companies also research existing or prospective markets by analyzing sales and distribution methods, performing sales forecasts, or surveying target consumers. Moreover, organizations interested in expanding operations rely on sound fiscal and strategic planning to generate financial backing from capital investors. An organization's research and development (R&D) division might investigate ways to shorten the lead time needed to move a product from the drawing board to production, just as the manufacturing division of the same company might study methods for speeding operations and reducing material costs while also improving quality assurance. Furthermore, to understand better the professional needs, attitudes, and motivations of their workers, organizations currently invest millions of dollars into the research of crucial human resource issues, including employee training, labor laws, morale, safety, wages, salaries, advancement, and working conditions.

Research Sources in Managerial Report Writing ————

Regardless of the specific type of research you may be asked to perform for your organization, you will collect your research from either secondary or primary sources. **Secondary sources** contain information that other researchers have already collected, analyzed, and reported in either published or unpublished form. Books, journals, magazines, and newspapers comprise the bulk of secondary sources; however, your research should not overlook unpublished works, such as business reports, operating and procedural manuals, and doctoral dissertations, which often provide highly specific and detailed information that could be valuable to your report.

Primary research involves the synthesizing, analyzing, and evaluating of data or information culled from your own observations or studies through such methodologies as experimentation, surveys, and interviews. Such investigations are designed to answer questions and to solve problems surrounding the specific focus of your document. Consequently, primary sources can provide extremely detailed and relevant data and information. Planning and performing the kind of primary research that will provide you with accurate and reliable data can, however, be prohibitively time-consuming and expensive for researchers with tight deadlines and restrictive budgets.

Researching secondary or primary sources will normally be the most time-intensive phase of your report-writing process. To use your time efficiently, it is important that you design a logical and ordered system for collecting, organizing, and evaluating information. This chapter provides you with such a strategy for researching secondary sources, as Chapter 8 does for primary research. In examining the secondary research process and its role in managerial reports, this chapter discusses

benefits of secondary research.

research strategies.

organization of libraries and their research capabilities.

sources of data and information available through secondary research.

advantages and limitations of computer data-based searches.

selecting and evaluating sources collected from secondary research.

compiling bibliography and note cards.

Benefits of Secondary Research ————————

Before collecting data or information from secondary sources, you should first consider how those sources might best serve your research and writing process. First, by conducting a thorough search of secondary sources, you can determine if other researchers have already completed and published similar research on a subject. Uncovering and using such related research in your report can save you considerable energy, time, and money that you might otherwise have spent in performing your own primary study (Emory, 1980, p. 192). In effect, investigating secondary resources is primary research by proxy.

Secondary sources can also help you better define and focus your report topic. Inexperienced writers too often select topics that are so broad and ill-defined that they would have to fill volumes to cover their subjects sufficiently. You can learn much about the research and writing process of effective communication by reading how noted authors in your field have limited the parameters of their own studies. Although the general subject of your report may have already been decided for you by superiors, examining how other authors handle topics related to your topic helps you to (a) decide what specific content should be included in your report and (b) determine how that information might best be organized to meet your audience's informational needs, technical backgrounds, professional interests, and intended uses of the information.

In addition, secondary sources provide you with contextual background on the subject(s) of your research, as well as related topics that might deserve coverage in your report. In this way, the research process is, in essence, a method of self-education, and the collected information may prove central to analyzing and solving the problem(s) addressed in your report.

When used as substantive evidence in your report, secondary sources also lend credibility and authority to your discussion of issues. A thorough investigation of secondary sources tells readers that you've done your homework and that you understand the significance of your own research as it relates to the work of other authors in the field. By discovering where other researchers stand on the subject, you can determine where your approach to and research on the same, or a related, issue fit into the general pool of knowledge. In addition to their value as supportive evidence, many secondary sources provide bibliographies of still more useful references pertaining to your topic.

Finally, your investigation of secondary sources can reveal areas within your field of study that deserve further attention. You may decide to redefine the focus or expand the scope of your report to cover those unexplored topics. If you cannot alter the scope of your report to address uncovered but important areas relevant to your research, at least the recognition of these shortcomings in coverage might help generate future reports on the subject.

Research Strategy _____

Normally, researchers perform either pure research or applied research. Investigators involved in **pure**, or **basic**, **research** study topics of professional interest or import. Such research can add much to the field of knowledge in which the researchers are working. However, because these studies often hold little work-world application, they are seldom used in the business world. Projects of pure research are rarely designed to produce results of practical value.

Applied research, on the other hand, is born out of a pragmatic need to solve real-world problems. Its intent, from its very inception, is to make practical use of the study's findings and conclusions. Central aims of investigators performing applied research are to educate themselves in the problem, to report subsequent findings and analyses of the data, and, frequently, to recommend appropriate courses of action.

Most business reports are the products of applied research. Their primary purpose is not to provide readers with an exhaustive study of sources written on a specific topic but, rather, to study and present enough reliable and relevant information on which management can base important business decisions. Thus, your objective in performing secondary research for a managerial report is to collect accurate and objective data that are directly related to the focus and scope of your project. To do this, you must select only sources that contribute significantly to solving the problem at hand (Zikmund, 1991, pp. 59–70).

Before beginning your secondary research, you should plan a logical and cost-effective strategy for collecting only the data you need to complete a thorough and accurate report on or before its deadline and within its budget. The following preresearch steps should aid you in starting your research off on the right foot.

1. Clearly define the focus, scope, and purpose of your report. Try to state your purpose in a single sentence. (Stating the purpose in the form of a question often helps to identify the report problem as well as possible solutions.)
2. Estimate how much of the total time and money available to the report project should be allocated to the research phase.
3. Select a method for researching secondary sources that offers you the best chance of finding the required information quickly and conveniently.
4. Decide if you will need special research expertise, such as a librarian knowledgeable in computer data-based searches, in order to complete the research phase successfully by a predetermined deadline.
5. Begin your research at a point that immediately attracts you and where you have some basic knowledge or preliminary understanding. (Blank, 1984, Chaps. 2–3; Sekaran, 1984)

Location of Secondary Sources

University and public libraries are the most common source of secondary information and may prove to be the most productive resources for your research. However, many professionals often benefit significantly by beginning their research in company libraries as well as those of private organizations.

Company and Private Libraries

Company and private libraries could prove invaluable to your research, as they may well represent the only source of company-specific information on such topics as your organization's financial condition, management, personnel, production, and R&D. While company libraries are corporate property, private libraries are often maintained by professional associations and trade organizations. Company libraries can be especially useful, as they often contain relatively complete archives of in-house (internal) information (e.g., annual reports, company memoranda, employee handbooks and manuals, company newsletters and newspapers, policy and procedural directives, sales proposals, and strategic planning reports) as well as recorded interviews with company personnel. Company libraries also contain external materials (including books, government documents, journals, newspapers, and trade magazines) that, although generated outside the company, are often directly related to the organization's mission (Lavin, 1987, pp. 7–9).

In the past, internal documents were traditionally archived on hard copy and subsequently filed. Today, however, many of those documents are stored on computerized data bases, affording the researcher more convenience, faster access, and a more complete document search.

Planning the Search

Before rummaging haphazardly through company file cabinets or data bases, you should first

- define the exact focus of your study or the problem to be addressed in your report.
- decide which internal documents will provide you with the needed data and information on which to build a thorough, accurate, and decisive report.
- determine the location of those sources within the company as well as the most effective method of accessing and using them.
- restrict study to only information directly relevant to your report topic.

Collecting Internal Secondary Sources

The kinds and number of internal documents available to the researcher depend on the nature, size, and management structure of the company. Rarely will all divisions of a company open all their files to you. Although security clearances might occasionally prevent you from examining company-sensitive information, corporate politics often loom as the central reason that researchers are denied information. This obstacle, however, can normally be overcome. You'll obtain greater access to internal documents by (a) formally requesting and receiving support and authority from senior-level management to perform the study and (b) briefing managers within the areas of study on the goals of your research and ways the study will benefit not only the company as a whole but, perhaps, those same managers and their departments.

Ordinarily, the nature of your report problem will determine the types of company sources required to research a report subject properly. For example, let's assume that you are preparing a strategic plan for the R&D division of a pharmaceutical firm. You recognize the need for your company to introduce a new drug to compete with others of its kind currently being marketed by competitors. Company documents show that the firm's R&D division has experimented with drugs similar to the proposed new drug, yet no internal study or report addresses the issue of whether the company could successfully develop, much less produce, the new drug. The logical research avenue to explore might be the personnel files of the firm's scientists. Do they have the backgrounds and qualifications necessary to develop the drug? Do company records suggest that the R&D division is properly tooled and sufficiently staffed to handle new testing demands? Investigation of various internal documents might answer those questions.

To select only relevant and accurate company sources, be certain that the documents are timely and up-to-date. You should also confirm the accuracy and reliability of the information. What are the expertise and qualifications of the authors of these internal documents? Were their research and analysis methods sound?

To understand the full context surrounding these documents, you may supplement your investigation of internal documents with interviews of current or former employees affiliated with the planning, writing, or production of the documents. In cases where no internal documents exist, interviews might be the only remaining source of information on the type of detailed, company-specific material needed for your report. In other instances, discussing the report problem with colleagues could be significantly faster than performing a search of company documents. You might also depend on your observation of company operations for supplemental information when no relevant internal documentation or employee expertise is available. More about primary research methods, including interviewing and observation research, is provided in Chapter 8.

Advantages and Disadvantages of Internal Sources

Investigating secondary sources within your company can be valuable to your research because internal sources are

- often the only method of uncovering detailed, company-specific information.
- convenient to the researcher and possible interviewees.
- relatively inexpensive.

The disadvantages, however, of investigating secondary sources within your company are that such research can be difficult to perform because

- company records are notoriously disorganized, by and large, and often incomplete.
- the company- or industry-specific focus of internal resources invariably means that researchers must look elsewhere for information on external matters.
- employees whose expertise could be a valuable complement to company records are no longer with the organization.
- company turf battles constrict a researcher's access to important information (Emory, 1980, pp. 61–67).

Apart from a company's central library facilities, departments within the firm might support smaller, decentralized libraries that provide information specific to the regular duties of those organizational units. No research investigation within your company is complete, however, until you make use of the expertise of colleagues. If your research concerns department- or company-specific issues, the notes, files, bookshelves, and compiled research of fellow employees can save you significant time and energy. Some of your colleagues may already have performed studies similar to your own and can provide insights into your topic that you could gain nowhere else.

If research into your own company's records produces insufficient material, you might explore the libraries of other organizations conducting business in allied fields (Schlessinger, 1983, pp. 129–167). Many companies provide outside researchers with access to nonclassified information housed in their libraries.

Public and Research Libraries

After you have thoroughly researched relevant materials available in private libraries, you should investigate the resources of public and college or university libraries. **Public libraries** are sometimes referred to as **general libraries,** as they satisfy the varied reading needs of diverse audiences. Public libraries typically offer materials on a broad range of topics and at various reading levels to meet the informational needs of their users. However, you might find that the coverage offered by general library resources is inadequate for extensive research in specialized areas, as normally required by business research projects.

Because they must support faculty and students in their research efforts, college and university libraries can provide a vast array of resources on general as well as specialized topics. Also referred to as **research libraries,** college and university libraries normally offer modern search methods, including computerized card catalogs and data-based searches, for locating sources. In addition to providing standard secondary sources (e.g., books, newspapers, periodicals), research libraries maintain useful unpublished materials, including brochures, theses, dissertations, manuals, and pamphlets. Some college and university libraries are also depositories for federal government documents covering such areas as congressional legislation, scientific and technical research, committee findings, and public service records. Take advantage of these valuable resources and determine if your local college or university library is a depository of federal documents.

For an extensive listing of private, public, college and university, and government libraries, consult the *Directory of Special Libraries and Information Centers* published by Gale Research Company.

Organization of Libraries

Most libraries use either the Dewey Decimal System or Library of Congress System for cataloging and shelving their books. In the past, some libraries have actually used both systems to organize different types of secondary resources.

However, the large majority of libraries are now converting totally to the Library of Congress System.

Dewey Decimal System

The **Dewey Decimal System** classifies books into 10 different categories and references each by a call number. The classifications under the Dewey Decimal System are noted below:

000–099	General Works	500–599	Pure Science
100–199	Philosophy	600–699	Technology (Applied Sciences)
200–299	Religion	700–799	Fine Arts
300–399	Social Sciences	800–899	Literature
400–499	Language	900–999	History

You may find the 300 (Social Sciences) and 600 (Technology) divisions to be the most useful when performing business or technical research. Each of these 10 classes is further divided into groups of 10 subclasses, which are then divided into additional subclasses. The 10 subclasses of Technology, for example, are

600	Technology (Applied Sciences)	650	Management
610	Medical Sciences	660	Chemical Technology
620	Engineering	670	Manufacturers
630	Agriculture	680	Miscellaneous Manufacturers
640	Home Economics	690	Buildings

Library of Congress System

Developed to offer more categories than the Dewey Decimal System, the **Library of Congress System** references books by letters and classifies the works into 20 distinct classes:

A	General Works	L	Education
B	Philosophy, Psychology, and Religion	M	Music
		N	Fine Arts
C	History and Auxiliary Sciences	P	Language and Literature
D	History and Topography (except North and South America)	Q	Science
		R	Medicine
E–F	History: North and South America	S	Agriculture
		T	Technology
G	Geography and Anthropology	U	Military Science
H	Social Sciences	V	Naval Science
J	Political Science	Z	Bibliography and Library Science
K	Law		

(As they are not currently in use, the classes I, O, W, X, and Y are omitted from the list.)

For performing general business research, you may find the H (Social Sciences) category most helpful. Class H contains 16 subclasses. The first two subclasses (subclasses H and HA) constitute the generalia (general works and statistics) section for the social sciences. Seven subclasses (HB–HJ) form the economics section. The HB subclass contains works on economic theory; HC and HD contain economic history and agricultural, industrial, and national production; HE is transportation and communication; HF is finance, money, banking, and insurance; and HJ is public finance. The remaining seven subclasses comprise the sociology section, which includes general works and theory relating to sociology, social history, social problems and reform, and social groups.

Guidelines for Selecting Secondary Sources _____

As you collect secondary sources, remember the context and purpose of your research. By failing to select and keep only the most promising sources you uncover, you will likely find yourself with far more sources than you need. Moreover, a large percentage of the sources you gather may be only obliquely related to your subject and, thus, only marginally useful to your study or not useful at all.

You can save yourself from having to sort through mountains of relatively useless sources at the end of your research by evaluating each secondary source, as you find it, against some basic criteria. Scan the source's table of contents or read its abstract and ask yourself the following questions:

- Are the topics discussed in the source sufficiently related to my report subject(s)?
- Will the work provide me with reliable background or context to the problem as I have identified it? Could it provide insights into the viewpoints of other authors on the same subject?
- Will the source's information meet the informational needs and professional interests of my audience(s)?
- Does the source contain unique information that should be covered in my report and that no other source has yet delivered?
- Does the information seem readily accessible? Would the time and energy spent reading the source prove cost-effective for the quality and depth of the material that I might receive from it?

Secondary Sources _____

Although the Information Age has significantly increased the amount and variety of information available to researchers, it has also made the search process to access that wealth of material more complex. How do you go about locating the considerably greater reservoir of information now available on your topic?

Fortunately, the techniques and technologies for accessing library information have kept pace with the growing sea of secondary resources. To expedite research, most publications are indexed; that is, their titles, authors, and contents are noted in separate publications called **indexes.** Many specialized indexes list sources that pertain exclusively to business issues. However, though your research normally focuses on business-oriented topics, don't dismiss indexes that are more general in scope. They can provide a meaningful context for more focused and detailed data and information on your report subject.

Locating Sources with the Card Catalog

The card catalog contains 3- × 5-in. cards that list all books in the library and is typically located on the building's main floor. Many libraries have two sets of card catalogs: one that lists books alphabetically by the work's author and title, the other by the work's subject. Some libraries also store the contents of their card catalogs on computer, microfilm, or microfiche media to save space and speed search time.

The call number noted on each card serves as the book's identification number and also helps you to locate the document on the library shelf. Locating a needed source is easy if you know the author and title of the work. You simply find the book's index card in the catalog and make a note of its call number in the card's upper left-hand corner (Figures 7.1, 7.2, and 7.3). If your library offers a computerized search system, the same book referenced in the card catalog can also be found by entering a subject heading into the computerized card catalog. For example, Patrick Below's *The Executive Guide to Strategic Planning* can be referenced by entering the author's name, the title of the book, or an appropriate subheading, such as "strategic planning," as illustrated in Figure 7.4.

```
                        Strategic Planning

     HD          Below, Patrick J.
     30.28            The executive guide to strategic
     .B45         planning / Patrick J. Below, George L.
     1987         Morrisey, Betty L. Acomb. -- 1st ed. --
                  San Francisco, Calif. : Jossey-Bass,
                  c1987.
                      xxiii, 136 p. : ill. ; 24 cm. -- (The
                  Jossey-Bass management series)
                      Bibliography: p. 127-131.
                      Includes index.
                      ISBN 1-555-42032-x (alk. paper)

                      1. Strategic planning.  I. Morrisey,
                  George L.  II. Acomb, Betty L.

                  III. Title  IV. Series

     TXEU    29  JUN  87     14716762     TXUMsc     86-27863
```

FIGURE 7.1

Index card referenced by author.

```
HD                    The executive guide to strategic
30.28                     planning
.B45        Below, Patrick J.
1987            The executive guide to strategic
            planning / Patrick J. Below, George L.
            Morrisey, Betty L. Acomb. -- 1st ed. --
            San Fransisco, Calif. : Jossey-Bass,
            c1987.
                xxiii, 136 p. : ill. ; 24 cm. -- (The
            Jossey-Bass management series)
                Bibliography: p. 127-131.
                Includes index.
                ISBN 1-555-42032-X (alk. paper)

                1. Strategic planning.  I. Morrisey,
            George L.  II. Acomb, Betty L.
            III. Title  IV. Series

TXEU     29  JUN  87      14716762      TXUMnt      86-27863
```

Figure 7.2

Index card referenced by title.

In addition to supplying a book's author and title, index cards include important bibliographic information, such as the publisher of the work, the book's date, and its place of publication. Some cards also provide a short abstract of the book's contents.

When you have no particular book in mind, or if you're unsure of a book's author and title, you can try referencing works by subject (Figure 7.3). For ideas

```
                Strategic Planning
HD          Below, Patrick J.
30.28           The executive guide to strategic
.B45        planning / Patrick J. Below, George L.
1987        Morrisey, Betty L. Acomb. -- 1st ed. --
            San Francisco, Calif. : Jossey-Bass,
            c1987.
                xxiii, 136 p. : ill. ; 24 cm. -- (The
            Jossey-Bass management series)
                Bibliography: p. 127-131.
                Includes index.
                ISBN 1-555-42032-X (alk. paper)


                1. Strategic planning.  I. Morrisey,
            George L.  II. Acomb, Betty L.
            III. Title  IV. Series
```

Figure 7.3

Index card referenced by subject.

```
LUIS SEARCH REQUEST:  A=BELOW
BIBLIOGRAPHIC RECORD -- NO. 2 OF 2 ENTRIES FOUND

Below, Patrick J.
     The executive guide to strategic planning /
Patrick J. Below, George L. Morrisey, Betty L. Acomb.
-- 1st ed. -- San Fransisco, Calif. : Jossey-Bass, c1987.
     xxiii, 136 p. : ill. ; 24 cm. -- (The Jossey-Bass
     management series)
     Bibliography: p. 127-131.
     Includes index.
   SUBJECT HEADINGS (Library of Congress; use s=)
        Strategic planning.


LOCATION:  MAIN
CALL NUMBER:  HD30.28 .B45 1987
CIRCULATION STATUS:  Not charged out. If not on shelf,
ask at Circulation Desk.


TYPE : TO RETURN TO INDEX.
TYPE e TO START OVER.
TYPE h FOR HELP.
TYPE COMMAND AND PRESS ENTER
```

FIGURE 7.4

Search of "Patrick J. Below" using the LUIS computerized card catalog.

on possible topics to explore in the catalog, you might consult the subject card located at the beginning of each subject area. The subject card provides cross-references to topics relating to your subject. If the subject headings you're using do not produce enough relevant books, you should refer to *Subject Headings Used in the Dictionary Catalog of the Library of Congress*, which offers an extensive list of subjects for card catalogs using the Library of Congress System, or consult the *Sears List of Subject Headings* (for the Dewey Decimal System).

If you have difficulty using any of the referencing systems discussed in this chapter, consult the reference librarian. She or he typically will not only explain the reference resources provided by that specific library but also direct you to sources that will serve as good starting points for your research.

Keep in mind that the card catalog is only a beginning point for your research. Although the card catalog offers a sound foundation of research information, the lag time associated with updating the catalog means that often the most recent books on a topic are not listed. Moreover, though listed in the catalog, some books may already be checked out, otherwise unavailable, or outdated for your project purposes. In addition, many sources vital to your research—periodicals, journals, government documents—will not be noted in the card catalog and, thus, must be referenced through other indexes.

Due to the rising costs associated with buying new resource materials, many libraries must now be selective when purchasing new works and maintaining subscriptions to such critical secondary sources as periodicals, newspapers, and computer search services. If your local library does not have a source needed in your research, you might be able to receive a copy of the document via the interlibrary loan system, through which participating libraries lend materials to one another. Before requesting a work through interlibrary loan, however, be sure that you've completed a thorough search of your own library for the source.

Locating Sources Using Your Library's Reference Section

The following sections of this chapter address secondary sources that can be useful to your research:

almanacs	annual reports
atlases	bibliographies
biographies	books
business services	corporate annual reports
dictionaries	directories
encyclopedias	government publications
guides	newspapers
pamphlets	periodicals

The intended purposes of, and information provided by, these secondary sources vary greatly. It is important that you carefully select the types of sources best suited for your research needs.

Almanacs, Atlases, and Dictionaries

Almanacs and atlases are key sources of current demographic, geographical, and historical information on a variety of subjects, including population, business, government, agriculture, commerce, and education. The following list offers some of the more useful almanacs and atlases.

Commercial Atlas and Marketing Guide. New York: Rand, 1969 to date.

Dow Jones-Irwin Business and Investment Almanac. Homewood, IL: Dow Jones-Irwin, 1977 to date.

The Economic Almanac. New York: National Industrial Conference Board, 1940 to date.

Goode's World Atlas. New York: Rand, 1922 to date.

Information Please Almanac, Atlas and Yearbook. New York: Simon, 1947 to date.

Reader's Digest Almanac and Yearbook. New York: Norton, 1966 to date.

The World Almanac and Book of Facts. New York: Doubleday, 1868 to date.

Of these sources, the *Dow Jones-Irwin Business and Investment Almanac* may prove most useful to your research, as it provides a range of information on such subjects as industry surveys; general business and economic indicators; taxes; stocks; real estate investment; employee benefits in large firms; government budgets, receipts, and deficits; and financial statement ratios of major corporations.

Dictionaries are frequently invaluable when performing any type of research, especially when investigating subjects outside your area of expertise. Leading unabridged dictionaries include the *Oxford English Dictionary, Funk and Wagnall's New Standard Dictionary, Random House Dictionary of the English Language,* and *Webster's Third New International Dictionary.* Useful abridged dictionaries include the *Random House College Dictionary, Webster's New Collegiate Dictionary,* and *Webster's New World Dictionary.*

Dictionaries particularly useful in business research include the *Dictionary for Accountants, Dictionary of Banking and Finance, Dictionary of Business and Management, Dictionary of Economics and Business, Dictionary of Finance,* and *Encyclopedic Dictionary of Business Law.* Business handbooks such as the *Accountant's Desk Handbook, Business Executive's Handbook, Handbook of Financial Management,* and *The Business Writer's Handbook* are also helpful for quick reference on a variety of business topics. The *Business Executive's Handbook,* for example, provides information on sales by direct mail, advertising, employee benefit plans, and credit and collection.

Bibliographies

Normally, you will accumulate a sufficient working bibliography as you research sources in your area of investigation. Many books and journal articles, for instance, include helpful bibliographies. On occasion, however, you may need to create a list of research sources from bibliographical indexes that cite all significant titles published on a given topic up to the indexes' year of publication.

The *Bibliographic Index: A Cumulative Bibliography of Bibliographies,* for example, lists subjects from perhaps the widest range of disciplines (Figure 7.5). It cites books and other sources that provide bibliographies on a given subject. Specialized bibliographic indexes such as the following provide bibliographies on subjects from specific fields of research:

> *Administration Management: A Selected and Annotated Bibliography.*
> Normal, OK: U of Oklahoma P, 1975.
>
> *Business Reference Sources: An Annotated Guide for Harvard Business School Students.*   Boston: Grad. School of Bus. Admin., Harvard U, 1976.
>
> *Economics Information Guide* series.   Detroit, MI: Gale, including *Economics of Minorities: A Guide to Information Sources* (1975); *History of Economic Analysis* (1976); *Labor Economics: A Guide to Information Sources* (1976); and *Money, Banking, and Macroeconomics: A Guide to Information Sources* (1977).
>
> *Management Information Guide* series.   Detroit, MI: Gale, including such titles as *Business Trends and Forecasting Information Sources* (1965); *Commercial Law Information Sources* (1970); *Computers and Data Processing Information Sources (1969); Ethics in Business Conduct:*

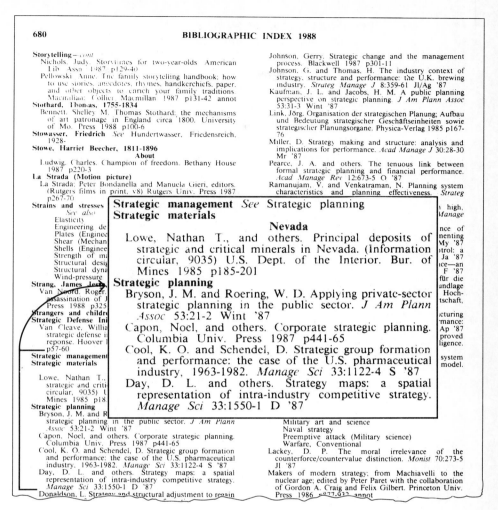

FIGURE 7.5

Search of sources relating to subject "Strategic Planning" using bibliographic index—*A Cumulative Bibliography of Bibliographies.*

Selected References from the Record: Selected Problems, Attempted Solutions, Ethics in Business Education (1970); *International Business and Foreign Trade* (1968); *Public Relations Information Sources* (1970); and *Real Estate Information Sources* (1963).

Small Business Bibliographies.   Washington, DC: SBA, 1977 to date.

The Source Directory.   Cleveland, OH: Predicasts, 1970 to date.

Thompson, Marilyn Taylor.   *Management Information: Where to Find It.*   Metuchen, NJ: Scarecrow, 1981.

Walsh, Ruth M., and Stanley J. Birkin.   *Business Communication: An Annotated Bibliography.*   Westport, CT: Greenwood, 1973.

Biographical References

For background information on prominent people, consult a biographical reference. While some biographical directories, such as the *Who's Who* series, provide a wealth of information on individuals (including their place of birth, parents, education, civic and political activities), directories of directors restrict their biography to business-related information. Commonly used biographical directories include

Biography Index. New York: Wilson, 1946 to date.

Current Biography. New York: Wilson, 1940 to date.

Dictionary of American Biography. New York: Scribner, 1928 to date.

Ingham, John W. *Biographical Dictionary of American Business Leaders*. Westport, CT: Greenwood, 1983.

Who's Who series (e.g., *Who's Who in America, Who's Who in American Jewry, Who's Who in American Law, Who's Who in American Education, Who's Who in Finance and Industry, Who's Who in Insurance*). Wilmette, IL: Macmillan Marquis Who's Who, 1899/1900 to date.

Figure 7.6 provides a sample page from *Who's Who in Finance and Industry*.

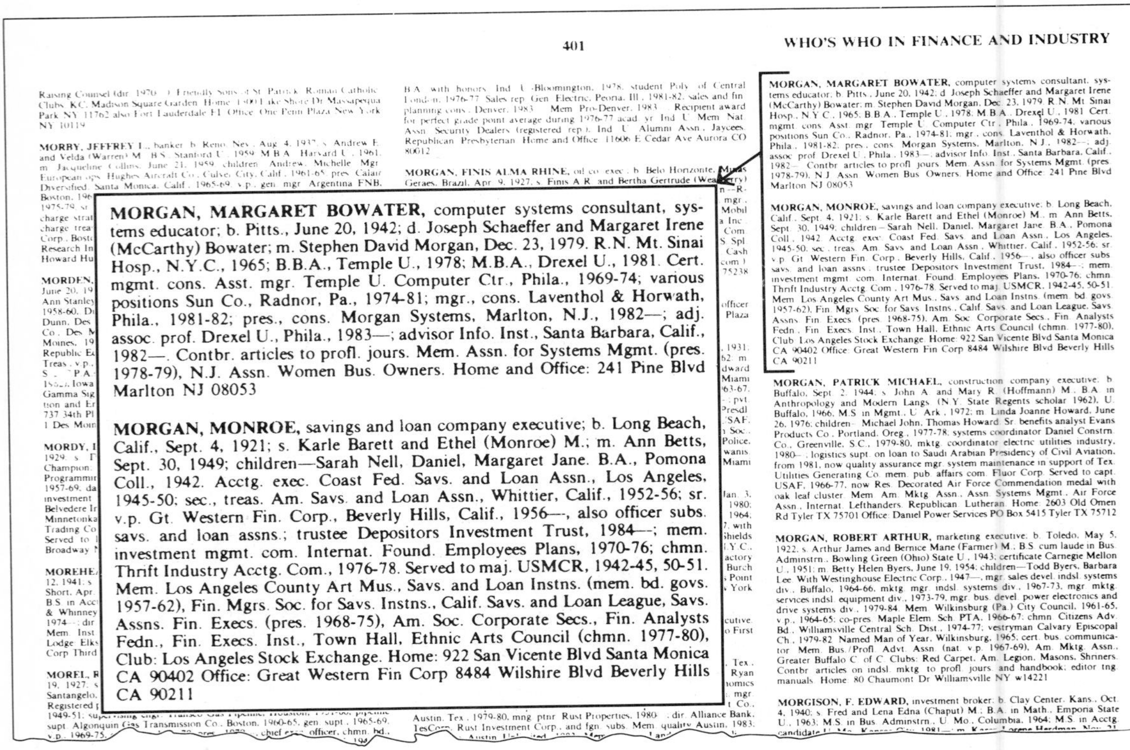

401 WHO'S WHO IN FINANCE AND INDUSTRY

MORGAN, MARGARET BOWATER, computer systems consultant, systems educator; b. Pitts., June 20, 1942; d. Joseph Schaeffer and Margaret Irene (McCarthy) Bowater; m. Stephen David Morgan, Dec. 23, 1979. R.N. Mt. Sinai Hosp., N.Y.C., 1965; B.B.A., Temple U., 1978; M.B.A., Drexel U., 1981. Cert. mgmt. cons. Asst. mgr. Temple U. Computer Ctr., Phila., 1969-74; various positions Sun Co., Radnor, Pa., 1974-81; mgr., cons. Laventhol & Horwath, Phila., 1981-82; pres., cons. Morgan Systems, Marlton, N.J., 1982—; adj. assoc. prof. Drexel U., Phila., 1983—; advisor Info. Inst., Santa Barbara, Calif., 1982—. Contbr. articles to profl. jours. Mem. Assn. for Systems Mgmt. (pres. 1978-79), N.J. Assn. Women Bus. Owners. Home and Office: 241 Pine Blvd Marlton NJ 08053

MORGAN, MONROE, savings and loan company executive; b. Long Beach, Calif., Sept. 4, 1921; s. Karle Barett and Ethel (Monroe) M.; m. Ann Betts, Sept. 30, 1949; children—Sarah Nell, Daniel, Margaret Jane. B.A., Pomona Coll., 1942. Acctg. exec. Coast Fed. Savs. and Loan Assn., Los Angeles, 1945-50; sec., treas. Am. Savs. and Loan Assn., Whittier, Calif., 1952-56; sr. v.p. Gt. Western Fin. Corp., Beverly Hills, Calif., 1956—, also officer subs. savs. and loan assns.; trustee Depositors Investment Trust, 1984—; mem. investment mgmt. com. Internat. Found. Employees Plans, 1970-76; chmn. Thrift Industry Acctg. Com., 1976-78. Served to maj. USMCR, 1942-45, 50-51. Mem. Los Angeles County Art Mus., Savs. and Loan Instns. (mem. bd. govs. 1957-62), Fin. Mgrs. Soc. for Savs. Instns., Calif. Savs. and Loan League, Savs. Assns. Fin. Execs. (pres. 1968-75), Am. Soc. Corporate Secs., Fin. Analysts Fedn., Fin. Execs. Inst., Town Hall, Ethnic Arts Council (chmn. 1977-80), Club: Los Angeles Stock Exchange. Home: 922 San Vicente Blvd Santa Monica CA 90402 Office: Great Western Fin Corp 8484 Wilshire Blvd Beverly Hills CA 90211

MORGAN, PATRICK MICHAEL, construction company executive; b. Buffalo, Sept. 2, 1944; s. John A. and Mary R. (Hoffmann) M.; B.A. in Anthropology and Modern Langs. (N.Y. State Regents scholar 1962), U. Buffalo, 1966; M.S. in Mgmt., U. Ark., 1972; m. Linda Joanne Howard, June 26, 1976; children—Michael John, Thomas Howard. Sr. benefits analyst Evans Products Co., Portland, Oreg., 1977-78; systems coordinator Daniel Constrn. Co., Greenville, S.C., 1979-80, mktg. coordinator electric utilities industry, 1980—; logistics supt. on loan to Saudi Arabian Presidency of Civil Aviation, from 1981, now quality assurance mgr. system maintenance in support of Tex. Utilities Generating Co. mem. pub. affairs com. Fluor Corp. Served to capt. USAF, 1966-77, now Res. Decorated Air Force Commendation medal with oak leaf cluster. Mem. Am. Mktg. Assn., Assn. Systems Mgmt., Air Force Assn., Internat. Lefthanders. Republican. Lutheran. Home: 2603 Old Omen Rd Tyler TX 75701 Office: Daniel Power Services PO Box 5415 Tyler TX 75712

MORGAN, ROBERT ARTHUR, marketing executive; b. Toledo, May 5, 1922; s. Arthur James and Bernice Marie (Farmer) M.; B.S. cum laude in Bus. Adminstrn., Bowling Green (Ohio) State U., 1943; certificate Carnegie Mellon U., 1951; m. Betty Helen Byers, June 19, 1954; children—Todd Byers, Barbara Lee. With Westinghouse Electric Corp., 1947—, mgr. sales devel. indsl. systems div., Buffalo, 1964-66, mktg. mgr. indsl. systems div., 1967-73, mgr. mktg. services indsl. equipment div., 1973-79, mgr. bus. devel. power electronics and drive systems div., 1979-84. Mem. Wilkinsburg (Pa.) City Council, 1961-65, v.p., 1964-65; co-pres. Maple Elem. Sch. PTA, 1966-67; chmn. Citizens Adv. Bd., Williamsville Central Sch. Dist., 1974-77; vestryman Calvary Episcopal Ch., 1979-82. Named Man of Year, Wilkinsburg, 1965; cert. bus. communicator. Mem. Bus./Profl. Advt. Assn. (nat. v.p. 1967-69), Am. Mktg. Assn., Greater Buffalo C. of C. Clubs: Red Carpet, Am. Legion, Masons, Shriners. Contbr. articles on indsl. mktg. to profl. jours. and handbook; editor tng. manuals. Home: 80 Chaumont Dr Williamsville NY w14221

MORGISON, F. EDWARD, investment broker; b. Clay Center, Kans., Oct. 4, 1940; s. Fred and Lena Edna (Chaput) M.; B.A. in Math., Emporia State U., 1963; M.S. in Bus. Adminstrn., U. Mo., Columbia, 1964; M.S. in Acctg. ...

Figure 7.6
Sample page from *Who's Who in Finance and Industry*.

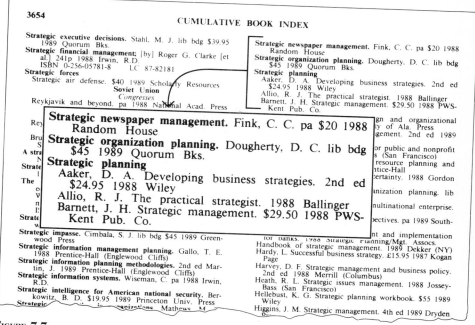

Strategic newspaper management. Fink, C. C. pa $20 1988 Random House

Strategic organization planning. Dougherty, D. C. lib bdg $45 1989 Quorum Bks.

Strategic planning
Aaker, D. A. Developing business strategies. 2nd ed $24.95 1988 Wiley
Allio, R. J. The practical strategist. 1988 Ballinger
Barnett, J. H. Strategic management. $29.50 1988 PWS-Kent Pub. Co.

FIGURE 7.7

Search for sources relating to subject "Strategic Planning" using *Cumulative Book Index*.

Book Indexes

For a list of books currently available on your topic, consult a book index. Book indexes such as the following note the author, title, subject, price, and publishers of works that are still in print.

Books in Print. New York: Bowker, 1948 to date.

Cumulative Book Index. New York: Wilson, 1928 to date.

National Union Catalog. Totowa, NJ: Rowan, 1973 to date.

Paperbound Books in Print. New York: Bowker, 1971 to date.

Publisher's Weekly. New York: Bowker, 1873 to date.

Subject Guide to Books in Print. New York: Bowker, 1957 to date.

The *Cumulative Book Index* (Figure 7.7) lists works published since 1928, while *Publisher's Weekly* lists books (including paperbacks) and pamphlets published each week. The *Subject Guide to Books in Print* lists only books that are currently in print in the United States.

Whereas these general indexes cite books on any subject, some book indexes specialize in specific disciplines, including such business fields as economics, finance, management, marketing, and computer information systems. The following specialized book indexes may prove useful to your research:

Business and Economics Books and Serials in Print. New York: Bowker, 1981 to date.

Business and Economics Books, 1876–1983. New York: Bowker.

FIGURE 7.8

Search for sources relating to subject "Production Planning" using *Business and Economics Books 1876–1983.*

Figure 7.8 provides sample citations on the subject of strategic planning from *Business and Economics Books, 1876–1983.*

Business Services

Subscription or syndicated business services provide a variety of financial and investment information on national and international companies, many of which are traded on a Wall Street exchange. Business services normally distribute this information to subscribers through mailed publications or through telecommunications networks to home or business computers. Some of the leading services are provided here:

Investment Companies. New York: Wiesenberger, 1944 to date.

The Kiplinger Washington Letter. Washington, DC: Kiplinger, 1923 to date.

Labor Relations Reporter. Washington, DC: Bureau of Nat'l. Affairs, 1948 to date.

Moody's series. Including such areas as *Bank and Finance,* 1955 to date; *Industrial,* 1954 to date; *International,* 1981 to date; *Municipal and Governmental,* 1955 to date; *OTC Industrial,* 1970 to date; *Public and Utility,* 1954 to date; *Transportation,* 1954 to date. New York: Moody's.

Standard & Poor's Corporation Records. New York: Standard & Poor's, 1940 to date.

Standard & Poor's Register of Corporations, Directors, and Executives: United States and Canada. New York: Standard & Poor's, 1928 to date.

Standard Federal Tax Reports. Chicago: Commerce Clearing House, 1913 to date.

Value Line Investment Service. New York: Arnold Bernhard, 1969 to date.

Figure 7.9 provides a sample page from *Moody's Bank and Finance Manual.* Figure 7.10 provides a sample page from *Standard & Poor's Register of Corporations, Directors, and Executives.*

In addition to the above sources, *Federal Taxes* (New York: H. W. Wilson, 1952) offers weekly updates of federal tax laws and regulations, while also providing tips on tax planning. *Investment Companies* (New York: A. Wiesenberger, 1941 to date) and *Labor Relations Reporter* (Washington: Bureau of National Affairs, 1976) provide current news and trends in investment and labor relations, laws, and practices. *Editor & Publisher Market Guide* (New York: Editor & Publisher Company, 1959 to date) is a daily newspaper that reports financial information about banks, manufacturers, and retail businesses in U.S. and Canadian cities.

Corporate Annual Reports

Each year corporations report their financial performance of the previous year to a variety of readers—bankers, corporate employees, financial journalists, investment analysts, shareholders, U.S. federal oversight agencies (e.g., the Securities and Exchange Commission). By closely examining the financial statements contained in an annual report, you can generally surmise the current economic health of the reporting business as compared with its financial condition in prior years. Text components of the annual report, such as the "Letter to Shareholders" and "Management's Discussion and Analysis" sections, also frequently reveal the company's own perspective on its finances as well as its progress in meeting established corporate goals in such areas as effective management, manufacturing, production, R&D, sales, and service.

You can obtain the annual reports of specific corporations by writing directly to the company. Some business magazines, including *Dun's, Fortune,* and *Forbes,* regularly feature request forms for annual reports of selected corporations. You might also access the annual reports of major corporations by using *Corporate Microfile,* a service that provides copies of companies' yearly reports on microfiche.

MORGAN GUARANTY TRUST CO. OF NEW YORK

(Controlled by J.P. Morgan & Co. Incorporated)
Incorporated in New York April 13, 1864, as New York Guaranty & Indemnity Co.; name changed to Guaranty Trust Co. of New York Jan. 2, 1896; present name adopted Apr. 24, 1959 on merger with J.P. Morgan & Co., Inc. (see below).

On Jan. 27, 1910, the Morton Trust Co. (which in 1900 absorbed the State Trust Co. on a share for share basis) and the Fifth Avenue Trust Co. were merged with the Guaranty Trust Co. On Oct. 16, 1912, Standard Trust Co. of New York was merged. On May 6, 1929, merged Bank of Commerce in New York, formerly National Bank of Commerce in New York (chartered in 1865 originally incorporated in 1839).

On Apr. 24, 1959 merged with J.P. Morgan & Co., Inc., incorporated Mar. 21, 1940 under New York State banking law as successor to partnership of J.P. Morgan & Co. (originally established in 1861). Commenced business under new designation on Apr. 1, 1940. Under merger plan Morgan stockholders received 4⅖ shares for each share held. Guaranty Trust stock was exchanged share for share.

In Nov. 1979, Morgan Guaranty International Finance Corp., a subsidiary of J.P. Morgan acquired 20% interest in Inversiones Finalven S.A. of Venezuela for an undisclosed amount. Morgan announced it also plans to sell its 20% interest in Sociedad Financiera Valinvenca, a Venezuelan investment bank to Inversiones.

In May 1981, sold 29.32% interest in Morgan Grenfell Holdings Ltd.

On Jan. 5, 1987, sold its 50% interest in Banco Inter-Atlantico De Investimento S.A. and an associate company, Companhia De Arrendamento Mercantil, to its former partners in the joint venture. Terms of the transactions were not disclosed.

Divisions: Banking, Financial and Information Systems Operations, Treasurer's Private Banking, and Administration.

Member of Federal Reserve System and Federal Deposit Insurance Corp.

Operates banking offices in New York, and one each in Brussels, Buenos Aires, Frankfurt, Geneva, Hong Kong, London, Madrid, Milan, Nassau, Paris, Rome, St. Helier, Seoul, Singapore, Taipei, Tokyo and Zurich.

Also has representative offices in Jakarta, Los Angeles, Manila, Melbourne, Mexico City, San Francisco, Sao Paulo and Sydney.

Subsidiaries

Wholly owned:
J.P. Morgan Interfunding Corp. Manages a portfolio of capital equipment leases.

Morprop Incorporated Holds real estate acquired in connection with loans.
Morgan Guaranty International Bank with offices in Miami and Nassau. "Edge Act" bank, headquartered in Miami, performing international services for clients in the United States and abroad.
Morgan Guaranty International Finance Corporation "Edge Act" company holding interests in overseas banks, investment firms, and other businesses.
J.P. Morgan Overseas Capital Corporation finances overseas activities.
J.P. Morgan Argentina S.A. Financial services and off-stock market dealer.
J.P. Morgan Australia Ltd. Merchant bank.
J.P. Morgan Belgium S.A. Finance company.
J.P. Morgan Commissionaria S.p.A. Securities company.
Morgan Bank of Canada; J.P. Morgan Securities Canada Inc. Provides financial advisory, securities, and wholesale banking services.
J.P. Morgan (Suisse) S.A., with offices in Geneva and Zurich provides banking services, including investment management for individuals.
J.P. Morgan Investment Management Pacific Limited. Markets international investment services, manages portfolios, and conducts regional investment research.
J.P. Morgan Nederland N.V. Merchant bank.
J.P. Morgan & Cie S.A. Merchant bank.
J.P. Morgan Espana S.A. Merchant bank.
J.P. Morgan Securities (Switzerland) Ltd. Finance company; also engages in underwriting.
J.P. Morgan GmbH., Investment bank.
J.P. Morgan Securities Ltd. with offices in London and Tokyo. Underwriters, distributes, and trades international securities, including Eurobonds, commercial paper, foreign government bonds, and international equities.
J.P. Morgan S.p.A. Finance company.
J.P. Morgan (Hong Kong) Limited Merchant bank.
J.P. Morgan Investimentos e Financas Ltda. Financial advisory company.
JPM Corretora de Cambio, Titulos e Valores Mobiliarios S.A., J.P. Morgan Distribuidora de Titulos e Valores, Mobiliarios S.A. with offices in Sao Paulo and Rio de Janeiro. Equities and securities dealers.
J.P. Morgan Sterling Securities Ltd. Primary dealer in UK government securities.
J.P. Morgan Securities Asia Ltd. with offices in Singapore, Tokyo and Hong Kong. Licensed securities dealer.
J.P. Morgan Singapore Ltd. Merchant bank.

Morgan Bank Chile Commercial bank.
Morgan Guaranty y Cia Ltda. Securities dealer/
Morgan Guaranty Cia, de Inversiones y Servicios Ltda. Investment company.
Morgan Trust Bank Ltd. Trust bank.

Associated companies

(% ownership in parentheses)
Bank of the Phillipine Islands (20.4%). Commercial bank.
Nivard Flornoy S.A. (49%). Stock brokerage company.
Saudi International Bank (Al-Bank Al-Saudi Al-Alami Ltd.), London (20%). Merchant bank.

MANAGEMENT

Executive Officers
Dennis Weatherstone, Chmn.
D.A. Warner, III, Pres.
L.T. Preston, Chmn., Executive Committee
J.F. Ruffle, Vice-Chmn.
R.G. Mendoza, Vice-Chmn.
K.F. Viermetz, Vice-Chmn.
A.B. Brackenridge, Group Exec.
R.G. Engel, Group Exec.
J.T. Flynn, Executive Vice President
D.L. Hopkins, Jr., Managing Director
J.B. Mayer, Managing Director
R.G. Mendoza, Managing Director
J.T. Olds, Managing Director
M.E. Patterson, Executive Vice President & Gen. Counsel
D.B. Riefler, Chmn., Market Risk Committee
P.B. Smith, Chmn., Credit Policy Comm.
R.B. Wagner, Vice Chmn., Credit Policy Committee
D.A. Warner III, Managing Director
T.H. Fox, Senior Vice President & Controller
P.A. Flugger, Senior Vice President & Auditor
J.J. Lewis, Senior Vice-Pres. & Princ. Acctg. Off.
E.P. Rogers, III, Senior Vice President & Resident Counsel
B.S. Stokes, Sec.

Directors: See under J.P. Morgan & Co. Incorporated, preceding statement.

Offices:
Banking: 23 Wall St., New York, N.Y. 10015.
522 Fifth Ave., New York, NY 10015.
616 Madison Ave., New York, NY 10022.
9 West 57th St., New York, N.Y. 10019.
Stock Transfer Agent: First Chicago Trust Company of New York, 30 West Broadway, New York, N.Y. 10036. **Tel.:** (212) 791-6422.

COMPARATIVE STATEMENT OF CONDITION, AS OF DEC. 31

(in thousands of dollars)

Resources:	1989	1988	(1)1987	(1)1986	(1)1985
Cash & due from banks	1,931,000	2,556,000	2,602,000	4,727,000	4,381,000
Interest-earning deposits with banks	11,213,000	12,775,000	11,478,000	9,679,000	7,073,000
Investment securities	15,469,000	15,639,000	14,193,000	12,063,000	9,918,000
Trading account assets	2,726,000	1,618,000	1,059,000	3,416,000	2,870,000
Secur. purch. under agreements to resell and fed. funds sold	1,104,000	2,214,000	1,303,000	710,000	2,406,000
Net loans and lease financing	22,383,000	24,950,000	26,717,000	31,532,000	34,307,000
Premises and equipment, net	1,556,000	1,320,000	1,051,000	587,000	466,000
Customers' acceptance liability	1,243,000	1,163,000	1,189,000	1,348,000	1,641,000
Accrued interest & accts. receiv.	3,100,000	2,327,000	2,601,000	902,000	994,000
Other assets	2,913,000	2,597,000	2,183,000	2,899,000	1,715,000
Total	63,638,000	67,159,000	64,376,000	67,863,000	65,771,000

FIGURE 7.9
Moody's Bank and Finance Manual listing for J. P. Morgan & Co., Inc.

Directories

Business directories provide general information about companies and organizations, names of chief officers or directors and a brief description of the company's operations and products. Some of the more often used directories include the following:

Business Organizations and Agencies Directory. Detroit: Gale, 1980.

Directory of American Firms Operating in Foreign Countries. 10th ed. New York: Uniworld Business Publications, 1983.

FIGURE 7.10

Standard & Poor's Register listing for J. P. Morgan & Co., Inc.

Directory of Business and Financial Services. 7th ed. Eds. Mary M. Grant and Norma Cote. New York: Special Libraries Assn., 1976.

Directory of Corporate Affiliations. Skokie, IL: National Register, 1967 to date.

Dun & Bradstreet International Principal International Businesses. New York: Dun & Bradstreet, 1982 to date.

Dun & Bradstreet's Million Dollar Directory. New York: Dun & Bradstreet, 1964 to date.

Dun & Bradstreet's Reference Book of Corporate Managements. New York: Dun & Bradstreet, 1967 to date.

Dun & Bradstreet's Standard Register. New York: Dun & Bradstreet, 1965 to date.

> *National Trade & Professional Associations of the U.S. and Canada.* Washington, DC: Columbia, 1966 to date.
>
> *Standard & Poor's Register of Corporations, Directors and Executives.* New York: Standard & Poor's, 1928 to date.
>
> *Thomas' Register of American Manufacturers and TOMCAT File.* New York: Thomas, 1905 to date.
>
> *Trade Directories of the World.* Queens Village, NY: Croner, 1952 to date.
>
> *United States Government Manual.* Washington, DC: Office of the Federal Register/GSA, 1973/74 to date.
>
> *Who Owns Whom: Continental Europe.* London: Dun & Bradstreet, Ltd., 1991.
>
> *Who Owns Whom: North America.* London: Dun & Bradstreet, Ltd., 1991.
>
> *World Guide to Trade Associations.* 2nd ed. Detroit: Gale, 1980.

Some directories furnish a listing of other business directories. In effect, they contain directories within a directory:

> *Directory of Directories.* Detroit: Gale, 1980 to date.
>
> *Guide to American Directories.* 10th ed. New York: B. Klein, 1978.

Encyclopedias

Encyclopedias are most effectively used at the start of your research as they provide background data and information on a vast range of subjects. Three well-known encyclopedias are

> *Encyclopedia Americana.* International ed. Danbury, CT: Grolier, 1829 to date.
>
> *The New Encyclopedia Britannica.* 15th ed. Chicago: Encyclopedia Britannica Education, 1981.
>
> *World Book Encyclopedia.* Chicago: World Book, 1990.

Encyclopedias specializing in business-oriented subjects include the following:

> *Encyclopedia of Associations.* Detroit, MI: Gale, 1973 to date.
>
> *Encyclopedia of Banking and Finance.* 7th ed. Boston: Banker's, 1973.
>
> *Encyclopedia of Business Information Sources.* Detroit, MI: Gale, 1986.
>
> *Encyclopedia of Economics.* Guilford, CT: Dushkin, 1985.
>
> *Encyclopedia of Information Systems and Services.* Detroit, MI: Gale, 1983.
>
> *Encyclopedia of Management.* New York: Van Nostrandt Reinhold, 1973.

Government Publications

Federal, state, and local governments publish thousands of documents each year on business-related topics. This continual flood of information can, understandably, make the task of finding specific sources considerably difficult.

The following indexes, however, will help you to locate most of the documents printed each year by federal and state governments:

American Statistics Index. Washington, DC: Congressional Information Service, 1973 to date.

Checklist of State Publications. Englewood, CO: Information Handling Services, 1977 to date.

Congressional Information Service. Washington, DC: Congressional Information Service, 1970 to date.

Economic Report of the President. Washington, DC: Office of the President, 1950 to date.

Federal Index. Cleveland, OH: Predicasts, 1977 to date.

Guide to United States Government Publications. Ed. John L. Andriott. McLean, VA: Documents Index, 1981 to date.

Handbook of Business Statistics. Washington, DC: Economic Analysis Bureau, 1935 to date.

Handbook of Labor Statistics. Washington, DC: U.S. Dept. of Labor, 1924 to date.

Index to United States Periodicals. Chicago: Infodata, 1970 to date.

Monthly Catalog of United States Government Publications. Washington, DC: U.S. Supt. of Documents, 1896 to date.

Monthly Checklist of State Publications. U.S. Library of Congress, Processing Department. Washington, DC: GPO, 1910 to date.

Standard Industrial Classification Manual (SIC). Washington, DC: Office of the President/OMB, 1972 to date.

Statistical Abstract of the United States. Washington, DC: GPO, 1878 to date.

United States Industrial Outlook. Washington, DC: U.S. Dept. of Commerce, 1984 to date.

In addition to the above sources, the U.S. Bureau of Census offers a variety of publications addressing an assortment of business subjects, including *Census of Manufacturers, Census of Retail Trade, Census of Service and Industries,* and *Census of Wholesale Trade.*

Although this section places much of its emphasis on federal documents, most state commerce departments provide publications reporting economic and financial information on both state and local levels. If your report research requires such material, you might, in addition to consulting the *Checklist of State Publications,* investigate the state documents section of a university library. Figure 7.11 provides a sample page from the *Checklist of State Publications.*

Guides

Most libraries offer a range of general reference guides that explain how to locate useful sources of business data and information, for example:

CHECKLIST/1977: SUBJECT INDEX

ECONOMIC MANAGEMENT
FLO443:2 MARKET EXPANSION AND PROMOTION FEEDBACK

ECONOMIC OPPORTUNITY
AK0121:2 REPORT OF THE URBAN HOUSING CONFERENCE MAY 1975
AK0122:2 SUMMARY OF RURAL LEGISLATIVE PRIORITIES CONFERENCE
AR0230:2 THE ACTION
IL0847:2   ILLINOIS INITIATIVES STATE ECONOMIC OPPORTUNITY OFFICE JUN 13 1975
IL0848:2   ILLINOIS INITIATIVES STATE ECONOMIC OPPORTUNITY OFFICE JUN 30 1975
IL0849:2   ILLINOIS INITIATIVES STATE ECONOMIC OPPORTUNITY OFFICE JUL 31 1975
IL0850:2   ILLINOIS INITIATIVES STATE ECONOMIC OPPORTUNITY OFFICE AUG 25 1975
IL0851:2   ILLINOIS INITIATIVES STATE ECONOMIC OPPORTUNITY OFFICE SEPT 22 1975
MA0544:2 ECONOMIC OPPORTUNITY OFFICE INFORMATION SERVICE
MA0545:2 LEGISLATIVE ACTION BULLENTIN
MN0725:2 ECONOMIC OPPORTUNITY OFFICE SEPP VIEWS NEWS AND OTHER NOTES
MN0726:2 THE MEDIATOR MEDIA
SD0422:2 BEFORE DEATH JUN 1975
SD0423:2 POVERTY IN SOUTH DAKOTA JUL 1975

ECONOMIC OUTLOOK
IL0812:2   REVENUE ESTIMATE AND ECONOMIC OUTLOOK FISCAL 1976
KY0189:2 KENTUCKY ECONOMIC OUTLOOK
KY0190:2 KENTUCKY ECONOMIC OUTLOOK SUPPLEMENT

ECONOMIC PLAN
TX0330:2 OVERALL ECONOMIC PLAN SAN SABA COUNTY 1975-1976

ECONOMIC PLANNING
WY0035:2 WYOMING PROGRESS REPORT

FIGURE 7.11
Search for sources relating to subject "Economic Opportunity" using *Checklist of State Publications.*

Brownstone, David M., and Gorton Curruth.   *Where to Find Business Information: A Worldwide Guide for Everyone Who Needs the Answers to Business Questions.*   2nd ed.   New York: Wiley, 1982.

Daniells, Lorna M.   *Business Information Sources.*   2nd ed.   Berkeley: U of California P, 1985.

Fiqueroa, Oscar, and Charles Winkler.   *A Business Information Guidebook.* New York: AMACOM, 1980.

Johnson, H. Webster.   *How to Use the Business Library: With Sources of Business Information.* 5th ed. Cincinnati: South-Western, 1984.

Piele, Linda J., John C. Tyson, and Michael B. Sheffey.   *Materials and Methods for Business Research.* New York: Neal-Schuman, 1980.

Schlessinger, Bernard S., ed. *The Basic Business Library: Core Resources.* Phoenix: Oryx, 1989.

Strauss, Diane Wheeler. *Handbook of Business Information: A Guide for Librarians, Students, and Researchers.* Englewood, CO: Libraries Unlimited, 1988.

Wasserman, Paul, Charlotte Georgi, and James Way. *Encyclopedia of Business Information Sources.* 5th ed. Detroit: Gale, 1983.

Newspaper Indexes

You can collect a significant amount of current and important information from a range of mainstream business newspapers and journals, including *The Wall Street Journal, Barron's, Business Week, Dun's Review, Forbes, Fortune, Harvard Business Review,* and *U.S. News and World Report.* However, many lesser-known newspapers and periodicals—such as *Accounting Review, Business Horizons, Management Review,* and *Monthly Labor Review*—are equally worthy of attention during your secondary research. As their subject areas are more focused than those of the mainstream publications, these scholarly, professional, and trade publications typically include articles that also are more thorough and research-based.

The biggest obstacle in researching newspapers and periodicals is accessing relevant articles from the wealth of publications. Newspaper and periodical indexes, however, usually make the search much easier. Newspaper indexes list news articles by subject, author, or publication. The most commonly used newspaper indexes include the following:

Bell & Howell Newspaper Index. Wooster, OH: Bell & Howell, 1972 to date.

Los Angeles Times Index. Wooster, OH: Bell & Howell, 1973 to date.

The New York Times Index. New York: The New York Times, 1913 to date.

The Wall Street Journal Index. New York: Dow Jones, 1958 to date.

Figure 7.12 provides a sample page from *The Wall Street Journal Index.*

While *The New York Times, The Wall Street Journal,* and *Los Angeles Times* indexes cite only articles from their respective newspapers, the *Bell & Howell Index* lists articles published in various newspapers across the country, including the *Chicago Sun-Times, Chicago Tribune, The Christian Science Monitor, Denver Post, The Houston Chronicle, New Orleans Times Picayune, San Francisco Chronicle,* and *The Washington Post.* The *National Newspaper Index* of Information Access Corporation, Menlo Park, California, offers monthly and yearly listings (on microfilm or microfiche media) of articles published in various national newspapers.

Periodical Indexes

Periodicals, or **serials**, are regularly published journals, magazines, and newspapers. Periodicals are typically published at monthly, quarterly, or semiannual intervals and index articles by subject. Periodical indexes reference articles from a spectrum of fields, such as education, law, medicine, politics, science, and

THE WALL STREET JOURNAL INDEX

DEREGULATION & REGULATION *(Cont.)*
racy of medical laboratories, including those in doctors'
offices. 10/12-B4;5

Many providers of child care go unregulated under a
hodgepodge of state laws, while a controversial proposal to
impose federal child-care standards recently met defeat in
the Senate; part of the controversy was whether a 'mother
down the block' should be regulated as a day-care pro-
vider. 10/18-A16;1

The Democrats: Better for Business. Editorial page
article by Roger Altman and Lawrence Summers suggests
business support for Vice President Bush is ironic since his
economic views are out of step with the business community; instead, business would be better off with Dukakis in
the areas of budget and trade policies and in government
regulation. 10/31-A18;3

Small California recycler, Rho-Chem Corp., is profiting as concern rises about toxic pollution; it recycles
sells solvents. (First of two articles about smaller co
nies profiting from stricter environmental regula
11/9-B2;3

Stricter oil-tank rules lead to buried treasure for p
leum marketing firm of J.W. DeWitt Inc., which now
healthy subsidiary business in storage tank renovation
testing. (Second of two articles about smaller comp
profiting from stricter environmental regulat
11/14-B2;3

Canadian deregulation sparks a dogfight; cou
three major airlines—Air Canada, Wardair Inc. and
Corp.—battle for passengers. 12/8-A18;1

Even as lawmakers debate legislative action on
aged buy-outs, they pressure regulators to improv
forcement of existing laws and seek other ways to ti
up. (Washington Wire) 12/9-A1;5

Major detergent makers invested heavily in the early
1980s to package soap, fabric softeners and even bleach in
single, no-fuss packages; now it seems a flop; consumers
are discouraged by perceived higher cost and technical
problems. 7/29-20;4

Whether soaps and shampoos damage the eyes of
children could become an area of controversy; researchers
at the Medical College of Georgia are testing the long-
terms effects on the eyes of sodium lauryl sulfate, an
ingredient of many soaps and shampoos. (Lab Notes)
11/1-B1;1

DEUKMEJIAN, GEORGE
War of Succession for California's Bond Empire: Editorial page article by Dan Walters on the battle over
naming a successor to the late Jesse Unruh in the politically powerful post of treasurer; at issue is control of the
state's bond business. 3/2-28;3

since newspapers state that Mich
win election; for one thing, Je
radical, potentially crippling to D
Bentsen are campaigning for the s

DIABETES
Unproven remedies, especiall
and headaches, tempt the ailing;
flourish despite lack of scientific
5/27-19;3

Immunex Corp.'s researchers
receptor, a development that could
treating such diseases as rheumat
8/1-20;4

It's too risky, says the Insuran
Safety, to let people using insu
drivers; group urges Federal Hi
reject a petition for waivers fron
Labor Letter) 8/9-1
ces challenge to its
t as two rivals star
es, a Squibb-Novo
solinpen, a lightwe
untain pen, while N
nada. 8/17-26;5
recently approve
abetics to adjust th
System, device w
ost about $300, a
are Corp. (Techno
ETER
A and Publication
mandis Communi
Prudential Insuran
lis. for $712 million
agreed to acquire

DEREGULATION & REGULATION *(Cont.)*
racy of medical laboratories, including those in doctors'
offices. 10/12-B4;5

Many providers of child care go unregulated under a
hodgepodge of state laws, while a controversial proposal to
impose federal child-care standards recently met defeat in
the Senate; part of the controversy was whether a 'mother
down the block' should be regulated as a day-care pro-
vider. 10/18-A16;1

The Democrats: Better for Business. Editorial page
article by Roger Altman and Lawrence Summers suggests
business support for Vice President Bush is ironic since his
economic views are out of step with the business community; instead, business would be better off with Dukakis in
the areas of budget and trade policies and in government
regulation. 10/31-A18;3

FIGURE 7.12
Sample page of *The Wall Street Journal Index*.

technology. Nonspecialized, popular indexes that reference a broad range of
subjects include

Applied Science and Technology Index. New York: Wilson, 1958 to date.

Education Index. New York: Wilson, 1929 to date.

Engineering Index. New York: Engineering Index, 1928 to date.

Index to Legal Periodicals. New York: Wilson, 1908 to date.

P.A.I.S. (Public Affairs Information Service Bulletin). New York: P.A.I.S., 1915
    to date.

Reader's Guide to Periodical Literature. New York: Wilson, 1900 to date.

Social Sciences Citation Index. Philadelphia: Institute for Scientific
    Information, 1973 to date.

Social Sciences Index. New York: Wilson, 1974 to date.

The Standard Periodical Directory. 7th ed.   New York: Oxbridge, 1981–82.

Ulrich's International Periodical Directory. New York: Bowker, 1988.

Almost every professional field within business has its own periodical index. Some of the more frequently used indexes specializing in business subjects
include

Accountant's Index. New York: American Institute of CPAs, 1921/23 to date.

Accountant's Index Supplement. New York: AICAO, 1921 to date.

> *American Statistics Index.* Washington, DC: Congressional Information Service, 1973 to date.
>
> *Business Index.* New York: Information Access, 1979 to date.
>
> *Business Periodicals Index.* New York: Wilson, 1958 to date.
>
> *Funk and Scott (F & S) Europe.* Cleveland, OH: Predicasts, 1978 to date.
>
> *Funk and Scott (F & S) Index of Corporations and Industries.* Cleveland, OH: Predicasts, 1960 to date.
>
> *Funk and Scott (F & S) International.* Cleveland, OH: Predicasts, 1978 to date.
>
> *Journal of Economic Literature.* Nashville, TN: American Economic Assn., 1963 to date.

Figure 7.13 provides a sample page from the *Business Periodicals Index* displaying references for the researcher exploring periodical sources relating to "strategic planning."

For a complete listing of periodicals and libraries that carry these indexes, you might consult a periodical directory, such as the *Union List of Serials in Libraries of the United States and Canada, Ulrich's International Periodicals Directory,* and *Gebbie Press House Directory.* *N. W. Ayer's Directory of Newspapers and Periodicals* provides an index of newspapers and periodicals.

Pamphlets

An often overlooked resource for business research is the library pamphlet file, also referred to as the **vertical file**. The file contains pamphlets printed by a vast range of businesses; federal, local, and state government offices; political parties; lobbying groups; religious factions; and so on. Perhaps the most useful indexes for accessing information in the pamphlet file are *Business Pamphlets and Information Sources* (New York: Exceptional Books, 1987), *The Vertical File Index* (New York: H. W. Wilson, 1935 to date), and *Corporate Publications in Print* (New York: McGraw-Hill, 1980).

Locating Information with Computerized Data-Based Searches

As time is a critical factor in an organization's ability to compete in business today, the speed with which a researcher can access essential information during a search of secondary sources can make the difference between a document's succeeding or failing to deliver timely, relevant, and complete information. Just as the use of computers has been integral in enabling organizations to become more efficient and effective in all areas of business, computer technology is also playing an increasingly important role in expediting a researcher's library search (Strauss, 1988, pp. 150-181).

The **on-line** search of secondary sources is an interactive, computerized method of accessing bibliographic citations and complete abstracts on particular subjects. On-line searches enable researchers to query large computer data bases that can electronically store literally millions of pages of data. A data base,

Strategy, Corporate—cont.

Build flexibility — not power plants. J. C. Sawhill and L. P. Silverman. graphs tabs *Public Util Fortn* 111:17-21 My 26 '83

Build, hold, harvest: converting strategic intentions into reality. A. K. Gupta and V. Govindarajan. graphs tab *J Bus Strategy* 4:34-47 Wint '84

Business development strategies. N. Johnson. *Manage Plann* 32:52 N-D '83; 32:51+ Ja-F '84

Business is turning data into a potent strategic weapon [strategic information management systems] *Bus Week* p92+ Ag 22 '83

The business portfolio approach—where it falls down in practice. R. A. Bettis and W. K. Hall. graphs tab *Long Range Plann* 16:95-104 Ap '83

Business unit strategy and changes in the product R&D budget. D. C. Hambrick and others. bibl tabs *Manage Sci* 29:757-69 Jl '83

Business unit strategy, managerial characteristics, and business unit effectiveness at strategy implementation. A. K. Gupta and V. Govindarajan. bibl (p39-41) tabs *Acad Manage J* 27:25-41 Mr '84

Can a hands-on executive learn to take a strategic view? [J. van Dijk of Van Nelle-Lassie BV; Holland] *Int Manage* 39:57-8+ Mr '84

Capital budgeting: linking financial analysis to corporate strategy. J. V. Rizzi. *J Bus Strategy* 4:81-4 Spr '84

The CEO and corporate strategy in the eighties: back to basics. W. W. Lewis. tab *Interfaces* 14:3-9 Ja-F '84

CEOs' views on strat... McDaniel. tabs *J B*...

Chase: from lending ... *Euromoney* p36-51 ...

Collective strategy: s... environments. W. G... tabs *Acad Manage*...

Company rescue—an ... T. Janzen. graphs t... D '83

Competitive strategies ... based industries [inv... G. Tassey. bibl grap... '83

Competitive strategy v... *Bus Strategy* 4:36-4(...

A concept of entrepren... sion making] J. A. ... *Strateg Manage J* ...

Constituencies, conflict,... in acquisition strateg... graph *Interfaces* 14:...

Content analysis of annual reports for corporate strategy and risk. E. H. Bowman. bibl tabs *Interfaces* 14:61-71 Ja-F '84

Corporate culture and human resource management: two keys to implementing strategy. S. M. Davis. *Hum Resour Plann* 6 no3:159-67 '83

The corporate culture vultures. B. Uttal. *Fortune* 108:66-70+ O 17 '83

Corporate entrepreneurship and strategic management: insights from a process study. R. A. Burgelman. bibl flowchart graphs *Manage Sci* 29:1349-64 D '83

The corporate strategic planning process. A. C. Hax and N. S. Majluf. bibl tabs *Interfaces* 14:47-60 Ja-F '84

Corporate strategies. See issues of Business Week

Corporate strategies for an uncertain world economy. H. B. Malmgren. *Can Bus Rev* 10:6-8 Wint '83

Corporate strategy and the power of competitive analysis. R. E. MacAvoy. flowcharts graphs *Manage Rev* 72:9-19 Jl '83

Cutting costs, strategic management stre... *Underwrit (Prop Casualty Insur Ed)* 87:74...

Decision-oriented information. V. E. Mill... *Datamation* 30:159-62+ Ja '84

Decision support systems—strategic plannin... L. Rector. *Manage Plann* 31:36-40 My-Je...

Designing organizations to compete. I. C. ... and P. E. Jones. flowchart tabs *J Bus Strat*... Spr '84

Developing sites near water: running a govern... tlet. L. C. Tarlton and others. il *Ind Dev*... Mr-Ap '83

Developing strategic capability: an agenda for t... ment [with discussion] C. K. Prahalad. bibl... *Resour Manage* 22:237-55 Fall '83

Developing strategic information systems. ... 22:1-12 My '84

Developing strategic thinking [getting managers to contribute effectively to strategic planning] M. Easterby-Smith and J. Davies. flowchart *Long Range Plann* 16:39-48 Ag '83

Divestment as a corporate strategy. S. S. Singhvi. *J Bus Strategy* 4:85-8 Spr '84

Domain maintenance as an objective of business political activity: an expanded typology. B. D. Baysinger. bibl...

Don... L... Effec...dy...ta... Effec...an...co... A...an...Al... An...en...-Ac... Emp...R... End...ril... Jl-Ag '83

Environmental forecasting: key to strategic management...

S 23 '83

High profit strategies in mature capital goods industries: a contingency approach. D. C. Hambrick. bibl graph il tabs *Acad Manage J* 26:687-707 D '83

How the experts plan [chemical industry] tab *Chem Week* 134:11-12 Mr 28 '84

Business unit strategy, managerial characteristics, and business unit effectiveness at strategy implementation. A. K. Gupta and V. Govindarajan. bibl (p39-41) tabs *Acad Manage J* 27:25-41 Mr '84

Can a hands-on executive learn to take a strategic view? [J. van Dijk of Van Nelle-Lassie BV; Holland] *Int Manage* 39:57-8+ Mr '84

Capital budgeting: linking financial analysis to corporate strategy. J. V. Rizzi. *J Bus Strategy* 4:81-4 Spr '84

The CEO and corporate strategy in the eighties: back to basics. W. W. Lewis. tab *Interfaces* 14:3-9 Ja-F '84

A framework for retail planning. R. F. Lusch and M. G. Harvey. *Business* 33:20-6 O-N-D '83

From the shadows [role for linear programming in corporate strategic planning] D. S. Hirshfeld. flowchart *Interfaces* 13:70-4 Ag '83

The future catches up with a strategic planner [Boston Consulting Group] *Bus Week* p62 Je 27 '83

Gaining insights through strategy analysis. G. Day. *J Bus Strategy* 4:51-8 Summ '83

Getting physical: new strategic leverage from operations. W. Skinner. *J Bus Strategy* 3:74-9 Spr '83

A guide to short-term strategic planning. D. V. Austin and T. J. Scanpini. *Bankers Mag* 166:62-8 N-D '83

A framework for retail planning. R. F. Lusch and M. G. Harvey. *Business* 33:20-6 O-N-D '83

From the shadows [role for linear programming in corporate strategic planning] D. S. Hirshfeld. flowchart *Interfaces* 13:70-4 Ag '83

The future catches up with a strategic planner [Boston Consulting Group] *Bus Week* p62 Je 27 '83

Gaining insights through strategy analysis. G. Day. *J Bus Strategy* 4:51-8 Summ '83

Getting physical: new strategic leverage from operations. W. Skinner. *J Bus Strategy* 3:74-9 Spr '83

A guide to short-term strategic planning. D. V. Austin and T. J. Scanpini. *Bankers Mag* 166:62-8 N-D '83

Corporate entrepreneurship and strategic management: insights from a process study. R. A. Burgelman. bibl flowchart graphs *Manage Sci* 29:1349-64 D '83

The corporate strategic planning process. A. C. Hax and N. S. Majluf. bibl tabs *Interfaces* 14:47-60 Ja-F '84

Corporate strategies. See issues of Business Week

Corporate strategies for an uncertain world economy. H. B. Malmgren. *Can Bus Rev* 10:6-8 Wint '83

Corporate strategy and the power of competitive analysis. R. E. MacAvoy. flowcharts graphs *Manage Rev* 72:9-19 Jl '83

FIGURE 7.13

Search for sources relating to subject "Strategic Planning" using *Business Periodicals Index*.

in a conceptual sense, is like a filing cabinet into which people place files of information pertaining to an assortment of subjects. Files containing secondary sources can be organized in any number of ways, but are typically ordered by author, date of publication, subject, document title, and title of publication.

A growing number of companies design and build data bases that reference sources on a vast range of subjects. The companies lease or sell their data bases to **data-based search services**, which in turn sell access to the data bases to on-line customers, such as libraries, businesses, government, and private individuals. Most data bases are updated monthly and serve as the computerized counterpart of printed abstracts and indexes.

Researchers access the **host computer** where data-based files are stored by using computer networks. The researcher works from a site, such as a business or library, that offers on-line search capabilities. Users identify themselves to the on-line service by entering a unique password provided to them by personnel of the research institution (e.g., a reference librarian in charge of on-line searches). The service then queues the search tasks requested by the user along with jobs of other researchers. Because the powerful host computers used by data-based service companies process multiple search tasks within billionths of a second, you will rarely sense that thousands of other researchers are querying the same data base at the same time. Information is transferred in digital form between the researcher's terminal and the data base computer, which may be at opposite ends of the country, through various telecommunication technologies, including microwave systems, satellites, and telephone land lines (Schlessinger, 1989, pp. 101–109).

On-line information retrieval services began in the late 1960s as a way of compiling, in bibliographic form, the massive growth in technical and scientific data and information. Since the early 1970s, this process of converting information in hard copy form to digital form has spread to commercial use. In 1973, there were only two commercially available on-line retrieval services, which offered access to about half a dozen bibliographic data bases. Today, data-based search services offer individual users thousands of electronic data bases from which to cull sources for their research.

As many users of data-based searches have little expertise in the technical side of computers, search services have simplified the data-based search to the point that researchers, in most cases, need only respond to a series of menus. The charge to the researcher for using a search service's data bases is typically based on a formula that considers the amount of time spent on the on-line system, the number of titles found, and the number of abstracts requested (if any). On-line search fees normally range from about $50 to $150 per hour. An average search for a business report might cost from $75 to $100, depending on your skill at performing data-based searches and the complexity of your topic.

Advantages of On-Line Searches

Perhaps the biggest advantage of on-line searches is speed. The time and energy saved by researchers, who otherwise might have invested days or weeks in manual searching, can make data-based searches well worth the fee charged by search service companies. Within minutes of accessing an on-line data base, you can accumulate an extensive bibliography on your topic and print off the list of citations on your terminal's printer. Even if the search results have to be printed at an on-line service's computer facility, you can receive the citations by mail within a few days. Some libraries can also provide electronic facsimiles of documents (FAX services) accessed through the data-based search.

Data-based searches are also extremely comprehensive, as they offer the researcher access to far more sources than a typical library could support in printed form. Some data bases provide exclusive information that has no printed form equivalent and thus can be accessed only through on-line searches. One hour of on-line searching might provide a range of sources and information that a manual search would require weeks to collect. During one on-line session, the user can access citations on nearly all sources available on a specific topic, including books, periodicals, newspapers, government documents, doctoral dissertations, conference papers, and patents.

Moreover, as they are updated monthly, biweekly, or even weekly, data-based searches provide some of the most current information available. Some on-line services even list sources before publishers can print and distribute hard copies of the documents. On-line searches also provide users with added flexibility and convenience. Thousands of researchers, for example, can concurrently search the same data base independently of one another and from different locations.

Types of Data-Based Searches

You can perform on-line searches in a variety of different ways. A **retrospective search,** for example, is meant to collect an exhaustive amount of historical data or information from one or more data bases on a particular topic, author, or type of document (e.g., journal, newspaper, government publication). A retrospective search typically investigates a topic back to the earliest dates covered by the data base. A **comprehensive** search investigates a specific topic, but, unlike the retrospective search, it references *all* authors and documents relevant to the subject being searched regardless of whether sources are historical or nonhistorical in nature.

A **selective** search provides a bibliography of only those sources *recently* published on a specific author or topic, whereas the **state-of-the-art** search seeks to find the most up-to-date information on current *research* in a particular area or industry. Some on-line services actively support selective state-of-the-art data-based searches by offering current bibliographies on frequently searched topics. A **selective dissemination of information** (**SDI**) provides researchers with citations on a specific search profile. The on-line service then periodically retrieves and sends the user (via computer or mail) updated bibliographies on the selected topic over a specified length of time. Business and industry researchers may also use a **patent** search to speed their investigations into past and current patent issues and applications within the United States and abroad.

Types of Data Bases

During your data-based search, you will interact with either reference or source data bases. **Reference data bases** have either a bibliographic or a directory structure, and they provide lists of reference and secondary sources on specific topics. **Bibliographic** data bases are the most frequently used type of data base. They provide bibliographic citations (with abstracts if requested) of secondary sources, including books, journals, magazines, newspapers, and reports. **Directory** data bases contain references (with abstracts if requested) to activities of given fields, including professional organizations, contracts, grants, and important people.

Unlike reference data bases, **source data bases** provide the actual information contained in the source. Source data bases are either numeric, full-text, or dictionary in structure. **Numeric** data bases contain numerical or statistical data, often organized into formal tables or figures to enhance reader comprehension. Whereas numeric data bases occasionally contain a minimum of text, **full-text** data bases normally contain the entire text of a document along with supporting numeric data. **Dictionary** data bases, in essence, function as on-line handbooks or dictionaries in providing users with concise, accurate information regarding their professions or areas of research.

Using On-Line Data Bases

Regardless of the type of data base you choose in your research, the process used to access stored information is fundamentally the same. After logging onto the data-based system, you must enter a key word or phrase, called a **descriptor,** that describes specifically the subject for which you wish the data base to supply sources. Most computer data bases apply **Boolean logic** to interpret your descriptors. Boolean logic responds to key relational terms, or **operators,** used in the search descriptor. The most commonly used operators are *and, or,* and *not.* The *and* operator suggests intersection, the *or* equivalency, the *not* exclusion.

LIMITING YOUR DATA-BASED SEARCH

The *and* operator works well in restricting the number of references posted by the data base. For instance, requesting the data base to search for sources with the subject descriptor "computers AND education AND Macintosh" would limit the number of sources the system would list, while also saving you much time you would otherwise spend sorting through numerous sources that were not exactly related to your topic of computer-aided instruction with Macintosh computers. Using the *and* operator, however, has its drawbacks. If you overuse it in a single-subject descriptor, there's a good chance that the data base will find *no* sources relevant to such a narrow subject descriptor. Moreover, using the *and* operator to narrow the data-based search will not necessarily produce those sources that are the most relevant or even the most specific to your topic.

The *or* operator requests that the data base retrieve sources, or citations of those sources, related to at least one of the terms included in the subject descriptor. A subject descriptor phrased as "PCs OR microcomputers OR laptops OR portables" would produce from the data base a list of only those sources that were relevant to one, or several, or all of those terms.

The *not* operator is used to subtract a subject for which the data base would otherwise search sources. If, for example, you were to enter a subject descriptor "computers NOT PCs," the range of your search would be greatly reduced by eliminating the massive library of literature pertaining to IBM and IBM-compatible personal computers.

Clearly, your research of secondary sources through a data-based search will be thorough and productive only (1) if you choose the appropriate type of data base (e.g., bibliographic, numeric, full-text) in which to perform the search and (2) if you provide the computer with well-defined search parameters by entering the right descriptors. Subject descriptors whose terms are too broad, vague, or restrictive and inappropriate operators can significantly restrict the effectiveness of your data-based search. If you do not have experience in on-line search procedures, you should consult a reference librarian skilled in computerized data-based research.

Guided by the right descriptors targeted at the appropriate data-base type, the computer typically produces a thorough list of bibliographic citations that you can then locate in your library or obtain through interlibrary loan. Most data-based services offer complete abstracts of cited articles. In addition, printing the list of citations from the screen to hard copy provides you with not only a good working bibliography but also a convenient reference sheet for locating the sources. To print the citations on your library printer, you must first **capture** the information presented on the screen and **download** it through the on-line computer network to your personal computer. If you are unsure of how to perform this procedure, consult the reference librarian trained in data-based searches.

SELECTING SEARCH SERVICES AND ON-LINE DATA BASES

You can access a data base in one of two ways. You might buy access directly through the company that owns the database—such as Dow Jones, Dun & Bradstreet, Moody's, or Predicasts—or you could work through a vendor that sells access to a range of data bases. Some vendors offer access to a wide assortment of data bases and, consequently, provide considerable depth and range of coverage in many subject areas. The largest search services are Dialog Information Systems (DIALOG), Bibliographic Retrieval System, Inc. (BRS), and Systems Development Corporation (SDC).

DIALOG offers access to more than 167 data bases, many of which specialize in providing business, financial, or economic information. Depending on the data base you are searching, you can obtain bibliographic and full-text information through DIALOG. A portion of a bibliographic search performed with DIALOG is shown in Figure 7.14.

In this search, DIALOG accessed the *ABI/Inform* data base and searched for all sources relating to the descriptor "strategic planning." The citation includes such key bibliographic information as the work's title, author, source, number of pages, and date. You might also request that DIALOG provide abstracts for sources, as shown in Figure 7.15. These data-based citations note the type of document (e.g., book, journal, newsletter, dissertation), the language in which it is written, and index terms the researcher might use for future searches on the same subject. In addition, the citations provide a descriptive abstract of the document.

```
     s strategic( )planning
              14173  STRATEGIC
              56729  PLANNING
     S1         5444  STRATEGIC ( ) PLANNING
     ?s s1/ti
     S2          684  S1/TI
     ?t2/3/1–10


     2/3/1
     89034878
        Characteristics of Strategic Planning in Selected Service Industries
     and Planner Satisfaction with the Process
        Ginter, Peter M.; Rucks, Andrew C.; Duncan, W. Jack
        Management International Review (Germany) v29n2 PP:
     66–74   Second
     Quarter 1989
        AVAILABILITY:  ABI/INFORM


     2/3/2
     89034082
        Fitting the Strategic Planning Process to Organization:  A Clinical
     Study of Burroughs Wellcome Co.
        Burton, Richard M.; Namm, Donald H.
        Technovation (Netherlands)  v8n1–3   PP:  143–152    1988
        AVAILABILITY:  ABI/INFORM


     2/3/3
     89033975
        The Information Media Matrix: A Strategic Planning Tool
        Diers, Fred V.
        ARMA Records Mgmt Qtrly  v23n3  PP: 17–23  Jul 1989
        AVAILABILITY:  ABI/INFORM


     2/3/4
     89032237
        Strategic Planning for MIS
        Kessner, Richard M.
        Bankers Magazine  v172n4  PP:  40–44  Jul/Aug 1989
        AVAILABILITY:  ABI/INFORM


     2/3/5
     89031708
        Enterprisewide Information Management: State-of-the-Art
     Strategic Planning
           Parker, Marilyn, M.; Benson, Robert J.
           Jrnl of Information Systems Mgmt   v6n3    PP: 14–23 Summer 1989
        AVAILABILITY:  ABI/INFORM
```

FIGURE 7.14

Printout from ABI/INFORM on-line search for sources on subject "Strategic Planning."

Source: ABI/INFORM, 1989.

2/5/1
89034878
Characteristics of Strategic Planning in Selected Service Industries and Planner Satisfaction with the Process
Ginter, Peter M.; Rucks, Andrew C.; Duncan, W. Jack
Management International Review (Germany) v29n2 PP: 66–74
Second Quarter 1989 CODEN: MINARY ISSN: 0025-181X JRNL
CODE: MIR
DOC TYPE: Journal Paper LANGUAGE: English LENGTH: 9 Pages
AVAILABILITY: ABI/INFORM

Three interrelated aspects of the strategic planning process--rationality and completeness, formality, and participation--were examined in 3 service sectors. Using a mail survey, responses were obtained from planners in 24 offices of national and international public accounting firms, 40 insurance companies, and 16 health care organizations. Despite evidence that strategic decision makers do not always behave in a logical manner, the planners believed that there was an attempt to be as logical as possible. The normative model of strategic planning was perceived to be an accurate description of strategic planning with the greatest exception occurring relative to the health care organizations. The degree of satisfaction of the planners, with respect to the strategic planning process, was positively related to completeness–rationality, formality, and participation. Again, only health care planners were less satisfied with the degree of participation. Planners were supportive and positively disposed to managerial participation in the process of strategic planning. Tables. References.

DESCRIPTORS: Strategic planning; Service industries; Satisfaction; Perceptions; Questionnaires; Studies
CLASSIFICATION CODES: 2310 (CN=Planning); 9130 (CN=Experimental/Theoretical); 8300 (CN=Service industries not elsewhere classified)

2/5/2
89034082
Fitting the Strategic Planning Process to Organization: A Clinical Study of Burroughs Wellcome Co.
Burton, Richard M.; Namm, Donald H.
Technovation (Netherlands) v8n1–3 PP: 143-152 1988 ISSN: 0166-4972 JRNL CODE: TCH
DOC TYPE: Journal Paper LANGUAGE: English LENGTH: 10 Pages
AVAILABILITY: ABI/INFORM

The successful implementation of strategic planning requires managerial skill that transcends formulas. For successful strategic planning, an organization's first goal is to develop a process that fits the organization and makes successful implementation the first priority. A clinical analysis of Burroughs Wellcome Co. (Research Triangle Park, North Carolina) provides insight and understanding of the strategic planning process. Some suggestions for successful strategic planning are: 1. Strategic planning questions and procedures must fit an organization's style. 2. Balance and cohesion have to be considered and maintained. 3. Strategic planning must be taken seriously, and the chief executive officer's leadership is mandatory. Gresham's Law suggests that short-term demands drive out long-term considerations. Someone must make a commitment so that Gresham's Law does not become a reality. Charts. References.

COMPANY NAMES: Burroughs Wellcome Co. (DUNS 05-254-7635)
DESCRIPTORS: Strategic planning; Case studies; Implementations; Organizational structure; Chief executive officer; Questions; Commitments
CLASSIFICATION CODES: 2310 (CN=Planning); 9110 (CN= Company specific)

FIGURE 7.15
DIALOG abstracts of sources relating to subject "Strategic Planning."
Source: ABI/INFORM, 1989.

Begun in 1976, BRS is an established vendor of search services and offers on-line users access to more than 100 data bases which provide an extensive number and range of sources in such areas as business, education, and the sciences. Like DIALOG, BRS can provide bibliographic and full-text information on cited sources. For research during off-time hours, BRS offers BRS After Dark, a lower-cost service that accesses dozens of data bases from BRS's full assortment. SDC's services are comparable to those of DIALOG and BRS.

Of the hundreds of available data bases offered through data-based service companies, *Abstracted Business Information (ABI/Inform)* is one of the most productive data bases for researching periodical literature. Its data base contains more than 260,000 citations published within the past five years. Many of the citations come from more than 540 domestic and international journals in the areas of business, economics, and management. *ABI/Inform* is distinctly easy to use, or *user-friendly,* for nontechnical users. Consequently, it might be a good place to begin for researchers who are new to data-based searches. You can access the *ABI/Inform* data base through various data-based services, including DIALOG, BSR, SDC, and NewsNet.

Management Contents Inc.'s *Management Contents Database* provides worldwide coverage of significant business and industry literature (1974 to present) published in newspapers, magazines, journals, government documents, and bank reports. The data base contains 228,000 citations that cover a wide range of business areas, including banking, decision science, operations research, and public administration. Like many data bases, *Management Contents* is updated monthly. The data base can be accessed through the DIALOG, BRS, DATA-STAR, and SDC.

The *Accountants' Index* data base, produced by the American Institute of Certified Public Accountants, is the on-line counterpart of the company's *Accountants' Index* directory. The data base contains approximately 111,500 citations and can be accessed through SDC and SDC-Japan. Although the index does not provide abstracts for cited articles, its data base does offer a wealth of sources relating to accounting, data processing, financial reports, industrial securities, management, and taxation.

Dow Jones & Company, Inc. offers business-oriented research sources through the *Dow Jones News* data base and *Dow Jones Text-Search Services.* Whereas most data bases are updated periodically with current sources, *Dow Jones News* is updated continuously, allowing it to provide late-breaking news stories at the same time they are printed by the Dow Jones News Service. The data base keeps track of business news surrounding 6,000 domestic and international companies. *Dow Jones Text-Search* provides access to 250,000 articles (1979 to present) on such topics as management, investments, finance, and government legislation affecting the business world. You can search either data base by using company stock symbol or industry and government codes. The *Text-Search* data base also lets you search the entire text of sources using descriptors. Access both data bases through Dow Jones and Company, Inc.

Like Dow Jones, Dun & Bradstreet offers a variety of data-based services. The *Dun's Million Dollar Directory* is Dun & Bradstreet's data-based version of the company's hard-copy directory that goes by the same name. The 121,000 citations in the data base contain data and information on private and public companies having net worths of $500,000 or more. Each data-based record includes such information as the company's address, area of business, SIC code, and the stock exchange on which the company's stocks are traded. The *Dun's Financial Profiles* data base presents detailed financial statement data in spreadsheet format on 1,000,000 firms in the United States. You can access both data bases through Dun & Bradstreet (Williams, 1985, p. 586).

Moody's answers the entry of Dun & Bradstreet and Dow Jones into the data-based search market with two of its own data bases: *Moody's Corporate Profiles* and *Moody's Electronic Information Service*. The two data bases complement each other to offer thorough coverage on a range of business topics. *Moody's Corporate Profiles*, for example, presents full-text descriptions of companies on the New York and American Stock Exchanges as well as 1,300 Over-the-Counter (OTC) companies, while *Moody's Electronic Information Service* offers historical financial statistics on 4,000 corporations and 144 industries. Access both data bases through Moody's.

PREDICASTS F & S Indexes, produced by PREDICASTS, Inc., offers a data base containing 2,587,000 citations of sources published since 1972. *PREDICASTS* is strongest in its coverage of important business information on countries and industries. The data base can be accessed through DIALOG, BRS, and DATA-STAR. Other business-centered data bases include *Harvard Business Review*, which contains the full text of all articles published in the *Harvard Business Review* since 1976. The data base also provides bibliographic citations and abstracts for those articles published between 1971 and 1976, as well as 700 selected articles published prior to 1971. Articles retrieved by the data base cover such topics as accounting, finance, decision making, information systems, and management. Access *Harvard Business Review* through DIALOG or BRS (Williams, 1985, p. 665).

Other useful data bases include Standard & Poor's *Compustat*, Arthur D. Little's *Arthur D. Little/Online, Consumer Information Service (CIS)* from Compuserve, Inc., *NEXIS* from Mead Data Central Inc., Trinet Inc.'s *Trinet Company Database*, and *Value Line Database II* from Arnold Bernhard & Company. As economics and finance must now be monitored and managed on a global level, you might consider accessing the *Public Affairs Information Service Bulletin (P.A.I.S.)* data base for monthly updates on international coverage of economic, political, and social affairs around the world. For the author, subject, title, and abstract of every dissertation approved by accredited colleges and universities since 1861, access *Dissertation Abstracts Online* (University Microfilm International) through BRS or SDC.

For a complete listing of available data bases, consult Greg Byerly's *Online Searching: A Dictionary and Bibliographic Guide*, Martha E. Williams' *Computer-Readable Data-Bases: A Directory and Data Sourcebook*, or Capital Systems Group Inc.'s *Directory of Online Information Resources*. Information USA's *Federal Data Base Finder* identifies data base sources relating to federal government activities, legislation, and public services.

Limitations of Data-Based Searches

Despite its advantages of speed and convenience, the data-based search, like all research techniques, has its limitations. Data bases were first made commercially available in the late 1960s; however, the large majority of data bases were established in the early 1970s. Consequently, material published before that time is often not listed in the data base. For that reason, you will have to search sources in those earlier years manually (e.g., using the card catalog or indexes).

Second, although data bases normally provide remarkably current information, the process of transferring printed information to electronic media is time-consuming. Because lag times for information transfer can vary from a matter of days to weeks or months, depending on the search service, you might occasionally have to use alternative research techniques to obtain the most current information on a topic.

Third, the effectiveness of a data-based search is dependent on your effectiveness as an on-line researcher. In short, your data-based search can give you only what you've asked it to find, as defined by your descriptors and operators. Your descriptors, then, must be focused and properly phrased to generate a productive search. But even the success of a so-called productive search is relative. What about the side of the issue, or other related issues, that you haven't even considered? Too often our ignorance in a subject restricts the scope and direction of our research. Frequently, we know so little about a topic that we haven't the foundation of knowledge from which to pose a functional research question.

Sometimes a manual search of sources can help to educate us in a subject while also providing a working bibliography. Although the data-based search can supply you with the type of information you had already expected or hoped to find, it cannot completely substitute for manually searching such traditional sources as the card catalog, indexes, or rows of shelved books. Many veteran researchers will readily attribute a key part of their research success to inadvertent discoveries made while flipping through books as they wandered, half lost, through the stacks, or as they idly paged through a periodical index while waiting for a library's data-base computer terminal to become free.

Evaluation of Secondary Sources _____

Although you may have collected many promising secondary sources of information, not all will be useful to your purposes in writing the report. Consequently, you must evaluate each source to determine which ones should be read in full. You might evaluate the usefulness of the source by asking the following questions:

- Is the source truly useful in substantiating the thoroughness and validity of your report analyses and conclusions?
- Are the data current or dated? If less current, does the source's information necessarily lose its validity or usefulness to your project?

- Are the data accurate and reliable? Have they been collected and analyzed with proven methodologies?
- What is the expertise of the author? Has she or he published other works in the same or related area?
- How reputable is the publication in which the work appears? How can you tell?

Although current and timely information on a topic is often the most useful, older material can also be integral to developing background on a subject. For instance, if you were researching the public's reaction to the stock market crash of 1929, contemporary news reports of that time period might provide invaluable information regarding not only the financial devastation of the event but also the social, psychological, and emotional hysteria created by the event. Of course, you can easily determine how current the information is by noting the work's most recent publication date.

The credibility and validity of a source often depend on the degree of expertise that authors bring to their collection and analysis of the information. To help establish an author's qualifications, some articles and books provide author profiles that illustrate the author's expertise in the area of her or his writing, including the writer's professional affiliations, teaching or career experience in the field, noted awards, and other works by the same author on related subjects. However, you might also consult the *Who's Who* series of directories for more background on the author's qualifications.

To evaluate accurately the journal, book, or even the publisher of the work in which the information appears, you should spend time researching other articles that have been published in the same journal or by the same publisher. Do they seem well researched, complete, consistent, and objective in their findings? Do they include substantive bibliographies? Are their authors recognized experts in their fields? If yes, you might infer that the journal or publisher is respected by professionals in the area. You might also determine the journal's affiliation. Is it an academic journal published by a university press or a journal produced by a private think tank, such as the Brookings Institute? Or is it a slick, commercially oriented magazine owned by a publishing company and intended for special-interest groups (e.g., insurance or medical associations, political parties, or religious denominations)? The professional affiliation of a journal or publishing company may suggest the presence of bias (and, thus, the lack of objectivity) in the articles it publishes.

Bibliography and Note Cards

After locating your sources, you should formulate a logically organized method for recording not only the key information gleaned from those sources but also the important information needed to cite those sources later in your report.

Before deciding what information to use from the sources you've collected, you might build an expandable bibliographic system with note cards.

Bibliography Cards

To compile a list of bibliography cards, use 3- × 5-in. note cards or electronic note cards produced on a computer screen by special applications software. Record on the cards all pertinent bibliographic data from your sources, including such items as

> names of author(s).
> title of source (e.g., article, book, annual report).
> edition number (if applicable).
> volume number (if applicable).
> page numbers (if applicable).
> date of publication.
> name of publisher.
> city and state location of publisher.
> library call number of source.

Order the bibliography cards (usually alphabetically) and number them in the upper left-hand corner of the card, as shown in Figure 7.16. Many researchers also include the source's call number just below the card number so they can easily reference and locate the source later.

Use a separate card for each source, as you will later need to arrange the cards alphabetically, or in some other order, when building your bibliography page. Placing more than one source on a card complicates this task. On each card, include the essential bibliographic information across the top of the card, perhaps using the bibliographic format outlined in your documentation style guide (e.g., Modern Language Association, American Psychological Association, University of Chicago). Information on how to document your report using accepted documentation styles is provided in Chapter 11.

Note Cards

Many researchers use 5- × 7-in. note cards for recording essential information from their sources. Use a separate card for each key topic; related subtopics may be noted on a single card, or on separate cards for easier reading. Place a subject heading (a descriptive word or phrase) at the top of the card so that you can identify its topic at a glance, as shown in Figure 7.17. This also simplifies the task of organizing the cards easier.

You might also include either the complete bibliographic citation of the source from which you obtained the information or the number of the source's bibliography card. In either case, be certain to include the page number on which you found the data.

FIGURE 7.16
Sample bibliography cards citing books by Below and Taylor on subject "Strategic Planning."

Some researchers prefer note pads or sheets to cards when taking notes. This method can make notetaking easier and faster, as you can cull on a single sheet a number of notes from one source, or multiple sources, on a common topic. However, as researchers rarely know the complete organization or content of their reports, multiple notes on a single sheet can make more difficult the task of ordering cards and organizing research data or information later in the writing process.

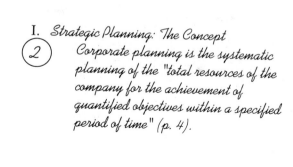

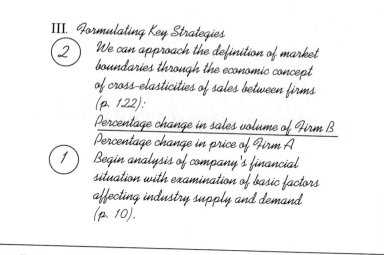

FIGURE 7.17

Sample note cards on the works of Below and Taylor.

Methods for Recording Information

Report writing often requires that the author refer to sizable amounts of information from secondary sources. To ensure that you give proper attribution to authors of these original works, it is important that you identify on your note cards or sheets the method by which you recorded the information. The three fundamental methods of reporting information from sources are to quote, paraphrase, or summarize.

Original Text:

Managers were generally satisfied with how rhetorical components of the sample annual reports were used to ensure the corporate message matched audiences' informational needs and demographic backgrounds. Reports earned the highest marks for style, with 31% of surveyed managers granting them "excellent" ratings and 60% giving either "good" or "fair" ratings. Managers also found the format and layout of reports to be effective in promoting the corporate image and in making content as accessible to the reader as possible. We find it worth noting here that, while 21% of managers rated the format/layout of the reports as "excellent" and 78% as "good" or "fair," no manager thought the reports' design and contruction were "poor."

Direct Quote:

The study conducted by Ortega (1991) shows that managers are generally satisfied with the style of U.S. corporate annual reports. Ortega adds that, "while 21% of managers rated the format/layout of the reports as "excellent" and 78% as "good" or "fair," no manager thought the reports' design and construction were "poor" (p. 116).

Summary:

According to Ortega (1991), managers are generally satisfied with how U.S. corporations match the rhetorical components of their annual reports with the informational needs and demographic backgrounds of targeted audiences.

Paraphrase:

Managers in this country are generally satisified with how U.S. corporations match the rhetorical components of their annual reports with the informational needs and demographic backgrounds of targeted audiences. In a recent study, surveyed managers gave report style the highest overall rating. Thirty-one percent of the managers rated report style as excellent. Report format/layout components also received positive marks with 99% of the managers granting these with excellent, good, or fair ratings (Ortega, 1991).

FIGURE 7.18
Direct quote, summary, and paraphrase with appropriate APA documentation.

Direct quotation is a verbatim copy of another author's words (Figure 7.18). When you quote material from another source, be sure to maintain the punctuation and spelling of the original passage. If you omit parts of the original, use ellipses points, as represented by three periods (. . .), to signify the deletion of material. Be careful, however, not to distort the original meaning or intent of the passage when using ellipses.

Whenever you put the ideas of another author into your own words, you are **paraphrasing.** If you paraphrase ideas unique to an author, you must cite that source with a footnote or use an in-text citation. Also, include the source in your report's bibliography, works cited, or reference section.

A **summary** is a distillation or condensation of information from another author. As with paraphrasing, when you summarize ideas of other authors, you should cite the source.

Paraphrasing and summarizing are effective tools to employ in notetaking. To produce accurate and precise paraphrases and summaries whose topical thrusts are directly relevant to your own report subject, you must have (a) understood the source material; (b) understood how that information, if only generally, relates to topics or arguments raised in your report; and (c) speculated on how that secondary source material might best be used in the context of your report. In short, writing substantive and accurate paraphrases and summaries of relevant source data and information is a valuable method for informally formulating the organization and content of your own report.

When including quotations, paraphrases, or summaries in your notes, be sure that you specify on your note cards which of the three forms the recorded information takes. For either brief or lengthy quotations, use quotation marks. For paraphrased or summarized material, you might make a simple notation at the end of the passage.

Photocopies

The novice researcher quickly learns the value of photocopied source information and the importance of bringing an ample supply of nickels, dimes, and quarters to the library. Photocopies are the easiest way of accurately recording secondary information. Having a photocopy of a document also enables the researcher to review the wording of the original work at a later time. All full-service libraries provide either photocopy service or access to photocopy machines.

Photocopies are also a convenient and accurate method of recording graphic aids such as tables and figures that you might decide later to use in your own work. If you do incorporate graphics from other sources, be sure to document them, as discussed in Chapter 12.

Summary

In Chapter 7, we have asserted that research is central to the successful planning and execution of all business activities. Regardless of the specific type of research you perform for your business, you will collect your research from either **secondary** or **primary sources.**

Secondary sources are critical to the report-writing process, as they provide you with contextual background on the subject(s) of your research while you determine if other researchers have already completed and published similar research on the subject. Uncovering and using such related research in your report can also save you considerable energy, time, and money that you might otherwise spend in performing your own primary study. In addition, when used as substantive evidence in your report, secondary sources lend credibility and authority to your discussion of issues in the report. They can also help you better define and focus your report topic. Finally, your investigation of secondary sources can reveal areas within your field of study that deserve further attention.

Before beginning your secondary research, you should plan a logical and cost-effective strategy for collecting only the information you need to complete a thorough and accurate report on or before its deadline. We have suggested that in your preresearch preparation you (a) clearly define the focus, scope, and purpose of your report; (b) estimate the total time and money needed to complete the research project; (c) select a method for researching secondary sources that offers you the best chances of finding the required information quickly and conveniently; and (d) decide if you will need special research expertise, such as a professional reference librarian experienced in computer data-based searches, in order to complete the research phase by a predetermined deadline.

University and public libraries may prove to be the most productive sources of secondary research; however, you should not forget to examine collections in such private libraries as that of your own company. Most libraries use either the **Dewey Decimal System** or **Library of Congress System** of cataloging and shelving their books.

To save yourself from having to sort through mountains of relatively useless sources at the end of your research, we have recommended evaluating each secondary source against some basic criteria, such as (a) whether the topics discussed in the source are sufficiently related to your report subject(s); (b) if the work will provide you with reliable background or context to the problem; (c) whether the source's information meets the informational needs and professional interests of your audience(s); (d) if the source contains unique information that no other source has yet shown and that should be covered in your report; and (e) whether the information seems readily accessible.

In addition to its card catalog, the library offers a variety of methods for finding secondary sources, including almanacs, annual reports, atlases, bibliographies, biographies, books, business services, dictionaries, directories, encyclopedias, government publications, guides, indexes, newspapers, pamphlets, periodicals. The on-line data-based search can be a significant help in your secondary research process because of the speed, comprehensiveness, and flexibility it offers in accessing current data and information on your topic.

We have reviewed a variety of on-line search techniques, including retrospective, comprehensive, selective, state-of-the-art, SDI, and patent searches. During your data-based search, you will interact with either **reference** or **source data bases.** There are two types of reference data bases (bibliographic and directory) and three types of source data bases (numeric, full-text, and dictionary.)

Use **descriptors** to describe the subject on which you wish the data base to supply sources. The data base uses Boolean logic to respond to key relational terms, or **operators,** used in the search descriptor. The most commonly used operators are *and, or,* and *not.* The *and* operator suggests intersection, the *or* equivalency, the *not* exclusion. You will probably search one or more of the largest data-based services, including DIALOG, BRS, and SDC.

After collecting your sources, you should evaluate which sources should be read. Consider the accuracy and reliability of the source's data and information, the author's expertise in the subject area, and the reputation of the publication in which the work appears. While reading the sources you've decided are valuable and relevant to your report, you should build an expandable bibliography system and use note cards to paraphrase, summarize, or quote information that you will later use in your report.

Related Reading

BAXTER, CAROL McFARLAND. *Business Report Writing: A Practical Approach.* Boston: PWS, 1983.

BLANK, STEVEN. *Practical Business Research.* Westport, CT: AVI, 1984.

BOWMAN, JOEL P., and BERNADINE P. BRANCHAW. *Business Report Writing.* 2nd ed. New York: Dryden, 1988.

BROWNSTONE, DAVID M., and GORDON CARRUTH. *Where to Find Business Information.* 2nd ed. New York: Wiley, 1982.

BUCKLEY, JOHN W., MARLENE H. BUCKLEY, and H. F. CHIANG. *Research Methodology and Business Decisions.* New York: Nat'l. Assn. of Accountants, 1976.

BYERLY, GREG. *Online Searching: A Dictionary and Bibliographic Guide.* Littleton, CO: Libraries Unlimited, 1983.

CLOVER, VERNON T., and H. L. BALSLEY. *Business Research Methods.* 2nd ed. Columbus, OH: Grid, 1979.

COYLE, WILLIAM. *The Macmillan Guide to Writing Research Papers.* New York: Macmillan, 1990.

Directory of Special Libraries and Information Centers. Detroit: Gale, 1963 to date.

DOMINOWSKI, ROGER L. *Research Methods.* Englewood Cliffs, NJ: Prentice, 1980.

EMORY, C. WILLIAM. *Business Research Methods.* 2nd ed. Homewood, IL: Irwin, 1980.

Federal Data Base Finder. Potomac, MD: Information U.S.A., 1985.

GLOSSBRENNER, ALFRED. *How to Look It Up Online: Get the Information Edge with Your Personal Computer.* New York: St. Martin's, 1987.

HOOVER, RYAN E. *Executive's Guide to Online Information Services.* White Plains, NY: Knowledge Industry, 1984.

HUCK, SCHUYLER W., WILLIAM H. CORMIER, and WILLIAM G. BOUNDS. *Reading Statistics and Research.* New York: Harper, 1974.

JOHNSON, H. WEBSTER, ANTHONY J. FARIA, and E. L. MAIER. *How to Use the Business Library, with Sources of Business Information.* 5th ed. Cincinnati: South-Western, 1984.

LAVIN, MICHAEL R. *Business Information: How to Find It, How to Use It.* Phoenix: Oryx, 1987.

LEEDY, PAUL. *How to Read Research and Understand It.* New York: Macmillan, 1981.

———. *Practical Research: Planning and Design.* New York: Macmillan, 1985.

MOYER, RUTH, ELEANOUR STEVENS, and RALPH SWITZER. *The Research and Report Handbook.* New York: Wiley, 1981.

POPOVICH, CHARLES J. *Business and Economics Database Online: Environmental Scanning with a Personal Computer.* Littleton, CO: Libraries Unlimited, 1987.

SCHLESSINGER, BERNARD S., ed. *The Basic Business Library: Core Resources.* 2nd ed. Phoenix: Oryx, 1989.

Sears List of Subject Headings. Ed. Barbara M. Wertby. 11th ed. New York: H. W. Wilson, 1977.

SEKARAN, UMA. *Research Methods for Managers.* New York: Wiley, 1984.

SMITH, CHARLES B. *A Guide to Business Research: Developing, Conducting, and Writing Research.* Chicago: Nelson, 1981.

STRAUSS, DIANE WHEELER. *Handbook of Business Information: A Guide for Librarians, Students, and Researchers.* Englewood, CO: Libraries Unlimited, 1988.

TREECE, MALRA. *Effective Business Reports.* Boston: Allyn, 1982.

UNITED STATES LIBRARY OF CONGRESS. *Subject Headings Used in the Dictionary Catalog of the Library of Congress.* 11th ed. Washington, DC: Cataloging Distribution Service, 1988.

WILLIAMS, MARTHA E., ed. *Computer-Readable Databases: A Directory of Data and Sourcebook.* 2 vols. Chicago: American Library Assn, 1985.

ZIKMUND, WILLIAM G., ed. *Business Research Methods.* 3rd ed. Chicago: Dryden, 1991.

CHAPTER 8

Conducting Primary Research for Management Reports

Secondary research, as we discussed in the previous chapter, can contribute invaluable data and information to your report. By providing you with relevant material on your report topic, secondary research can also save you significant energy, time, and money you might otherwise have invested in performing primary research. However, rarely will you be able to collect all the data and information you need for your managerial report from secondary sources. Although you might be fortunate in finding secondary sources that investigate your report topic in a general fashion, chances are those sources will not provide enough current, accurate, or substantive information relating to the company-specific concerns of your report.

Whereas secondary research can provide excellent background and contextual information on industrywide, national, or international issues, it is **primary research** that typically supplies the up-to-date information necessary for making intelligent managerial decisions in an increasingly dynamic business environment. This chapter examines three fundamental methods for conducting primary research:

1. Observation research
2. Survey research
3. Experimental research.

Observation research and **survey research** are passive and descriptive in nature; that is, the researcher using one or both of these methods gathers data—whether through analytical observation, personal or phone interviews, or mail surveys—without altering the research environment and, thus, without influencing the results of the study. In effect, the researcher simply describes events as an interested but objective observer. This type of research is often called *descriptive* research.

The methods for conducting **experimental research** are intrinsically different from those of descriptive research. Experimental researchers test hypotheses on which a report is based by (a) intentionally controlling and modifying the research environment and (b) measuring how the altered or static environment has succeeded or failed to produce evidence to support the hypothesis. Often hypotheses are only vague, speculative theories or hunches. But they can also be specific, studied, yet still unproven, explanations. Whether speculative or studied, however, all hypotheses require corroboration through empirical testing before managers feel confident enough to base decisions on them.

Regardless of which primary research method(s) you employ in conducting your study, you will normally perform your investigation in five basic steps:

1. Planning the report focus and research method
2. Collecting data
3. Organizing data
4. Analyzing data
5. Reporting the synthesized and interpreted information.

Chapter 9 examines effective methods for organizing and analyzing the data collected through primary or secondary research. Appendix A provides detailed information on statistical methods for manipulating and analyzing data collected specifically through primary research.

Benefits of Primary Research

Primary research offers business researchers various benefits. First, primary research often brings to light new information that cannot be found in secondary sources. For example, how could strategic planners thoroughly investigate and accurately assess current hiring needs within their company if they did not use interviews with company managers and labor leaders as part of their research methods? No secondary source could provide this type of immediate, company-specific information, nor could secondary information cover the production and sales ends of the equation that would invariably influence the company's future hiring needs. When performing primary research for the first time on an organizationwide level, many companies are shocked to discover the large discrepancy between how they *thought* their businesses operated and how their businesses *actually* operate.

Second, if you have properly conceived, controlled, and executed your primary research, the resulting information should reveal ways to make the report organization more effective and efficient. Often the investigation produces cost-saving results that pay the price of the primary research many times over. Moreover, primary research, especially experimental research, is conducted on a smaller and less expensive scale than would normally be required if the same information were to be gleaned from years of ordinary experience.

Third, primary research provides information that is significantly more accurate than data collected haphazardly by managers using their own business experience to eyeball a problem or by researchers extrapolating data collected from secondary sources. Finally, some business situations simply cannot be studied in work-world situations because of associated costs, time constraints, or inherent dangers. Many companies, for example, when formulating projected sales for the upcoming fiscal year, would not limit their investigation only to secondary research, such as a study of sales figures recorded in company archives. Instead, prudent organizations would supplement that secondary research with market surveys (survey research) to obtain more realistic corroborative evidence of sales estimates.

Observation Research

Observation research involves the systematic visual monitoring of observable data or phenomena related to your report topic or problem (Emory, 1980, pp. 312–330). The researcher basically watches with a purpose in mind, without altering the observed data. The procedures and techniques used to gather this observed data and information will vary, depending on the purpose and occasion of your report as well as the nature of your subject. Observation research often proves most useful when used to monitor the behavior of people in business situations, such as studying customers' reactions to marketing and sales techniques, examining the work habits of production staff in order to streamline operations, or just counting the number of shoppers to determine the fluctuations in store traffic over a period of time.

For example, to determine how a department store could improve its sales of expensive perfumes, a researcher might observe (a) the types of people who window-shop as opposed to those who actually purchase perfumes and (b) the kinds of perfumes they buy. Observation of customer behavior can reveal a great deal regarding how effectively the store is attracting and winning consumers. Do the displays of the perfume section seem to spark customer interest? If so, why? If not, why not? Do sales techniques of the section's salespeople appear effective? What are the customers' reactions to those techniques? To supplement this observation research, the researcher might also consider administering a survey (discussed later in this chapter) to obtain detailed information that is not observable.

The observer conducting such research would have to be trained to know exactly *what* she or he is looking for in customer behavior and to possess a thorough knowledge of customer demographics as well as the sales techniques and products of the store. In some cases, however, observation research serves to teach observers in situations where researchers do *not* know what they're looking for. The security personnel of the same department store, for instance, may observe customers via remote-control cameras not merely to catch shoplifters but also to learn about shoplifting methods. From the collected information, the store could document how shoplifters steal, enabling security personnel to formulate a profile of potential shoplifters that salespeople might use to anticipate and avoid shoplifting situations.

To ensure that the observation process produces reliable and accurate data, you should

define the objectives of the observation research.

plan the research design and observation instrument.

select and train reliable observers.

collect and organize the data.

analyze and report the data.

repeat the observation process to corroborate the reliability and accuracy of the results.

Planning the Research Design and Observation Instrument

Before you can structure the research design and construct the observation instrument with which to perform your research, you must ensure that observation is the best method for researching for the types of data and information needed. In addition, you must define and focus the purpose and objectives of your study. When performing any kind of research, you should always consider if alternative research methodologies might not be more effective in obtaining the information needed for your report. You should be certain that observation research—rather than, say, survey or experimental research—offers you the best chance of obtaining the necessary results. Moreover, you should consider a combination of research methods for gathering a thorough mix of relevant data.

After determining the focus of your investigation, construct an **observation instrument** (also called *schedules*, *score cards*, or *observationnaires*) on which observed data can be recorded accurately and completely by observers. The structure of the form should enable researchers to tabulate the data quickly and easily, as illustrated by the sample observation instrument in Figure 8.1.

When preparing the instrument, you should remember to include

an identification box in which the observer can record a number for each case observed as well as her or his own name (or ID number), the location of the observation, time, and date.

OBSERVATION SURVEY 36: CUSTOMER RESPONSE TO PERFUME DISPLAYS

Observer: _____   Date of Observation: _____

Location: _____   Time of Observation: _____

Special Conditions/ Occurrences: _____

	Recognition			Duration of Observation (in seconds)					Focus of Observation			Response		Purchase	
	None	Minimal	Full	0–5	5–10	10–20	20–30	30+	CD	MD	GD	Left	DS	Yes	No
1															
2															
3															
4															
5															
6															
7															
8															
9															
10															

Instrument Key

Locations: A—Arlington, VA   B—Bethesda, MD   CC—Chevy Chase, MD
             H—Hyattsville, MD   W—Washington, D.C.   WF—White Flint, MD

Recognition: None=No recognition at all from customer.
               Minimal=Passing glance by customer.
               Full=Brief pause (or longer) by customer. May not result in customer's stopping.

Focus of Observation: CD=Counter display.
                        MD=Mannequin display.
                        GD=Display in glass case.
Response:
               Left=Customer left display area.
               DS=Customer paused to discuss products with salesperson.

FIGURE 8.1
Sample observation instrument.

- all the explanatory information and instructions needed for the observer to record and for the compiler to tabulate the data accurately.

- sufficient space for the observer to record results of each standard item as well as space for unforeseen yet relevant findings that the observer feels should be noted.

- logical groupings of related items ordered in the sequence in which the observer is likely to observe them. (Clover, 1984, pp. 159–170; Emory, 1980, pp. 221–223, 287–296)

Instruments should list every possible item directly related to the study's focus that can be observed. Incomplete instruments force observers to improvise, often haphazardly, ways of recording data not covered on the form, which not only lengthens the observation process but also distracts observers from the point of the research—that is, to observe accurately. Moreover, logically and sequentially organized instruments enable observers to record data quickly, a key ingredient of any form if the observer is to perform a thorough, accurate, and efficient observation.

When conducting the research, observers should be certain to note each observation occurrence on the instrument. To expedite the tabulation and interpretation of collected data, observers should also identify themselves by name or an identification number. Should researchers later discover any omissions or errors on the instrument, they can easily identify the appropriate observer and ask for assistance.

Training observers is an important component in successful observation research. You should carefully prepare and distribute to observers detailed instructions on conducting observations that produce accurate and reliable data. Instruct observers on each part of the instrument so that they know how to locate, identify, observe, and record items under study. Test observers by using trial observations, which have proven to be an effective method for preparing observers for the kinds of data they should look for as well as the field conditions in which they will be working. If trial tests are inappropriate or impossible, pictures, samples, or models of the event or item to be observed might prove to be the next best thing (Blank, 1984, pp. 184–192). If your research budget allows, the exceptionally accurate representations of real-world situations provided by computer simulations, such as those used in the training of ship captains, airline pilots, and National Aeronautics and Space Administration (NASA) shuttle crews offer infinite possibilities in the training of observers.

Finally, the observer should be trained to read people's facial expressions and body language. Such data can actually reflect the thoughts and emotions of test subjects more accurately than data collected from formal surveys of those same subjects. However, only qualified experts—as those involved in **kinesics** research (the study of body language)—should attempt to interpret the psychological and emotional states of subjects based on observable expressions, behavior, and actions alone.[1]

Collecting and Organizing Findings

After you have distributed to observers a well-structured and complete instrument, ensure that the observation is performed under conditions that will

---

[1]For additional reading on the subject of interpreting facial expressions, we refer you to Ray L. Birdwhistell's *Kinesics and Contexts* (1970) and to some of the numerous works of Paul Ekman: *Unmasking the Face: A Guide to Recognizing Emotions from Facial Clues* (1984), *Emotion in the Human Face* (1982), *Telling Lies: Clues to Deceit in the Marketplace* (1985), and *Approaches to Emotions* (1984).

produce the most accurate and reliable results possible. Position observers in a location from which they can clearly see the items, people, or phenomena they are to record. Select the appropriate time of day, week, and year during which to observe the subject or phenomena. The observer should stay alert to record *precisely* what occurs, without adding or deleting details. As tired and restless observers often make inattentive researchers, also consider discomfort and fatigue factors associated with observation when determining the work hours of observers.

On occasion, observers are greatly aided in performing their jobs if supplied such supporting mechanical devices as hand counters; photoelectric-eye counters; pocket calculators; tape recorders; X-ray scanners; closed-circuit television; still, motion, or sound cameras or other specialized cameras equipped with infrared filming, microscopic or telescopic lenses, and lens filters (Emory, 1980, Chap. 10). When using mechanical devices in your observation research, be certain that your observers know how to use them properly. Furthermore, make sure that the devices are used uniformly throughout the research by all observers to prevent artificial discrepancies between data recorded by observers equipped with devices and by those not equipped.

In addition, ensure that your observation covers a sufficient number of cases from which you can generalize about the larger population. The number of cases to be observed depends on the heterogeneity of the items being observed and how many cases are necessary to make the sample **representative** of the general population. Your observation research should encompass a representative cross-section of the sample. Choose the times and conditions during which to perform the research that ensure that your study will include a representative sample. More about sampling designs and procedures is provided later in this chapter.

Analyzing and Reporting Results

Before beginning your analysis, check for the accuracy and completeness of the data. Follow-up observations of the same items by different observers will often expose possible contamination of the data that might have occurred for any number of reasons, including observer bias or improper observation technique. You might use a different set of mechanical devices to corroborate the findings collected with mechanical assistance. If your research budget allows, you might use two separate sets of observers or mechanical devices in tandem and later cross-check the findings of each set to uncover any discrepancies that could invalidate the data.

Logically organized observation instruments, if completed by well-trained observers, should make the tabulation and synthesis of the data easier. From careful analysis of the findings, you should be able to infer if the data show any patterns on which you might base subsequent conclusions or recommendations. When reporting the results, be sure to double-check the accuracy of your interpretation of the data and present the information in an organization most useful for the reader.

Advantages and Disadvantages

Carefully controlled observation research has several major advantages. Observation research

> is often the only way to study people, events, and phenomena under real-life conditions without manipulating the research environment (as field-based research does).
>
> is relatively inexpensive, convenient, and fast to plan, execute, and duplicate.
>
> provides data that are normally easy to tabulate.
>
> typically produces reliable and accurate data by minimizing researcher interaction with test subjects, thus reducing the possibility of human error and the level of subjectivity.
>
> is flexible in its use of mechanical devices, which can increase the efficiency and convenience of the observer as well as the reliability and accuracy of research findings.

Observation research, however, has a variety of limitations as well.

- The technique realistically allows an observer to measure only one type of problem or phenomenon, as an observer can't be expected to view and record everything that occurs during her or his watch.
- Certain psychological data, such as thoughts and motivations, are typically impossible to observe.
- The accuracy and reliability of data collected from observation research depend largely on the level of proficiency of the observers, requiring that researchers expend the time and money to carefully train observers.
- Obtaining permission to perform observations can be time-consuming and expensive.
- Some mechanical devices used to measure and record data in observation research are not only expensive to purchase or rent but also difficult to obtain, operate, and transport. These complications often necessitate the hiring of experts to either train observers or operate the devices themselves. (Blank, 1984, pp. 192–195; Walizer & Wiener, 1978)

Survey Research

When attempting to uncover certain types of information from people, you can make the best use of your research efforts by simply *asking* them. Survey research is most productive in business research when you query people on information that is difficult, if not impossible, to gather any other way, including their opinions, emotions, motivations, experiences, and interests. As today's businesses increasingly press for up-to-the-minute information through survey research, you must ensure that your survey methods are sufficiently sound and valid to produce reliable and accurate data on which to base successful managerial decisions.

Before planning your survey strategy and sampling procedure, you should consider the following steps:

1. Clearly define the information for which you are searching, the use of that information, and the people who can provide the data or information.
2. Determine what survey research will be the most effective method for collecting the needed information.
3. Decide which type of survey technique—mail questionnaire, personal interview, or telephone interview—will best meet the informational needs, time constraints, and budget of the study.

Planning Survey Strategy and Sampling Procedure

Small, well-defined populations are relatively easy to survey as a whole. For example, let's assume that your report intends to investigate the views of 30 employees regarding how they might be more productive in their work. In performing primary research for the report, you could easily survey all relevant production personnel on site, including floor supervisors and midlevel managers.

For a variety of reasons, other populations would not be so convenient to survey. Many target populations prove to be too large to survey each individual. In addition, respondents may be too scattered geographically to survey cost-effectively and within the time limitations of the report project. When surveying an entire population is impractical, you might consider generalizing about the whole population by querying a **sample** of people (through a survey questionnaire) who are a representative subset of that larger group. A representative sample, then, should serve as a microcosm of the larger population. Understandably, surveying a representative sample is often less expensive, less time-consuming, and more efficient than trying to canvas an entire population.

The target population of your survey depends entirely on the objectives of your report. To delimit your sample population accurately, you must first define the demographics of the general population, such as their socioeconomic, educational, occupational, ethnic, racial, and religious backgrounds. More about building random samples and deciding on appropriate sample sizes is provided later in this chapter.

Questionnaires used to survey a sample population must be clearly written and appropriately organized so that respondents know exactly what they are being asked. The questionnaire should, of course, include questions that address all the issues in your study. The second part of this chapter explains how to construct an effective questionnaire.

Initially, you might not be able to narrow your target population sufficiently to delimit a representative sample. For instance, suppose you're the manager of the perfume section of the same department store discussed earlier in this chapter. As it is the holiday season, you are planning inventory levels for perfumes to ensure that the store is not caught short on customers' favorite fragrances. You've considered mailing a questionnaire to all of your regular customers; however, you realize that many either do not buy perfume or do not have enough knowledge in perfumes to provide you with much guidance in your inventory planning.

In this case, you decide to include a **filter question** in your survey, which you might conduct through the mail or by personal or telephone interviews. Filter questions screen sample subjects who do not rightly belong in the desired sample population and whose views, if included in the study, might distort your findings. This particular survey might contain a filter question such as: "Do you regularly purchase the perfumes available at HAGER & SCHEIBER'S DEPARTMENT STORE?" Subsequent questions might survey respondents for their perfume preferences. To obtain accurate data from which to surmise which perfumes might sell well during the holiday season, you should tabulate and analyze results from only those surveys whose respondents answered "yes" to the filter question.

Developing Interview Techniques and a Survey Schedule

The type of information sought, the nature of the sample population, and the conditions surrounding the research will determine how, where, and when you conduct the survey. As an example, let's continue with our hypothetical perfume survey. If less than a month remained before the holiday, you would probably rule out doing a mail survey, as there would be insufficient time for the questionnaires to be returned, the results tabulated and analyzed, and perfume inventories adjusted in time for the onslaught of holiday customers in search of a pleasing fragrance. In this case, you would wisely opt for either a telephone or a personal interview. If you decide to query shoppers from the store's list of regular customers, you might find the phone interview most convenient. However, you might also choose to narrow the survey and interview only those customers who happen to shop the perfume section.

To construct an effective survey that queries the most appropriate respondents from whom to gather the types of information required by your research, you must

> develop items to be included in the survey.
> determine the procedures and techniques for analyzing the collected data.
> run a test questionnaire on a test sample.
> revise the questionnaire items and format based on changes dictated by the test run.
> complete a final draft of the questionnaire.

Instructions for constructing a sound questionnaire are provided later in this chapter.

Collecting and Organizing Findings

When collecting survey data through telephone or personal interviews, interviewers must be

objective in their presentation of the questionnaire.

courteous to respondents.

complete and meticulous in their recording of data (Gottlieb, 1986; Lavrakas, 1987).

Before collecting information, interviewers should be properly trained in how to administer the survey. Training sessions conducted by field supervisors can significantly improve the proficiency of interviewers in their presentation and recording of survey data. Each interviewer should understand the objectives of the survey, the meaning of questions being asked of respondents, the technique of presenting the questionnaire, and the procedures for recording results. Interviewers need not know the entire context surrounding the research, however. In some instances, interviewers perform more impartial work if they are ignorant of the project's specific aims and methodologies that, if known by them, might prejudice their presentation of the survey and thus invalidate the results.

Interviewers must do more than collect the required information from survey subjects; they must record that data or information accurately. When conducting any type of survey (e.g., phone or personal interview), interviewers must note responses *precisely* as they are given, without omission or interviewer bias, and record those responses in the appropriate space on the questionnaire. In certain cases, however, respondents, especially businesspersons representing their respective firms, will prefer to complete the questionnaire themselves to avoid errors (Clover, 1984, pp. 111–155).

Maintaining and imparting to interviewees a professional impartiality during the interview is not a simple or easy matter. Interviewers should know the interviewing process in detail to avoid having to interject their own interpretations of questions that can mislead or bias interviewees. During their training, interviewers must also learn to recognize those people targeted by the survey to avoid interviewing inappropriate subjects and thus contaminating survey results.

In addition, training sessions should instruct interviewers to wear clothing that is appropriate for conducting interviews. An interviewer who is overdressed or underdressed for the occasion can make an unfavorable impression that might prejudice the interviewee for or against the questionnaire. Moreover, make telephone or personal interviewers aware that a pleasant tone of voice and clear speech are required to avoid offending respondents or prejudicing their responses.

Before closing the interview and dismissing the interviewee, interviewers should edit the questionnaire to ensure that all questions were answered clearly and correctly. If your budget allows, you might consider sending interviewers out in pairs so that each can audit the other's interview sessions to uncover possible flaws in the administering of the questionnaire, including inaccurate or biased explanations of questions, incomplete responses, or omissions of information.

Survey supervisors should observe interviewers on the job to verify that the questionnaires are being administered properly. Knowing that their work may be monitored by supervisors, interviewers typically perform more effective field work and take their role in administering the survey more seriously. In turn, the seriousness with which the survey is handled by the interviewers is imparted to the interviewee, who, as a result, tends to offer more complete and thoughtful responses. To validate the accuracy and reliability of the survey results, you might choose to run a follow-up survey with the same questionnaire, but with new sample subjects (drawn from the same sample) and a different team of interviewers.

Analyzing and Reporting Results

After tabulating survey results, consider the significance of the data or information as it relates to your report topic and scope. If you have appropriately chosen your survey sample, you should be able to generalize from the sample to the larger target audience. (Additional methods for analyzing data and information are provided in Chapter 9 and Appendix A.) Finally, communicate to target readers the results of your research, as well as the anaylsis of those findings, in written or oral reports.

Mail Surveys

Mail surveys represent a convenient, inexpensive method for collecting survey data and information. Consequently, their use in business has grown considerably over the years.

To conduct an effective and efficient mail survey, consider the following procedure:

1. Prepare a questionnaire that elicits from respondents accurate and honest answers to all questions central to the research.
2. At the top of the questionnaire or in a cover letter, clearly state the survey's objective.
3. Define the survey sample.
4. Collect current addresses for respondents.
5. Stuff the survey envelope with a cover letter; questionnaire; return self-addressed, stamped envelope; and response incentive, if appropriate.
6. Mail questionnaires.
7. Follow up the questionnaire, if the sample is not too large, by phoning respondents to urge for their cooperation and prompt response.

Advantages and Disadvantages

Surveys conducted by mail have several major advantages. They reach a great number of respondents scattered over a large geographical area at a relatively low cost.

allow respondents to complete the forms at the time and place most convenient to them, which normally produces more thoughtful and accurate responses.

provide respondents with the necessary anonymity and privacy not available in telephone or personal interviews to respond honestly to questionnaire items that may be personal in nature.

require no interviewers to be present, thus reducing the chances of interviewer bias or errors in either the administering of the questionnaire or recording of information. (Emory, 1980, pp. 307–312)

Mail surveys, however, can prove disadvantageous to your research, as they

normally produce relatively low response rates of only 10 to 50%.

tend to elicit responses from a subgroup of respondents who are not necessarily representative of the sample or general population. (They may not, for example, elicit responses from people who don't like to, or cannot, write; are often away from their mailing address; don't have the free time to respond; or are not even part of the sample group but who were included due to a dated or otherwise inaccurate mailing list.)

produce results whose accuracy and honesty can be difficult to confirm, as the researcher cannot even be sure that the intended respondent is actually the person who completes the questionnaire.

prevent would-be interviewers from recording respondents' nonverbal communication, such as expressions and body language, which may add important evidence to the research.

allow respondents to answer the items without supervision, which can result in incorrect or incomplete responses.

require that the questionnaire be extremely well written, as it must stand on its own without the benefit of an interviewer to alleviate the possible confusion of respondents. (Dillman, 1978; Eredos, 1983)

Due to the unique demands placed on the clarity, completeness, and organization of mail questionnaires, such surveys might not, in the final analysis, be as inexpensive as they first appear. You may need to spend additional money to hire professional writers to prepare a reader-centered mail questionnaire that is arranged and written on a technical level appropriate for the sample respondents. The questionnaires may also require special paper and printing, which can significantly increase the cost per questionnaire.

Moreover, mailing lists that appropriately cover your target sample can be expensive, not to mention difficult, to obtain. Getting people to respond to questionnaires can also require that you include some incentive: discounts on products or services, small tokens of appreciation (e.g., pens, bookmarks, publications sent under separate cover), or even small monetary awards. Finally, if the rate of questionnaire returns seems significantly lower than needed or expected, you might have to invest additional funds in mailing follow-up letters urging a response or even in conducting personal interviews.

Personal Interviews

If your budget and time schedule permit, personal interviews may represent the most effective survey method of gathering accurate, complete, and detailed information about your sample population. As with mail and telephone interviews, the success of the personal interview depends largely on a properly prepared questionnaire. However, unlike the other two survey methods, personal interviews also rely heavily on the skill of their interviewers, which, as we shall see, creates both advantages and disadvantages in constructing effective personal interviews. Personal interviews, we should emphasize, are often used in conjunction with other survey techniques for collecting accurate data or information those survey methods are not able to supply.

There are two types of personal interviews: the **structured interview** and the **unstructured interview.** In conducting a structured survey, the relaxed interviewer poses items to respondents exactly as they are stated in a prepared questionnaire. The interviewer is allowed to repeat questions but not to change their order or to rephrase or explain them, even if respondents become confused.

In conducting an unstructured interview, the interviewer attempts to create a relaxed atmosphere by posing questions as appropriate during the guided flow of conversation. If the respondent becomes confused, the interviewer may repeat and even clarify an item. To obtain more complete answers, the interviewer may depart from a prepared set of items and ask follow-up questions to elicit more detailed and accurate responses.

Contrary to what its name might imply, however, the unstructured interview is (and should be) based on a well-organized questionnaire whose items the interviewer expects to answer more effectively by first putting the respondent at ease with the relaxed interview format. Although interviewers occasionally wait to record responses of short questionnaires until after the interview, they normally take notes on or tape longer interviews, as do their counterparts conducting structured interviews. As in any interview situation, the interviewer should avoid posing leading questions or influencing the respondent's answer in any way.

To conduct an effective and efficient personal interview, consider the following procedure.

1. Understand completely the precise objectives of the survey.
2. Rehearse the delivery of questionnaire items and the recording of responses.
3. Consider expected responses and prepare probing follow-up questions.
4. Contact respondents in advance: Ask for their cooperation in your survey, make an appointment for the interview, notify respondents of the expected duration of the interview, and ask if you might tape their responses.
5. Arrive promptly and be courteous when conducting the interview.

6. Clearly restate the purpose of your survey at the beginning of the interview (you should have already mentioned this in your preinterview phone conversation).

7. Stay on topic (i.e., the predetermined items of the questionnaire).

8. At the close of the interview, thank the respondent for her or his cooperation; offer to furnish results of the survey, if appropriate. Should you later decide to quote the respondent, ask for her or his permission first.

Advantages and Disadvantages

Personal interviews have several major advantages, as they

> enable interviewers to clarify complex or ambiguous items in a questionnaire, thus increasing the overall accuracy of responses.
>
> often produce a high rate of complete and reliable questionnaires. Interviewers are able to check the form for errors before the respondent is permitted to leave.
>
> allow the interviewer to elicit more detailed information that the respondent probably would not offer in a mail or telephone survey.
>
> allow the interviewer to observe respondents' nonverbal communication and to include in the research any observed data that could prove valuable to subsequent analysis.
>
> realize considerably higher response rates than do mail or telephone surveys. Interviewers can confirm the identify of targeted respondents and travel to respondents' locations to complete the survey.

Personal interviews, however, can prove disadvantageous to your research in certain aspects because they

> require that interviewers undergo extensive training in properly administering the questionnaire and accurately recording complete responses.
>
> introduce possible human bias into the survey through the comments, tone of voice, dress, expressions, or body language of insufficiently trained interviewers.
>
> might not obtain accurate or complete data from respondents who, feeling pressed or inhibited by the interviewer's presence, supply information they have not fully considered or find too personal to share with an unfamiliar interviewer.
>
> can produce resentment from respondents who find the personal interview an intrusion into their lives, which typically results in their giving inaccurate or incomplete responses.
>
> can become time-consuming and expensive if respondents are located at distant or scattered geographical sites.
>
> tend to be more initially expensive than mail or telephone surveys due mostly to the cost of training interviewers. (Blank, 1984, pp. 167–182; Clover, 1984, pp. 83–85)

Although the cost for conducting a survey based on personal interviews is higher than that of other survey methods, many researchers argue that the superior accuracy and completeness of the data produced by the personal interview, as well as the representative sample it provides, make the method actually less expensive per usable item in the long run than either mail or telephone surveys.

Telephone Interviews

Telephone interviews have become a major survey technique due mainly to their convenience and low cost to the researcher. However, because of this rise in the use of telephone surveys, the research method has become increasingly unpopular among respondents, perhaps ultimately making it a less effective survey technique.

To conduct a successful telephone interview, consider the following procedure:

1. Understand completely the precise objectives of the survey.
2. Rehearse delivery of questionnaire items and recording of responses and estimate length of interview; it typically should be no longer than 10 minutes.
3. Consider expected responses and prepare probing follow-up questions.
4. Phone at a time convenient for respondents.
5. Ask respondents for their cooperation in your survey, notify them of expected duration of the interview, and ask if you might tape their responses. If the interview is lengthy, set up an appointment time in advance.
6. Clearly identify yourself and state the purpose of your survey.
7. Be courteous during the interview, stay on topic (i.e., the predetermined items of the questionnaire), and avoid personal questions not directly related to the study.
8. At the close of the interview, thank the respondent for her or his cooperation; offer to furnish survey results, if appropriate. Should you later decide to quote the respondent, ask for her or his permission first. (Frey, 1989, Chap. 4; Bradburn & Sudman, 1979, Chap. 4)

Advantages and Disadvantages

Major advantages of telephone interviews are that they

offer interviewers a chance to clarify complex or ambiguous questions and to include follow-up questions, thus improving the accuracy and completeness of some responses.

are significantly more convenient for the interviewer than are mail surveys or personal interviews, as names and addresses of potential respondents are readily available in a telephone directory.

are easily structured for probability or random sampling by using the telephone directory as a source.

are relatively fast and inexpensive to perform.

can be used as a supplemental survey technique to elicit responses from people who did not return mail questionnaires. (Emory, 1980, pp. 305–307)

Telephone interviews, however, may not always provide your research with dependable, reliable, or complete data, as

respondents who become annoyed at what they perceive is an intrusive phone call sometimes give inaccurate or incomplete responses.

respondents feel pressured into giving immediate answers that may prove unreliable.

respondents who doubt the authority or authenticity of the interviewer sometimes provide misleading information.

interviewers cannot observe respondents' nonverbal communication, including dress, expressions, and body language, which restricts the amount of meaningful data the researcher can collect from respondents.

some respondents will not provide faceless interviewers with answers to personal questions.

interviewers can introduce human bias into the survey through comments or voice intonation. (Clover, 1984, pp. 86–87)

In addition to those disadvantages, telephone surveys often cannot cull the views from a representative sample, as they can collect data only from people with listed telephone numbers. By their very nature, telephone surveys must also be short, leaving interviewers only enough time to ask 5 or 10 questions on average, which significantly restricts the breadth and depth of questioning researchers can undertake. Finally, as in performing a mail survey, telephone interviewers cannot verify that the person who is responding to the questionnaire at the other end of the line is truly the respondent targeted for the sample population.

Experimental Research

Traditionally a stalwart research method in the sciences, experimental research has also become an effective and highly accurate means for businesses to collect, evaluate, and analyze data or information that can be quantified. Experimental research centers on the testing of a hypothesis under controlled conditions by manipulating one factor, or **variable,** surrounding the subject, or **item,** being investigated, while all other factors are kept constant. Researchers then determine if the manipulation of the variable causes short- or long-term effects on the item by measuring any resulting changes in the item.

There are two types of experimental research: **laboratory-based experimental research** and **field-based experimental research.** As it is normally the least costly as well as the quicker method of the two for obtaining precise and reliable quantitative data, laboratory research, whenever feasible, is often the preferred experimental method. Field research, however, allows researchers to test hypotheses and to collect data within work-world conditions such as the actual operation of a business. This research orientation allows field researchers to gather data that are more closely aligned with work-world situations than data collected through laboratory research, which must rely on simulated work-world conditions.

Planning Experiment Strategy

To conduct experimental research that is both efficient and effective in providing useful information for your report, consider the research process outlined below.

1. Define and clearly state the central and associated problems to be studied in the report.
2. Formulate your hypothesis.
3. Determine research variables (dependent and independent) and their relationships.
4. Develop the experiment strategy that will provide you the best opportunity to test the hypothesis.
5. Select an appropriate sample population and determine control and experimental groups.
6. Begin your research. (Clover, 1984, pp. 170–184; Emory, 1980, Chap. 4)

Formulating Your Hypothesis

A hypothesis goes beyond the statement of the report problem. It is a calculated, yet still unproven, explanation of a problem or phenomenon. A hypothesis is, in effect, an educated guess based on experience and knowledge. A clearly stated and properly focused hypothesis will help you to determine and direct your research methods. When forming the hypothesis for your study, state the hypothesis in declarative form without injecting value judgments that cannot be scientifically measured or tested. The hypotheses presented below, for example, prejudice the research from the very start:

> The United States *should* insist on a lower foreign exchange rate for the dollar in order to lower the cost of American goods overseas and, thus, increase the export of its goods to foreign markets.

> The United States *ought* to increase the export of American goods to help balance the nation's foreign trade deficit.

These hypotheses might be more useful in directing research if they were stated more objectively, as illustrated below:

A lower foreign exchange rate for the U.S. dollar can lower the cost of American goods overseas and, thus, increase the export of American goods.

An increase in the export of American goods to foreign markets can help balance the nation's foreign trade deficit.

A hypothesis always suggests a relationship between variables, such as a lower foreign exchange rate for the U.S. dollar's affecting the cost of American goods overseas, thereby lowering the U.S. trade deficit. Your hypothesis should be posed so that relationships between variables can be quantitatively measured and then proved or disproved on the basis of probability, as reflected in the results from a randomly selected sample. A **positive hypothesis** suggests a relationship between variables. A **null hypothesis,** on the other hand, negates any relationship between variables. When testing the hypothesis, you are measuring, documenting, and analyzing the relationships between related variables.

Determining Variables

Variables are characteristics that can be quantified, measured, and analyzed. Any hypothesis you formulate will contain at least two related variables. There are two types of variables in experimental research: **dependent** and **independent variables.** The changes in dependent variables result from the influence of independent variables. Researchers determine the strength of influence exerted on the dependent variable by altering, or *manipulating*, the independent variable during the experiment. For example, if you were to perform a simple field experiment to determine if a specific type of counter advertisement increased perfume sales, the central independent variable would be the advertisement itself. The dependent variable—the level of sales—might change by manipulating the independent variable. If you took the counter display away, would sales drop? If so, perhaps there is a correlation between the advertisement and higher sales.

To manipulate variables effectively without invalidating your experiment and thereby contaminating results, you should be careful to

manipulate only independent variables.
never manipulate dependent variables.
manipulate only one independent variable at a time.
keep all other variables constant.

Before planning the research design of your experiment, follow these steps:

1. Isolate all possible variables relating to the hypothesis and identify them as either dependent or independent variables.
2. Ensure that the variables are specific, quantifiable, and, thus, testable.
3. Determine the best method for measuring the change in variables during the course of the experiment.

Developing the Experiment Design

The experiment design is the systematic strategy for testing an experiment's hypothesis and then analyzing test results. The design you choose will normally be determined by the nature of the research problem and the resulting hypothesis. There are three basic designs of experimental research: the before-after design, the controlled before-after design, and the time design.

Regardless of the design you choose for your experimental research, you should consider the following steps to improve your chances of collecting accurate and usable data.

1. Accurately and thoroughly record the conditions of related variables before testing.
2. Ensure that testing conditions are as close to work-world conditions as possible.
3. Validate test results by repeating the experiment.

Changes in the values of variables as a result of the test cannot be fully understood or appreciated unless you first accurately observe and record the conditions of those variables before the experiment. Moreover, findings of experimental research are of little application value in work-world situations if they result from experiment conditions only obliquely similar to those of the actual workplace. Finally, corroborate test results by repeating the experiment under the same conditions. Replication of an experiment, however, can be costly, time-consuming, and, at times, impossible. Consequently, if the first or second duplication of the experiment does not produce results that corroborate those of the initial experiment, attempts to validate with further testing might be impractical and imprudent (Clover, 1984; Emory, 1980; Mishler, 1986).

Before-After Design

The **before-after design** is the most basic method of experimental research. After distinguishing the dependent variable(s) from the independent variable(s) in a test group, measure the values of the two variables, then manipulate one independent variable, as we did in the earlier example when we removed the counter advertisement to measure its effect on perfume sales. Next, measure the dependent variable to determine how much change was caused by the influence of the manipulated variable. Figure 8.2 offers a flow chart of the before-after design.

The primary drawback of the before-after design is that you cannot attribute the entire change in the dependent variable (if one is observed) to the manipulation of the independent variable. There may be too many variables that cannot be controlled and any one, or a combination, of those variables could have contributed to the changing of the dependent variable's value.

Controlled Before-After Design

The **controlled before-after design** is a variation of the before-after design. Instead of experimenting with only one group, this second design studies at

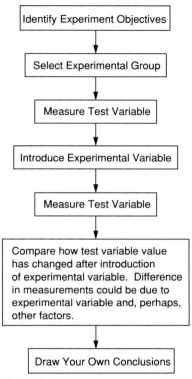

FIGURE 8.2
The before-after design.

least two groups: a **control group** and an **experimental group.** Before manipulating any variables in either group, you must measure the dependent variable in both groups. Following this pretest, manipulate the independent variable in the experimental group only (Figure 8.3). At the end of the experiment, perform a posttest on both groups to measure changes in dependent variables between the two groups. Then analyze the results to determine if the degree of change in variables is significant.

The controlled before-after design has its drawbacks. The validity of the data collected through this design, for instance, is largely dependent on the two groups' being very similar. However, because experimental groups are often randomly selected, you cannot be sure that both groups will be sufficiently comparable. Groups also naturally tend to change over time regardless of the introduction and manipulation of independent variables. As a result, you must become adept at recognizing when the margin of change in the dependent variable is truly significant or just incidental.

Time Design

Although structured much like the controlled before-after design, the **time design** involves closer monitoring of the dependent variable over time by using

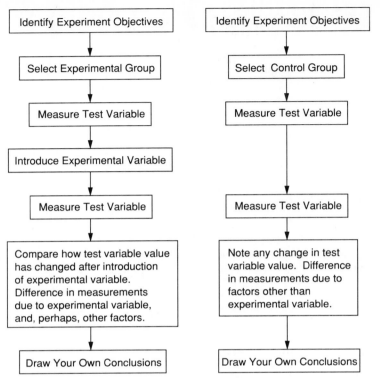

FIGURE 8.3

The controlled before-after design.

additional testing (Figure 8.4). Time designs, for example, include an extra test following the posttest to measure any latent changes in the dependent variable. Some time designs also measure the dependent variable twice before the independent variable is manipulated.

By including additional measurements, you are able to determine the degree to which the dependent variable has undergone short- or long-term changes, if any. Suppose, for example, that you hypothesize that manipulating one particular variable (e.g., salary) will measurably influence another variable (e.g., productivity) in a group of workers. To test your hypothesis, you divide the workers into two groups. Those in the control group receive no salary incentives during the experiment, while those in the experimental group do. You begin the experiment by measuring the values of the two variables of both groups. You then measure the same variables several months later. Each group should show comparable change in the variable values between the first and second measurements. You subsequently manipulate the independent variable (salary) in the experimental group. From a third measurement of the variables, you would expect to see that the dependent variable (worker productivity) of the experimental group had changed from that of the control group. By measuring the variables a fourth time, you would be able to determine if the influence of the independent variable on the dependent variable were short- or long-term in nature.

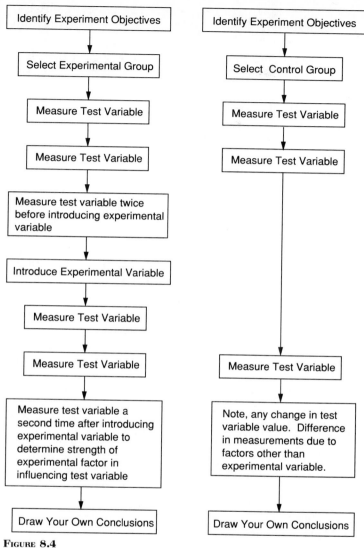

FIGURE 8.4
The time design.

Advantages and Disadvantages of Laboratory-Based Research

Major advantages of laboratory experiments are that they

provide relatively effective and exact control of dependent and independent variables.

reduce the element of human error to a minimum, lending considerable objectivity and precision to the experiment.

allow researchers to manipulate independent variables under simulated conditions that would be too expensive, dangerous, or impossible in an actual business situation.

often prove less time-consuming than waiting for the occurrence of comparable work-world situations to observe.

can be performed by specially equipped and staffed labs, relieving businesses of major logistical concerns.

are easily authenticated as the experiment can be duplicated under the same conditions as many times as needed.

Laboratory experiments, however, can be limited in their effectiveness, as they

normally can only simulate conditions that may not correlate with actual work-world situations.

often cannot sufficiently manipulate and control variables associated with human subjects as demanded by test requirements.

may produce results that cannot be generalized to a larger, work-world situation or population.

are limited in their ability to quantify and measure such key human variables as emotions, motivations, opinions, and thought.

may require expensive equipment and high-salaried test personnel. (Clover, 1984, pp. 164–165; Kerlinger, 1986, pp. 367–369)

A key limitation of laboratory-based experimental research is that it does not allow researchers to manipulate and control important variables associated with human subjects. This can significantly reduce the accuracy and reliability of findings derived from that research. For example, a laboratory experiment meant to determine the relationship between the high cholesterol levels of human subjects and their diets would undeniably produce misleading results if the demographic, cultural, and other variables surrounding those subjects' lives outside the laboratory were not thoroughly investigated. In other words, to provide valid findings, an experiment with those and comparable objectives would have to involve field-based research.

Advantages and Disadvantages of Field-Based Research

Field-based experiments offer unique advantages, as they (a) allow researchers the flexibility to investigate the relationship of variables and to test a hypothesis in actual work-world situations, and (b) provide researchers some freedom in randomly selecting groups.

In addition to some of the disadvantages associated with laboratory-based experiments, field-based experiments also

are not conducive to defining, controlling, and manipulating the range and variety of variables that can arise in work-world conditions.

make selecting random groups difficult.

might require large or immobile equipment that is difficult, expensive, impractical, or impossible to move to test sites. (Kerlinger, 1986, pp. 370–372)

Sampling and Questionnaire Design

The research designs discussed to this point offer a general view of methods for collecting specific, accurate, and reliable data and information on which to build intelligent managerial decisions. They provide you with the *means* of gathering primary information from people. However, in order to *collect* the data and information, you need an instrument that not only prompts people to surrender the information but also stores that information logically for easy retrieval, tabulation, synthesis, and analysis. In short, you need a **questionnaire.**

After you have determined the types of data required for your research, your research method, and which sample population would best represent the whole population, you're ready to

choose the most appropriate sampling method (i.e., random, systematic random, stratified random, cluster, or quota).

develop a well-designed and effectively written questionnaire that will collect the data or information needed for the research.

compose a cover letter.

conduct a pilot questionnaire survey.

distribute the questionnaire to the sample population through the preferred presentation method (e.g., mail surveys, personal interviews).

Sampling

Rarely will you have enough time or money to survey or test a hypothesis on each person in your target population. Consequently, you will normally test the hypothesis on a smaller subset of the whole population—a **sample.** The basis for an effective sample is that you select at random and survey as many subjects or items as possible from the whole population. The accuracy and usefulness of results from such a survey, however, are totally dependent on the degree of reliability and representativeness inherent in the survey.

Sample Reliability

Sample **reliability** requires that you select a large enough number of survey subjects or items to *stabilize* your sample results. In other words, if you base your survey on too few items, your sample might not provide the range of responses the entire population would supply, if it were possible to survey them all. As you include a greater number of items, the sample will reflect a

TABLE 8.1.

Statistically Reliable Sample Sizes for Varying Degrees of Precision

	Confidence Limits	
Degree of Error	95 of 100 Samples	99 of 100 Samples
1%	9,604	16,587
2	2,401	4,147
3	1,067	1,843
4	600	1,037
5	384	663
6	267	461
7	196	339

Source: Adapted from *Survey Research* (p. 33) by C. H. Backstrom and G. D. Hursh, 1963, Chicago: Northwestern University Press.

growing mix of responses in proportion to the whole population. In essence, the larger your sample, the better chance you have of obtaining a sample that will not distort the overall views and characteristics of the larger population. You should be able to reproduce results collected from a reliable sample by subsequent, identical tests.

To determine an appropriate sample size, you might refer to sample sizes that are considered statistically reliable, as illustrated in Table 8.1. For example, if you wanted the reliability of your survey to have a margin of error no greater than 3% in 95 out of 100 samples, you would have to sample at least 1,067 persons from that population. To obtain from the same population a survey with a margin of error no greater than 3% in 99 out of 100 samples, you would have to survey 1,843 people.

You might also measure the reliability of your sample by selecting and testing several key questions. Using the **standard deviation** of the responses for each question is one statistical method for measuring sample reliability. The standard deviation measures the distance that the majority of responses fall from the arithmetic average, or **mean,** of the sample. To determine the reliability of your sample, you would test for the standard deviation of responses given to a question. If the standard deviation for each question is small, then you probably have a fairly reliable sample population. More about standard deviation and statistical analysis is provided in Appendix A.

While standard deviation testing requires that you have some understanding of statistics, the **cumulative frequency** test can measure the reliability of a question, questionnaire, or sample just by adding numbers and determining percentages. To test reliability using the cumulative frequency, follow these steps:

1. Divide your completed questionnaires into randomly grouped stacks of equal numbers (e.g., 25, 50, 100).
2. Select a question from the questionnaires in stack 1.

TABLE 8.2.

Cumulative Frequency Test for Sample Reliability

Stack Number	YES Answers to Question 1	Cumulative YES Answers	Cumulative Percentage of YES Answers
1	67	67	67
2	52	119	59
3	61	180	60
4	75	255	64
5	69	324	65
6	44	368	61
7	55	423	60
8	77	500	63
9	74	574	64
10	56	630	63
11	66	696	63
12	70	766	64
13	57	823	63
14	78	901	64
15	65	966	64

3. Tabulate the responses to that question from all of the questionnaires on that stack.

4. Convert the total number of responses to each answer into percentages.

5. Perform the same process on the same question from surveys piled in the remaining stacks.

Now add the total number of responses for each answer obtained from stack 2 to the corresponding responses obtained from stack 1. Table 8.2 provides a cumulated listing of responses from 15 different stacks of survey results.

Next, convert these new total figures into percentages. Plot these percentages on a line graph (Figure 8.5). The line might move sharply up and down through the responses of the first few stacks; however, as you tabulate more stacks, their totals should flatten the line that charts the running percentages for each answer. The responses to the question are reliable if the percentage line becomes more or less parallel to the chart's base line. To prove that your questionnaire and sample are reliable, you'll need to test several more questions in the same manner.

The reliability of survey results should not be confused with their **validity.** To be valid, a questionnaire must test for what it actually intends to measure. For example, the SAT examination is widely used in the United States to measure the intelligence of high school students preparing for college. Can that standardized test, however, truly measure what it purports to quantify? Many educators now question how the SAT could ever reliably and validly measure a population as diverse in culture and language as that of the United States.

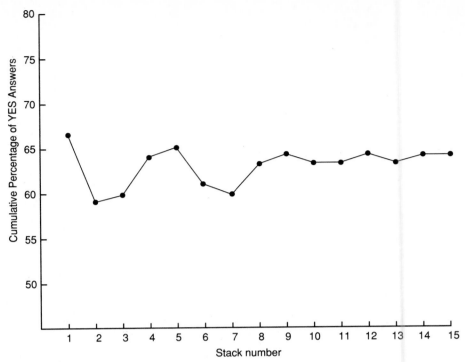

FIGURE 8.5
Plot of values from cumulative frequency test.

To improve the validity of your questionnaire, always consider how your survey questions address the central problems of the study and how, or if, those concerns can be accurately quantified and measured.

Sample Representativeness

The size or reliability of your sample does not automatically make your sample representative. To draw accurate conclusions about the entire population based on your study of the sample population, you will have to select a sample that is comparable to or representative of the whole population. Sample **representativeness** requires that you include in the survey subjects or items that (a) reflect the cross-section of characteristics shared by the larger population and (b) include those characteristics in the same proportions as exhibited in the whole population. The most common sampling methods for selecting subjects and ensuring a high degree of representativeness are random sampling, systematic sampling, stratified sampling, cluster sampling, and quota sampling.

Random Sampling

The notion of **randomness** in any study using scientific research methods is far from the common understanding of the word *random*, which is to be haphazard, aimless, or accidental. To produce a sample that is random actually requires that you be so systematic and deliberate that, ironically, you can *not* predict which subjects or items will ultimately be selected for the research sample.

Random sampling is the basic technique assumed in any sampling that claims to be representative. The random sampling technique gives every member of the whole population an equal chance of being chosen as a member of the sample group. One simple method of random sampling is to write the name of all subjects on separate cards and drop them into a large bowl. For example, let's assume that you want a random sample of a company's 500 employees. If you folded the 500 cards (each holding the name of a different employee) in exactly the same fashion and mixed the bowl well, each member of the company should have an equal chance of being chosen for your research.

Many researchers use tables of random numbers (available in most statistical research texts) to achieve random samples. Computer software packages can also provide you with randomly selected numbers.

Systematic Random Sampling

Systematic random sampling is similar to random sampling, yet this sampling method randomly chooses subjects or items at regular intervals (i.e., every *n*th unit). The interval you select will depend on the size of the whole population and the desired sample size. For example, if you wanted to include in your sample 500 university students from a graduating class of 5,000, you might select every 10th name from the alphabetized list of seniors. This method is clearly systematic, yet not exactly random or representative, as you have not given every student an equal chance of being chosen—only every 10th student. To improve the randomness of the sample, you might pull a number (from 1 to 10) out of a hat and use that as the interval, such as 3. Thus, the sampling would consist of those students who were listed 3rd, 13th, 23rd, 33rd, and so forth on the roll of 5,000 graduating students.

Stratified Random Sampling

In a **stratified random sample,** the sample population is divided into groups that represent different characteristics of the whole population (e.g., income, education level, ethnicity, religious affiliation, buying habits). The size of each group is normally proportionate to that group's size in relation to the larger population. If, for example, you were studying the types of employment chosen by business students just graduating from a specific university, you might divide the students into groups according to their majors, such as accounting, computer information systems, economics, finance, management, and marketing. You might further divide students in each group by grade point averages, then survey the types of employment the students in each group chose.

Occasionally, the small proportion of the group in the whole population will cause its respective sample group to have too few subjects to make a reliable sample. In such cases, you may arbitrarily increase the number of that sample group. To amass a truly representative stratified sample, you must identify characteristics of the whole population that are important to the study and, thus, should be shared by survey subjects or items. To identify those relevant characteristics, you must possess a thorough knowledge of your target populations as well as the conditions and variables that affect them in order to identify central characteristics deserving attention and investigation.

Cluster Sampling

Cluster sampling, sometimes called *area sampling,* is a technique of selecting items for a sample in successive steps. It is most useful when the population is large enough to divide into a continuum of smaller and more specific subgroups.

If you were surveying the salaries of oil industry employees in the United States, for example, you might first randomly select a list of oil companies, then progressively divide that group into smaller subgroups until you reached your desired sample. You might divide the list of oil companies by randomly selecting employees from different operations—exploration, human resources, oil refining, sales—within those firms. You could further divide the sample by randomly selecting jobs within each group. You ultimately would end up with a sample of specific job titles and their salaries from a range of industry operations of many different companies in the United States.

Quota Sampling

This sampling technique surveys only those groups that have characteristics of the whole population being studied. Consequently, quota sampling is not random. **Quota sampling,** also called *controlled sampling,* is meant to ensure that only groups with specific traits are represented and that they are represented in the same proportion as they are in the larger population. For example, if you were quota sampling oil industry employees working on derricks in the Gulf of Mexico, you could choose various types of subjects to analyze, as illustrated in Table 8.3.

Whichever items or people (and their associated characteristics) you decide to include in this specific sample of 600 derrick workers, you would have to ensure that

- subjects within each trait group chosen for the survey are given an equal chance to be selected.
- the percentage of subjects within trait groups chosen for the sample corresponds to the percentage of subjects sharing the desired characteristics within those respective trait groups from the entire population.
- the percentage of subjects chosen to represent a trait group in the survey corresponds to the percentage each group represents in the whole population.
- the total number of surveyed subjects equals 600.

Questionnaire Design

The questionnaire is the research instrument that should (a) prompt subjects for specific and accurate answers to focused questions and (b) provide subjects an organized and inviting form on which to record their answers. You should be

TABLE 8.3.

Quota Sample Categories of Derrick Workers

	Number in Total Population	Percent of Total	Number to Be Surveyed
DERRICK WORKERS	10,000	100	600
SEX			
Male	9,500	95	142
Female	500	5	8
AGE			
18–24	2,500	25	37
25–34	4,500	45	68
35–44	2,000	20	30
45–54	700	7	10
55 and older	300	3	5
MARITAL STATUS			
Married	7,500	75	113
Unmarried	2,500	25	37
JOBS AREAS			
Platform workers	4,500	45	68
Support staff	3,000	30	45
Middle and upper management	1,000	10	15
Lower management	1,000	10	15
Petrogeologists	500	5	7
TOTAL NUMBER OF SAMPLED RESPONDENTS			600

able to apply the data or information collected from the questionnaire directly toward the testing of your research hypothesis.

Begin the design of your questionnaire by first making a list of questions it might contain. Consider which questions are necessary in solving the research problem; then structure the questions so that they can effectively elicit from survey subjects the precise data or information needed. Questionnaires should normally be limited in length so that they can be completed in 15 minutes or less. When administering longer questionnaires, you should take extra steps to prepare survey subjects for the questionnaire, such as making appointments to conduct personal interviews. For a long mail questionnaire, you should consider mailing a prefatory letter to subjects asking for their cooperation and introducing them to the mail survey that they are to receive under a separate cover.

The process for developing a functional questionnaire follows:

1. Determine what survey questions need to be asked.
2. Decide what type(s) of survey question is most appropriate for the kinds of questions being posed.
3. Compose clear and precise questions.

4. Sequence the questions in a logical order.

5. Design the survey with an inviting and professional format.

Types of Survey Questions

The basic types of survey questions are the fixed-alternative, free-response, fill-in, scale, and ranking questions. The following discussion explains the most common variations of these question forms.

Fixed-Alternative Questions

Fixed-alternative questions provide the respondent with a choice of responses for each question posed. The most popular types of fixed-alternative questions are dichotomous, multiple choice, and checklist questions.

DICHOTOMOUS QUESTIONS

Dichotomous questions, also called *either-or* questions, present the respondent with a question that can be answered in one of two ways, such as "yes" or "no," or "true" or "false." The question may be designed so that respondents could write in their answer:

Do you believe in UFOs? _____

Although you may add a third choice for subjects, you are still implicitly offering respondents an either-or choice.

Do you believe in UFOs?
Yes _____ No _____ Don't Know _____

The dichotomous question has several key advantages. First, it can be answered quickly, which encourages respondents to complete the survey. Second, responses can be rapidly and accurately coded and tabulated because of the form's uniformity, which in turn increases the survey's reliability. A major disadvantage of dichotomous questions, however, is that they typically cannot address complex questions that, to be answered accurately, must offer respondents more than just two or three standard choices. Too many questions that researchers need to ask subjects require varying degrees of agreement or disagreement not allowed by the dichotomous question format (Blank, 1984, Chap. 8; Clover, 1984, pp. 112–126).

MULTIPLE-CHOICE QUESTIONS

This type of question provides respondents any number of prepared answers from which they are to choose one. Respondents make their selection by placing a check mark or number in the appropriate box or blank. Some **multiple-choice questions** can be little more than methods of collecting demographic information:

In what region of Madrid is your permanent residence?

_____ Central   _____ Northeast
_____ West Side   _____ East Side
_____ Northwest

Or a question might be more ambitious, soliciting respondents' thoughts and beliefs:

What do you think is the most logical explanation for UFOs? (Please check only _one_ answer from the following choices.)

_____ They are misidentified natural phenomena, such as lightning, reflections of the moon on cloud coverage, or falling meteors.

_____ They are really U.S. or Soviet aircraft performing secret missions whose existence cannot be shared with the general public.

_____ They are beings from another planet who are visiting our planet for any number of reasons.

_____ They are the creations of people who are unhappy and bored with their lives and who are seeking attention from the press and the community in which they live.

_____ Other. Please specify: _____

You should include answers to survey questions that respondents would most probably mark to avoid their having to write-in their "Other" response. The advantages associated with multiple-choice questions are similar to those of dichotomous questions. The results from multiple-choice questions are convenient for respondents to answer and are easy for compilers to tabulate, if prepared choices are appropriately selected. Multiple-choice questions also tend to generate reliable data. Moreover, multiple-choice questions may, in some cases, be superior to dichotomous questions as they can address topics that require more than a "yes" or "no" answer.

However, like the dichotomous question, the multiple-choice question does not allow respondents to explain the psychology—e.g., the reasons, motivations, or emotions—behind their answers. Moreover, sometimes out of apathy or ignorance respondents will check answers haphazardly, thus lessening the survey's reliability.

CHECKLIST

The **checklist question** is very similar to the multiple-choice question, although it allows respondents to choose more than one answer from the prepared list of answers, as illustrated here:

From the selections provided below, please check manufacturer(s) of personal computer(s) you currently own. (You may check more than one.)

_____ Epson
_____ Hewlett-Packard

_____ IBM

_____ Apple Computers

_____ Sun Microsystems

_____ Zenith

_____ Other. Please specify: _____

Free-Response Questions

Free-response questions (also called **open-ended** questions) provide respondents no prepared list of answers, but, rather, allow respondents to answer the question in their own words. The central advantage of free-response questions over fixed-alternative questions is obvious: respondents can tell researchers the psychological side of the story. Free-response questions offer subjects the chance to answer "Why?" Why do you think this way? Why did you do that? Why do you want to do that? As they provide no prepared answers, free-response questions dramatically reduce the potential for biasing respondents' answers. The following is an example of a free-response question:

What is your explanation for UFOs? _____

_____

_____

Free-response questions also have their drawbacks. Many less motivated respondents will not take the time and energy to write full answers to such questions. Some may not bother to answer at all. Furthermore, if the free-response question is even slightly vague in meaning, respondents will be more confused than they would be if the same question offered prepared answers that helped clarify the kind of information the unclear question was soliciting. Finally, the answers given by respondents to free-response questions can be widely disparate, which can complicate and make difficult the coding, tabulation, compilation, and analysis of the findings.

Fill-In Questions

A **fill-in question** is a hybrid between a multiple-choice and a free-response question. Respondents are asked a free-response question that they can answer any way they please with only one word or a short phrase. Fill-in questions, then, ask respondents to fill in the blanks, as illustrated below:

What type of auto(s) do you now drive? _____

How many miles does your auto's odometer currently show? _____

Fill-in questions are most appropriate for situations in which only short responses are needed. They also share the general advantages and disadvantages of open-ended questions.

Scales

Scales enable researchers to gauge the intensity of respondents' opinions or feelings on different topics. Respondents select the number on the scale that corresponds to the intensity of their feelings. The following is a sample scale-based survey question:

The general quality of education at your university is

Excellent	Good	Fair	Poor	Very Poor
1	2	3	4	5

Respondents marking 1: 100

Respondents marking 2: 200

Respondents marking 3: 400

Respondents marking 4: 200

Respondents marking 5: <u>100</u>

Average Score: 3

By tabulating and averaging scores registered by survey subjects, researchers receive a general sense of subjects' views. Averages, however, do not always offer a representative picture of most respondents' perceptions. For example, the average score of 3 would accurately reflect the overall view of respondents regarding the previous question. However, highly skewed scores, such as the following, would provide the same average, yet would not reflect the distance between the two groups' perceptions:

Respondents marking 1: 500

Respondents marking 2: 0

Respondents marking 3: 0

Respondents marking 4: 0

Respondents marking 5: <u>500</u>

Average Score: 3

As a result, you should also consider the standard deviation of scores when analyzing results from scale questions.

Ranking Questions

Ranking questions ask respondents to compare and rate their feelings toward a stated topic or situation. The following ranking question, for example, asks respondents to rate college business majors in terms of their difficulty.

Rank the following College of Business majors in terms of their academic difficulty (1 being the most difficult and 5 being the least difficult). You must use all the numbers 1 through 5 with *no* ties:

_____ Accounting
_____ Computer Information Systems
_____ Economics and Finance
_____ Management
_____ Marketing

Because no two answers can be given the same ranking, respondents often discover it difficult to rank answers for which they feel no strong reaction. For that reason, ranking questions, as with scale questions, tend to be more accurate and useful in indicating extreme rather than neutral reactions from respondents.

Question Phrasing

The questions you include in the questionnaire should be stylistically clear, precise, and specific to ensure that respondents (a) are able to understand fully what is being asked of them and (b) are, thus, able to provide complete, reliable data or information on which to base effective managerial decisions. Writing a clear and precise questionnaire requires much time in revising and testing the wording of each question. It also requires that you have a great degree of clarity in your own mind regarding the kind of information you are really seeking from respondents. The absence of those two ingredients will invariably produce ambiguous, confusing, or invalid questions that do not ask respondents for the right kind of information, or are incapable of clearly articulating what exactly the researchers are asking.

Pretesting should flag most ineffective questions in a survey, yet all questionnaires are vulnerable to the most common stylistic problems, such as the

ambiguous question.
double question.
leading question.
misleading question.
overlapping question.
invalid question.

The **ambiguous question** has no clear meaning and can be understood to be asking a number of different things. For example, the question

Are you interested in employment at the National Aeronautics and Space Administration?

might be asking respondents if they would like to apply for employment with NASA. Respondents could also interpret the question as asking them if they are simply curious about NASA activities surrounding employment.

The **double question** is also intrinsically ambiguous as it actually contains at least two questions in one. For example, respondents may find the following question difficult to answer accurately:

> Would you like to volunteer your time to the prevention of the major social problems currently affecting our community—alcohol abuse, drug abuse, and child abuse?

The question is asking respondents at least three related questions that should be asked separately:

- Would you volunteer your time to the prevention of the alcohol abuse problem that is currently affecting our community?
- Would you volunteer your time to the prevention of the drug abuse problem that is currently affecting our community?
- Would you volunteer your time to the prevention of the child abuse problem that is currently affecting our community?

The wording of the **leading question** is such that it influences the respondent's answer, which biases and thus invalidates the response. For example, the following question leads the respondent into answering affirmatively:

> Wouldn't you like to buy a new German automobile?

To avoid leading the respondent, the question should be phrased more objectively, as in the following revision:

> Would you like to buy a new German automobile?

Whereas the leading question is unintentional, the **misleading question** is a deliberate attempt by the researcher to encourage survey subjects to respond in a certain way. Misleading questions make suspect the researcher's ethics and cast doubt on the reliability of all data and information collected from the study. Misleading questions normally contain blatantly subjective wording. With the addition of appealing adjectives, the leading question offered earlier could easily be converted into a misleading question that clearly presses the respondent into answering "yes":

> Would you be willing to invest in a sound, elegant, and superbly engineered German automobile?

Such emotionally charged questions, however, can backfire on the researcher. They may evoke a negative reaction from respondents who sense that they're being manipulated by the question, the survey, and, indirectly, the researcher. This may antagonize respondents to the point that they, intentionally or unwittingly, provide inaccurate answers not only to the leading question but, perhaps, to other questions as well.

Overlapping questions ask respondents for basically the same information. For instance, the following two questions are essentially asking for answers that could be tabulated under the same category:

> Would you characterize senior management's attitude toward the introduction of new technologies into the workplace as enthusiastic and supportive?

> Would you characterize senior management's attitude toward the introduction of new technologies into the workplace as passive?

Both questions could easily be combined into one:

> How would you characterize senior management's attitude toward the introduction of new technologies into the workplace? (Check all that apply.)

> [ ] Enthusiastic   [ ] Passive
>
> [ ] Supportive   [ ] Nonsupportive

By eliminating overlapping questions, you simplify the tabulation of your research results, shorten your questionnaire, and save respondents' time. You also avoid injecting doubt into respondents' minds. Overlapping questions can lead respondents to believe that either you committed a sloppy oversight in preparing the questionnaire or you are attempting to double-check the consistency in, and the truthfulness of, their answers.

Invalid questions are those that ask respondents for information that (a) is not relevant to the research or (b) cannot be provided by respondents, as they require respondents to possess information that they do not, or cannot, have. For example, if you were surveying Cadillac owners for their willingness to make their next new car a Mercedes Benz, the following invalid question would provide you with no useful data:

> Do you appreciate quality in a new automobile?

Such an empty question produces predictable and equally empty responses. What person *wouldn't* appreciate quality in a new car?

Although empty questions typically do not provide your study with unreliable data, questions requesting information that is not available to respondents will often encourage respondents to offer rough, inaccurate estimates or simply to fabricate answers. For example, the following question would be incomprehensible to a respondent with no introductory knowledge of microcomputers:

> Check the type of PC you would like to order:
> _____ 12 megahertz with 40 megabytes of hard-disk storage
> _____ 16 megahertz with 40 megabytes of hard-disk storage
> _____ 16 megahertz with 70 megabytes of hard-disk storage
> _____ 25 megahertz with 70 megabytes of hard-disk storage
> _____ 25 megahertz with 130 megabytes of hard-disk storage

Such a question posed to respondents who are not computer-literate would produce either unreliable data or no responses at all.

Question Sequence

The ordering of questions can directly influence the accuracy with which respondents interpret and respond to those questions. As respondents move from one question to another, the topic and nature of the first question are still on their minds, if only subconsciously. The influence of the first question, then, lingers on into respondents' reading and interpretation of subsequent questions. Consequently, the sequencing of questions creates a thematic pattern that tends to influence how respondents answer questions. For instance, a question that prompts respondents for their reactions to Middle East terrorism might well influence how respondents answer a subsequent question: Do you think the United States should continue purchasing oil from Persian Gulf countries?

Because of the associative quality created by question patterns, researchers normally place **profile questions** at the beginning of the questionnaire. Profile questions are neutral in nature as they typically prompt respondents for such demographic information as sex, age, race, income, and educational level. If profile questions were placed later in the survey, respondents might assume an unintended relationship between the thrust of previous questions and the profile questions. Such an incorrect assumption could bias respondents' answering of the profile questions (Emory, 1980, pp. 237–240).

While carefully sequenced questions can enhance the reliability of data collected by clarifying for respondents the meaning and relevance of some questions, questions improperly ordered can make respondents feel manipulated. Let's take, for example, a survey that opens with questions concerning shortcomings of European cars and closes with questions regarding the strengths of Japanese cars. Based on the sequence of questions in this questionnaire, respondents might sense researcher bias, even when the researcher intends no manipulation. When logically ordering your questions, keep in mind the associative power of question patterns.

Moreover, you should consider the fatigue factor when ordering your questions. Respondents will tire at different rates, depending on the time of day, the length of the questionnaire, and the nature of the survey questions. Don't clump together survey questions that require extensive thought. Alternate blocks of such questions with blocks of questions requiring less concentration so that respondents have regular intervals to relax. Some questionnaires also contain humorous questions strategically located throughout the survey to relieve fatigue. Finally, consider a clear and limiting title for the questionnaire, one that specifies precisely for respondents the exact focus of the study.

Questionnaire Format

The questionnaire should be professional in appearance so that it draws respondents' attention and encourages them to provide complete and accurate answers to survey questions. The format should include plenty of white space between survey components, such as the title and questions, to distinguish the different items and to make the survey more appealing. Moreover, the format of questions should be logical and consistent. Scale questions, for example, might consistently place lower values on the right end of the scale. Dichotomous questions might uniformly place the "Yes" answer on the left and the "No" on the right.

Furthermore, the questionnaire should be neatly typed or produced on a letter-quality or laser printer. Use quality paper and provide a stamped, self-addressed envelope. Although survey lengths vary, remember that respondents should normally be able to complete the survey in 15 minutes or less. All pages should include an identification block (that includes the page number and abbreviated survey title) at the top or bottom of the page.

Cover Letter

The **cover letter,** or **letter of transmittal,** introduces the survey to respondents. Its content and tone should clarify for the sample population (a) the intent of the survey, (b) their role in the research project, and (c) the importance of their responding with complete and accurate answers. A well-organized and stylistically clean cover letter can significantly increase your chances of convincing respondents to participate in the research project.

Keep the tone of the cover letter friendly and positive. In the letter's introduction, identify yourself (or your organization) and establish the purpose of the survey. You might include the name of the authorizing organization that is directing or funding the survey project (if applicable). Subsequent paragraphs might explain why those respondents in particular were chosen to participate in the study and how you plan to use survey results. You can also increase respondents' interest by mentioning the benefits participants will realize (directly or indirectly) by completing and returning the survey. Emphasize the significance of the survey and the importance of the respondents' contribution.

Close the letter by assuring respondents that all results from the survey will be kept in strict confidence as outlined by the ethical codes of professional research. Assume that readers will complete the survey and thank them for their valuable participation. Remind respondents to use the enclosed self-addressed, stamped envelope and tactfully urge them to return their surveys by a specified date. Mention also that they will receive the results of the survey within a certain time frame. The sample cover letter in Figure 8.6 effectively integrates a number of these components. Figure 8.7 provides a work-world questionnaire designed and distributed by the American Management Association.

Pilot Questionnaire

Pilot tests of the questionnaire often uncover weaknesses in the survey—in its sampling method; the form(s), wording, or sequencing of its questions; or its format. You might consider testing the survey on company professionals experienced in constructing effective surveys in order to gain knowledgeable

1991 AMA SURVEY

THE MANAGEMENT OF TECHNOLOGY

Dear Friend:

In exchange for a few minutes of your time, we offer you an exclusive look at the fully tabulated results of this AMA research effort on the management of technology. All AMA corporate members will share an executive summary of key findings, but only survey respondents will receive the complete data—in print, or, if you wish, on computer disk—at no charge.

The management of technology is a topic of rising interest. As with any new concept, it requires definition. In answering the questions below, we ask you to consider the *full range* of technology at work in your organization—not only your production facilities (if any), but also your telecommunications and information systems, your data processing, and your office automation. All these forms of technology affect your competitive position; each of them, managed well, can enhance that position.

The results of this survey will tell us not only *how* respondent firms are managing technology, but *why* certain approaches provide a competitive edge. We are as eager to share these results with you as we are to have your completed questionnaire.

Your response will be held in strictest confidence; no respondent will be identified to any outside party. We ask for your name and address so that we can send you some data, but if you wish to remain anonymous, your response is still welcome. We expect to deliver the tabulated data no more than three months after you receive this questionnaire.

It should take you less than ten minutes to complete this questionnaire. Please return it in the enclosed post-paid envelope. Thank you very much for your participation.

Sincerely,

Eric Rolfe Greenberg
Editor
AMA Research Reports

FIGURE 8.6

Sample questionnaire cover letter—AMA Research Reports.

Source: Courtesy of American Management Association.

advice regarding technical aspects of the questionnaire, such as the representativeness of its sample population, its capacity to collect reliable data, or the validity of its questions.

You might then present a pilot questionnaire to a small group of respondents who share key characteristics with your target sample. Once the responses have been tabulated, analyze them to uncover possibly weak survey questions or poor question sequencing—two flaws that can evoke unreliable and unrepresentative responses. Supplementing the pilot questionnaire with a posttest interview allows you to survey respondents' feelings toward the questionnaire in general as well as toward specific questions.

Ethical Concerns

While it can be a significantly useful method for producing report data, primary research can also be a powerful tool when applied to decision making that might affect thousands or even millions of people. Because information is a very real form of power, some researchers—under certain political, social, or economic conditions—may be tempted to manipulate data or exploit research findings so that report results might promote the interests of the researchers themselves or their organizations.

Many professional societies now sponsor formalized codes of ethics to prevent the misuse of primary data and to protect the rights of individuals associated with surveys and experimental research. The American Sociological Association (ASA), for example, outlines in its code of ethics issues ranging from objectivity in research to disassociation from unethical research arrangements. The following guidelines (abstracted from the ASA's code of ethics) are important considerations for anyone performing primary research:

- *Objectivity and integrity in research:* You should remain objective in your planning, execution, analysis, and reporting of your research. You should also recognize your own limitations and not perform research or analysis of research beyond your level of competence without the assistance of other experts.
- *Abuse of research authority:* You should consistently and clearly identify for research associates, as well as survey subjects, your authority for and purpose in performing the research and not use this authority to obtain data for any purpose outside of that research mandate.

I. THE COMPETITIVE IMPACT OF TECHNOLOGY

1. With its present technology, your organization's competitive position within your industry is:
   [ ] Ahead of the competition with leading edge technology
   [ ] Equal to the competition with up-to-date technology
   [ ] Trailing the competition with out-of-date technology

2. Does your present technology provide your *products* or *services* with a *market* advantage over your competition?
   [ ] No
   [ ] Yes, by enhancing product performance or service delivery
   [ ] Yes, for reasons other than product performance or service delivery

Those other reasons include:
_____
_____
_____

3. Does your present technology provide your *business* with a *cost* advantage over your competition?
   [ ] No
   [ ] Yes, by enhancing productivity
   [ ] Yes, for reasons other than productivity

Those other reasons include:
_____
_____
_____

FIGURE 8.7
Sample questionnaire—AMA Research Reeports.

Source: Courtesy of American Management Association.

4. Does your business plan include technological upgrades?

[ ] No, not at present

[ ] Yes, to develop or acquire *leading-edge* technology within _____ years

[ ] Yes, to develop or acquire *up-to-date* technology within _____ years

5a. How much time do you allot for new technology to have an impact on your competitive position within your industry?

[ ] Less than six months   [ ] Two years

[ ] Six months to one year   [ ] Three to five years

[ ] One year   [ ] More than five years

5b. With new technology installed, how long will it give you a competitive advantage within you industry?

[ ] Less than six months   [ ] Two years

[ ] Six months to one year   [ ] Three to five years

[ ] One year   [ ] More than five years

6a. In terms of the operation of your *present* technology, your annual costs are:

[ ] Below average for your industry

[ ] Just about average for your industry

[ ] Above average for your industry

6b. Over the next three years, you expect these *operational* costs:

[ ] To *rise*, at an *annual* rate of _____ percent

[ ] To remain at present levels, adjusted for inflation

[ ] To *decrease*, at an *annual* rate of _____ percent

7a. In terms of the development or acquisition of *new or upgraded* technologies, your annual costs are:

[ ] Below average for your industry

[ ] Just about average for your industry

[ ] Above average for your industry

7b. Over the next three years, you expect the costs of *development or acquisition*:

[ ] To *rise*, at an *annual* rate of _____ percent

[ ] To remain at present levels, adjusted for inflation

[ ] To *decrease*, at an *annual* rate of _____ percent

8. What is the projected useful life of new technologies being introduced into your firm today?

[ ] Less than one year   [ ] Five to ten years

[ ] One to two years   [ ] More than ten years

[ ] Three to five years   [ ] No projections made

II. THE ORGANIZATIONAL ENVIRONMENT

1. How well does your organization deal with technological change?

[ ] Not well; there are high levels of resistance

[ ] Fairly well; there are pockets of resistance, but change is generally accepted

[ ] Very well; technological change is welcome

2. How well does your organization deal with other, non-technological forms of change or innovation?

[ ] Not well; there are high levels of resistance

[ ] Fairly well; there are pockets of resistance, but change is generally accepted

[ ] Very well; change and innovation are welcome

3. How would you characterize senior management's attitude towards the introduction and utilization of new technologies?

[ ] Enthusiastic   [ ] Passive

[ ] Supportive   [ ] Non-supportive

4. Where does the impetus for technological change most often originate in your company?

[ ] User departments   [ ] Senior management

[ ] Technical staff   [ ] Customer base

5. Please indicate on the scale below how well your current technological position matches up with your business strategy. (A 7 would indicate a perfect match; a 1 would indicate no match at all.)

7   6   5   4   3   2   1

6. On the scales below, please evaluate your organization's needs for training in the use of new technologies. (A 7 would indicate a very high training need; a 1 no need at all.)

Training needs in use of new technologies for:

a. Senior management   7   6   5   4   3   2   1

b. Technical staff   7   6   5   4   3   2   1

c. Mid-management, staff positions   7   6   5   4   3   2   1

d. Mid-management, line positions   7   6   5   4   3   2   1

e. Supervisory staff positions   7   6   5   4   3   2   1

f. Supervisory line positions   7   6   5   4   3   2   1

g. Non-management staff positions   7   6   5   4   3   2   1

h. Non-management line positions   7   6   5   4   3   2   1

i. Sales management & personnel   7   6   5   4   3   2   1

7. What, specifically, is your organization's greatest training need in the *use* or *management* of new technology?

_____

_____

_____

III. ABOUT YOUR ORGANIZATION

1. Your organization's total annual sales (or budget, if nonprofit):

[ ] Under $2 million   [ ] $50-$249 million

[ ] $2-$10 million   [ ] $250-500 million

[ ] $10-$49 million   [ ] $500 million or more

2. The number of people your organization employs, world-wide:

[ ] Fewer than 100   [ ] 1,000 to 2,499

[ ] 100 to 249   [ ] 2,500 to 4,999

[ ] 250 to 499   [ ] 5,000 to 9,999

[ ] 500 to 999   [ ] 10,000 or more

3. Your organization's primary business or industry classification: _____

So that we may share the fully tabulated results of this survey with you, please provide this information (or attach your business card):

Name: _____

Title: _____

Organization: _____

Address: _____

City, State: _____ Zip: _____

FIGURE 8.7

Continued

- *Research subjects' rights to privacy and dignity:* All research subjects have a right of privacy and dignity of treatment. They must understand fully the purpose of your research and the intended uses of its results. You must ensure that the identity of all subjects will remain confidential during and after the study.
- *Protection of subjects from personal harm:* Subjects should not be placed in conditions that may be dangerous to their health or lives; neither should they be coerced into participating in the study.
- *Acknowledgment of research collaboration:* To give credit to all individuals involved in the research project, you should acknowledge in your report the professionals or institutions that contributed to your study.
- *Disclosure of sources of financial support:* You should report all sources of financial support as well as your affiliation with those supporting individuals or institutions.
- *Full reporting of the facts:* You must include in your report all significant findings whose omission would distort the actual meaning of the data.

Summary

This chapter has explained how primary research can supply the up-to-date information necessary for making intelligent managerial decisions in an increasingly dynamic business environment. The three fundamental methods of primary research are observation, survey, and experimental research.

We have stated that primary research often brings to light new data and information that could not be found in secondary sources. If it has been well conceived and properly controlled and executed, primary research can reveal to an organization ways to make itself more efficient, often producing cost savings that pay the price of the primary research many times over. Moreover, primary research can be conducted on a smaller and less expensive scale than that required for the same information to be gleaned from years of ordinary experience.

Primary research also provides information that is significantly more accurate than data collected haphazardly by managers using their own business experience to eyeball a problem or by researchers extrapolating data collected from secondary sources. Finally, some business situations simply cannot be studied in work-world situations because of associated costs, time constraints, or inherent dangers.

Observation research is the systematic visual monitoring of observable data or phenomena related to your report topic or problem. In this chapter we have explained that effective observation research requires that you define the objectives of the observation research, plan the research design and observation instrument, select and train reliable observers, collect and organize the data, analyze and report the data, and repeat the observation process to corroborate the reliability and accuracy of the results.

Survey research is most productive in business research whenever you query people on information that is difficult, if not impossible, to gather any other way, including opinions, emotions, motivations, experiences, and interests. The survey process requires that you clearly define the information for which you are searching, the use of that information, and the people who can provide the data or information. You should also determine what survey research is the most effective method for collecting the needed information and decide which type of survey technique (i.e., mail questionnaire, personal interview, or telephone interview) best meets the informational needs, time constraints, and budget of the study.

Mail surveys represent a convenient, inexpensive method for collecting survey data and information. **Telephone interviews** have become another major survey technique due mainly to their convenience and low cost to the researcher. If your budget and time schedule permit, however, **personal interviews** may represent the most effective survey method for gathering accurate, complete, and detailed information about your sample population. The two fundamental types of personal interviews we have discussed are the **structured interview** and **unstructured interview.**

Experimental research centers on the testing of a hypothesis under controlled conditions by manipulating one factor, or variable, surrounding the subject, or item, being investigated, while all other factors are kept constant. There are two types of experimental research: **laboratory-based experimental research** and **field-based experimental research.** To conduct experimental research that is both efficient and effective in providing useful data and information for your report, we have recommended that you define and clearly state the central and associated problems to be studied. You should also formulate your hypothesis, identify the research variables (dependent and independent) and their relationships, select an appropriate sample population, and determine control and experimental groups.

Survey research also requires that you choose the most appropriate sampling method (i.e., random, systematic random, stratified random, cluster, or quota), develop a well-designed and effectively written questionnaire that will collect the data or information needed for the research, compose a cover letter, conduct a pilot questionnaire survey, and distribute the questionnaire to the sample population through the preferred presentation method (e.g., mail surveys, personal interviews).

Information is a form of power. To ensure its appropriate use and protect the rights of individuals affected by it, we have concluded Chapter 8 with an overview of the ethical concerns associated with primary research.

Related Reading

ALRECK, PAMELA L., and ROBERT B. SETTLE.   *The Survey Research Handbook.* Homewood, IL: Irwin, 1985.

BLANK, STEVEN C.   *Practical Business Research Methods.* Wesport, CT: AVI, 1984.

BRADBURN, NORMAN M., and SEYMOUR SUDMAN. *Improving Interview Method and Questionnaire Design.* San Francisco: Jossey-Bass, 1979.

BROWN, LELAND. *Effective Business Report Writing.* 4th ed. Englewood Cliffs, NJ: Prentice, 1985.

CLOVER, VERNON T., and HOWARD L. BALSLEY. *Business Research Methods.* 3rd ed. New York: Wiley, 1984.

DILLMAN, DON A. *Mail and Telephone Surveys: The Total Design Method.* New York: Wiley, 1978.

EMORY, C. WILLIAM. *Business Research Methods.* 2nd ed. Homewood, IL: Irwin, 1980.

EREDOS, PAUL L. *Professional Mail Surveys.* Malabar, FL: Krieger, 1983.

FOWLER, FLOYD J., JR. *Survey Research Methods.* 2nd ed. Vol. 1. Newbury, CA: Sage, 1988.

FREY, JAMES H. *Survey Research by Telephone.* 2nd ed. Beverly Hills, CA: Sage, 1989.

GOLDMAN, ALFRED E., and SUSAN SCHWARTZ McDONALD. *The Group Depth Interview: Principles and Practices.* Englewood Cliffs, NJ: Prentice, 1987.

GOTTLIEB, MARVIN. *Interview.* New York: Longman, 1986.

GROVES, ROBERT M., and ROBERT L. KAHN. *Surveys by Telephone: A National Comparison with Personal Interviews.* New York: Academic Press, 1979.

JOLLIFE, F. R. *Survey Design and Analysis.* New York: Wiley, 1988.

KERLINGER, FRED N. *Foundations of Behavioral Research.* 3rd ed. Chicago: Holt, 1986.

LANNON, JOHN M. *Doing Field Research.* New York: Free Press, 1985.

LAVRAKAS, PAUL J. *Telephone Survey Methods: Sampling, Selection, and Supervision.* Beverly Hills, CA: Sage, 1987.

LUCAS, WILLIAM A., and WILLIAM C. ADAMS. *An Assessment of Telephone Survey Methods.* Santa Monica, CA: RAND, 1977.

MISHLER, ELLIOT G. *Research Interviewing: Contest and Narrative.* Cambridge: Harvard University, 1986.

SMITH, MARY JOHN. *Contemporary Communication Research Methods.* Belmont, CA: Wadsworth, 1988.

VARNER, IRIS I. *Contemporary Business Report Writing.* New York: Dryden, 1987.

WALIZER, MICHAEL H., and PAUL L. WIENER. *Research Methods and Analysis.* New York: Harper, 1978.

CHAPTER 9

Assembling and Analyzing Information for Management Reports

After collecting data and information from secondary or primary sources, you will need to organize the material in a logical order before attempting to analyze its significance to the report problem at hand. If you have followed an orderly methodology in performing your research, much of the collected information should already have some general organization. However, as we near the outlining and drafting stages of the report-writing process (as discussed in Chapter 10), you should now consider more specifically (a) what information should be included in the report, (b) how that material should be arranged, and (c) how the information should be interpreted in order to present report readers with clearly defined and well-founded conclusions and recommendations.

This chapter discusses the fundamental steps involved in arranging and analyzing data in the report-writing process:

1. Classifying data
2. Coding and editing data
3. Tabulating results
4. Applying tools of effective analysis
5. Understanding statistical analysis
6. Overcoming obstacles to effective analysis
7. Drawing conclusions
8. Making recommendations

Classifying Data

Classifying data and information involves the logical grouping of data into manageable blocks of information that are topically related. Classification provides the researcher an opportunity to assess

- whether enough research has been collected from which cogent and substantive conclusions on report topics can be drawn.
- if the research suggests a shift in topical emphases of the report.
- if areas of the report require further research.

You began your research efforts with a coherent plan as to what topics should be studied and how those topics should be grouped. You may even have decided the number and types of sources needed to provide enough evidence on which to base report conclusions and recommendations. However, neither the secondary nor primary research process can produce data that are sufficiently ordered to begin your analysis of the material. The classification stage affords you a chance to reexamine the quantity and quality of the information you've collected. It helps you to determine if more investigation is needed to fill any gaps in your research that would undermine the reliability, validity, and thoroughness of your study (Cox, 1987; Daniel & Terrell, 1983).

Moreover, classification can assist you in clarifying the focus of your report. Rarely can you accurately anticipate at the start of your research the topical groups for all of the data and information you will ultimately collect. To perform effective research, you must first define the central subject and associated topics of your report. However, as you investigate your sources, these topics and, perhaps, even the focus of your report will change as you uncover information that supports or refutes your initial hypothesis. Findings from your investigation may urge you to modify the amount of space and depth of coverage originally allocated to different topics. For example, some topics previously thought to be only of secondary importance may, in fact, become central to your study, requiring proportionally more space and analysis, while topics that seemed more important at the start of your research may actually warrant less coverage.

Classifying information into logical, topically homogeneous blocks of evidence also simplifies the task of analyzing the collected material. Information not relevant to the study may be discarded, while useful evidence is reduced and shaped into workable chunks that can be analyzed one at a time before being compared.

Classification involves two basic steps: (1) sorting macro report components and (2) ordering micro components. **Macro components** include the large and often standard parts of your report, such as the introduction, review of literature, research methods, collected data (or results) section, analysis of findings (or discussion) section, summary, conclusion, and recommendations. When classifying, first understand what *major*, or macro, components such as these should be included in your report. Much of your data will be placed in the collected data section of the report, while your analysis of the data will often come in a subsequent analysis of findings section.

Micro components are subsections of each macro component. For example, an introduction for a managerial report typically contains a statement of the report's purpose, scope, and methodology. Introductions may also include a history of the subject or problem under study. After you have decided what information belongs in the introduction, order that information on a micro level by placing it in the most logical subsection using one or a combination of classification methods, such as time, place, quantity, or criteria.

The collected data section of a business report often proves the most difficult component to organize on the micro level. Normally you will open this section with findings relating to the most important topic of your report, followed by a discussion of topics in descending order of importance or significance. You might, however, organize findings chronologically in terms of time or spatially in regard to geographic location, or by using both classification methods. For example, if your report focused on retail sales of your company's low-calorie beer in five different regions of the country over the past 10 years, you might choose to begin the collected data section with sales data from the East Coast, followed by sales from the Southeast, the Midwest, the Southwest, and finally the West Coast. You might logically order the data within each region chronologically, starting with the first and ending with the most recent year of beer sales. You could also classify this same information by quantity, starting with the region with the most beer sales and ending with the region with the lowest sales. You might classify the information in the following analysis section of the report according to the criteria against which you evaluate the sales campaigns run over the past 10 years in those five regions.

Regardless of the classification method(s) you use to partition your collected data and information logically, be sure your classifications adhere to the rules of *uniqueness*, *inclusivity*, and *exclusivity*. Decide first if the information deserves its own section—or subsection—as indicated by its importance, significance, and distinct nature. If the information does indeed appear unique from other topics, are you including all the information from your study that is relevant to that classification? Classifications that are conspicuously *noninclusive* may be a clear tip-off that more research is needed on the subject to ensure your report is thorough. Finally, are the topical focuses of each classification mutually exclusive of one another? In short, don't mix apples with oranges within a single classification. Mixing beer sales data of the East Coast region with those of the Southeast would not only confuse readers but also make your analysis of the data more difficult. As we discuss in Chapter 10, logically ordered classifications that are unique, inclusive, and exclusive simplify for readers the task of outlining, reading, and comprehending your report.

Coding and Editing Data

After classifying data into their respective groupings, you will need to code all quantifiable results from any questionnaire you administered or experimental research you performed. Coding involves assigning a number (or letters or symbols) to each individual response. For example, if you were surveying shoppers at a local ice cream store, you might code each classified item of a particular question like this:

How often do you buy SuperDuper brand ice cream?

Often (at least once a week)	1. _____
Regularly (at least twice a month)	2. _____
Occasionally (at least once every two months)	3. _____
Rarely (fewer than once every two months)	4. _____
Never	5. _____

While coding is useful when preparing for analysis of data from even small surveys, it is absolutely essential whenever using a computer to manipulate the numerical results of a large survey or complex experiment.

After coding, edit the data of your primary research so that they are in the proper form for subsequent tabulation and analysis. In editing, look for and correct, if possible, any irregularities, omissions, or errors in the collected data. For example, when editing the responses to a survey, you may discover that a number of respondents failed to answer a pair of related questions. Consequently, you decide to qualify the results and interpretations based on those report questions. Editing of survey results is also necessary when respondents do not understand what the question is asking of them. Sometimes, for example, respondents might incorrectly rate the answers to a ranking question such as giving two or more answers the same ranking. In this case, you can choose to disregard those individual responses that were in error. If a large percentage of respondents committed the same error, however, you might decide to dismiss the question entirely from analysis and reporting.

The reliability and validity of your results after tabulation depend largely on your skill in editing the raw data. The more invalid pieces of data you can uncover and correct or discount, the more accurately the final results of your primary research will reflect the perceptions of your sample population as collected through a survey or experiment.

Tabulating Results

Tabulation is the process of counting or measuring the results of your observation, survey, or experiment and compiling that information in an orderly form that allows you easy and quick access when analyzing the results. To count the responses to each survey question, use a simple cross-five tallying technique you probably learned in grade school (卌), with every fifth occurrence represented by a diagonal mark across the prior four occurrences, as illustrated in the following example:

1. What is your sex?
   Male: 卌 卌 卌 III
   Female: 卌 卌 卌 卌 卌 卌 I

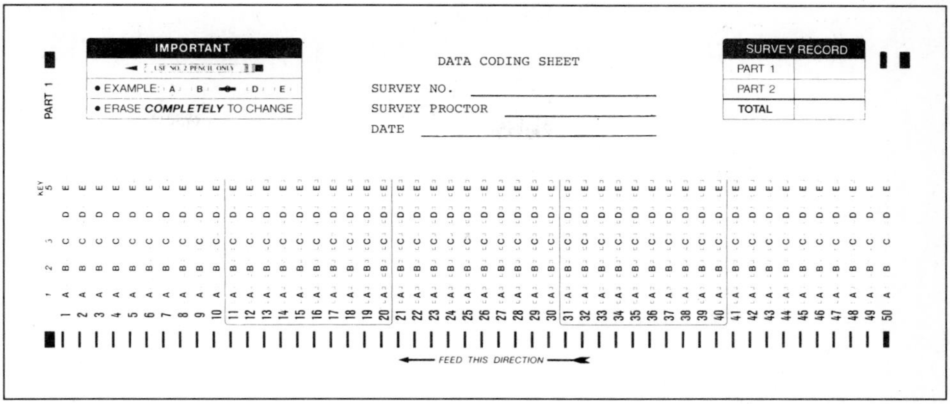

FIGURE 9.1
Computer-readable data coding sheet.

Computers, however, offer a much faster and more efficient method of tabulating data than manual tabulation. You should exploit the savings in speed and time offered by computer tabulation, especially when tabulating surveys of large sample populations. Computer tabulation basically involves the storing of survey results in a computer's memory and then running a computer program that manipulates those data in any number of ways. Requesting that your respondents answer questions on computer-readable answer sheets will save you the time and energy you would have otherwise spent inputting the responses yourself (Figure 9.1).

In some instances, surveys can be administered through computer terminals so that respondents read questions displayed on the terminal monitor and then enter their answers directly into the computer through the terminal keyboard. This tabulation option can significantly reduce the time required to input and count responses. Today's word-processing and statistical software packages also make the task of editing survey results before tabulation much easier.

A computerized surveying method requires that your organization have access to relatively powerful computers, or even a network of computers. If your company lacks the needed computer hardware or software, or the necessary computer expertise in computer-assisted tabulation, you can receive help from a growing list of companies that provide computer services in such areas as survey tabulation and statistical analysis. Later in this chapter we discuss how you might use computers and their accompanying software to perform statistical analyses of primary research data.

Applying Tools of Effective Analysis

The following objectives are central to your analysis of the tabulated results from your research:

- Interpret the exact meaning of the data.
- Determine their significance in addressing your report problem.
- Formulate conclusions based on the significance of those results and make recommendations based on those conclusions.

The amount of time and resources available to your research can influence the degree to which you are able to meet those objectives. However, your ability to achieve those goals will depend largely on your knowledge of the subject area and your ability to analyze—that is, to delve beneath surface meanings, recognize important and relevant relationships between pieces of data, and define patterns and trends among factors within your study. Practiced and finely honed analytical skills are essential not only to your providing shape and significance to business report information but also to your succeeding in the business world. Successful organizations require that you do far more than simply amass data and information. Computer and telecommunications technologies can provide organizations with a continual flood of data and information both day and night, yet *how* that information is interpreted and the way its significance is analyzed and reported are integral responsibilities of the business report writer. We can expect this emphasis on analytical skills to increase dramatically as we confront the technological and intellectual challenges of the 21st century.

You can improve your chances of deriving accurate conclusions and appropriate recommendations by understanding and regularly applying the tools central to accurate analysis, which include

maintaining a critical point of view.

remaining objective and fair.

consulting with others.

testing your analysis.

recognizing the fallacies of logic.

understanding statistical analysis.

Maintaining a Critical Point of View

A critical point of view should not be treated like a minor afterthought considered only when trying to give meaning to research findings but, rather, integrated throughout the entire report-writing process. Although critical thinking requires that you be skeptical of others' ideas as well as your own work, it is not negative thinking. On the contrary, the critical point of view requires that you examine as many other sides of the issue as possible before making up your mind. This approach not only provides you with greater contextual knowledge of the subject but also frequently produces more positive and constructive results (Ruggiero, 1990, pp. 12–20).

You can lose your critical edge for any number of reasons. Perhaps by investing a considerable amount of time and effort in the project you have lost your objectivity and distance. As a result, you become sensitive to criticism, including your own. You or your organization might have a vested interest in the outcome of the report, which could influence the degree to which you question report findings and interpretations. Fatigued from a long report project, you might also have lost the energy necessary for thoughtful reevaluation.

All of those excuses aside, it is essential in the analysis phase of the report process that you reevaluate each component of the report process, such as your research methods, findings, and classification of data. As you evaluate the accuracy and thoroughness of your interpretation of the findings, you will normally uncover questions regarding the process leading up to the analysis phase. For example, although you have already considered the appropriateness of your research methods, you discover when interpreting the findings from your telephone survey that an overwhelming majority of respondents favored placing an economic embargo on foreign countries that support international terrorism. However, two weeks after conducting the survey, you sense from speaking with policymakers and reading the news that public opinion has shifted. You hypothesize that earlier barrages of negative press against terrorist countries and terrorist bombings around the world caused a knee-jerk response from survey subjects. In this case, if time and budget permit, you might consider performing a follow-up telephone survey to test the representativeness and validity of the earlier results.

Remaining Objective and Fair

To remain objective and fair in your interpretation of data, you must first distinguish between fact, inference, and opinion and determine if any confusion among the three has produced bias in your analysis. A **fact** is an assertion that has been proven to be true. An **inference,** although a logical deduction based on facts, is not a fact but an assumption whose truth has yet to be proved. An **opinion** is basically a view or belief founded on what seems to be true or probable in one's own mind. An opinion is typically based on only a casual examination of the evidence, if indeed facts which are collected from objective research are considered at all (Ruggiero, 1990, pp. 37–44). **Bias** is partiality and prejudice, a perception maintained even when the facts support views to the contrary. Objectivity and fairness in report writing demand that we determine how, if at all, our opinions and inferences can distort the facts and, thus, weaken the accuracy, honesty, and usefulness of our interpretations.

Biased thinking, whether intentional or unintentional, can significantly reduce the effectiveness of your report in three ways. First, a prejudiced view of the report problem could force you to dismiss or distort important findings that affect your conclusions or recommendations. Second, although you might initially persuade readers to share this distorted or biased view of the report problem, other report writers will ultimately offer more accurate and objective views on the same issue. As a result, you and your organization could suffer a backlash of distrust and negative sentiment from associates and the public. Many years devoted to building a reputation of credibility and accuracy could quickly be erased by a single biased report (Jaffe & Spirer, 1986). Third, by not accurately researching or analyzing a problem due to your bias, both you and your organization will be deprived of a complete and truthful view of the facts.

Any decision based on a report containing such a biased view will invariably be flawed.

To avoid injecting bias into your report analysis, ask yourself if you hold any preconceptions as to what results the research will, or should, eventually reveal. Have you, in fact, already manufactured an answer to your report problem before the research and analysis are completed? Does your organization have anything to gain from a particular report result? Would *you* gain, from a specific outcome? Do you feel pressured into presenting results that the firm would consider favorable? If you answer "yes" to any of those questions, you should critically review all phases of your report process for bias.

We cannot, nor would we want to, always avoid bias in report writing. In some cases, bias might represent an important and valid variable in your analysis. For example, suppose your organization were deciding whether to purchase personal computers from Company A or Company B. Workers' preference for, or bias toward, working on computers from Company B might well be the determining factor for your choosing to recommend that the organization buy from that company. Be sure, however, to note to readers whenever you include bias—or inference, for that matter—in your report.

Consulting with Others

Rarely will you be able to recognize all the factors associated with the report problem that should be studied and interpreted during the analysis phase. Moreover, you will inevitably require some technical assistance when analyzing information outside your area of expertise. Consequently, it's a good idea to consult with colleagues or others you feel would contribute to your producing a more accurate and thorough analysis of report findings.

The same people who have offered you expertise and new ideas regarding work in earlier stages of the report process (e.g., planning, research methods, classification of data, coding, tabulating) might prove to be helpful resources when interpreting the meaning and significance of the data and information. Be sure not to limit your search for assistance to people within your immediate area of study or to those who tend to share your views. Experts from allied areas in your organization or from outside organizations can often provide objective advice and constructively critical interpretations. For example, a strategic planning report for their company's research and development division could no doubt strengthen the interpretation of findings contained in that document by receiving useful criticism from experts in such related divisions as production, marketing, management, and human resources. Consulting with knowledgeable others will not only give you a sense of confidence in your interpretations but also produce more accurate and thorough analyses of findings.

Testing Your Analysis

The testing of your analyses is an extension and product of the critical thinking that you've been using throughout the report-writing process. Before drawing conclusions founded on your interpretations of the collected data and information, you should consider the accuracy and significance of your analyses as a whole. Based on your business experience, knowledge in the area of study, and critical skills, do the interpretations (a) imbue the data with meaning that is accurate and insightful, (b) seem thorough in covering all significant findings, and (c) provide you with sufficient information with which to answer the report problem?

For some report problems, testing can be performed with relative ease and with few negative results should the analyses prove faulty. For example, assume you have completed your study regarding the effectiveness of a counter display in attracting customers to buy a specific type of perfume, as discussed earlier in Chapter 8. You have surveyed customers and interviewed salespeople in the perfume department for their views on the display's usefulness. After analyzing the results, you decide that the display attracts only a negligible number of window-shoppers, the majority of whom do not actually buy perfume, and that the counter space could be better used in other ways. The interpretations of the data seem accurate and reasonable to you. You believe you have examined the data thoroughly and that the analyses lead you to a clear conclusion. You might easily give your interpretations a final test by removing the display for several months. If perfume sales do not change appreciably, your analyses were probably right.

In other testing situations, however, such final tests of your interpretations might be too costly, impractical, or impossible to perform. For instance, suppose you had completed a three-year strategic plan for your small business. Waiting one or two years to realize that your analyses were incorrect could jeopardize the financial health of your company. Consequently, in most cases you will have to depend entirely on your critical skills to immediately recognize and possibly correct any inconsistencies or inaccuracies in your analyses.

Finally, be sure that you have considered all other reasonable interpretations of the data. Are there other interpretations that may better explain them?

Recognizing Logical Fallacies

You can improve your chances of providing your readers with sound interpretations of data by understanding some of the basic rules of logic. Any interpretation or argument that you wish to present in a managerial report should be founded on a logical progression of premises. A **premise**, or **proposition**, is an assertion that may, or may not be, based on fact. A conclusion, as a component in an argument, is, in effect, a type of premise that not only is derived from but also concludes a logical sequence of preceding premises. If removed from that causational context of supporting premises, a conclusion would be indistinguishable from those premises. Assumptions, hypotheses, and statements of fact can all function as premises in constructing an argument (Geach, 1976, Chap. 16).

While complex arguments can contain a number of premises and more than one conclusion, **syllogisms** are simple logical arguments that usually contain only two premises and a single conclusion. Larger arguments can normally be factored into several related syllogisms. The following syllogism suggests a logical relationship between the first proposition, the **major premise**, and the second proposition, the **minor premise**, which then leads to a reasonable conclusion:

Major Premise

Our store has too large an inventory of shoes ordered specifically for the December holidays.

Minor Premise

After-holiday sales can quickly reduce unneeded stock while also providing business with a modest profit.

Conclusion

Let's hold an after-holiday sale to reduce inventory.

To be true and valid, an argument must contain premises that are (1) proved to be true and (2) logically sequenced. You can effectively evaluate any argument by addressing the following four questions (Nickerson, 1986, p. 88):

1. Is it complete?
2. Is its meaning clear?
3. Is it valid? (Does the conclusion follow logically from the preceding premises?)
4. Do I believe the premises?

First, consider if the argument is complete. In other words, is it missing any required premises, or a conclusion? Second, evaluate the argument's clarity. Is the meaning of each component (premises and conclusion) clear and exact?

Third, check the validity of the argument. In short, does the conclusion follow logically from the sequence of supporting premises? Conclusions based on true and logically organized premises are always true and valid. However, it is interesting to note that valid conclusions can also follow from premises that, although not true, are logically sequenced.

Finally, determine if the argument is plausible. What degree of doubt surrounds the argument? If all premises are true, and if the premise sequence is logical, then, clearly, the conclusion is true. However, the fact that one premise (or more) is false does not preclude the possibility that the conclusion is perhaps (by chance) true. Thus, if a premise is false, you must still consider the possible truth in the conclusion. Herein lies the gray area of evaluating an argument's plausibility (Nickerson, 1986, pp. 36–37, 72–89).

Some common argumentation strategies are offered below (Nickerson, 1986, pp. 80–93; Olson, 1969, p. 401):

All A are B	No A are B
<u>All B are C</u>	<u>No B are C</u>
Therefore, all A are C	Therefore, no A are C

All A are B	Some A are B
<u>No B are C</u>	<u>Some B are C</u>
Therefore, no A are C	Therefore, some A are C
No A are B	If X then Y
<u>All B are C</u>	<u>Not Y</u>
Therefore, no A are C	Therefore not X
No A are B	If X then Y
<u>All A are C</u>	<u>X</u>
Therefore, no B are C	Therefore Y

Premises that imply positive absolutes (e.g., "All men are mortal") are called **universal affirmative propositions** (Geach, 1976, Chap. 7; Olson, 1969, p. 63). **Universal negative propositions** (e.g., "No men are immortal") express negative absolutes. Premises that positively qualify their propositions (e.g., "Some men are tall") are **particular affirmative**; propositions negatively qualified are **particular negative** (e.g., "Some men are not tall").

Unfortunately, too many arguments voiced in business today are not based on logic but, rather, on fallacious reasoning. An argument contains a **logical fallacy** when it attempts to convince using false or invalid inferences (Olson, 1969, pp. 179–192). Logical fallacies are normally the result of premises that are false statements or that are not logically sequenced. Although fallacious reasoning can occasionally and accidentally result in a true and valid conclusion, such flawed logic typically undermines the integrity of your argument, as well as your study and any further studies based on that reasoning. The logical fallacies presented in the following subsections represent some of the most commonly committed errors in logical thinking.

Sweeping Generalizations

When we generalize to an entire population based on too narrow a sample, we are making a **sweeping generalization.** Simply because one person or variable reacted in a certain way to a condition or situation does not mean that the whole population will react the same way in similar circumstances. Aristotle referred to this type of narrow analysis as "reasoning by example" with, clearly, an insufficient number of examples (Willard, 1989, Chap. 10).

EXAMPLES

The real estate market in our community has been extremely soft recently. Therefore, the real estate industry across the entire nation must be suffering also.

The two United States–made automobiles I've owned were as dependable as I could have hoped for. Thus, all American cars must also be of equal quality.

Sweeping generalizations often lead to faulty **extrapolations,** or predictions. For instance, let's assume that you generalize from the softness of the real estate market in your own community that the market is weak across the nation. Armed with this flawed generalization, you incorrectly predict that the country's real estate industry will disintegrate if steps (such as the Federal

Reserve's and banks' lowering of interest rates for home mortgages) aren't taken to spark the interest of prospective home buyers. Although such an extrapolation might be logical, the fact that it is based on insufficient data may well make your recommendation not only inaccurate but perhaps counterproductive.

Sweeping generalizations and unsound extrapolations are typically the result of haste. Don't be in a hurry to prove or disprove a hypothesis. Consider the report problem, define all important and influential variables, and research enough data to make educated, sound interpretations.

Circular Reasoning

Logical reasoning should normally be linear. You begin with a major premise ("All people must eat"), add a minor premise ("Jane is a person"), and draw a conclusion based on those related propositions ("Jane must eat"). However, when the evidence for a conclusion is merely a restatement of that conclusion, we are guilty of **circular reasoning,** or *circulus in probando,* meaning "arguing in a circle," as illustrated in the following examples:

EXAMPLES

The new advertising campaign is bound to work because it will give the product more exposure through advertising.

We need to broaden our research and development interests because our current R&D projects are too narrow in scope.

Faulty arguments such as these are said to be **begging the question** as they beg, or assume, the very conclusions they purport to prove (Capaldi, 1971). Flawed reasoning that begs the question can also be based on a single word. For example, arguing that any *reasonable* person would agree with the new ad campaign only prompts the obvious question: Why would a reasonable person support the new campaign? And, further, why would the campaign be successful?

Tu Quoque

The logical fallacy of *tu quoque* is a distant cousin of circular reasoning. Reasoning based on the strategy of *tu quoque,* meaning "you too," is to defend an argument by turning a counterargument back against itself. It is a defense against a counterargument that provides no evidence but, rather, accuses the accuser. Normally, the *tu quoque* defense against the counterargument has little relevance to the original argument or the point of the counterargument:

Argument

Lumber Company A should continue logging trees from the Amazon Basin in Brazil.

Counterargument

Such heavy harvesting of trees in the Amazon Basin, the "lungs of the world," will significantly deplete a primary source of oxygen in the world and severely restrict the forest's capacity for alleviating the increasing amounts of carbon dioxide in our ecosphere. Such disregard for natural resources may well jeopardize the entire world's very survival.

Tu Quoque *Defense*

By preventing Lumber Company A from harvesting and making practical use of a natural resource, conservationists would be threatening the livelihoods of thousands of workers around the world while also preventing the lumbering industry from providing the world with necessary lumber products that enrich and make possible our daily lives.

As illustrated above, our *tu quoque* strategy contends that the accuser is guilty of the very errors or misdeeds for which we were accused in our initial argument.

Red Herring

When we attempt to support a proposition by introducing a piece of evidence that is only peripherally related to that proposition, we are committing another flaw in logical reasoning called the **red herring.** If we feel our argument lacks sufficient evidence on which to convince our audience, we might buttress the argument with a second proposition that, though irrelevant to the strengths or weaknesses of the initial argument, will win readers' emotional support, as illustrated here:

First Proposition

We should move the shelter for the homeless to a suburb of the city, where the residents will enjoy a better quality of life, and demolish the inner-city shelter (which is built on property recently targeted for booming real estate speculation).

Evidence to the Contrary

Such a suburb site for the shelter would restrict the movement of the homeless and, thus, actually prevent them from seeking support services located in the city center.

Red Herring

Opponents of this resettlement of the homeless really do not understand these people's plight and are insensitive to their right to live in clean, modern facilities rather than the dilapidated inner-city ghetto.

False Analogy

Analogies are comparisons between two items that are similar in at least one important respect. Logically, the more similarities involved in the comparison, the stronger the analogy. A **false analogy,** on the other hand, compares two things that are not similar in any meaningful way.

EXAMPLES   Our assembly line approach toward producing machine-made shoes streamlined operations dramatically last year; perhaps we can take the same approach in redesigning our production of handmade shoes.

Our marketing approach to owners of Luxury Car A in the United States should work equally well to owners of Luxury Car A in Japan.

The analogy made in the first example overlooks the many and important differences between producing machine-made and handmade shoes. An assembly line approach, as used in making shoes by machine, probably would not work with their handmade counterparts. A marketing executive making the analogy shown in the second example will quickly realize that consumers in Japan and the United States can often share more dissimilarities than similarities. Comparing the buying habits of consumers in two countries having significantly different cultures and associated perceptions of purchasing needs is an error in comparison that could easily cause an international marketing group substantial frustration and failure.

Reasoning Based on Emotional Appeal

Some researchers resort to appeals based on emotion rather than logic and fact. Advertisers often use emotional appeals to reach target consumers. They play on the entire range of their audience's emotions, such as romance, prestige, fear, patriotism, sense of competition, honor, prejudice, and pride. Emotional appeals may be appropriate in some of your business communications; however, you should be sensitive to how such appeals can create a backlash against the writer of a managerial report that is assumed by readers to be objectively researched and presented.

First, while an argument based on emotional appeal may initially succeed in winning a desired action from your report audience, readers will ultimately sense that they have been unfairly manipulated through their emotions. Abused or misused appeals based on emotion can lead to antagonism between the reader, writer, and often the organization represented by the writer. Second, arguments based on emotional appeal also tend to distort or ignore facts surrounding the report problem. Without these facts and an objective analysis of the data, managers have little chance of making well-informed, sensible decisions.

Third, emotional appeals reflect writer bias. After readers have discovered the prejudice, they question the accuracy and reliability of the whole report. They distrust the degree of objectivity used by the writer to analyze the data. They wonder how thoroughly the data were researched and collected. Finally, such distrust between reader and writer tends to erode the credibility of the writer in performing objective and professional research and analysis. The most prevalent forms of emotional appeal include the personal attack, appeal to fear, appeal to pity, bandwagon appeal, and appeal to authority.

PERSONAL ATTACK

The personal attack argues against an opposing position by discrediting its advocate. The attack is typically against a person, or **ad hominem,** meaning "against the man," rather than against the merits or weaknesses of a previous argument (Nickerson, 1986, Chap. 7).

EXAMPLES Frank White will not be able to take Airline B out of Chapter 11 bankruptcy for the very same reasons he wasn't able to save Airline A from that same fate: He lacks the kind of insight, intelligence, and charisma needed in a successful leader.

Mary is supporting the proposal only because it will net her a new office and more authority in the organization.

APPEAL TO FEAR

We appeal to the reader's sense of fear (i.e., ***argumentum ad baculum***) when we argue that undesired consequences to the reader are imminent if our arguments, or interpretations of the data, aren't accepted.

EXAMPLES Have you noticed the vast destruction of recent hurricanes and earthquakes? Do you realize that more than 50% of homes destroyed each year in the United States by natural disasters are *not* insured against such calamities? Have you reviewed your insurance coverage lately?

If we do not act immediately, we will lose the largest share of the market.

APPEAL TO PITY

When we appeal to an audience's sense of pity, we are playing on a nobler trait of humankind—that is, the empathetic quality to feel for others less fortunate than we. Through our appeal to pity (i.e., ***argumentum ad misericordiam***), we hope to win readers' support for our argument by manipulating their sympathies (Willard, 1989, Chap. 10).

EXAMPLES If we don't modify our loan policies toward developing nations, those countries will be forced to repay the loan and mounting interest at the expense of the working class whose standard of living perpetuates the cycle of irrevocable poverty.

If I do not get a substantial raise this year, I won't be able to put my child through a special school for the severely handicapped.

BANDWAGON APPEAL

The **bandwagon** appeal is an attempt to persuade an audience by playing on their need to feel a part of the community and crowd, rather than by presenting an argument based on reason. The success of an ***argumentum ad populum***—literally, an "appeal to the people"—depends on the strength of readers' propensity to jump on the bandwagon of popular sentiment instead of standing alone to consider the persuasiveness and validity of the facts presented.

EXAMPLES Most Americans are switching from Cola A to Cola B. Why don't you?

An increasing number of major computer companies are moving manufacturing operations to Pacific Rim countries to lower production costs and, at the same time, increase product quality. Why not make that same move?

APPEAL TO AUTHORITY

When we base our argument on the reputation of experts within a field of study in order to convince readers of the validity of that argument, we are appealing to authority. This logical fallacy is called *ad verecundiam*—meaning "appeal to revered authority." Citing authorities in a work is important in establishing the credibility of an argument; yet, when the basis for the argument rests soley on the reputation of an associated expert, we are expecting readers to accept blindly the voice of authority without weighing the merits or weaknesses of the argument.

EXAMPLES

Many high-ranking and influential congressional leaders read the *National Review*. It must be a reputable and worthwhile magazine.

Airline A must be the best shuttle between New York and Boston because Michael Jordan flies it regularly.

Black-or-White Arguments

Rarely, if ever, are the causes and solutions of problems in the business world, or in the world at large for that matter, either black or white. When we ignore the varying shades of gray that surround and define a problem, we are at great risk of missing the more subtle but significant variables associated with that problem and its possible solution. Placing issues in such a black-or-white context also oversimplifies complex problems that demand complex solutions. As in life, few things in business are absolute and fully knowable. Pretending that we can shape all the irregular data discovered in our research into a neat package of answers can produce only a superficial, inaccurate, and incomplete report.

EXAMPLES

We must expand our vacation offerings to include the St. Kitts route, or forget about ever gaining a substantial share of the Caribbean cruise market.

After 1992, the European Economic Community must maintain its high tariffs on products imported from Japan and the United States or suffer high trade imbalances.

Arguments Based on Self-Evident Truths

Occasionally, we all tend to assume the truth of premises on which we build arguments. Because the premise is perhaps based on another premise made by an earlier researcher or has been long accepted as a proven fact, you might simply consider the proposition as a self-evident truth. Such assumptions in a management report, however, can seriously undermine the accuracy and credibility of the report's analyses, conclusions, and recommendations.

EXAMPLES

The IBM Corporation is clearly the largest and most powerful computer manufacturer in the world. [This will need some clarification and evidence to convince skeptical readers.]

As Eastern Europe recovers from its years of economic hibernation under communist regimes, it will provide Western Europe with a source of cheap labor just as Japan, Singapore, and Taiwan once offered U.S. companies a source of cheap labor. [Besides raising a comparison of questionable accuracy, this self-evident truth is without substantiating proof.]

You might unknowingly employ self-evident truths as a form of evidence with which to support your interpretations and conclusions. For example, as the research project has made you an expert on the report subject, you might forget that your audience lacks the same depth of knowledge in the area of study. Consequently, you might incorrectly assume that the interpretive process of readers has somehow advanced at the same pace and in the identical direction as your own and that they have formulated interpretations of the data that are similar to your own analyses. The best advice, then, is not to assume (a) the truth of premises contained in your report or (b) the level of knowledge or technical expertise of your audience.

Understanding Statistical Analysis

Because of recent advances in computer hardware and software, statistical analysis is no longer restricted to large organizations equipped with expensive computers and accompanying technical expertise. Besides simplifying the procedure for performing and interpreting statistical analyses of report data, powerful personal computers have dramatically reduced the cost of statistical analysis. Consequently, even small businesses can profit from this valuable research tool.

Some of the most popular statistical software packages are SPSS® (Statistical Package for the Social Sciences), SPSSx®, STAT/BASIC®, SAS® (Statistical Analysis System), Minitab®, and BMDP®. Regardless of the nature or complexity of your statistical analysis, your study would probably profit greatly from the various statistical measures that these statistical packages provide—including data generation, regression and correlation analysis, multivariate analysis, and analysis of variance.

An explanation covering all the statistical methods for analyzing data is beyond the scope of this text. However, as you should be aware of the most common statistical methods, we offer an introductory discussion of statistical analysis in Appendix A. When composing a report that relies heavily on statistics, consult some of the suggested texts noted at the end of this chapter and Appendix A.

Overcoming Obstacles to Effective Analysis

Although you might have applied the strategies discussed here to produce analyses that are accurate, thorough, and insightful, your report may still fall short of its goals due to common obstacles to effective analysis, including the exaggeration of findings for the sake of the sensational.

faulty cause–effect relationships.

comparisons of noncomparable data.

emphasis on unimportant data.

insufficient reliable data.

insufficient analysis.

forced conclusions.

The following discussion defines these obstacles and suggests ways to circumvent them.

Exaggeration of Findings

After thoroughly researching a report problem, it is only natural that you would seek a return on your investment of time, effort, and money. It would be wonderful if your report could substantiate significant discoveries that would make your organization more efficient and effective, save it sizable amounts of money, or enhance its reputation. Perhaps management is pressing you for fresh perspectives on old ideas, and you feel pressured into making the report meet their expectations. You might see a report that shakes the industry as a means for moving up the corporate ladder.

Faced with those and other expectations or pressures, you may tend to study only those variables that will support a favorable conclusion, overstate unimportant findings, or even ignore data that contradict a popular interpretation. Such perceptions, and actions based on those perceptions, place a disproportionate emphasis on results, to the extent that expectations might distort the facts and the interpretation of the data in order to ensure a desired outcome. You should recognize and minimize these tendencies toward the sensational, the new, and the unexpected. Effective analysis is invariably slow, tedious, and unglamorous. Only the objective, thorough, and accurate analysis of data is of any use to managers having to make insightful, intelligent decisions.

Faulty Cause–Effect Relationships

Because two pieces of data may share some incidental similarities, you might incorrectly imagine a causal relationship where there is none. Whenever we assume a causal relationship between variables, data, or events because they occur sequentially, our reasoning is vulnerable to the logical fallacy of ***post hoc, ergo propter hoc*** — meaning "after this, therefore because of it." You might discover, for example, that the increase in shoe sales in your department store seems to correlate with the increase in shoplifting throughout the store. However, the fact that shoplifting increases the week after each shoe sale does not prove that the occurrence of shoe sales influences the frequency of shoplifting. Shoes sales and shoplifting may have variables in common, but the cause(s) of increased shoplifting lies elsewhere. Similarly, the fact that events occur simultaneously does not necessarily imply causation. If shoplifting increases during the same time period of a shoe sale, the relationship may well be coincidental or perhaps related only indirectly to a third event that is the actual cause of the rising incidence of shoplifting.

Comparisons of Noncomparable Data

Despite whatever care we might take in conducting secondary or primary research, we must recognize that not all the data we might collect will be comparable. Unless the data share fundamental and meaningful similarities, any inferences you draw from the comparison to solve the report problem will be unfounded and probably inaccurate.

For example, comparing the effectiveness of health care systems in the United States and Sweden would require that you first examine the many differences between the two systems, the most conspicuous being that Sweden maintains a system of socialized medicine. Even when comparing countries that maintain national health care systems—such as Great Britain, France, Germany, Spain, and Sweden—you would have to recognize the many differences between countries in terms of how each structures its own form of socialized medicine.

Emphasis on Unimportant Data

Rarely are all data in a report of equal importance. Thus it would be inappropriate and counterproductive to give equal coverage to different sets of data that hold varying degrees of importance in solving your report problem. Consequently, you should be discriminating in determining the emphasis in your report, providing coverage proportionate to the significance of the information. Including in your report data and associated interpretations that have little relevance to solving your report problem only slows the pace of the report and loses readers in a flood of minor details. Moreover, when awash in details, readers often are unable to differentiate between important and less important findings, interpretations, and conclusions.

You should give priority to the data that are most relevant to solving the report problem. Allocate more time and energy to interpreting those data, and give that interpretation more space in your report to ensure that the information is covered thoroughly. Understandably, the information with greatest relevance and highest priority should be placed first in the report, followed by information that is less significant but still important to solving the problem.

Insufficient Data

During your analysis, you might find that the depth or breadth of your data fails to provide you with enough information from which to make a sound and justifiable interpretation. As you classify and interpret collected data, you may discover that you have overlooked key topics or that the information you have gathered is not sufficiently thorough or varied. In such a case, you would have to return to the library to collect data that would fill those gaps or, if you have relied on primary sources, repeat the research done through observation, surveys, or experimentation (Capaldi, 1971; Kalton, 1983).

As you analyze data, you may also find that, while you seem to have enough data, the information collected through primary research is too unreliable to support accurate interpretations. You might even question the validity of your research methodology. This situation is much more serious than the problem of insufficient data, as it obliges you to reexamine all phases of your research. Quiz yourself on the fundamentals of effective research, as discussed in Chapters 7 and 8 and Appendix A. Did you choose the most appropriate research method, considering the nature of your report problem and research constraints, such as time and budget? Did you use correct sampling procedures? Are the samples random? Are they large enough? Are they representative of the target population? Are the responses reliable? Were the questionnaires properly prepared and administered? Are the findings verifiable? Did you use the most appropriate method of statistical analysis?

A reassessment of your research data might result in your having to make minor adjustments, such as stopping off at the library to double-check a few sources before continuing your analysis. However, problems with unrepresentative samples, unreliable data, or flawed questionnaires can mean major adjustments to the report process as you repeat parts, or all, of your primary research.

Insufficient Analysis

The quality of your analysis depends on any number of variables. The amount of knowledge in the field of study and experience in analysis that you bring to the problem greatly determine the success of your analysis. Your ability to remain the skeptic, to maintain the critical eye, when analyzing each piece of evidence also significantly influences the degree to which your analysis plumbs the deeper recesses of a problem.

To improve your chances of building accurate and valuable interpretations of data, consider the following questions throughout the analysis phase:

- Have you considered all the key data and information pertaining to the report problem?
- Have you avoided oversimplification of the issue at hand?
- Have you addressed the different sides of the issue?
- Have you differentiated between the most and least important data?
- Have you organized the topics and their associated data in descending order of importance?
- Have you carefully assessed the meaning and significance of the important data and information?
- Are your interpretations objective and fair?
- Are your interpretations based on verifiable and reliable data?
- Have you based your analysis on sound reasoning rather than fallacies of logic?
- Have you considered the obstacles to sound and accurate analysis that are discussed in this text?

Keep in mind that arguments are founded on evidence, not on the absence of any proof to the contrary. Simply because there are no arguments against your own does not prove the validity of your interpretation. The fact that you can find no reason for not establishing an Italian restaurant within your local mall does not guarantee that the restaurant is a good idea and that it will turn a profit.

Forced Conclusions

To assume that all reports must conclude with clear-cut solutions is to invite biased or otherwise distorted interpretations and unsound speculation for the sake of wrapping up research in a neat package. You may, at one time or another and for numerous reasons, feel pressured into closing a report with insightful conclusions supported by incontrovertible evidence. You have worked for months on the project, and you want something substantive to show for all your hard work. Management is expecting you to solve current problems and to chart a new course for the organization.

Regardless of those pressures, not all research can produce reports with emphatic, definitive conclusions. For example, although stores in the local mall seem to be thriving and your survey of shoppers suggests support for Italian cuisine, you cannot define and consider all the possible variables that may influence the success of the Italian restaurant, were it to be built. In such cases, you may speculate on the appropriateness of starting the restaurant. You would then qualify your conclusions by informing the reader that other interpretations of the same data may be appreciably different.

You need not always tie up all loose ends surrounding a report problem. The passage of time and discoveries of new data regularly make previous conclusions obsolete. Business operates in an ever-fluid environment of changing events, facts, and variables; it is unreasonable to expect that conclusions reached today and based on past data will be equally decisive and seen in the same light tomorrow with the introduction of new data and information. If your research suggests that further research in the area is needed, then state it. If your conclusion is that there is no single conclusion but, rather, numerous possibilities, then state that. The success of management decisions based on your report relies largely on the degree of competence, objectivity, and honesty you have brought to the analysis and presentation of the facts, opinions, and speculation.

Drawing Conclusions

The conclusion section of your report synthesizes and summarizes your major interpretations of collected data and information. It leaves the reader with your final impressions as to the *significance* of what the study has uncovered and what those findings *mean* to solving the report problem. The conclusion also prepares readers for any subsequent recommendations you might include in the report. Because of the conclusion's importance to the overall success of your report, you should plan its content and organization carefully.

The conclusion looks back into the past to tell us the current state of things. It answers the question: Where are we now? Thus, you should begin your planning of the conclusion by examining the ground you have, or should have, already covered. Take an inventory of the key steps that have brought you to this point, such as those considered in the following checklist:

- Have you properly classified the data?
- Have you appropriately tabulated the data?
- Have you applied the most relevant statistical method for analyzing your data?
- Does your analysis suggest that further investigation is required? For example, has the sample produced what seem to be unrepresentative data? Does statistical analysis of the data suggest that they are, for some reason, unreliable?
- Are your interpretations of the data complete and objective? Are they relevant to solving the report problem?

If you feel that the report process has been weak in any of these areas, you should not begin planning the conclusion. Instead, review and correct any shortcomings within the area in question.

Most conclusions contain two key components. First, the conclusion presents readers with an accurate summary of interpretations of data and information that are central to solving the report problem. Second, the conclusion provides readers with a bottom line regarding the solution(s) for the report problem. It, in effect, interprets the interpretations just presented, as illustrated in the following example:

Summary of Interpretation of Topic 1

Interest rates will continue to drop over the next six months before jumping sharply as higher inflation prompts the Federal Reserve to tighten the money supply.

Summary of Interpretation of Topic 2

The organization should purchase advanced, and very expensive, telecommunications and computer equipment if it is to boost productivity and meet increasing business demands.

Final Conclusion

One solution to the problem is to purchase the needed equipment by acquiring a major loan within the next few months.

Organize the conclusion hierarchically by discussing your interpretations in descending order of importance. Thus the most significant interpretations are examined first and the least important last. This is often, but not always, the same order in which you interpreted those data in the analysis section of the report.

Remember that conclusions must be based on sound evidence presented and analyzed earlier in the report. Therefore, do not introduce new data that have not already been interpreted and evaluated. Conclusions should also be logical extensions of that evidence and resulting interpretations. If you make assumptions, note them as such; if you intentionally inject bias into your conclusion, note that also. The following conclusion, for example, is based at least partially on the writer's personal view and this bias is so noted:

Summary of Interpretations

Computer A and Computer B have comparable computing capabilities and would be equally easy to install onto our organization's existing network.

Final Conclusion

In the past, we have purchased all our computers from Computer Company A, and we have been satisfied with computer performance and company support of the equipment. Based on this preference, the most appropriate decision might be to purchase the needed equipment from Company A rather than from Company B.

Keep in mind that not all research leads to decisive or definitive conclusions. As discussed earlier, forced conclusions are more counterproductive than no conclusions at all.

Making Recommendations

Whereas the conclusion is concerned with summarizing the past and present states of affairs, the recommendation section of your report should tell readers the future of things to come. The conclusion tells readers what the data mean; the recommendation section tells readers what they should do in light of the conclusion and provides a specific plan for action. For example, the following:

The organization *should* seriously consider purchasing the needed equipment by acquiring a major loan within the next few months.

should be supplemented with additional recommendations that offer as detailed a plan for action as possible, such as

Recommendation 1

We recommend that the organization consider securing a substantial loan of $500,000 from one of the following four sources:

1. Investment Management Company A
2. Investment Management Company B
3. Bank A
4. Bank B

Recommendation 2

The loan should be secured within the next four months to safeguard against a sudden and unexpected rise in inflation and subsequent tightening of money supplies by the Federal Reserve.

Recommendation 3

The organization should draft a proposal for purchasing specific telecommunications and computer equipment. The proposal should address such design and analysis issues as

cost of equipment and associated support costs.

compatibility of hardware and software.

equipment expandability (and cost thereof).

process for integrating new equipment.

impact of new equipment on current policies and procedures.

Remember that recommendations should provide managers with all practical options that offer reasonable chances of success in solving the report problem. Like conclusions, recommendations should be arranged hierarchically, with the most significant recommendation offered first. The recommendation section is the final stage in a highly interdependent process. Recommendations must be based on your conclusions, which are founded on your interpretations, which are based on the evidence, which should have been collected with appropriate research methods to ensure the reliability and accuracy of the data.

Summary

After completing your research, you will need to provide the material with a logical organization before attempting to interpret or analyze its significance to the report problem. In preparing for the outlining and drafting stages of the report, you should consider specifically (a) the content of the report, (b) the arrangement of that content, and (c) the analysis of that information. As we have explained in this chapter, the fundamental steps in arranging and analyzing data are classifying data, editing and tabulating the results, using tools of effective analysis, overcoming obstacles to effective analysis, performing statistical analysis, drawing conclusions, and making recommendations.

Classifying data and information into logical groupings that are topically related offers the researcher an opportunity to assess whether enough research has been collected from which cogent and substantive conclusions on report topics can be drawn, in what areas further research might be needed, and whether the research suggests a needed shift in the topical emphases of the report. **Editing** data ensures that the material is in the proper form for subsequent tabulation and analysis. When editing, you look for and correct, if possible, any irregularities, omissions, or errors in the collected data.

When you **tabulate** data, you count or measure the results of your research and then compile those results in an orderly form that allows you easy and quick access when analyzing the results. Your objectives in **analyzing** the tabulated results are to (a) interpret the exact meaning of the data, (b) determine their significance in addressing your report problem, (c) formulate conclusions based on the significance of those results, and (d) make recommendations based on those conclusions.

For the most part, your ability to provide readers with meaningful information that can help solve the report problem depends largely on your knowledge of the subject area and your ability to analyze—that is, to delve beneath surface meanings, recognize important and relevant relationships between pieces of data, and define patterns and trends among factors within your study. To improve your chances of making accurate conclusions and proper recommendations, we have stressed the importance of understanding and regularly applying the tools central to accurate analysis, which include maintaining a critical point of view, remaining fair and objective, consulting with others, testing your analysis, recognizing logical fallacies, and understanding statistical analysis.

Obstacles to your effectively analyzing report data include exaggeration of findings for the sake of the sensational, faulty cause–effect relationships, comparisons of noncomparable data, emphasis on unimportant data, insufficient reliable data, insufficient analysis, and forced conclusions.

The **conclusion section** of your report synthesizes and summarizes your interpretations of data and information. It leaves the reader with your final impressions about the significance of what the study has uncovered and what those findings mean to solving the report problem. The conclusion also prepares readers for any subsequent recommendations you might include in the report. Remember that conclusions must be based on sound evidence presented and analyzed earlier in the report. Conclusions should be logical extensions of that evidence and resulting interpretations.

While the conclusion is concerned with summarizing the past and present state of affairs, the **recommendation section** of your report should tell readers the future of things. The conclusion tells readers what the data mean; the recommendation section tells readers what they should do in light of the conclusion and provides a specific plan for action. Remember that recommendations should provide managers with all the options that are practical and that offer reasonable chances of success in solving the report problem.

Related Reading

CAPALDI, NICHOLAS. *The Art of Deception.* New York: Brown, 1971.

CONWAY, DAVID A., and RONALD MUNSON. *The Elements of Reasoning.* Belmont, CA: Wadsworth, 1990.

COX, C. PHILIP. *Handbook of Introductory Statistical Methods.* New York: Wiley, 1987.

DANIEL, WAYNE W., and JAMES C. TERRELL. *Business Statistics: Basic Concepts and Methodology.* 3rd ed. Boston: Houghton, 1983.

FALMAGNE, RACHEL JOFFE. *Reasoning: Representation and Process.* New York: Wiley, 1975.

FREUND, JOHN E., F. J. WILLIAMS, and BENJAMIN M. PERLES. *Elementary Business Statistics: The Modern Approach.* 5th ed. Englewood Cliffs, NJ: Prentice, 1988.

GEACH. P. T. *Reason and Argument.* Berkeley: U of California-Berkeley, 1976.

HAYAKAWA, S. I. *Language in Thought and Action.* New York: Harcourt, 1978.

HUFF, DAVID, and IRVING GEIS. *How to Lie with Statistics.* New York: Norton, 1954.

JAFFE, A. J., and H. SPIRER. *Misused Statistics: Straight Talk for Twisted Numbers.* New York: Dekker, 1986.

KALTON, GRAHAM. *Compensating for Missing Survey Data.* Ann Arbor, MI: U of Michigan, 1983.

LESIKAR, RAYMOND V., and JOHN O. PETTIT. *Report Writing for Business.* 8th ed. Homewood, IL: Irwin, 1991.

LIN, NAN. *Foundations of Social Research.* New York: McGraw, 1976.

LIN, NAN, RONALD S. BURT, and JOHN C. VAUGHN. *Conducting Social Research.* New York: McGraw, 1976.

MACKIE, J. L. *Truth, Probability, and Paradox.* London: Oxford, 1973.

NICKERSON, RAYMOND S. *Reflections on Reasoning.* Hillsdale, NJ: Laurence Erlbaum, 1986.

OLSON, ROBERT G. *Meaning and Argument: Elements of Logic.* New York: Harcourt, 1986.

PERELMAN, CHAIM, and L. OLBRECHTS-TYTECA. *The New Treatise on Argumentation.* Trans. J. Wilkinson and P. Weaver. Notre Dame, IN: U of Notre Dame, 1969.

RUGGIERO, VINCENT R. *Beyond Feelings: A Guide to Critical Thinking.* 3rd ed. Mountain View, CA: Mayfield, 1990.

TOULMIN, STEPHEN. *The Uses of Argumentation.* Cambridge, England: Cambridge UP, 1989.

TOULMIN, STEPHEN, RICHARD RICKE, and ALLAN JANIK. *An Introduction to Reasoning.* New York: Macmillan, 1979.

VARNER, IRIS I. *Contemporary Business Report Writing.* New York: Dryden, 1987.

WILLARD, CHARLES ARTHUR. *A Theory of Argumentation.* Tuscaloosa, AL: U of Alabama, 1989.

ZIEGELMUELLER, G., and J. KAY. *Argumentation: Inquiry and Advocacy.* 2nd ed. Englewood Cliffs, NJ: Prentice, 1990.

CHAPTER 10

Organizing and Outlining Management Reports

With the bulk of your research and analysis behind you, now is a good time to take note of all the influences and changes that have altered the purpose and focus of your report. You have gathered data and information through secondary or primary research and then tabulated and analyzed those data. In researching the subject of your report, you have probably formulated a general organization to which you might have assumed your final report would conform. But during the research and analysis phases a number of factors surrounding your project could have changed, requiring modifications to the initial organization.

For example, as you uncovered new information or reexamined existing data, you might have altered the purpose, focus, or scope of your report. Moreover, your interpretations of the data and information could have revealed that earlier assumptions were incorrect or inappropriate, which could also have produced changes in the direction, content, and organization of your report.

Review the steps you've taken thus far in the report-writing process. In light of all the modifications you've made to the emphasis and direction of your research over the past days, weeks, or months, you might now redefine the purpose and scope of your work. Review and, if necessary, redefine the report's target audience:

- Has the shift in report focus increased or reduced the number or range of potential readers?
- Do you have multiple audiences?
- Is the audience(s) hierarchical?
- What are the readers' intended uses of the report's information?

- What are their informational needs?
- What is their expertise in the area under study?
- How are they disposed toward the report?
- Are they neutral, receptive, hostile?
- What social or cultural traits of the audience might restrict or enhance your communication design and delivery?

Addressing all of these considerations will help you to

> organize your report findings and interpretations of those findings into a logically ordered presentation for your target readers.
>
> place the key topics of your research into a detailed and formal outline.

After you have organized and outlined your report, you will be ready to begin drafting the document.

Organizing Your Report

A logically ordered report enables readers to access information more easily and, thus, enhances readers' comprehension of the material. Well-organized components of a report also provide better transition between report sections, as each section falls naturally in line with the logical flow of the entire document's overriding organization.

Reports are organized according to their purpose and scope, as well as the informational needs, expertise, and expectations of the target audience. The overall organization of a report (e.g., introduction, body, and conclusion) is called the macro organization. When we speak of the smaller components of a report—such as individual sections, paragraphs, and even sentences—we are referring to its micro organization. There are many organizational patterns for sequencing the macro and micro components of your report; however, the most common and fundamental patterns are the inductive arrangement and the deductive arrangement.

Inductive Organization

An **inductive arrangement** of information begins with data and information collected during primary or secondary research, followed by the interpretations of that evidence. For example, after its introduction section, a report organized inductively on the macro level would present data and information relevant to the work's central thrust. The report would then offer the author's interpretations of this evidence and, in many cases, a conclusion and recommendation section. The organization of the inductive report, then, roughly follows the same order in which the author performed the research and analysis. The author is, in essence, walking the reader through the most significant phases of the research process. The inductive organization is frequently referred to as the *indirect* approach.

The following example presents the central evidence and conclusions based on the evidence, or proofs, that might serve as the body, conclusion, and recommendation sections of a short memo:

Central Evidence

1. Personal computers provide significant improvements in employees' speed in solving office problems, thus increasing workers' productivity.
2. Increased employee productivity due to the use of personal computers in the business environment has led to lower production costs.
3. Research shows that computers markedly improve the quality of employees' work.
4. Because today's personal computers are significantly more user-friendly, employees will find substituting new personal computers for their old typewriters an easy transition to make.
5. Technology companies continue to make major advances in their research and development and to streamline the manufacturing process, which ultimately means that we can expect less expensive yet more powerful and versatile computers on the market in the near future.

Conclusion/Recommendation

Our organization has been searching for methods to improve employee productivity while also cutting production costs. We would like to accomplish this without large infusions of money for new offices, expensive technology, and training. Based on the findings outlined above, I suggest we consider personal computers as a major step in solving our production problems.

The inductive organization is most useful when you feel the target audience may be unreceptive to the interpretations, conclusions, or recommendations presented in the report. Leading readers through the key evidence behind your interpretations will make them more inclined to accept your conclusions and recommendations than simply opening the report with your conclusions and recommendations. By using the inductive approach, you maximize your chances of keeping readers' minds open long enough to provide them with a full picture of the facts and to convince them of the fairness and validity of your interpretations, the logic of your conclusions, and the appropriateness of your recommendations.

Deductive Organization

A **deductive arrangement** of information begins with a statement of the central topic of discussion, followed by specific facts, details, and interpretations that support and develop that topic statement. The introduction of a deductively arranged work serves as a contextual framework for the data or information that is to follow. In effect, it introduces us to the subject at hand and forecasts for us the topical focus of the evidence that is to follow.

Unlike an inductively arranged work, deductively organized text, whether a paragraph, report section, or entire report, is not presented in the same sequence in which the research was performed. Deductive organization requires that you, after synthesizing the collected information, place your interpretations and conclusions before the findings on which those analyses are based. For example, a deductively organized report would present the author's conclusions and recommendations immediately after the introduction section. The presentation and analysis of the facts would follow as evidence. The deductive organization is often referred to as the *direct* approach.

The next example presents the same evidence and conclusions from the earlier illustration, but in a deductive arrangement with the order of the proofs and conclusion sections reversed:

Conclusion/Recommendation

Our organization has been searching for methods to improve employee productivity while also cutting production costs. We would like to accomplish this without large infusions of money for new offices, expensive technology, and training. Based on the findings outlined below, I suggest we consider personal computers as a major step in solving our production problems.

Central Evidence

1. Personal computers provide significant improvements in employees' speed in solving office problems, thus increasing workers' productivity.
2. Increased employee productivity due to the use of personal computers in the business environment has led to lower production costs.
3. Research shows that computers markedly improve the quality of employees' work.
4. Because today's personal computers are significantly more user-friendly, employees will find substituting new personal computers for their old typewriters an easy transition to make.
5. Technology companies continue to make major advances in their research and development and to streamline the manufacturing process, which ultimately means that we can expect less expensive yet more powerful and versatile computers on the market in the near future.

The deductive organization is most appropriate whenever you anticipate that the target audience is receptive or, at worst, neutral to your message. Because readers of management reports are normally eager to examine conclusions provided by the documents, the deductive organization is more commonly used than the inductive arrangement in the business environment.

Introduction and Conclusion Sections

The organizational strategies discussed in this chapter are most applicable to use in the body of your report, where you will present the significant findings of your research as well as your interpretations of those data. Your report, however, will include at least two other major sections in addition to the body: the introduction and conclusion.

The **introduction** typically defines and explains the purpose and scope of a report. The introduction should specifically explain, though briefly, how the report problem is addressed later in the document's analysis, discussion, and conclusion sections. It may also provide contextual information regarding the background of the report problem. Many introductions also include the research methods used by the researcher to investigate the report problem. Moreover, if researchers were somehow restricted from achieving all the goals of the research, they might note the limitations of the study in the introduction.

The **conclusion** includes a summary of the major interpretations that you have formulated from your analysis of collected data and information. The conclusion section may also contain recommendations (i.e., suggested plans for action) based on those interpretations that will solve, or move toward solving, the report problem. Chapters 13, 14, and 15 provide more detailed information about the specific components comprising the introduction and conclusion sections of various management reports.

Selecting Organizational Strategies

Choosing just the right organizational strategy, or combination of strategies, for your report is critical if you are to develop sufficiently the body of your report and to provide readers with a clear and logical route through the premises, evidence, and interpretations presented in the complete work. However, a discussion of organizational strategies should always begin with a word of caution. No organizational strategy should be selected and subsequently applied in a contextual vacuum. Your decision for choosing an organizational strategy for your report should be based on such rhetorical concerns as

the purpose and scope of the report.

the nature of the report content.

the hierarchy of your audience.

readers' informational needs and their intended uses of the information.

readers' receptivity toward your message.

readers' technical expertise in the area of study (Spatt, 1987).

This discussion defines the most common organizational strategies and explains briefly their use in management reports. All the strategies may be applied in reports that are inductively or deductively arranged. The use of one strategy does not preclude the use of several others in your report. You will often find that your report requires a combination of strategies to communicate information most effectively.

Chronological Order

A **chronological**, or sequential, organization is most commonly used to document a sequence of events, either past, present, or future in time. A report topic organized chronologically may begin with the first occurrence of an event and move to the last and most recent occurrence. The same topic might also be discussed in reverse chronology, with the most recent occurrence developed first and other occurrences covered in reverse order. In reverse chronology, the first occurrence is, in effect, discussed last.

Chronological organization is routinely used to document the minutes of meetings, procedures, and processes. In recording historical background on a report subject, researchers also regularly apply a chronological strategy to present the sequence of past events, as shown below:

EXAMPLE　　Threats to Penelope Ice Cream sales began in May 1988 when Joliet Desserts opened a new franchise in the Central City district, which had, up to that point, been our strongest market. By October 1988, our sales had dropped by 10%. Our increased marketing activities from April 1989 to August 1989 have not significantly improved sales. On March 1, 1990, Judith Lancaster, president and CEO of Penelope Ice Cream, authorized the firm's marketing division to thoroughly research the causes behind the company's stagnant sales and to recommend plans for capturing a larger share of the Central City market.

As everything in life is inextricably linked to time and as time can be viewed as a linear phenomenon, all events, processes, and even thoughts can be seen as linear—and thus chronological. Processes, such as instructions for performing a computer data-based search or conducting a marketing survey, lend themselves naturally to chronological or sequential organization. The stages of research in advertising development, as shown below, could easily be divided into sequential, or chronological, steps:

EXAMPLE　　　Stage 1: Strategy Determination
　　　　　　　A. Define the product class.
　　　　　　　B. Select the prospect group.
　　　　　　　C. Select the message element.
　　　　　　　D. Study consumer attitude and advertising usage.
　　　　　　Stage 2: Concept Development
　　　　　　　A. Test concept.
　　　　　　　B. Test name.
　　　　　　　C. Test slogan.
　　　　　　Stage 3: Pretesting
　　　　　　　A. Pretest print.
　　　　　　　B. Pretest TV storyboard.
　　　　　　　C. Pretest radio commercial.
　　　　　　Stage 4: Posttesting
　　　　　　　A. Evaluate advertising effectiveness.
　　　　　　　B. Measure change in consumer attitude.
　　　　　　　C. Measure increase in sales.

If your report includes a recommendation section, you might find that your plans for action should be completed in sequential order.

To increase the sales of Penelope Ice Cream in the Central City district, the firm should adopt and adhere to the following plan for action:

1. Expand the current line of Penelope ice cream flavors to match the assortment of flavors currently offered by Joliet Desserts.

2. Reduce the price of standard Penelope ice creams (i.e., vanilla, chocolate, and strawberry) to a level 5% lower than current prices of corresponding Joliet ice creams.

3. Perform follow-up marketing and sales studies to determine how much subsequent sales have increased.

Order by Geographical Location

If your report contains information related to location, you may decide to divide the body of your document by geographical boundaries. For example, if your report were evaluating the productivity of your firm's 10 manufacturing facilities around the country, you might first group the facilities into five separate geographical areas and then evaluate each facility against common criteria:

<pre>
Northeast Region
  Facility 1
    Criterion A
    Criterion B
  Facility 2
    Criterion A
    Criterion B
Southeast Region
  Facility 3
    Criterion A
    Criterion B
  Facility 4
    Criterion A
    Criterion B
Midwest Region
  Facility 5
    Criterion A
    Criterion B
  Facility 6
    Criterion A
    Criterion B
Southwest Region
  Facility 7
    Criterion A
    Criterion B
  Facility 8
    Criterion A
    Criterion B
West Region
  Facility 9
    Criterion A
    Criterion B
</pre>

Facility 10
  Criterion A
  Criterion B

Order by Division

Many of the topics discussed in your report may be best organized by dividing, or **factoring**, them into parts. These parts, in turn, may be further factored into subparts, depending on the complexity of your topic and the level of detail required in your study. For example, researchers considering the potential safety problems of constructing a nuclear power plant at a particular site may factor the relevant section of their report in the following way:

Potential Problems Stemming from Site Location
  On-Site Problems
      Inadequate bedrock to ensure integrity of facility
      Uncertain water supply
      Insufficient waste disposal capabilities
  Off-Site Problems
      Inadequate emergency evacuation plans for public
      Incomplete environmental impact studies
          1985 EPA study
          1990 EPA study

The above informal outline combines several organizational strategies: order by division as well as chronological order.

Order by Classification

Order by classification is the complete opposite of order by division. Rather than factoring a topic into its subparts—or dividing a problem into smaller problems—researchers ordering their report by classification seek a commonality among separate topics or problems so that those subparts might be unified into a larger problem or topic. A group of engineers, for example, recently faced the following list of seemingly disparate and unrelated topics:

- Incomplete environmental impact studies
- Inadequate bedrock to ensure integrity of facility
- On-site problems
- Insufficient waste disposal capabilities
- Inadequate emergency evacuation plans for public
- Uncertain water supply

They used order by classification to organize their report into a logical sequence of on-site and off-site problem areas:

On-Site Problems
    Inadequate bedrock to ensure integrity of facility
    Uncertain water supply
    Insufficient waste disposal capabilities
Off-Site Problems
    Inadequate emergency evacuation plans for public
    Incomplete environmental impact studies

As you have noticed, this outline looks very much like the sample outline for order by division, and it should. Keep in mind that we are discussing *processes* for organizing information. It is possible to achieve the same general organization of the same information by using two different organizational processes.

Order by Contrast–Comparison

When faced with having to make a decision between two or more items, you might consider comparing the items with, or contrasting them to, each other. In the following outline, researchers compare three sites to determine which one would be the best location for a new chemical plant. The outline divides discussion into three major parts (Site 1, Site 2, and Site 3) and then evaluates the three sites against a common set of five criteria:

Site 1
    Availability of Skilled Labor
    Proximity to Transportation Arteries
    Strike Orientation of Labor
    View of Local and State Officials Toward Chemical Plant
    Special Tax Incentives for Locating at Particular Site
Site 2
    Availability of Skilled Labor
    Proximity to Transportation Arteries
    Strike Orientation of Labor
    View of Local and State Officials Toward Chemical Plant
    Special Tax Incentives for Locating at Particular Site
Site 3
    Availability of Skilled Labor
    Proximity to Transportation Arteries
    Strike Orientation of Labor
    View of Local and State Officials Toward Chemical Plant
    Special Tax Incentives for Locating at Particular Site

The above outline is organized according to the different sites. Each site is subsequently measured against a set of criteria. The same information could also be organized with an alternating pattern according to criteria. In this case, the discussion fully evaluates one site against a criterion before moving on to the next site. After all three sites have been evaluated against a common criterion, the discussion moves on to a subsequent criterion and the cycle continues thus until all three sites have been measured against all five criteria:

      Availability of Skilled Labor
        Site 1
        Site 2
        Site 3
      Proximity to Transportation Arteries
        Site 1
        Site 2
        Site 3
      Strike Orientation of Labor
        Site 1
        Site 2
        Site 3
      View of Local and State Officials Toward Chemical Plant
        Site 1
        Site 2
        Site 3
      Special Tax Incentives for Locating at Particular Site
        Site 1
        Site 2
        Site 3

When ordering your comparison–contrast of items in long reports, alternating criteria is often most effective, as readers normally find it convenient to compare the performance of all items against one criterion at a time. The division pattern, however, works well in short reports where the alternating pattern can produce choppy transitions, preventing a smooth flow of ideas.

Order by Cause-to-Effect

Ordering the body of a report according to cause and effect provides decision makers information on which (a) to understand the causes that led to an action and (b) to forecast the possible outcomes of the same causes if placed in a different context. Thus, organization by cause-to-effect can provide decision makers a basis from which to answer the quintessential question of speculation: *What if?*

Strategic planning reports are fundamentally ordered according to cause and effect. A firm involved in planning its financial course for the next 5 years knows well the territory it has already travelled. But how can it predict which business opportunities will best help it to meet its goals and objectives? The partial outline that follows is from a 5-year strategic plan for a utilities company. The outline opens with a statement of the strategic plan's purpose and scope, presents the current financial condition of the company, and ends with a suggested 5-year forecast of the organization's growth:

      Introduction
        Background
        Purpose

Scope
Methods
Current Condition of Company
  Base Rates
  Cost Control
  Cost Recovery
  Marketing Division
  Diversification
Conclusions and Recommendations
  1992 to 1993
    Base Rates
    Cost Control
    Cost Recovery
    Marketing Division
    Diversification
  1993 to 1994
    Base Rates
    Cost Control
    Cost Recovery
    Marketing Division
    Diversification
  1994 to 1995
    Base Rates
    Cost Control
    Cost Recovery
    Marketing Division
    Diversification
  1995 to 1996
    Base Rates
    Cost Control
    Cost Recovery
    Marketing Division
    Diversification
  1996 to 1997
    Base Rates
    Cost Control
    Cost Recovery
    Marketing Division
    Diversification

Order by Effect-to-Cause

Order by effect-to-cause is the opposite of order by cause-to-effect. Reports organized by effect-to-cause attempt to uncover and explain the cause(s) of a particular action or situation. In reports organized by cause-to-effect, researchers initially know the causes but not the results. In reports organized by effect-to-cause, researchers know the results, but are left to discover the causes.

Troubleshooting reports commonly adhere to an effect-to-cause organization. Let's assume, for instance, that you are a computer systems programmer and you have been requested by the manager of the computer facility to determine why one of the five mainframe computers tends to go off-line more often than normally expected. You probably begin your study by researching and documenting the current situation. Exactly how often does the computer go off-line? What types of computing tasks does the computer perform on a regular basis? Are those tasks the sorts of tasks performed on other computers? What are the technical differences between this computer and the others? When does the computer tend most to go off-line? Is there a connection between any of these variables?

After assessing the current situation, you would begin your search for the causes of the excessive downtime by examining the history of the problems and then drawing connections between the incidents. You might, for example, find that the computer consistently "crashes" every Friday afternoon at the end of each month. By investigating the types of tasks performed by the computer, you learn that one of its main duties is to serve as a backup system for the other mainframes. On the last Friday of each month, managers of 10 different divisions of the company back up their important computer files to the central computing facility—specifically to the mainframe in question. By interviewing those managers, you discover that the amount of information to back up each month has grown substantially over the past year. As the computer is not equipped to handle such a workload in addition to its normal duties, you determine that outdated backup practices and mounting storage needs are the causes for the increased downtime of the failing mainframe.

Arranging a report body by effect-to-cause is much like describing to readers the shards of a shattered vase as a basis for explaining how the vase came to be pushed from the table to the tile floor and its destruction. In using the effect-to-cause organization, you are, in fact, conducting a process of reverse engineering wherein you present the known product or result first, followed by the discovery of how it came to be.

Order of Importance

When choosing to order your report findings and interpretations according to their importance, you begin with the most significant item and end with the least significant, or begin with the least significant and close with the most important item. Researchers normally open the body of their report with their biggest gun—the most significant topic of the study. Most readers want to be told first the information that is most significant and central to the research.

However, in some cases, researchers hold the most important item until the end of the report body if contextual information, though less important, is needed to lay a foundation for the more significant item that is to follow. Such a strategy also leaves readers with the most important item fresh in their minds. The sample outline that follows provides the general topics included in a strategic report for a cellular telecommunications company. The outline begins with what the researchers consider to be the most important topics and ends with the least significant items:

Increase product sales.
Enhance sales techniques.
Lower product cost.
Improve products.
Enter new markets.
Recognize competition in new markets.
Expand and meet demand for products.
Adhere to new regulations in cellular industry.

Formally Outlining Your Report

An **outline** is an orderly plan for arranging most effectively the ideas you wish to include in your report. The outline should illustrate the relationships between the ideas as well as their significance in relation to each other. A properly designed outline clearly shows which ideas are most important to the report and which are subordinate. In a longer report, the outline often serves as the work's table of contents. In both long and short reports, outline entries can also function as headings in the report itself.

Outlines are invaluable in helping you determine not only the organization but also the content of your document. Outlines function as the architectural blueprint of your report. They keep the entire report and its individual sections thematically unified. Outlines, in effect, can prevent you from digressing from the focus of discussion and from including irrelevant information. A well-structured outline also helps you to maintain coherence in your writing so that ideas flow in a smooth and logical progression of related topics and evidence.

Outlines also provide you with "the big picture" of your report. Acting as the report's framework, the outline illustrates how the parts of the report fit together. The use of an outline can reveal sections of the report that are inadequately developed and must be modified before you begin drafting your report. Outlines can also suggest ways in which you might restructure the report by moving entire sections or subparts of sections.

As writing itself is a process, so is constructing an effective outline. You will probably spend most of the outlining process formulating multiple **informal outlines** whose primary purpose is to place ideas into a logical sequence and to show the subordination of less important ideas. Once you have fine-tuned an informal outline to the point that unified ideas progress logically and coherently toward solving the report problem, you will want to formalize the blueprint by placing it into the format of a **formal outline**. The two most commonly used outline forms are the topic outline and descriptive outline.

Topic Outlines

The entries in a **topic outline** consist of single words or short phrases that identify the general subject of discussion. The following section of a topic outline was prepared for a strategic planning report of a telecommunications firm:

II. Financial position of ABC Telecommunications
    A. Product sales
        1. Sales techniques
            a. Advertising
            b. Customer service programs
            c. Sales incentives
        2. Production costs
            a. Automation
            b. Product material costs
    B. Product quality
        1. Reception of cellular phones
        2. Cellular innovation
        3. Radio paging
    C. New markets
        1. Competition in new markets
        2. Regulations in cellular industry
III. Summary of five-year strategic plan

As topic outlines do not consist of complete sentences, no end punctuation is used to close each entry.

Descriptive Outlines

While the entries of topic outlines identify only the general topic of discussion, entries of **descriptive outlines** (also called **sentence outlines**) express a complete thought or slant toward the subject being reported. Descriptive outlines do more than indicate the topic being covered; they reflect the author's viewpoint on the topic. In the following example, the topic outline provided earlier has been converted into a descriptive outline:

II. ABC Telecommunications must identify and apply workable methods for improving its financial position.
    A. Increase lagging product sales.
        1. Incorporate innovative and much needed sales techniques.
            a. Abandon traditional advertising techniques and adopt high-tech media.
            b. Modify and update unresponsive and inefficient customer service programs.
            c. Introduce attractive incentives for sales staff.
        2. Lower, then maintain, rising production costs.
            a. Introduce high-tech automation and retrain production personnel.
            b. Reexamine and restructure product material costs to make prices more competitive.

    B. Improve unsatisfactory product quality.
      1. Improve reception of cellular phones.
      2. Promote cellular innovation.
      3. Provide broader coverage of radio paging.
    C. Enter new markets within current regions and in new regions.
      1. Match strengths and exploit weaknesses of products from competing firms in new markets.
      2. Research and understand increasingly complex and restrictive regulations in cellular industry.
  III. Five-year strategic plan should include concerted efforts in marketing and sales, research and development, and human resources.

From the entries of the descriptive outline, you—as both a reader and a writer—can readily anticipate not only the specific topics that are to be discussed in each section of the report but also the particular slant the author is taking on the subject at hand. Because descriptive outlines require that you know very clearly the tack you plan to take in each section of the report, they are typically more difficult to compose than topic outlines. However, once constructed, descriptive outlines can aid you in the drafting process significantly more than topic outlines by constantly reminding you of the specific slant you should adhere to in each section. Each entry of a descriptive outline consisting of sentences should end with a period.

Outline Formats

Most formal outlines adhere to either the Roman-Arabic outline format, or the decimal format. The **Roman-Arabic numeral-letter outline** uses Roman numerals and letters as well as Arabic numerals to show subordination of ideas, as shown in the following sample outline:

    I. First-level entry
      A. Second-level entry
      B. Second-level entry
        1. Third-level entry
        2. Third-level entry
          a. Fourth-level entry
          b. Fourth-level entry
            (1) Fifth-level entry
            (2) Fifth-level entry
              (a) Sixth-level entry
              (b) Sixth-level entry
   II. First-level entry
     [etc....]

The **decimal outline** uses only numbers and decimal extensions of those numbers to show divisions of topics. Each main item in a decimal outline is assigned an arabic numeral. Subordinate topics under that item are assigned the same numeral followed by a decimal point and additional numerals to indicate subdivisions, as illustrated in the following sample decimal outline:

1. First-level entry
    1.1 Second-level entry
    1.2 Second-level entry
        1.2.1 Third-level entry
        1.2.2 Third-level entry
            1.2.2.1 Fourth-level entry
            1.2.2.2 Fourth-level entry
                1.2.2.2.1 Fifth-level entry
                1.2.2.2.2 Fifth-level entry
                    1.2.2.2.2.1 Sixth-level entry
                    1.2.2.2.2.2 Sixth-level entry
2. First-level entry
    [etc. . . .]

The outline format that you employ will normally depend on personal preference; however, before reaching the formal outline phase of the report-writing process, you should determine whether your organization supports one form or the other. While neither outline format enjoys any significant advantage over the other, some researchers prefer the decimal outline format because it allows them to factor their topics into an infinite number of subdivisions. Technical and scientific reports tend to contain more subdivisions than reports from nontechnical fields. This may partially explain why many researchers in business and science have traditionally considered the decimal outline as the accepted outline format of their disciplines.

Outline Style

Constructing an effective outline that will direct you through the drafting of your report involves more than identifying topics that are central to solving your report problem and then ordering them into a logical sequence that adheres to a topic or descriptive outline format. To construct an outline that is clear, precise, and accurate, you should consider

its consistency of form.

its balance and symmetry.

the parallelism of its construction.

the variety, conciseness, and precision of its wording.

Consistency of Form

One of the most important rules of outlining is to keep the format of your outline consistent in its form. If, for example, you choose to construct a topic outline, do not introduce descriptive sentences into the outline; the reverse is true when working with descriptive outlines. When formatting either a topic or a descriptive outline, you should address the following considerations:

- Keep the spacing and alignment of outline entries consistent. Double space throughout the outline to provide room for revision. Keep all Roman and Arabic numerals or letters aligned according to their respective level of subordination. Place each symbol directly beneath the first word of the preceding entry.
- If divided, an outline section must have at least two subsections. If a section in your outline has an *A*, it must also have a *B*. If it has a 1, it must also have a 2.
- Capitalize the first letter of the first word following each symbol. Subsequent words are normally capitalized only if they are proper nouns (e.g., names of people, places, and business or governmental organizations). However, all words (except articles and prepositions) are normally capitalized when part of a first- and even second-level heading.
- Place a period after every symbol in an outline—with two exceptions: not after final symbols in decimal outlines and not after fifth-level entries and above in traditional outlines. Skip two spaces after each symbol and period (if present) before beginning the entry.
- Properly punctuate sentence entries of a descriptive outline.

Balance and Symmetry

Rarely will you construct an outline for a report in which all of the sections contain the same number of subdivisions. Normally, neither topics nor problems lend themselves to such neat and balanced factoring. However, outlines composed of sections that are significantly unbalanced in terms of the depth of division might suggest that you have not factored the topics in the most advantageous manner.

Outlines typically reflect the amount of development and emphasis a topic will receive in the report by the number of entry levels assigned to it. Topics that run five or six levels deep will normally be more developed than those assigned only two or three levels of entries in the outline. An outline like the one shown here is relatively symmetrical:

```
  I. XXXXXXXXXX
     A. XXXXXXXXX
     B. XXXXXXXXX
        1. XXXXXXXXX
        2. XXXXXXXXX
 II. XXXXXXXXXX
     A. XXXXXXXXX
        1. XXXXXXXXX
        2. XXXXXXXXX
     B. XXXXXXXXX
        1. XXXXXXXXX
        2. XXXXXXXXX
           a. XXXXXXXXX
           b. XXXXXXXXX
           c. XXXXXXXXX
```

```
            C. XXXXXXXXX
                1. XXXXXXXXX
                2. XXXXXXXXX
                3. XXXXXXXXX
       III. XXXXXXXXX
            A. XXXXXXXXX
            B. XXXXXXXXX
```

The balanced portioning of this outline's entry levels suggests that the researcher has isolated the most significant topics relating to the report problem. Each topic appears to require approximately the same depth of discussion. The following outline, however, is conspicuously asymmetrical in the development of section II and its constituent topics when compared with sections I and III:

```
         I. XXXXXXXXX
            A. XXXXXXXXX
            B. XXXXXXXXX
                1. XXXXXXXXX
                2. XXXXXXXXX
        II. XXXXXXXXX
            A. XXXXXXXXX
                1. XXXXXXXXX
                2. XXXXXXXXX
                    a. XXXXXXXXX
                    b. XXXXXXXXX
                    c. XXXXXXXXX
                        (1) XXXXXXXXX
                        (2) XXXXXXXXX
            B. XXXXXXXXX
                1. XXXXXXXXX
                2. XXXXXXXXX
            C. XXXXXXXXX
       III. XXXXXXXXX
            A. XXXXXXXXX
                1. XXXXXXXXX
                2. XXXXXXXXX
            B. XXXXXXXXX
```

An outline as unbalanced as this one should serve as a red flag. Outlines that are significantly asymmetrical should prompt you to reexamine the proposed organization and development of your report. You may need to reconsider the focus of each section in order to evaluate its role in solving the report problem. This reevaluation will allow you to consolidate less important topics under a common division or to further divide larger and more important topics so that significant details are fleshed out.

Parallelism of Entry Construction

The structure of the entries in your outline must be parallel; that is, entries on the same level within a division must share the same grammatical construction. For example, if entry A is a complete sentence, then entries B, C, and D within that same division must also be sentences. If entry 1 is a noun phrase, then entries 2, 3, and 4 must be noun phrases. The following entries, for instance, are not parallel:

A. ABC Telecommunications should abandon traditional advertising techniques and adopt high-tech media. [sentence]
B. Modifying and updating unresponsive and inefficient customer service programs. [participial phrase]
C. Incentives for sales staff. [noun phrase]

The most common entry constructions are complete sentences, "decapitated" sentences, noun phrases, and participial phrases. The following sample entries are sentences:

A. High-tech media should replace traditional advertising techniques.
B. Unresponsive and inefficient customer service programs should be modified and updated.
C. Sales staff require more attractive incentives.

The same topics could also be stated as decapitated sentences, as illustrated below:

A. High-tech media replacing traditional advertising techniques
B. Unresponsive and inefficient customer service programs being modified and updated
C. Sales staff requiring more attractive incentives

As noun phrases, the entries might be structured as follows:

A. Traditional advertising techniques versus high-tech media
B. Unresponsive and inefficient customer service programs
C. Attractive incentives for sales staff

The topics could also be rewritten as participial phrases:

A. Abandoning traditional advertising techniques and adopting high-tech media
B. Modifying and updating unresponsive and inefficient customer service programs
C. Introducing attractive incentives for sales staff

Variety of Entry Wording

Although outline entries of a common level should maintain the same grammatical structure, they should not be so repetitious in structure that they appear to be dull, monotonous carbon copies of each other. Such "cloned" entries, if later used as headings in your report, might suggest to readers that you've failed to invest sufficient time in constructing specific headings that are unique to the topics they signal. The examples below illustrate such carbon-copy entries:

A. Evaluating advertising campaigns in Region 1
B. Evaluating advertising campaigns in Region 2
C. Evaluating advertising campaigns in Region 3

If you identify accurately and specifically the information that is signaled by the entry, or heading, your entries should contain naturally distinct structures and wording. Because you have factored your report's topics into exclusive and unique divisions, entries that accurately describe each of those topics should always produce entries with distinct wording.

Conciseness and Precision of Entry Wording

Entries of topic outlines are normally short, consisting of one or two words or a short phrase at most. Descriptive outlines, however, tend to contain longer entries whose purpose is to provide readers with a clear idea of not only the topics discussed under each entry but also the particular slant on the topic the author is pursuing. Although detailed and specific descriptive entries can significantly increase reader insight into the information contained in each section of a report, entries crammed with too many details can easily overload readers with information that may ultimately confuse them. The following entries, for example, include too much information about the topics they are intended to signal:

A. High-tech media should replace traditional advertising techniques in all three campaign regions because of the cost savings and greater efficiency afforded such advanced technology as video conferencing, QUBE, and computer video networking.
B. Unresponsive and inefficient customer service programs in all three regions should be modified to conform to current industry standards and then updated to enable ABC Telecommunications to compete with emerging competitors.
C. All sales staff in the three regions require more attractive incentives that will motivate them to increase sales to the expected level of $243,000,000 in the upcoming fiscal year.

Such long descriptive entries have a number of drawbacks. First, they are tedious to read and, in their tangle of detail, make it difficult for readers to easily recognize the focus of the section. Second, the entries contain repetitious and obvious information that should be omitted. The phrase "in the three regions," for instance, would best be noted in the report's title or the section entry (e.g., I, II, III) under which the three subsections in the above example fall. Third, the fact that "attractive incentives" are meant to motivate sales personnel "to increase sales" is an obvious point that does not need mention in the entry. Lastly, such overly detailed entries can be so specific that the author narrows the scope of a section too much. The entry for section C, for example, may unnecessarily restrict the author to discussing sales incentives only for the three regions that can increase company sales to $243,000,000.

The above entries would be more effective if they were pared down to the few key words that reflect the essence of both the section topics and the slants taken by the author, as shown in this sample descriptive outline:

A. High-tech media should replace traditional advertising techniques.
B. Unresponsive and inefficient customer service programs should be modified and updated.
C. Sales staff require more attractive incentives.

Developing Your Outline

While outlines are invaluable prewriting tools, they are worthless if not properly developed and applied toward solving your report problem. After you have determined the macro organization of your report, consider how you intend to develop the outline topics on a micro level. Each topic in your outline must be accompanied by data or information—in other words, evidence.

Chapters 13, 14, and 15 discuss the nature of the content often contained in the introduction, body, and conclusion sections of short and long reports. The specific content to be included in the body of your report is, of course, up to you; however, it will be helpful if you know the general micro organization of how evidence is inserted into each topical section of the report body. Figure 10.1 illustrates how blocks of evidence (e.g., examples, statistics, definitions, interpretations) are typically incorporated into a report to support topics and subtopics.

When writing the body of your report, you should be sure to distinguish between findings (collected data or information) and interpretations based on that material. You have collected your findings by using unbiased research methods. You should, therefore, communicate those same findings in an equally objective manner. Simply put, your findings are what you *found* during your research. The findings that are significant to solving your report problem are included in the report body. Your analysis of the findings are what the collected data and information *mean* in regard to solving the report problem, as shown in the following example:

Findings

HL&P has engineered two plans to deal with its need to compensate for costly investments in nuclear generator plants. One method of relief is through rate increases. A rate increase request has been filed, but a final decision is not expected until mid-1992. The second plan is to seek relief by deferring costs associated with nuclear power projects until rate increases are approved.

Interpretation

Whatever the method used, it is imperative that HL&P obtain relief from the high costs associated with their investments in alternative energy sources.

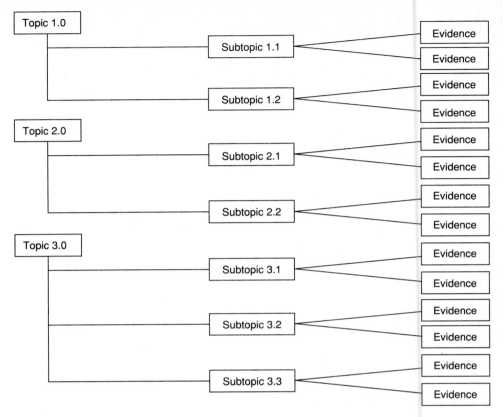

Figure **10.1**
Integration of evidence into report body.

Although you choose to organize the body of your report according to major topics, you might decide to divide the body section into two parts—"Collected Data" and "Analysis of Data"—to emphasize the distinction, for both yourself and your readers, between data and interpretations. The following outline offers one way of maintaining the distinction between findings and analysis:

    II. Collected Data
       A. Research and Development
          1. Cardiovascular Medications
          2. Imaging
       B. Financial Planning
          1. Existing Operations
          2. New Acquisitions
       C. European Markets
          1. United Kingdom
          2. Germany
          3. Italy

        4. France
        5. Spain
III. Analysis of Findings
    A. Research and Development
        1. Cardiovascular Medications
        2. Imaging
    B. Financial Planning
        1. Existing Operations
        2. New Acquisitions
    C. European Markets
        1. United Kingdom
        2. Germany
        3. Italy
        4. France
        5. Spain

While this organization is appropriate for longer reports, such a duplication of the topical sections may be impractical for short reports. The following outline includes the same information as that of the previous one, but integrates the findings and analysis under each topic:

II. Research and Development
    A. Cardiovascular Medications
        1. Findings
        2. Analysis
    B. Imaging
        1. Findings
        2. Analysis
III. Financial Planning
    A. Existing Operations
        1. Findings
        2. Analysis
    B. New Acquisitions
        1. Findings
        2. Analysis
IV. European Markets
    A. United Kingdom
        1. Findings
        2. Analysis
    B. Germany
        1. Findings
        2. Analysis
    C. Italy
        1. Findings
        2. Analysis
    D. France
        1. Findings
        2. Analysis

      E. Spain
         1. Findings
         2. Analysis

Summary

During the research and analysis phases of report writing, a number of factors surrounding your project might have changed. As you uncovered new information or reexamined existing data, you might have altered the purpose, focus, or scope of your report. Moreover, your interpretations of the data and information may reveal that earlier assumptions are incorrect or inappropriate, which could also produce changes in the direction, content, and organization of the report. During your research, the political and economic climate of your organization could have changed. All of these factors might influence the organization and content of your report. We have introduced Chapter 10 by demonstrating the importance, before drafting your report, of organizing your report findings and interpretations into a logically ordered presentation for your target readers and then placing the key topics of your research into a detailed and formal outline.

A logically ordered report enables readers to access information more easily, thereby enhancing reader comprehension of the material. Any report, whether short or long, is either **inductive** or **deductive** in organization. Choosing the right organizational strategy, or combination of strategies, for your report is critical if you are (a) to sufficiently develop the body of your report and (b) to provide readers a clear and logical route through the premises, evidence, and interpretations presented in the report.

Your decision for choosing an organizational strategy for your report should be based on such rhetorical concerns as the purpose and scope of the report; the nature of the report content; the hierarchy of your audience; and readers' informational needs, intended uses of the information, receptivity toward your message, and technical expertise in the area of study. This chapter has explained the most common methods for organizing reports—by chronology, geographical boundaries, division, classification, contrast–comparison, cause-to-effect, effect-to-cause, and order of importance.

An **outline** is an orderly plan for effectively arranging the ideas you wish to include in your report. The outline should illustrate the relationships between the ideas as well as their significance in relation to each other and in solving the report problem. Outlines can also help you to determine the content of your document as well as enhance unity and coherence in the report's organization. The two most commonly used outline forms are the **topic** outline and **descriptive** outline. Most formal outlines, whether topic or descriptive, adhere to either the **Roman-Arabic letter-numeral** format or the **decimal** format.

To construct an outline that is clear, precise, and accurate, you should consider its consistency of form; its balance and symmetry; the parallelism of its construction; and the variety, conciseness, and precision of its wording.

Related Reading ⎯⎯⎯⎯⎯⎯⎯⎯⎯⎯⎯⎯⎯⎯⎯⎯

JOHNSON, JEAN. *The Bedford Guide to the Research Process.* New York: Bedford, 1987.

LESIKAR, RAYMOND V., and JOHN D. PETTIT. *Report Writing for Business.* 8th ed. Homewood, IL: Irwin, 1991.

LESTER, JAMES D. *Writing Research Papers.* 6th ed. Chicago: Scott, 1990.

MURPHY, HERTA A., and HERBERT B. HILDEBRAND. *Effective Business Communication.* 5th ed. New York: McGraw, 1988.

ROTH, AUDREY J. *The Research Paper: Process, Form, and Content.* 6th ed. Belmont, CA: Wadsworth, 1989.

RUCH, WILLIAM V., and MAURICE L. CRAWFORD. *Business Reports: Written and Oral.* Boston: PWS, 1988.

SAGEEV, PNEEMA. *Helping Researchers Write...So Managers Can Understand.* Columbus, OH: Batelle P, 1986.

SPATT, BRENDA. *Writing from Sources.* 2nd ed. New York: St. Martin's, 1987.

TREECE, MALRA. *Successful Business Communication.* 2nd ed. Boston: Allyn, 1984.

WASHINGTON RESEARCHERS LTD. *The Business Researchers Handbook: The Comprehensive Guide for Business Professionals.* Washington, DC: Washington Researchers, n.d.

WEIDENBOERNER, STEPHEN, and DOMENICK CARUSO. *Writing Research Papers: A Guide to the Process.* 3rd ed. New York: St. Martin's, 1990.

CHAPTER 11

Documenting Your Sources

During the writing of your management report, you will most likely include data or information taken from secondary sources—such as books, periodicals, government documents, and pamphlets—or from primary sources—such as surveys and interviews. Many of the ideas expressed in your report may be based on this borrowed material. **Documentation** is the formal acknowledgment of these sources of data or information. Whether you have incorporated borrowed material into your own work by using direct quotations or by paraphrasing or summarizing the original ideas of other people, you must acknowledge fully your debt to those authors and researchers.

When we speak of documentation, we are really referring to two separate but related activities:

1. Documenting the source of borrowed data or information in the report text where that material is actually used
2. Citing bibliographic information of all sources at the end of the report on the "References" page (also called the "Bibliography" or "Works Cited" page).

Purposes of Documentation

Thorough documentation is critical in preparing an accurate and professional report, as it

acknowledges your indebtedness to the ideas of other people.

provides corroborating evidence for your ideas.

extends the range and relevance of your report with supplemental biblio-graphical material.

strengthens the impact and unity of your work.

Acknowledging the Ideas of Others

Documentation distinguishes for readers of your report which information is derived from your own original research and which is taken from the work of others. Deciding whether to document a source from which you used data or information for use in your report is not always an easy choice. Clearly, when you quote directly (verbatim) from the source—whether a single word, phrase, sentence, or entire block of information—you must acknowledge your indebtedness by citing the source. But what if you're using the material indi-rectly by paraphrasing or summarizing points that are of particular relevance to your own work without quoting directly from it? How do you register your indebtedness in these cases?

Your decision to cite, or not to cite, a source would depend on whether the information expresses common knowledge or original ideas of the author of that specific work. Well-known facts that are easily verifiable and do not differ from one source to another are typically considered common knowledge. Sources from which such material has been taken, then, would not have to be cited. Ideas or opinions original to another individual, however, must be documented, whether incorporated directly or indirectly into your report. Failing to document your sources accurately and completely, whether intentionally or unintentionally, can result in **plagiarism,** the use of another individual's ideas or wording without proper attribution. Plagiarism is a serious violation of professional ethics and can result in legal action taken against your organization or you personally. When in doubt, it is always a good idea to document the source.

Providing Corroborating Evidence

A thorough and consistent documentation of sources also gives reports greater credibility. Readers recognize that authors of such reports have done their homework and have sufficiently researched the most relevant or significant texts on the report subject. Consequently, readers assume that the ideas ex-pressed in the report are based on verifiable data and information. Properly documented reports, then, can make readers feel more comfortable with the validity of the information contained in your report as well as the accuracy of the interpretations built on that material. In addition, the care and discipline you use in documenting sources in your report suggest to readers (a) the rigor-ous organization and discipline applied during your research and (b) the care and precision used to analyze the report problem(s) and associated solutions.

Supplementing the Report with Bibliographical Leads

By thoroughly documenting in your report the ideas you have borrowed from others, you enable your readers to use your bibliography as a foundation from which to conduct follow-up research in related subjects. Moreover, after their own investigation based on your reference, readers might in turn expand their understanding of your report's meaning and significance. The reference page at the end of the report, then, not only encourages readers to educate themselves further in your area of study but also can enhance the effectiveness of your report by raising readers' comprehension levels.

Strengthening Report Unity

Finally, consistent documentation throughout your report can help tighten the document's organizational unity. By referring to the same author, or set of authors, at strategic points throughout the report (or within particular sections of the report), you can remind readers of important ideas, while also illustrating to them the significant relationships between those ideas as you introduce new material. For example, a reference to Author A after you have just introduced the ideas of Author B can assist readers in comparing the two authors' ideas. Referring to both authors in the report's conclusion might aid readers in remembering the logical connections between the ideas of the two authors at a critical point of your report, its ending.

Internal Citation of Sources

The documenting of sources used in the text of your report is called **internal citation.** There are four forms of internal citation:

1. Footnotes
2. Endnotes
3. Parenthetical citation
4. Numbered citations.

The form of internal citation you use in your report will depend on the documentation style preferred by your audience or organization. The content and format of these citation forms differ among style guides, so it is important that you follow one documentation style to keep your citations consistent throughout the report. Many organizations and professional associations maintain their own documentation style manuals. However, three style manuals commonly used by professionals in their report writing are the *MLA* (Modern Language Association) *Handbook for Writers of Research Papers*, *The Chicago Manual of Style*, and the *Publication Manual of the American Psychological Association* (APA). Because a growing number of management publications now support the APA documentation system or variations on that system, this chapter focuses on the content and format of the APA documentation style for both internal citation and references.

Footnotes and Endnotes

Authors using the **footnote** system cite sources by placing superscript numbers where the borrowed information is mentioned in the report text. The numbers correspond to numbered footnotes at the bottom of the page where the source is justified. The partial quotation contained in the following passage, for example, is cited using the superscript [1] :

> Bovee and Arens define advertising as "the nonpersonal communication of information usually paid for and usually persuasive in nature about products, services, or ideas by identified sponsors through the various media." [1]

To determine the source of the quotation, a reader has only to glance to the appropriate footnote at the bottom of the page to find a complete bibliographical citation on the source (including name of author, title of work, facts of publication, date, and page number), as shown in the following sample footnote formatted according to *The Chicago Manual of Style:*

> 1. Courtland L. Bovee and Williams F. Arens, *Contemporary Advertising* (Homewood, IL: Dow-Jones-Irwin, 1986), 5.

When listed on a separate page at the end of the report, these same footnotes are referred to as **endnotes.** Endnotes are placed on the "Notes" page at the end of the report immediately preceding the bibliography. Virtually the same information contained in a footnote or endnote is also provided on the report's bibliography page (but in a somewhat different form).

It should be noted that, whereas footnotes and endnotes have traditionally been the standard choice for formally citing sources, the preferred citation method for contemporary report writing is the parenthetical citation system. Unless your organization, or the organization to which the report will be submitted, requests that you use footnotes or endnotes, we encourage you to incorporate the more streamlined and practical parenthetical system.

Parenthetical Citation System

Parenthetical, or **in-text, citation** is significantly different from footnotes and endnotes. Parenthetical citation is perhaps the most widely used form of internal citation in today's management report writing. Rather than repeating virtually the same information included on the bibliography page to document sources (as done by footnotes and endnotes), parenthetical citations normally include just the

last name of the source publication's author.

date of the source publication.

page number(s) of the source publication from which the information is taken (normally included only when citing a direct quote from the source).

Citation information is placed within parentheses, as illustrated in the following example formatted according to APA style:

Advertising is "the nonpersonal communication of information usually paid for and usually persuasive in nature about product, services, or ideas by identified sponsors through the various media" (Bovee & Arens, 1989, p. 5).

Readers can refer to the reference page at the end of the report to obtain complete bibliographic information on the source.

Numbered Citation System

The **numbered citation** method uses numbers to identify a source. Instead of citing a source in your text by noting the author's last name and publication date of the work, you would cite the number that corresponds to that source's bibliographical citation on the reference page of your report. Although it has traditionally been used in the applied sciences (e.g., chemistry, computer science, engineering, mathematics, and physics) and in the medical sciences (e.g., medicine and nursing), the numbered citation system has become increasingly popular in the field of business.

You can assign numbers to each source in one of two ways. First, after completing your list of references, you might arrange the references in alphabetical order and number them consecutively. You might also arrange the references in the order in which they appear in your text. The source noted first in your report text, for example, would be assigned the number 1 on the reference page. When referring to that source in your report, you would identify the work by placing that particular number in parentheses or brackets immediately after the cited matter.

When citing a single source, place the number citation (sometimes underlined or bold-faced) after the author's name or at the end of the cited information:

According to Bovee and Arens [1], advertising, often paid for by a client, is typically persuasive in nature as it attempts to sell a client's products, services, or ideas through a range of media.

If the text contains a direct quotation or paraphrase from the source, add page numbers to the citation and place the number citation at the end of the quoted material, followed by a period:

According to Bovee and Arens, "Advertising is the nonpersonal communication of information usually paid for and usually persuasive in nature about products, services, or ideas by identified sponsors through the various media"[1, 5].

APA and MLA Parenthetical Citation Systems _____

The APA, like the MLA, supports parenthetical citation. However, the two style guides require slightly different content in their forms of internal citation. For example, the APA method supports the **name and year** system of citation, which requires that the parenthetical citation include the last name of the person who wrote, or the organization that sponsored, the work, followed by the year the document was published. Page numbers are included whenever direct quotes are involved. The MLA method, on the other hand, supports the **name and page number** system, which includes the author, editor, or sponsor and page number for all citations. As later discussed in this chapter, the APA style for documenting references at the end of the report is also different from that of the MLA documentation method.

The major differences between the MLA system and APA system of parenthetical documentation center on content and format:

- In the APA system, you provide the year of publication in the citation, which is rarely done in the MLA system.
- In the APA system, you give the page numbers only when citing a direct quotation, not when paraphrasing or summarizing, from a source, as is done in the MLA system.
- The APA system stresses when a source was presented to the reading public, whereas the MLA system is primarily concerned with locating the information in a source through the regular inclusion of page numbers in the parenthetical documentation.

Punctuation and Integration of APA Citations

The way you integrate parenthetical citations into your text and how you punctuate those citations are governed by precise conventions outlined by APA. When placing your notes within your report text, you must follow these rules of punctuation and placement without deviation:

- As a parenthetical citation is considered part of the sentence, place the citation inside the final punctuation (e.g., period, semicolon, comma) of the relevant clause or sentence.
- If the citation follows a quotation, close the quotation before the parenthetical documentation, as the citation is not part of the quotation.
- If the quotation includes any terminal punctuation other than a period (e.g., question mark, exclamation point), retain that punctuation inside the quotation marks, but also place a period at the end of the sentence after the parenthetical citation.
- Commas must separate name from date when both appear within a citation.
- Use the abbreviations *p.* and *pp.* to indicate *page* and *pages*, respectively, in the citation, except after the volume and issue numbers (if any) of a periodical.
- When citing more than one author in your citation, use an ampersand (&) rather than *and* between authors' names.
- When citing more than one source in the same citation, alphabetize the sources and separate them with a semicolon.

Depending on the specific documentation guidelines supported by your organization or a target publication, you will use either the author–date format or number format of parenthetical documentation.

APA Name and Year System

The APA name and year citation system requires that you include the author's last name (or name of editor or sponsoring organization) and date of publication whenever citing a source. In the following example, the authors of a marketing report refer to a book by Bovee and Arens:

> The persuasiveness of advertising is a central element in any marketing strategy (Bovee & Arens, 1986).

On occasions when you note the name of the author in your text, the parenthetical citation need only include the date of the publication. In the following example, the author mentions the names of Bovee and Arens in the text and places the date of publication immediately following the reference to the two authors:

> Bovee and Arens (1986) confirm the persuasiveness of advertising in their own studies.

If you include both the author's name and the date of publication in the text, no parenthetical documentation is needed:

> In 1986, Bovee and Arens confirmed the persuasiveness of advertising in their own studies.

Paraphrase the ideas of others when you can integrate the information from the source more efficiently into your own report by putting the material into your own words. If the original wording of the information, however, is unique, you may decide to quote the material directly to add not only credibility to your own text but also the voice and tone of the original author's style. When quoting verbatim, you must include page numbers from the cited work. On occasion, however, you might also refer readers to specific pages in the source text when paraphrasing or summarizing information of special importance. When referring to page numbers, use the abbreviation for page(s) (p. or pp.):

> According to Bovee and Arens (1986), advertising, often paid for by a client, is typically persuasive in nature as it attempts to sell a client's products, services, or ideas through a range of media (p. 5).

If you do not mention the author's name in the report text where you are paraphrasing or summarizing information, include the name in the parenthetical citation along with the date and page number:

> Advertising, often paid for by a client, is typically persuasive in nature as it attempts to sell a client's products, services, or ideas through a range of media (Bovee & Arens, 1986, p. 5).

When integrating a verbatim quotation into your report, you might identify the source author in the text and place the publication date in parentheses immediately following that author's name. Place the page number in parentheses at the end of the sentence, outside the quotation marks but before the period:

> According to Bovee and Arens (1986), "Advertising is the nonpersonal communication of information usually paid for and usually persuasive in nature about products, services, or ideas by identified sponsors through the various media" (p. 5).

If your sentence contains a partial quotation, you might include the source author's name, publication date, and page number at the end of the sentence:

> Advertising can be defined as "the nonpersonal communication of information usually paid for and usually persuasive in nature about products, services, or ideas by identified sponsors through the various media" (Bovee & Arens, 1986, p. 5).

When including a partial quotation, as the previous sample illustrates, you should integrate the quoted material so that it fits seamlessly into the stylistic flow of your sentence structure as well as the logical progression of your ideas.

If you include the author's name within the text, cite the partial quotation by including the publication date after the author's name and the page number after the partial quotation:

> Bovee and Arens (1986) argue that advertising is a unique form of organizational communication as it is "usually paid for and usually persuasive in nature about products, services, or ideas by identified sponsors through the various media" (p. 5).

If your sentence includes both the author's name and the date of publication, place in parentheses only the page number:

> In 1986 Bovee and Arens argued that advertising is a unique form of organizational communication as it is "usually paid for and usually persuasive in nature about products, services, or ideas by identified sponsors through the various media" (p. 5).

When citing a source with more than three but fewer than six authors, include all names in the first reference. But in subsequent references to the same work, cite only the name of the first author and use *et al.* to represent the remaining authors left unnamed:

> The situational influences that will most affect your writing process and the style in which you write are "the medium you use, the company you work for, and the business image you choose to project" (Halpern et al., 1988, p. 3).

When citing a work with six or more authors, include only the last name of the first author and use *et al.* in all references to the source, including the very first reference.

If you refer in your report to two or more authors who share the same last name, include in the text, or the parenthetical documentation, the first initals to distinguish between the authors:

> The fundamental steps in preparing any business presentation are to establish objectives for the presentation, analyze your audience, prepare an outline, integrate into the outline the content of your discussion, and rehearse the entire presentation (A. Smith, 1991).

If you are citing a source that is listed on your reference page only by its title, include in parentheses a shortened version of the work's title. Remember that the title of a book is underlined (or, as done here, placed in italics); the title of an article is placed within quotation marks:

> The American Management Association reported that in 1985 the average computer information center spent, on average, $89,000 on upgrading existing mainframes and minicomputers and $58,900 on new terminals (*Information centers*, 1986).

When citing a work by a corporation or government agency, place the entire name of the organization in your first reference to the source. Use an abbreviation of the corporation or agency in subsequent citations:

> Because *innovation* is limited to a particular technology that is new to a given setting or organization, it is inseparable from the *process* of innovating—"that is, adopting and implementing new processes, products, or practices" (National Science Foundation, 1983, p. 9).

> . . . "that is, adopting and implementing new processes, products, or practices" (NSF, 1983, p. 9).

Use the accepted abbreviations of organizations whenever possible. For example, *GPO* for Government Printing Office, *EPA* for Environmental Protection Agency, and *NSF* for National Science Foundation.

When performing research in a specific area of business, you may find yourself referring to multiple works published by the same author. If citing more than one work by the same author, simply include the publication date of each publication in parentheses:

> The central reason for pretesting an advertising campaign is to increase the likelihood of preparing the most effective advertising messages for the target market (Mills, 1987, 1989, 1991).

If a cited author has published more than one work in the same year, distinguish between the publications by including an identifying letter to each date in the parentheses:

> Many of the difficulties in appreciating the current debt problem faced by third-world countries are linked to the fact that few loan institutions realize fully that these nations are not only poor but underdeveloped (Weinstein, 1990a, 1990b).

The letters will also appear in each work's bibliographical citation on the reference page of your report.

If you are referring to multiple authors, list the authors alphabetically, followed by the publication dates of the respective works. Separate each author–date pairing with a semicolon:

> There is still no science of effective managerial work and, despite the overwhelming influence computers have had on the business world in general, the boom of computer technology has had little effect on changing the working methods of the average manager (Mintzberg, 1989; Ornstein, 1975; Simon, 1977).

If one of your sources refers to another work and you also want to mention that second work in your report, use the following citation format:

> Harvard Professor Stirling Livingston (cited in Mintzberg, 1989) suggested the lack of relationship between students' grades at that university's business school and those same students' subsequent success in management positions.

Informational and Bibliographical Notes

At times you will want to say more on a topic than you feel should be included in a particular section of your report. Perhaps this supplemental commentary would disrupt the logical flow of central ideas or unnecessarily complicate the organization or development of a given passage. In such cases, you might decide to place the material in informational notes or bibliographical notes.

Informational, or **content, notes** contain supplemental information—such as incidental comments, corollary materials, notes of conflicting views, or technical definitions—that clarifies or amplifies the meaning and significance of ideas in your report. An example of an informational note follows:

> [1] In *Communication for Business and the Professions* (New York: W. C. Brown), Patricia Hayes Bradley and John E. Baird (1980) disagree, arguing that the perception process involves three successive stages: selecting, sorting, and interpreting.

A **bibliographical,** or **reference, note** cites sources that are relevant to the topic at hand but that you do not refer to directly in your report and, thus, do not cite on your report's reference page. Include bibliographical notes when readers might profit from investigating a source further. An example of a bibliographical note follows:

> [1] For a more detailed discussion of organizational development strategies, see B. Wells and N. Spinks, *Organizational Communication: A Strategic Approach* (2nd ed.) (Houston, TX: Dame Publishing, 1989); and G. Goldhaber, *Organizational Communication* (New York: R. W. Brown, 1989).

Whether you are using informational or bibliographical notes, be sure that the removal of the information from the report proper will not change your meaning or the logical organization of your ideas in the report text.

Reference Section

The APA "References" page at the end of a report is equivalent to the MLA "Works Cited" page; both include all sources cited in the report. The bibliographical information contained in a reference citation should be *functional* in that it enables readers to locate any source cited in your work quickly and easily.

Punctuation and Format

When documenting your sources according to APA style, the bibliographical entries on your report's reference page should adhere to the following punctuation conventions:

- Normally, list entries alphabetically by the first letter of the author's last name or, when the author is not known, by the first word of the source's title (excluding *a, an,* and *the*); however, when using the number system for citing your sources, number the entries and sequence them in the order in which they appear in your report.

- If your reference list includes two or more works by the same author, place the names in chronological order by date of publication, beginning with the earliest work.

- Place two or more works by the same author and published in the same year in alphabetical order by title; repeat the name of the author in each entry.

- Include only the initials of author's first names, unless two or more persons have the same surname.

- When the entry includes more than one author, list all authors by last names first, followed by their initials; remember to use the ampersand (&) before the surname of the last author.

- Place commas between authors' surnames and initials as well as between authors.

- Begin the first line of each entry at the left margin; indent each subsequent line three spaces from the left margin.

- Underline or italicize book titles, periodical titles, and the work's volume number (if any).

- Use no quotation marks around titles of essays, book chapters, or periodical articles.

- Capitalize only the first word, a word following a colon, proper nouns, and proper adjectives in essay and book titles; capitalize all main words in periodical titles.

Books

The bibliographical citation for a book includes

the last name of the author, followed by a comma, and the author's initials.

the date of the work's publication in parentheses, followed by a period.

the title of the book (capitalize only the first word of the title, the first word of the subtitle, if any, and proper names within the title and subtitle; the title is underlined or italicized and closed with a period).

the city in which the work was published (if the city is not commonly known or if it could be confused with another location, identify the city's state using U.S. Postal Service abbreviations).

the name of the book's publisher in brief.

A sample reference entry for a book with one author is shown here:

Mintzberg, H. (1989). *Mintzberg on management.* New York: Free Press.

For a book with more than one author, list the names of all authors (last names first) and use commas to separate the different surnames. An ampersand (&) is used instead of *and* before the last name in the series:

Bradley, P. H., & Baird, J. E. (1980). *Communication for business and the professions.* New York: W. C. Brown.

For a book, or any work, with more than six authors, list the first six only, followed by *et al.*:

Ritzman, L. P., Krajewski, L. J., Berry, W. L., Goodman, S. H., Hardy, S. T., Vitt, L. D., et al. (1979). *Disaggregation: Problems in manufacturing and service organizations.* New York: St. Martin's.

When documenting an article from a periodical, however, you must include *all* the authors' names.

For a book beyond its first edition, identify the specific edition number in abbreviated form within parentheses after the work's title:

Strickland, A. J., & Thompson, A. A. (1988). *Cases in strategic management* (3rd ed.). Plano, TX: Business Publications.

Identify a book that has been edited by adding the abbreviation for editor (*Ed.*) or editors (*Eds.*) in parentheses after the name of the editor at the beginning of the entry:

Moyer, R. (Ed.). (1984). *International business: Issues and concepts.* New York: Wiley.

When documenting multivolume books published over a span of years, separate the first and last years of publication with a hyphen and place them in parentheses after the author's name:

Kahn, A. E. (1970–1971). *The economics of regulation: Principles and institutions* (Vols. 1–4). New York: Wiley.

When referring to a particular volume in a book series, note the specific date of the work after the author's name and its volume number in parentheses after the title:

Kahn, A. E. (1971). *The economics of regulation: Principles and institutions* (Vol. 2). New York: Wiley.

Identify a book that has been translated by placing the name of the translator in parentheses followed by the abbreviation *Trans.:*

Perelman, C., & Olbrechts-Tyteca, L. (1989). *The new treatise on argumentation* (J. Wilkinson & P. Weaver, Trans.). Notre Dame, IN: University of Notre Dame Press. (Original work published 1958)

For books without an author or editor, begin the bibliographical entry with the title of the work:

The process of technological innovation: Reviewing the literature. (1983). Washington, DC: National Science Foundation.

The citation for a reprinted book contains the reprint date after the author's name and the date of the original printing after the name of the publisher:

Smith, A. (1964). *The wealth of nations* (Intro. Edwin Seligman). New York: Dutton. (Original work published 1910)

Periodicals

The bibliographical entry for a periodical (e.g., professional journals, magazines, and newspapers) includes

the last name of the author(s) followed by his or her initials.

the year of publication in parentheses (citations for newspapers and magazines also include the month and day of publication).

article title (not in quotation marks).

the title of the periodical (underlined or italicized).

the periodical's volume number (underlined).

inclusive page numbers of the cited article followed by a period.

Journals and Magazines

To cite an article appearing in a professional journal whose pagination begins anew with each subsequent issue, place the issue number in parentheses after the volume number:

> Bowman, J. P., & Renshaw, D. A. (1989). Desktop publishing: Things Gutenberg never taught you. *The Journal of Business Communication, 26* (1), 57–77.

An article appearing in a journal with running, or continuous, pagination from one issue to the next should be documented in the following format:

> Phelps, L. D., & DuFrene, D. D. (1989). Improving organizational communication through trust. *Journal of Technical Writing and Communication, 19*, 267–276.

The following entry is for an article that was published in a magazine having a volume number:

> Richards, T. (1990). Advances in technology and changing customer needs fuel trends in computer services. *Science, 3*, 37–38.

When documenting an article in a magazine with no volume number, include the month and day (if any) and the year of publication. Also include the abbreviation *p.* or *pp.* when citing the page numbers:

> Dobrzynski, J. H. (1990, February 12). LBOs fall to earth. *Business Week,* pp. 62–65.

Newspapers

A sample bibliographical entry for a newspaper article is offered below. Note that the section of the newspaper (indicated by a letter) is given with the article's page numbers, including any discontinuous pages on which the article may appear:

> Garth, J. (1990, January 22). Agencies faulted for latitude given to contractors. *The New York Times,* pp. A7, A14.

An entry for a newspaper or magazine article without an author begins with the article's title:

> Limited names Turpin to Lane Bryant, succeeding Ira Quint. (1990, January 5). *The Wall Street Journal,* p. B4.

Articles that are not news stories should be indicated within brackets following the title:

> Brady, J. (1989, July 11). No time to waive Gramm–Rudman [Letter to the editor]. *The Wall Street Journal,* p. A20.

Entries for book reviews include the subject of the work within brackets following the title:

Maddox, B. (1988, February 28). Where favoritism reigns [Review of *Where Favoritism Reigns*]. *The New York Times Book Review*, p. 18.

Monographs

Although **monographs** can be any work by a single author on a single subject, they are often more narrowly defined as noncommercial, bound works written by one author on a very specific topic. Monographs are normally published by university presses or other small presses devoted to the publication of scholarly or creative works.

Bibliographical entries for monographs are similar to those for periodicals, except that the nature of the work is always noted within brackets after the title. Any additional identifying numbers, such as issue and serial numbers, are placed in parentheses after the volume number:

Fleishman, E. A., Harris, E. F., & Burtt, R. D. (1955). Leadership and supervision in industry [Monograph]. *Ohio State Business Education Reserve Monographs*, *55*.

Abstracts

The bibliographical entry for an abstract of a published article looks much the same as that for a periodical article, except that the source of the abstract is provided in parentheses at the end of the entry. Reference to the abstract source should include the title of the abstract, date of publication, volume number (underlined or, as here, italicized), and abstract number:

McElroy, M. B., & Burmeister, E. (1988). Arbitrary pricing theory as a restructured nonlinear multivariate regression model: ITNLSUR estimates. *Journal of Business and Economic Statistics, 6*, 29–42. (From *Statistical Theory and Methods Abstracts*, 1988, *29* (3), Abstract No. 29-2311)

Book Chapters and Articles

When referring to a chapter or article in an edited book, place the author of the chapter at the beginning of the entry. The inclusive page numbers of the particular chapter or article are placed in parentheses following the title of the book:

Doe, P. (1984). Japanese business success. In R. Moyer (Ed.), *International business: Issues and concepts* (pp. 381–387). New York: Wiley.

If the chapter or article was previously published in another work, cite the original publication in parentheses at the end of the entry. The citation for the original source includes the work's title, year of publication, volume number (if any), and inclusive page numbers of the article:

> Cao, A. D. (1984). Non-tariff barriers to U.S. manufactured exports. In R. Moyer (Ed.), *International business: Issues and concepts* (pp. 85–96). New York: Wiley. (Reprinted from *Columbia Journal of World Business*, 1980, *15*, 93–102)

The bibliographical entry for a congressional testimony or proceedings that have also been published as a chapter in an edited book is offered here:

> Aho, M. (1980). U.S. export competitiveness. In R. Moyer (Ed.), *International business: Issues and concepts*. New York: Wiley. (Testimony before Joint Economic Committee, 96th Congress, 2nd Session, July 29, 1980, pp. 24–29)

Technical and Research Reports

Entries for technical and research reports are similar to those for a book, except that the name of the organization sponsoring the report as well as the report's series or number should be placed in parentheses after its title:

> Adams, J. A., & Rogers, V. C. (1978). *A classification system for radioactive waste disposal—What waste goes where?* (U.S. Office of Nuclear Material Safety and Safeguards Publication No. NUREG-0456). Washington, DC: U.S. Nuclear Regulatory Commission.

If the technical report is sponsored by an information service, such as the National Technical Information Service (NTIS) or Educational Resources Information Center (ERIC), include the name of the service and the report's document number in parentheses at the end of the entry:

> Burkmeyer, E., Mitchell, M., Mikkilineni, K. P. , Su, S. Y. W., & Lam, H. (1986). *Architecture for distributed data management in computer integrated manufacturing*. Gaithersburg, MD: National Bureau of Standards. (NTIS Document No. PC A04/MF A01)

Published Proceedings of Meetings

Papers that are printed in the proceedings of a meeting or conference adhere to the format of a chapter in a book:

> McLean, C. R. (1985, August). Architecture for intelligent manufacturing control. *Proceedings of international computers in engineering conference and exhibit* (pp. 391–397). Boston.

Bibliographical entries for meeting or conference papers that have not been published include the author's name, date of presentation, title, and location of the meeting or conference:

Smith, M. (1990, November 6). *The influence of writing on the classroom context in an introduction to management class.* Paper presented at the 54th National and 16th International Convention of the Association for Business Communication, Las Vegas, NV.

Doctoral Dissertations

When using a dissertation as a source for your report, you may cite either the typescript copy or the microfilm of the work. The citation of the microfilm version should include the microfilm number and the volume and page numbers of the dissertation's listing in *Dissertation Abstracts International:*

Smith, D. (1988). Corporate power, risk assessment, and the control of major hazards: A study of Canvey Island and Ellesmere Port. *Dissertation Abstracts International A: The Humanitites and Social Sciences, 50,* 2137A. (University Microfilms No. BRD–86498)

When citing the typescript copy of the dissertation, provide the name of the university granting the degree, the year the work was accepted, and the volume and page numbers in *Dissertation Abstracts International:*

Smith, D. (1988). Corporate power, risk assessment, and the control of major hazards: A study of Canvey Island and Ellesmere Port. (Doctoral dissertation, University of Manchester, United Kingdom, 1987). *Dissertation Abstracts International A: The Humanities and Social Sciences, 50,* 2137A.

A dissertation not included in *Dissertation Abstracts International* is cited as an unpublished work:

Utzinger, V. A. (1952). *An experimental study of the effects of verbal fluency upon the listener.* Unpublished doctoral dissertation, University of Southern California.

Newsletters

The entry format for articles from newsletters is the same as that for a general periodical article:

Paley, N. (1989, December). The Monday morning marketing memo. *Marketing Forum.* New York: American Management Association, pp. 9–11.

If the newsletter article has no author, place the name of the publisher in the author position:

Office of Sponsored Projects, The University of Texas at El Paso. (1990). Postdoctoral fellowship opportunities in science and engineering. *OSP Funding Newsletter.* El Paso, Texas, pp. 2–3.

Unpublished Materials

Document an unpublished manuscript much as you would a book, except that the entry for the unpublished work includes no publisher:

> Wiio, Osmo. (1971). *Contingencies of organizational communication: Studies in organization and organizational communication.* Unpublished manuscript.

The entry for a manuscript submitted for publication should adhere to the following format:

> Grant, C. P. (1991). *Economic development on the Pacific Rim.* Manuscript submitted for publication.

Nonprint Media

When citing sources from nonprint media—such as films, cassettes, and records—begin the bibliographical entry with the name of the work's primary organizer, director, creator, or producer. Note the type of medium in brackets following the work's title. The following entry is for a motion picture:

> Stone, O. (Director). (1987). *Wall street* [Film]. Twentieth Century Fox.

Sources from cassette tapes should adhere to the following format:

> *The Wall Street Journal on Management.* (1988). (Cassette Recording No. RH/SE 57). New York: Random House.

An entry for computer software should include the name of the author (or manufacturer), year of publication (or production), title (underlined or italicized), and any other information required to locate the program:

> Microsoft Corporation (Producer). (1983). *Microsoft Word* [Computer software]. Bellevue, WA: Microsoft Corporation. (Version 1.15)

Many of the entries discussed in this chapter are included in the sample reference pages provided in Figures 11.1 and 11.2. The entries are organized alphabetically (Figure 11.1) as well as by number in the order in which they appear in this chapter (Figure 11.2). Note that in some disciplines the numbered reference page may be different in format from its alphabetized counterpart in several key areas:

1. Placement of publication date
2. Underlining, quoting, and capitalization of titles
3. Abbreviation of periodical titles
4. Placement of publisher's location and name

Consult the *Publication Manual of the American Psychological Association* for the numbered reference format for your particular discipline.

REFERENCES

Adams, J. A., & Rogers, V. C. (1978). *A classification system for radioactive waste disposal—What waste goes where?* (U.S. Office of Nuclear Material Safety and Safeguards Publication No. NUREG-0456). Washington, DC: U.S. Nuclear Regulatory Commission.

Aho, M. (1980). U.S. export competitiveness. In R. Moyer (Ed.), *International business: Issues and concepts* (pp. 24–29). New York: Wiley. (Testimony before Joint Economic Committee, 96th Congress, 2nd Session, July 29, 1980)

Bovee, C. L., & Arens, W. F. (1986). *Contemporary advertising* (2nd ed.). Homewood, IL: Dow Jones-Irwin.

Bradley, P. H., & Baird, J. E. (1980). *Communication for business and the professions.* New York: W. C. Brown.

Brady, J. (1989, July 11). No time to waive Gramm–Rudman [Letter to the editor]. *The Wall Street Journal,* p. A20.

Cao, A. D. (1984). Non-tariff barriers to U.S. manufactured exports. In R. Moyer (Ed.), *International business: Issues and concepts* (pp. 85–96). New York: Wiley. (Reprinted from *Columbia Journal of World Business,* 1980, *15,* 93–102)

Dobrzynski, J. H. (1990, February 12). LBOs fall to earth. *Business Week,* pp. 62–65.

Doe, P. (1984). Japanese business success. In R. Moyer (Ed.), *International business: Issues and concepts* (pp. 381–387). New York: Wiley.

Garth, J. (1990, January 22). Agencies faulted for latitude given to contractors. *The New York Times,* pp. A7, A14.

Kahn, A. E. (1971). *The economics of regulation: Principles and institutions* (Vol. 2). New York: Wiley

McElroy, M. B., & Burmeister, E. (1988). Arbitrary pricing theory as a restructured nonlinear multivariate regression model: ITNLSUR estimates. *Journal of Business and Economic Statistics, 6,* 29–42. (From *Statistical Theory and Methods Abstracts,* 1988, *29* [3], Abstract No. 29–2311)

McLean, C. R. (1985, August). Architecture for intelligent manufacturing control. *Proceedings of international computers in engineering conference and exhibit* (pp. 391–397). Boston

Mintzberg, H. (1989). *Mintzberg on management.* New York: The Free Press.

Moyer, R. (Ed.). (1984). *International business: Issues and concepts.* New York: Wiley.

Figure 11.1

APA reference page organized alphabetically.

REFERENCES

1. Bovee, C. L., & Arens, W. F. (1986). *Contemporary advertising* (2nd ed.). Homewood, IL: Dow Jones-Irwin.
2. Mintzberg, H. (1989). *Mintzberg on management.* New York: The Free Press.
3. Bradley, P. H., & Baird, J. E. (1980). *Communication for business and the professions.* New York: W. C. Brown.
4. Moyer, R. (Ed.). (1984). *International business: Issues and concepts.* New York: Wiley.
5. Kahn, A. E. (1971). *The economics of regulation: Principles and institutions* (Vol. 2). New York: Wiley.
6. Dobrzynski, J. H. (1990, February 12). *LBOs fall to earth.* Business Week, pp. 62–65.
7. Garth, J. (1990, January 22). Agencies faulted for latitude given to contractors. *The New York Times,* pp. A7, A14.
8. Brady, J. (1989, July 11). No time to waive Gramm–Rudman [Letter to the editor]. *The Wall Street Journal,* p. A20.
9. McElroy, M. B., & Burmeister, E. (1988). Arbitary pricing theory as a restructured nonlinear multivariate regression model: ITNLSUR estimates. *Journal of Business and Economic Statistics, 6,* 29 – 42. (From *Statistical Theory and Methods Abstracts,* 1988, 29 [3], Abstract No. 29 – 2311)
10. Doe, P. (1984). Japanese business success. In R. Moyer (Ed.), *International business: Issues and concepts* (pp. 381–387). New York: Wiley.
11. Cao, A. D. (1984). Non-tariff barriers to U.S. manufactured exports. In R. Moyer (Ed.), *International business: Issues and concepts* (pp. 85 – 96). New York: Wiley. (Reprinted from *Columbia Journal of World Business,* 1980, *15,* 93–102)
12. Aho, M. (1980). U.S. export competitiveness. In R. Moyer (Ed.), *International business: Issues and concepts* (pp.24–29). New York: Wiley. (Testimony before Joint Economic Committee, 96th Congress, 2nd Session, July 29, 1980)
13. Adams, J. A., & Rogers, V. C. (1978). *A classification system for radioactive waste disposal—What waste goes where?* (U.S. Office of Nuclear Material Safety and Safeguards Publication No. NUREG–0456). Washington, DC: U.S. Nuclear Regulatory Commission.
14. McLean, C. R. (1985, August). Architecture for intelligent manufacturing control. *Proceedings of international computers in engineering conference and exhibit* (pp. 391–397). Boston.

Figure 11.2

APA reference page organized by number, in the order citations appear in chapter.

Summary

Documentation is the acknowledgment of those sources of data and information that you have used in your report. Whether you have incorporated borrowed material into your own work by using direct quotations, or by paraphrasing or summarizing the original ideas of other people, you must fully acknowledge your debt to those other authors and researchers.

We have described documentation as the process of (a) citing the source of borrowed data or information at the location in the report where that material is used and (b) documenting all sources cited in the report on the "Bibliography," "Works Cited," or "Reference" page. Thorough and accurate documentation is critical in preparing a professional report, as it (a) acknowledges your indebtedness to the ideas of other people, (b) provides corroborating evidence for your ideas, (c) extends the range and relevance of your report with supplemental bibliographical material, and (d) strengthens the impact and unity of your work.

The most commonly used documentation style manuals in report writing are the *MLA Handbook for Writers of Research Papers*, *The Chicago Manual of Style*, and the *Publication Manual of the American Psychological Association*. Most business reports use some form of the APA style for both parenthetical documentation within the text and for reference citations at the end of the report. This chapter has provided examples of APA bibliographical formats of various published and unpublished works.

Related Reading

AMERICAN CHEMICAL SOCIETY. *Handbook for Authors of Papers in American Chemical Society Publications.* Washington, DC: ACS, 1978.

AMERICAN INSTITUTE OF PHYSICS PUBLICATIONS BOARD. *Style Manual for Guidance in the Preparation of Papers.* 3rd ed. New York: AIP, 1978.

AMERICAN MATHEMATICAL SOCIETY. *A Manual for Authors of Mathematical Papers.* 7th ed. Providence: AMS, 1980.

AMERICAN PSYCHOLOGICAL ASSOCIATION. *Publication Manual of the American Psychological Association.* 3rd ed. Washington, DC: APA, 1983.

CAMPBELL, WILLIAM GILES, STEPHEN VAUGHAN BALLOU, and CAROLE SLADE. *Form and Style: Theses, Reports, Term Papers.* 8th ed. Boston: Houghton, 1990.

COUNCIL OF BIOLOGY EDITORS. Style Manual Committee. *CBE Style Manual: A Guide for Authors, Editors, and Publishers in the Biological Sciences.* 5th ed. Bethesda, MD: CBE, 1978.

FLEISCHER, EUGENE B. *Style Manual for Citing Microform and Nonprint Media.* Chicago: American Library Assn., 1978.

GARNER, DIANE L., and DIANE H. SMITH. *The Complete Guide to Citing Government Documents: A Manual for Writers and Librarians.* Bethesda, MD: Congressional Information Service, 1984.

GIBALDI, JOSEPH, and WALTER S. ACHTERT, EDS. *MLA Handbook for Writers of Research Papers.* 3rd ed. New York: MLA, 1988.

HARVARD LAW REVIEW ASSOCIATION. *A Uniform System of Citation.* 13th ed.   Cambridge: Harvard Law Rev. Assn., 1981.

INTERNATIONAL STEERING COMMITTEE OF MEDICAL EDITORS. "Uniform Requirements for Manuscripts Submitted to Biomedical Journals." *Annals of Internal Medicine* 90 (1979): 95–99.

JOHNSON, JEAN. *The Bedford Guide to the Research Process.* New York: St. Martin's, 1987.

LESTER, JAMES D. *Writing Research Papers.* 6th ed.   Chicago: Scott, 1990.

ROTH, AUDREY J. *The Research Paper: Process, Form, and Content.* 6th ed.   Belmont, CA: Wadsworth, 1989.

TURABIAN, KATE L. *A Manual for Writers of Term Papers, Theses, and Dissertations.* Chicago: U of Chicago P, 1955.

U.S. GEOLOGICAL SURVEY. *Suggestions to Authors of Reports of the United States Geological Survey.* 6th ed.   Washington, DC: GPO, 1978.

U.S. GOVERNMENT PRINTING OFFICE. *Style Manual.* Washington, DC: GPO, 1984.

UNIVERSITY OF CHICAGO. *The Chicago Manual of Style.* 13th ed.   Chicago: U of Chicago P, 1982.

CHAPTER 12

Designing and Integrating Graphic Aids

The quantity and complexity of data and information contained in today's managerial reports can occasionally overwhelm audiences. During the planning and writing of your report, you have discovered topics within the document that you believe require greater explanation, simplification, emphasis, or clarification. **Graphic aids** enable you to convert textual material into tabular or pictorial form. By properly designing and integrating graphic aids into your report, you can significantly enhance reader comprehension and use of the information in the document, thereby increasing the overall functionality and effectiveness of the document and its message.

Although the terms *graphic aids* and *visuals* are often used interchangeably, we can make one general, yet significant, distinction between the two. *Graphic aids* refers to nontextual material that (a) is tabular or pictorial in form, such as tables and figures, and (b) is used in hard-copy documents such as articles, reports, and books. *Visual aids*, on the other hand, refers to data or information (in tabular or pictorial form) that is integrated into oral presentations. Commonly used visuals include flip charts, overhead transparencies, slides, and computer graphics displays. This chapter examines graphic aids specifically and focuses on the

    important purposes for using graphic aids.

    guidelines for designing effective graphics.

    methods for integrating graphics into your report.

    commonly used types of tables and figures found in today's managerial reports.

Purposes of Graphic Aids

The purposes for using graphic aids are as varied as the types of reports in which they are placed. Well-designed and properly integrated graphics

explain and simplify for readers complex data and information contained in the report.

emphasize key material such as important figures, trends, and concepts.

summarize and condense vast amounts of material into a manageable and orderly form, thereby saving space while also increasing reader comprehension.

provide insights into the report problem and possible solutions that might otherwise have been overlooked if relevant data and information were buried in text form.

offer readers key information in an easily and quickly accessible form, enabling them to make sound decisions more quickly.

improve the quality of readers' decisions when based on accurately and thoroughly represented central issues, their significance, and the interrelationships between them.

reduce the level of reader resistance to reading page after page of text, which ultimately increases the readability of your report.

increase the credibility of your report and its findings by projecting a sense of order, preparedness, and professionalism.

As discussed throughout this chapter, the key to realizing some or all of the above purposes is that the graphic aid must be *functional*. Effective graphics are not decoration but, rather, communication tools whose central function is to supplement text so that the document might convey important data and information more efficiently and effectively.

Designing Graphic Aids

Today the visually oriented business world and its supporting technology oblige report writers to consider how best to design and present graphic aids that not only instruct but also attract readers accustomed to such dynamic visual forms of communication as television, motion pictures, laser video discs, and computer graphics. An important aim, for example, of corporate annual reports—a major component in an organization's projection of its public image—is to dazzle their audiences with color graphics in an assortment of forms, including photographs, pie charts, line graphs, and bar graphs. One international beer producer even included in its yearly report a sophisticated, as well as costly, hologram of its name superimposed over the company's eagle mascot.

Effective graphics, however, are more than visual acrobatics meant to decorate an organization's documents and attract the attention of readers. Well-designed graphics, once having sparked readers' interest, spur readers into delving more deeply into the data and ideas contained in the report. Effective graphics must always be functional; that is, they must serve a specific purpose in order to justify the time, expense, and expertise an organization invests in designing and producing them. Fully functional graphics are not, for instance, last-minute afterthoughts ill advisedly inserted into a report simply as filler or to make the document look more professional; nor are they used to retrofit a report that is short on substance with attractive "whistles and bells" in order to dress it up.

Effective graphics are designed and modified throughout the entire report-writing process—from researching the report subject to planning the report format to composing and revising the document's text. From the very beginning of the report-writing process, you should identify which topics require the assistance of graphic aids. You might make a running list of needed graphics, their planned placement in the report, and the type of information each graphic aid should contain. As you revise the text of your report, you will gradually refine the focus, content, and design of the document's graphics. During this development process, consider such central design concerns as

the number and size of graphics to be included in your report.

the system for labeling and numbering your graphics.

the most appropriate titles and captions for the graphics.

what footnotes and source lines might be required in the graphics.

the spacing and format of the graphics.

Number and Size of Graphics

The number of graphic aids contained in your report will depend on the particular needs of your document. Including superfluous graphic aids in your document is just as counterproductive as omitting helpful graphics necessary to supplement important data or concepts contained in the report text. The outlines you completed earlier in the report-writing process should assist you in identifying most of the major topics that warrant a graphic aid; however, more specific sections of key data or central ideas not included in the outline might require graphics as well.

The size of each graphic aid will depend on different variables surrounding the need and use of the graphic. How much information, for example, must the graphic contain? What is the physical size of the document in which the graphic is to be placed—standard 8.5- × 11-in. bond paper, legal-size paper, or paper offering special texture and consistency? What is the importance of the graphic? Should more important graphics in your report be larger for greater exposure and emphasis? How large must the graphic be to ensure appropriate readability of its content?

A graphic aid should normally fit on one page. Examine closely the need for any graphic longer than a page. When constructing multipage tables, repeat column headings on subsequent pages. You should also identify each multipage table or figure at the top of each additional page, usually in the upper left or right corner [e.g., "Table 1 (*continued*)"]. In addition, notify readers that the graphic continues onto a subsequent page by placing the note "(*continued*)" at the bottom of the previous page or at the top of the subsequent page. Oversized graphics—such as large diagrams, maps, and charts—can be folded (usually into thirds or quarters). Graphics with a vertical orientation on the page should be placed so that the top of the graphic runs along the left margin, the side of the report page that is normally bound.

Because long tables or multipage figures tend to interrupt the pace and flow of a report, you might place such graphics in an appendix. Readers interested in delving more deeply into the data relevant to a particular topic may refer to that section of the report for more extensive and specific information. Keep in mind that not all graphic aids may be immediately important enough to the topic at hand and, consequently, should be placed in an appendix rather than in the body of your report.

Label and Number System

Each graphic aid should be labeled and numbered. You can refer to graphics in various ways, depending on the different types and the combination of graphics contained in your report. For example, if your document includes numerous tables and figures, you will probably want to label the graphics as "Table 1," "Table 2," "Table 3" (or "Table I," "Table II," "Table III"); "Figure 1," "Figure 2," "Figure 3"; and so on. Any graphic aid that is not a table is referred to as a figure. Number all tables and figures in the order in which they appear in the report. If your report contains multiple chapters or sections, you may want to identify the graphic aid with its corresponding chapter by using a decimal point in the graphic label and number. The label and number "Figure 2.3," for example, identify the graphic as the third figure in the second chapter or section of a report. "Table 3.1" would be the label and number for the first table in the third chapter or section of a report.

Although your report may contain various types of figures (e.g., charts, diagrams, photos, maps), the encompassing label of "Figure" simplifies for readers your method of referencing them. If your report, however, contains numerous graphics in various figure formats, you may want to be more specific by using such label categories as "Chart 1," "Chart 2"; "Diagram 1," "Diagram 2"; "Map 1," "Map 2"; and so on. To simplify and standardize the labeling of all graphics, many report writers, especially in the sciences, have adopted the "Exhibit" label when referring to tables as well as the different types of figures (e.g., "Exhibit 1," "Exhibit 2").

The label and number for a table are normally centered above the graphic aid along with the table title, as illustrated in Figure 12.1. The label and number for figures have traditionally been placed below the figure and flush on the left margin as shown in Figure 12.2. Some contemporary managerial reports support a more uniform placement of labels, numbers, and titles *above* the graphic aid, regardless of whether it is a table or a figure.

Titles and Captions

You should determine the title for each graphic aid much as you select the title and headings contained in your report. Carefully word the title so that readers

TABLE 2. PERSONAL CHARACTERISTICS AND JOBS

	1 Problem-solving ability	2 Uses tools, machinery	3 Instructs others	4 Repetitious	5 Hazardous	6 Outdoors	7 Physical stamina required	8 Generally confined	9 Precision	10 Works with detail	11 Frequent public contact	12 Part-time	13 Able to see results	14 Creativity	15 Influences others	16 Competition on the job	17 Works as part of a team	18 Jobs widely scattered	19 Initiative
INDUSTRIAL PRODUCTION OCCUPATIONS																			
Foundry occupations																			
Patternmakers																			
Molders		●		●	●		●	●	●	●			●				●		
Coremakers		●		●			●	●		●			●				●		
Machining occupations																			
✓ All-round machinists	●	●		●			●	●	●	●			●				●		
Instrument markers (mechanical)	●	●		●			●	●	●	●			●	●			●	●	●
Machine tool operators	●	●		●	●		●	●	●	●			●	●			●		
Setup workers (machine tools)	●	●		●	●		●		●	●			●				●		
Tool-and-die makers	●	●		●			●	●	●	●			●				●		
Printing occupations																			
✓ Compositors		●					●	●	●				●				●		
Lithographers		●					●	●	●				●				●		
Photoengravers		●					●	●	●				●	●			●		
Electrotypers and stereotypers		●		●			●	●	●				●						
Printing press operators		●		●	●		●	●					●				●		
Bookbinders and bindery workers		●		●	●		●	●					●						
Other industrial production and related occupations																			
✓ Assemblers		●		●				●	●							●			
Automobile painters								●	●										
Blacksmiths		●		●	●		●		●		●	●					●		
Blue-collar worker supervisors	●		●							●					●		●	●	●
Boilermaking occupations	●	●		●	●		●		●	●			●				●		
Boiler tenders		●		●			●		●								●		
Electroplaters		●		●	●		●						●				●		
Forge shop occupations		●		●	●		●		●				●						
Furniture upholsterers		●		●			●		●				●	●			●		
Inspectors (manufacturing)	●	●		●			●	●	●				●				●		
Millwrights	●	●		●			●	●	●	●							●		
Motion picture projectionists		●		●			●		●	●		●					●		
Ophthalmic laboratory technicians		●		●			●	●									●		
Photographic laboratory occupations		●		●			●										●		
Power truck operators		●		●	●	●	●										●		
Production painters		●		●	●	●	●						●				●		
Stationary engineers	●	●		●			●										●		
Wastewater treatment plant operators	●	●			●		●										●	●	
Welders		●		●	●	●		●					●				●	●	
OFFICE OCCUPATIONS																			
Clerical occupations																			
Bookkeeping workers			●					●	●	●		●	●				●	●	
Cashiers			●					●	●	●	●	●			●		●	●	
Collection workers			●					●	●	●	●						●	●	●
File clerks			●						●	●	●	●					●	●	
Office machine operators		●	●					●	●	●		●					●	●	
Postal clerks		●	●					●	●	●	●						●	●	
Receptionists			●	●				●		●	●	●					●	●	
Secretaries and stenographers			●					●	●		●	●	●				●	●	

FIGURE 12.1

Sample table.

EXHIBIT 3: PAY EQUITY

INDEX OF OCCUPATIONS:

ALSO INCLUDES THE NUMBER OF MALE AND FEMALE WORKERS IN EACH FIELD.

MANAGERIAL AND PROFESSIONAL
SPECIALTY OCCUPATIONS
(MALE–11,555,000 — FEMALE–9,339,000)

SECRETARIES, STENOGRAPHERS,
AND TYPISTS
(MALE–68,000 — FEMALE–3,881,000)

ENGINEERS, ARCHITECTS,
AND SURVEYORS
(MALE–1,623,000 — FEMALE–115,000)

POLICE AND
DETECTIVES
(MALE–627,000 — FEMALE–80,000)

MATHEMATICAL AND
COMPUTER SCIENTISTS
(MALE–405,000 — FEMALE–222,000)

MAIDS AND
HOUSEMEN
(MALE–75,000 — FEMALE–291,000)

HEALTH ASSESSMENT
AND TREATING OCCUPATIONS
(MALE–243,000 — FEMALE–1,309,000)

JANITORS AND
CLEANERS
(MALE–1,030,000 — FEMALE–297,000)

TEACHERS, ELEMENTARY
SCHOOL
(MALE–171,000 — FEMALE–1,002,000)

OPERATORS, FABRICATORS,
AND LABORERS
(MALE–10,926,000 — FEMALE–3,716,000)

MEDIAN WEEKLY EARNING OF WAGE AND SALARY WORKERS WHO USUALLY WORK FULL TIME, BY SEX, 1987 ANNUAL AVERAGES.

INDEX
● MALE
■ FEMALE

Figure 12.2

Sample figure.

Source: U.S. Department of Labor, Bureau of Labor Statistics; by B. Castrodale, 1988.

can easily and quickly recognize the focus of the information contained in the graphic aid. The title should present an accurate and complete picture of the significant message communicated by the graphic, yet it must also be concise. As with the report title (see Chapter 14), address the journalist's five *W*s: *who, what, where, when,* and *why.* The following sample title answers all five of the journalist's prompts:

> The Impact of the Army's 1983–1988 Media Campaign Using Broadcast National Media and Narrowcast Local Media

Although the *why* is not explicitly expressed in the title, readers have no difficulty inferring the purpose of the graphic: to illustrate the effectiveness of the Army's media campaign between 1983 and 1988. Including all five *W*s in your graphic title may occasionally prove impractical or unnecessary; however, the more specific and encompassing you can be in your wording, the more useful the title will be to the report audience(s).

Although the terms *title* and *caption* are often used interchangeably, the two are distinct in meaning and usage. A caption is normally used only with figures, while titles are required with tables and figures. Placed below a figure, a caption is in essence a focused title that draws reader attention to a specific item in a figure. For example, a bar graph illustrating the growth in car sales of an automobile company may carry the following title:

> Growth in Sales of Excalibur Models 1985 to 1990

To stress the significant growth in sales of one specific car model, the report writer may well include a caption in the same figure:

> Figure 1. Sales of the Excalibur Marbella Rise 73%

Titles of tables have traditionally been centered after the "Table" label two lines above the graphic, while those for figures have been placed after the "Figure" label two lines below the frame line. For greater uniformity, however, many present-day authors are choosing to center all titles and labels above the tables or figures.

When including a caption in your figure, you should normally center the figure title two lines above the graphic. Place the caption after the label and number, two lines below the frame line of the figure. If the title occupies more than one line, single- space and center the remainder of the title on the following line. Titles are normally printed in lowercase letters, with the first letter of the first word and all following key words (i.e., usually all words except prepositions and conjunctions) capitalized. Unless the title is a complete sentence, include no end punctuation (e.g., period, question mark).

Footnotes and Source Lines

You may occasionally decide to comment on information in a graphic aid for any number of reasons. Your research might have produced an incomplete array of data, making several important items unavailable for your graphic. Under such circumstances, you would want to briefly explain the absence of such data from your table. Moreover, perhaps a figure you provide in a table, though accurate, does not represent the full significance of your findings; thus, an explanation might be required. Perhaps your color-coded pie chart needs a brief legend or key to identify each color. In all these cases, you would probably make additional comments for the sake of clarity by including a footnote below the table or figure itself.

You can refer to information to be footnoted by placing special footnote symbols immediately after the item—such as one or more asterisks (*), a degree symbol (°), daggers (†), or lowercase letters (*a, b, c*). You may raise the special footnote symbols slightly above the line in superscript position for greater emphasis. Place the footnote itself two lines below the lowest part of the graphic (e.g., below the frame line of a table or the label, number, and title of a figure). Begin the footnote with the special footnote symbol on the left margin and close the notation with your brief comment.

You may also footnote graphics by using the term *Note* instead of the special footnote symbols. *Note* works well when commenting on the entire graphic, rather than several specific items. Begin the footnote with *Note*, followed by a colon. Skip two spaces and insert the notation.

In addition to commenting on the nature or significance of the information contained in a graphic aid, you may choose to note the actual source of the material. Whenever including in your graphics data or information gathered from secondary sources, you must cite those sources at the bottom of the graphic aid. The **source line,** like the sample that follows, should identify for readers the secondary source(s) from which you collected all (or part) of the information contained in the graphic. Source lines typically include the name of the work's author (or sponsoring organization), year of publication, and page number(s) where the information can be found:

Source: World Bank, 1991, pp. 298–301.

As with any footnote placed in the text of your report, the complete bibliographic citation for the reference (in this case, the World Bank source) should be included on the reference page.

Information that you have collected from primary research and included in your graphics does not have to be footnoted. However, you may choose to clarify the source of such material by using the following source line:

Source: Primary.

When including both footnote(s) and source line together in the same graphic, place the source after the footnote(s). Single-space within footnotes and source lines; double-space between each component and the graphic itself.

Rules and Frames

Rules and frames can enhance the appearance of your graphic aids, while also making it easier for readers to access and understand the information contained in the graphics. Vertical and horizontal **rules** are lines typically used within tables to separate columns and rows of tabulated data. Simple tables with few columns and rows of data often need no rules. However, the use of vertical or horizontal rules in complex tables can greatly help your readers to line up columns and rows of data and information in a table matrix.

Frames, sometimes called *borders*, are horizontal or vertical lines that set the graphic off from the text of the report. You should use frames whenever the graphic is inserted between passages of text. Graphics set off on their own pages may also require frames for emphasis. As a general rule, leave an inch between the text and frame line. Leave the same amount of spacing between the frame and the information within the graphic aid. You should not normally place frames slightly beyond the margin of the report.

Color

Readers have become increasingly demanding in their expectations of graphic aids in a professional report. Graphics must not only present meaningful data and information clearly and accurately but also convey this material in an appealing manner and with color. While color graphics, and graphics in general, have traditionally been left to the skilled and steady hand of corporate artists, computer graphics software now allows anyone to design and produce multicolor graphic aids of exceptional quality.

Color attracts reader interest while aiding audiences to better read and interpret the information contained in the graphic itself. Color-coded lines in a line chart, for example, assist readers in distinguishing between the lines, as well as in comparing their movement and values. Color-coded pie charts and bar graphs also simplify the task of reading the data and comparing the items contained in the graphic.

When selecting colors for a graphic aid, be sure that the colors stand out from each other. Choose from basic colors such as reds, greens, yellows, and blues. In addition, vary the colors and, if one color must be repeated, use distinctive shades of it. Five similar shades of blue in the same bar chart will probably confuse readers and either delay or prevent your audience from fully grasping the graphic's information and its meaning.

Furthermore, you should determine which colors and shades are most appropriate for the nature of information you are attempting to convey. Be conscious of the emotive and cultural associations that most colors carry. For example, red usually communicates a sense of importance, urgency, perhaps even danger, depending on the context in which it is used. Green and blue tend to serve as more neutral and soothing colors. In addition, before deciding on a color scheme for your graphic, test the colors for reproducibility. Some shades reproduce poorly when making photocopies or overhead transparencies.

If color proves too impractical as a graphic-enhancing tool, you might try **crosshatching** such graphics as pie charts, bar graphs, maps, and diagrams with diagonal lines (Figure 12.1). By varying the angle of the crosshatching, you can effectively distinguish for readers, for example, the wedges in a pie chart or the different states on a map graphic. When crosshatching is not possible, you might consider diversifying the format of the lines themselves. You could, for instance, use an unbroken line when showing the values of one item, a broken line for a second item, a dash-dot-dash line for a third, and a dot line for a fourth. A central disadvantage of both crosshatching and line diversification is their limited repertoire of variations. Graphics containing more than five or six different items make the use of crosshatching and line diversification unmanageable.

Integrating Graphics Into Your Report

After constructing the appropriate number and type(s) of graphic aids required in your report, you should take care to integrate them properly into the document. Misplaced or poorly introduced or explained graphics can easily weaken the clarity and credibility of a report. You can effectively integrate graphic aids by following three basic steps:

1. Refer to the graphic at least once in the report.
2. Insert the graphic as close to its first reference as possible (unless it is to be placed in an appendix). For example, if you refer to a table on page 3 of your report, you should place the table on the same page as that first reference or on the following page.
3. Explain the significance of the graphic as it relates to your topic.

Figure 12.3 illustrates how a graphic aid can be effectively integrated into a document by following these three steps.

Assay findings of the Shore Zone, as shown in Figure 3, suggest that the site may be considerably less profitable in gold production than the West Zone. Total tonnage (618,397) is lower than expected, as is the ounce-per-ton for gold (.268). However, with an average ounce-per-ton figure of 29.12 for silver, the Shore Zone promises to be a more productive source of silver (on a per-ton basis) for the company than the West Zone.

TABLE 3. Shore Zone Mineral Inventory

SHORE ZONE	TONS	GOLD (oz/ton)	SILVER (oz/ton)
Proven	105,044	.243	34.15
Probable	154,240	.337	31.22
Inferred	359,113	.225	21.99
	618,397 (Total)	**.268** (Average)	**29.12** (Average)

Source: American Mining Services, Inc., 1990.

Although the Shore Zone is in the proximity of Sprucejack Lake and its watershed, Newmont exploration and mining specialists (1) do not expect any complications to mining efforts caused by lake or watershed water, and (2) foresee no contamination of the lake or its dependent wildlife due to mining activities.

FIGURE 12.3

Effective integration of a graphic aid.

Always refer to your graphic at least once in your report. You can refer to the aid in various ways. You might, for example, make an explicit reference to the graphic in your text, as do the following references:

> ..., as illustrated in Figure 3...
> As shown in Table 1, ...
> ..., while Chart 14 suggests that ...
> Exhibit 5 indicates that ...

You might also refer to the graphic aid by placing its label and number in parentheses:

> ...(Figure 3).
> ...(Table 1),...

Remember that the graphic aid should be self-contained to convey effectively the appropriate information. The reader should not have to refer to the text to understand the fundamental meaning of the material contained in the graphic aid. However, graphic aids are communication tools designed to contain *supplemental* information that—although important in explaining, clarifying, or simplifying material contained in the report—should never be used as a substitute for the report itself. A reader should not have to depend on only a graphic aid to understand the central ideas and data expressed in the report.

Remember that *you* are the presumed expert on the topic of your report. You should sufficiently discuss in your text the key information contained in your report's graphic aids. You have included the graphic in your document because you believe it helps to clarify or emphasize important data and information contained in the report text.

Leaving readers to interpret for themselves the meaning of a graphic aid (a) deprives your audience of your valuable insights into the significance of the information and (b) invites inaccurate interpretations of the aid's function, meaning, or significance by readers who, for the most part, are less knowledgeable in the area of study than you. Therefore, help readers in their analysis of the data and information that you are providing in the graphic. Highlight for them in the text of your report the key pieces of information contained in the graphic. Then explain how and why that material is important when considering solutions to the problem at hand. Keep in mind that graphic aids that are not central to the discussion within the report proper should be placed in an appendix or omitted from the document entirely.

Tables

All graphic aids can be categorized as either tables or figures. The content contained in **tables** can range from general information relating to your report topic to specific information that offers a detailed focus on a particular issue within the report topic. Tables are most effective in providing readers with accurate, specific, and complex information (especially numerical values) in an easily accessible and compact package. In their physical format, as well as their content, tables are either tabular or textual in form.

Tables organize information graphically in orderly columns and, in most cases, rows. Tables composed of a matrix of both columns and rows of primarily nontextual information (e.g., numbers, symbols, equations) are called **tabular** tables, as illustrated in Figure 12.4. **Textual** tables consist of phrases or sentences and serve, for the most part, to summarize information discussed elsewhere in the text, as shown in Figure 12.5.

Both tabular and textual tables can be placed in either formal or informal formats. Besides having a label, number, title, and perhaps a footnote or source line, formal tables contain **stub lines** that separate the title, **column heads,** rows and columns of information, and often subtable material (i.e., footnotes and source lines), as illustrated in Figure 12.6. Your table may also require that some column heads contain subheadings. In such cases, you would probably choose to include a **spanner head** to unify the different subheads. Formal tables adhere, for the most part, to the table construction provided in Figure 12.6. They are included in the report's "List of Illustrations" and are typically framed and ruled.

As their name implies, informal tables do not adhere to the standard structure of a formal table. They normally contain small chunks of information (numerical or textual) specific to the passages on report text between which they are placed. Informal tables are not labeled, numbered, or titled, and they include no frames or rules as used by most formal tables. Moreover, informal tables are not noted on the "List of Illustrations" page. Most informal tables are relatively small clusters of data strategically integrated between relevant sections of text. They serve as easily accessible and comprehensible lists of key data that are set off from surrounding text by borders of white space, as shown by the sample informal table below:

	October	November	December
BankAmerica	$35.5*	$30.0	$27.5
Fannie May	42.0	40.7	41.0
Sotheby's Holdings	34.2	28.5	23.0

* (in millions of dollars)

Informal tables help emphasize to readers important information that might otherwise be overlooked if placed in a paragraph of text. In addition, informal tables serve as subtle layout tools, as their white space gives readers a break from often dense passages of textual material. To help readers align items with their corresponding values, some informal tables, like the sample provided above, include **leaderwork,** a line of dots that normally connect text with its respective numerical data.

When designing your table, consider some fundamental layout and format guidelines for this specific graphic aid:

- Organize the information logically in the graphic (e.g., by order of importance, alphabetically, chronologically).

Direction of Trade: Destination of Canadian Forest Product Exports (in millions of dollars)

	(1) Pulpwood		(2) Saw and Veneer Logs (C)		(3) Lumber Shaped (C)		(4) Woodpulp		(5) Newsprint		Total Columns (1) to (5)	
	Value	Percent Total	Value	Percent Total	Value	Percent Total	Value	Percent Total	Value	Percent Total	Value	Percent Total
1973 EXPORTS TO												
Europe (EEC)	1.6	6	—	—	136.2	9	258.3	24	94.8	7	490.9	15
United States	24.3	87	0.7	—	1263.0	81	624.0	59	1072.9	83	2335.9	71
Japan	—	—	4.5	—	116.6	7	97.5	9	6.6	1	225.2	7
Other	2.1	7	—	—	45.7	3	82.6	8	111.6	9	242.0	7
Total	28.0	100	5.2	100	1561.5	100	1062.4	100	1285.9	100	3294.0	100
1977 EXPORTS TO												
Europe (EEC)	2.0	13	—	—	149.3	7	580.8	29	168.5	8	900.6	14
United States	12.7	83	16.3	39	1856.5	84	1113.2	55	1770.7	79	4769.4	73
Japan	—	—	23.8	58	126.5	6	150.5	7	—	—	300.9	5
Other	0.6	4	1.3	3	60.0	3	184.5	9	298.8	13	545.2	8
Total	15.3	100	41.4	100	2192.4	100	2029.0	100	2238.0	100	6516.1	100
1978 EXPORTS TO												
Europe (EEC)	3.3	15	—	—	165.7	6	538.4	28	182.7	7	890.1	12
United States	18.0	85	10.1	31	2393.2	86	1001.3	52	2081.6	81	5504.2	75
Japan	—	—	20.8	64	158.1	6	184.8	10	—	—	363.7	5
Other	—	—	1.6	5	70.3	2	206.9	10	292.8	12	571.6	8
Total	21.3	100	32.5	100	2787.3	100	1931.4	100	2557.1	100	7329.6	100

Source: FAO, Yearbook of Forest Products, 1978

FIGURE 12.4

Tabular table.

HOUSEHOLD DATA NOT SEASONALLY ADJUSTED QUARTERLY AVERAGES

A-57. Work-seeking intentions of persons not in the labor force and work history of those who intend to seek work within the next 12 months by sex, age, and race

(in thousands)

Work-seeking intentions, work history, and sex	Total		Age						Race			
			16 to 24 years		25 to 59 years		60 years and over		White		Black	
	II 1988	II 1989	II 1988	II 1989	II 1988	II 1989	II 1988	II 1989	II 1988	II 1989	II 1988	II 1989
TOTAL												
Do not intend to seek work	54,717	54,078	6,240	5,901	17,608	17,177	30,869	31,000	47,017	46,439	5,997	5,974
Intend to seek work in the next 12 months	8,316	8,319	4,122	4,025	3,670	3,752	524	541	6,397	6,358	1,583	1,596
Never worked	1,582	1,447	1,473	1,242	111	195	—	9	1,065	960	434	377
Last worked over 5 years ago	1,114	1,081	69	65	850	834	194	182	831	767	237	287
Last worked 1 to 5 years ago	1,752	1,851	438	508	1,142	1,176	173	166	1,271	1,408	400	358
Worked during previous 12 months	3,869	3,940	2,143	2,209	1,568	1,547	157	184	3,231	3,222	513	574
Men												
Do not intend to seek work	17,729	17,620	2,486	2,278	3,329	3311	11,914	12,030	15,027	14,907	2,122	2,133
Intend to seek work in the next 12 months	2,999	3,086	1,879	1,896	895	962	225	228	2,346	2,363	534	593
Never worked	708	658	695	623	12	34	—	1	472	428	211	192
Last worked over 5 years ago	233	219	26	18	134	140	65	—	178	142	30	71
Last worked 1 to 5 years ago	534	585	153	183	294	314	86	—	420	443	90	106
Worked during previous 12 months	1,535	1,624	1,005	1070	456	475	75	78	1,276	1,349	203	224
Women												
Do not intend to seek work	36,988	36,458	3,753	3,621	14,281	13,865	18,954	18,970	31,990	31,532	3,875	3,840
Intend to seek work in the next 12 months	5,317	5,233	2,224	2,131	2,773	2,790	299	313	4,051	3,995	1,049	1,003
Never worked	874	788	778	619	98	162	—	9	593	532	224	185
Last worked over 5 years ago	890	862	43	48	719	694	129	121	653	625	206	216
Last worked 1 to 5 years ago	1,219	1,266	286	326	845	863	86	78	851	851	310	251
Worked during previous 12 months	2,333	2,316	1,138	1,139	1,112	1,073	84	105	1,955	1,995	310	350

FIGURE **12.4**

Continued

- Identify each column and row of information with clear and accurate headings.
- Normally, place column and row totals at the end of each row or column, or as needed, though totals may appear at the beginnings of rows and columns as well for greater emphasis.
- Convert all fractions into their decimal equivalents.
- Align numerical data in columns by decimal point; round off numbers as the level of precision warrants.
- Where no data are available, use the dash (two hyphens), the abbreviation N.A., or three dots (...); do not use a zero as it can confuse readers in their interpretation of the data.

TABLE 10-II. PHOTOGRAPHIC MAPPING SITES

Site	Name	Objective
M1	Gulf Stream	The Gulf Loop Current and the Gulf Stream from eastern Florida to its confluence with the Labrador Current
M2	New Zealand	The Alpine Fault in South Island and the coastal waters between the two islands and north of North Island
M3	Southern California	Coastal waters off California, the San Andreas Fault system, and the Mohave Desert
M4	Himalaya Mountains	Ocean features in the Indian Ocean and Arabian Sea, the flood plain of the Indus River, drainage patterns, and snow cover in the Himalayas
M5	Arabian Desert	The Afar Triangle, dune patterns in Ar-Rub Al-Khali, and coastal processes at Doha, Qatar
M6	Australia	Dune patterns and erosional features in the Simpson Desert, the Great Barrier Reef, and eddies in the Coral Sea
M7	African drought	Vegetation and land use patterns in the Sahel, desert colors in northeastern Africa, the Nile River Delta, and the Levantine Rift
M8	Falkland Current	The Falkland Current and its confluence with the Brazil Current east of South America
M9	Sahara	Vegetation and land use patterns in the Sahel, desert colors and dune patterns in the Sahara, and coastal waters off Tripoli
M10	Northern California	Coastal waters off northern California and subsystems of the San Andreas Fault
M11	New England	Eddies and gyres in the Gulf of Mexico, the Mississippi River Delta, Chesapeake Bay, and coastal waters off New England

Source: National Aeronautics and Space Administration

FIGURE 12.5

Textual table.

- Place unit definitions (e.g., pounds, tons, gallons, years) of numerical data in column heads; use standard unit abbreviations and common symbols (e.g., %, #).
- Place the dollar sign (and that of other commonly known currencies) with the first column entry and the total entry only (Schmid & Schmid, 1979; Tufte 1983).

Table XX. Table Title

| Stub Head | Column Head | Column Head | Spanner Head | |
			Column Subhead	Column Subhead
Row Head*	XXXX	XXXX	XXXX	XXXX
Row Head**	XXXX	XXXX	XXXX	XXXX
Row Head	XXXX	XXXX	XXXX	XXXX
"	"	"	"	"
"	"	"	"	"
"	"	"	"	"
"	"	"	"	"
"	"	"	"	"
TOTAL	XXXX	XXXX	XXXX	XXXX

* Footnote 1
** Footnote 2
Source:

FIGURE 12.6
Formal table construction.

Tables—tabular and textual, formal and informal—are excellent graphic aids for communicating detailed and precise data and information. However, you should use tables only when you believe the collection of data will assist readers in understanding the meaning and significance of your message. For audiences with less knowledge or technical expertise on the subject of your report, large tables of complex data may prove more confusing and frustrating than instructive.

Moreover, as tables are primarily static in nature, they are not an effective means of illustrating dynamic trends or tendencies (e.g., significant growth, dramatic decline) in numerical values. To emphasize and clarify in a meaningful way important dynamic movements in numerical data, you might consider integrating into your managerial report one or a combination of figures.

Figures

When tables cannot appropriately convey the information you wish to present in a graphic aid, integrating a figure into your report might be the solution. The most commonly used figures in today's managerial reports include various types of charts, graphs, pictograms, diagrams, maps, and photographs.

Graphs

Perhaps the most popular and frequently used figures are the graph and chart. Although the two terms are often used interchangeably, they are, in fact, distinct in both meaning and function. **Graphs** are figures that plot values on a coordinate system (i.e., on a grid of columns and rows). **Charts,** on the other hand, depict relationships between items and their respective values without using a grid. Bar, line, and surface graphs are the most commonly used form of graph in managerial reports (Lannor, 1991, p. 254).

Line Graphs

Line graphs use a printed line to represent and plot the changing numerical values of an item. As the values change, the line rises and falls as it is plotted across a **grid,** a field of intersecting vertical and horizontal lines. Line graphs are most effective when used to illustrate the quantitative changes in one or more items over a period of time. Often dynamic quantities—such as prices, sales, and income—and the cause-and-effect relationships between them can be more clearly and quickly communicated through line graphs than in text.

As shown in Figure 12.7, the *X-* (horizontal) and *Y-* (vertical) **axes** provide the boundaries and measurement scale for the grid. The intersection of these two axes creates four quadrants. Because management reports deal, for the most part, with data of positive values, your line chart will probably include only the first quadrant of the whole grid.

A line connecting different coordinates plotted between the *X-* and *Y-*axes displays how the numerical value of an item changes over time. Time—often in

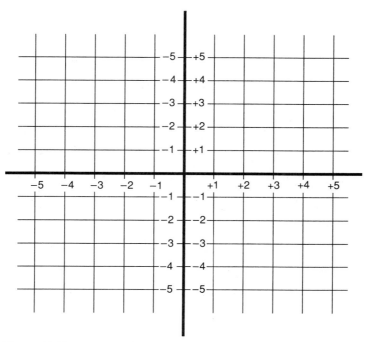

Figure 12.7
Grid of four line-graph quadrants.

the form of months, quarters, years—is commonly placed on the X-axis. The Y-axis frequently serves to quantify the amount of change an item undergoes over specific periods of time. For this reason, the Y-axis is scaled according to relevant measurements of the item being plotted, such as monetary amounts, distances, and weights. In Figure 12.8, the single plotted line represents the fluctuating point values of the Dow Jones Index from August 1986 to October 1989.

You can also plot the values of independent and dependent variables from, say, the results of experimental research you might have performed by using the X- and Y-axes. The X-axis (often referred to as the **base,** or **abscissa,** axis) is always reserved for independent variables. Dependent variables are placed on the Y-axis, also called the **scale,** or **ordinate,** axis.

In constructing your line chart, calibrate both the X- and the Y-axes with vertical (on the X-axis) or horizontal (on the Y-axis) **hash marks,** or **tick marks,** to denote each calibration. Be sure to leave equal space intervals between each hashmark to avoid distortion of the line. The lengths of both axes should be roughly equal. Label the axes, placing the caption below the X-axis and to the left of the Y-axis. Plot each point where data on the X-axis intersect data on the Y-axis. Connect those points to form a continuous line.

When plotting more than one line, distinguish between items by color-coding them. You might also use different line formats to differentiate lines in a multiple-line graph, including solid lines (———), broken lines (– – –), dash-dot lines (— · —), dots (· · · ·), or any combination of these. Identify the item or variable that each line represents by including a legend in a corner of the chart. If space limitations preclude the use of a legend, you might label the items by placing captions on a horizontal line near the items and connecting captions and item tag lines.

Line graphs can significantly expand readers' understanding of the data in your report as well as reduce the time required by readers to decode and

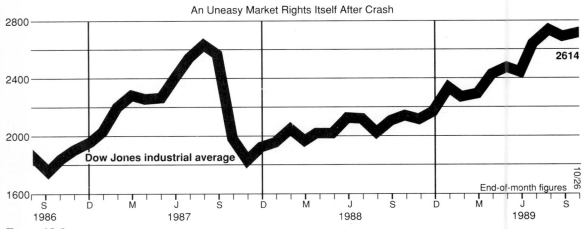

FIGURE 12.8
Simple line graph.

interpret your message. However, when not properly constructed, line graphs, like any graphic aid, can easily decrease the accuracy, accessibility, and effectiveness of your report. When designing and constructing your line chart, avoid some of the more common errors presented here:

- As a general rule, integrate no more than five lines into your line chart. A chart crammed with lines, regardless of the care you take in identifying each, invariably confuses readers.
- Begin your calibration of the *Y*-axis at zero. If the range from zero to the highest value on the axis is too great to be represented within the space of the chart, break the vertical axis by using a slash, zed, or graph break, as shown in Figure 12.9 (Bovee & Thill, 1986, p. 476; Cleveland & McGill, 1988; Murgio, 1969, p. 83).
- Calibrate values of an axis at equal increments. As Figure 12.10 illustrates, unequal increments distort the meaning of data (Lannon, 1991, pp. 249–254).

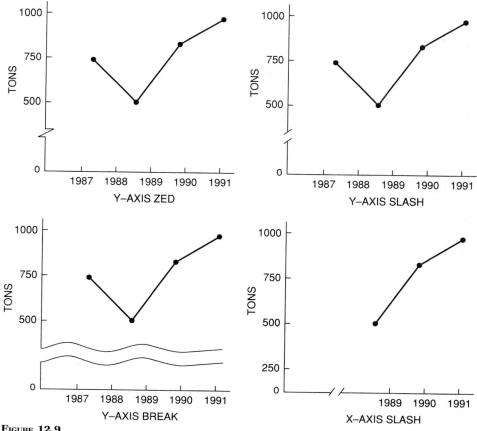

FIGURE 12.9

Methods for breaking *X*- and *Y*-axes.

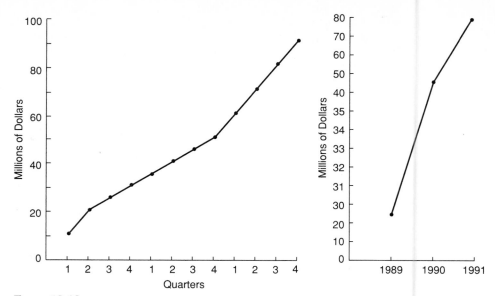

FIGURE 12.10

Distorted presentation of data using unequal calibration of *X*- and *Y*-axes.

- Choose increments that most accurately depict the true meaning and significance of your data. Because this is often a matter of discretion, it is important that you maintain your objectivity so as not to distort your presentation of the data. Figure 12.11 shows the same data plotted on two different charts, each with radically different value increments on the *Y*-axis.
- Omit grid lines most of the time, as they are not normally needed by readers in estimating the values of plotted items or variables (Spear, 1969).

When constructing a **multiple-line graph,** as that shown in Figure 12.12, be sure to label each line by using different colors, tag lines, or a legend placed in open space on the chart. To aid readers in determining the value of key coordinates, you might plot the points of coordinates at important locations on the chart.

Surface Graphs

On occasion, you may want to measure and plot multiple components of a single item. A **surface graph,** also called a **belt** or **band graph,** is a variation of the line chart that allows you to illustrate the numerical changes in each subcomponent of an item. As shown in Figure 12.13, the values of the components of a surface chart add up to 100% of the overall value represented on the item.

Although it resembles a multiple-line graph, the surface graph is read very differently. As you recall, the value of a line in a multiple-line graph is measured from the baseline of the graph to the position of any coordinate on that line. In a surface graph, however, each line represents a percentage of

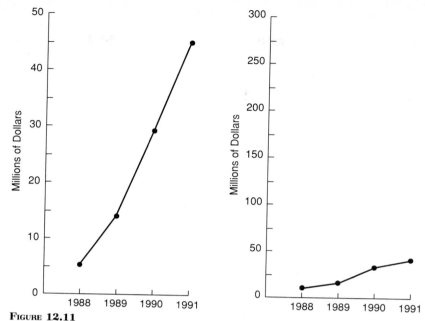

FIGURE 12.11

Distorted presentation of data using extreme ranges of values on *Y*-axis.

the total value of a single item, which is represented by the top line. Thus, the value of any coordinate on a line is determined by the distance between that coordinate and the same coordinate on the line below that of the first coordinate.

When constructing your surface graph, place the largest component at the base of the graph; then overlay subsequent components in descending order of size, with the smallest component plotted on the top line. Use different colors, crosshatching, or shading to distinguish between the various layers of components.

The surface graph, then, enables readers to estimate (a) the value of each subcomponent at any point along its plotted line and (b) the percentage of the whole represented by that component. The surface graph, however, is not without its disadvantages. You cannot plot components of an item when even a single subcomponent line intersects the line of a component above it, thus disrupting the consistent layering of items representing discrete percentages of the whole. Moreover, you can plot the components of only one item per surface graph. The surface graph is similar in many ways to the 100-percent bar graph, which is described, along with other types of bar charts, in the following section.

Simple Bar Graphs

By using **bar graphs,** you can compare quantities of different items by representing them as distinct bars of varying lengths—the longer the bar, the greater the quantitative value of the plotted item. Bar graphs are most effective in illus-

NET PURCHASES OF LONG-TERM DOMESTIC
SECURITIES BY SELECTED COUNTRIES

Calendar Years 1985 through 1989, Third Quarter

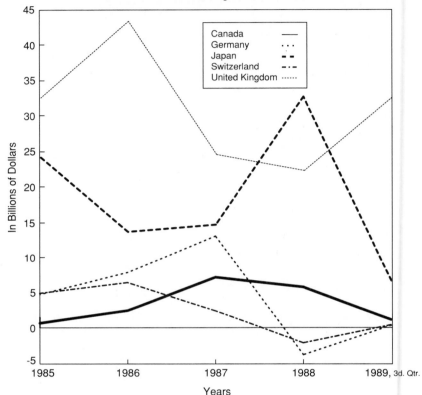

FIGURE 12.12

Multiple-line graph.

Source: Abstracted from U.S. Treasury Department.

trating the growth and decline in those quantities over time. The bars may be either vertical or horizontal but must be of the same width.

When constructing your bar graph, consider the following fundamental guidelines:

- Identify each bar at the graph's base, with an accurate, concise **item caption** below the *X*-axis or left of the *Y*-axis, depending on whether you are working with a vertical or horizontal bar graph.
- Identify the axis (*X* or *Y*) representing the quantities of the dependent variable(s) with a **scale caption** such as "Millions of Dollars," "Tons of Ore Shipped," "Kilometers Flown."
- Initialize the units of measurement along the *Y*-axis (for vertical graphs) or *X*-axis (for horizontal graphs) at zero.

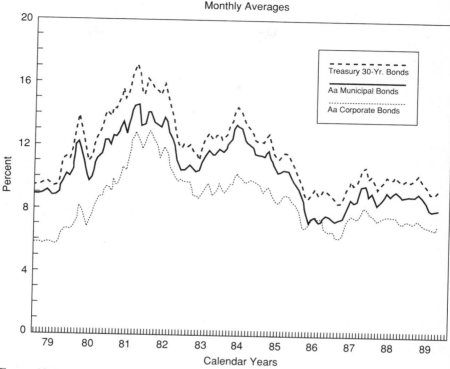

AVERAGE YIELDS OF LONG-TERM TREASURY,
CORPORATE, AND MUNICIPLE BONDS

FIGURE 12.12
Continued

- Use grid lines or figures to aid readers in determining the exact quantities of items. Grid lines should extend out from the *Y*-axis (for vertical bar graphs); place figures above or within bars (as in segmented bar graphs).
- Organize the bars in a logical sequence (e.g., according to importance, or chronologically, numerically, or alphabetically).
- Maintain equal distance and numerical increments along both axes to avoid distortion of measurements.
- Maintain equal space intervals (usually less than the width of a bar) between bars as well as equal bar width.
- Supply a legend to identify any special design effect such as different colors, crosshatching, or shading used to differentiate bars or segments within bars (Cleveland & McGill, 1988; Carlson & West, 1977).

Figure 12.14 illustrates a simple vertical bar graph that shows U.S. capital expenditures as a percentage of those outlays of five other industrialized countries.

On occasion, the numerical values on the *Y*-axis may possess a range too great for the size of your graph. In such instances, you can break the axis by using slash, zed, or graph break symbols, as illustrated earlier in Figure 12.9.

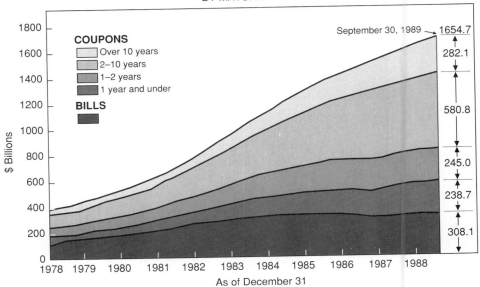

FIGURE 12.13

Surface graph.

Source: U.S. Treasury Department, Office of Market Finance.

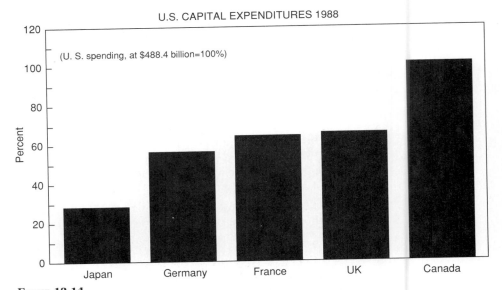

FIGURE 12.14

Simple bar graph.

Source: U.S. Department of Commerce.

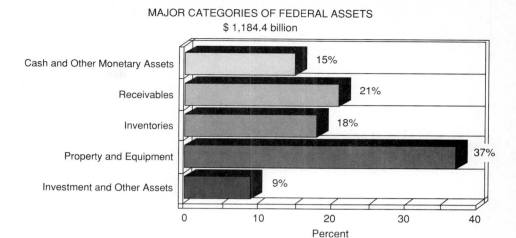

FIGURE 12.15

Horizontal bar graphs.

Source: U.S. General Accounting Office.

We commonly think of bar graphs as vertical in orientation, with the *X*-axis serving as the graph's base and the values of the plotted items represented in vertical bars. A **horizontal bar graph,** however, uses the *Y*-axis as its base (Figure 12.15). Because its bars run horizontally across the page, horizontal

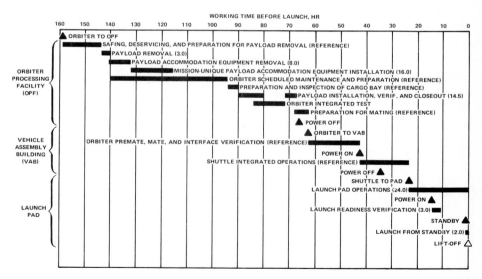

Shuttle Operational Processing Schedule; OPF Payload Installation

FIGURE 12.15

Continued

Source: Courtesy of Bill Shapbell, Jr., payload integration officer, National Aeronautics and Space Administration (NASA), Kennedy Space Center, Florida.

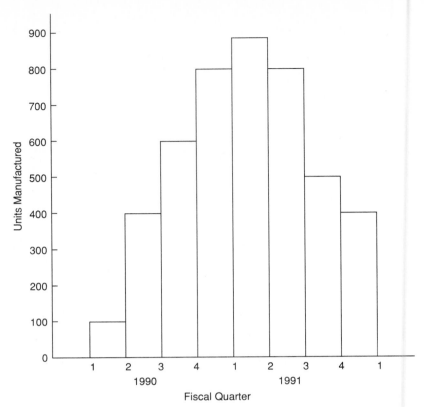

FIGURE 12.16
Histogram.

bar graphs are visually effective in illustrating items whose values increase or decrease significantly in terms of percentage change, time, or distance.

A vertical bar graph that depicts a frequency distribution of values is called a **histogram,** as shown in Figure 12.16. Histograms are useful for depicting frequency distributions of such demographic information as population, sex, age, and income (Zelazny, 1985, p. 79). Whereas the bars of a normal bar graph are separated by the width of a bar, a histogram leaves no space between the bars. As with all bar graphs, leave enough space (usually the width of a bar) at both ends of the X-axis so the bars won't appear squeezed against the Y-axis or frame lines (Schmid, 1983; Tufte, 1983).

Multiple-Bar Graphs

Multiple bar graphs enable you to compare the values of more than one item in a single graph. The first multiple-bar graph shown in Figure 12.17 represents fiscal results for federal agencies; the second multiple-bar graph represents net increases in major trust fund investments.

Because multiple-bar graphs can easily become cluttered with excessive bars, you should limit your graph to no more than three separate items. For

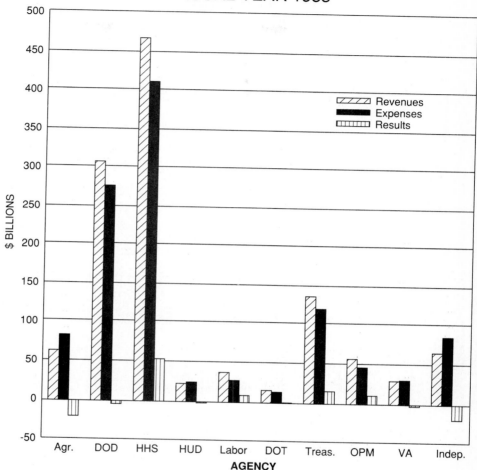

FIGURE 12.17

Multiple-bar graph.

example, if you wanted to compare in your multiple-bar graph the growth in your company's ice cream sales over the past 5 years you might want to provide sales figures for the flavors vanilla, chocolate, and strawberry for each year. Because multiple-bar graphs express more than one item or quantity, you should distinguish bars from one another by coding them with distinct colors, crosshatching, or shading. Identify each coded item in a legend.

Bilateral Bar Graphs

On occasion, some items depicted in your bar graph may have negative rather than positive values. In **bilateral bar graphs,** the axis pertaining to the independent variables (the *X*-axis in vertical graphs, the *Y*-axis in horizontal graphs)

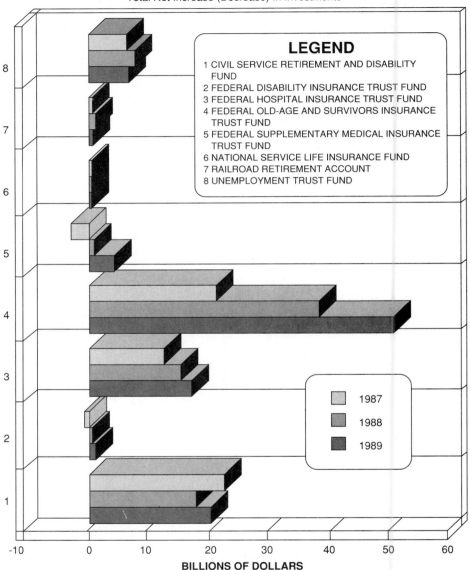

FIGURE 12.17
Continued

is extended to include negative values, as shown in Figure 12.18. The bilateral bar graph, then, uses a second quadrant of a grid.

When constructing your bilateral bar graph, place the zero value near the center of the graphic so that you have sufficient space for both positive and negative values and bars. Because bars in a bilateral graph can extend into

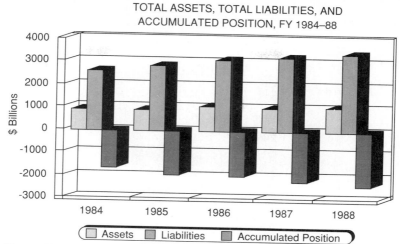

FIGURE 12.18

Bilateral bar graph.

Source: U.S. General Accounting Office.

all four quadrants of a bar grid, you should place the variable captions inside, above, or below the bars. Bilateral bar graphs are especially effective in depicting percentage changes in quantities.

Segmented Bar Graphs

To represent subdivisions of each item or bar in the graph, you might consider integrating into your report a **segmented bar graph** (also called a **component** bar graph). Instead of measuring the value of only one item with each bar, as done by simple bar graphs, segmented bar graphs allow you to divide each bar into subordinate components (Figure 12.19).

To distinguish between item divisions within each bar, use different colors, crosshatching, or shading. Start with darker colors and shades near the base axis and alternate contrasting colors and shades to make each segment as distinct as possible. Use distinct crosshatching angles for each segment and be sure to include a legend to identify these special design techniques. To avoid cluttering the graph, you should generally segment an individual bar into no more than three parts.

A special type of segmented bar graph called a **100-percent bar graph** shows the percentage change of different components within an item. In such a graph, the percentage values of the segments within each bar add up to 100%, as shown in Figure 12.20. The bars in a segmented percentage graph are the same length; however, the segments within each bar will vary in length, according to their percentage values. To identify the different components, label each segment (with a tag line) or include a legend. Aid readers in measuring the percentage changes in the various segments by placing the numerical percentage within each segment or by connecting the percent figure to the segment with a tag line.

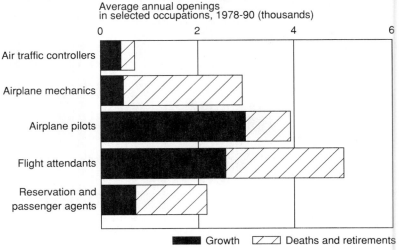

Keen competition is expected for the relatively small number of openings in air transportation occupations

FIGURE 12.19

Segmented bar graph.

Source: Bureau of Labor Statistics.

Pictograms

A **pictogram** is a horizontal bar graph that uses pictures, icons, or symbols instead of bars to represent numerical data and the relationships between data items. Because they are unique in design from other figures, pictograms can effectively attract readers' attention and communicate simple information quickly, as does the sample pictogram in Figure 12.21.

When constructing your pictogram, be sure to illustrate information that can be expressed accurately and easily with pictures. For example, you could represent the growth in population of City A over a 5-year period with rows of stick figures in a pictogram.

Because the pictogram is constructed of pictures, icons, or symbols, however, it cannot be segmented. Multiple-bar pictograms also prove to be confusing to readers. Thus, when representing the 5-year population growth of City A, you would not be able to segment the rows of figures to distinguish male and female populations. Moreover, arranging three rows of figures, say, to represent three different cities (as you might do with bars in a multiple-bar chart) would clutter the graphic aid and invariably confuse readers.

If you decide that a pictogram is the appropriate graphic aid with which to represent your data, choose a picture or symbol that is suitable for the information. Common symbols include coins, buildings, stick figures of people, and barrels. Measure the value or quantity of the item being charted in units rather than by symbol size. Make all units equal in size and identical in appearance to avoid distorting your presentation of the data.

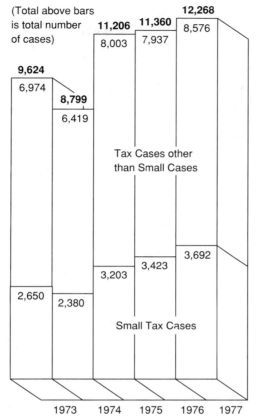

TAX COURT CASES RECEIVED
(1973 – 1977)

(Total above bars is total number of cases)

FIGURE 12.20

One hundred percent bar graph.

Source: U.S. Internal Revenue Service.

Charts

The most commonly used charts in managerial reports are the pie, organizational, and flow charts.

Pie Charts

One of the most appealing and easily interpreted graphic aids is the **pie chart.** As you might imagine, the pie chart resembles a pie, with each slice of the pie representing a subdivision or part of the whole item. The sum of the percentage or numerical values of the pie wedges equals 100% of the whole. Pie charts enable readers to compare the constituent parts not only to each other but also to the whole.

In constructing your pie chart, identify each of its parts by placing a label inside or to the side of each wedge. If space limitations prohibit your putting

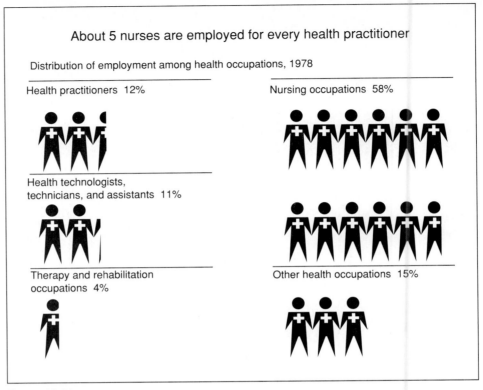

About 5 nurses are employed for every health practitioner

Distribution of employment among health occupations, 1978

FIGURE 12.21

Pictogram.

Source: Bureau of Labor Statistics.

the external label next to the wedge, use a tag line to connect the slice with its corresponding label, as shown in Figure 12.22. Keep all labels horizontal for easy reading. In addition, because estimating the numerical value represented by each wedge of a pie is frequently difficult for readers, you may include that value in parentheses below the percentage.

After drawing your circle for the pie chart, begin dividing the pie at the 12 o'clock position. First cut the slice representing the largest percentage of the pie; then subdivide the remaining pie in clockwise fashion and in descending order of largest to smallest slices. To distinguish between subdivisions of the pie, use different colors, crosshatching, or shading for each wedge.

Pie charts are most effective in representing simple percentage divisions of only one whole. They become confusing and thus counterproductive for readers when cluttered with too many wedges and numbers. As a result, you should normally divide your pie chart into no more than seven (and at least three) wedges. Combine smaller and less significant divisions into a single wedge, which you may label "Miscellaneous" or "Other."

Pie charts are least effective in communicating detailed data and information. For example, to convey the same information contained in the bar chart in

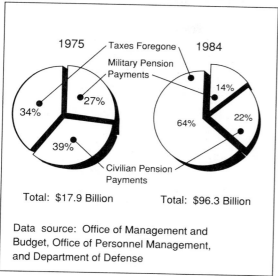

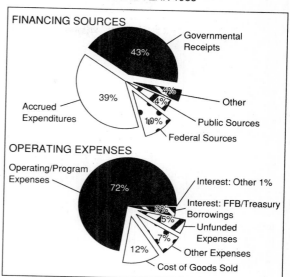

FIGURE 12.22
Pie charts.

Figure 12.2 would require 10 pie charts, one for each occupation plotted on the bar chart. Moreover, like tables, pie charts cannot illustrate the dynamic trends of values over time. Rather, pie charts serve as excellent introductory graphic aids that provide readers with a brief and attractive overview or forecast of more detailed, specific, or dynamic information presented elsewhere in the report and, typically, in the form of other graphics more effective in conveying such types of material (e.g., tables, bar graphs, line graphs).

Organizational Charts

An **organizational chart** graphically represents the hierarchy of authority and responsibility in an organization. Organizational charts use blocks and connecting lines to indicate the varying levels of authority and the relationships between the positions at different levels of an organization. Organizational charts enable readers of your report, especially new employees, to visualize the subordinate, lateral, or superior positions within an organization.

Like bar charts, organizational charts can be vertical or horizontal in structure. **Vertical organizational charts,** like the one shown in Figure 12.23, begin with top-level management positions (e.g., president, chief executive officer, chairman of the board) at the top of the chart, and then branch downward to subordinate positions.

Horizontal organizational charts begin at the left and branch toward the right, as illustrated in Figure 12.24. A third type of chart—the **circular organizational chart**—places the top level management positions in the center of a circle, with lower level positions or constituent divisions occupying

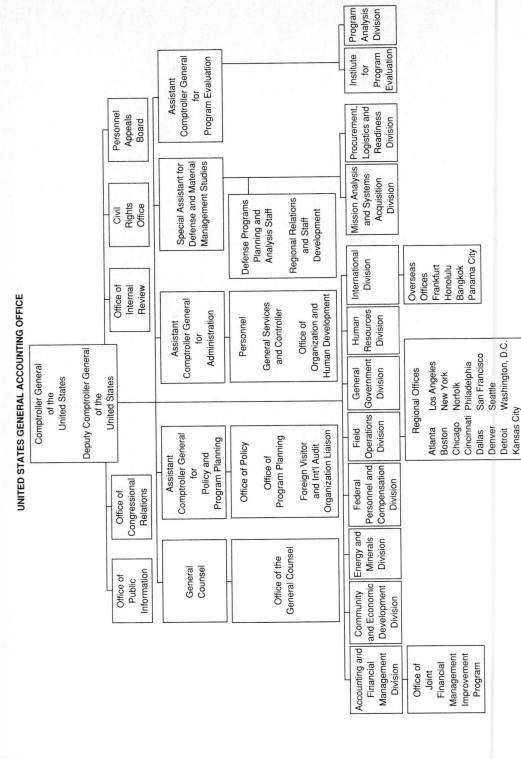

UNITED STATES GENERAL ACCOUNTING OFFICE

FIGURE 12.23

Vertical organizational chart.

Source: General Accounting Office.

FDIC ORGANIZATION CHART

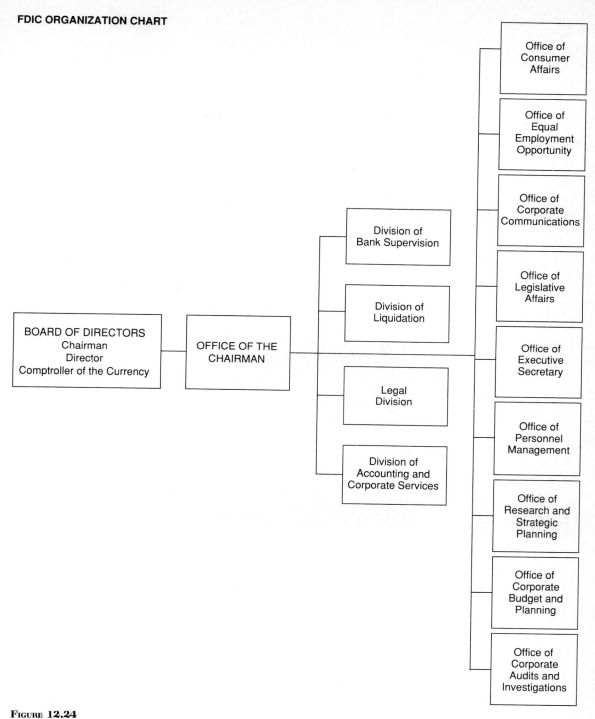

FIGURE 12.24
Horizontal organizational chart.
Source: U.S. Department of Commerce.

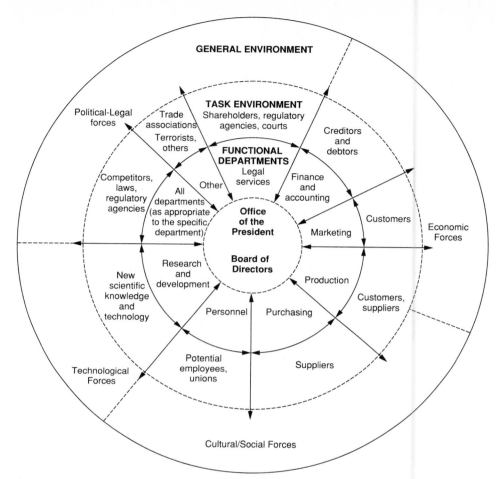

FIGURE 12.25

Circular organizational chart.

Source: Organizational Behavior (p. 396) by D. Hellreigel, J. W. Slocum, and R. W. Woodman, 1986, New York: West.

surrounding circles or blocks; the farther out from the center, the more subordinate the position or division in the chain of command and authority. Figure 12.25 offers a circular organizational chart that represents not only the general relationships between parts of an organization but also the relationships between those divisions and environmental forces. The arrows incorporated in the figure suggest a flow of communication and interdependence between the divisions much as flow arrows do in representing processes.

Flow Charts

Flow charts resemble organizational charts in that both present relationships between parts of a whole. However, whereas an organizational chart depicts the

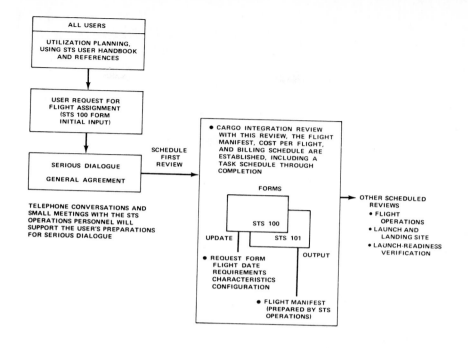

Steps to Flight Assignment

FIGURE **12.26**

Flow chart.

Source: Courtesy of Bill Shapbell, Jr., payload integration officer, National Aeronautics and Space Administration (NASA), Kennedy Space Center, Florida.

relatively static chain of command in an organization, a flow chart represents the flow of a dynamic process. Each relevant and significant step in the process is represented by a block (rectangular, square, or diamond); the flow of the process is indicated by lines and arrows connecting the blocks, as shown in Figure 12.26.

Flow charts are effective in representing an unlimited variety of processes, from depicting the logical flow of calculations in a computer accounts receivable program to tracing the flow of written messages in a communication audit of a major corporation. When constructing your flow chart, double-check the logical flow of the chart's sequence of steps. In addition, ensure that the chart contains no **endless loop**—a process (or routine) that has no logical end, but simply "loops" back on itself indefinitely.

Combination Graphs and Charts

The combination of graphs and charts is common in managerial reports that contain detailed or complex data. Figures 12.27 to Figure 12.29 illustrate how combined graphs and charts can effectively emphasize and clarify the relationships among data.

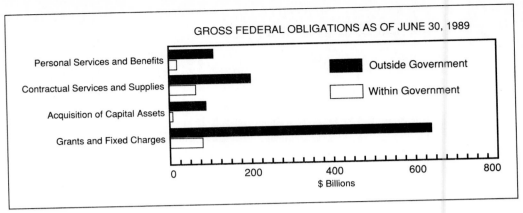

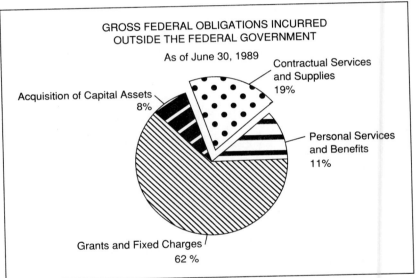

FIGURE 12.27

Combination graphics.

Source: U.S. General Accounting Office and U.S. Internal Revenue Service.

Diagrams

Simply stated, a **diagram** is a drawing of an object or process. It can depict not only the item itself but also the relationship(s) between that item, its components, and the items surrounding it. Diagrams are particularly useful in illustrating detailed objects and processes that are difficult or impossible to study in their real-world settings (Truran, 1975).

While drawings can be useful in showing lifelike external views of an object, as shown in Figure 12.30, you may occasionally need to provide readers with an internal view of a mechanism. An **exploded diagram** illustrates the

INTERNAL REVENUE COLLECTION SOURCES SHOWN IN TABULAR AND GRAPHIC FORM

Net Internal Revenue Collections

(Including tax rebates) through September 30, 1977

(Dollar in thousands)

			Net collections	
Source	**Collections**	**Refunds[1]**	**Amount**	**Percent of Total**
Grand total	**358,139,417**	**36,178,997**	**321,960,420**	**100.0**
Corporation income taxes	60,049,804	5,214,540	54,835,264	17.0
Individual income taxes	186,755,263	30,142,134	156,613,129	48.7
Employment taxes, total	86,076,316	436,189	85,640,127	26.6
Old-age, survivors, disability and hospital insurance	82,257,211	400,140	81,857,071	25.4
Railroad retirement	1,908,803	190	1,908,613	0.6
Unemployment insurance	1,910,302	35,859	1,874,443	0.6
Estate and gift taxes	7,425,325	98,737	7,326,588	2.3
Excise taxes	17,832,707	287,397	17,545,310	5.4

[1]Does not include interest paid on refunds.

The Tax Dollar: Where It Came From

Fiscal Year 1977 (Net Collections)

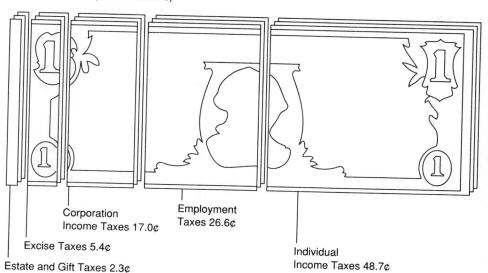

Corporation Income Taxes 17.0¢

Employment Taxes 26.6¢

Excise Taxes 5.4¢

Individual Income Taxes 48.7¢

Estate and Gift Taxes 2.3¢

FIGURE 12.28

Combination graphics.

Source: U.S. Internal Revenue Service.

FEDERAL DEBT

Total Federal debt held by the pulblic amounted to $2,047.8 billion in FY 1988, an increase of $141.5 billion from FY 1987. This chart has been presented to graphically show the increase in Federal debt and the interest expense.

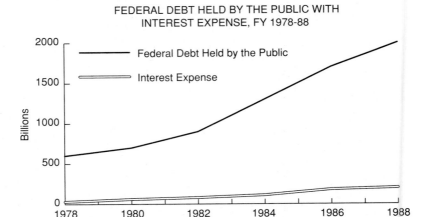

FEDERAL DEBT HELD BY THE PUBLIC WITH
INTEREST EXPENSE, FY 1978-88

The public debt table which follows reflects information on the borrowing of the Federal Government needed to finance the Government's operations. This table supports the balance sheet caption, "Debt issued under borrowing authority," which is shown net of intragovernmental holdings and unamortized premium or discount. Intragovernmental holdings represent that portion of the total Federal debt held by Federal entities, including the major trust funds.

The distribution of 1988 net borrowing from the public by major source category is graphically depicted.

NET BORROWING BY MAJOR SOURCE CATEGORY

FIGURE 12.29

Combination graphics.

Source: U.S. General Accounting Office.

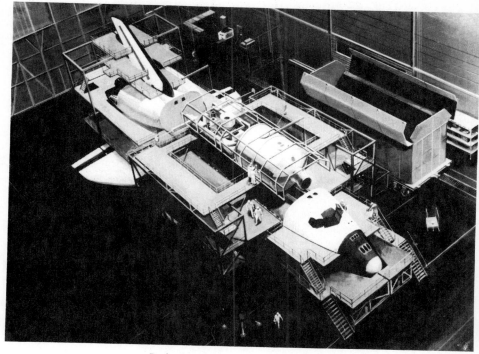

Payload Installation in the Orbiter Processing Facility

FIGURE 12.30

Drawing providing an external view.

Source: NASA, Kennedy Space Center, Florida.

distinct parts of a mechanism and how that object is assembled (Figure 12.31). Exploded diagrams are frequently used in technical operation, reference, and maintenance manuals. A second type of diagram is the **cutaway diagram,** which shows the components inside an object (Figure 12.32). Although they can be exhibited as a stand-alone graphic aid in your report, cutaway diagrams are often integrated into exploded diagrams.

The **procedural diagram** is closely related to the flow chart. Whereas the flow chart illustrates a process with blocks of text, connecting lines, and flow arrows, the procedural diagram presents sequential drawings of major steps in the process, as shown in Figure 12.33.

Other diagrams, called **conceptual diagrams,** illustrate the dynamic relationships between concepts that may or may not be evident or applicable to the physical world. Conceptual diagrams, like that shown in Figure 12.34, can be invaluable in clarifying for readers the often complex relationships between macro- and microeconomic forces and how those forces affect an organization.

Similar to the conceptual diagram is the **schematic diagram.** While both attempt to present abstract ideas or forces, schematic diagrams illustrate ac-

SRB/ET Aft Separation System, Lower and Diagonal Struts

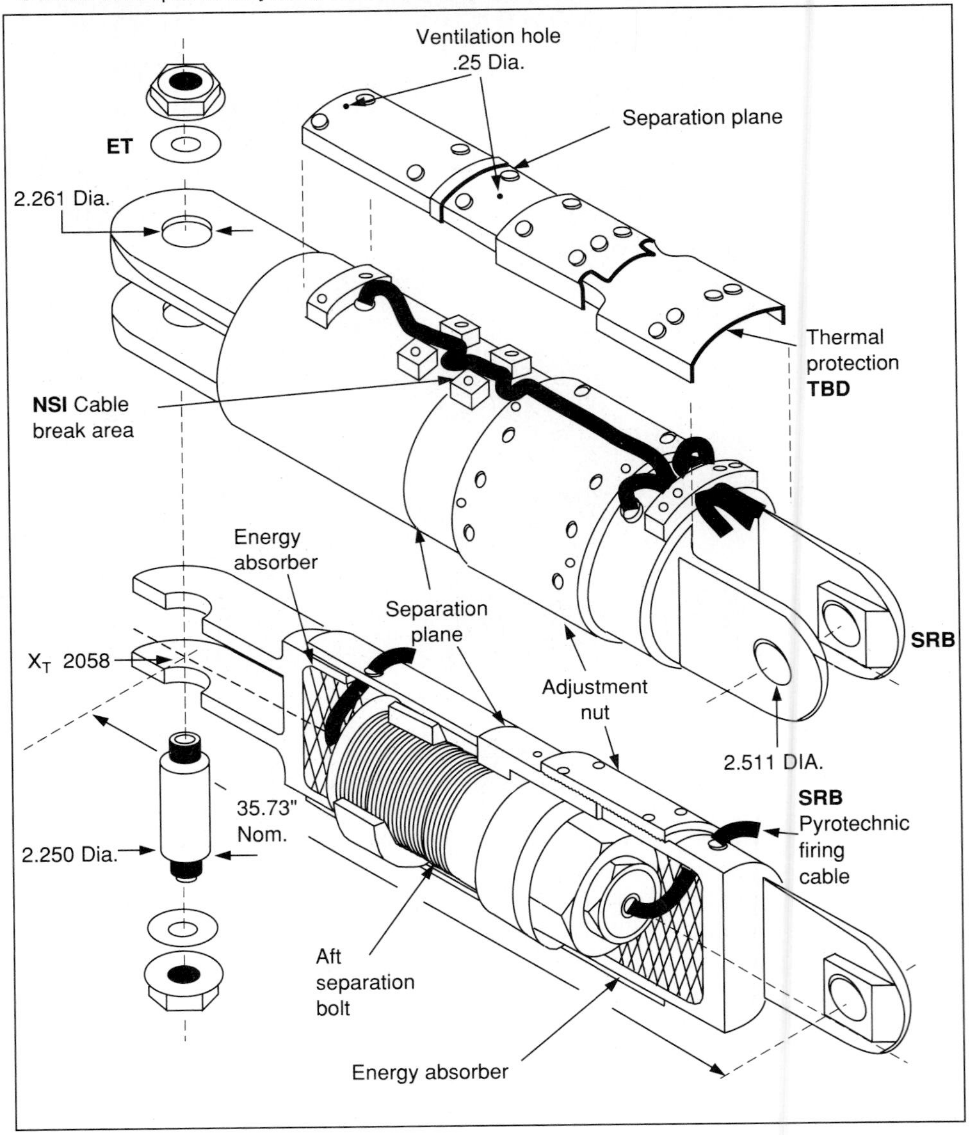

FIGURE 12.31
Exploded diagram.
Source: NASA.

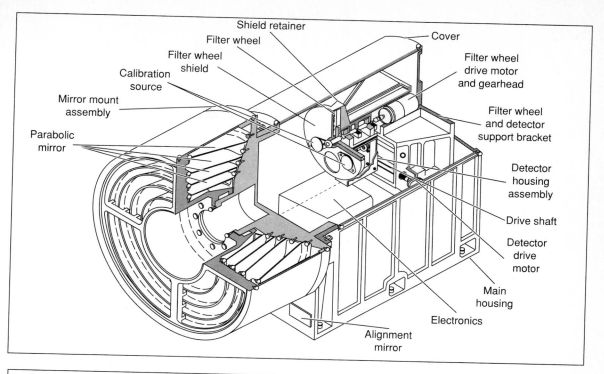

Shield retainer
Filter wheel
Filter wheel
shield
Calibration
source
Mirror mount
assembly
Parabolic
mirror
Cover
Filter wheel
drive motor
and gearhead
Filter wheel
and detector
support bracket
Detector
housing
assembly
Drive shaft
Detector
drive
motor
Main
housing
Electronics
Alignment
mirror

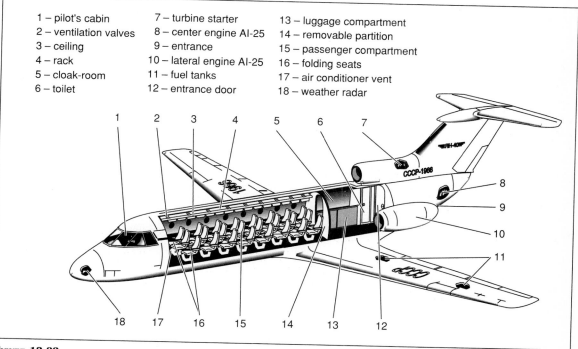

1 – pilot's cabin
2 – ventilation valves
3 – ceiling
4 – rack
5 – cloak-room
6 – toilet
7 – turbine starter
8 – center engine AI-25
9 – entrance
10 – lateral engine AI-25
11 – fuel tanks
12 – entrance door
13 – luggage compartment
14 – removable partition
15 – passenger compartment
16 – folding seats
17 – air conditioner vent
18 – weather radar

FIGURE 12.32

Cutaway diagrams.

Source: NASA.

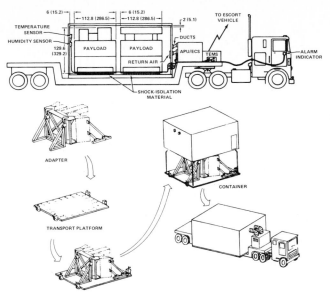

FIGURE 12.33

Procedural diagram.

Source: NASA.

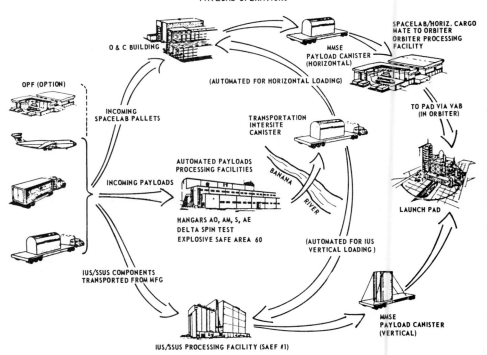

FIGURE 12.33

Continued

Forces Influencing Product Marketing

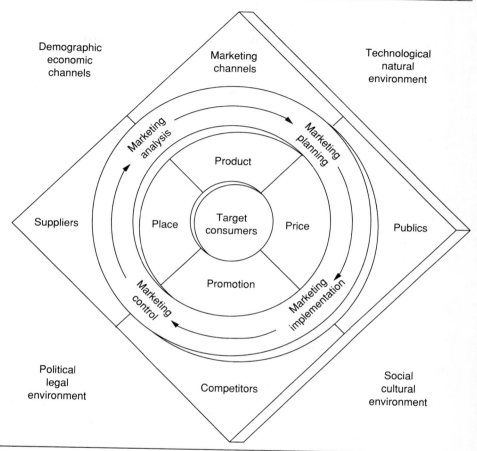

FIGURE 12.34

Conceptual diagram.

Source: Principles of Marketing (p. 49) by P. Kotler and G. Armstrong, 4th ed., 1989, Englewood Cliffs: Prentice-Hall.

tual physical objects or processes that, due to limiting factors (such as their complexity, size, location, scale of operation), are best studied in pictorial form (Figures 12.35 and 12.36).

Maps

When the data you wish to place in a graphic aid are geographically based, consider placing this information in a **map,** or **cartogram.** The maps you use should pertain to the specific geographical area (e.g., counties, cities, states,

Schematic Diagram of the Ground-support Electrical Checkout Equipment

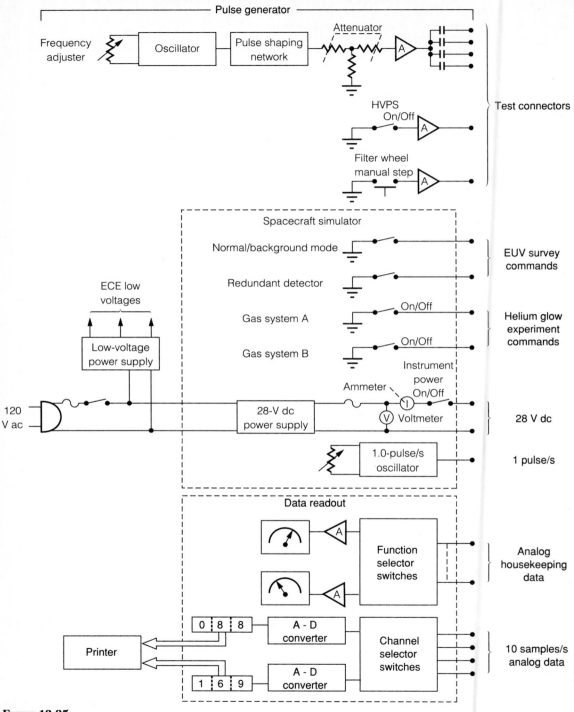

FIGURE 12.35
Schematic diagram.
Source: NASA.

372

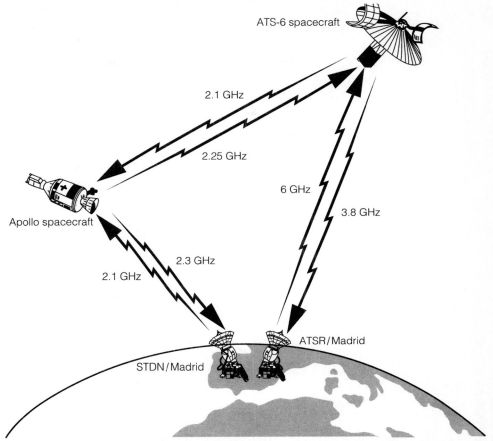

Schematic of the ATS–6/Apollo communication links for operations with ATS–6 in the Eastern Hemisphere. The ATS Ranging station is designated ATSR; the Spaceflight Tracking and Data Network station is designated STDN.

FIGURE 12.36

Schematic drawing.

Source: NASA.

countries, oceans) that is relevant to the data. Maps can accommodate a variety of data and information including population levels, employment statistics, types of agricultural and industrial products, production and sales figures, political districts, and meteorological information (see Figures 12.37 through Figures 12.39).

You may integrate data into your map by actually placing the numerical values into their respective geographic areas. A second choice is to use special graphic techniques such as color-coding, shading, or crosshatching to distinguish between regions having different numerical values. A third approach is

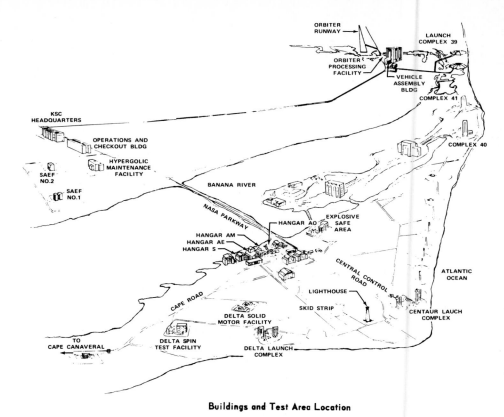

Buildings and Test Area Location

FIGURE 12.37

Map.

Source: NASA.

to integrate pictures (much as a pictogram does) into the map to represent the quantitative data relevant to the geographic region. Another alternative is to place dots on your map, with each dot representing a specific numerical value. When using such special graphic techniques, be sure to include a legend somewhere in the graphic aid to identify the value of each symbol.

Photographs

While other figures provide graphic representations of items, their quantities and significance, and the relationships between them, **photographs** offer readers a real-life image of the item itself. Photographs have additional advantages over other forms of figures, in that they

attract the attention of readers and invite closer reading of the text itself.

accurately record as evidence an overall or focused view of particular people, events, objects, or processes.

Map of Regions, Districts, and Service Centers

Key:
- ⊛ Commissioner of Internal Revenue (Washington, D.C.)
- ■ Regional Commissioner
- ○ District Director
- ● Service Center
- ★ National Computer Center (Martinsburg, W. Va.)
- ◆ IRS Data Center (Detroit, Mich.)
- —— Regional Boundary
- - - - District Boundary

Included in Western Region — Alaska — Hawaii

Office of International Operations, National Office

Puerto Rico and Virgin Islands

Region and District Legend:

Central Region
1 Cincinnati, Ohio
2 Cleveland, Ohio
3 Covington, Ky. (Cincinnati S.C.)
4 Detriot, Mich.
5 Indianapolis, Ind.
6 Louisville, Ky.
7 Parkersburg, W. Va.

Mid-Atlantic Region
8 Baltimore, Md.
9 Newark, N.J.
10 Philadelphia, Pa.
11 Pittsburgh, Pa.
12 Richmond, Va.
13 Wilmington, Del.

Southeast Region
14 Atlanta, Ga.
15 Birmingham, Ala.
16 Chamblee, Ga.
17 Columbia, S.C.
18 Greensboro, N.C.
19 Jackson, Miss.
20 Jacksonville, Fla.
21 Memphis, Tenn.
22 Nashville, Tenn.

Southwest Region
23 Albuquerque, N. Mex.
24 Austin, Tex.
25 Cheyenne, Wyo.
26 Dallas, Tex.

27 Denver, Colo.
28 Little Rock, Ark.
29 New Orleans, La.
30 Oklahoma City, Okla.
31 Wichita, Kans.

Midwest Region
32 Aberdeen, S. Dak.
33 Chicago, Ill.
34 Des Moines, Iowa
35 Fargo, N. Dak.
36 Kansas City, Mo.
37 Milwaukee, Wis.
38 Omaha, Neb.
39 Springfield, Ill.
40 St. Louis, Mo.
41 St. Paul, Minn.

North Atlantic Region
42 Albany, N.Y.
43 Andover, Mass.
44 Augusta, Maine
45 Boston, Mass.
46 Brooklyn, N.Y.
47 Buffalo, N.Y.
48 Burlington, Vt.
49 Hartford, Conn.
50 Holtsville, N.Y. (Brookhaven S.C.)
51 Manhattan, N.Y.
52 New York, N.Y.
53 Portsmouth, N.H.
54 Providence, R.I.

Western Region
55 Anchorage, Alaska
56 Boise, Idaho
57 Fresno, Calif.
58 Helena, Mont.
59 Honolulu, Hawaii
60 Los Angeles, Calif.
61 Ogden, Utah
62 Phoenix, Ariz.
63 Portland, Ore.
64 Reno, Nev.
65 Salt Lake City, Utah
66 San Francisco, Calif.
67 Seattle, Wash.

FIGURE 12.38

Map.

Source: U.S. Internal Revenue Service.

NATIONAL PROTECTED AREAS AND PARKS

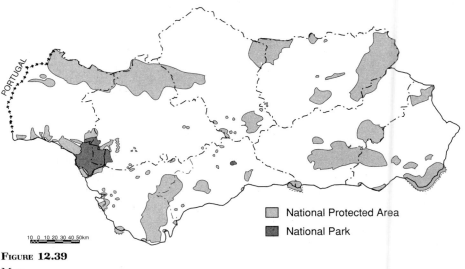

☐ National Protected Area
■ National Park

FIGURE 12.39
Map.

enhance the effectiveness of a report by contributing a sense of professionalism and sophistication.

Despite these advantages, however, photographs have their limitations. Photographs cluttered with too many details appear too busy and lose their focus, confusing readers as to the meaning and significance of the graphic
aid. Therefore, when using photographs, be sure to limit carefully the focus of the object, person, or process. In addition, because photographs cannot provide readers with a clear sense of an object's third dimension (i.e.,
depth), you should include in the photograph a second object (e.g., a pen-
cil, hand, person) whose scale is easily recognizable. Aided by this second object, readers can then calculate the size of the primary object more
accurately.

Be certain that the nature of the item is appropriate for a photograph
as well. For example, complex, intricate, or large objects—such as computer chip circuitry or the eastern coastline of the United States—can hardly
be photographed and reproduced except with highly sophisticated and expensive camera technology. Furthermore, while some processes like wine-
making, golf swings, and production line tasks can be effectively illustrated
with sequential photographs of key steps, processes more conceptual in nature (e.g., the educational process in the United States, effective management training, and the steady growth in the inflation rate) might be better communicated through other types of figures such as flow charts or
diagrams.

Computer Graphics _____

Computer graphics software has significantly simplified the process of designing and producing sophisticated, professional graphic aids. The attractive yet complex graphics that traditionally had been reserved for the steady hand of seasoned graphics designers can now be completed by report writers with just hours of prior training in the use of a graphics application program.

Depending on the nature of your business and the kinds of data and information with which you work, you may have access to a range of computer systems and their accompanying graphics software. In the past, only large computer systems such as mainframes and minicomputers had the power and memory capacity required to run graphics programs. However, the phenomenal advances in the miniaturization and speed of computer hardware (e.g., microcomputers, portable computers, laptops, briefcase computers) as well as the efficiency and assortment of software programs (e.g., word processors, text editors, graphics application programs, desktop publishing programs) since the mid-1980s have dramatically opened the world of computer graphics to report writers. Managers, for example, now have the computing power, speed, and flexibility to design and construct a wide variety of professional graphics in the office, at home, or during travel.

The greatest advantages computer graphics programs have over manually created graphics are speed and versatility. Graphics programs allow you to choose from a range of existing graphics constructs (e.g., tables, pie charts, line graphs, bar graphs). After selecting the graphic for your report, you simply enter the data into the graphics construct, save the new graphics aid in the memory of the computer much as you would file a folder in a cabinet, and later insert the graphic (when convenient) into your report. If you use a word-processing program to compose your managerial report, make sure that your graphics software is compatible with that program so that you can easily transfer the graphics directly into your report. Some graphics software packages also allow you to create your own specialized configurations, such as drawings of objects or processes specific to your organization.

The benefits of using graphics software to design and produce your graphics aids are numerous. Some of the most central and universal benefits follow:

- You can learn how to use most graphics programs easily and in a matter of hours. Graphics software packages typically include user manuals that contain detailed information for first-time users, as well as on-line tutorials that teach you step-by-step how to create graphics.
- You can update and modify graphics on screen at any time and with the same level of accuracy and precision afforded you by the graphics program you used to create the graphics.
- You can save yourself and your organization considerable time and cost with the fast updating and revision capabilities of graphics programs.
- Because graphics programs used in conjunction with sophisticated printers can produce hard copy that appears as good as or better than manually pro-

duced graphics (and in a fraction of the time), you can significantly speed production time for your report and accompanying graphics while also lowering production costs.

- You can choose from an attractive assortment of colors for use in your graphics. Many graphics programs offer far more colors than most printers. For this reason, the purchase of an advanced color laser printer is a wise investment for the manager committed to producing sophisticated, multicolor graphics.
- You can select from the program's assortment of special formatting features, including different type sizes, fonts, and various designs of rules, frames, and bars.
- You can produce three-dimensional effects in your graphic aids with shading, overlays, scale changes, and other perspective-enhancing techniques.
- You can design complex models of objects, processes, or systems (e.g., the planning of production, costs, marketing, and sales) and—by using the speed, power, and memory of the computer—forecast and monitor the condition of those models when different variables are inserted into their formulas.

Moreover, the accuracy in graphics representation that had previously been offered only in advanced computer-aided design/computer-aided manufacturing (CAD/CAM) work stations is now available in computer hardware and graphics software at the laptop level. Today any 32-bit microcomputer (16-bit in some cases) can provide you with WYSIWYG ("what-you-see-is-what-you-get") graphics that appear on the screen exactly as they will appear (e.g., in the same scale, spacing, and font) once printed on hard copy in your report.

Despite the advantages of speed, accuracy, and advanced graphics capabilities offered by graphics application software, however, computer-generated graphics are not without their drawbacks. First, once surrounded by an appealing array of computer-supported graphics capabilities, you might be tempted to overuse graphics in your report. Second, with the advanced graphics capabilities of graphics programs, you might attempt to integrate too many special features into your graphics, cluttering them and reducing their effectiveness. Keep in mind that your use of a graphic aid, and each component within it, must be justified by how effectively that graphic performs its specified function in the report. Finally, although the prices of computer hardware and accompanying graphics software continue to fall with the continual arrival of new and less expensive computer technologies, investment in a quality graphics system (both hardware and software) can still be expensive.

Summary

As this chapter has discussed, properly designed and integrated graphic aids not only enhance your readers' comprehension of the information contained in your report but also expand their use of that information. Specific purposes of graphic aids are numerous. Graphics, for example, can explain and simplify for readers complex data and information contained in the report; emphasize key material, such as important figures, trends, and concepts; and summarize and condense vast amounts of material into a manageable form.

Effective graphics also provide readers with important insights into the report problem and possible solutions. Moreover, because they place information in an easily accessible form, graphics enable readers to make sound decisions more quickly. Because those decisions are based on graphics that accurately and thoroughly represent central issues focusing on the report problem, the quality of those decisions is often enhanced. Finally, apart from making your report more attractive to readers, well-designed graphics can enhance the credibility of your report and its findings by projecting a sense of order, preparedness, and professionalism.

We have stressed throughout Chapter 12 that the key to realizing some or all of the above purposes is that the graphic aid be *functional*. Graphics should not be used as mere decoration but, rather, as communication tools whose central function is to supplement text so that the document conveys significant data and information efficiently and effectively. To make your graphic aids fully functional, you must design and modify your graphics throughout the entire report-writing process—from researching the report subject to planning the report format to composing and revising the document's text.

Related Reading

BOVEE, COURTLAND L., and JOHN W. THILL. *Business Communication Today.* New York: Random, 1986.

CARLSEN, ROBERT D., and D. L. WEST. *Encyclopedia of Business Charts.* Englewood Cliffs, NJ: Prentice, 1977.

CLEVELAND, WILLIAM S., and MARYLYN E. McGILL. *Dynamic Graphics for Statistics.* Pacific, CA: Wadsworth, 1988.

DICKINSON, GORDON CAWOOD. *Statistical Mapping and the Presentation of Statistics.* New York: Crane, 1973.

GLAU, G. R. *Business Graphics with the IBM PC/XT/AT.* Homewood, IL: Dow Jones-Irwin, 1986.

LANNON, JOHN M. *Technical Writing.* New York: HarperCollins, 1991.

McCOMB, GORDON. *Executive Guide to PC Presentation Graphics.* New York: Bantam, 1988.

Making the Most of Charts: An ABC of Graphic Presentation. New York: American Mgmt. Assn., Finance Div., 1960.

MURGIO, MATTHEW P. *Communications Graphics.* New York: Van Nostrand, 1969.

OSGOOD, WILLIAM C. *Using Business Graphics: Lotus 1-2-3 on the DEC Rainbow.* Burlington, MA: Digital, 1985.

SCHMID, CALVIN F. *Statistical Graphics: Design Principles & Practices.* New York: Wiley, 1983.

Schmid, Calvin F., and S. E. Schmid. *Handbook of Graphics Presentation.* 2nd ed. New York: Wiley, 1979.

Sigband, Norman B., and Arthur H. Bell. *Communication for Management and Business.* 5th ed. Glenview, IL: Scott, 1989.

Spear, M. E. *Practical Charting Techniques.* New York: McGraw, 1969.

Truran, H. C. *A Practical Guide to Statistical Maps and Diagrams.* London: Heinemann, 1975.

Tufte, Edward R. *The Display of Quantitative Information.* Cheshire, CT: Graphics, 1983.

Zelazny, Gene. *Say It with Charts: The Executive's Guide to Successful Presentations.* Homewood, IL: Dow Jones-Irwin, 1985.

PART IV

Presenting Short and Long Mangerial Reports

CHAPTER 13

The Short Report: A Useful Form for Communicating in the Managerial Arena

Our discussion in Chapter 4 classified and explored managerial reports according to their subject and contents, purpose(s), intended audience, and the components they share. We concentrated on the forms, the functions, the organizational elements, and the uses to which readers might put a variety of reports. In this chapter we will focus on the short report as an effective form for communication to, from, and through the manager who, earlier in this text, we identified as the organizational nexus for a broad spectrum of decisional and informational documents (see Figure 2.1).

Key Elements

We define **short reports** as brief managerial documents limited to five pages or less of report text, frequently coupled with relevant attachments or appendixes. Based on that text limit, though, short reports comprise the largest and most diverse group of decisional and informational documents written, read, responded to, and acted on in every contemporary business environment. Short managerial reports are an efficient mode of communicating important information—facts, decisions, analyses, actions, recommendations—to audiences of all kinds and at all levels in the organizational hierarchy.

Efficient Means of Communicating

The short report is a particularly efficient mode of communication because it can usually be read in a matter of moments; processed, pondered, and internalized by a reader in just a few more moments; and answered orally or in a follow-up document shortly thereafter. Of importance to report writers, short reports are likely to be read because they do not make inordinate demands on their reader's time.

Unlike lengthy analytical reports, short reports will be read in full, and probably from beginning to end, not only by technical specialists or managers whose self-interest will propel the reading of a document, but also by readers in at least two other organizational audience groups: busy senior-level executives with very real constraints on their reading time and second-level staff or line supervisors whose immediate priorities might not include careful attention to a particular report's content. The brevity of these documents alone might, if not arouse a reader's interest, at least supply the necessary nudge to read through a document whose title or subject line would otherwise repel even a well-intentioned senior manager, not to mention a somewhat indifferent staff supervisor.

Therefore if short reports will be read more completely by more readers more of the time, managerial report writers have a built-in incentive—perhaps even an organizational imperative—to produce short reports wherever and whenever possible. After all, to paraphrase Malcolm Forbes, former president and editor-in-chief of *Forbes*: Who's going to benefit if your report is quick and easy to read?

Format, Formality, and Function

Just as all categories of managerial reports differ one from another, short reports also differ according to the same six interrelated variables:

1. Location of reader(s)
2. Format
3. Degree of formality—in style and structure
4. Time frame or business interval
5. Subject matter or content
6. Function.

In Chapter 4 we explored these six variables in depth as we examined the most commonly produced managerial reports used to satisfy a diversity of organizational communication situations. Here, we will briefly review only format, formality, and function variables and concentrate on examining the nature and structure of the short report in general. We will highlight and examine three individual reports written for different organizational audiences, purposes, and uses.

As we have suggested, short reports might differ in a number of overlapping ways; chiefly, though, short reports differ in **format**, degree of **formality**, and **function**. Depending on (a) the nature of the communication situation to be satisfied with a document and (b) whether the reader(s) resides within or outside of the organization, short reports might take one of the following forms:

- **Informal**
  format
  memo- or letter-report
  block (flush left), indented paragraph, or manuscript (handwritten) form
  function — to inform, sell, direct, clarify, recommend
- **Formal**
  format
  memo- or letter-report
  headings or key structural elements identified by numbers, letters, or bullets
  function — to inform, document, direct, clarify, examine, analyze, propose, persuade, study/recommend
- **Formal**
  format
  standard report (nonmemo, nonletter)
  brief cover or transmittal letter attached
  headings or key structural elements identified by numbers, letters, or bullets
  function — to inform, document, direct, clarify, examine, analyze, propose, persuade, study/recommend
- **Informal** or **formal** (based on company style policy)
  format
  preprinted company form (see Chapter 4, Figures 4.8a and 4.8b)
  brief cover letter might be attached
  headings or key structural elements identified and built into report form
  function — to inform, document (with sales, labor, statistical, expenditure data); to present routine (weekly, monthly, quarterly) data and information

We should point out that certain organizations, depending on the nature of the enterprise and its leadership, might encourage the blending of both formal and informal stylistic and structural features within a given document, such as a letter-report (see Figure 13.1). Other organizations might consistently require their report writers to carefully choose either formal or informal approaches, depending on the communication situation within which they were constructing a document (see, for example, Figure 13.2).

Three Models

In Chapter 4 we exhibited a wide range of report types. For the most part, we presented only very brief reports or illustrative portions of long reports.

Here we will take a closer look at three short reports. The three short reports we present in Figures 13.1, 13.2, and 13.3 are complete documents that reflect typical short report formats. We will examine these short documents in terms of their structures and styles, the writers' purposes, and the uses to which readers might have put each short report.

Model 1—Letter-Report

As we have noted above, memo- and letter-reports might be informal or formal documents, or even a blending of the two. An organization's written documents may reflect either an informal, a formal, or a mixed posture, depending on the following: (a) the manner in which a given organization wishes to project itself to clients/customers, other organizations, and its own executives and employees (i.e., on the culture and the communication climate of the organization) and (b) the types of communication situations that regularly arise and to which report writers respond within, and external to, the organization.[1]

At Betz Process Chemicals, Inc., for example, management report writers routinely appear to blend together both informal and formal stylistic and structural features in their short documents. Their short memo- and letter-reports reflect a variety of verbal characteristics—for example, use of first names (throughout), friendly and familiar tone, casual clauses and sentences—that, when coupled with more formal lists of itemized recommendations or options, illustrate a mixed, informal-formal posture to their readers. Figure 13.1 shows a typical **letter-report** written by a Betz district manager to a client, in this case Mr. D. A. Joss—addressed, simply, as "Dan"—representing Chevron USA, a client firm.

The letter-report in Figure 13.1 tends to be somewhat more formal than some Betz short memo- and letter-reports. It is not uncommon for Betz report writers to sprinkle casual phrases, clauses, and sentences like the following throughout their documents:

- "Just wanted to drop you a line and go over a few things that we discussed last week while I was in the Woodlands."
- "Things are still looking pretty good at Conoco, Bobby."
- "Generally, the people at CRC feel pretty positive about the 3F8 program."
- "I'm sure that by the time you read this letter, a lot of work regarding these two accounts will already be done and be in our district office."
- "Ron, after reviewing this packet, if there are any other questions that I may be able to address . . ."

---

[1] For a detailed and rigorous examination of the concept of corporate culture—what it is and is not, how it develops and changes—see Edgar H. Schein, *Organizational Culture and Leadership* (San Francisco: Jossey-Bass, 1988). For a brief introduction to corporate culture and related employee, organizational, and communication issues, see Terrence E. Deal and Allen A. Kennedy, *Corporate Cultures: The Rites and Rituals of Corporate Life* (Reading, MA: Addison-Wesley, 1982), particularly pages 85–103, "Communications: Working the Cultural Network."

**BETZ PROCESS
CHEMICALS, INC.**

11059 E. Bethany Dr.
Suite 113
Aurora, Colorado 80014
Telephone:(303) 368-7782

August 24, 19--

Chevron USA
P.O. Box 20002
El Paso, TX 79998

Attention: D. A. Joss

Informal greeting

Dan,

**Introduction to
letter-report**

    This correspondence serves to follow-up on our recent conversation regarding the possible options in addressing the current high caustic demand for chloride control in No. 6 C.U. As we discussed, there is no suitable existing valve for installation of a new retractable crude/caustic injection quill. It is not desirable that caustic be injected upstream of any crude preheat exchangers due to the potential for caustic-related fouling and loss of heat transfer. For this reason, caustic injection needs to take place between the last preheat exchanger and the furnace inlet. The ideal location is in the area of the exising caustic injection point. The only problem is that we have reason to believe that the existing quill is not in proper working condition. This being the case, some viable options include:

**Review of options
discussed**

**Purpose 1 —
Series of options**

(1) Hot tap a new 2-inch valve near the existing crude/caustic injection point. The valve can be used for installation of a retractable crude/caustic injection quill.

(2) Install an in-line static mixer on the crude/caustic line prior to injection into the main crude line.

(3) Eliminate caustic injection for the control of chlorides in the C-1601 overhead water altogether.

**Purpose 2 —
Recommendation to conduct
stepwise evaluation**

    I recommend that we conduct a stepwise evaluation to determine the feasibility of complete caustic removal prior to doing any hot tapping or installing any additional mixing equipment. This would involve a three-month study correlating chloride control range to coupon corrosion rates and initial condensate point pH. Below is a detailed step-wise plan for this survey.

Step 1: Reduce caustic injection sufficient to increase the chloride content of the D-1601 water to between 30 and 40 ppm. The range should be maintained for a 30-day coupon period. A titanium and admiralty coupon will be monitored. Further, Betz will conduct frequent D-1601 water analyses

FIGURE 13.1

Letter-report—Betz Process Chemicals, Inc.

**Purpose 3 —
List three steps
in stepwise plan**

and a C.O.L.A dew point survey to identify any effect on pH at the initial condensate point (ICP). Drops in ICP pH will be corrected by increasing the 4H1 injection rate to the C-1601 overhead line.

Step 2: Reduce caustic injection further to increase the chloride content of the D-1601 water to 50-70 ppm. A new set of corrosion coupons will be monitored. This time they will consist of carbon steel and admiralty. As before, a C.O.L.A. survey of the ICP pH and detailed water analyses will be conducted.

Step 3: Complete elimination of caustic injection, which would allow chloride content in the D-1601 water to increase to approximately 90 ppm. Again, a new set of corrosion coupons (carbon steel and admiralty) will be monitored. Another C.O.L.A. survey of ICP pH will be monitored along with detailed water analyses.

**Additional data and
information**

Throughout all three steps it will be necessary to maintain the ICP pH between 5.0 and 5.5 with the use of the C.O.L.A. device. This maintenance will be done with the injection of 4H1 to the C-1601 overhead.

**Review and restatement of
survey recommendation**

We feel that the above plan will result in eliminating the need for caustic injection and the associated penalties at the FCCU without significant change in the corrosion activity in the C-1601 condensing system. Maintaining proper control of the ICP pH will be the key. I strongly recommend that this survey be done prior to any work that is begun on the crude/caustic injection facilities. I can begin this survey at any time; obviously, the sooner the better.

**Call for action plus
helpful close**

We can discuss this survey further during my next routine service visit or at your earliest convenience.

Sincerely,

BETZ PROCESS CHEMICALS, INC.

Tim Macharrelli
District Manager

cc: R.M. Maddaford
      L.A. Wilson
      T.E. Stapelkamp
      R.R. Kooiman
      W.S. Bousman
      Area III SS

Figure 13.1
Continued

Generally in its short memo- and letter-reports, as in the letter-report shown in Figure 13.1, Betz effectively projects an organizational image of casual, interested, easy-going authority to its clients and employees. A short report from a Betz manager seems to say "you can certainly rely on us because we know what we're doing," coupled with the attitude of "we are interested in *you*, friend, in *your* organization, and in *your* problems."

The reader of the document (Dan) in Figure 13.1 will have readily understood the writer's (i.e., the district manager's) three major purposes in sending him a short letter-report:

1. To outline in full a short series of options for determining whether an "existing quill" is "in proper working condition" for use in the "caustic injection" process.

2. To provide him with a recommendation "to conduct a stepwise evaluation [survey] to determine the feasibility of complete caustic removal prior to doing any hot tapping or installing any additional equipment."

3. To list the three steps in the "stepwise plan" for a possible (necessary) study/survey.

After having read the short letter-report, the reader, Dan (of Chevron USA), perhaps in consultation with other Chevron managers and technical specialists, must use Tom's concise analysis—options, recommendation, and items listed in the stepwise plan—to make a decision based on all current data and information and to take the necessary action. In short, then, Tom's letter-report has called for some kind of action (an agreement to begin the feasibility survey) on the part of Dan and his organization, Chevron.

Model 2—Memo-Report

The next short organizational document we will examine and exhibit (see Figure 13.2) exemplifies in both format and content the typical formal, internal **memo-report**. The document begins with formal memorandum elements: the date; TO, FROM, and SUBJECT lines. Formal memo-reports, as is the case here, do not require letters of transmittal. Major sections of the body or text of this procedures-based document have been identified by numbers; subsections are identified with letters. The primary purpose of the writer, Ms. D. R. Merrill (of the general accounting department), is to request "approval for the adoption of corporate-wide procedures for controlling [accounting] journal entries" from the reader of the document, Mr. Gordon Heggem, the corporate comptroller.

The memo-report also functions to inform (and announce), to clarify, and to document general accounting procedures "for controlling journal entries" within various sections or departments of the organization (a quasipublic utility). On the final page of the document, the writer, Ms. Merrill, aiming to move Mr. Heggem to action, urges him to approve the "recommended control procedure[s]" for distribution and general organizational use.

Memo-report —
Formal elements

MEMORANDUM

SEPT. 4, 19--

TO: Mr. Gordon Heggem, Comptroller

FROM: Ms. Donna Merrill, General Accounting Department

SUBJECT: PROCEDURE FOR CONTROLLING JOURNAL ENTRIES

Primary purpose —
Request for approval
(action)

I am requesting approval for the adoption of corporate-wide procedures for controlling journal entires. The following functions occur in processing manual journal entries:

1. Removing the month's preprint entries from the file.
2. Distributing the entires to the preparers.
3. Preparing and approval.
4. Batch control for interface with Data Entry.
5. Filing of journal entries.

Secondary purposes —
Inform, announce,
clarify, document

Several records or files also display and/or control manual journal entries:

1. General Ledger System authorization file (G.L. File). Contains the journal entries (machine and manual) authorized by number and title.
2. Journal Entry Authorization form. Used to initiate, approve, and document changes made to the General Ledger System above.
3. Journal entry record and numbering system. A typed document of manual and machine entries by number, title, preparing department/section, and month(s) prepared.
4. Journal entry record book. Records journal entries by number, title, and authorization/deactivation month and year.
5. Record of journal entries sent to/from Data Entry.
6. Batch control form. Records journal entries and control totals for each batch.

procedures,
functions,
additional
information
for readers
and users

To document the control system, simplify the process, and reduce the number of records, the following control procedure for manual journal entires is recommended:

Memo-report sections —
Identified by numbers

1. A numbering system used for all journal entries
   5001 – 5099 Machine-generated entries
   6101 – 6229 Monthly entries
   6230 – 6249 Periodic (quarterly, semi-annual,
                     annual, etc.) entries

Responsibility for all entries rests with General Accounting Department—Records and Reports Section and all requests for new journal entry numbers or deletion of existing entries must be sent to that section.

Memo-report
subsections —
Identified by letters

2. Authorizing (deactivating) of journal entries
   a. The Journal Entry Authorization form (see attached) will be completed, approved and entered to the G.L. File (including

FIGURE 13.2

Memo-report—general accounting department.

Page 2
Ms. D. R. Merrill
September 4, 19--

documentation of entering on the form).
  b. The person entering the change to the system will also record this on the Journal Entry Control Record which is discussed in 4. below.
  c. The person entering the change to the system will also make any changes necessary to the file folders discussed in 3a. below.
3. Process of preparing entries
  a. The monthly and periodic entries will be preprinted and retained in individual file folders in Records and Reports Section files. The month's entries will be removed for distribution using the Journal Entry Control Record as the guide for showing the entries necessary and authorized. As each journal entry for the month is removed from the file, a check will be placed in the appropriate space on the Journal Entry Control Record. This step will also be documented by signing in the appropriate space. A review will be made of the Control Record and the file to ensure that all entries for the month have been accounted for prior to distribution.
  b. The individual entries will be prepared and checked by the department/section assigned this responsibility. The entries will be approved by the supervisor or department head of the preparing section or department.
  c. If there are no transactions to be recorded on a Monthly or Periodic entry, the entry must be marked to indicate this. A discounted (deactivated) Monthly or Periodic entry will be marked to indicate this until it is reassigned. The discontinued entry will *not* be reassigned until 25 months after the month of discontinuation.
  d. In order to maintain the continuity of the numbering system, all Monthly and Periodic entry numbers not used must be accounted for by indicating the applicable condition in 3c. above and filing with the month's entries.
4. Journal Entry Control Record (Record)
  a. This Record (see attached) will be kept by Records and Reports Section and retained in a Follow-up Folder for the purpose of documenting journal entry numbers and their description, recording the business month and year of deactivation, providing a source document for removing the appropriate journal entries from file in order to distribute to the preparers, documenting of sending and receiving the entries to and from Data Entry and documenting of the journal entries being contained on the Journal Entry Register (see 5. below).
  b. A separate workpaper sheet will be used for each year.
  c. All changes to the G.L. File in the General Ledger System will be recorded on this Record as discussed in 2b. above. When a journal entry is discontinued, the word "Discontinued" will be recorded on the Record in the column for the business month of discontinuance.
  d. This Record will be used as the guide for removing the month's journal entries as discussed in 3a. above.

FIGURE 13.2
Continued

Page 3
Ms. D. R. Merrill
September 4, 19--

    e. When the journal entries are received by Records and Reports Section for forwarding to Data Entry, a review is made for proper documentation (on *each* page of the journal entry) of preparing, checking and approving, as well as for proper accounts, cost centers, charges and credits to proper accounts, and reasonableness of amounts.

    f. As properly approved and reviewed journal entries are organized into batches (see attached batch control procedure) prior to forwarding to Data Entry, the batch number for the entries will be entered in the appropriate space on the Record. When the batches are returned from Data Entry, the individual entries will be recorded as returned by placing a check in the appropriate space on the Record. Completion of sending and receiving of all journal entries will be documented by signing in the appropriate space on the Record.

    g. If there are no transactions for an active Monthly or Periodic entry, "NT" will be entered in the space on the Record provided for recording the entry being sent to Data Entry.

    h. At minimum, a cross-review of the Record with G.L. File will be made every four months.

5. Tie of Record to Journal Entry Register

    a. The Pre-Tax Journal Entry Register output and the Post-Tax Journal Entry Register output will be cross-reviewed with Record so as to ensure that all journal entries (both machine and manual) that should have had activity for the month are contained in the output. This will be accomplished by ensuring that the output contains information for each journal entry that is documented on the Record as having activity for the month. This review will be completed as soon as the output is received and documented by placing a mark in the appropriate space on the Record.

    b. After the Post-Tax review is complete, the Record will be signed in the appropriate space and given to the Supervisor of Records and Reports for approval and signature.

6. Filing of Journal Entries

    a. After the month's business is closed and the manual journal entries are assembled and prepared for filing, a final review of all journal entries is made for proper documentation of preparing, checking, approval and data entry. The Record and the Post-Tax Journal Entry Register will be used as the guide to determine that all journal entries processed for the month are being filed and/or bound. Any discrepancies must be resolved prior to filing and/or binding. The Record will be returned to its Follow-up Folder file until required for the following month.

Restatement of memo-report purpose — Request for approval (action)

Approval of the above recommended control procedure is requested.

APPROVED:

_____

Figure 13.2
Continued

Memo-report —
Attachment 1

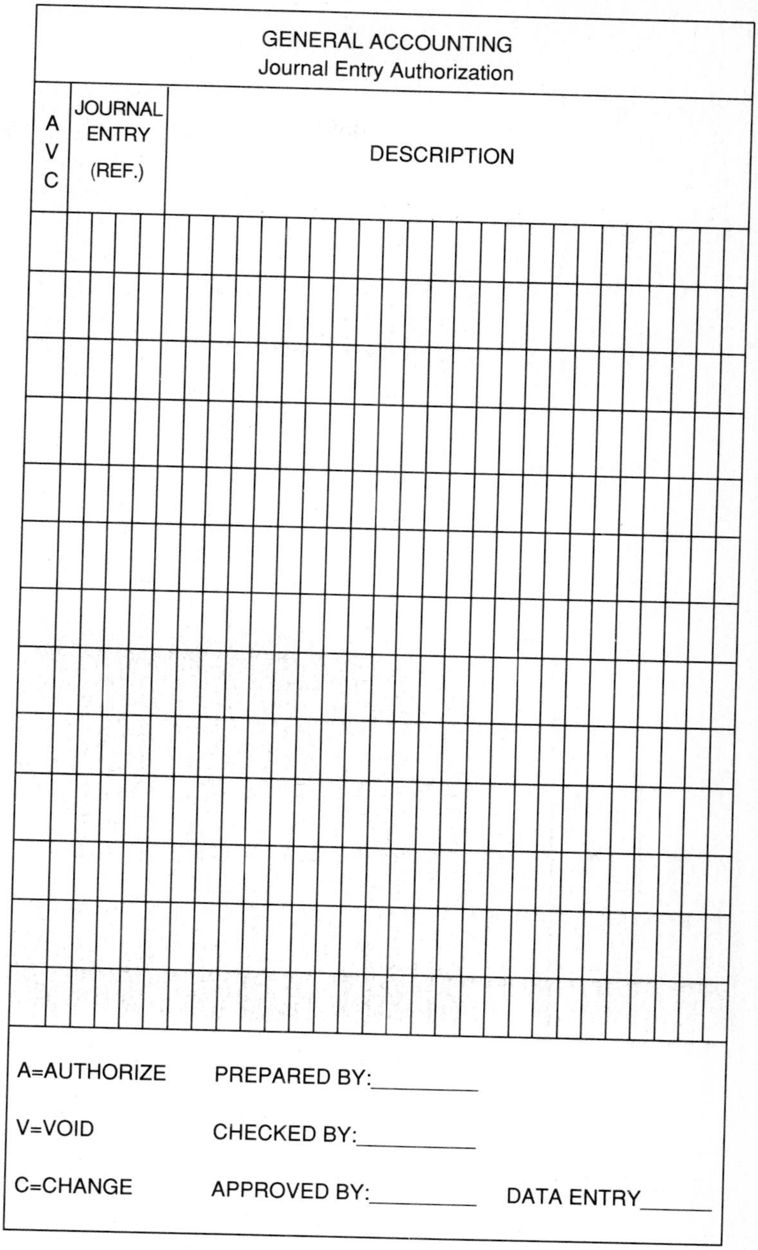

A V C	JOURNAL ENTRY (REF.)	DESCRIPTION

GENERAL ACCOUNTING
Journal Entry Authorization

A=AUTHORIZE   PREPARED BY:_____

V=VOID   CHECKED BY:_____

C=CHANGE   APPROVED BY:_____   DATA ENTRY_____

FIGURE 13.2
Continued

JOURNAL ENTRY BATCH CONTROL PROCEDURE

A. As approved journal entries are prepared and/or received by Plant Accounting Section (Plant) and Records and Reports Section (R & R), they are assembled into batches. These batches should not be large (in number of records to be entered) so that checking of hash and dollar totals is facilitated.

B. Batch preparation and checking

1. The following batch numbers are to be used:

   Pre-tax: Plant   1–49
                R & R 50–89
   Tax (Federal income tax and other journal entries) 90–99

2. Completion of the Journal Entry Batch Control form (Form) in duplicate (see attached)
   a. Batch numbers are to be sequentially assigned using the above series.
   b. The journal entry numbers included in the batch should be written in the appropriate spaces. The batch number will also be entered on the journal entry forms, which are included in the batch.
   c. The hash totals and dollar totals will be determined by aggregating the items from the records contained in the journal entries included with the batch. All hash and dollar value totals are to be entered on the Form.
      (1) The month and year are successively added and then subtracted to yield a hash total value equal to zero or the value included on one record.
      (2) All other hash totals and the dollar totals are determined by adding all the values (excluding the alphabetic digits for designation, tag and property numbers).
   d. The Form will be signed by the preparer.
   e. The batch will be detail-checked by another individual and documented by signing.
   f. The date and time submitted are to be completed.

3. The journal entries along with the duplicate Form will be forwarded to Data Entry. The duplicate Form remains in Data Entry for their records.

4. After the journal entries have been inputted by Data Entry, a Batch Control List G004 GEN (List) computer output is produced.

   a. The hash totals and dollar totals from the Form are compared to similar totals on the List. Any discrepancies must be investigated in order to correct the journal entry input and achieve a match of all hash and dollar totals.
   b. If there are no errors on the List, the Form is signed in the space provided and the List and Form are retained.
   c. If there are errors on the List, they must be submitted to Data Entry for correction. After corrections are inputted, another List must be produced and the above 2 steps (B4a. and B4b.) are completed.

5. The actual physical journal entries in a correct batch are retained as a batch in a temporary file in R & R.

6. The last List run before Pre-Tax closing and the final Tax closing will be reviewed for all batches as insurance that no Data Entry errors were made in inputting or correcting a record included in a batch number that was already correct and complete. The last List for the final Tax closing will only need to be reviewed for the batch numbers of 90 or greater.

7. The Forms and the corresponding Lists as well as the final Pre-Tax and Tax Lists will be retained on file in R & R for two months.

FIGURE 13.2
Continued

Memo-report —
Attachment 3

JOURNAL ENTRY BATCH CONTROL
BATCH NO. _____

DATE & TIME SUBMITTED _____
DATE & TIME RETURNED _____

JOURNAL ENTRIES SUBMITTED:

_____ _____ _____ _____ _____ _____ _____ _____ _____

_____ _____ _____ _____ _____ _____ _____ _____ _____

HASH TOTALS

MO. _____   YEAR _____   SOURCE _____   REF. _____

FERC NO. _____   DES. NO. _____   COST CENTER _____   TAG NO. _____

PROP. NO. _____   EST. YEAR _____   EST. NO. OR SUB/LINE NO. _____

SCHOOL DIST. _____   QUANTITY _____

DOLLAR TOTALS:

DEBITS $ _____   CREDITS $ _____

BATCH PREPARED BY: _____

BATCH CHECKED BY: _____

BATCH ENTERED BY: _____

HASH TOTALS AND DOLLAR TOTALS BALANCED TO BATCH CONTROL
LISTING BY: _____

HASH TOTALS AND DOLLAR TOTALS BALANCED TO *FINAL* BATCH CONTROL
LISTING BY: _____

FIGURE 13.2
Continued

In addition to the text of her memo-report, three **attachments** complete Ms. Merrill's package of report materials:

1. A "Journal Entry Authorization" form (designed by the general accounting department)
2. A formal outline of "Journal Entry Batch Control Procedure"
3. A "Journal Entry Batch Control/Batch No." form.

These attachments are copies of forms and further guidelines or procedures that will be used or referred to later by members of the wider corporate audience who will actually need to follow the listed journal entry control procedures.

Model 3—Proposal-Report

Brief, formal proposals like the research-based **proposal-report** we exhibit in Figure 13.3 are written to persuade their readers of a recommended policy, program, study, strategy, solution, new direction, or new idea. Based on preliminary research (pilot studies) and future research based on data collection/analysis, proposals must, as we suggested in Chapter 4, sell their ideas, solutions, new directions, or recommendations for change(s) to leaders within their own organizations or to institutional audiences within national, regional, or statewide funding agencies.

What's more, the selling function that proposals must demonstrate frequently needs to be performed in a very short space—the limited format of the short report. The proposal writers' case, therefore, must often be (a) argued quickly and concisely and (b) structured inductively so that neutral or even hostile readers might become educated, in some sense, while they are being persuaded to adopt a particular point of view, new direction, strategy, method, or recommendation for change.

The arrangement, section by section, of the formal proposal has been illustrated in Chapter 4. Here we will illustrate and examine the format of a typical inductively arranged short proposal-report (shown in Figure 13.3). Formal proposals, even those that are brief in scope and length, are generally accompanied by **letters** (or **memos**) **of transmittal** that introduce, summarize, and/or abstract the text portion of the project proposal.

The text portion of the short, formal proposal begins with the **introduction**, involving the following subsections:

1. A statement of the problem to be solved or a proposal purpose statement
2. A statement of project needs and proposed project scope
3. A brief discussion of the data to be collected and analyzed, the method of the research to be conducted (e.g., survey, experimental), and the size of the population under study or the sample
4. A list of the proposal writers or researchers involved in the project and their qualifications for undertaking the proposed research.

University of Texas Health
   Science Center at Houston
6431 Fanin St., Suite G.024 MSMB
Houston, Texas 77225

(713) 792-4732

March 6, 19--

Dr. Peter Regah, Director
National Research Foundation
10017 Constitution Avenue
Washington, D.C. 20001

SUBJECT: A Proposal for Epidemiologic Research on the Use of Psychoactive
           Drugs by Medical Students and Physicians

Dear Dr. Regah:

Letter of transmittal for proposal-report

As I mentioned to you in our telephone conversation on Monday, February 27, the University of Texas Health Science Center (UTHSC) at Houston Committee on Physician Impairment and the Harvard School of Public Health propose to conduct an 18-week survey of drug use among medical students and practicing physicians in Massachusetts.

The question of drug dependency among health care providers is of great concern to the medical profession and the general public. Practicing and future physicians who are drug addicts not only harm themselves, but may illegally channel drugs to others, and risk the health and life of their patients because they practice in an impaired state. Impaired-physician programs have been organized to deal with these problems. At this point, however, we believe that it is imperative to conduct a statistical analysis to provide base-line data for evaluating the adequacy and progress of these programs.

The projected cost for this 18-week epidemiologic research is $36,200. This seems to be a very small price to pay considering the consequences of not investigating this very serious problem.

FIGURE 13.3

Sample proposal-report—epidemiologic research on the use of psychoactive drugs.

INTRODUCTION

Subject and Purpose

Proposal-report —
Text portion

|

Purpose statement

In order to arrive at a clear picture of the extent of drug dependency among future physicians and those currently practicing in the profession, a comprehensive statistical analysis of drug abuse among medical students and physicians is considered essential. The UTHSC Committee on Physician Impairment, in conjunction with the Harvard School of Public Health, proposes to undertake a survey of drug use in a cross-section of physicians and medical students in Massachusetts.

Need

Project needs

With the recent concern over misuse of psychoactive drugs among medical professionals, all 50 states have developed impaired-physicians programs. In addition, the American Medical Association sponsors conferences addressing this problem. Without a statistical analysis of physicians' and medical students' drug use, the success of such programs will be difficult, if not impossible, to evaluate. Data on drug-use will serve as a basis for measuring the progress of these programs.

Scope

Project scope

The proposed research will focus on four general areas: (1) the frequency of drug use among medical students and physicians; (2) the recency of drug use by these groups; (3) the kinds of drugs used; and (4) the purpose of use. The purpose of use includes instrumental (to perform better or longer in sports, work, or study), recreational, and self-treating. The survey will cover the following drug categories: marijuana, cocaine, hallucinogens, stimulants, sedatives, analgesics, tranquilizers, and opiates. As a means of comparison, drug use among pharmacists and pharmacy students also will be investigated.

In addition to drug use, general information, such as the practice, specialty, the availability of drugs, and the extent of drug education, will be surveyed.

Data Sources

Project data sources

A questionnaire will be sent to: 500 physicians; 504 medical students; 510 pharmacists; and 470 pharmacy students randomly chosen from professional societies and professional schools in Massachusetts. The sample sizes are based on the percentage of each group in the state, relative to the number of physicians surveyed.

FIGURE 13.3
Continued

Project personnel —
qualifications brief

Qualifications of Personnel

The UTHSC Committee on Physician Impairment was one of the first programs of its kind in the country. The Committee comprises 8 members who have spent most of their careers studying the causes and effects of drug abuse. Three are physicians with specialties in psychiatry, emergency medicine, and internal medicine; and five hold doctoral degrees in the behavioral sciences. This committee will be working in conjunction with Dr. William E. McAuliffe and his associates at the Harvard School of Public Health. Dr. McAuliffe is a distinguished researcher in the area of drug abuse and has contributed significantly in evaluating the severity of drug dependency in other professions.

Project proposal —
central focus

PROPOSED RESEARCH

Method of data
collection and
analysis

Method

Each subject will receive (a) a cover letter explaining the research and the importance of his/her participation, (b) the multiple-choice questionnaire, and (c) a response postcard. The questionnaires are to remain unsigned so that the respondents will feel free to answer truthfully. The response postcard is to be returned separately. If a postcard is not returned within 3 weeks, a second questionnaire packet will be mailed out. Three more weeks will be allowed to elapse before a third and final questionnaire is mailed out and a telephone call is made to remind the subject.

The information will be compiled by Dr. McAuliffe and his team of statisticians. The data will then be analyzed by the UTHSC Committee on Physician Impairment, and recommendations will be made based on our findings. The study will take 18 weeks to complete.

Project budget

Projected Costs

Printing Costs

1.	$.05/cover letter 5,960 cover letters	$298.00
2.	$.15/3-page questionnaire 5,960 questionnaires	894.00
3.	$.10/response postcard 5,960 response postcards	596.00
4.	$.05/envelope 5,960 envelopes	298.00

Figure 13.3
Continued

Project budget
(continued)

Mailing Costs
  1. Postage $1,312.00

Telephone Expenses
  1. Local calls (Boston)   20.00
  2. Long-distance calls   2,260.00

Salaries
  1. UTHSC Committee members 5,522.00
  2. McAuliffe and associates 25,000.00
           —————
    TOTAL $36,200.00

CONCLUSION

Proposal conclusions —
Summary of project
and restatement of
project needs

  Drug use by medical professionals is an important issue affecting all of society. Our proposed 18-week survey will provide an accurate picture of the extent of this problem. The instruments for this investigation are already in place, the UTHSC Committee is organized, and Dr. McAuliffe and his research team are fully committed to the project. The $36,000. in funding which we are requesting is essential for the successful completion of our research and for our comprehensive report.

Respectfully,

Maria A. Halsted, M.D.
Chairperson, the UTHSC Committee
  on Physician Impairment

MAH:gba

FIGURE 13.3
Continued

The next section of the short proposal, necessarily brief and abbreviated, is its center or focus—the outline of the **proposed research** itself. This section frequently includes all or some of the following subsections:

1. Information, facts, and additional details on method(s) to be followed
2. Data collection, analyses, and procedures
3. The proposed solution(s) and method of, or directions for, implementation
4. Estimates of project-related costs (for printing, mailing, salaries).

Finally, short, formal, research-oriented proposals often close with a **summary** or **conclusions** section involving all or a portion of the following subdivisions:

1. An overview or summary of the project
2. A restatement of project needs
3. Results of a pilot study or previous studies
4. Future research to be conducted and goals for related research projects.

The short proposal-report exhibited in Figure 13.3—"A Proposal for Epidemiologic Research on the Use of Psychoactive Drugs by Medical Students and Physicians"—generally conforms to the format, inductive structure, and section (heading /subheading) requirements of typical short research proposals. The proposal is compact, yet complete; it carefully and precisely (a) identifies the subject or problem to be studied, (b) discusses the proposed research, and (c) itemizes the monies requested and considered necessary in order to carry out that research.

This short proposal-report informs, explains, and clarifies the ideas, method of data collection, and procedures for data analysis behind the study that Dr. Halsted and her colleagues at the University of Texas Health Science Center and the Harvard School of Public Health plan to conduct if funding is provided by the National Research Foundation. Dr. Halsted's proposal-report also effectively *persuades* her audience—Dr. Peter Regah and proposal readers at the National Research Foundation—of the urgency of the research study and the pressing need for the funding agency to commit requisite monies to the project.

A Final Word on Short Reports

As we noted earlier in this chapter, short reports of all kinds, unlike long informational or analytical reports, will often be read by their readers from beginning to end. Writers of short reports, then, must carefully

fine-tune, focus, and arrange the content or subject matter of their documents so that the most important information (e.g., a request for action) is presented first.

tailor their documents to meet the needs and priorities of busy readers, as well as ensure that their documents clearly articulate the writers' own purposes.

provide interested, neutral, or potentially hostile readers with sufficient data and information—in a short space—with which to make a decision and take action.

Managerial report writers who generate successful short documents must clarify and document information; in addition, they must frequently persuade their audiences of the value and importance of a particular position, strategy, idea, method, or project. Writers of short reports must discuss their ideas quickly and package them concisely for busy, and possibly inattentive, readers. In sum, successful writers of short managerial reports of all kinds must *sell* their ideas and requests in a relatively short space, convincing their readers to "buy"—decide on, act on, fund, adopt, and recall—what they are selling.

Summary

The short report is an effective means of transmitting information, decisions, and requests to, from, and through the manager in any organizational setting. We have viewed **short reports** as brief managerial documents of five pages or less of report text, often coupled with attachments or appendixes. Because of their length, short reports are frequently read from beginning to end; and because of their length they tend to arouse the interest of even unmotivated readers. Organizational readers and writers alike will benefit from short documents that are quick and easy to read.

As we saw in our discussion of managerial reports in general (see Chapter 4), reports differ in a number of overlapping ways. Short reports, though, differ chiefly in **format**, degree of **formality**, and **function**. Depending on the communication context and whether readers reside within or outside of organizations, short reports adhere to one or a combination of the following major forms: informal memo- or letter-reports, formal memo- or letter-reports, formal standard short reports, and informal or formal preprinted short reports.

To illustrate the variety of short-report forms, we have presented three model documents that typify those most commonly used in business and professional settings: a short **letter-report**; a brief, formal **memo-report**; and a short, formal **proposal-report**. As you have seen, these model reports have been examined in terms of their structures and styles, the writers' purposes, and the uses to which readers have put them. In the case of the proposal, we emphasized how the report writer must sell an idea, strategy, new method, or project to an organizational reader or external proposal evaluator.

Writers of short reports must routinely clarify and document information; they must also persuade their audiences of the value of their requests and ideas. Writers of short reports must articulate their requests, recommendations, and proposals concisely, packaging their contents for busy readers. Successful managerial report writers generate short documents that sell their ideas, information, and data-based proposals to readers in a short space, quickly convincing readers to buy what they are selling.

Related Reading

BELL, ARTHUR, and ROGER WYSE. *The One-Minute Business Writer.* Homewood, IL: Dow Jones-Irwin, 1987.

BLICQ, RON S. *Writing Reports to Get Results: Guidelines for the Computer Age.* New York: IEEE, 1987.

BOOHER, DIANNA. *Would You Put That in Writing? How to Write Your Way to Success in Business.* New York: Facts On File, 1983.

BOVEE, COURTLAND L. *Techniques of Writing Business Letters, Memos, and Reports.* 2nd ed. Los Angeles: Roxbury, 1989.

DEAL, TERRENCE E., and ALLEN A. KENNEDY. *Corporate Cultures: The Rites and Rituals of Corporate Life.* Reading, MA: Addison, 1982.

DUMAINE, DEBORAH. *Write to the Top: Writing for Corporate Success.* Rev. ed. New York: Random, 1989.

GATIEN, GARY. "Managing in the New Corporate Environment." *Technical Communication* 37 (1990): 415–419.

PAXSON, WILLIAM C. *The Business Writing Handbook.* New York: Bantam, 1981.

PFEIFFER, WILLIAM S. *Proposal Writing: The Art of Friendly Persuasion.* Columbus, OH: Merrill, 1989.

PIPES, ROSS, and ASSOCIATES. *The Pocket Proposal Style Manual—For Writers and Editors of Government Proposals.* Chapel Hill, NC: Tekne P., 1989.

REDISH, JANICE C., ROBBIN M. BATTISON, and EDWARD S. GOLD. "Making Information Accessible to Readers." *Writing in Non-Academic Settings.* Ed. Lee Odell and Dixie Goswami. New York: Guilford P., 1985. 129–153.

SCHEIN, EDGAR H. *Organizational Culture and Leadership.* San Francisco: Jossey, 1988.

THOMSETT, MICHAEL C. *The Little Black Book of Business Letters.* New York: AMACOM/American Mgmt. Assn., 1988.

——. *The Little Black Book of Business Reports.* New York: AMACOM/American Mgmt. Assn., 1988.

WASHINGTON RESEARCHERS, LTD. *Business Researcher's Handbook: The Comprehensive Guide for Business Professionals.* Washington, DC: Washington Researchers, n.d.

CHAPTER 14

Assembling the Long Formal Report

By the time you have reached this stage of assembling your report, you have invested considerable time, energy, and probably money into planning, researching, interpreting, and outlining data and information for your long report. So that you can illustrate fully and clearly the depth of your research, the significance of your findings and conclusions, and the decisiveness of your recommendations, you must select a report organization that is most appropriate for the content and degree of formality of your document.

The infinitely varied purposes, audiences, and contents of management reports produce a wide variety of report organizations, formats, and lengths. As we have already seen in Chapter 13, short management reports normally focus on very specific problems or topics of limited scope and immediate concern to an organization. Consequently, they rarely run more than a few pages in length. Likewise, their formats, as a rule, are simple—normally placed within the framework of a memo or letter, or constructed as a truncated report with only a title page to preface the report proper.

The scope of the typical formal report, on the other hand, is wider than that of the short report; thus, the research, analyses, and conclusions are often more involved, which naturally makes the formal report significantly longer. Moreover, because the formal management report is typically designed as the organization's definitive work on a specific subject, it adheres to a more formal format, which might include a range of prefatory parts and appended matter.

It is impossible to account for all the possible formal report formats. However, most formal management reports, regardless of their content, organization, and target audience(s), will contain some, if not all, of the basic

Long Formal Report	Report of Average Length	Short Report
Prefatory Parts		
Cover	Cover	
Title Fly		
Title Page	Title Page	Title Page
Letter of Authorization		
Letter of Acceptance		
Letter of Transmittal	Letter of Transmittal	
Acknowledgments		
Table of Contents	Table of Contents	
Table of Exhibits	Table of Exhibits	
Executive Summary	Executive Summary	
The Report Proper		
Introduction	Introduction	Introduction
Body	Body	Body
Conclusion	Conclusion	Conclusion
Appended Matter		
Appendix	Appendix	
Glossary		
References	References	References
Index		

FIGURE 14.1
Degrees of formality in different reports.

components of that specific report genre, depending on where they fall along the spectrum of formality (Figure 14.1). For example, while an organization's 150-page strategic planning report may incorporate all of the parts of a formal report, a three-page troubleshooting report on a particular problem within that same company may contain only one prefatory part (e.g., a title page) preceding the report proper. If placed in a memo or letter format, that same report would probably contain no prefatory parts and no appended matter at all.

Whereas Chapter 13 addresses the organization of short reports, this chapter examines the components of long formal reports:

Front Matter
Title Fly
Title Page

Letter (Memo) of Authorization
Letter (Memo) of Acceptance
Letter (Memo) of Transmittal
Acknowledgments
Table of Contents
Table of Exhibits
Executive Summary
The Report Proper
  Introduction
  Body
  Conclusion
Appended Matter
  Appendix
  Glossary
  References
  Index

Purposes of Formal Formats

The most obvious reason for formal formats is that they are necessary in making the most effective communication possible between writer and reader. The common macro components of the report proper—introduction, body, and conclusion—parallel the beginning, middle, and end of any process. Such a consistent macro organization shared by nearly all management reports maintains and promotes the predictability of report structures.

The emphasis of your report should focus on its *content*, not on creative but distracting organizational schemes. You can reinforce this aim by keeping the organization of your report so logical and coherent that it becomes transparent to the reader. By factoring the **report proper** into its organic parts (i.e., introduction, findings, analysis, conclusions, and recommendations), you (a) provide the basic elements of the report planning and research process and (b) increase reader comprehension by incorporating predictable yet critical organizational components. Standardization of the report proper enables readers to concentrate on content because of the deliberately transparent nature of the document's organization.

The **front matter** (or **prefatory parts**) and **appended matter** (e.g., appendixes, glossary, references, and index) of a formal report are intended to make the document more accessible to readers. Such front matter as the title page, table of contents, and executive summary, for example, provide readers with a preview of the report's content. The different readers of your management report, while perhaps sharing some purposes in reading the document, will most likely differ in their own individual interests, technical needs, and intended uses of the report information. Thus, by forecasting the report's content in the prefatory parts, you assist readers in deciding if the report is relevant to their informational needs.

which report parts, if not all, of the document should be read.

in what sequence those parts should be read.

Regularly pressed for time, managers, for instance, commonly scan the executive summary for key findings, conclusions, and recommendations from a report, postponing their reading of the complete report (if they read it at all) to a more convenient time. While some managers may eventually examine a report in its entirety, other managers will have the time, interest, or technical expertise to read only the central parts of the document such as its introduction, conclusion, and recommendation sections. The sections of the report containing detailed findings and interpretations on which the document's conclusions and recommendations are based are subsequently analyzed by other members of the organization whose interests or job duties are directly focused on or related to those findings and interpretations.

For example, a manager of a pharmaceutical firm would likely study the conclusions and recommendations of a troubleshooting report analyzing the recent difficulties the company has experienced in its production of a new medicine. The manager would probably then distribute the report to personnel in related technical areas of the firm, such as research and development (R & D) and production, to obtain their expert views on the accuracy and thoroughness of the report's findings, validity of its conclusions, and feasibility of its recommendations. Based on information provided in the report and corroborating or contradictory views expressed by technical personnel, the manager would plan his or her response to the production problem.

Appended matter often includes supplemental information that can help readers to understand more fully the material in the report proper, thereby increasing the effectiveness and relevance of the document. Your report, for example, might include in one of its appendixes a related study written on a problem similar to that addressed in your report to provide readers with a helpful context on the history of that problem. Likewise, a complete glossary can significantly enhance the effectiveness of a technical report especially if a segment of the audience consists of nontechnical or semitechnical readers.

The next section examines the organization, content, and format of major formal report components:

Front matter

Report proper

Appended matter

Front Matter

In this section we discuss the front matter, or prefatory parts, in the order in which they are normally presented at the beginning of a formal report. However, you will most likely plan and compose these short documents after you have completed the report. The reason for this is simple: Prefatory parts provide readers with a complete overview of the report contents, and you cannot possess this full overview until you have finished writing and revising the report.

Front matter consists of the

cover.

title fly.

title page.

letter (memo) of authorization.

letter (memo) of acceptance.

letter (memo) of transmittal.

acknowledgments.

table of contents.

table of exhibits.

executive summary.

Cover

The **cover** distinguishes a formal report as an important document in its significance to the organization. The cover should include such key information as

the report title.

name of author.

name of organization that authorized the writing of the report.

date the report is submitted.

Although there are many different cover formats, you should normally center the report title three to four inches down from the top of the cover page. The title is often typed in uppercase and underlined. Center your name as well as that of the authorizing organization receiving the report just below the center line of the cover. Capitalize only the first letters of your name as well as the key words of your organization. Center the date on which the report was submitted near the bottom of the cover.

As the report cover should maintain the neat appearance of the report through the handling over time by multiple readers, it should be constructed of durable material and bound, for example, by a ring notebook, plastic or wire spiral, or binding clip. To maximize reader convenience, choose a binding system that allows the opened document to lie flat.

Title Fly

Although it is not numbered, the **title fly** is formally considered the first page in the prefatory parts section of a report. It typically contains only the report title, which clearly states the purpose and subject of the report.

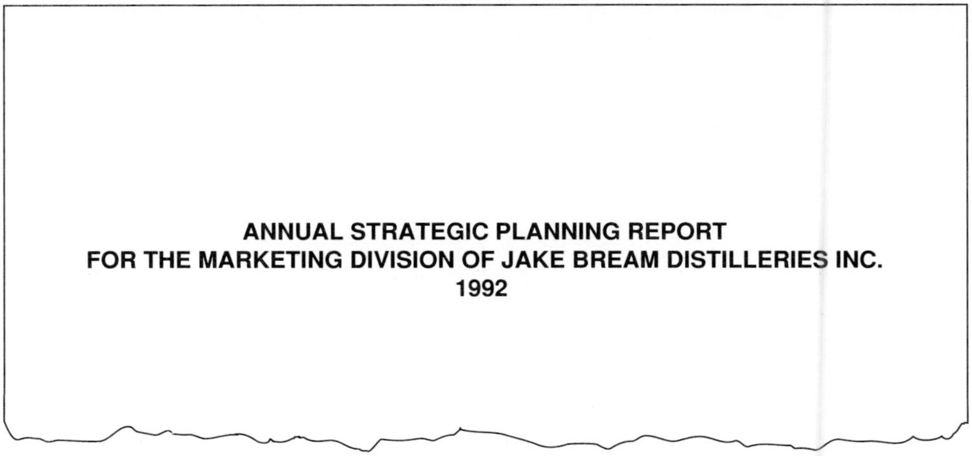

**ANNUAL STRATEGIC PLANNING REPORT
FOR THE MARKETING DIVISION OF JAKE BREAM DISTILLERIES INC.
1992**

FIGURE 14.2
Title fly.

You should carefully word the title so that readers can easily and quickly recognize the central thrust of the report. To ensure that you have included in the title the main elements of the report's purpose and scope, you might address the *who, what, where, when, and why*—commonly referred to as the journalist's five *W*s—surrounding your report. Although rare, some report titles even hint as to *how* the report problem was studied.

A major weakness of many report titles is that they are not specific enough to provide readers with a clear idea of the document's focus, such as the following title, which is too general and vague:

STRATEGIC PLANNING REPORT

This title fails to answer key questions any reader would bring to this report: *Whose* strategic plan is it? For what time period? Is it a strategic plan for the entire company or for particular divisions within the organization? What key issues are addressed? The report title presented on the sample title fly in Figure 14.2, on the other hand, clearly identifies the central thrust of a strategic planning report, the organization for which the document is written, and the time period being examined. The title also implicitly tells *why* the report was written: to supply the distillery a sound plan for future growth in its marketing division.[1]

While a report title must be clear, accurate, and comprehensive, it must also be concise. The sample title below is so detailed and specific that its wordiness could easily confuse readers regarding the report's specific focus and scope:

[1]We would like to thank Yoliette Galarza, Jack Johnston, Tywain Segaline, and John Thompson for the use of their report on which many of the sample report components contained in this chapter are based.

ANNUAL STRATEGIC PLANNING REPORT FOR 1991
ON TAXATION, REVENUE, AND POLITICAL LOBBYING ISSUES
AND RELEVANT RESEARCH & DEVELOPMENT CONCERNS
RELATING TO THE MARKETING AND SALES DIVISION
OF JAKE BREAM DISTILLERIES, INC.

Constructing an effective title that provides readers with a clear window to your report's purpose and scope is not a simple, last-minute afterthought but, rather, an important process requiring that you (a) fully define and understand the objectives and parameters of your report and (b) revise repeatedly to produce a highly precise, specific, and yet concise distillate of the report's parameters. If the title runs more than seven or eight words in length, you might consider dividing and placing it on two separate lines.

Title Page

The **title page** of a formal report consists of four components:

1. The report title
2. The names and addresses of people or the organization to whom the report is being submitted
3. The names and addresses of authors of the report and their affiliations
4. The date on which the report was submitted.

Figure 14.3 provides a sample title page for Jake Bream Distilleries' 5-year strategic planning report.

Like the title fly, the title page is not numbered. It is, however, considered page ii of the prefatory parts (page i if your report contains no title fly). Center all four components of the title page, with the title beginning approximately two inches down from the top of the page. Double-space components on the page, giving additional space between the four major components.

The recipient component is typically introduced with the phrase "Submitted to" or "Written for," while the author component is identified by the opening phrase "Submitted by" or "Written by." The recipient component should include the names and titles of the people (if known) who are to receive the report, the name of the organization for which the report is written, and the city and state location of the organization. The author component includes the name of the author, his or her title, and the name and address of his or her organization (and, occasionally, division). Center the date of submission at least an inch up from the bottom of the page.

As illustrated in Figure 14.3, the entire title is normally printed in uppercase and underlined for emphasis. However, with the type font and special formatting capabilities of today's word processing and desktop publishing software, you may create your own consistent system for highlighting not only your document's title but also report headings and subheadings. Finally, reports that do not include an executive summary may place an abstract of the document's purpose, scope, and conclusions on the lower half of the title page.

ANNUAL STRATEGIC PLANNING REPORT

FOR THE MARKETING DIVISION OF JAKE BREAM DISTILLERIES, INC.

1992

Submitted to

Wilhemina J. Atley, President and
Chief Executive Officer

Frederick M. Dobson, Executive Vice-President
of Domestic Operations

Thomas C. Haynes, Vice-President for Marketing and Sales

Marketing and Sales Headquarters
Jake Bream Distilleries, Inc.
Nashville, Tennessee

Submitted by

Tyrone Swenson, Chief Analyst for Marketing and Sales

Frances Drummond, Marketing and Sales Coordinator

Marketing and Sales Division
Jake Bream Distilleries, Inc.
Memphis, Tennessee

August 1, 1991

FIGURE 14.3
Title page.

Letter (Memo) of Authorization

The **letter** (or memo) **of authorization** is the document that originally granted you the responsibility to research and write the report (Figure 14.4). The letter, or memo, usually states the general purpose and scope of the proposed report as well as possible methods for researching the report problem. Although both the letter and the memo of authorization are comparable in content and organization, the memo of authorization (like memos of acceptance and transmittal) is used for correspondence inside the organization. The letter of authorization is appropriate for corresponding with readers outside the organization.

The authorization letter written by Thomas C. Haynes, vice-president of marketing and sales (Figure 14.4), authorizes Tyrone Swenson to supervise the design, research, and preparation of the 1992 annual strategic plan for the marketing and sales division of Jake Bream Distilleries, Inc. Moreover, Haynes outlines the scope of the project and mentions specific issues that the report writer might address. The letter also notes why the report is needed and where Swenson's report fits into the larger context of a companywide strategic plan. Furthermore, Haynes announces the deadline for the report's scheduled completion.

The letter of authorization, like most formal business letters, normally adheres to a block, modified block, or simple block letter format. Figure 14.4 illustrates the letter in a standard block format. The format requirements for letters vary widely from one organization to another. Business letters, however, are typically written on the organization's letterhead stationery and are single-spaced. The first line of each paragraph may, or may not, be indented, depending on the letter style preferred by your organization. Maintain at least one-inch margins on all four sides of the letter, with the left margin preferably one-half inch wider than the other three margins.

Letter (Memo) of Acceptance

In the **letter** (or memo) **of acceptance**, the author formally accepts the assignment and the related responsibilities of planning and completing the report (Figure 14.5). The letter of acceptance typically states the author's commitment to the report project, confirms the report's scope, and closes with a positive plan for action. In addition to including these components, the sample letter of acceptance in Figure 14.5 also summarizes the methodology that the author intends to follow in researching the report problem. Moreover, the author notes important dates regarding the report-writing schedule. In the sample letter of acceptance offered here, Swenson is implicitly offering a plan for action by specifying a deadline for submitting to Haynes a work plan for the project.

As the letter of acceptance and letter of authorization share many major components, you will normally include one of these two documents in the front matter of your report, but rarely both. Your letter of acceptance should adhere to the same letter format guidelines noted in our discussion of the letter of authorization.

JAKE BREAM DISTILLERIES, INC.
Marketing and Sales Headquarters
1618 Bolton Avenue, Suite 310
Nashville, Tennessee 32719
(615) 555-1234

March 16, 1991

Tyrone Swenson
Chief Analyst for Marketing and Sales
Jake Bream Distilleries, Inc.
1220 Oleander Boulevard
Knoxville, TN 38103

Dear Mr. Swenson:

During its second-quarter meeting, the Board of Directors for Jake Bream reemphasized the firm's goal to significantly increase sales of its distilled spirits for the next fiscal year. Based on the excellent strategic planning reports your marketing research group has produced for the past two years, I would like you to supervise the research and preparation of the 1992 annual strategic plan for the Marketing and Sales Division.

Although sales of Jake Bream distilled spirits have risen steadily since 1985, a number of recent events may well influence <u>what</u> distilled spirits products Jake Bream decides to market next year and how those spirits will be marketed. As in previous reports, your strategic planning group should address key challenges our marketing and sales division will face during the upcoming year. In this particular report, however, you might devote special attention to federal and state regulation and legislation activities that pose a growing threat to the company's marketing efforts toward younger consumers.

So that our strategic planning report can be merged and printed with those from other divisions by September 1, please submit your report to my office by August 1.

If I can offer your group any assistance, please don't hesitate to call on me.

Sincerely,

Thomas C. Haynes

Thomas C. Haynes
Vice-President for Corporate Marketing and Sales

TCH/mg

FIGURE 14.4
Letter of authorization.

JAKE BREAM DISTILLERIES, INC.
Marketing and Sales Division
1220 Oleander Boulevard
Memphis, Tennessee 38103
(901) 234-8899

March 23, 1991

Thomas C. Haynes
Vice-President for Corporate Marketing and Sales
Jake Bream Distilleries, Inc.
1618 Bolton Avenue, Suite 310
Nashville, TN 37219

Dear Mr. Haynes:

I look forward to working once again with the strategic-planning group for the Marketing and Sales Division in preparing our 1992 strategic plan. Having already briefed group members regarding project parameters and schedule, I am certain that we can complete and submit the final report by the August 1 deadline.

As in past years, the strategic planning group will investigate central issues surrounding the marketing and sales of our distilled spirits, such as current demographics of target markets, level of competition in general as well as select markets, pricing strategies, and marketing strategies. As you suggested, we will also study ongoing regulation and legislation activities of federal and state governments. One particular area of concern is the influence lobbyists (such as MADD) are having in persuading federal legislators to establish a national legal drinking age at 21 or higher.

Research methods for this project will vary, as they have in previous reports, to fit the nature of the material being sought. We will use various telephone and mail surveys, as well as personal interviews, to obtain market demographics information. Secondary research into government documents and personal interviews, at this time, appear to offer the best chances of culling timely and accurate information regarding future federal and state legislation.

I will send you a copy of the strategic planning group's work plan and document schedule by April 1. All of us here look forward to yet another successful glimpse into next year's strategies, goals, and objectives of the marketing and sales division.

Sincerely,

Tyrone Swenson

Tyrone Swenson
Chief Analyst for Marketing and Sales

Figure 14.5
Letter of acceptance.

Letter (Memo) of Transmittal

The **letter** (or memo) **of transmittal** formally submits, or "transmits," the finished report to its target reader(s). Also referred to as the *cover letter*, the letter of transmittal, like the one shown in Figure 14.6, should follow a direct organization scheme. That is, it should immediately open with the point of the letter; no prefatory information is necessary to explain or justify the document's purpose.

The letter of transmittal is typically no more than one page in length. Its introduction should acknowledge the person who, or organization that, authorized the report, as well as when and why the report was authorized. The *why* may be integrated into the second component of the introduction paragraph: a clear statement of the report's purpose. If possible, incorporate the scope of the report into the purpose statement. However, if the scope is too complex for such distillation, place the parameters of the report in the letter's second paragraph.

The letter's second paragraph should refer very briefly to the most significant findings, conclusions, or recommendations contained in the report. If the report's scope is too large and complex to include in the letter's introductory paragraph, the second paragraph will consist solely of the scope, and the findings, conclusions, or recommendations will be moved to the third paragraph. A subsequent paragraph might also comment on other important issues surrounding the report, such as

limitations of the study.

ideas on how the report might be most effectively used.

the need for follow-up investigations.

acknowledgment of people who assisted you in the planning, researching, or writing of the report.

The letter of transmittal and executive summary do somewhat overlap in the information they provide. However, the executive summary expands on these same topics with significantly more detail. These documents, however, are not redundant, as they serve two different functions: The letter of transmittal transmits the report and notes the document's purpose, scope, and major conclusions; the executive summary forecasts for the reader and previews the content of each major section of the report. In addition, because the letter of transmittal is directed toward a specific person and may contain sensitive information meant only for that reader, the report recipient may remove the letter before distributing the document to other readers in the organization, making an executive summary necessary as a synopsis of the report.

You should close the letter with a warm note of appreciation for having had the opportunity to work on the report project. In the closing paragraph you might also urge the reader toward action based on report findings and conclusions. Although you might end the letter by suggesting that the reader contact you should he or she have questions concerning the document's

JAKE BREAM DISTILLERIES, INC.
Marketing and Sales Division
1220 Oleander Boulevard
Memphis, Tennessee 38103
(901) 234-8899

August 1, 1991

Thomas C. Haynes
Vice-President for Corporate Marketing and Sales
Jake Bream Distilleries, Inc.
1618 Bolton Avenue, Suite 310
Nashville, TN 37219

Dear Mr. Haynes:

Here is the 1992 strategic-planning report for the Marketing and Sales Division that you requested March 16.

The strategic-planning report bases its strategic plan for the fiscal 1992 on our examination and analysis of the division's current financial condition, recent changes in the firm's target market for distilled spirits, level of competition in general as well as select markets, pricing strategies, marketing strategies, and government regulation and legislation.

Among other recommendations, the report suggests that the division increase its marketing efforts (via celebrity endorsements) toward younger and more ethnically and racially varied consumers and to consider the marketing of new products—such as low-alcohol spirits and spritzers—to attract this growing segment of the consumer market.

The report also recommends that the division continue lobbying campaigns to maintain federal and state excise taxes at current levels, institute education programs at primary and secondary levels to prevent alcohol abuse, and form professional lobbyist groups to argue against a national drinking age of 21.

Members of the division's strategic planning group and I appreciate having had the opportunity to prepare the planning report. I will contact you within the week to answer any questions you might have regarding the report's findings, conclusions, and recommendations.

Sincerely,

Tyrone Swenson

Tyrone Swenson
Chief Analyst for Marketing and Sales

TS/ao

FIGURE 14.6
Letter of transmittal.

content, you might, instead, follow common professional courtesy and note that you will phone the reader during a specified period of time to answer any possible questions regarding the report. Even if the reader has no major questions, the follow-up call allows you to maintain a positive business relationship with the reader, who, in many cases, is your superior. Furthermore, because you are not forcing the reader to expend the time and energy to contact you, you are showing the reader an appropriate degree of respect and courtesy.

The letter of transmittal is similar in structure and content to a traditional *preface* and *forward*. The tone of all three documents should be personable, courteous, and positive. Your use of first-person personal pronouns, such as "I" and "we" and the second-person pronoun "you" will contribute to the warmth and friendliness of a prefatory document. Although the preface and forward tend to place more emphasis on such research concerns as methodology and assistance provided the study by colleagues and other experts, all three prefatory parts aim to help the reader better understand the report by focusing readers' attention on key findings and conclusions.

Acknowledgments

If you have received significant help from other people in planning, researching, or writing the report, you may want to acknowledge them formally on the **acknowledgments** page (Figure 14.7). Although the letter of transmittal offers you the chance to mention the assistance of others, you may need the extra

---

ACKNOWLEDGMENTS

We deeply appreciate the flexibility provided us by Thomas C. Hayne, Vice-President for Corporate Marketing and Sales, to research, write, and revise this report as we felt would best lay the foundations for an effective 1992 strategic plan for the division. We also would like to acknowledge Elizabeth Rand and Roger Auckland of the Special Projects Division for their expertise in statistical analysis, which enabled our investigation team to produce accurate and reliable data from our series of administered questionnaires. Lastly, we wish to thank our excellent support staff of researchers and writers—Diane Bates, Robert Cain, Antonio Garcia, and Carmen La Blanc—who invested many long hours to make this a successful report.

FIGURE 14.7
Acknowledgments page.

space to explain the special help that you've received from people in such areas as secondary research, interviewing, experimental research, surveying, revision and editing, and document design.

As illustrated in Figure 14.7, the title for the acknowledgments page is centered approximately two inches down from the top of the page and printed in upper case. The acknowledgments page also is normally double-spaced and has the same margin settings as those for the report proper (i.e., at least one inch on all sides, with the left margin being approximately one-half inch wider).

Table of Contents

Constructed from your formal outline, the **table of contents**, also called the *contents page*, serves as a road map for readers as it forecasts the general organization of your report as well as the depth of coverage provided for each report topic (Figure 14.8). The table of contents normally includes

- all major headings and subheadings in the order in which they appear in the report proper.
- the page numbers on which the headings and their respective subsections appear in the report.
- rows of dots, or leaders, to connect headings with their respective page numbers.

The table of contents may be single- or double-spaced. If you single-space, be sure to double-space between major headings as a formatting device to emphasize the transition between these distinct sections. Although each prefatory part included in the report is counted as a page in the overall report (except the cover), the table of contents normally lists only the following front matter: the table of exhibits, preface or forward (if any), and executive summary. All front matter noted in the table of contents is numbered in small roman numerals. The table of exhibits page, then, in a formal report that includes a title fly, title page, letter of authorization, and letter of transmittal would be listed as page vi on the table of contents page, and the executive summary as page vii. All pages from the report proper (the introduction, body, and conclusion of the report) and appended matter (e.g., reference page, appendixes, glossary, and index) are listed in arabic numerals, with the first page of the report proper serving as page 1.

All major headings and subheadings (usually first-, second-, and sometimes third-level headings) must appear in the table of contents, and the placement of the heading should reflect its level of importance. The sample table of contents in Figure 14.8, for example, includes decimal numbers and indentions to illustrate the subordination of heading levels. All primary headings are also placed in uppercase to underscore their importance. All headings noted in the table of contents must be phrased exactly as they are in the report. Chapter 15 discusses in greater detail headings and formatting devices used in document design.

TABLE OF CONTENTS

v

FIGURE 14.8
Table of contents.

Table of Exhibits

Your management report will most likely contain graphic aids such as tables, graphs, charts, diagrams, and photographs. If your report contains more than four or five graphic aids, you should list them by title on the **table of exhibits** page (Figure 14.9). The table of exhibits page is frequently referred to in a variety of different ways, including *table of charts and illustrations*, *list of illustrations*, and *list of tables and figures*. Formatted like the table of contents, the table of exhibits includes

the number of each graphic aid presented in the report.

the title of the graphic aid.

the page on which the graphic aid appears in the report.

leaders to connect the graphic's title with its respective page number.

The sample table of exhibits in Figure 14.9 includes decimal numbers to identify the chapter and section where each graphic aid appears in the report. As discussed in Chapter 12, the two major types of graphics are tables and figures. Because a report might contain several of each graphic type, the table of exhibits uses subheadings to distinguish between tables and figures. Like the table of contents, the table of exhibits may be single- or double-spaced, with single-spaced tables being double-spaced between exhibit titles and their respective page numbers. Note that the table of exhibits, like the table of contents page, is numbered with a roman numeral at the bottom of the page.

Executive Summary

Rarely will managers have the time to sit down and read a recently completed and submitted report from cover to cover. Typically, management reports are read when readers consciously create a wedge of time during a busy schedule. The **executive summary** assists managers in fully and quickly recognizing the importance of your report and in estimating how much time should be allocated to reading the document (if the entire report is read at all).

The executive summary is an accurate and representative distillation of the report proper (Figure 14.10). In addition to stating the purpose, scope, and background of the report, the executive summary summarizes its major findings, conclusions, and recommendations. You may also briefly explain the research methodology used to investigate the report problem. Although placed near the beginning of your formal report, the executive summary, like the other front matter, is written only after you have completed the report proper.

Because it is targeted toward managers who require a brief synopsis of conclusions and recommendations (if any), you should normally arrange the information deductively, or directly. First introduce the purpose and scope of the report, followed by its key conclusions and recommendations. Then close the summary with a summary of the report's most important findings and,

TABLE OF EXHIBITS

vi

FIGURE 14.9
Table of exhibits.

perhaps, the research methods used to collect report data and information. When composing your executive summary, add no information that is not covered in the report itself.

Although most executive summaries are deductively organized, some report writers choose to arrange the summary inductively, or indirectly— providing information in the order in which it is discussed and analyzed in the report. The executive summary of an inductively organized report would begin with a statement of purpose and scope, a discussion of research methods (if relevant), followed by key findings, conclusions, and, lastly, recommendations.

In condensing the report, keep your summary of report sections proportionate to the amount of coverage given those sections in the report itself. A 10-page findings section and a 5-page analysis section of a 20-page report, for example, would warrant approximately 50 and 25 percent, respectively, of the space in the executive summary. The executive summary maintains the margin settings of the report proper and is single- or double-spaced, but it rarely exceeds more than one page in length, never more than two pages. You may find listing key findings, conclusions, and recommendations a useful method for compressing information. The integration of major headings into your executive summary can assist readers in quickly accessing specific types of information, while ensuring smooth transitions between topics.

If your report does not contain an executive summary, you may decide to include a **descriptive** or an **informative abstract** on a separate page before the report proper, or at the bottom of the title page. A descriptive abstract merely describes what the report is about. Normally no longer than one or two sentences, the descriptive abstract mentions the purpose and the scope of the report. An informative abstract, on the other hand, tells readers what the report contains. Informative abstracts typically run two to three paragraphs in length and include a summary of the report's key findings and conclusions.

The sample executive summary in Figure 14.10 uses a deductive organization, as it places the conclusions and recommendations of the report immediately after a short introduction. Major findings and a highly compressed analysis of those findings appear last in the summary. As it is an optional component in the executive summary, the key findings section is frequently omitted for the sake of conciseness.

On a micro level, the introduction of the executive summary states the purpose and scope of the report, briefly explores critical components for orienting readers to the general context of the report problem, and identifies the report's parameters. The conclusions section summarizes the overall assessment of major issues under study (i.e., the firm's financial condition, recent changes in its target market, current status of government taxation of distilled spirits, and opponents of the distilled spirits industry), while the recommendations section specifies important plans for action. Each paragraph in the findings and analysis section notes only the most crucial facts and analyses on which those conclusions and recommendations are based.

EXECUTIVE SUMMARY

Introduction

This strategic planning report for the Marketing and Sales Division of Jake Bream Distilleries, Inc., recommends a strategic plan for fiscal 1992 based on our examination and analysis of the division's current financial condition and recent changes in the firm's target market for consumers of distilled spirits. The report also studies the current status of government taxation of distilled spirits as well as opponents of the distilled spirits industry—two central issues that could significantly affect future Jake Bream marketing and sales strategies.

Conclusions

Shifts in consumer demographics and political sentiment toward the distilling industry require new marketing and sales goals and techniques.

Women and minorities continue to represent a growing percentage of distilled spirits consumers. By 1993, the majority of consumers of Jake Bream products will be female, black, or Hispanic. The age group from 18 to 35 continues to represent our largest consumer segment. Marketing strategies should be aimed directly at attracting and holding a dominant segment of this younger and more ethnically-racially varied population of consumers.

As the rates of federal and state taxation of distilled spirits will remain constant for at least the next 12 months, no modification of current pricing is required.

Efforts by federal and state lobbyists to reduce drinking by younger consumers may result in weaker sales to consumers between the ages of 18 and 21. Jake Bream, along with others in the distilled spirits industry, should solidify its impact on state and federal governments through increased lobbyist activity.

Recommendations

The marketing and sales strategic report recommends that the division

- increase marketing efforts (via celebrity endorsements) toward younger and more ethnically and racially varied consumers

- consider the marketing of new products, such as low alcohol spirits and spritzers, to attract this growing segment of the consumer market

FIGURE 14.10
Executive summary.

- increase bonuses to leading retailers of Jake Bream products

- continue lobbying campaigns to maintain federal and state excise taxes at current levels

- form professional lobbyists groups to argue against a national drinking age of 21

- institute education programs at primary and secondary school levels to prevent alchohol abuse

- establish an annual university scholarship of 10,000 to be awarded by selected local chapters of MADD across the country.

Findings and Analysis

Jake Bream sold more than six million cases of distilled spirits in 1990, placing the corporation as the third largest U.S. producer and distributor of distilled spirits. Consumption of Jake Bream spirits continues to grow steadily, increasing nearly 35% since 1985. The firm is the leading producer of bourbon whiskey in the United States, controlling nearly 34% of the market in 1990, an increase of 2% from 1989.

Our demographic survey of Jake Bream consumers suggests that men purchased 73% of the spirits produced by the firm in 1990. This figure is slightly down from the 78% level recorded for fiscal 1989. Women and minorities between the ages of 18 and 35 represent the fastest growing market for Jake Bream distilled spirits.

Since 1937, federal and state governments have consistently increased tax rates on distilled spirits. Federal taxes have increased an average of 3.8% annually during that time, with Federal Excise Tax on a gallon of distilled spirits currently at 12.5%. State taxes on distilled spirits vary, with the average state tax ranging from 3.06 to 3.25% per gallon. Six states—New York, California, Florida, Texas, Pennsylvania, and Ohio—account for 40% of all state tax revenues.

Effective lobbyists, such as Mothers Against Drunk Drivers (MADD), continue to influence government regulators of the distilled spirits industry. MADD's call for stricter drinking laws is having an impact on Congressional leaders. While Jake Bream publicly supports stiffer penalties for those who abuse the use of alcoholic beverages, we believe the solution to alcohol abuse lies in educational programs and not in more government legislative interference.

FIGURE 14.10
Continued

The Report Proper

The possible organizations of management reports are unlimited, as they are determined according to the (a) unique and varied informational needs of report audience(s); (b) purpose, scope, and content of each document; and (c) arrangement requirements established by groups sponsoring the reports. Despite this seemingly confusing abundance of report organizations, however, the large majority of management reports follow one of two general, or macro, arrangement plans: indirect and direct.

The **inductive**, or indirect, organization presents the report in much the same order in which you have planned, researched, and composed your study. An inductively arranged report opens with the introduction section, which provides the reader with a clear context for reading and understanding the report. The introduction forecasts the report's organization and content by noting such key elements of the study as its purpose, scope, methods, and limitations. The findings of your research follow the introduction. The results are then interpreted as they relate to the report problem in the analysis section of the report, followed by the conclusion, which contains a summary of major findings and interpretations and, often, recommendations for solving the report problem.

The inductive approach is especially useful when presenting the report to an audience who you believe might be unreceptive to your conclusions or recommendations. Placing findings and interpretations before the conclusion has several important advantages. First, findings and interpretations serve as the groundwork and justification for subsequent conclusions and recommendations, preparing unreceptive readers for possibly unwelcome news. Also, by delaying your conclusions and recommendations, you stand the best chance of keeping the minds of hostile readers open to your views as long as possible. Introducing your conclusions and recommendations before explaining the evidence on which you base those ideas will usually meet with a sudden, negative reaction from readers who will not recognize your rationale regardless of how high and wide you subsequently pile the evidence.

A report organized according to the **deductive**, or direct, arrangement opens with the document's introduction, followed by its conclusions and any accompanying recommendations. The findings and analysis sections come last in a deductively organized report. Documents arranged deductively are most effective when written to receptive audiences who require your conclusions and recommendations fast. Many managers, pressed for time, welcome deductively organized reports from which they can quickly glean the "bottom line" of the writer's argument and make initial decisions based on the report's conclusions and recommendations. The report can then be distributed to other personnel in related fields for further analysis, discussion, and decision making.

Examples of the report proper and their constituent components—including the introduction, body, and conclusion—are provided in Chapter 15 and Appendix B.

Report Introduction

The report introduction orients readers to the purpose and scope of your report, while also containing other components—such as background of the problem, methods, key research sources, limitations of the study, term definitions, and report preview—that provide the reader with important contextual information for understanding the report problem. By stating the nature and parameters of the research, your introduction *forecasts* for readers not only the content of your report but also its organization. You may decide to place each introductory component, depending on its length and significance, in a distinct subsection with an accompanying heading, or merge shorter, less important components under a combined heading (Maki & Shilling, 1987).

Introduction sections typically include the following components:

1. Purpose of the report
2. Report scope
3. Background of the problem addressed in the report
4. Research methods
5. Sources
6. Limitations to the study
7. Definitions of technical terms
8. Report preview.

Purpose

In the **purpose** component of the introduction section, you clearly state primary and secondary goals of the report. In effect, the purpose component answers *why* you have researched and reported on a particular problem and *what* you expect to accomplish by completing the project.

Normally the purpose statement requires only one or two sentences. Some authors phrase the purpose statement as a question (e.g., "What is the fourth-quarter marketing forecast for the Belleville operation?"). However, a straightforward, declarative wording of the report purpose (e.g., "The purpose of this marketing forecast report is to...") often proves even more effective, as it

specifies the purpose of your report in unmistakable terms.

forces you to understand fully the aims of the report in order to capsulize its focus precisely for readers.

provides you with a clear and confidently declared mission from which you should not deviate in the writing and presentation of the report.

Scope

The **scope** component should outline the parameters of your research and the resulting report. By defining the report's parameters, you clarify for the reader the issues surrounding the report problem. In some cases, you may need to explain why you have narrowed, or broadened, the topic as you have. The scope of your report should be both inclusive and exclusive. That is, your report should include all topics that are significant to solving the report problem; you should exclude topics that, while related to the problem, are not central to its solution.

Background

To appreciate fully the scope, significance, or urgency of a report problem, readers often need to understand its historical background. The **background** component of the introduction, then, should offer readers answers to this question: How did the subject being researched and studied get to the point of becoming a problem or an important area of concern for your organization? Once aware of the historical source, context, and causes of the report problem, readers are better able to recognize the appropriateness of the research methods selected by the writer as well as the validity of the report's findings, interpretations, conclusions, and recommendations.

In addition to presenting the relevant issues and their significance to the central problem addressed in the report, the background component might also explain how the problem evolved into a subject requiring investigation. Questions that you might answer in the background section include the following:

- Who authorized the researching of the problem and the subsequent report? When? Why?
- How was the authorization given—by formal letter of authorization, by telephone, or by interoffice memo originating from a committee decision?
- What were the purpose and parameters given for the authorized study?
- Which departments, divisions, or offices were involved in the study and to what degree?

Such information proves invaluable in reports that include no letter of authorization, acceptance, or transmittal.

Research Methods

In researching the report problem, you might have used a variety of **research methods**. For example, you could have conducted extensive secondary research on the subject in your local university library and found that its computerized data-based sources proved extremely helpful in understanding past and current literature on the problem. You could also have performed primary research. For instance, you might have consulted with colleagues within your organization regarding their understanding of the problem and possible solutions. Moreover, you might have incorporated any combination of other primary research methods such as surveys (e.g., mail surveys, telephone, and personal interviews) and experiments to obtain the most current data and information from specific sources within your organization or industry.

In the methods component, documenting the research methods you have employed to study your particular report problem is important for several reasons:

- Clearly and thoroughly documented methods indicate to readers the validity and appropriateness of your research design as well as the reliability of your findings, interpretations, and conclusions.
- By documenting how you collected your data and information, you enhance the credibility and, thus, the importance and usefulness of your report, as you have carefully and objectively investigated the report problem according to accepted research standards.
- A report containing a precise and detailed explanation of the researcher's methodology is helpful to readers who hope to perform similar research and require some understanding of how others conducted parallel work on comparable problems.

Your methods component should provide enough information for readers to recognize the value and validity of your research, if not reproduce the research and obtain similar results. If you have performed secondary research, for example, you should note the types of works (e.g., books, trade journals, government documents, microfilm-based dissertations) that provided you with the most significant information. You should also identify the name and location of the libraries—such as your organization's private library, a local university library, or public library—where you performed the secondary research, as well as the dates when the research was done.

If your report introduction does not contain a sources component, you might also want to refer to the specific titles of major secondary works that proved most useful in your research. However, because the methods component is not meant as a bibliography or reference section, limit your listing of titles to only those considered most central to your project.

If you have conducted interviews as part of your research methods, you should include information to answer such fundamental primary research questions as these:

- Under what conditions were the interviews performed (e.g., when, where, with whom)?
- What was the size of the sample population?
- How was that population selected (e.g., using random sampling techniques, stratified random sampling techniques)?
- How was the questionnaire designed?
- How were the collected data tabulated?
- What statistical analyses were used (if any) on your data?
- How was the reliability of the sample and results verified?

For reports whose results and conclusions depend heavily on the methods employed, you may choose to emphasize the methods component by separating it from the introduction and allocating to this component its own major heading immediately after the introduction section. When report data or information is collected from surveys, you should include a sample of the questionnaire in an appendix at the end of your report.

Sources

The **sources** component of your introduction may be a part of the methods component, or it may be placed under its own heading, serving as an extension of the methods component. The sources component identifies for readers the most (and least) useful sources of data and information that you encountered during your research into the report problem. The component's primary purpose is to provide fellow researchers with an accurate idea of which sources they might find most (and least) helpful in performing research on the same or related subjects.

Like the methods section, the sources component is not meant as a bibliography; rather, it is only a reference to and brief discussion of selected sources. The sources component should refer readers to useful secondary sources. The component also might be equally effective in directing readers toward helpful primary sources such as valuable interviewees and sample survey populations. If you wish to include a source component in your report, remember to refer to no more than three or four sources that were (or were not) significant in your research. Be sure also to explain briefly why they were particularly helpful or not helpful.

Limitations

Rarely does a report attain everything its author hoped to achieve when planning the document. Conditions surrounding the research and writing of the report may change without notice and, consequently, affect the success and impact of the report in unpredictable ways. The **limitations** component identifies the major influences that may have, to a significant degree, impeded the report or somehow prevented it from realizing its anticipated level of success. As limitations of the report can directly influence the document's scope, you may decide to discuss both scope and limitations under a joint heading.

Limitations might include inadequate time allotted to the project, a loss or reduction of funding, or unforeseen difficulties in collecting the required sources through either secondary or primary research. Perhaps only later, during the course of your investigation, you recognized that the very nature of the report problem prevented you from realizing any definitive conclusion to the study. A marketing survey, for example, that attempts to answer why a specific target population of women prefer one fashion of pleated skirts over another may quickly run up against the enigmatic answer "Because we just like it" or "We look better in this fashion, that's all." Clearly, that's *not* all, but the research demands required to understand fully the psychology on which the respondents base their tastes in fashion would rarely fit into the time schedule and budget of the average management report.

Definitions

If your report contains terminology with which some, or all, of your readers may not be familiar, you might consider including a **definitions** component in the introduction section. Even though your readers may be knowledgeable in the general field in which you are writing, they may not have the technical expertise in the specific area of study. Include in the definitions component all terms that you feel target readers with the least amount of background in the report area might find difficult to understand; then provide a thorough definition of each term.

If you discover that numerous words need defining, you should consider placing the terms in a glossary section (as an appendix) at the end of the report. A long definitions component should be avoided as it tends to disrupt the flow of the introduction section. If only a few words need defining, you might simply define them where they are first used in the context of your report and forego a definitions components.

Report Preview

Longer, more complex reports may contain a **report preview** component that forecasts for readers the major topics addressed in the document. Topics, often listed, are previewed in the order in which they appear in the report. Your preview might also include a brief summary of key issues discussed in your report's analysis section. Such a forecast of the report topics provides readers with a clear sense of how subsections of the document's micro organization (e.g., purpose, scope, background, methods) fit logically, as well as chronologically, among sections of the report's macro organization (e.g., introduction, findings, analysis, conclusion, recommendations).

Body of the Report

The **body** of your report contains (a) the actual findings collected from your research and (b) your analysis of those findings. The body must supply the evidence on which the report's conclusions and recommendations are based. Consequently, the findings and analysis sections are normally the longest sections of the report, often representing 50 to 75% of the document's total length.

Clearly, you could not, nor would you want to, include in the findings sections all of your research findings; rather, include only the results of your secondary or primary research that are most relevant to your report problem and significant in determining solutions to that problem. Similarly, you would include in the report's analysis section only the most important interpretations of those findings. The findings and analysis sections of your report are normally separated under different headings or chapters. The findings section is referred to in a variety of ways (e.g., "Findings," "Collected Data," "Results"), as is the analysis section (e.g., "Analysis," "Interpretations," "Evaluation," "Discussion").

Because it presents the core of your research results, the report body will probably contain the majority of graphic aids contained in your report. Graphic aids properly integrated into the text of your report, as discussed in Chapter 12, can conspicuously strengthen the effectiveness of your findings and analyses by clarifying, simplifying, emphasizing, and explaining complex data and information.

Chapter 15 provides sample findings and analysis sections as part of a complete managerial report.

Report Conclusion

Components of the **conclusion** section of a report are the summary, conclusions, and recommendations. The ideas expressed in these three components are based on the findings and interpretations provided in the report body. You should include in the conclusion section no information that you have not already discussed, or at least referred to, in the body of your report.

Summary

The **summary** component contains exactly what its name implies: a brief summary of major findings and interpretations examined in the body of the report. You should summarize the key findings and interpretations of each major topic addressed in the report in the same order in which they were discussed in the report body, giving proportionately more space and emphasis to the more important subjects you covered.

Conclusions

Conclusions are fundamentally different from a summary in that they do not summarize but, rather, tell readers the meaning of the interpretations noted in the summary component. The **conclusions** component, then, is a vital extension of the summary, as it clarifies for readers the significance of the interpretations you derive from solving your report problem. Normally you will conclude topics in the order in which they were discussed in the report body; however, on occasion, you may decide to highlight topics central to solving the report problem by addressing them first in your conclusion.

Recommendations

Whereas some management reports serve solely as informational documents (providing, for example, information on the background of a report problem, corporate policies and procedures, or results of experimental research), many reports tell managers what to do on the basis of collected findings, interpretations, and conclusions. **Recommendations** are not summaries or conclusions; rather, they are specific, detailed plans for managerial *action*.

You, along with perhaps a team of writers and researchers, have researched a problem and determined what should be the most prudent and effective means of attaining a solution. Consequently, *you* are the expert regarding that particular problem, and thus it is you who must suggest, in a confident tone and persuasive style, the steps needed to realize this solution. Studying and proposing solutions to organizational problems are, in effect, why you were chosen to perform the study in the first place. The summary, conclusions, and recommendation components may be placed under a single heading, "Conclusion," or separated under distinct subheadings.

Appended Matter

The effectiveness of your report may occasionally depend on the inclusion of material that, for any number of reasons, does not belong in the introduction, body, or conclusion of the report. Your report conclusions, for example, may be based on results from a survey, but to include the actual survey in the report body would disrupt the flow of your document. In such a case, the survey, to which readers will most likely want to refer, should rightfully be placed as **appended matter** at the end of the report. The most common appended matter includes the appendix, glossary, reference page, and index.

Appendix

Your report may contain one or more **appendixes** in which you might place supplemental material that is important, but not necessary, to understanding the meaning or significance of ideas expressed in the body of the report. Types of documents that are often included in an appendix include

sample questionnaires.

interview questions and responses.

audit tables.

details of an experiment.

maps.

statistical information.

related correspondence.

related reports referred to in the text of your report.

other relevant but not essential visuals.

working papers.

suggested readings.

Avoid making your appendixes a catch-all for needless information. Include only material that is relevant to the purpose of your report. Use an appendix for each major item and title each appendix with a clear heading, such as "Appendix A: Sample Questionnaire."

Glossary

A **glossary** lists, in alphabetical order, specialized words and their definitions. When writing to a hierarchical audience with varying levels of technical expertise, you should consider including a glossary at the end of your report. Many of your readers, although highly educated in their specific disciplines, may not possess the technical knowledge and experience in the particular area of study covered in your report.

Midlevel managers and VPs may have a clear understanding of macro concerns facing the organization but often do not have the time or need to study the organization's workings on a micro level (i.e., micromanagement). For example, your firm's chief accountant, while aware of the big picture of the organization's finances, may require a glossary of computer terminology to understand and appreciate fully a report's recommendation that your company purchase a new relational data-based computer system to reduce operating costs.

If you have only a few words that need defining, you should probably define the terms at their first point of reference in the report text or within a definitions component in the report introduction. However, if a glossary is appropriate, construct useful definitions by following these guidelines:

- Avoid defining a term by using the term itself.
- Define all terms unfamiliar to the least technical reader of your report
- Define all terms that have unique or unorthodox meaning in the context of your report (e.g., "In this report, a *contractual agreement* is defined as . . . ").
- List terms in alphabetical order for easy reference.
- Underline all terms and place a colon to separate them from their respective definitions.
- Define all terms by first providing their class, or **genus**, and their distinguishing features, or **differentia** (e.g., "Theory X is a perspective on an organization's structure that (1) implies an autocratic approach toward managing people and (2) maintains that most people dislike work and will try to avoid it if possible"); define operational terms such as *manager obsolescence* and *point of purchase* by their specific functions.
- Place an asterisk after the term at its first mention in the text to notify readers that the word or phrase is defined in the glossary.

You can incorporate your glossary as either an appendix or, for greater emphasis, as its own section under the heading of "Glossary."

References

You should cite all secondary sources referred to in your report on the **"References"** page (according to the APA) or the **"Works Cited"** page (in MLA vernacular). Depending on the format requirements of your specific organization and its accepted style guide, the reference page can be single- or double-spaced, but the second and subsequent lines of each citation should always be indented three spaces (five spaces in MLA format) from the left margin. A complete and properly formatted reference page not only aids readers in locating works for their own research in the subject area of your report but also reflects the care and precision in your identification and use of sources.

Index

An **index** alphabetically lists the key words contained in the report text along with the page numbers on which the words can be found. A complete index should contain all important terms that express ideas central to the thrust of the report.

contain all terms included in a definitions component or glossary.

provide sublistings beneath general terms to help readers locate specific subtopics relating to those terms.

cross-list terms so that readers might locate a topic under more general subjects, thus allowing them to find terms without actually having to know their exact phrasing or spelling.

Although indexes are useful for formal reports of medium length (e.g., 10–30 pages), normally only long formal reports (e.g., 30 pages or more) include an index to aid readers in locating references to key words in the text.

Summary

To illustrate the depth of your research, the significance of your findings and conclusions, and the decisiveness of your recommendations, you must select a report organization that is most appropriate for the content and formality level of your document. Understandably, the infinitely varied purposes, audiences, and contents of management reports produce a countless variety of report organizations, formats, and lengths. However, most formal reports, regardless of their content or the rhetorical situation in which they are written, will contain some, if not all, of the central components of the management report, such as front matter, report proper, and appended matter.

This chapter has emphasized the necessity of formal formats to ensure the most effective communication possible between writer and reader. Consistent organization reflects the basic elements of the report planning and research process, while increasing reader comprehension by incorporating central organizational components. This standard nature of report organization enables readers to concentrate on content and not on complex and possibly confusing arrangement schemes.

The **front matter** and **appended matter** of a formal report are intended to make the document more accessible to readers. The different readers of your management report, while perhaps sharing some purposes in reading the document, will most likely differ in their own individual interests, technical needs, and intended uses of the report information. By using the front matter, or prefatory parts, to forecast the report's content, you assist readers in deciding if the report is relevant to their informational needs; which parts, if not all, of the document should be read; and in what sequence the report parts should be read. **Appended matter** often includes supplemental information that can help readers to understand more fully the material in the **report proper**, thereby increasing the effectiveness and relevance of the document.

The large majority of management reports follow one of two general organization plans: inductive or deductive. The **inductive**, or indirect, organization presents the report in much the same order that you have planned, researched, and composed the study. An inductively arranged report opens with the introduction section, which provides the reader with a clear context for reading and understanding the report, followed by the report's findings, interpretations, conclusions, and recommendations (if any). The inductive approach is especially useful when presenting the report to an audience who you believe might be unreceptive to your conclusions or recommendations. Placing the findings and interpretations before the conclusion section serves as the groundwork for subsequent conclusions and recommendations, preparing unreceptive readers for possibly unwelcome news. Also, by delaying your conclusions and recommendations, you stand the best chance of keeping the minds of hostile readers open as long as possible to your views.

A report organized according to the **deductive**, or direct, arrangement reverses the order of the report body and conclusion. In a deductively arranged report, the conclusion and any accompanying recommendations immediately follow the introduction section. The findings and analysis sections are the last part of such a report. Deductively arranged reports are most effective when written to receptive audiences who prefer conclusions and recommendations fast.

Finally, the effectiveness of your report may occasionally depend on the inclusion of material that, for any number of reasons, does not belong in the report's introduction, body, or conclusion. The most common appended matter includes the appendix, glossary, reference page, and index.

Related Reading

ANDREWS, PATRICIA A., and JOHN E. BAIRD, JR. *Communication for Business and the Professions.* 3rd ed. Dubuque, IA: Brown, 1986.

BOVEE, COURTLAND L., and JOHN V. THILL. *Business Communication Today.* 2nd ed. New York: Random, 1989.

CULLINAN, MARY. *Business Communication.* Chicago: Holt, 1989.

DUMONT, RAYMOND A., and JOHN LANNON. *Business Communications.* 2nd ed. Boston: Little, 1990.

HIMSTREET, WILLIAM C., and WAYNE M. BATY. *Business Communications.* 7th ed. Boston: Kent, 1987.

MAKI, PEGGY, and CAROL SHILLING. *Writing in Organizations: Purposes, Strategies, & Processes.* New York: McGraw, 1987.

MURPHY, HERTA A., and MARY J. PECK. *Effective Business Communications.* 4th ed. New York: McGraw, 1980.

SIGBAND, NORMAN B., and ARTHUR H. BELL. *Communication for Management and Business.* 4th ed. Glenview, IL: Scott, 1986.

15

Designing the Formal Report

In addition to containing meaningful content that is logically organized and communicated in a clear, concise style, your formal report should have an inviting format that makes information easily accessible to readers. The **format**, or *information design*, of a report is its appearance—how report components such as text, headings, and graphic aids look on the page. A report whose information is appropriately designed makes you a direct, efficient, and effective communicator by

enabling readers to recognize and access key information quickly.

reducing the effort needed by readers to convert important report ideas into usable information.

accelerating the learning curve of readers—helping them to understand and remember your message more easily.

raising and maintaining reader interest in the document.

providing you with more control over how your message is read and processed by your audience(s).

You should begin designing the format for your document much as you began planning its content and graphic aids—by considering the purpose of the report as well as the informational needs and background of your audience. Remember that reports exist to communicate to readers. As the content, organization, and style of your report should be reader-centered, so should its format. Because they communicate to managers with various needs and constraints, managerial reports require functional formats that are audience-tailored. The general context in which managerial reports are written and read is presented here. Consider how these influences relate to the purpose and audience of your particular report and how they might help you to determine the format most appropriate for your document.

- Managers are busy people. They must be able to identify the most important points in your report quickly and easily.
- The time and energy of managers are normally pulled in many directions. Consequently, managers rarely read a report from cover to cover in one sitting. Thus, they need a report that they can refer to easily.
- The content of managerial reports is often complex and technical. Managers need breaks (i.e., white space or graphic aids) between dense sections of text.
- Like the competitive world from which it comes, the managerial report, through its attractive and orderly format, must also compete for the manager's attention.
- Managers are professionals who expect reports to look professional.

As suggested by this general context, effective and functional formats must be accessible, orderly, attractive, and inviting.

Format Components

When designing the format of your report, work from the macro (general) to the micro (specific) level of your document. First consider the overall format of the entire report, including its title style and placement, margins, headers and footers, and page numbering. Then work on the smaller units, such as sections, paragraphs, and sentences. Components that are central to constructing an effective format for your document include paper types, ink, type sizes and fonts, margins, line spacing, page numbering, headers and footers, headings, and special highlighting techniques.

Paper, Ink, and Legibility

You should normally type or print your report on white rag-bond paper (20 pound or heavier) of the standard $8\frac{1}{2} \times 11$-inch dimensions. To give the report a feel of substance, make sure the paper has a high-fiber content (e.g., cotton). Use black ink whether typing or printing the report text and use a fresh ribbon.

If you type the report, be sure that the keys are sufficiently clean to produce sharp print. Clearly, mistakes in typing are inevitable, but you should make the errors as invisible to the reader as possible. Use typewriters with correction ribbons; opaquing fluid and erasures are messy and their use results in reports that look less than professional. Printing your report on a laser or letter-quality printer is the best choice. You can quickly and easily correct mistakes with your computer word processor or text editor before printing an error-free final copy of the report. Keep in mind that software programs that check the spelling or grammar of your writing do not eliminate the need for you to proofread your document carefully.

Type Sizes and Fonts

Most word-processing software and accompanying printers will provide you with a variety of typefaces, type sizes, and type weights from which to choose.

Typeface refers to the general appearance of the letters and numbers on the page. Each typeface has its own name, such as Courier, Helvetica, Times, Swiss, and Venice (Figure 15.1).

You can modify the character size of your report text by changing the pitch or point size of the type. The size of monospaced characters is measured in their **pitch**, or as characters per inch (CPI). **Monospaced** characters are printed with the same horizontal width, with each letter given equal space on the line. The letter *i*, for example, would use just as much space as the letter *w* in a monospaced report (Figure 15.2). A 10 pitch means that 10 characters are printed per inch on the line. **Proportionally spaced** characters use only as much space on the line as they require. The letter *i*, for example, would take about half the space of the letter *w* in proportionally spaced text. **Point** measures proportionally spaced characters vertically, as each letter occupies a different amount of horizontal space. One point equals $\frac{1}{72}$ inch. For greater emphasis, you may use larger type sizes for titles, headings, graphic aid captions, or other special information (e.g., notes, cautions, warnings).

The **weight** of type is the thickness or slanting of the characters. **Boldface**, for example, is heavier in appearance than *italic*, which is light and slanted. A complete set of characters with a particular typeface, size, and weight is called a **font**. The font you select for your report can affect the document's readability. The characters of some fonts, for example, have small tails (called **serifs**) at their corners that lead readers' eyes to the next character (Figure 15.3). Characters of serif fonts typically make reading faster and easier. The characters of **sans serif** fonts have no tails and normally appear cleaner—though, perhaps, more austere—than their serif counterparts. **Decorative** fonts are the extreme opposite of sans serif fonts. Characters of decorative fonts are embellished with ornamental and often intricate flourishes that, though attractive, are hard on the eyes for general reading. Consequently, they are typically reserved for titles and signs.

You should choose more conservative fonts (e.g., Courier, Helvetica, Roman) for the general text in your report. However, it's a good idea to experiment with more ornate typefaces for highlighting and distinguishing such textual components as headings, notes, cautions, and warnings.

Margins, Line Spacing, and Page Numbering

Maintain generous margins throughout your report. Narrow margins make a document look cramped and uninviting. Wider margins prevent your report from having long line lengths. Long lines make it more difficult for readers to locate the following line. Most effective line lengths average from 9 to 12 words, or 50 to 65 characters. As a general rule, leave at least $1\frac{1}{4}$ inch on the top, right, and bottom margins. Allocate more space—about 2 inches—on the left margin for binding the report.

If you are using a word processor to print your document, you will probably be able to choose between justified and unjustified right margins. A **justified** right margin is one that is even, while an **unjustified** margin is ragged. Although justified margins are preferred for such published documents as

This is Clarinda at 12 pt.
This is Helvetica at 12 pt.
This is Times Roman at 12 pt.
This is New Century Schoolbook at 12 pt.

This is *Zapf Chancery Medium* at 14 pt.
This is Helvetica Bold Italic at 14 pt.
This is Times Roman Italic at 14 pt.
This is New Century Schoolbook at 14pt.

This is Garamond at 24 pt.
This is Helvetica at 24 pt.
This is Times Roman at 24 pt.

This is Cloister Black at 36 pt.
This is Helvetica at 36 pt.
This is Times Roman Bold at 36 pt.

FIGURE 15.1
Sample typefaces and fonts.

```
     This is monospaced text, each letter given the same amount of vertical and
horizontal spacing regardless of whether the letter requires that much space.
The point and font of these characters are Clarinda Typewriter at 8 pt.
```

This is proportionally spaced text, each letter given only as much space as it needs. The point and font of these characters are Times Roman at 8pt.

FIGURE **15.2**

Examples of monospaced and proportionally spaced type.

annual reports, brochures, and periodicals, communications research shows that unjustified right margins make it easier for readers to move their eyes from the right to left margin when searching for the next line. Right justification can also produce wide spaces between words on a line.

Reports can be single- or double-spaced. When double-spacing the lines of your report, indent the first line of each paragraph five spaces. While most managerial reports are still double-spaced, the growing worldwide concern to cut paper costs makes single-spacing increasingly attractive to present-day organizations. When single-spacing, double-space between paragraphs. In addition, you may indent or not indent the first line of each paragraph.

Number the prefatory pages of your formal report with lowercase roman numerals (ii, iii, iv). Though not numbered, the title page is counted as page one (i). The first page and all subsequent pages of the report proper are numbered with arabic numerals (1, 2, 3). Page numbers (both roman and arabic numerals) of most reports are either placed in the upper right corner or centered at the bottom of the page. Double-space the numbers from the top, or bottom, of the page.

This is the serif font called Bauer Bodoni.

This is the sans serif font called Gill Sans.

This is the decorative font called Cloister Black.

FIGURE **15.3**

Examples of serif, sans serif, and decorative fonts.

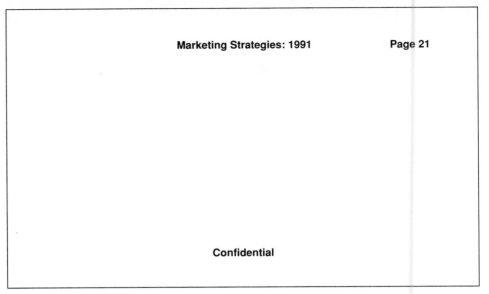

Marketing Strategies: 1991   **Page 21**

Confidential

FIGURE 15.4
Use of both header and footer.

Headers and Footers

Headers and footers identify the title, author(s), or date of your report. A **header** is normally a block of text placed at the left corner, center, or right corner at the top of each page of the report (except the title page). A **footer** is placed at the bottom of each page (except the title page) and usually contains information that further identifies the source or nature of the report, such as the name of the author's organization or the society publishing the report, the series of publications of which the report is a part, or the level of the document's confidentiality. You may use both headers and footers in the same report, such as when the footer contains information regarding the document's classification or clearance status within the organization, such as the "Confidential" footer illustrated in Figure 15.4.

Headers and footers are usually placed in boldface for emphasis and, when containing more than one line, they are single-spaced. Because they can occupy the same line on the page as page numbers, headers and footers are frequently placed next to the numbers.

Heading Placement

Effective headings work as road signs to aid readers in their passage through your report. As emphasized in Chapter 10, descriptive and concise headings are essential in making sections of topically unified information easily accessible to readers. They let readers know in a glance the subject of the report section and if that topic is of immediate interest to them. Although later refined after multiple revisions of the report, general headings inserted into the report early in the writing process also can make writing and revising the document easier and faster as they keep you on the topic at hand. Moreover, headings indicate the subordinate divisions of the report organization and serve as transitions between those sections. Finally, headings simplify for readers the task of referencing information.

There is no one standard for highlighting and placing headings on the page. Whether you are aided by heading guidelines prescribed by your organization or creating your own, you can significantly enhance the effectiveness of your headings by following the widely accepted formatting guidelines for headings noted here.

- Keep your highlighting techniques and placement of headings consistent throughout the document. All level-one headings should look and be placed the same way regardless of where they are in the document.
- Normally use no more than four heading levels (e.g., section, major topic, minor topic, subtopic) in your report. Too many heading levels can confuse readers trying to determine the relationship between deeply embedded headings and their respective sections.
- Never leave a heading stranded without text at the bottom of a page; carry it over to the following page.
- Skip three or four lines before a heading; skip two lines after a heading and before its respective text.
- Show subordination of headings and their respective sections by using appropriate highlighting techniques and placement.

The final point just mentioned involves the use of such highlighting techniques as:

Capitalization
Underlining
Bold lettering
Italics
Typeface
Type size
Type weight

By placing your headings in the center or on the left margin of the page and using some or all of the highlighting techniques noted previously, you can provide your readers with a clear and consistent view of topic subordination. One example of a heading hierarchy is offered in Figure 15.5.

You can, of course, experiment with different heading arrangements, depending on the number of heading levels contained in your report and your access to additional highlighting techniques. A desktop publishing system, for example, would provide you with a wide variety of highlighting options such as italics and double underscore and various type sizes and fonts.

FIRST-LEVEL HEADING

Center, capitalize, and bold section headings.

<u>Second-Level Heading</u>

Center, bold, and underline major topic headings. Capitalize the first word and all key words in the heading.

<u>Third-Level Heading</u>

Third-level headings are formatted exactly as second-level headings, except that they are placed flush on the left margin. Bold and underline minor topic headings. Capitalize the first word and all key words.

   <u>Fourth-Level Heading</u>

Fourth-level headings look much like second- and third-level headings, except that they are indented five spaces. Bold and underline all subtopic headings. Capitalize the first word and all key words.

FIGURE 15.5
Sample hierarchy for four levels of headings.

Sample Formal Reports

The sample formal report provided here is a strategic planning report written for a small gold mining firm. For ideas on how to present scientific and technical information, refer to the sample report in Appendix A. That report examines the use of psychoactive drugs by medical students and practicing physicians in Massachusetts.

The two reports are similar on a macro level. Both are formal in format and are written to audiences with some technical background in the subject area of the report. Moreover, both reports use APA documentation style. The reports, however, are quite different in their arrangement of information. The following business report, directed primarily toward managerial readers, uses a deductive organization so that its conclusions and recommendations are presented immediately following the introduction section. Authors of the technical report in Appendix A, on the other hand, assume that reported findings and discussion information would be as important to primary readers as the report's conclusions. That report, then, employs an inductive arrangement and places the conclusion and recommendation sections at the end. [1]

[1]We would like to thank Maria A. Halsted, Renee Job, and Christina Sanchez for the use of their reports on which the sample reports presented in this chapter and in Appendix A are based.

Title Page

GOLD NUGGET MINING, INC.

FIVE-YEAR STRATEGIC PLANNING REPORT

Submitted to

J. P. MacIntyre, President and Chief Executive Officer

D. Grant, Chairman of the Board

M. A. Ortega, Vice President of Exploration

C. Packard, Vice President of Finance

Submitted by

Gold Nugget Mining Strategic Planning Group
Corporate Headquarters
Missoula, Montana

March 16, 1991

MEMORANDUM OF TRANSMITTAL

Memo of Transmittal

TO: J. P. MacIntyre, President and Chief Executive Officer

FROM: Strategic Planning Group: K. Phillips, C. Garcia, P. Jordan, B. Rassmussen

RE: 1992–97 Strategic Plan for Gold Nugget Mining, Inc.

DATE: March 16, 1991

Statement of transmittal and reference to earlier authorization

Gold Nugget's Strategic Planning Group is pleased to submit the 1992–97 Strategic Plan which you authorized on October 12, 1990.

Purpose and scope of report

This report projects a 5-year expansion plan in technological exploration to advance mining productivity. The report focuses on two central components of new exploratory initiatives: (1) Gold Nugget's current financial condition, and (2) increased attention to human resources as it relates to exploration and productivity.

Summary of key findings and conclusions in exploration and associated recommendations

As detailed in the following report, Gold Nugget now has the opportunity to improve significantly its competitive position in the gold mining industry through expanded exploratory operations. Research findings show that estimated gold ore and mineralization reserves located on Gold Nugget properties can support an increase in our exploratory operations by 60% over the next 5 years. To maximize productivity of these operations, the firm should invest in advanced exploratory equipment.

Summary of key findings and conclusions in company's human resources along with associated recommendations

In addition to expanding exploration and incorporating advanced mining technologies, Gold Nugget should implement efficient, cost-effective measures to recruit and retain productive and highly-trained employees. Previous and ongoing ventures have been relatively profitable for Gold Nugget, resulting in markedly higher net incomes in both 1990 and 1991. Gold Nugget should reinvest a larger percentage of these profits back into programs to heighten job satisfaction among its employees:

Confidential

J. P. MacIntyre Page — iii

- An employee stock purchase plan that allows a portion of an employee's salary to go directly toward the purchase of Gold Nugget common stock
- Employee bonuses and other incentives for crews that meet and surpass mining quotas
- Frequent workshop meetings to keep communication channels open between Gold Nugget management and the labor force
- A more comfortable and "at home" atmosphere at worker barracks of mining facilities

Summary of key findings and conclusions regarding company's financial health

Gold Nugget's financial health will serve as a sound foundation on which to increase exploration. During fiscal 1991, Gold Nugget surpassed all production goals. Total assets at the end of the year cash position have improved appreciably with an increase of more than $29 million over that same position in 1990. Costs and expenses, however, were also up $24.4 million from the year before. Gold Nugget's profits for 1991 exceeded $2.5 million.

Expression of appreciation

Plan for future action

The Gold Nugget Strategic Planning Group appreciates the opportunity for having researched, written, and presented this report. Ms. K. Phillips, Group leader, will contact you within the week to address any questions you might have regarding the report.

TABLE OF CONTENTS

Confidential

Confidential

vi

LIST OF ILLUSTRATIONS

Confidential

EXECUTIVE SUMMARY

Executive Summary

Purpose and scope

    The following report provides a 5-year expansion plan and tentative annual plans for Gold Nugget Mining, Inc. It focuses primarily on (1) the need to increase the number of mining sites and the use of advanced mining technologies to raise production levels at those locations, (2) the importance of recruiting and retaining a skilled labor force, and (3) the company's financial condition.

Exploration

Topic sentence introducing objectives of company's exploration efforts

    A central goal of Gold Nugget is to reduce production costs and reduce exploration-to-drilling time by remaining current with advanced exploration and mining technologies.

Key findings

    Gold Nugget's current agenda involves both surface and underground exploration in the most promising mining areas—Sprucejack Lake's West Zone, Shore Zone, and Beaver Hill Zone—all of which are located in northern Minnesota. Although further drilling will be necessary to evaluate total results, a 52% increase in gold grade has made the West Zone an excellent prospect for exceptionally profitable mining. All three drilling zones offer rich reserves in other mining areas as well:

- They are superior fields for silver mining.
- Underground excavation and diamond drilling have increased markedly since 1987 not only in number of sites but also in profitability.
- Findings from our analysis of diamond drilling operations suggest that mineralization in the southeastern section of Beaver Hill Zone is significantly larger than previously expected.

Conclusions

Recommendations

    Our study indicates a solid upturn in the need for additional exploration. For the next 5 years, Gold Nugget will be in the position to increase its exploratory and drilling operations by 60%. Because company properties are vast and ore/mineral-rich, additional exploration should appreciably strengthen Gold Nugget's already sound financial condition. To achieve these exploration goals, however, the company must significantly increase its investment in advanced exploratory technologies.

Confidential

Executive Summary—viii

Human Resources

Topic sentence

Focus placed on key
conclusions as well
as recommendations
for improving
company's human
resource component

The importance of recruiting and retaining skilled
employees at Gold Nugget cannot be stressed enough. Our
analysis of Gold Nugget's human resources shows that more
initiatives are needed to guarantee the continued safety and
job satisfaction of the company's human resources:

- an employee stock purchase plan that allows a portion
  of an employee's salary to go directly toward the
  purchase of Gold Nugget common stock
- employee bonuses and other incentives for crews that
  meet and surpass mining quotas
- frequent workshop meetings to keep communication
  channels open between Gold Nugget management and
  the labor force
- upgraded living conditions at mining site barracks to
  produce a more comfortable and "at home" atmosphere.

Financial Condition

Topic sentence

Key findings
and conclusions

Based on our evaluation of Gold Nugget's financial
condition, we conclude that the company has attained a sound
financial foundation from which to expand its mining ventures:

- increased corporate assets, shareholder capital, and
  investments have produced a 10% net increase in profits
  of $2.5 million, more than 10% over 1990
- end-of-the-year cash position has risen more than $2.4
  million
- losses relating to write-off costs of obsolete equipment
  and abandoned properties rose by only $2,600
- a rise in salaries, diamond drilling, and the cost of field
  supplies increased the total costs for exploration to just
  under $24 million.

Key recommendations for
strengthening financial
condition of company

This report recommends that Gold Nugget create a
retained earnings account to accumulate more working capital,
allowing it to declare and pay higher dividends to common
stock shareholders.

Confidential

INTRODUCTION

Introduction

Background regarding
authorization of report

On October 12, 1990, Mr. J. P. MacIntyre, President and Chief Executive Officer of Gold Nugget Mining, Inc., authorized the Strategic Planning Group to prepare the company's 1992–97 Five-Year Strategic Plan. Gold Nugget believes that continued successful operation depends largely on

- increasing exploration of new mining sites and gold production through the use of advanced exploratory and drilling technologies.
- improving management-labor relations.
- achieving a clear and accurate view of the company's ability to upgrade and expand its operations through regular reviews of its financial health.

The Gold Nugget Strategic Planning Group presented its report to J. P. MacIntyre on March 16, 1991.

Purpose

Purpose of report

The purpose of this report is to assess the financial condition of Gold Nugget Mining, Inc., and, based on that analysis, to project a 5-year expansion plan in technological exploration for advanced productivity in our gold mining operations.

Scope

Scope of report

The report focuses on surface and underground drilling as it pertains to Gold Nugget mining sites; it also emphasizes access to the sites and providing electrical power to exploration areas. Moreover, the report examines labor conditions as they relate to productivity, safety and health standards, and worker living environments at Gold Nugget mining facilities. Finally, the report studies the financial condition of the company, concentrating on assets/liabilities,

Confidential

Five-Year Strategic Plan — 2

shareholder equity, losses and deficits, property costs, and working capital.

Sources, Methods, and Limitations

Key sources

Many of the revenue data, cost analyses, and cost projections used in this report were provided by the Accounting Department and the Budgetary Planning Office at Gold Nugget Duluth Headquarters as well as the Corporate Public Relations Office in Vancouver, Canada.

Methods

The Strategic Planning Group also relied heavily on interviews with management and labor representatives at all 10 Gold Nugget mining facilities in its collection of data and information pertaining to on-site safety and health conditions and employee satisfaction. The Group conducted personal interviews of Gold Nugget personnel from November 12 through December 14, 1990. (A copy of the survey is provided in the appendix of this report.)

Analysis of the company's use of exploration technologies is based on information gathered from technology experts at Gold Nugget as well as from the Vancouver-based Association for the Exploration and Mining Industry.

Limitations of study

The forecasting accuracy of this report is limited by two key unknowns, both of which could result in positive repercussions for Gold Nugget. First, the rate of innovations in mining technologies is dramatic. As new technologies regularly enter the market, it is difficult to anticipate how much these innovations might help Gold Nugget reach its production goals at a more accelerated pace than that forecasted here. Second, current unrest in the Middle East significantly increases the value of precious metals and oil products while world confidence in monetary currencies deteriorates. Significant political unrest would clearly reverse the recent down trend in gold and silver prices and provide Gold Nugget with additional capital for reinvesting in such areas as exploration and human resources.

Confidential

Five-Year Strategic Plan — 3

CONCLUSIONS

Conclusions

Forecasting statement
for conclusion section

The following sections summarize and evaluate the company's activities in exploration and human resources as well as its financial condition.

Exploration Summary and Evaluation

Topic sentence

Findings collected for this report clearly indicate the success of Gold Nugget's 1990–91 ventures in exploration and drilling. Based on recent geologic studies, Gold Nugget's exploratory techniques are enabling the company to realize an extremely high hit ratio (3:10) of holes explored to mineral-rich mines discovered. The use of modern exploratory strategies and advanced mining technologies has also significantly helped Gold Nugget to maintain its edge among other gold mining firms in the cost-effectiveness of exploration activities.

Human Resources Summary and Evaluation

Topic sentence

Recent efforts by Gold Nugget to improve the workplace safety for all company employees as well as the living conditions for mining workers have achieved positive results. Key advancements in Gold Nugget's goal of recruiting and retaining skilled professionals are listed below.

Key conclusions

- All safety and sanitary standards outlined in the Occupational Safety and Health Act (OSHA) have been met and, in some cases, surpassed by Gold Nugget projects to improve on-site conditions for mining crews.
- Accident rates have dropped dramatically since Gold Nugget's implementation of safety-awareness programs.
- Discussions with labor leaders and mining crews suggest general worker satisfaction with new company policies pertaining to and negotiation postures toward employees.

Confidential

Five-Year Strategic Plan — 4

Despite these advances in improving management-labor relationships, Gold Nugget will continue to enhance safety, sanitation, and living conditions to ensure progressively high marks for on-the-job satisfaction.

Financial Condition Summary and Evaluation

Topic sentence

Due to Gold Nugget's progressively stringent requirements over the past few years that its accounting procedures present precise and accurate financial position, the company now possesses consolidated financial statements that report useful inflow and outflow indicators of moneys as well as other numerous components of Gold Nugget's finances.

Key findings and conclusions

Gold Nugget is currently in a very positive revenue position, with an increase of more than $26 million over that of 1990 due to increases in assets, shareholder capital, and investment activity. Cash position has risen more than $2.4 million, while Gold Nugget's net profit for 1991 of $2.5 million is better than earlier projected.

Company losses relating to write-off costs of obsolete equipment and abandoned properties rose only minimally. Moreover, higher property costs were due mainly to an increase in the number of drilling sites as well as rising costs in salaries and wages, field supplies and expenses, diamond drilling, equipment, and transportation.

Recommendations

RECOMMENDATIONS

Forecasting statement for entire recommendations section

This section recommends a 5-year strategic plan for Gold Nugget as well as an annual plan for each of those years.

Five-Year Strategic Plan

Forecasting statement for 5-year strategic planning subsection

The 5-year plan is divided into recommendations regarding exploration, human resources, and financial condition.

Confidential

Exploration

Topic sentence

It is vital that Gold Nugget plan for the future using a consistent, realistic, and flexible strategic design. Increased exploration is a central element in building more efficient and cost-effective operations.

For the next 5 years, Gold Nugget will be in the position to increase its operations by more than 60%. Estimated gold and mineral reserves on Gold Nugget properties are vast and should support much growth for the company. To make the best use of these reserves, Gold Nugget should

Recommendations

- step up its implementation of advanced exploratory and mining technologies.
- train mining crews on these new technologies.
- train crews to mine effectively surface and underground ore deposits.
- increase the number of mining projects through more joint ventures.

Human Resources

Topic sentence

Gold Nugget must attract and retain skilled professionals in order to meet its mining and production goals. The company can continue to improve management-labor relationships by implementing the following recommendations:

Recommendations

- Initiate an employee stock purchase plan in which a portion of an employee's salary can go toward the purchase of Gold Nugget common stock. This option gives Gold Nugget employees the opportunity to invest their money in safe, high-yield stock. Such a program would improve employee morale by making the individual worker a part owner of the company.
- Provide employee bonuses and incentives for the crews that meet and surpass their quotas. Employees who meet yearly quotas should be rewarded with a salary increase at the end of that year. In addition, the crew with the highest productivity rate at each Gold Nugget

Confidential

Five-Year Strategic Plan — 6

mining site should receive a cash bonus or additional shares of the company's common stock. Bonuses for crew productivity should be given every 6 months.

- Establish frequent management-labor workshops to keep communications open. Monthly or bimonthly meetings will provide workers the opportunity to express their concerns, complaints, and suggestions. Such meetings may also enable management to make more effective business decisions once it has understood clearly employee's views on related issues. More open communication between management and labor will help the two factions to synchronize their work efforts and improve production.
- Continue striving to provide on-site mine workers an at home atmosphere in their living quarters. Gold Nugget might consider, for example, upgrading landscape around living quarters, interior and exterior decor of residences, and mining sites' recreation facilities.
- Press for even safer working conditions through employee training and more frequent safety inspections.

Financial Condition

Topic sentence

Few major changes are needed to improve Gold Nugget's financial condition. However, the company might consider several initiatives to make Gold Nugget more profitable.

Recommendations

- Because Gold Nugget achieved higher net incomes in 1989 and 1990, a budget increase is necessary to enact more efficient and cost-effective mining projects, spur revenues even more, and ultimately bolster net incomes.
- Modify slightly the company's accounting procedures to make financial statements more functional in assessing capital levels.
- Begin and maintain a retained earnings account to build capital.

Confidential

Five-Year Strategic Plan — 7

Annual Strategic Plans

Forecasting statement for annual strategic planning

The following annual strategic plans, while serving as building blocks toward achieving 5-year goals, offer Gold Nugget management flexibility in modifying goals and objectives as economic conditions change.

Year 1: 1992–93

Recommendations for Year 1

During the first year of the strategic plan, Gold Nugget should implement the following steps in order to achieve a 20% increase in revenues.

- Increase exploration activities at Sprucejack Area mining sites by 20%.
- Offer and promote the employee stock purchase plan on January 1, 1992.
- Begin the employee bonus and incentive program on January 1, 1992.
- Schedule monthly and bimonthly management-labor meetings at various levels of the organization.
- Start retained earnings account and project $2.5 million for an end-of-year balance.

Year 2: 1993–94

Recommendations for Year 2

The second year of the strategic plan emphasizes increased mining activity to achieve the planned 15% increase in revenues.

- Open complete mining operations at the Shore Zone and Beaver Hill Zone.
- Evaluate progress of all joint ventures and consider expanding those and other joint projects.
- Research and incorporate into Gold Nugget mining projects leading-edge exploration and drilling technologies.
- Continue the employee stock purchase plan, bonus and incentive programs, and management-labor communications meetings.
- Renovate recreation facilities at all Sprucejack Area sites.

Confidential

Five-Year Strategic Plan — 8

Year 3: 1994–95

Recommendations for Year 3

In Year 3, Gold Nugget management should continue its support of the employee stock purchase plan, bonus and incentive programs, and management-labor communications meetings. In addition, the following actions will help the company to increase revenues by the projected 10%.

- Expand Gold Nugget's use of computer technologies to streamline administrative duties in all areas of the company (e.g., accounting, management, marketing) as well as robotics to raise production levels while lowering production costs.
- Declare dividends on its shares of common stock.
- Begin paying dividends on a 2% quarterly rate.
- Continue renovations of Sprucejack facilities.

Year 4: 1995–96

Recommendations for Year 4

During Year 4, the employee stock purchase plan, bonus and incentive programs, and management-labor communications meetings continue as established for earlier years. In addition, the following actions will help the company to increase revenues by the projected 10%.

- Retool worn or outmoded equipment at all Gold Nugget sites.
- Increase quarterly dividends for common stock holders at a 0.75% rate per quarter, raising yearly dividends to 11%.
- Complete renovation of Sprucejack Area facilities.

Year 5: 1996–97

Recommendations for Year 5

The final year of the strategic plan stresses increased exploration of prospective sites and productivity of mines.

- Level dividend payments to a 12% rate.
- Appoint a committee to evaluate the success of the employee stock purchase plan, bonus and incentive programs, and management-labor communications meetings.
- Begin research and writing of next 5-year strategic plan.

Confidential

Related Research

RELATED RESEARCH

Forecasting statement
for entire section

Findings collected in exploration, human resources, and financial condition are provided in the following sections.

Exploration: Gold for the Future

Major Topic
#1: Exploration

Forecasting statement
for subsection and
scope statement

Today gold mining involves scientific and highly technological methods for exploring and drilling for valuable ores and minerals. To establish a context for the types of technologies needed now and in the future at Gold Nugget sites, the following discussion summarizes (1) the status of surface and underground exploration at company mining sites, (2) underground diamond drilling and reserve calculations, (3) access and power supply to mining facilities, and (4) mining activities at other facilities.

Surface and Underground Exploration

Topic sentence

Gold Nugget has completed surface and underground exploration on the Sprucejack Area Property, a major undertaking that cost the company more than $5.5 million. This expense, however, has resulted in a hit ratio of three mineral-rich reserves discovered for every 10 explored—one of the highest ratios in the mining industry.

Related findings

Topic sentence

The bulk of the surface exploration also is concentrated on the ore-rich Sprucejack Area (Figure 1). The primary exploration and mining zones on that site are the

Division of Sprucejack
Area into three zones

- West Zone.
- Shore Zone.
- Beaver Hill Zone.

Background on zones

The three zones have a combined total of 94 drilled holes. Gold Nugget has begun underground exploration in those zones to allow for the use of larger and more efficient equipment. The step requires that the dimensions of the existing decline be extended to 10 × 13 ft to accommodate the large-size machinery (Hodder, 1982). The extension also enables mining crews to achieve greater underground development.

Confidential

Forecasting statement

Topic sentence

Supporting evidence

The following three subsections examine exploration and mining activities in the West Zone, Shore Zone, and Beaver Hill Zone.

Drilling on the West Zone. The West Zone, located 35 miles directly west of Sprucejack Lake, is a significant site for drilling (Figure 1). Of the 94 holes drilled in the Sprucejack Area, 71 are located on this site. Gold Nugget has targeted

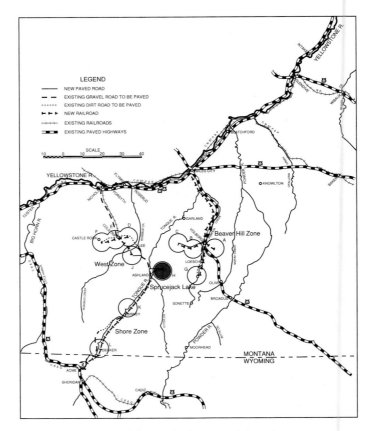

FIGURE 1.   Map of Sprucejack area mining sites.

Confidential

Five-Year Strategic Plan — 11

the West Zone for further exploration because its potential appears to be much greater than anticipated. A 52% increase in gold grade-mined at West Zone sites has made that area an excellent prospect for extended mining ventures (Cousineau, 1979).

Reference to Table 1 and topic sentence

As illustrated in Table 1, the West Zone currently offers the greatest mining promise of all three Sprucejack Area sites in terms of total tonnage and ounce-per-ton of gold and silver mined thus far.

TABLE 1. SPRUCEJACK AREA MINERAL INVENTORY

Zone	Tons	Gold (oz/ton)	Silver (oz/ton)
West Zone	1,535,928	0.505	20.97
Shore Zone	618,397	0.268	21.92
Beaver Hill Zone	252,356	2.270	15.68
2,406,681 (total)		1.014 (average)	19.52 (average)

Source: American Mining Services, Inc., 1991.

Background on exploration in West Zone

Gold Nugget has performed and continues to conduct exploratory work in the West Zone. During the summer of 1988, Gold Nugget drilled four deep surface holes to test the structure at a greater depth than that of previous drilling. Hole 1 deviated south and did not fully test the structure in the target area. Exploratory crews abandoned Hole 2 when it made a similar deviation. Holes 3 and 4, however, did intersect at 1,650 feet below the surface. Analyses of test findings from those two holes verify that significant gold mineralization lies deeper—approximately 2,000 to 2,750 feet below the ground surface. As comparable studies suggest, further exploratory tests are needed to determine specific mineralization depths (Hodder, 1982; Hoffman, 1947; Robinson, 1935).

Table 2 factors the West Zone findings into *proven*, *probable*, and *inferred* tonnage and ounce-per-ton of gold

Confidential

Discussion of key
data in Table 2

and silver. The 869,447 inferred tons of gold and silver and the high 0.503 ounce-per-ton of gold figures make the West Zone one of the most promising mining areas of all Gold Nugget fields. The 20.97 average ounce-per-ton figure for silver reflects the potentially high profitability of silver mining in the West Zone as well.

TABLE 2. WEST ZONE MINERAL INVENTORY

West Zone	Tons	Gold (oz/ton)	Silver (oz/ton)
Proven	310,141	0.517	28.27
Probable	356,340	0.495	13.76
Inferred	869,447	0.503	20.88
	1,535,928 (total)	0.505 (average)	20.97 (average)

Source: American Mining Services, Inc., 1991.

Drilling on the Shore Zone.   The Shore Zone is located 10 miles southwest of Sprucejack Lake, as shown in Figure 1. Of the 94 holes drilled in the West Zone, 12 were made on the Shore Zone. Gold Nugget has limited drilling on this zone because work crews and equipment have been diverted to exploration of the West Zone. However, despite the relatively low drilling activity conducted on the Shore Zone, all 12 of the exploratory holes confirm high-grade intercepts. The drilling of 5 to 10 additional holes will verify the full mining potential of this zone (Verity, 1957).

Assay findings of the Shore Zone, as shown in Table 3, suggest that the site may be considerably less profitable in gold production than the West Zone. Total tonnage (618,397) is lower than expected, as is the ounce-per-ton for gold (0.268). However, with an average ounce-per-ton figure of 29.12 for silver, the Shore Zone promises to be a more productive source of silver (on a per-ton basis) for the company than the West Zone.

Confidential

TABLE 3. SHORE ZONE MINERAL INVENTORY

Shore Zone	Tons	Gold (oz/ton)	Silver (oz/ton)
Proven	105,044	0.243	34.15
Probable	154,240	0.337	31.22
Inferred	359,113	0.225	21.99
	618,397 (total)	0.268 (average)	21.92 (average)

Source: American Mining Services, Inc., 1991.

Although the Shore Zone is in the proximity of Sprucejack Lake and its watershed, Gold Nugget exploration and mining specialists (1) do not expect any complications to mining efforts caused by lake or watershed water and (2) foresee no contamination of the lake or its dependent wildlife due to mining activities.

Drilling on the Beaver Hill Zone.   The Beaver Hill Zone is located 25 miles northeast of Sprucejack Lake (Figure 1). Exploratory samples of the site taken from 11 test holes drilled on the Beaver Hill Zone suggest that the property contains important gold and silver reserves as well as mineralization. As much of the exploratory drilling has been concentrated on the testing of the West Zone, the full extent of the mining potential of the Beaver Hill Zone will remain unclear until more tests are conducted (Hoffman, 1947).

According to assay results, the Beaver Hill Zone may represent the least productive and profitable site in the Sprucejack Area (Table 4). Total tonnage is low (252,356), as are average ounce-per-ton figures on both gold (2.270) and silver (15.68), compared to figures in those same test categories for the West Zone and Shore Zone. Gold Nugget, however, has conducted relatively little exploration in the Beaver Hill Zone, and more testing is needed before determining definitive mineralization estimates (Hodder, 1982).

TABLE 4. BEAVER HILL ZONE MINERAL INVENTORY

Beaver Hill Zone	Tons	Gold (oz/ton)	Silver (oz/ton)
Proven	30,111	2.583	18.30
Probable	67,233	1.915	11.06
Inferred	155,012	2.313	17.68
	252,356 (total)	2.?70 (average)	15.68 (average)

Source: American Mining Services, Inc., 1991.

Underground Excavation. Increased underground excavation at the West Zone, Shore Zone, and Beaver Hill Zone has made mining efforts easier and more productive. Excavation has created greater access and space for large equipment, allowing miners to extract more gold and silver. Many samples taken from 141 feet of mineralization show a strong correlation with ore blocks. Assays from a depth of 52.5 feet averaged 0.840 ounces of gold per ton and 81.82 ounces of silver per ton. Expanded underground excavation has proven significantly cost-effective.

Underground Diamond Drilling and Reserve Calculations
Detailed diamond drilling has provided exploration teams with valuable information regarding the location of diamond-rich fields. Teams have drilled 170 holes for a total of 25,900 drilled feet. In accordance with company assay procedures, data collected from all surface diamond drilling and underground drilling were submitted to American Mine Services, Inc., of Denver to determine reserve calculations.

Results from underground diamond drilling indicate that mineralization is increasing in width in a southeasterly direction from the Beaver Hill Zone toward the eastern edge of the Sprucejack Area (Verity, 1957; Robinson, 1935). Gold Nugget geologists and engineers are currently testing eastern

Confidential

Sprucejack to determine the depth and quantity of this mineralization.

Access and Power Supply

As the Sprucejack Area is located in an isolated area in northern Minnesota, entry into and exit from the fields should be made easy to avoid unnecessary delays. To date, temporary access routes consist of a tote road and barge link. These routes play an integral part in Gold Nugget's gold mining operations, as they are the primary means of transporting to the 40-person camp large quantities of fuel, machinery, and food and medical supplies. They also serve as the main transportation channel for shipping ore and minerals from mining sites to Klondike, Minnesota—the central transport junction for northern Minnesota.

The only other transport to and out of the Sprucejack Area is the airstrip in the West Zone. Scheduled and chartered flights are used to transport crews to and from the mining sites. Plane transport is essential for supplying emergency power, supplies, and medical staff to the camps.

Thus far, road and barge transport have effectively hauled all the supplies (gasoline, propane, diesel, and plane fuel) necessary to support mining and living energy needs. However, increasing fuel requirements are placing growing demands on this transportation system. Gold Nugget engineers, as well as outside consultants, are studying the feasibility of supplying hydroelectric power to the mining area by harnessing the outflow of water from Sprucejack Lake. Hydropower has the potential of supplying enough energy to support a 500-ton daily mining operation (Cousineau, 1979). Though the estimated cost of constructing a small-scale hydroelectric facility might reach $2 million, power supplied by the facility could pay for the outlay in less than 2 years.

Activities at Other Properties

Gold Nugget currently owns two mineral properties located in the United States: the Dove Canyon Property and

Brimstone Property. They are held by Grant Resources, Inc., under option from Nordic Mining Corporation. Gold Nugget has entered into agreement with these two corporations to earn interest in the mineral properties.

Dove Canyon Property.   Dove Canyon Property is located 160 miles northeast of Wenatchee, Washington. The most recent Gold Nugget venture at that site was a 1,500-foot, eight-hole surface diamond drilling program whose results indicate the presence of significant gold mineralization. The exploratory drilling revealed 7.65 ounces of gold per ton deeper than 5 feet and 1.94 ounces of gold per ton deeper than 4.5 feet. In addition, the study found 7.5% copper at both depths.

Gold Nugget plans to conduct further exploration studies that include geochemical sampling, trenching, and 6,000-foot drilling. Taking current sampling into consideration, these projected exploratory programs should provide Gold Nugget with sufficient data and information on which to base definitive strategic plans for expanded mining ventures.

Brimstone Property.   Brimstone Property is located 26 miles east of Missoula, Montana. Gold Nugget holds a 30% interest in the site and has drilled 13 holes along 900 feet of the Brimstone Property. During the exploration of 11 holes, Gold Nugget crews discovered gold values in excess of 0.01 ounces of gold per ton. The remaining two holes showed 0.150 ounces of gold per ton and 0.190 ounces per ton. Moreover, previous exploration programs have indicated a large gold soil geochemical anomaly, which suggests that significant mineral deposits may exist on the Brimstone Property.

Major Topic #2:
Human Resources

Human Resources

Human resources is a central part of all Gold Nugget exploration and mining. Gold Nugget employs from 50 to 65 crew members at its 15 mining camps and an additional staff of 950 at its Duluth, Vancouver, and Seattle business offices. As Table 5 illustrates, about half (47.9%) of Gold Nugget

Confidential

employees (e.g., engineers, scientists, mining technicians, skilled laborers) work directly with exploration or extraction programs. The remaining 52.1% of Gold Nugget employees are involved in daily business activities, including management, marketing, accounting, mining analysis, computer information systems, services, and clerical positions.

TABLE 5. GOLD NUGGET EMPLOYEE CATEGORIES

Category	Number	% of Total
Mining Staff		
Engineers	75	8.7
Scientists (geologists, chemists, physicists)	23	2.6
Ecologists	17	1.9
Mining technicians	240	27.4
Skilled laborers	520	59.4
TOTAL	875	100.0
Business Staff		
Executive management	20	2.1
Middle management	69	7.2
Marketing professionals	106	11.2
Accounting professionals	85	8.9
Mining analysts	127	13.3
Data processing and computer information professionals	95	10.0
Human resources professionals	83	8.8
Service staff	125	13.2
Clerical	240	25.3
TOTAL	950	100.0

For the past 8 months, Gold Nugget has been operating with a work force 98% complete. The company continues

Confidential

to stress recruitment of college graduates at leading universities to obtain competitive employees in professional positions (Hodder, 1982). To enhance its recruitment package to prospective employees, Gold Nugget is considering new benefit and stock purchase incentive programs and improvements to working conditions.

Safety and Health Standards

Gold Nugget management is committed to ensuring the safety and well-being of all company employees. Heavy equipment and dangerous underground operations pose a continual threat to workers' health; however, Gold Nugget strictly adheres to all relevant state and federal employee safety regulations (most notably those outlined by OSHA) to minimize health risk to employees. Such a policy has resulted in the lowest annual accident rate (five incidents) in company history.

In addition to reducing risk to employees' health, Gold Nugget strives to upgrade worker satisfaction to lower absenteeism. Recent improvements in sanitary and living conditions at mining facility barracks have resulted in a 65% decrease in illnesses requiring attention at facility clinics. Furthermore, on-site interviews with Gold Nugget workers suggest a meaningful rise in employee satisfaction with not only their salary and benefit package but also their roles and duties within the company. Though only one variable, the upturn in employee job satisfaction is a key reason for increased production at nearly all Gold Nugget mining sites.

Major Topic #3:
Financial Condition

Financial Condition

Because of Gold Nugget's progressively stringent requirements regarding its accounting procedures, the company now possesses consolidated financial statements that report the firm's useful inflow and outflow indicators of moneys as well as other numerous components of Gold

Confidential

Nugget's finances. Besides offering coverage of Gold Nugget accounts, current financial statements contain accounts from its wholly owned subsidiary Oaxaca, Inc. (Tucson, AZ), which is accounted for by the proportionate consolidation method.

At this time, Gold Nugget is evaluating the cost-effectiveness of its mineral properities. Costs for mineral development and exploration are capitalized on a site-to-site basis until ore is found. Once mining begins, the site is evaluated on a unit-of-production basis that estimates the life of the reserves. Costs of abandoning the exploration site are written off. Gold Nugget uses a declining balance sheet method for depreciating its fixed assets at a rate of 30% for equipment and 15% for transportation vehicles.

Gold Nugget investment in marketable securities is carried at cost. Dividend income is reported when received, interest income is recorded on an accrual basis, and capital gains are reported as realized.

Consolidated Balance Sheet

During a 1-year period, current assets increased to five times the total from the previous year of production. Profits from resource properties, Gold Nugget's exploration sites in Canada and the United States, escalated by almost $24 million. Investments rose significantly (24%), and fixed asset value tripled for the year. Similarly, liabilities advanced to record figures for the company.

Accounts payable increased from $18,526 to $623,883 within a 1-year period (1990–91). Shareholder's equity grew 31% due to increased issuance of no-par share of common stock. All of these factors left Gold Nugget in a very positive position in terms of profits, an increase of more than $26 million.

Consolidated Statement of Loss and Deficit

Deficits for the beginning of the year were up slightly from those of the previous year. Losses for the year (write-off costs

Five-Year Strategic Plan — 20

and costs of abandoning sites) actually dropped from those figures of the previous year by more than $24,000. The deficit at the end of the year rose by approximately $2,600.

Consolidated Statement of Changes in Financial Condition
The total for Gold Nugget used-in working capital increased 340% from that of 1990. In addition, working capital rose $1.5 million from 1990 to 1991. Net increase in cash added to the beginning-of-the-year cash balance netted Gold Nugget nearly $3 million.

Consolidated Statement of Resource Property Costs
An increase in the number of drilling and exploration projects has contributed greatly to higher property costs. Rising costs in salaries and wages, field supplies and expenses, diamond drilling, equipment, and transportation were additional causes for the higher property costs as well. Property costs for 1991 totaled just over $27 million. In addition, Gold Nugget recently acquired all outstanding shares of Oaxaca, Inc., and issued 4,035,000 common shares of its own stock at a value of $7.50 per share.

ANALYSIS

Analysis | Analysis of findings collected on exploration, human resources, and financial condition are provided in the following sections.

Forecasting statement for entire section

Exploration
Topic sentence

Overall evaluation of exploration findings provided in Related Research section.

Exploration is a Gold Nugget mainstay. The company's exploration program, which includes surface and underground drilling, has achieved outstanding results. Gold Nugget crews have continued to perform with no work stoppages. The Sprucejack Area is emerging as a profitable gold camp. The

Confidential

Five-Year Strategic Plan — 21

three zones within Sprucejack (West, Shore, and Beaver Hill) are establishing themselves as exceptional mining sites.

The following discussion examines mining procedures, drilling, and excavation; improvement in road access and power supply; and activities in other properties.

Forecasting statement for following exploration subsections

Mining Procedures, Drilling, and Excavation

Gold Nugget has taken numerous and sufficient measures for drilling and excavation through increasing its number of working mines and incorporating modern equipment and exploratory technologies. The company's commitment to expanding its exploration efforts and the valuable data and information drawn from those efforts have placed Gold Nugget in an excellent position to mine sites having the greatest mineral potential.

Evaluation of findings from corresponding subsection in Related Research subsection

Improvement in Road Access and Power Supply

Tote road and barge transport have been Gold Nugget's central supply links between the remote Sprucejack Area and the outside world. Plane transport, however, has become an increasingly important means for moving freight to and from mining sites. Air transport will steadily support the brunt of transporting needs. Whereas only 10% of transport requirements were met by air freight in 1991 (65% by tote road and 25% by barge), plane transport is expected to handle more than 30% of mining freight in 1992.

Evaluation of findings from corresponding subsection in Related Research subsection

Gold Nugget's decision to consider the use of hydroelectric power in the Sprucejack Area may result in significant power savings. While outside power sources have increased steadily (45%) over the past few years, water power is an energy-efficient and economical method for providing year-round power to the company's mining camps.

Activities at Other Properites

Gold Nugget's joint venture sites regarding its U.S. gold properties show large mineral deposits. Assay results from the

Confidential

Five-Year Strategic Plan — 22

Dove Canyon Property and Brimstone Property were extremely encouraging. The company's agreement to form joint ventures illustrates the firm's ability to use creative finance management to bring growth to Gold Nugget. The success of these two properties suggests that the company should conduct further joint venture exploration and mining.

Human Resources

The value of recruiting and retaining a skilled work force has not been lost on Gold Nugget management. Much has already been done to improve the safety and living conditions at Gold Nugget mining sites. These steps appear to have been successful in significantly raising worker satisfaction and productivity. Moreover, 1991 on-site injuries are markedly down from 1990. To improve on these accomplishments, Gold Nugget should consider staffing mining sites with full-time medical staffs and more complete clinics. More frequent safety inspections of site facilities and exploration and mining procedures would enable the firm to reduce injury risks even further (Hodder, 1982; Verity, 1957).

Financial Condition

Overall net worth of Gold Nugget production has increased dramatically since 1990. Revenues increased more than $26.5 million due to increases in assets, shareholder capital, and investment activity. Company losses relating to write-off costs of obsolete equipment and abandoned properties rose only minimally. Cash position has risen more than $2.4 million due, for the most part, to the general increase in working capital that boosted Gold Nugget's cash position in 1991.

A rise in production will bring an increase in costs. Total costs for Canadian and U.S. exploration sites have risen to nearly $24 million. This increase in costs is partially due

Confidential

to rising salaries, diamond drilling costs, and field supply expenses. Administrative costs and miscellaneous fees have also risen by $81,000. The company's net profit of $2.5 million in 1991 is better than the projected figure.

REFERENCES

Cousineau, E. (1979). *The world industry and Canadian corporate strategy*. Ontario, Canada: Center for Resource Studies.

Hodder, R. W. (1982). *CIM gold symposium*. Montreal: Canadian Institute of Mining and Metallurgy.

Hoffman, A. D. (1947). *Free gold: The story of Canadian mining*. New York: Rinehart.

Robinson, A. H. A. (1935). *Canada mines branch (1901–36)*. Ottawa, Canada: Printer to the King.

Verity, T. W. (1957). *A survey of the gold mining industry in Canada*. Ottawa, Canada: Department of Mines and Technical Surveys.

Summary

The **format** of a report is its appearance—the way report components such as text, headings, and graphic aids look on the page. We have stressed in this chapter that a well-formatted report not only raises and maintains reader interest in the document but also aids your audience in understanding and remembering your report's message.

The format of your report should be reader-centered. Because they communicate to managers with various needs and constraints, managerial reports require functional formats that are audience-tailored. Managers are busy people who face sizable demands on their time and energy. This chapter has described managerial reports as competing for the manager's attention, just like the rest of the competitive world from which they come. To meet the special requirements of report audiences, attractive and functional formats must be accessible, orderly, inviting, attractive and well designed.

We have recommended that, when designing the format of your report, you work from the macro to the micro level of the document. First consider the overall format of the entire report, including its title style and placement, margins, headers and footers, and page numbering. Then work on the smaller units, such as sections, paragraphs, and sentences. Components that are central to constructing an effective format for your document include paper types; ink, typefaces, type sizes, and type weights; margins; line spacing; page numbering; headers and footers; headings; and special highlighting techniques. Many of these considerations are demonstrated in a sample report that we have included in full, from title page to references.

PART V

Preparing and Delivering Oral Presentations for Management Decisions

CHAPTER 16

Preparing Oral Presentations

As we have discussed throughout this text, the data and information critical to the decision-making process within an organization are typically communicated in written documents, often in short or long reports. The communication of such material, however, is not restricted to the written medium. The **oral presentation** can be as important and effective as the written report in aiding managers in making wise management decisions.

The ability to communicate orally in an effective manner is essential to any professional in a present-day organization. During any business day, you might be called on to speak on a range of topics to different audiences and in various communication contexts. You may, for example, find yourself needing to brief staff on new goals and objectives, exchange ideas informally with a small group of colleagues, or deliver a formal oral presentation on the progress of your division to a committee of senior-level executives. Your understanding of how to prepare and deliver formal oral presentations will enable you to communicate more effectively in both formal and informal speaking situations.

Business Presentations versus Public Speaking

While oral presentations within business environments have much in common with the larger and more generic field of public speaking, business presentations are unique in several important ways. As noted by Paul R. Timm (1981), oral presentations in organizations can be classified as private speaking:

> That is, it takes place "within the family," among people who know each other and who share common organizational language and understanding. Presumably, they

also have common goals—those relating to the advancement of the organization. Listener analysis, a crucial factor in speaking effectiveness, can be enhanced by simply going to those with whom you will speak and gathering data about their specific wants and needs. (p. 13)

Speakers within organizations must be especially conscious of how their messages will (a) succeed when applied to work-world situations, (b) advance the organization in achieving its goals and objectives, and (c) fly in the political winds within the organization. If the speaker's message is approved by the organization's management, the speaker will probably earn the reputation of being an effective communicator and, in turn, a valuable member of the organization, perhaps even one marked for accelerated advancement. The reverse can also be true. If the business speaker's message flops as an applicable solution to an organizational problem or is poorly received as a politically unattractive or untimely solution, the speaker may suffer both in reputation and advancement (Frank & Ray, 1987; Glenn & Forman, 1990).

When delivering a business presentation within an organizational family, the speaker must recognize how the content of the presentation might affect both the business and the social atmosphere within the organization. Defining the audience often proves more difficult for the public speaker who does not share the family orientation with his or her listeners. Public speakers, however, who fail to communicate their messages effectively to their audiences may regret that the talk didn't go better, but rarely will they suffer the loss of business or their own jobs (Timm, 1981, pp. 13–14).

In addition, business presentations and public speaking engagements often differ in how their topics are chosen and in the sizes of their audiences. Whereas public speaking situations normally leave you free to choose from a range of topics, the subject of your business presentation will likely be decided for you by upper management or organizational situations. Audiences of public presentations also tend to be larger and more diversified in their backgrounds than those for business presentations. Thus, topics for public presentations are typically more general in scope, development, and recommendations (Applebaum & Anatol, 1984; Samovar et al., 1981, pp. 13–16).

Oral Presentation Situations

Managers at all levels of an organization regularly use a variety of oral presentation formats in many different communication situations, such as

- an oral briefing to upper management on the progress of a current project.
- a planning presentation to explain to upper management the benefits of approving a major project that you have designed.
- an oral overview of an organization's financial projections to upper management from various divisions or departments.
- a sales presentation to prospective clients.

a presentation to subordinates to identify and explain future goals and objectives of the organization, division, department, or office.

a training presentation to introduce new employees to their respective tasks and responsibilities within the organization.

a public presentation to strengthen bonds between the community and the organization.

a recruiting presentation to attract qualified prospective employees to the organization.

One very important communication situation not included in the above list, but one that is perhaps the most critical in beginning a management career with an organization, is the employment interview. The notable job qualifications of a job applicant mean little if he or she is unable to communicate them clearly and persuasively in the interview. The following list provides some of the key benefits realized through effective oral presentation skills:

- Your ability to present meaningful information orally to peers, subordinates, and superiors in a logical and convincing form significantly enhances your effectiveness in winning approval and support for your ideas.
- By getting things done, and done well, through superior oral communication skills, you distinguish yourself as a "shaker and mover"—a professional who, through his or her skills in maximizing the collaboration of peers, subordinates, and superiors to achieve organizational objectives and goals, is identified as a manager certain to rise in the organization.
- The planning, researching, organizational, and analytical skills that you have employed in preparing and delivering an effective oral presentation ultimately make you a better thinker and overall communicator in and out of the workplace. (Johnson, 1990)

Oral Presentations versus Written Reports

Oral presentations and written reports have much in common in regard to how they are planned and constructed. Both speakers and writers, for example, must brainstorm and identify, research, outline, and ultimately compose their messages. Despite these similarities, however, the two forms of communication also differ in a number of significant ways. First, the dramatic nature of oral reports provides the speaker with unique visual and aural dimensions that help impress upon listeners the meaning and importance of his or her message. The speaker, for example, might alter the tone, rhythm, or pitch of his or her voice to emphasize key points in the presentation. The speaker's personality and appearance also influence how the audience evaluates the credibility of the speaker and significance of the message (Capp & Capp, 1990).

Moreover, by using appropriate facial expressions, gestures, and body movements, speakers can demonstrate their interest in the subject matter as well as their sensitivity to the views of the target audience. A speaker who projects enthusiasm for the message being delivered encourages listeners to approach the topic with similar interest. Such shared enthusiasm produces a bond between speaker and audience that invariably increases an audience's attentiveness to the message as well as their receptiveness to and retention of the information. Listeners who can be made more interested in a speaker's message are also more willing to participate actively in the presentation, such as during the question-and-answer period (Knapp, 1978).

In addition, the oral presentation offers the presenter flexibility in altering the form of the message during its communication. The speaker, for example, can modify the organization or content of a presentation according to verbal and nonverbal feedback received from the audience. Furthermore, oral presentations tend to be shorter and more condensed than written messages. Whereas written reports can be read by readers at their leisure when they can direct their full attention to the message, the success of oral presentations often depends on the speaker's ability to limit the scope of her or his message to only a few key points. An audience whose attention span has been exhausted by a long-winded speaker will hardly be attentive listeners.

The temporal nature of business presentations, however, can be a major shortcoming. Unlike written reports, the actual presentation of an oral report cannot be reviewed later by the audience (unless electronically stored by audio or video technologies). Consequently, if the success of the message relies heavily on the audience's assessment of complex and numerous pieces of data, you might consider communicating the information in written rather than oral form. Moreover, while oral presentations offer you the flexibility to extemporize the presentation and thus enhance its effectiveness, this same freedom of structure and expression may occasionally tempt you to express ideas that would better have been left unspoken. Whereas written reports provide you with the revision time often needed to recognize and delete inappropriate comments from the message, off-the-cuff remarks slipped into a business presentation can quickly sour the audience's perception of you and reduce (if not destroy) the effectiveness of the presentation.

Finally, because an important part of a successful oral presentation is the dramatic presence of the speaker, an insightful and valuable message might easily be overlooked and discarded by the audience if the presenter lacks the needed composure and communication skills. Recognizing the power and importance of a speaker's stage presence in delivering an effective presentation does not devalue the central importance of the cohesion, unity, and accuracy of the message itself but, rather, confirms the complexity of preparing and delivering a convincing and well-organized oral message.

Appropriateness of Oral Presentations

Oral presentations are not always the most appropriate medium for communicating your report message. Often a written report (or a letter, memo, or telephone call) may prove more efficient and effective in conveying particular information to your target audience. Before deciding on whether to present your report orally, consider

the nature of the information.

the informational needs of your audience and their intended uses of your message.

time and budget restrictions.

Some data and information cannot be easily or effectively communicated orally. Information that is highly complex or substantial in quantity might well be communicated more efficiently through a written report rather than an oral presentation. In addition, knowing how your audience intends to use the information you offer them will help you to decide whether to present the material orally. If your audience, for example, will need to refer back to the information at a later date, you should provide the material in hard copy such as a report, letter, or memo. This would allow them to refer to the material at their leisure or when the material is most relevant. Remember that hard copy can also be archived and later retrieved as proof of record for legal purposes.

Your decision to present, or not to present, your message orally may also depend on your ability to convey such information in a clear, meaningful, and logical manner. If you feel that you lack the specific knowledge and experience required to deliver complex or specialized information effectively, you would be prudent to choose another form of communication.

The informational needs of your audience and their background in the topic being presented may also influence your decision to communicate your message orally. Audiences, for example, with little background in the topic to be presented will invariably be aided in their understanding of the material if you distribute hard copies of the information. In such a situation, you might choose to disseminate written reports in lieu of an oral presentation or to distribute hard-copy handouts of key information as a visual aid during your oral presentation.

Finally, preparing and delivering an oral presentation can be expensive in terms of both time and money. For example, the cost of a business trip involving cross-country plane transportation, along with room and board for 2 days at a downtown hotel for your presentation staff (not to mention the cost of designing and producing professional visual aids), could easily run into thousands of dollars. Before choosing an oral presentation mode of communication, consider the hours that would be invested by all those involved in writing the presentation script, designing and preparing visual aids, and orchestrating details of the presentation event itself (e.g., mailing invitations or notices, managing travel arrangements, reserving rooms for the presentation, coordinating the arrival and assembly of visual aids at the presentation site). Despite the many advantages oral presentations have over written communication, the particular time demands and budget constraints surrounding a possible presentation may make the oral medium impractical.

Presentation Preparation

The basic steps in preparing your presentation include the following:

1. Determine the purpose of your presentation.
2. Identify the objectives of your presentation.
3. Select the presentation format.
4. Analyze your audience.
5. Organize the presentation.
6. Choose and integrate visual aids.

Determine the Purpose of Your Presentation

The fundamental purposes of oral presentations are to inform, instruct, entertain, and persuade. These four purposes are not exclusive of one another. The content, organization, and delivery of many oral presentations are designed with aspects of more than one of the above purposes in mind. However, as explained in the following sections, most presentations have only one central purpose.

Presentations That Inform

Informational business presentations provide listeners with objective data or information that is meaningful in helping the audience to become more effective members of the organization. Essentially, informational presentations educate listeners on relevant and important topics. They normally contain compiled facts, figures, and analyses on which managers can make fast and intelligent organizational decisions.

Informational presentations do not attempt to persuade an audience to accept the views of the speaker or to adopt a specific action, as persuasive presentations do. Neither do informational presentations provide information with which the audience is expected to perform a particular task or procedure, as do instructional presentations. Rather, informational presentations offer findings and, on occasion, interpretations of those findings. The action taken by listeners as a result of learning this information is left up to the audience.

The informational approach might be used, for example, to

orient new employees to their job duties as well as the goals and objectives of the organization.

brief management on the current status of business activities, such as research and development (R & D), production, and sales.

update clients on improvements in the services or products they have already purchased from the organization.

present findings from an investigation you have just completed regarding an ongoing organizational problem.

provide background information on prospective investment options to a special task force of capital investment analysts.
(Capp & Capp, 1990)

Presentations That Instruct

The primary objective of instructional presentations is to teach an audience how to *do* something based on the information provided in the presentation. Instructional presentations are chiefly pragmatic in both intent and content, as listeners expect to be able to perform a task or procedure based on instructions received from the presentation.

Because of its practical nature, the instructional presentation heavily encourages audience interaction and collaborative team exercises, often in the form of audience workshops in which participants gain hands-on experience in performing a task. Instructional presentations are typically used to

teach employees how to operate new equipment.

introduce employees to methods of implementing and adhering to new policies and procedures.

train employees in work habits that will increase their productivity while also enhancing their job satisfaction.

demonstrate to clients how to operate your company's products or to apply your services in their professional or personal use.

Presentations That Entertain

Presentations that are well ordered, based on sound research, buttressed with objective and accurate information, and attractively and efficiently presented are normally entertaining to attentive listeners. Clearly, no speaker who wishes to maintain the attention and receptiveness of his or her audience would choose to deliver an unentertaining presentation. However, rarely is entertainment the central purpose of a business presentation. Rather, entertainment is typically used to increase the effectiveness of informational, instructional, and persuasive reports.

Entertainment can significantly strengthen a presentation by

putting listeners at ease with you as a speaker, making them more interested in and receptive to your message.

emphasizing key points throughout the report.

providing a break from complex, lengthy, and, perhaps, stressful passages of the talk.

injecting humor to reduce audience fatigue or boredom. (Kushner, 1990)

Entertaining an audience effectively requires considerable tact and knowledge of your listeners—their values, professional interests, shared experiences, and goals. Humor in the hands of an insensitive speaker can easily become counterproductive to the point, causing listeners to lose interest in the presentation, reject your message, or even leave the talk feeling insulted.

Presentations That Persuade

All presentations are, to varying degrees, persuasive in intent. As a speaker, you want to establish as much credibility with your audience as possible. You can achieve this in a number of ways, such as by

ensuring that all arrangements for the presentation (e.g., room, time, invitations, refreshments) are in order.

arriving on time and being prepared with all necessary notes and visual aids.

dressing appropriately.

delivering a message that is well organized and meaningful.

handling audience feedback with sensitivity and tact. (Snyder, 1990, Chap. 2)

An oral presentation whose primary purpose is to persuade, however, aims to do more than win audience trust and respect. The focus of a persuasive presentation is to gain the support of an audience and to succeed in convincing them to adopt your point of view. To persuade your audience, you might appeal to their sense of reason by offering logical arguments supported by substantive evidence. You might also appeal to the psychological needs of your listeners, such as their pride, fears, hopes, and sense of self-esteem, as well as their sense of ethics.

The appeals you use in your presentation will depend on the nature of your message and the character of your audience. A psychological appeal to an audience's sense of self-esteem and elitism may be productive when attempting to sell luxury foreign cars to upper-income consumers. The same strategy, however, would probably be inappropriate for convincing financial executives to invest their organization's time and money in an expensive and unproven advertising campaign. Often your business presentation can be made more persuasive by combining a mixture of logical, psychological, and ethical appeals.

Some common business situations in which persuasive presentations would be appropriate include the following:

- Entice existing clients to increase their purchase of your firm's products or entice prospective clients to begin purchasing from your company.
- Convince your firm's rank and file that the new policies and procedures you have proposed and implemented will prove profitable to them as well as to the organization.
- Persuade multilevel managers from various departments to commit more funding and company resources to a project you believe will significantly advance the organization in realizing its goals and objectives.
- Impress upon superiors at periodic merit reviews that your professional accomplishments should be recognized in the form of salary and position advancement.

Identify Presentation Objectives

Once you have determined the purpose of your presentation, you should complete the most important step in the predelivery phase—establishing realistic objectives for the presentation. Before considering what you should say or how you should say it in the presentation, you must first answer *why* you are delivering the presentation. You might start by addressing the following questions:

- *Under what circumstances was the idea for the presentation born?* For instance, was the task thrust upon you by superiors and can you count on the organization's support? Or was it a result of your own brainstorming, and do you expect limited, or no, support from power brokers within the organization?
- *What ideas do I need most to get across to the audience?* If you had to choose one or two points most central to your message, what would they be? Do you have a clear idea of what information the audience must comprehend fully in order to consider the presentation a success?
- *Do I know* how *I might get my point across?* Have you thought through your ideas enough to know what data and information will be needed to make your point? Do ideas in the presentation require the assistance of visual aids?
- *How do I want the audience to respond to the presentation?* What short- or long-term impact do you want your presentation to have on the audience?
- *What tasks or procedures, if any, do I want the audience to perform as a result of the presentation?* If you are delivering an instructional or persuasive presentation, you may well expect the audience to perform some procedure or to follow some plan of action. What might that be? And why? (Applebaum & Anatol, 1984)

Keep in mind that your objective(s) in presenting the message may not be the same as the objective(s) of the message itself. Your objective in a proposed advertising campaign, for example, would be to expand sales to a particular region of the country. However, the central objective for delivering that same proposal would be to persuade upper management to approve funding and resources for the plan (Snyder, 1990, pp. 20–27).

George L. Morrisey and Thomas L. Sechrest (1987) suggest four criteria that you might use to identify successful objectives for your presentation:

1. Be realistic in determining the scope of your oral report. Don't attempt to convey too much information, or information that is too technical, for the amount of presentation time available. In other words, don't bite off more than you, or your audience, can chew. It is better to excel in presenting two crucial points of a report than to rush through all five points of the report, overwhelming and turning off the audience in the process.

2. Be realistic in view of the audience's knowledge of, and background in, the presentation topic. Does the audience have sufficient knowledge, experience, or expertise to understand fully what you are attempting to communicate? A detailed and technical analysis of fiber optics would be far less effective on

an audience of sales executives than would, say, a general discussion of the extraordinary communication speed and capacity offered by the technology.

3. Be realistic in view of the audience's ability to act. Do members of your audience possess sufficient knowledge, experience, or expertise in the report's subject area for them to perform the task, procedures, or plan of action that you expect of them? Do they have the authority to make the decisions and to act on those decisions? For example, if you were presenting a sales briefing on your company's line of personal computers to first-line managers of a prospective client, it might be unrealistic in many instances to expect the presentation to elicit immediate orders for the computers, as the authority to make such decisions is frequently the domain of purchasing departments or managers farther up the chain of command.

4. Be realistic regarding what you can reasonably expect to accomplish from the presentation. Often the enthusiasm for and commitment to what we feel is the best solution to a problem are not shared by decision makers in the audience. Many factors central to the decision-making process within your audience's organization are beyond your control as well as the scope of your presentation. Factors such as constrained budgets, limited personnel, insufficient floor space, or resistance from key decision makers can override the most cogent and convincing arguments of a presentation. Consequently, it may be more prudent to offer your audience a "second-best" alternative, one that, though not the optimum solution, will solve the major portion of the problem. More complete solutions can be proposed at a later date when specific obstacles are absent or less problematic. (pp. 13–14)

Select the Appropriate Delivery Technique

You can present your oral report using one or a combination of the four basic delivery techniques:

1. Read from a prepared script.
2. Extemporize from prepared notes.
3. Memorize.
4. Present information through an impromptu format.

Reading from a prepared script is most appropriate when delivering a presentation whose content is highly complex or technical and when there is no room for error in the precision and accuracy of the communicated information. Reading also prevents the speaker from digressing from the topic at hand. Moreover, reading from a script enables the presenter to estimate the length of the presentation closely if time is a major consideration. Presentations delivered at scientific or technical conferences are often read. Formal briefings in industry, government, and the military are also normally read from a prepared statement. The primary, and considerable, disadvantage of reading your presentation is that the speaker is unable to maintain eye contact with the audience for most of the presentation, which markedly increases the chance of losing the attention of your listeners. Reading at a lectern also prevents the speaker from moving about the stage to draw listeners' attention and punctuate topical movements in the presentation. Moreover, reading, unless done by exceptionally skilled speakers, normally results in dull, monotone presentations that quickly transform attentive, participatory listeners into bored, passive observers (Smith, 1984, Chap. 7).

Extemporizing from prepared notes allows the speaker to modify the content and organization of a presentation, if needed, during delivery to communicate the message more effectively. At the same time, brief notes or an outline of the presentation helps keep the speaker on course. In addition, because the speaker's eyes are not pinned to a page of text, regular eye contact can be maintained with the audience. Although the preferred delivery method among most professionals, extemporizing can be an invitation to the speaker to digress too far from the presentation message. Moreover, gauging the length of an extemporized presentation is more difficult than it is for a read presentation.

Memorizing a business presentation requires appreciable skill and work; however, memorizing your message has some distinct advantages. First, because you need no lectern on which to place prepared notes or a written report, you are free to move about the room and maintain continual eye contact with listeners. Like an extemporized presentation, a memorized presentation also permits you the flexibility to change the content or organization of your message during the course of the presentation.

A major drawback to memorization, however, is that it generally requires substantially more preparation time and practice than do the other three delivery techniques, and time in the business world is typically a scarce commodity. Although mnemonic techniques can increase a speaker's skill in memorization, rarely will an individual have the time, aptitude, and skill to memorize all the facts, figures, and details that might be required during the presentation or question–answer period. Often, the time invested in memorizing a presentation is better spent in reviewing the critical points of the message as well as its peripheral issues. Even after memorizing a presentation, a speaker is not guaranteed that she or he will remember it during the stress of a presentation. A single forgotten sentence or word can disrupt or stop even the most carefully planned and memorized presentation. Moreover, speakers who memorize their presentations can easily sound wooden or staged.

The **impromptu** presentation is the least formal of the four delivery formats. Presenters using the impromptu delivery do not memorize their messages; nor do they work from note cards. Rather, they draw from general outlines of key ideas that they have memorized, delivering the ideas as they seem appropriate during the presentation. Although key phrases of the message may be memorized, most of the presentation is off the cuff. By using an impromptu delivery, presenters can establish an informal and personal tone for their presentations. Impromptu formats are also employed to encourage listeners to interact with the speaker by asking questions or commenting on topics during the presentation.

Successful impromptu presentations, however, demand a great deal of the speaker. Presenters who deliver their ideas in an impromptu format must depend on a sound knowledge of the material, an ability to retrieve information rapidly from memory, excellent listening skills, a quick mind, and significant composure. A second drawback to impromptu presentations is that they often lure the speaker into a false sense that exhaustive preparation time is not needed. On the contrary, impromptu presentations, when effectively delivered, appear fluid and communicate exactly the information needed by the audience only because the presenter has thoroughly researched the presentation topic; methodically defined listeners' needs, interests, and backgrounds; anticipated a general organization of the material; and achieved a polished delivery style.

Analyze Your Audience

Knowing the purpose of the presentation as well as your objectives in delivering the oral report are major steps in planning a successful business presentation. However, structuring your presentation so that it meets the informational needs and background of your listeners is impossible unless you take the time to analyze, or **delimit,** your audience. After all, the central purpose of presentations, like written reports, is to *communicate.* A fundamental component in the communication equation, as we have stressed throughout the written report chapters of this text, is the audience. If you are unable to design the topic, content, organization, and delivery of your presentation so that your listeners understand the meaning and significance of your message, then you have failed in the most basic goal of the communication process.

Oral presentations, then, like written reports, should be audience-centered, not speaker-centered. The greater your understanding of your listeners, the more effective your presentation will be. The needs and background of your audience will not only suggest to you *what* you need to say in the presentation but also *how, why, when,* and even *where* you should say it. After determining the purpose and objectives of your presentation, examine carefully and thoroughly your audience. You might begin by determining their

informational needs.

intended uses of the information provided by the presentation.

knowledge in the field of the presentation topic.

range of experience in the topic area.

preconceptions of you and the presentation itself.

demographic characteristics.

size.

Effectively delimiting your audience will help you to

alter the topic, content, organization, and delivery of your presentation well in advance so that it fits the needs of your listeners.

anticipate and prepare for unavoidable obstacles (e.g., factions of unreceptive or hostile listeners, changing audience sentiments that may turn contrary to your message, hidden prejudices that even your listeners might not be aware of) that could hinder the communication of your message.

modify your message more adeptly during the presentation so that alterations to the original presentation appear seamless to the audience.

select the most appropriate visual aids to clarify, simplify, or explain key ideas in your presentation.

The presentation predesign worksheet illustrated in Figure 16.1 is an effective method for delimiting an audience and clarifying objectives, as is the "Presentation Predesign" used by presenters at General Dynamics in Figure 16.2 (Frank & Ray, 1987; Samovar et al., 1981, pp. 22–33; Timm, 1981, Chap. 3).

You probably have many points that you consider significant enough to warrant the attention of your listeners, and that may very well be the case. But what are the specific informational needs of your audience? Make distinctions between what they *want* to hear as opposed to what they *need* to hear. Major stockholders invariably want to hear that their firm is in excellent financial health, but what they need to hear may be something quite different. Deciding what information your listeners should know will depend largely on the purpose(s) and objective(s) of your presentation (Meuse, 1980, Chap. 3).

In addition to analyzing your listeners' informational needs, consider their intended uses of the information you provide in the presentation. How general or specific should the information be so that the audience might use it as they had hoped? If you were delivering an instructional presentation on a new text-editing program to data-processing personnel, for example, you would want to provide enough information and in sufficient detail for your listeners to use the software as they had expected and as the objectives of the presentation had promised.

Your listeners' knowledge and experience in the field of the presentation topic can also greatly determine the organization and content of your presentation. What general base of knowledge and experience can you expect your audience to share? What specific knowledge and experience do your listeners possess in relation to the presentation topic? How much do they already know about your message? How much more do they need to know? How many years of training or experience have they had in such areas? Where did they receive this experience? With your organization? With a competing organization? What is the general or specific technical level of their education or training?

Speakers deeply immersed in the topic of their report frequently make the mistake of assuming that their audience is equally knowledgeable about that topic. Armed with this misconception, speakers often launch into a presentation too advanced or specific in content for their audience. Unless the occasion for the presentation attracts a select group of listeners with shared backgrounds in the topic area, such an assumption will invariably leave most, if not all, of the audience feeling confused and disappointed.

Suppose, for example, that you are attempting to persuade a group of nontechnical managers from marketing, sales, and accounting to purchase a par-

PRESENTATION PREDESIGN WORKSHEET

Presentation Essentials

Presentation Topic: _____

Occasion for Presentation: _____

Presentation Date and Time Limit: _____

Location of Presentation: _____

Contact Person with Host Department or Organization (and phone number): _____

Purposes of the Presentation

What is my central purpose in doing this presentation?

To inform: ____ Why? _____
To instruct: ____ Why? _____
To entertain: ____ Why? _____
To persuade: ____ Why? _____

Presentation Objectives

What do I expect to achieve by delivering my presentation?

Objective 1: _____
_____

Objective 2: _____
_____

Objective 3: _____
_____

Audience Overview

What kinds of general information does my audience need in order to perform the desired actions, change their own attitudes and ideas, etc.?

_____
_____
_____

Review of Objectives

Consider presentation objectives in light of the informational needs of your audience. How would I alter, if at all, my initial presentation objectives to meet my audience's informational needs?

_____
_____
_____

Figure 16.1

Presentation predesign worksheet.

Source: Adapted from Morrisey and Sechrest, 1987, pp. 30–32.

Main Topics

List the key ideas my audience must understand if I am to achieve my presentation objectives.

Idea 1:

_____

_____

Idea 2:

_____

_____

Idea 3:

_____

_____

Supporting Evidence That Corresponds to Main Ideas

List key pieces of evidence that I will use to support the main ideas expressed in the presentation.

Evidence 1:

_____

_____

Evidence 2:

_____

_____

Evidence 3:

_____

_____

Expected Results

What do I expect my audience to <u>do</u> based on the information presented?

_____

_____

_____

Figure 16.1

Continued

PRESENTATION PREDESIGN		
SUBJECT OF PRESENTATION:	DATE TO BE GIVEN:	
	LOCATION:	
AUDIENCE:	LENGTH:	
	MEDIA:	
OCCASION/EVENT:	GENERAL COMMENTS:	
PRESENTER(S):		

My (Our) <u>MAIN PURPOSE</u> is to (CONVINCE OR PERSUADE) (INFORM) (ENTERTAIN) this audience.
THE MAIN <u>IDEA</u> I (we) want to get across is: (one simple action statement)

The 3 to 4 <u>KEY POINTS</u> I feel best prove or illustrate that main idea are: (simple action statements)

What <u>ACTION</u> do I want to bring about? What specific step do I want the audience to take?

What other <u>CHOICES</u> or options do they have?

What must I not forget to do or say? What does the audience want or expect to hear? Does the occasion demand anything special (e.g., protocol)? What should I definitely avoid?

FIGURE 16.2

Presentation worksheet.

Source: Courtesy of General Dynamics Electric Boat Division.

Who are the KEY INDIVIDUALS in the audience?	Who makes up the rest of the audience?
How KNOWLEDGEABLE are they about our subject? What topics are they most or least familiar with?	How does this influence our presentation?
How INTERESTED are they in this subject?	How does this influence our presentation?
What are their ATTITUDES toward our proposition, our speakers, or the competition proposals? Why do they have these attitudes?	How does this influence our presentation?

What primary NEEDS or concerns does the audience have regarding our subject?

What does our proposal do for them? What BENEFITS does it offer them? Why is ours better than the competition's?

What major OBJECTIONS might they have? How do we answer or overcome them?

FIGURE 16.2
Continued

ticular personal computer networking software package that would connect the data bases of all their divisions, thereby improving efficiency while also cutting operational costs within the organization. In such a presentation, you would probably choose to focus your discussion on the specific needs of the three divisions, rather than provide a detailed and computer-technical analysis of the three leading networking systems. The technical level and lack of focus of such an analysis would fail to express the practical applications and benefits of the software.

Because oral presentations involve the interaction of people, they tend to be more personal than written reports. Consequently, as a speaker, you should consider psychological and emotional perceptions that your audience may have of you and the presentation itself. Might your listeners, for example, bring to the presentation any positive or negative perceptions of you professionally or personally? Might these perceptions affect the audience's receptiveness to your message? What is the psychological and emotional state of your audience? Has any unique incident prior to the presentation affected them emotionally and might this influence how they react to your message or portions of your message? Do you perceive any underlying or blatant prejudice on the part of your audience for or against you or your message? Is your message the one your listeners are expecting? If not, you should structure your presentation to minimize any negative reaction and resistance that arise as a result.

The psychological and emotional state of an audience is often affected by the occasion of the presentation. Is the occasion, for instance, one that invites a receptive audience or one that may make listeners resentful toward the presentation or you? Employees, for example, might well resent having to attend a presentation addressing future cuts in employee benefits. Delivering such a presentation effectively would require that you (a) accurately assess the depth of possible hostility listeners might feel toward the presentation, as well as you, and (b) select methods for diffusing the resentment. In Chapter 17 we discuss how you might handle unreceptive, resentful, or otherwise hostile audiences.

Another important component of audience delimitation is listener demographics. What, for example, is the male-to-female ratio of your audience? What is their average age? What is the average income and educational level of your audience? What are their general occupations (e.g., physicians, professors, lawyers, computer scientists)? What are their specialties (e.g., endocrinology, U.S.-European trade agreements, corporate tax law, design and analysis of banking computer systems)? What are their cultural and religious backgrounds? What are their political, social, or labor affiliations? What are their hobbies? Consider these demographic characteristics when choosing the content and constructing the arguments of your presentation.

The size of your audience can also affect how you plan your presentation. Audience size will depend on the purpose of your presentation. Naturally, you will want to present your message to all the people who have a vested interest in your message. A sales presentation meant to persuade a small company to purchase two new photocopiers may include only you and the firm's president. Other presentation purposes may involve tens or even hundreds of people.

An unnecessarily large audience, on the other hand, can easily become counterproductive for a number of reasons. First, the basic logistical requirement of making yourself heard may become difficult in a large conference hall packed with people. Acoustics may be poor, the sound system may not effectively reach outlying areas of the hall, and large audiences simply tend to produce more noise against which your own voice must compete. Second, large audiences also make the presentation environment less personal. Exchanging ideas on a one-to-one level is difficult when addressing more than 15 to 20 listeners; this personal touch becomes virtually impossible with more than that number of listeners. Moreover, rarely are large audiences homogeneous in terms of their informational needs, knowledge and experience levels, and demographic profiles. A more diverse audience will normally require that your presentation be more general in content than an oral report delivered to a smaller and often more homogeneous audience.

Knowing *what* to look for in analyzing your listeners is only half the task in delimiting your audience; you must also know *where* to look for answers during your investigation. One of the most obvious ways to find out more about your audience is to ask them. Although this technique may be possible when delivering presentations to small audiences whose members are regularly accessible to you, such as colleagues within your organization, a personal, direct approach is normally impractical when addressing large audiences or listeners with whom you will have little or no contact before the presentation, as in the case of conference presentations.

Other methods of investigating your audience include

extrapolating from your experiences with other audiences in similar presentation situations to formulate a general sense of the informational needs, background, and interest of your current audience.

consulting other speakers who have delivered presentations to comparable audiences in similar speaking situations.

reviewing the work (e.g., professional accomplishments, notable awards, publications) of representative audience members.

using your common sense and your experience in dealing with professionals like those in your audience to construct an audience profile. (Meuse, 1980, Chap. 3)

To help yourself in getting a clear picture of your audiences, you might complete an audience analysis worksheet, which prompts you for key descriptors of your listeners. The audience analysis worksheet provided in Figure 16.3 consists of four major components:

1. Identifying presentation objectives.
2. Analyzing audience demographics.
3. Examining audience motivations and expectations.
4. Applying your knowledge of your audience to determine what content, organization, delivery techniques, and visual aids would be most appropriate for use in the presentation.

AUDIENCE ANALYSIS WORKSHEET

Presentation Objectives

1. What do you want listeners to learn from your presentation?

_____

_____

2. What do you expect listeners to be able to do with the information given in the presentation?

_____

_____

Audience Demographics

1. What is the size of your audience?

_____ Fewer than 10 _____ 10–25 _____ 25–50 _____ More than 50

2. From what levels of the organization's hierarchy do your listeners come?

_____ Executive Management _____ Midmanagement

_____ Supervisors _____ Office Professionals

_____ Line Workers and Staff _____ Other (Please specify: _____)

3. What is the average education level of your audience?

_____ High School _____ Master's Degree

_____ Bachelor's Degree _____ Doctoral Degree

4. What are listeners' technical level(s) of expertise in the subject area covered by the presentation?

_____ Nontechnical _____ Semitechnical _____ Technical

5. What experience do listeners have in the subject area of the presentation?

_____ None _____ Limited _____ Moderate _____ Substantial

FIGURE 16.3
Audience analysis worksheet.

Audience Motivations and Expectations

1. Why is your audience attending the presentation?

   _____

   _____

2. What are their expectations of the coverage, tone, and applicability of the information provided in the presentation?

   _____

   _____

3. How receptive will the audience be to your message?

   _____ Very receptive _____ Moderately receptive _____ Neutral

   _____ Unreceptive _____ Hostile

4. What audience-related barriers do you anticipate in successfully communicating your message?

   _____

   _____

Application

1. What areas of content should you communicate in order to achieve your presentation objectives and meet audience needs?

   _____

   _____

2. What organization should you employ to communicate this information?

   _____ Deductive _____ Inductive

   _____ Other (Please specify: _____)

3. What presentation technique(s) are most appropriate for communicating this content for your particular audience?

   _____ Lecture _____ Demonstrations _____ Workshops

   _____ Panel Discussion _____ Other (Please specify:_____)

4. What visual aids will you need to convey the information effectively:

   _____

   _____

FIGURE 16.3
Continued

Understanding the informational needs, interests, backgrounds, and attitudes of your listeners is critical if you are to plan and deliver an oral presentation whose organization, content, and style are appropriately tailored to your audience. Presentations that do not tell listeners what they need to know when they need to know it inevitably waste the time of the speaker as well as the audience.

Organize the Presentation

After determining the purpose of your presentation, analyzing your audience, and performing any needed research, you are ready to organize the content of your oral report. The steps involved in organizing an oral presentation are fundamentally the same as those for structuring a written report, which are discussed in Chapter 10.

The business presentation, like the written report, normally contains an introduction, body, and conclusion. Furthermore, as with the written report, the organization of the presentation depends on the purpose, audience, and occasion of the report. In addition, the general organization of the presentation is usually deductive or inductive in structure, as in written reports. If, for example, you expected your audience to be receptive to your message, you would probably state your conclusions or recommendations early in the report, followed by the evidence and analysis of your research material. This would be a direct, or deductive, organization. However, if you anticipated that your listeners might be unreceptive or even hostile to all or some of the information in the presentation, you might well use an indirect, or inductive, approach—that is, to explain the evidence and analysis before presenting your conclusions or recommendations.

The organizational approach of the oral presentation, however, is also notably different from that of the written report. In the following discussion we examine organizational and content considerations that are unique to the introduction, body, and conclusion of oral presentations.

Report Introduction

The primary purposes for the introduction of your presentation are to

grab the attention of your listeners.

generate audience interest in the presentation topic.

establish a sense of mutual respect and goodwill between you and your audience.

establish your credibility as a trustworthy and objective expert in the topic area of the presentation.

state the central focus and scope of the presentation.

relate that focus to the informational needs and interests of your audience.

An effective introduction depends largely on preparing listeners for the information that is to follow in the body and conclusion of the presentation.

You, in effect, *forecast* for the audience the order of topics that will be covered in your oral report. While formulating concise and clear thesis and scope statements is central to building an effective introduction, grabbing listeners' attention is critical if you are to hold your audience's interest long enough to introduce the topic.

Keep in mind that the attention span of audiences is limited and that listener interest will fluctuate throughout your presentation. The audience retention curve shown in Figure 16.4 illustrates how audience retention normally drops dramatically following the introduction of a presentation as the level of listener attention tends to wane. Audience attention and retention remain low throughout the body of the presentation, but then both rise during the conclusion to approximately the same level as that of the introduction. Obviously, you can significantly change the attention and retention curve of your particular audience by carefully organizing and focusing the presentation content to meet audience needs and interests. Moreover, the more you can involve your audience in the presentation itself, such as through the use of audience-directed questions, the more they will listen and retain.

You can grab and hold the attention of your audience by integrating into the introduction of your presentation

a thought-provoking question.

a meaningful and relevant quote.

a vivid example that illustrates the central point of your message.

significant statistics.

a bit of humor.

an insightful story or anecdote.

a report of an unusual or startling event.

Whenever you use these or other techniques for winning audience attention, there is always the chance that such dramatic strategies might go awry and reduce the effectiveness of your introduction and the presentation following it. To avoid the abuse or mismanagement of attention-getting techniques, you might consider these guidelines:

• Whatever the technique, be certain that its subject is directly related to the topic of your report.

• Construct and incorporate the technique so that it leads smoothly into the purpose and scope statements of the introduction.

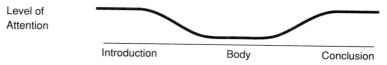

FIGURE 16.4

Audience retention curve.

- Never use profanities.
- Avoid humor that may be construed by your audience as racist, sexist, or otherwise inappropriate for the occasion.
- Avoid criticizing people or activities associated with the presentation, such as its occasion, presentation facilities, the audience for your or other presentations, and other speakers.
- Keep the attention-getting component short; its purpose is to increase the listeners' attention while also directing it toward the purpose and scope forecast section, not to dominate the introduction.
- Don't be in a hurry to begin the introduction; take the time to thank the person who has just introduced you to the audience.
- Don't apologize for inadequacies in the content or delivery of your presentation.
- Avoid gimmicky openings that are conspicuously included in the presentation merely to draw listeners' attention.
- Don't use the same old, worn-out opening (e.g., "Ladies and gentlemen," "Glad to see so many of you here").

(Glenn & Forman, 1990; Kushner, 1990; Morrisey & Sechrest, 1987, Chap. 5).

Report Body

The body of your report furnishes listeners with the evidence and analyses that have led you to your conclusions or recommendations. If you are using a deductive (direct) organization for your presentation, your report's conclusions and recommendations will immediately follow the introduction. If your oral report has an inductive (indirect) organization, the findings and analyses of that evidence will follow the introduction, followed by conclusions and recommendations.

You should explain the findings and analyses contained in the presentation body in whatever detail is required to attain the objectives of your oral report. Your evidence may take many forms, such as explanations, descriptions, definitions, examples, and statistics. You should sequence your ideas and evidence using an organizational pattern that allows your presentation to progress in a logical and coherent fashion toward your conclusion. These organizational patterns are the same arrangement strategies used in written reports, such as chronology, comparison–contrast, cause–effect, effect–cause, evaluation by criteria, order of importance, and problem–solution. Chapter 10 offers a closer study of these organizational patterns. How you organize the body of your presentation will depend on the nature of your findings and analyses, the purpose and objectives of the presentation, and your audience.

When organizing the body of your presentation, consider the following questions:

- Specifically what information is needed by your audience for you to realize the objectives of your presentation?
- In what order does the audience need to know this information and in what detail?

- How much information can be effectively communicated in the total amount of time available for the presentation? Divide that time by the number of key points you must cover in the body of your presentation. Remember also to subtract the time needed to introduce and conclude your presentation.
- At what points during the presentation body should you work in the needed visual aids? Remember that visual aids are effective in highlighting key points for listeners.
- Is there a need for a question–answer period? Is there time?

The thesis and scope statements at the end of your introduction should forecast for listeners the general order in which you will discuss the major points of the presentation. Each key point is then examined in appropriate detail in the presentation body. Introduce each subtopic with a clear topic sentence that prepares listeners for the relevant information to follow. Because your audience may miss important or complex information the first time it is mentioned in the presentation, you might remind your listeners of the key points that you've just covered by summarizing the central ideas handled in each subtopic section. The **iterative organization strategy** allows you to do exactly that.

A presentation body using an iterative organization is constructed in building block fashion. After dividing your presentation into major subtopics, you should introduce each subtopic with a mini-introduction (i.e., topic sentence) that has already been forecasted in the introduction of your presentation. Follow each subtopic's mini-introduction with relevant findings and analysis. A mini-conclusion consisting of one or two sentences that stress central ideas just covered closes your discussion of each subtopic. Figure 16.5 provides a conceptual diagram of the iterative organization strategy.

Besides aiding listeners in their retention of key information, the iterative organization strategy enhances the transition in your presentation body by clearly delineating subtopic sections. Other transitional techniques, as discussed in Chapter 10, include the use of pronouns, transition sentences, and transition words and phrases (e.g., *accordingly, furthermore, moreover, now, therefore, as a result, for this reason, on the other hand, as you would expect*).

Report Conclusion

The conclusion of your business presentation should summarize the central points of your report that you want your audience to remember most. Conclusions in oral presentations, like those in written reports, normally

> restate the thesis of the presentation.
> identify for the audience the meaning and significance of key points presented in the body of the report.
> recommend plans of action based on the conclusions.
> leave the audience with a sense of goodwill toward the speaker and an interest in remaining current on the presentation topic.

```
┌─────────────────────────────────────────────────────────┐
│                                                         │
│   PRESENTATION BODY                                     │
│                                                         │
│                    Topic 1 Introductory Sentence        │
│                                                         │
│                         ●   Evidence                    │
│                                                         │
│                         ●   Analysis                    │
│                                                         │
│                         ●   Conclusions                 │
│                                                         │
│                                                         │
│                                                         │
│                    Topic 2 Introductory Sentence        │
│                                                         │
│                         ●   Evidence                    │
│                                                         │
│                         ●   Analysis                    │
│                                                         │
│                         ●   Conclusions                 │
│                                                         │
│                                                         │
└─────────────────────────────────────────────────────────┘
```

FIGURE 16.5
Iterative organization strategy.

A presentation that has captured listeners' attention and provided an interesting discussion of topics of direct concern to the audience will usually simplify the task of concluding the oral report. Guidelines for preparing your conclusion are offered below:

- Include no new information in the conclusion that has not already been discussed, mentioned, or implied earlier in the presentation.
- Keep the conclusion summary brief. The summary is meant to recap only key points and analyses, not to rehash the entire body of the presentation.
- Be specific when recommending a plan of action; a persuasive analysis is of little use if your listeners don't know exactly how (or where) they should apply the information.

To aid listeners in understanding the scope and sequence of your recommendations, you might list suggested actions highlighted in a visual aid for greater emphasis.

Selection and Integration of Visuals

Visual aids are the oral presentation counterpart of graphic aids in written reports. Like graphic aids, visual aids can be integral in helping your audience (a) recognize the meaning of the message being communicated, (b) understand its significance, and (c) comprehend how that message can be applied to meeting their informational needs and interests. Visual aids are also an important supplement to the text of an oral presentation in enhancing listeners' retention of information. While audiences remember about 30% of what they hear and only 20% of what they see, their retention of information rises to approximately 50% whenever a presentation is supported by visual aids.

Visual aids can strengthen the effectiveness of your presentation by

increasing the impact of your message by simplifying, emphasizing, clarifying, or explaining your ideas.

attracting attention to the presentation in general and to specific points.

enhancing listener interest in the presentation.

providing a change of pace for the audience by diverting their attention from you (the speaker) to the point of discussion, thereby increasing listener comprehension and retention.

supplying transitions between topics.

keeping you on topic.

providing you with a short break from audience scrutiny so that you might take a deep breath, relax, assess the progress of the presentation, make any needed modifications to the report itself, and, in the process of all this, increase your self-confidence.

Many of the graphic aids discussed in Chapter 12 can be integrated into your presentation as various forms of visual aids such as chalkboards, computer display screens, flip charts, handouts, models, overheads, slides, audio tapes, videos, and teleconferencing. When choosing and designing visual aids for your presentation, consider

your purpose in using the visual aid.

the informational needs and technical background of your audience.

the nature of the information to be displayed.

the appropriate placement of the visual aid in the presentation.

the extent to which the visual is visible or audible to the entire audience.

the ease of accessing the visual aids during the presentation.

the ease of presenting or operating the visual aid.

A slide show at the beginning of your presentation, for example, might prove very effective in gaining your audience's attention while also providing a general overview of the report topic. Flip charts of bar charts could be a useful way to illustrate dynamic changes in several items being discussed in the body of your report. Highly complex or technical data and information, however, might be better presented in handouts distributed before the presentation.

Once decided on the number and kinds of visual aids required in your presentation, construct effective visuals by following the general guidelines offered below:

• Use visual aids to emphasize, clarify, simplify, or explain only the most important ideas in your message; don't waste your listeners' time or your organization's money by cluttering your presentation with superfluous visual aids.

- Keep them simple.
- Keep them accurate and clear.
- Keep them professional in appearance; obtain the help of a graphics professional if necessary.
- Place them where everyone can see them, and stand out of the way.
- Maintain eye contact with your audience; don't talk to the visual aid.
- Don't distract the audience by introducing a visual aid before it is needed in the presentation. (Capps et al., 1981, pp. 195–209; Timm, 1981, Chap. 9)

Chalkboards

The chalkboard is probably the most familiar visual aid, and, whether portable or wall-mounted, it offers the speaker a number of advantages:

- It is widely available (a basic component in most conference rooms) and inexpensive to use.
- The chalkboard provides speakers with the flexibility of writing key points on space that can easily be erased for new information.
- By noting key points on a chalkboard as the presentation progresses, speakers inject into their talk a sense of spontaneity and immediacy; listeners often view the information as more current than information prepared beforehand and presented on such visual aids as handouts, audiotapes, records, and videos (Vardaman, 1981, p. 60).
- Speakers can modify presented information whenever they sense the disposition of the audience and outside conditions change; if an audience, for example, had difficulty understanding a specific point, then you might want to inject more explanatory information into your talk through the use of the chalkboard.
- Speakers can use the chalkboard to encourage audience participation in the presentation by recording listener responses to questions on the board.
- Chalkboards allow the speaker to control the flow of the discussion, as an idea can be written at the time it is needed and not before.
- Chalkboards aid speakers in identifying and emphasizing relationships between key points by allowing the presenter to draw connecting lines between important ideas relevant to the discussion (Applebaum & Anatol, 1984; Capp & Capp, 1990; Glenn & Forman, 1990).

The most important rule when using the chalkboard in your presentation is to write legibly and large enough so that all viewers can read the information easily. While writing on the board, try to maintain the pace and direction of your presentation. Don't leave the audience with dead silence while you take time-out to fill the board with text, which leads us to another guideline in chalkboard use: Highlight the key ideas of your presentation by noting in a logical structure only important terms or phrases on the board. Writing dense passages of text or cramming the board with spaghetti trails of figures or equations will only confuse your audience. Use color chalk to emphasize only *key* ideas. In addition, when writing, try to stand to the side of the board so as not to block your audience's view of the information.

Moreover, make sure not to erase information before your listeners have had time to read it carefully or to copy it into their notes. On the other hand, promptly erase information once it is no longer relevant to the discussion. If you have large amounts of information to place on the board, write the information before the presentation and cover the chalkboard so as not to confuse your listeners with the purpose of the material before it is needed in the discussion (Morrisey & Sechrest, 1987, Chap. 3).

The central disadvantages of using a chalkboard include the following:

- It demands neat handwriting, a criterion that, for some of us, may make the chalkboard an impractical if not a counterproductive visual aid.
- The process of writing information on a board breaks your eye contact and, to a certain extent, your rapport with your listeners.
- Complex diagrams or drawings are difficult to reproduce on a chalkboard.
- Chalkboards are often seen as mundane because of their widespread use.

Flip Charts

Used much like the chalkboard, the flip chart is a large pad of paper mounted on an easel. The speaker can write key words or phrases or make simple drawings on the flip chart using felt-tip marking pens. One advantage flip charts have over chalkboards is that you need not erase key information that you have written as you normally would on a board in order to make room for new information. Having made your point and on completing a flip chart page, you merely flip to the next page. A second advantage to using flip charts is that old material can be reviewed by simply flipping back to previous pages, or those same pages might be detached from the pad and taped to the wall for ongoing reference. In addition, like chalkboards, flip charts provide a sense of spontaneity and immediacy to the oral report, because the speaker is able to visually highlight key ideas as they arise during the presentation.

Flip charts offer additional advantages, in that they

are inexpensive.

are easily portable and accessible during the presentation.

can be prepared before the presentation.

effectively conceal information contained on subsequent sheets to prevent the audience from jumping ahead of the discussion.

The disadvantages of using flip charts are the same as those of chalkboards. Flip charts require that your handwriting be neat and attractive. Writing on flip charts also forces you to turn from your audience, thus breaking eye contact with your listeners. In addition, because of their size, flip chart pages are limited in the amount of information they can hold. For that same reason, they might not be appropriate for large audiences. You might also find that you spend more time flipping pages than writing or drawing. Such constant interruptions in your presentation may reduce the continuity in your message.

Opaque Projectors

Opaque projectors enable you to integrate portions of a document such as a book or periodical by projecting its image onto a screen with mirrors and light. The advantages of using opaque projectors in your presentation are that they

> are easy to use and relatively simple to transport.
>
> require no special preparation of the document (such as transparencies required by overhead projectors).
>
> save you the cost of duplicating the information in handout form.

Before delivering your presentation, place the documents next to the machine in the sequence in which they are to be displayed. When it is time to refer to the documents, simply turn on the projector and integrate the document's material into your discussion. In addition, try not to minimize the loss of eye contact with your listeners by looking down at the projector for long periods of time. When referring to items on the screen, stand to the side of the screen and use a pointer to highlight specific information for the audience.

Fundamental disadvantages in using an opaque projector include the following:

- The speaker often cannot face the audience unless he or she uses a projectionist.
- The projector also may obstruct the audience's view of the screen.
- The projector's strong light may blind the audience whenever the projection stage is lowered.
- The projector's fan is often noisy, making it difficult for listeners farther from the speaker to hear.
- Opaque projectors require darkened rooms, making it difficult for listeners to consult their notes.
- Opaque projectors, even in a darkened room, often do not produce sufficiently sharp and clear images.
- Projector bulbs occasionally burn out during a presentation (thus carrying an extra bulb is always a good idea).

Overhead Projectors

Like opaque projectors, overhead projectors use mirrors and lights to project portions of a document onto an overhead screen. However, instead of projecting images from a book or other paper-based document, overhead projectors reflect images written on a **transparency**—a transparent sheet of plastic. Overhead projectors come in all sizes, from compact models that fit into briefcases to console models designed to project large images for bigger conference or meeting rooms.

Overhead projectors and the use of transparencies have a number of advantages over other visual aids:

- Overhead projectors, like opaque projectors, are easy to use and relatively simple to transport.
- Overhead transparencies are inexpensive and easy to produce.
- Personal computers, graphics software, and high-resolution color printers enable you to create highly professional transparencies in the convenience of your own home or office.
- Unlike opaque projectors, overhead projectors allow the speaker to face the audience when reading the transparency and, thus, to retain eye contact with listeners.
- Overhead projectors can be used in various degrees of lighting—from a fully lit room to a darkened one—which enables listeners and speaker to refer to their notes or handouts.

In using an overhead projector, set up the projector and place your overhead transparencies in sequence next to the machine before the presentation. When it is time to refer to a transparency, simply turn on the projector and continue your discussion. To prevent listeners from reading upcoming transparencies and getting ahead of the presentation, you might lay a sheet of paper over the transparency to cover its contents until you are ready to discuss them (Meuse, 1980, pp. 58–59).

Overlays are also effective in controlling the pace of discussion. Overlays are sheets, or strips, of transparencies that can be layered over previous transparencies. They normally introduce a new topic related to that of the previous transparency.

When working with overlays or transparencies, be sure not to look down at the projector for long periods of time, as you lose considerable eye contact with your audience. To refer to items on the screen, stand to the side of the screen and use a pointer to draw listeners' attention to specific information.

Most office supply stores can make overhead transparencies from your **master copy,** which contains the text, figures, borders, graphics, or art as you want them to appear on the transparency. Transparencies are made in one of two ways. A transparency-making machine uses a thermal carbon-lifting process to burn images onto an acetate sheet. Some of today's more sophisticated photocopiers can also produce high-quality transparencies. When preparing your master copy, be sure to keep all graphics and text large enough for the audience to read them. Typewriter-size letters, for example, are often not large enough to be read by audiences in a medium to large conference room. Consequently, you may need to use special computer graphics programs or press-on letters from a lettering machine to produce sufficiently large print (normally 18-point type size or larger). In addition to employing large lettering, you may use uppercase type to increase readability of transparencies (Morrisey & Sechrest, 1987, pp. 74–78).

Overhead projectors share many of the disadvantages of opaque projectors. Some of the disadvantages unique to using overhead projectors are listed below:

- Images can become distorted if conditions require that the projector be placed too near the screen.
- Transparencies can be misused when long passages of text are included, which the speaker laboriously reads to the audience, instead of only key words or short phrases.

Audiotape Recorders and Record Players

Using recorded voices or sounds may occasionally add valuable prestige to, or create an appropriate mood for, your presentation. An audiotape of an influential person's commentary on a relevant topic, for example, could well increase the credibility of the ideas expressed in your presentation. Likewise, recorded sounds of machinery or animals could help your audience to understand and accept your message. For instance, a record of whales communicating to one another could effectively illustrate to an audience the intelligence of those mammals and indirectly exemplify the importance of protecting those animals from fishing and possible extinction.

Among their advantages, audiotape recorders and record players are

relatively inexpensive for even high-quality systems.

convenient to transport and use during a presentation.

dependable.

easy to use.

flexible in synchronized use with such visual aids as slides and videos (Vardaman, 1981, pp. 65–67).

One disadvantage in using audiotapes is sound projection. If you do not intend to use a tape that is professionally produced, be sure to record the voice or sound effects in a controlled and acoustically superior studio to eliminate background noise and enhance the sound quality of the tape. A major disadvantage to using record players is content selection. Often you will not be able to locate a professionally produced and commercially distributed record whose sounds are exactly what you need for your presentation.

Slides

The versatility, resolution, and attractiveness of slides have made them a popular form of visual aid for business presentations. With the wide availability of slide-producing technology—such as cameras, computer-graphics programs, and slide-developing equipment—slides have become a primary visual aid to illustrate a variety of graphic aids from simple pie charts to diagrams to photographs of people, processes, or products. The use of slides offers a number of advantages to your presentation, but perhaps the most central advantage is that they can incorporate a range of dynamic images, such as photographs of corporate chiefs from a recent annual report, lines and bar charts of economic indicators from a financial periodical, or drawings of your firm's new product line. In addition, slides and accompanying equipment are easy to transport and can be controlled during the presentation by remote control, leaving you free to move about the room, make gestures, and maintain eye contact.

Despite their notable ability to attract and hold viewers' attention and to present a range of images, slides also have their drawbacks. A common flaw of many slides is that they are crammed with too much information. Keep your slides simple and well focused. Moreover, take extra care when loading the slide carousel to avoid placing slides out of sequence. In addition, the layout of slide masters and the production of slides from those masters are often complex operations and can require the help of computer-graphics systems and graphics professionals. The use of graphics professionals also can increase significantly the cost of the visual aid and, indirectly, your presentation, while also extending the preparation time needed for the presentation.

Videotapes and Teleconferencing

Video systems such as videotapes and teleconferencing can enhance the effectiveness of your presentation by

- illustrating dynamic processes or events that require continuous action and sound in order to capture their essential meaning and significance.
- grabbing the attention of today's audiences, who are accustomed to visual media, such as television and movies, and the dynamic video images those media project.
- projecting video images to remote sites with the help of telecommunications satellites.
- recording and archiving a process or discussion for later examination.
- injecting a high degree of professionalism into your talk.
- including still-action shots of charts, diagrams, tables, and photographs.

In addition to videocassettes that contain prerecorded images, video aids (viewed on regular or closed-circuit television) also include the use of **real-time** video that can record events and, at the same time, broadcast images of those events as they are actually happening to local or remote sites through the use of telecommunications networks. Teleconferencing has become an important real-time video system for communicating actual images of processes or discussions as they happen. Real-time video such as teleconferencing normally involves the use of closed-circuit cameras, satellites, monitors, accompanying cables, and complex computer software that connects and manages the telecommunications network.

When using a video system in your presentation, consider carefully the size of your audience and the size of the image that your video monitor can project. Most video aids are designed for use with smaller audiences, as they project their images with 20- to 30-in. monitors or television screens, an image that can easily be seen by 15 to 20 people in a small conference room. Audiences any larger than that will have difficulty reading the image. Some video and teleconferencing systems do support large wall screens; however, their resolution typically is murky for viewers close to the screen (Cowan, 1984; Hilton & Jacobi, 1986).

If you have decided that commercially available videotapes and movies do not meet your visual needs, you may choose to make your own video. If so, keep in mind that the images projected by effective video aids should be **compressed images** (i.e., images that capture only essential information). There is no room in videos for superfluous movement or discussion. If, for example, you are using a videocassette system to illustrate the procedure for loading a computer program onto personal computers, you might show a person performing the key steps, but *without* the coffee breaks and chatter of the typical workplace. Moreover, although it is broadcast in real-time and is, thus, unavailable for editing, teleconferencing video must still be better planned and more tightly organized than a normal 15-minute office conference involving no high telecommunication costs.

In designing your video, be sure to inject movement into the film. The simplest type of movement is motion—that is, physical movement of people or objects. The most common flaw in in-house videos (those made by the speaker or an organization without the help of a professional cinematographer) is the static scene of people sitting, or standing, and talking without any movement at all. In some cases, the content of your video will be intrinsically static, and the introduction of dynamic, physical movement might be impractical or appear artificial. In such instances, you might give the appearance of movement by regularly changing camera angles of a static scene or by splicing together different but related scenes that, though static, give the sense of movement due to their varying settings, characters, or messages.

Some of the disadvantages of using video aids in a business presentation include the following:

- Designing and producing a technically and dramatically appealing and successful video presentation require the use of complex technology as well as the assistance of video experts.
- The use of such technology and video consultants can significantly increase the cost of your presentation.
- Videotapes or movies whose topics are directly related to your presentation message may not always be available.
- Video aids tend to transform listeners into passive observers, thus reducing audience participation.
- Like slides, videotapes are not easily changed when you decide modifications to your presentation are needed.

Computer Display Screens

The pervasive use of computers has also filtered into oral presentations in the form of a visual aid. A combination of overhead screen, projector, personal computer, and interfacing software will enable you to project whatever information is on your personal computer monitor onto the overhead screen, where it can be viewed by your audience. Clearly, computer display screens can be invaluable when the presentation pertains to computer-related topics, such as on-line tutorials and the operations of a personal computer or supporting software, as viewers can see the actual operation during the speaker's real-time demonstration.

Moreover, computer display screens work especially well when the presentation deals with process-oriented topics such as techniques in planning, composing, and revising documents or illustrating the dynamic movement of an item's value. Many graphics programs, for example, offer motion much like a video, allowing you to create various graphics (e.g., line and bar graphs, pie and flow charts) on the screen and then enter new values to examine their influence in modifying the graphic. A workstation personal computer equipped with special graphics capabilities can project stunning motion graphics that will grab any audience's interest.

A major advantage of the computer display screen is that its dynamism and high-tech appeal pull listeners into the discussion. Presentations delivered in a room equipped with computer terminals can even make an audience actual participants by allowing them to respond to the discussion through their own keyboards; their responses are instantly displayed on the overhead screen. However, because it is normally projected onto an overhead screen of standard dimensions, the computer display screen is best used with a relatively small audience. In addition, the technology involved with running a computerized visual aid often requires that the speaker have computer experience or training. Finally, depending on the budget available to your presentation, the cost of the computer hardware and software necessary to support a computer display visual may be prohibitive.

Samples and Models

Occasionally, you will find that descriptions or pictorial representations of an object or process are insufficient in communicating the full meaning and significance of your message. At such times, you might supply your listeners with a sample of the actual object or process being discussed. If, for example, you were proposing marketing strategies for a new product, you might strengthen your presentation by demonstrating or distributing samples of the actual product itself. Similarly, if you were explaining to a group of scientific programmers how they might build a new computer-aided design/computer-aided manufacturing (CAD/CAM) software package using the C programming language, then you would probably want to locate your presentation in a computer lab where programmers might actually use the necessary computer systems in writing the new program.

Sometimes, however, integrating samples into your presentation, even though they are important in communicating your message, is impractical or impossible. In such instances, you might consider using working models, small-scale versions of the real thing. For instance, let's change slightly the example just given and suggest that you direct your instructional presentation to a group of computer systems analysts who need to know how to integrate this new software package into their organization's large and complex computer network. Moving the entire computer network to the conference room is obviously out of the question. Instead, you might use a made-to-scale model of the system in order to illustrate to the analysts the steps necessary in integrating the software and how the inclusion would require the modification of the computer system.

The primary advantage of using samples and models is that both visual aids provide listeners with a three-dimensional view of the object or process under discussion. In addition, samples and models encourage audience participation. However, they can also distract listeners from your presentation if not properly integrated into your discussion or demonstration. Consequently, you should distribute the samples or models, or refer to them, only when they are to be examined or used. In addition, try to have on hand enough samples or models so that listeners don't have to pass the visual aids around. This invariably draws listeners' attention away from the presentation at different times as each examines the aid during his or her turn. Manage samples and models so that the attention of all listeners is either on the visual aid or on you and your message.

Handouts

Handouts are effective visual aids when used to communicate complex or technical information to your audience. The advantages of distributing handouts to your listeners are two-fold: (1) your audience can closely examine complex, detailed, or technical information when it is in hard copy in front of them, and (2) they can refer back to the information at a future time, a convenient time, or when the material is more relevant.

Exactly when you should distribute handouts during the presentation will depend on the purpose and nature of the handout information and your intended use of it in the presentation. Normally, handouts should be distributed before or after the presentation. The distribution of hard-copy handouts during the presentation typically wastes time, distracts listeners from the topic at hand, and interrupts the flow of the talk. If you expect to actively work with the material during the presentation, you should distribute the relevant handouts before the presentation. Handouts that might be distributed before the presentation might include sample documents to be analyzed and evaluated during the discussion, printed guidelines of workshop objectives and procedures, or key figures or passages of text that serve as the groundwork on which the rest of the presentation builds. Be aware, however, that handouts distributed before the presentation may tempt listeners to read the information rather than pay attention to the presentation.

If the purpose of the information is to provide listeners with important details supplemental to the presentation, then the handouts might be distributed after the presentation. Material that might be best handed out after the presentation includes tables of financial data, copies of overhead transparencies used during the presentation, audience response forms, a "Works Cited" page of experts referred to in the talk, or a bibliography of selected readings. Whether the handouts are distributed before or after the presentation, be sure to refer to them during the talk and to explain their purpose in realizing the objectives of your presentation. If they are handed out during the presentation, arrange for someone else to distribute the copies so as not to interrupt the flow of the discussion.

The central disadvantage of handouts is abuse. It is often tempting to depend too much on handouts, to the point that nearly the entire presentation is provided in handout form. In addition, the excessive use of handouts not only increases significantly the cost of the presentation but, to a large extent, makes the oral presentation superfluous. Be selective in deciding which information, if any, should be conveyed in handout form.

Summary

Most written reports that address issues central to an organization will, in one context or another, be presented orally to audiences inside or outside the company. Consequently, your ability to prepare effective oral presentations will provide you with numerous and significant benefits in your professional career. Successful business presentations, for example, can help you win approval and support for your ideas from decision makers at all levels of an organization. As an effective speaker, you also distinguish yourself as a shaker and mover who can maximize the collaboration of peers, subordinates, and superiors to achieve organizational objectives and goals. Moreover, the planning, researching, organizing, and analyzing skills you employ in preparing and delivering an effective oral presentation ultimately make you a better thinker and overall communicator in and out of the workplace.

Chapter 16 has stated that the fundamental purposes of oral presentations are to inform, instruct, entertain, and persuade. In preparing your presentation, you should determine your purpose, identify your objectives, select the presentation format, analyze your audience, organize the presentation, and choose and integrate visual aids. We have emphasized that structuring your presentation so that it meets the informational needs and background of your listeners is impossible unless you take the time to analyze your audience. If you are unable to design the topic, content, organization, and delivery of your presentation so that your listeners understand the meaning and significance of your message, then you have failed in the most basic goal of the communication process. Oral presentations, like written reports, must be audience-centered.

Visual aids are an integral component of most oral presentations, as they can increase the impact of your message by simplifying, emphasizing, clarifying, or explaining your ideas. Effective visuals also attract listeners' attention to the presentation in general and to specific points, thus enhancing listener interest in the presentation. Finally, visuals can (a) provide a change of pace for the audience by diverting their attention from you (the speaker) to the point of discussion, (b) keep you on topic, and (c) provide you with a short break from audience scrutiny so that you might take a deep breath, relax, assess the progress of the presentation, make any needed modifications to the report itself, and, in the process of all this, increase your self-confidence.

Related Reading

APPLEBAUM, RONALD L., and KARL W. E. ANATOL. *Strategies for Persuasive Communication.* Columbus, OH: Merrill, 1984.

CAPP, GLENN R., and CAROLYN C. Capp. *Basic Oral Communication.* 5th ed. Englewood Cliffs, NJ: Prentice, 1990.

CAPPS, RANDALL, CARLEY H. DODD, and LARRY J. WINN. *Communication for the Business and Professional Speaker.* New York: Macmillan, 1981.

COWAN, ROBERT, A. *Teleconferencing: Maximizing Human Potential.* Restin, VA: Reston, 1984.

FRANK, MILO O. *How to Get Your Point Across in 30 Seconds or Less.* New York: Simon, 1986.

FRANK, TED, and DAVID RAY. *Basic Business and Professional Speech Communication.* Englewood Cliffs, NJ: Prentice, 1987.

GLENN, ETHYL C., and SANDRA H. FORMAN. *Public Speaking: Today and Tomorrow.* Englewood Cliffs, NJ: Prentice, 1990.

HILTON, JACK, and PETER JACOBI. *Straight Talk about Videoconferencing.* Englewood Cliffs, NJ: Prentice, 1986.

JOHNSON, DAVID W. *Reaching Out: Interpersonal Effectiveness and Self-Actualization.* 4th ed. Englewood Cliffs, NJ: Prentice, 1990.

KAPLAN, BURTON. *The Manager's Complete Guide to Speech Writing.* New York: Free Press, 1988.

KNAPP, MARK L. *Nonverbal Communication in Human Interaction.* 2nd ed. New York: Holt, 1978.

KUSHNER, MAUREEN. *The Light Touch: How to Use Humor for Business Success.* New York: Simon, 1990.

MAYER, KENNETH R. *Well Spoken: Oral Communication Skills for Business.* New York: Harcourt, 1988.

MEUSE, LEONARD F. *Mastering the Business and Technical Presention.* Boston: CBI, 1980.

MORRISEY, GEORGE. L., and THOMAS L. SECHREST. *Effective Business and Technical Presentations.* 3rd ed. Menlo Park, CA: Addison, 1987.

SAMOVAR, LARRY A., STEPHEN W. KING, and MYRON W. LUSTY. *Speech Communication in Business and the Professions.* Belmont, CA: Wadsworth, 1981.

SMITH, TERRY C. *Making Successful Presentations: A Self-Teaching Guide.* New York: Wiley, 1984.

SNYDER, ELAYNE. *Persuasive Business Speaking.* New York: American Mgmt. Assn., 1990.

TIMM, PAUL R. *Functional Business Presentations.* Englewood Cliffs, NJ: Prentice, 1981.

VARDAMAN, GEORGE T. *Making Successful Presentations.* New York: AMACOM, 1981.

ZELAZNY, GENE. *Say It with Charts: The Executive's Guide to Successful Presentations.* Homewood, IL: Dow Jones-Irwin, 1985.

CHAPTER 17

Delivering Oral Presentations

The delivery is the moment of truth for any presentation. Many long hours of research and preparation may be wasted if you cannot draw upon your oral communication skills, poise, and presence to present the information effectively. The major steps in the delivery phase of your presentation are to

> rehearse.
>
> plan and review presentation logistics.
>
> deliver the oral report.

Rehearse

A common weakness in many presentations is that speakers, while knowing what they want to say, are not sufficiently prepared before the presentation in *how* they are going to say it. Rehearsing your presentation allows you to

> improve your delivery skills.
>
> practice integrating each visual aid so that it is smoothly introduced at the most efficacious point in the presentation.
>
> expand your knowledge and understanding of the presentation content.
>
> time the length of the oral report as well as its pace and assess where it might be shortened or expanded.

identify possible problem areas in the presentation and make any last-minute adjustments to such presentation components as content, organization, or visual aids.

increase confidence in yourself.

Rehearse your presentation as many times as needed until you are comfortable with how you plan to deliver the information to your audience. If possible, practice in the same room where the presentation will be held. Rehearsing the report in front of someone whose background and interests closely match those of the target audience can also provide you with valuable ideas on how the delivery could be improved.

Plan and Review Presentation Logistics

You may be lucky enough to have someone within your organization whose central responsibility is to plan the logistics surrounding company presentations. Often, however, this is not the case and you will be left to make your own arrangements for the oral reports you present inside or outside your organization. Regardless of whether there are others to help you prepare, it's always a good idea for you personally to review the arrangements for your talk. Remember that, regardless of who forgot to do what, *you* are the one who will be criticized if the presentation fails as a result of poor preparation (Morrisey & Sechrest, 1987, pp. 101–109).

When planning and reviewing the logistics of your presentation, make sure to double-check that

the notification or invitation list of your audience is complete and that it is sent out in plenty of time before the presentation.

the presentation room is properly set up with needed furniture and visual aids.

all potential problems with the presentation site (e.g., catering capabilities, heating/cooling, seating capacity, room setup) are formally identified and solved well in advance.

personnel are assigned to handle the registration of the audience and yourself (as presenter).

you have airline or hotel reservations, if needed, and ground transportation.

(Kaumeyer, 1985; Murray, 1983; Smith, 1984, Chap. 8)

The fact that presentation logistics are commonly referred to as "last-minute" details may well indicate the insufficient attention we pay to them. Don't leave presentation logistics to the last minute. Plan and review logistics earlier than you think necessary to prevent last-minute problems from reducing the effectiveness of your presentation.

Deliver the Presentation

The human element is significantly more crucial in communicating effectively through oral presentations than it is in written reports. The speaker's poise and appearance, body movement, and voice are central components of the presentation delivery and can greatly affect the audience's perception of both the presenter and the information presented.

Poise and Appearance

By projecting an air of relaxed self-confidence, a poised speaker places the audience at ease and implicitly asserts his or her credibility. A speaker who appears nervous or ill at ease in front of listeners can lose credibility as a knowledgeable authority on the report topic, which tends to significantly reduce, or even eliminate, the presentation's impact.

Perhaps the most common problem for speakers in presenting oral reports is nervousness and stage fright. A moderate amount of nervousness is normal and can actually be rechanneled as positive energy to make you more alert and enthusiastic during the presentation. Excessive nervousness, however, can distract you from your message and thereby significantly reduce the effectiveness of your delivery (Meuse, 1980, pp. 105–109; Snyder, 1990, Chap. 13). You can reduce your nervousness while also enhancing the degree of poise that you project to audiences by applying the following guidelines:

- Remember that all except the most hostile audiences want you to succeed in the presentation. They want to hear what you have to say. They don't want to waste their time or suffer embarrassment for you as you nervously bumble through the presentation. Don't forget that you have well-wishers out there in the audience.

- Concentrate on ideas. Think about your message and how you can most effectively communicate that message.

- Be prepared to present your message, to defend it, to compromise, and to respond to listeners' reactions (some of which may be negative).

- Make a good first impression. Stride confidently into the room. Pause before speaking to look your audience over and to give them a chance to look you over.

- Set a relaxed tone for the presentation. Address the audience with the same respect and courtesy as you would colleagues. Smile. Use wit, if appropriate. Show that you enjoy sharing your time and ideas with your listeners.

- Increase your self-confidence by moving and speaking in a professional manner. Avoid appearing stiff or distant, but allow your good posture, controlled and relaxed movement, and clear, well-modulated voice to build your self-assurance. (Timm, 1981)

Your appearance has much to do with the impression you make on your audience. The formality of your dress will depend on the occasion; however, regardless of whether the situation calls for a three-piece suit or casual shirt or blouse, you should always dress neatly with a minimum of accessories. Consider the expectations of your audience along with the image you want to project; then dress accordingly.

Body Movement

The way you move during the presentation can communicate to the audience a great deal about you as well as the message you're trying to convey. By the eye contact you maintain with your audience, facial expressions, gestures, and posture, you can strengthen the content of your presentation (LeRoax, 1984, pp. 18–23). For example, you can

> project your enthusiasm toward the topic (and thus encourage the same enthusiasm and attention from your listeners).
>
> illustrate your confidence in the importance of your message as well as your ability to express that message effectively.
>
> create a friendly and relaxed atmosphere.
>
> establish credibility for you and your message.

Eye Contact and Facial Expressions

Maintaining **eye contact** with your audience is an important technique in managing how your message is received by listeners. Consistent eye contact, for example, allows you to

> establish a personal connection with each person in the audience.
>
> draw listeners' interest and hold their attention.
>
> receive nonverbal audience feedback from which you can decide to adjust the content, organization, or delivery of your message to meet the changing needs of your audience (Smith, 1984, pp. 114–115).
>
> establish goodwill with your listeners by showing them that you care about how they react to your message, which builds listeners' confidence in you and your ideas (Snyder, 1990, pp. 127–130).

Maintaining eye contact with your audience is not always easy. For instance, looking into the eyes of your listeners, especially hostile ones, can produce stage fright or otherwise distract you from your line of thought. In addition, some visual aids (e.g., opaque projectors) may make eye contact difficult, and any exaggerated attempt to maintain eye contact might appear mechanical and false. Furthermore, visual aids requiring a dark room (e.g., slides) make eye contact impossible (Preston, 1979).

The primary rule in using eye contact is regularity. Don't ignore your listeners. If you are prone to nervousness or stage fright, pick out a few friendly faces in different areas of the crowd and talk to them until you are more relaxed. Rehearse your use of visual aids so that there is time to look up and make regular eye contact with your audience. Establishing a positive rapport with your listeners through the use of eye contact will make you more relaxed and your listeners more receptive to your message.

As with eye contact, your **facial expressions** communicate powerful messages to your audience that can either aid or impede your presentation. Unlike eye contact, however, facial expressions are difficult to manage consciously. Although you could fake the basic expressions—such as a smile, a scowl, a look of surprise, a grimace—such histrionics are difficult to maintain and keep consistently convincing, even for the best of actors (Snyder, 1990, pp. 126–127). More importantly, why would you want to waste energy trying to fool your listeners instead of concentrating on your message and delivery? The most effective expressions are those that are genuine and that come from a positive attitude. To project warm, genuine facial expressions, try to relax, enjoy the chance to discuss important ideas, and share this enthusiasm with your audience. The positive and authentic facial expressions will follow naturally.

Gestures

Well-timed **gestures** that are appropriate to the situation can effectively (a) emphasize key points in the presentation, (b) serve as transitions between topics, (c) increase audience interest, and (d) encourage listeners' participation in the talk (Samovar et al., 1981, pp. 86–88; Smith, 1984, p. 113). An extended hand held above the head, for example, can draw the audience's attention to a crucial message, while a short chopping motion with the hand can emphasize a point or suggest a change of topic. By holding your open palms up, you can encourage active participation from your audience; palms down implies the emphatic closure of an idea. Nodding the head can suggest affirmation of an idea or thoughtfulness, depending on the situation. A clenched fist increases the sense of urgency in your message by creating an air of aggression.

When using gestures in your presentation, consider the following guidelines:

- Use only those gestures that seem natural to you and the message at hand. Gestures that don't match your personality or the topic and that don't seem spontaneous usually appear rehearsed and artificial.
- Use only functional gestures that emphasize your message. Superfluous gestures distract audiences.
- Coordinate the gesture with corresponding words.
- Don't overuse a gesture.
- Avoid gestures that may be considered by your audience to be offensive.

Posture

Your **posture** can convey much to your audience about your emotional attitude toward them as well as your message. A speaker with poor posture often projects a lack of interest, energy, discipline, or orderliness. Slouching, for example, is associated with indifference, laziness, or even disrespect. Moreover, the halting movements of a speaker's walk may suggest a lack of confidence or imply his or her uncertainty in the meaning or accuracy of the message. The projection of such negative images reduces both the value and the effectiveness of your message in the eyes of your listeners.

Good posture, on the other hand, emphasizes that you are alert, interested, and confident. Brisk, energetic movements project confidence and decisiveness. Consider your posture throughout the presentation. Sit erect. Stand and walk straight with your shoulders back and head up. You should obviously avoid rigid movements that may imply you are nervous or uncomfortable with your message, the audience, or both. Always present to your audience a posture that projects a relaxed confidence.

Voice

Your voice is perhaps the most important delivery tool for clearly and persuasively communicating your message. Whereas a slow monotone can quickly put listeners to sleep, a moderately paced and modulated voice can just as quickly draw and hold an audience's attention through even the most complex discussions. Although most of us do not have the speaking skills of a Winston Churchill, John F. Kennedy, or Martin Luther King, Jr., we can significantly enhance the clarity, attractiveness, and persuasive power of our voices by better managing the volume, rate, pitch, pronunciation, and enunciation.

Volume

The **volume**, or intensity, of your voice should be sufficient so that all your listeners can hear your message, but not so loud that it distracts them. In addition, use varying degrees of voice volume as a dramatic device (Snyder, 1990, Chap. 11). Obviously, speaking in louder tones draws listeners' attention to key points. Your use of such visual aids as overhead projectors or slides may also require that you significantly raise your voice to be heard over background noise. But you can also emphasize parts of your message by modulating your voice volume. A sudden drop in voice intensity, for example, can quickly spark an audience's interest.

Rate

The **rate**, or tempo, at which you speak can directly affect how much of your message your audience hears and comprehends. As in managing your voice volume, you should vary the rate of your presentation to keep listeners' interest. A one-speed presentation can bore listeners, and bored listeners whose minds wander tend to miss key points in a presentation. Moreover, by using the same voice rate throughout the presentation, you cannot emphasize key points or distinguish central points from subordinate ones (Samovar et al., 1981, pp. 78–83).

A slower voice rate can emphasize ideas by giving the audience time to hear and comprehend the complete message. A fast voice rate, while perhaps effective when summarizing well-established points, is normally inappropriate when communicating information that is new to listeners. Furthermore, a fast voice rate used to communicate technically complex information can significantly reduce audience comprehension of your message.

Short presentations invite voice rate problems. Regardless of how much information you feel is vital to the presentation, don't cram so much material into your report that you are forced to rush frantically through it. Slow down. Avoid a rate so slow that listeners' attention wanes, but let your audience hear the full message. A well-placed pause when discussing key ideas can also give an audience just enough time to digest the significance of your message.

Pitch

The **pitch**, or tone, refers to the voice's lows and highs. Maintain a pitch that is natural to you. A conversational tone is typically most effective. Avoid a monotone pitch. As with voice volume and rate, modulate your pitch to keep listeners interested in not only your voice but, more importantly, your message. If you are energetic about the information expressed in your presentation, the enthusiasm noted in the pitch of your voice will draw listeners into the discussion at hand.

Pronunciation and Enunciation

Often overlooked by inexperienced or unprepared speakers, **correct pronunciation** can be a subtle, though important, voice element in effectively communicating your message. First, mispronunciation prevents listeners from immediately recognizing the mispronounced words, if they can recognize them at all (Meuse, 1980, pp. 90–97). Listeners who miss a word or phrase due to the speaker's poor pronunciation are often distracted enough to miss the entire idea expressed in that sentence.

In addition to reducing listener comprehension, poor pronunciation erodes speaker credibility. From an audience viewpoint, speakers who do not take the time to check the pronunciation of words in their presentations may also fail to double-check the accuracy of the information being presented. Ensure that your listeners hear your message. If you aren't sure how to pronounce a word, look it up in a dictionary. If you don't know how to pronounce someone's name, ask a colleague.

Enunciation is the articulation of words. While a speaker may pronounce a word correctly, he or she may not enunciate it properly. Poor enunciation, as with faulty pronunciation, can prevent listeners from hearing and understanding your message. Achieving clear, crisp enunciation takes practice. Some fundamental but too often ignored guidelines toward better enunciation include the following:

- Don't mumble. Open your mouth.
- Don't bite off the ends of words. Complete the entire word. Watch out for those words that end in consonants; they're commonly chewed at the end (e.g., "goin' " for "going").
- Don't round off your *t*s into *d*s (e.g., "liddle" for "little").
- Don't muddle through diphthongs (e.g., "yur" for "your").

Maximize Audience Participation

It is important that you involve your audience in your discussion from the very beginning of the presentation. A participatory audience will typically be more attentive and receptive to your message. Involved listeners tend to comprehend more because they are constantly examining and relating the information to their own base of knowledge and perceptions. Participatory audiences can also provide you with valuable reactions to your message that can help you in improving the content or organization of the message and even aid you in preparing and delivering better presentations later.

Ways in which you can increase audience participation in your presentation include

asking listeners questions.

maintaining eye contact with your audience (as if to say, "I am genuinely interested in your reaction to my message").

encouraging audience participation during the presentation's question–answer period.

Occasionally, not all audience participation is welcome. At one time or another you will face an unreceptive or even hostile listener or group of listeners. Perhaps you will face the argumentative listener who wants to corner you into a one-on-one debate. Such an individual is typically looking for attention or recognition from you and members of the audience. Your first reaction to the **argumentative questioner**, as with any hostile member of your audience, should be to remain calm. Don't turn the presentation into a war of conflicting points of view or, worse, personal insults. Recognize the idea put forth by the argumentative listener by thanking the individual for raising the idea. Then direct your response so that you can continue with your presentation; suggest to the listener that the two of you discuss the issue in greater detail *after* the presentation (Vardaman, 1981, pp. 107–109).

The **loaded question** often has no clear answer and is basically meant to put you on the spot. The best solution to a loaded question is to turn the question back on the questioner. Suppose that you are delivering a presentation on the current state of oil production in Texas that makes no recommendations on how to increase oil production. How would you react to a loaded question like the following: "Your solution to the oil shortage, then, is to raise the cost of April crude $2.25 per barrel?" You might do well to clarify that you have guaranteed no such solution in your presentation and that any answer to the oil shortage, although it would involve higher crude prices, would be dependent on many variables. You might then quickly remind the questioner of the central variables.

How many times have you seen a presentation come to a grinding halt because someone in the audience insists on posing a **long-winded question**?

You can cut short the long-winded question by asking the questioner to actually state his or her question so that the presentation can continue: "Do you have a question?" or "Can we have your question, Alice?"

Regardless of how experienced and knowledgeable you might be in the subject area of your presentation, inevitably a question will arise from your audience that you cannot answer. When this happens, don't panic or make up an answer whose inaccuracy will be discovered during or after the presentation, leaving you embarrassed and your credibility tainted. Instead, pause to give yourself the time to formulate a prudent answer (LeRoax, 1984, p. 136). Some of the most popular and successful pause tactics include

asking the questioner to repeat his or her question.

prompting the questioner for his or her own view on the issue (much as you would do with the loaded question).

sounding the audience for their answers to the question.

writing the question down on a visual aid such as an overhead transparency or flip chart until you have had time to construct your answer. (Morrisey & Sechrest, 1987)

Finally, if time is running out and you are asked a question for which you have no answer, you might simply postpone the discussion by saying, "That's an interesting and thought-provoking question. I wish I could tell you that I have a quick answer to it, but I don't. Could we get together after the presentation and discuss it when we have more time?"

Record and Interpret Audience Feedback

You can evaluate the effectiveness of your presentation by recording and interpreting the reaction of your listeners throughout the report. Based on the nonverbal or verbal feedback of your audience, you can modify your report so that (a) the content, organization, or delivery of your message remain in line with changing audience needs, (b) presentation objectives are achieved, and (c) visual aids are more effectively used.

Nonverbal audience feedback is most often reflected in the body language of your listeners, such as their facial expressions and body movement. Are their eyes glazed over with sleep, or do they look alert and interested? Are they weighed down by boredom and slouched deep in their chairs or attentively perched on the edge of their seats? Are they restlessly fidgeting or calmly glued to each word you speak? Read the nonverbal messages of your audience. They are trying to tell you something. You can influence the nonverbal feedback of your audience so that it is consistently more positive by altering and improving the content, organization, and delivery of your presentation (Knapp, 1978).

You can elicit **verbal** feedback from your audience by milling about the room before the presentation to get a sense of their informational needs and interests. You can also encourage feedback during the presentation by asking your listeners questions relating to the topic at hand. The most useful verbal feedback, however, comes during the question–answer period when listeners have heard all or part of your message and can intelligently respond to it.

Placement of the question–answer period will depend on your personal preference. Question–answer periods placed at the end of the presentation may be most effective in obtaining an accurate sense of listeners' views as the audience has had the chance to hear the entire message prior to responding. While questions or responses accepted before or during the presentation can contribute valuable responses to topics as they are addressed, such verbal feedback is invariably registered by listeners who are unfamiliar with the part of the message that is to follow. Consequently, this type of audience response is often short-sighted or misinformed—thus, invalid. In addition, verbal feedback during the presentation can disrupt the oral report by (a) anticipating topics that the speaker will address at a more appropriate point later in the presentation and (b) forcing the speaker to digress in order to address a side issue.

Another popular method of obtaining audience feedback is the **postpresentation questionnaire**. The survey, distributed either before or after the presentation, prompts listeners for their evaluation of presentation components—such as the value of its content, the appropriateness of its organization, and the effectiveness of the speaker's presentation style and use of visual aids—as well as a self-analysis of their own expectations of and participation in the presentation. A sample postpresentation survey is provided in Figure 17.1.

Summary

Your delivery is key to a successful **oral presentation**. Many long hours of planning your presentation may be wasted if you cannot draw upon your oral communication skills, poise, and physical presence to present information effectively. In Chapter 17 we have presented the major steps in delivering your presentation—rehearse, plan, review presentation logistics, and then give the oral report with attention to your appearance, body movement, enunciation, and pronunciation.

It is important that you involve your audience in your discussion from the very beginning of the presentation. A participatory audience will typically be more attentive and receptive to your message. Involved listeners tend to comprehend more because they are constantly examining and relating the information to their own base of knowledge and perceptions. Participatory audiences can also provide you with valuable reactions to your message that can help you in improving the content or organization of the message and even aid you in preparing and delivering better presentations in the future.

PRESENTATION EVALUATION SURVEY

Topic: _____

Presenter: _____

Occasion of Presentation: _____

CONTENT AND ORGANIZATION

INTRODUCTION

1. How effectively did the introduction create interest in the presentation?
Very well _____ Good _____ Fair _____ Poor _____

2. Was the purpose of the presentation clearly stated?
Yes _____ Somewhat _____ No _____ Not sure _____

3. Did the introduction sufficiently forecast for you the key
topics that would be addressed in the body of the presentation?
Yes _____ Somewhat _____ No _____ Not sure _____

Comments _____
_____
_____

BODY

1. Were all the key topics promised in the introduction later presented in the body?
Yes _____ Somewhat _____ No _____ Not sure _____

2. Were the speaker's ideas clearly and convincingly presented?
Yes _____ Somewhat _____ No _____ Not sure _____

3. Were the supporting data and information

Interesting?   Yes _____ Somewhat _____ No _____

Varied?   Yes _____ Somewhat _____ No _____

Diectly related?   Yes _____ Somewhat _____ No _____

Figure 17.1
Postpresentation survey.
Source: Adapted from Morrisey and Sechrest, 1987, Appendix.

4. Were the content and organization of the presentation successful in meeting your

Informational needs?   Yes _____ Somewhat _____ No _____

Interests?   Yes _____ Somewhat _____ No _____

Area of training/expertise?   Yes _____ Somewhat _____ No _____

Technical level?   Yes _____ Somewhat _____ No _____

Comments:_____

_____

_____

CONCLUSION

1. Did the conclusion summarize the purpose(s) of the presentation as well as the central interpretations of the data and information presented?

Yes _____ Somewhat _____ No _____ Not sure _____

2. If the conclusion included recommendations, did they effectively urge a plan of action and did the action seem appropriate and feasible?

Yes _____ Somewhat _____ No _____ Not sure _____

Comments: _____

_____

_____

DELIVERY

Visual Aids

1. Were the supporting visual aids

Interesting?   Yes _____ Somewhat _____ No _____

Varied?   Yes _____ Somewhat _____ No _____

Directly related?   Yes _____ Somewhat _____ No _____

2. Were they easy to read and understand?

Yes _____ Somewhat _____ No _____

3. Were they introduced into the presentation at the appropriate time?

Yes _____ Reasonably so _____ No _____

Figure 17.1
Continued

4. Were the aids sufficiently discussed in order to make their relevance and significance to the message clear?

Yes _____ Reasonably so _____ No _____

Comments: _____

_____

_____

DELIVERY TECHNIQUES

1. Did the speaker seem poised and relaxed, in control of the situation?

Yes _____ Reasonably so _____ No _____

2. Were the speaker's posture and body movements appropriate?

Yes _____ Reasonably so _____ No _____

3. Were gestures appropriate in communicating the speaker's message?

Yes _____ Reasonably so _____ No _____

4. Did the speaker maintain sufficient eye contact with the audience?

Yes _____ Reasonably so _____ No _____

Comments: _____

_____

_____

VOICE

1. How was the presenter's pitch and voice quality?

Good _____ Too high _____ Too low _____

2. How was the rate of the presenter's speech?

Good _____ Too fast _____ Too slow _____

3. How was the volume intensity of the presenter's speech?

Good _____ Too loud _____ Too soft _____

4. How was the presenter's pronunciation and enunciation?

Good _____ Fair _____ Poor _____

Comments: _____

_____

_____

FIGURE 17.1
Continued

GENERAL

1. How would you evaluate the overall effectiveness of the presentation's content and organization?

Outstanding _____ Good _____ Fair _____ Poor _____

2. How would you evaluate the overall delivery of the presentation?

Outstanding _____ Good _____ Fair _____ Poor _____

Please offer any additional comments that might help improve the presentation:

_____

_____

_____

_____

_____

_____

_____

_____

_____

Figure 17.1
Continued

Related Reading

Barker, L. *Communication.* 5th ed. Englewood Cliffs, NJ: Prentice, 1990.

Bonner, William H. *Communicating in Business: Key to Success.* 6th ed. Houston: Dame, 1990.

Burnett, Mary Joyce, and Alta Dollar. *Business Communication: Strategies for Success.* Houston: Dame, 1989.

Golen, Steven P., C. Glenn Pearce, and Ross Figgins. *Report Writing for Business and Industry.* New York: Wiley, 1985.

Hays, Richard. *Practically Speaking—In Business, Industry, and Government.* Reading, MA: Addison, 1969.

Kaumeyer, Richard A. *How to Write and Speak in Business.* New York: Van Nostrand, 1985.

Knapp, Mark L. *Nonverbal Communication in Human Interaction.* 2nd ed. New York: Holt, 1978.

LeRoax, Paul. *Selling to a Group: Presentation Strategies.* New York: Harper, 1984.

MEUSE, LEONARD F. *Mastering the Business and Techincal Presentation.* Boston: CBI, 1980.

MONTGOMERY, ROBERT L. *A Master Guide to Public Speaking.* New York: Harper, 1979.

MORRISEY, GEORGE L., and THOMAS L. SECHREST. *Effective Business and Technical Presentations.* 3rd ed. Menlo Park, CA: Addison, 1987.

MURRAY, SHEILA L. *How to Organize and Manage a Seminar.* Englewood Cliffs, NJ: Prentice, 1983.

PRESTON, PAUL. *Communication for Managers.* Englewood Cliffs, NJ: Prentice, 1979.

QUBEIN, NIDO R. *Communicate like a Pro.* Englewood Cliffs, NJ: Prentice, 1983.

ROBBINS, L. M. *The Business of Writing and Speaking: A Managerial Communication Manual.* New York: McGraw, 1985.

SAMOVAR, LARRY A., STEPHEN W. KING, and MYRON W. LUSTY. *Speech Communication in Business and the Professions.* Belmont, CA: Wadsworth, 1981.

SMITH, TERRY C. *Successful Presentations: A Self-Teaching Guide.* New York: Wiley, 1984.

SNYDER, ELAYNE. *Persuasive Business Speaking.* New York: AMACOM, 1990.

TIMM, PAUL R. *Functional Business Presentations.* Englewood Cliffs, NJ: Prentice, 1981.

VARDAMAN, GEORGE T. *Making Successful Presentations.* New York: AMACOM, 1981.

Appendix A:

Conducting
Statistical Analysis

Many business reports you write will require some degree of statistical analysis. A central benefit of statistical analysis is that it enables you to reduce large amounts of data into a manageable form that can be closely scrutinized for meaning and significance in regard to solving your report problem. Statistical analysis also allows you to evaluate numerically both qualitative and quantitative data and to determine the probability of error associated with those data. By understanding the level of reliability of your findings, you are then able to draw more accurate conclusions and to make sound recommendations based on those conclusions.

Although you may not conduct statistical analysis of your collected data or even analyze the results from such a study, you will find at least a general understanding of statistics invaluable for several reasons. First, to know which types of statistical analysis should be used on your data, you must understand the different statistical techniques available to you and which of those techniques would be most appropriate to your study. Some statistical techniques will prove to be more useful than others, depending on your chosen research methods, the nature and size of the sample, and the complexity of the data and required analyses. Though you may do well to consult professional statisticians when considering the statistical analysis for your data, *you* are the person who best knows the purpose, scope, research methods, and findings of your report. Your expertise, then, is vital in choosing which statistical techniques would produce the most relevant, penetrating, and accurate results from your research.

You should also understand the uses of statistical techniques in order to recognize and interpret the meaning and significance of your analysis results.

For example, how useful would the mean of a bimodal distribution of values be to your interpretation without a supplemental discussion of the standard deviation of those same values? How much meaningful insight would the median of a severely skewed distribution of values offer your analysis? Knowledge of statistical techniques would quickly provide you with the answers to these fundamental questions.

This discussion of statistical analysis is meant to provide you with a brief overview of commonly used statistical tools and their applications in managerial reports. It examines the differences between qualitative and quantitative data and how those data can be statistically analyzed with descriptive and inferential statistics. Your report objectives and subjects might require that you incorporate more advanced statistical methods than those studied here. Thus we encourage you to consult the suggested readings at the end of this chapter to gain a more thorough understanding of statistical analysis and its applications in business-related research.

Quantitative Data

Unlike qualitative data, which are subjective, **quantitative data** are objective and, as they are in number form, require no conversion to numerical values. The incomes of computer programmers within an organization, for instance, are examples of quantitative data, as are their ages, heights, and weights. Quantitative data are integral to all stages of statistical analysis. In Chapter 8 you read how sample populations for your primary research can be quantified to be statistically representative of the general population. The statistical analysis of quantitative data can also help you ultimately to test the accuracy and reliability of your findings.

Qualitative Data

The term **qualitative data** refers to the quality or descriptive characteristics of the data being examined. Whether your collected data are numeric or nonnumeric in form, those data would be qualitative if used to describe the attributes of an item under study. For example, if you were searching for the personal computer most appropriate for your organization's office personnel, you might begin by evaluating the capabilities of comparable computers. Many of those capabilities would be numerical in form, such as the systems' hard disk storage capacities, random-access storage, clock speeds, and microprocessor types. However, to make those data meaningful, you would have to rate the numbers subjectively, specifying which numerical values were most, or least, favorable. You might, for instance, decide that hard disks with 150 megabytes of storage capacity were significantly more appropriate than those with 70, 40, or 20 megabytes for the type of computer tasks done within your organization.

TABLE A.1.

Calculation of Weighted Averages

		Computer A		Computer B	
	Weights	Points	Average Value	Points	Average Value
Appearance	0.1	50	5	70	7
Ergonomic design	0.3	70	21	80	24
Keyboard	0.1	70	7	60	6
Monitor color	0.2	80	16	70	14
Warranty	0.3	60	18	80	24
TOTAL			**67**		**75**

The process of analyzing nonnumeric qualitative data adds an extra step to that of analyzing numeric data. Nonnumeric data must first be converted to numerical values (a process called *quantifying* data), then evaluated. For example, if you had surveyed office personnel for their preferences in personal computers, you might have received judgments based on a variety of attributes, such as appearance, ergonomic design, keyboard arrangement, monitor color, and warranty—all qualitative data. To quantify those data, you would have to assign a numeric value to each item based on your evaluation of that item's importance in making the chosen computer most effective and useful within your specific organization. A commonly used method of quantifying qualitative data is the calculation of **weighted averages**.

Table A.1 illustrates how you might weigh the value of each evaluated computer attribute. The figure includes the evaluation of only 2 of 10 computers compared in the study. All weight values must add up to one. You may assign whatever point value you wish for each item. In this example, the highest point value for each of the five items is 100.

The quantifying of qualitative data is highly useful when analyzing items that may be emotionally charged for respondents. Assigning numerical values to those items can help you more clearly define their place and significance in your analysis.

Descriptive Statistics

After you have collected and classified your data, you will need some quantitative method for comparing general similarities and dissimilarities among different sets of data. **Descriptive statistics** characterize different sets of data by first defining the center of each set's distribution of numbers or values. You can then describe the relationships between those groups by how those sets of numbers are grouped in relation to the central point of distribution. The most useful descriptive methods are measures of central tendency, dispersion, and correlation.

Measures of Central Tendency

You can measure and analyze the relationship(s) between one set, or differing sets, of data through measures of **central tendency**. The most frequently used indexes of central tendency are the mean, weighted mean, mode, median, and midrange (Stevenson, 1985; Hoel & Jessen, 1982).

Mean

The **mean**, also called the **arithmetic average**, is a frequently used measure of central tendency. It is the sum of all values in the distribution divided by the total number of values. The mean is represented by $\overline{X}$ or the Greek letter *mu*, or μ. The mean can be calculated with the following equation:

$$\overline{X} = \frac{\Sigma x}{n}$$

In the equation, x represents each individual value and n refers to the total number of scores in the distribution. The symbol Σ means "the sum of." The following informal table illustrates the procedure for determining the mean for 10 test scores:

Test Scores	Frequency	Total Scores
65	1	65
70	2	140
73	2	146
81	1	81
84	1	84
87	2	174
95	1	95
		785/10 = 78.5

If you divide 785 by the number of values in the distribution (10), you find that the mean test score for the class is 78.5.

Weighted Mean

The **weighted mean** is used when values of a distribution are not weighted equally, as in the case of our earlier evaluation of the qualitative characteristics of Computer A and Computer B. You can compute weighted means by using the following formula:

$$\text{Weighted Mean} = \frac{\Sigma wx}{w}$$

Multiply the sum of the scores by their weighted values. Then divide the sum by the weighted values.

Mode

The **mode** is the number that most frequently occurs in a distribution. For example, the mode value from the following distribution of income ranges for entry-level and junior computer programmers in one organization is $25,000 to $30,000:

Income Categories	Frequency
Below $20,000	5
$20,000–25,000	10
$25,000–30,000	20
$30,000–35,000	15
$35,000–40,000	10
$40,000–45,000	10
$45,000–50,000	5
Above $50,000	5

In this case, the distribution is **unimodal** as it has one value that occurs most often. When taken alone, the mode gives little context to the significance of the data. To recognize any depth of central tendency among the data, you will also need to calculate the median and mean.

Median

The **median** is the midpoint in a distribution of numbers arranged in ascending or descending order. In effect, half the scores will fall above and the other half below the median value. If the distribution contains an uneven number of items but with the same number of occurrences for each item, you can simply count to the middle score to determine the median. For example, the median income of the salaries in the following list is $25,500, as the incomes of half the number of surveyed employees (4) are less than $25,500, while the incomes of the other half are above that amount:

Incomes	Frequency
$20,000	1
$22,500	1
$23,000	1
$25,000	1
$25,500	1
$28,000	1
$30,000	1
$33,000	1
$35,000	1

If the distribution has an even number of items with the same number of occurrences, average the two central scores. For example, to determine the median income of the following 10 values, calculate the average of the fifth and sixth values: $25,500 + $28,000 = $53,500/2 = $26,750.

Incomes	Frequency
$20,000	1
$22,500	1
$23,000	1
$25,000	1
$25,500	1
$28,000	1
$30,000	1
$33,000	1
$35,000	1
$37,000	1

If the number of occurrences of an item are not equal, however, you will need to count the number of responses (n), add 1, and divide by 2, as illustrated in the following formula:

$$\text{Median} = \frac{n + 1}{2}$$

Using this formula, you could calculate the median of a distribution of responses of varying frequencies such as those illustrated below by calculating the total number of responses (79), adding 1, and then dividing that number by 2, leaving you with 40. Beginning at either end of the distribution, count the number of responses until you reach 40 and determine the central income category. The median for this specific distribution, then, is the $30,000 to $35,000 income range:

Income Categories	Responses
Below $20,000	5
$20,000–25,000	10
$25,000–30,000	20
$30,000–35,000	15
$35,000–40,000	10
$40,000–45,000	10
$45,000–50,000	5
Above $50,000	4

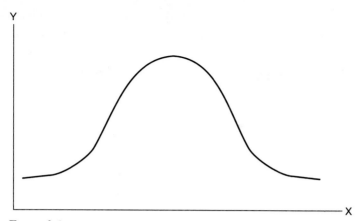

FIGURE A.1
Unimodal distribution.

Midrange

The **midrange** is the value occurring midway between the lowest and the highest numbers in a distribution. To calculate the midrange, add the low score and the high score. Then divide that number by 2. For example, if the lowest income in your organization were $15,000 and the highest were $75,000, the midrange for that distribution would be $45,000 ($15,000 + $75,000 = $90,000/2 = $45,000).

Unimodal and Bimodal Distributions

Distributions are **unimodal** when they contain only one frequently occurring score or value (Figure A.1). The scores 1, 2, 3, 4, 4, 5, 6, and 7 represent a unimodal distribution. A **bimodal** distribution, on the other hand, contains two groups of frequently occurring values (Figure A.2). For example, the scores *1, 1*, 2, 3, 4, 5, 6, *7*, and 7 represent a bimodal distribution.

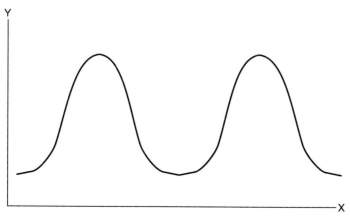

FIGURE A.2
Bimodal distribution.

An examination of bimodal distributions reveals how the pattern of data is weighted and, as a result, often provides more useful descriptions of the data than the mean or median. For instance, the mean of the following test scores is 78.23:

$$2 \times 63 = 126$$
$$1 \times 64 = 64$$
$$4 \times 66 = 264$$
$$5 \times 69 = 345$$
$$4 \times 72 = 288$$
$$2 \times 78 = 156$$
$$1 \times 85 = 85$$
$$4 \times 91 = 364$$
$$6 \times 93 = 558$$
$$1 \times 97 = \underline{97}$$

Mean: 78.23
Median: 72.0

In this case, however, the mean offers little insight into the significance and meaning of these scores that are distributed in a markedly bimodal fashion.

Multimodal Distributions

A **multimodal** distribution contains three or more clusters of frequently occurring scores (Figure A.3). For example, the scores *1, 1, 2, 3, 4, 4, 5, 6, 7,* and *7* would represent a multimodal distribution because three values—1, 4, and 7—occur most frequently and the same number of times (twice). A distribution of scores that occur the same number of times is called a **flat** distribution—for example, 1, 1, 2, 2, 3, 3, 4, 4, 5, and 5. Thus flat distributions, such as the one shown in Figure A.4, have no mode.

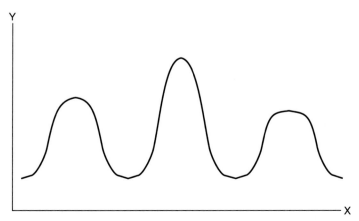

Figure A.3
Multimodal distribution.
Source: Adapted from Dietrich and Shafer, 1984, p. 254.

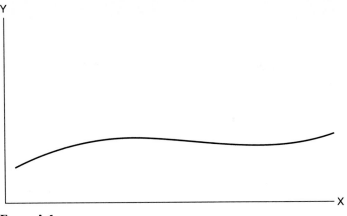

FIGURE A.4
Flat distribution.

Skewed Distributions

Scores that are exaggerated to one end of the distribution range constitute a **skewed** distribution (Figure A.5). For example, the scores 1, 2, 3, 4, 5, 5, 5, and 5 represent a skewed distribution at the high end of the scale.

Skewed distributions pose a problem to analyzing data through measures of central tendency, as mode, mean, and median typically offer no meaningful insight into the significance, or unimportance, of the data. The list of the following test scores is heavily skewed to the low end of the distribution, making

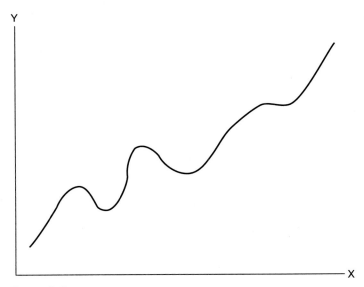

FIGURE A.5
Skewed distribution.

Source: Adapted from Dietrich and Shafer, 1984, p. 93.

its mean of 72.57 and median of 66.0 virtually useless as statistical analysis tools:

$$
\begin{array}{rcl}
6 \times 63 & = & 378 \\
7 \times 64 & = & 448 \\
5 \times 66 & = & 330 \\
4 \times 69 & = & 276 \\
3 \times 72 & = & 216 \\
1 \times 78 & = & 78 \\
2 \times 85 & = & 170 \\
1 \times 91 & = & 91 \\
1 \times 93 & = & 93 \\
1 \times 97 & = & \underline{97}
\end{array}
$$

Mean: 72.57
Median: 66.0

Measures of Dispersion

Indexes of dispersion measure how widely data are scattered, or dispersed, along the range of values. Often measures of central tendency do not provide sufficiently accurate or detailed information with which to determine the meaning and significance of the data. You might, for example, need to examine the relationships within and among sets of data having different bimodal and multimodal distributions. In such cases, you might supplement the measures of central tendency with measures of **dispersion**. Commonly used measures of dispersion include the range, variance, and standard deviation (Dietrich & Shafer, 1984).

Range

The **range** represents the difference between the highest (H) and the lowest (L) values in a distribution:

$$\text{Range} = H - L$$

The range of the sample test scores used in our earlier discussion of bimodal distributions, for example, is $97 - 63$, or 34.

Because the range disregards all values between the highest and lowest scores of a sample, it often is not a useful index for describing the pattern of distribution, or dispersion, of scores. The range of 34 for our sample distribution suggests a wide amplitude of test scores, but it does not reflect the heavy clustering of scores at the low end of the range. Your report data might also include scores distributed across such extreme ranges. To provide readers with a less distorted view of such polarized data, you might identify in your report the range in which most of the values fall. In any case, the range score, then, is most useful when considered with other measures such as mean, median, variance, and standard deviation.

Variance

The **variance** of values in a distribution is the average distance between each value and the mean. The variance, in effect, measures the deviation of scores from the mean by adding the squared deviations of all scores distributed around the mean. You can calculate the variance of a sample (*s*) with the equation below:

$$s^2 = \frac{\Sigma d^2}{n - 1}$$

The deviation of each score from the sample mean $(x - \bar{x})$ is represented by *d*, and *n* is the total number of scores in the sample. First, calculate the sample mean $\bar{x}$; then calculate the deviation of each score from the mean $(d = x - \bar{x})$. Square each value of *d* and sum all values of d^2. Finally, divide that sum by $n - 1$.

To calculate the variance of a whole population (σ), use the following equation:

$$\sigma^2 = \frac{\Sigma D^2}{N}$$

To find *D*, calculate the deviation of each score (*x*) from the population mean $(\bar{x})$, or $D = x - \bar{x}$. The total number of scores in the distribution is represented by *N*. Note that the symbol for the variance of a population is σ^2, as opposed to s^2 for that of a sample. The equations for computing the variance for a sample and population are identical, except for the denominators. The denominators are different to avoid distorting the computing of s^2. Theoretically, computing for s^2 with *N* can produce results that are too high or too low when compared with the variance of the population (σ^2).

The following is the calculation of variance for test scores from a sample distribution with a mean score (*x*) of 83.0:

$(x - \bar{x})$		Absolute Value *d*		d^2
73 − 83	=	−10	=	100
75 − 83	=	−8	=	64
75 − 83	=	−8	=	64
81 − 83	=	−2	=	4
82 − 83	=	−1	=	1
86 − 83	=	3	=	9
87 − 83	=	4	=	16
88 − 83	=	5	=	25
90 − 83	=	7	=	49
93 − 83	=	10	=	100
				432

$$s^2 = \frac{432}{10} = 43.2 \text{ square points}$$

A major shortcoming of variance in analyzing both a sample and a whole population is that variance measures the average distance between the mean and distribution values in units different from those of the sample or population. The variance of the test scores above, for example, is given in units of square points, rather than in points. Such a measurement is often of little relevance to research done in the context of managerial report problems.

Standard Deviation

The **standard deviation** is perhaps the most frequently used and most relevant index of dispersion for managerial report writing and research. The standard deviation is basically the square root of a distribution's variance. Because it is expressed in the same unit as the distribution data, the standard deviation is normally easier for researchers to work with and from which to draw meaningful inferences. Understandably, researchers tend to favor the use of standard deviation over that of variance. When analyzing samples, the standard deviation is represented by s and the lowercase Greek sigma (σ) when examining populations.

To calculate the standard deviation of a sample, use the following formula:

$$\text{Standard Deviation} = s = \sqrt{\frac{\Sigma(x - \bar{x})^2}{n - 1}} \text{ or } s = \sqrt{\frac{\Sigma d^2}{n - 1}}$$

In this formula, x represents the values in the distribution and $\bar{x}$ represents the mean. The procedure for calculating the standard deviation of a sample set of 10 test scores with a mean of 82.5 is provided here:

Frequency	$(x - \bar{x})$	Absolute Value*		$(x - \bar{x})^2$	
1	$(73 - 82.5)$	=	-9.5	= 90.25 × 1 =	90.25
2	$(75 - 82.5)$	=	-7.5	= 56.25 × 2 =	112.50
1	$(81 - 82.5)$	=	-1.5	= 2.25 × 1 =	2.25
2	$(82 - 82.5)$	=	-0.5	= 0.25 × 2 =	0.50
1	$(86 - 82.5)$	=	3.5	= 12.25 × 1 =	12.25
1	$(88 - 82.5)$	=	5.5	= 30.25 × 1 =	30.25
1	$(90 - 82.5)$	=	7.5	= 56.25 × 1 =	56.25
1	$(93 - 82.5)$	=	10.5	= 110.25 × 1 =	110.25
				$\Sigma(x - \bar{x})^2 =$	414.5

*Negative signs are disregarded when calculating the absolute value.

$$s = \sqrt{\frac{414.50}{9}} = \sqrt{46.06} = 6.79$$

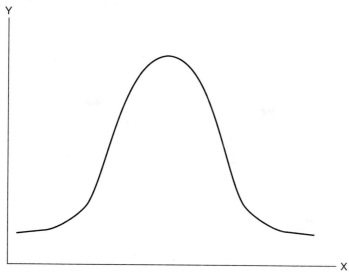

Figure A.6

Normal, or bell, curve.

Source: Adapted from Freund and Williams, 1972, p. 256.

You can calculate the standard deviation of a whole population by using a slightly modified formula:

$$\sigma = \sqrt{\frac{\Sigma D^2}{N}}$$

Charting the dispersion of distribution data on a line chart can produce a meaningful graphic illustration of how much the data deviate from the sample mean. A **normal distribution** of data would produce a gently sloping curve on a line chart, creating what is often referred to as a **bell curve**, as shown in Figure A.6. Within a normal distribution, approximately 68% of all scores will fall within ± 1 standard deviation of the mean, about 95.5% within ± 2 standard deviations of the mean, and 99.7% within ± 3 standard deviations of the mean (Figure A.7). According to a normal distribution, then, the standard deviation of the test scores would mean that

> 68% of test scores fall within 6.79 points, or within ± 1 standard deviation, of the mean,
>
> 95.5% of test scores fall within 13.58 points, or within ± 2 standard deviations, of the mean,
>
> 99.7% of test scores fall within 20.37 points, or within ± 3 standard deviations, of the mean.

The normal distribution of data can provide you with predictive capabilities to infer certain characteristics regarding the sample or population under study. For example, assume that your company has just introduced a new interior

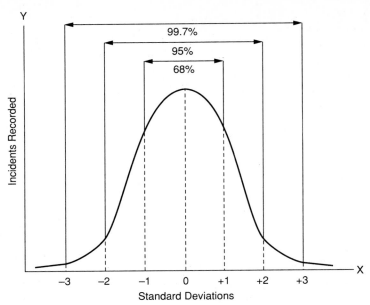

Figure A.7
Distribution of data under a normal curve.

design package for higher-income households. Your task is to price that package according to what you think the market will bear. Consequently, you decide to determine the mean household income of a more affluent neighborhood in your community and calculate the standard deviation of incomes. You find that the mean household income is $60,000 with a standard deviation of ± $3,000. Using the normal distribution curve, you could assume that

68% of the households have incomes that fall within ±1 standard deviation of the mean, or between $57,000 and $63,000.

95.5% of the households have incomes that fall within ±2 standard deviations of the mean, or between $54,000 and $66,000.

99.7% of the households have incomes that fall within ±3 standard deviations of the mean, or between $51,000 and $69,000.

From this distribution you could determine a pricing range for the interior design package that would be appropriate for the incomes of the target market. You might also infer that this new pricing range would dictate changes in the structure of relevant areas within the firm, including production methods, recruitment of skilled labor, and marketing techniques.

Besides providing you with the foundation on which to forecast business opportunities, the normal distribution curve enables you to isolate and solve existing problems within your organization. For example, your interior design department manufactures its own wallpaper, and recent inspections imply that production is turning out an increasing amount of wallpaper that falls below established quality levels. You would have a clearer sense of the extent of the potential problem by analyzing the standard deviation of wallpaper quality. A high standard deviation would suggest that rejected wallpaper rolls are missing the quality mark by a wide distance and that your organization probably will need to institute significant changes in the way it manufactures its product and maintains quality control.

Measures of Correlation

Measures of central tendency and dispersion are useful methods for describing the degree of association between two or more variables from a sample or population (Clover & Balsley, 1984; Groebner & Shannon, 1981). Your report problem might, however, require that you investigate the degree of association between numerous sets of data. You might, for example, need to explore the implied relationship between the introduction of computers into the workplace and the subsequent increase in productivity of workers. Your report problem might also focus on possible relationships between a number of road construction projects recently begun in your area of the city and the noticeable drop in your firm's sales. Perhaps your organization has noticed that employees with degrees from Ivy League universities consistently receive significantly higher merit raises each year compared with those of employees without Ivy League degrees.

You can study the possible relationships between those different variables within a sample or population by using measures of **correlation**. Correlations between variables are useful for

- defining the existence and nature of relationships between variables.
- measuring the strength of those relationships.
- suggesting *possible* causation between variables on which to project future business decisions.

A positive correlation between variables can also help you to screen out variables that are not related or appear unproductive to your study. By discriminating against less important variables, you can invest more of your energies in the testing of variables that seem most fruitful and meaningful in providing a solution to the report problem.

Correlation, however, should not be used as proof that (a) the variables are related or (b) the relationship is causal. A correlation between road construction and dropping sales may just be coincidental. The two variables may not be related at all, except temporally (as they both occurred at approximately the same time). A correlation between Ivy Leaguers and high merit raises should not be considered hard proof that employees' alma maters are the cause of their marked rise in the organization. Other variables are probably affecting the relationship. For example, the employees may be ambitious, hard-working people who chose what they perceived to be the esteem and academic challenge of Ivy League schools. The employees' drive for success, then, would be a central cause for their extraordinary performance with your firm, which ultimately won them high merit raises.

If applied and interpreted properly, measures of correlation can be a valuable decision-making tool in the report-writing process. On the other hand, if interpreted incorrectly as a guarantee of relationship or causation, correlation can lead to counterproductive and costly business decisions. The following discussion examines the most commonly used measures of correlation: linear correlation, simple regression analysis, and multiple regression analysis.

Linear Correlation

Data that are divided into two variables are called **bivariate** data (e.g., high merit raises and Ivy League degrees). **Linear correlation** measures the strength and direction of any possible relationship between the bivariate data. A clearly directed and strong correlation between two variables can enable you to predict appropriate solutions to your report problem.

In a positive linear correlation, the value of one variable (X) would increase or decrease at the same rate as the second variable (Y). In a negative linear correlation, the value of X might increase as Y decreases, or vice versa. Correlation values can range from +1 to −1, with a +1 representing a perfect linear correlation. For example, if the use of computers in the workplace (X) increased at the same rate as the productivity of employees supplied with those computers (Y), you would have a perfect linear correlation of +1 (Figure A.8). A correlation value of −1 indicates an inverse correlation. A value of 0 indicates that the variables share no relationship. To illustrate the strength and direction of possible

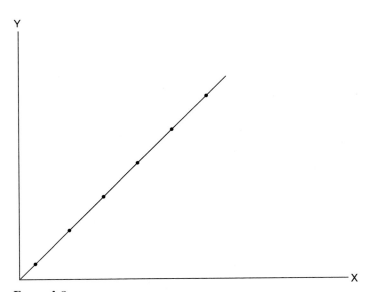

Figure A.8
Perfect linear correlation.

Source: Adapted from Groebner and Shannon, 1981, p. 425.

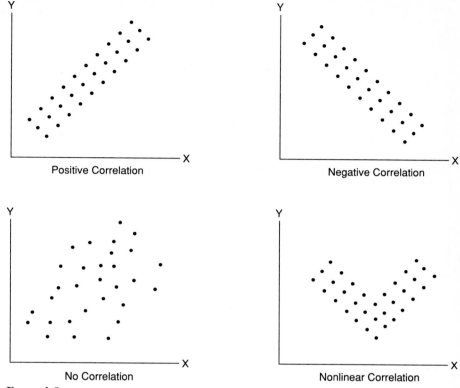

FIGURE A.9

Possible linear correlations and noncorrelations.

Source: Adapted from Groebner and Shannon, 1981, p. 425.

correlations, values of both *X* and *Y* are usually plotted on a scattergram, as shown in Figure A.9.

Simple Regression Analysis

Whereas linear correlation measures the strength and direction of bivariate data, **simple regression** analysis measures the *nature* of a possible relationship between two variables. Simple regression analysis allows us to predict the significance and behavior of one variable once we have measured the value of a second variable that shares a correlation with the first (Mansfield, 1983). The formula for a simple regression is

$$Y = a + bX$$

where

X is a selected *X* value to predict a corresponding value for the *Y* variable.

a is the *Y* intercept (estimated value of *Y* when *X* = 0), which is the estimated value of *Y* where the regression line crosses the *Y*-axis and when *X* = 0.

b is the estimated slope of the line.

The formulas for calculating a and b are

$$a = \frac{(\Sigma Y)(\Sigma X^2) - (\Sigma X)(\Sigma XY)}{n(\Sigma X^2) - (\Sigma X)^2}$$

$$b = \frac{n(\Sigma XY) - (\Sigma X)(\Sigma Y)}{n(\Sigma X^2) - (\Sigma X)^2}$$

where

X is the independent variable.

Y is the dependent variable.

n is the number of items in the sample.

$\bar{X}$ is the mean of the independent variable.

$\bar{Y}$ is the mean of the dependent variable.

To illustrate a simple regression analysis, let us assume that you have recognized a correlation between the level of university education held by each member of your firm's sales staff and the amount of weekly sales each achieves. You decide to measure the strength of this correlation so that you might (a) project what types of employment candidates would best suit the company, (b) examine what types of incentives the company might offer employees to further their college education, and (c) predict future sales. You designate sales as the dependent variable and years of university education as the independent variable (Table A.2). To make the correlation more visually evident, you plot the values of both variables on a scattergram (Figure A.10).

Table A.3 provides a tabulated illustration of regression values for $\bar{X}$ and $\bar{Y}$. In calculating the simple regression, you first determine the mean for each variable:

$$\bar{Y} = 4.2$$

$$\bar{X} = 6{,}600$$

TABLE A.2.

Data on Years of Education and Weekly Sales

Salesperson	Years at University	Weekly Sales
Ms. M. Adams	5	$8,000
Ms. L. O. Bunch	2	4,000
Mr. J. P. Cole	4	6,000
Dr. C. Golding	10	12,000
Mr. S. Proctor	0	3,000

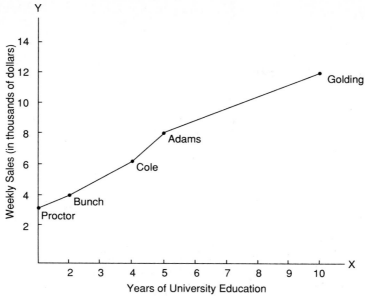

FIGURE A.10

Plot of education levels and weekly sales.

You calculate b and a as

$$b = \frac{5(192,000) - (21)(33,000)}{5(145) - (21)^2} = \frac{960,000 - 693,000}{725 - 441} = \frac{267,000}{284} = 940.14$$

$$a = \frac{(33,000)(145) - (21)(192,000)}{5(145) - (21)^2} = \frac{4,785,000 - 4,032,000}{441} = \frac{753,000}{441} = 1,707.48$$

Finally, you compute the simple regression:

$$Y = a + bX = 1,707.48 + 940.14(6) = \$7,348.32$$

TABLE A.3.

Regression of X and Y Values

X	X^2	Y	Y^2	XY
0	0	3,000	9,000,000	0
2	4	4,000	16,000,000	8,000
4	16	6,000	36,000,000	24,000
5	25	8,000	64,000,000	40,000
10	100	12,000	144,000,000	120,000
$\sum X = 21$	$\sum X^2 = 145$	$\sum Y = 33,000$	$\sum Y^2 = 269,000,000$	$\sum XY = 192,000$

From the calculation of the simple regression, you might predict that a salesperson with 6 years of college could expect to achieve approximately $7,348.32 in sales each week. When interpreting the results of a simple regression, as with any measurement of correlation, remember that these statistics can only suggest relationships between variables. Any implied causation is simply that: *implied*. Keep in mind that the variables could be influenced by outside forces and that associations between variables may only be coincidental. You can improve the validity and accuracy of forecasts based on a simple regression by considering all significant independent variables that might influence the values of the dependent variables.

Multiple Regression Analysis

Most relationships between variables of a report problem, like the correlation between Ivy League education and high merit raises, involve more than one dependent and one independent variable. **Multiple regression** analysis allows us to measure the nature and strength of the associations between a dependent variable and multiple independent variables.

Performing multiple regression analysis is highly complex and outside the scope of this text. While we do provide here the general forms of the multiple regression equation, you should consult the selected readings offered at the end of this chapter for more complete instructions on performing the type of multiple regression that is most appropriate for your configuration of data.

The multiple regression formula for analyzing a correlation between one dependent variable and two independent variables is

$$Y = a + b_1X_1 + b_2X_2$$

where

X_1 and X_2 are the two independent variables.

a is the Y intercept.

b_1 is the net change in Y for each unit change in X_1.

b_2 is the net change in Y for each unit change in X_2.

The multiple regression equation for analyzing three independent variables is the following:

$$Y = a + b_1X_2 + b_2X_2 + b_3X_3$$

Computing the multiple regression for any number of independent variables is usually beyond the capacity of electronic calculators. To perform such calculations, you normally need to use the speed and number-crunching power of a computer and the know-how of statistical analysis software such as SPSS®, SPSS-X®, SAS®, STAT/BASIC®, or BMDP®. A note of warning should accompany the mention of these software packages. Although their use is essential for performing complex statistical analysis, these packages require that you have a sound understanding of computers and statistics. Improper use of the software will invariably produce inaccurate results that might lead to inappropriate managerial decisions.

Inferential Statistics

Descriptive statistics describe the relationships among data within a population. In many business situations, however, you will need to test the validity of your analysis by better understanding the differences among the data. **Inferential statistics** examine samples to determine if significant differences probably exist between a study's sample population and its parent population. In Chapter 8, we discuss how experimental research employs control and experimental groups to test the influence of an independent variable on a dependent variable. Inferential statistics test for differences between results gathered from such control and experimental groups. Based on those measurements, you can (a) estimate the probability that real differences exist between the sample and parent population and (b) infer that forecasts based on the sample are true at a particular **level of significance** (Harnett & Murphy, 1985).

Inferential statistics can never ensure that findings from your sample are 100% typical of those from the parent population, if such a survey of the whole population were possible. Rather, inferential statistics suggest that the findings have a high probability of being typical. If your test results have a low level of significance, you can safely infer that the means of the sample and parent population do not differ much, if at all. A low level of significance, then, lends a certain level of validity and credibility to your data and logical interpretations drawn from those data. On the other hand, a high level of significance implies that the sample may not be representative of the population, suggesting that the data may not be reliable or accurate. The conventional level of significance is 0.05. This means that there is a 5% chance that your sample is not typical of the parent population.

Like the multiple regression equations, the complex procedure for computing inferential statistics is outside the scope of this text. However, brief descriptions of the three most frequently used measures of inferential statistics—the *t* test, z test, and chi-square test—are provided below.

t Test

The *t* **test** measures the significance of difference between two population means calculated from two random samples. The mean of samples with more than 30 scores is typically close enough to the mean of the parent population for use in most statistical analyses. The *t* test is used when one of the samples contains fewer than 30 scores.

The numerator of the *t* test equation represents the mean difference between the two samples. The denominator of the equation represents the estimate of sampling error (standard error of difference between the two samples).

The formula for calculating the t score for a sample having two independent variables is

$$t = \frac{\bar{x}_1 - \bar{x}_2}{\sqrt{\frac{\Sigma d_1^2 + \Sigma d_2^2}{n_1 + n_2 - 2} + \frac{n_1 + n_2}{n_1 n_2}}}$$

where

$\bar{x}_1$ and $\bar{x}_2$ are the means of the two samples.

$\Sigma d_1^2 + \Sigma d_2^2$ are the sums of the squared deviations of the two samples from their respective means.

n_1 and n_2 are the numbers of scores in the two samples.

z Test

The **z test** is used to estimate the significance of difference between large random samples (30 scores or more). Like the t test, the z test equation takes the form of a ratio. The formula's numerator represents the mean differences, while its denominator represents the estimated chance differences between the two samples. The general z test formula is as follows:

$$z = \frac{\bar{x}_1 - \bar{x}_2}{s_{\bar{x}_1 - \bar{x}_2}}$$

The values $\bar{x}_1$ and $\bar{x}_2$ are the mean scores of the samples, respectively. The value $s_{\bar{x}_1 - \bar{x}_2}$ is an estimate of the sampling error called the **standard error of difference between means**. Compute the standard error using the following formula:

$$s_{\bar{x}_1 - \bar{x}_2} = \sqrt{\frac{s_1^2}{n_1} + \frac{s_2^2}{n_2}}$$

where

s_1^2 and s_2^2 are the squared standard deviations of samples 1 and 2, respectively.

n_1 and n_2 are the numbers of scores in each sample, respectively.

Chi-Square Test

Due to its versatility, the **chi-square test** is used more often than the z test. Chi-square (x^2) measures differences between two or more samples that are moderate to large in size. The chi-square test indicates significant differences between the observed distribution of data and the expected distribution as constructed from previous observations, or based on a standard mathematical distribution. It is essentially a "goodness-of-fit" test. Using the chi-square, you can determine if a variance is within acceptable limits. The general formula for computing the chi-square is

$$x^2 = \Sigma \left[\frac{(O - E)^2}{E} \right]$$

where

O is the observed frequency in a sample group.

E is the expected, or theoretical, frequency in the same sample group.

If you decide that your statistical analysis could profit from chi-square testing, you might consider using and, thus, research in greater detail two of the most common chi-square measures: the single-sample chi-square and the multiple-sample chi-square (also called the **contingency table** analysis) (Stevenson, 1985; Hoel & Jessen, 1982; Mansfield, 1983).

Summary

We have asserted in Appendix A that at least a general understanding of statistics will prove invaluable to you for several reasons. First, to know what types of statistical analysis should be used on your data, you must understand the different statistical techniques available to you and which of those techniques would be most appropriate to your study. Some statistical techniques are more useful than others, depending on your chosen research methods, the nature and size of your sample, and the complexity of the data and required analyses. Second, you should understand the uses of statistical techniques in order to recognize and interpret the meaning and significance of your analysis results.

Throughout this appendix, we have provided an overview of commonly used statistical tools and their applications. Descriptive and inferential statistics assist you in comparing similarities and dissimilarities among different sets of data. **Descriptive statistics** characterize different sets of data by first defining the center of those sets' distributions of numbers or values and then describing the relationships among those different sets. The most useful descriptive methods are measures of **central tendency**, measures of **dispersion**, and measures of **correlation**. **Inferential statistics**, on the other hand, examine samples to determine if significant differences exist between a study's sample population and its parent population. Three of the most frequently used measures of inferential statistics include the *t* **test**, **z test**, and **chi-square test**.

Related Reading

AGGARWAL, Y. P. *Statistical Methods: Concepts, Applications, and Computation.* New York: Advent, 1986.

BANCROFT, T. A. *Statistical Theory and Inference in Research.* New York: Dekker, 1981.

BECKER, WILLIAM E., and DONALD L. HARNETT. *Business and Economics Statistics with Computers.* Reading, MA: Addison, 1987.

CLOVER, VERNON T., and HOWARD L. BALSLEY. *Business Research Methods.* 3rd ed. New York: Wiley, 1984.

Computer Packages and Research Design with Annotations of Inputs and Outputs for the BMDP, SAS, SPSS, and SPSSx Statistical Packages. Ed. Robert S. Barcikowski. Lanham, MD: UP of America, 1983.

DEMING, WILLIAM EDWARDS. *Some Theory of Sampling.* New York: Dover, 1950.

DIETRICH, FRANK H. II, and NANCY J. SHAFER. *Business Statistics: An Inferential Approach.* San Francisco: Dellen, 1984.

DIXON, WILFRED J. *BMDP Statistical Software.* Berkeley, CA: U of California P, 1983.

EMORY, WILLIAM C. *Business Research Methods.* Homewood, IL: Dow Jones-Irwin, 1976.

FREUND, JOHN E., and FRANK T. WILLIAMS. *Elementary Business Statistics: The Modern Approach.* Englewood Cliffs, NJ: Prentice, 1972.

GROEBNER, DAVID F., and PATRICK W. SHANNON. *Business Statistics: A Decision-Making Approach.* Columbus, OH: Merrill, 1981.

HAMMOND, KENNETH R., JAMES E. HOUSEHOLDER, and JOHN CASTELLAN. *Introduction to the Statistical Method: Foundation and Use in the Behavioral Sciences.* New York: Knopf, 1970.

HARNETT, DONALD L., and JAMES L. MURPHY. *Statistical Analysis for Business and Economics.* 3rd ed. Reading, MA: Addison, 1985.

HEDDERSON, JOHN. *SPSSx Made Simple.* Belmont, CA: Wadsworth, 1987.

HOEL, PAUL GERHARD, and RAYMOND J. JESSEN. *Basic Statistics for Business.* 3rd ed. New York: Wiley, 1982.

HOWARD, JOHN A. *Computer Applications for Consumer Behavior in Marketing Strategy.* Englewood Cliffs, NJ: Prentice, 1988.

MANSFIELD, EDWIN. *Statistical Analysis for Business and Economics: Methods and Applications.* 2nd ed. New York: Norton, 1983.

NIE, NORMAN H., DALE H. BENT, and C. HADLAI HULL. *SPSS: Statistical Package for the Social Sciences.* New York: McGraw, 1970.

OSTLE, BERNARD, and LINDA C. MALONE. *Statistics in Research: Basic Concepts and Techniques for Research Workers.* 4th ed. Ames, IA: Iowa State UP, 1987.

SAS User's Guide. 5th ed. Cary, NC: SAS Institute, 1985.

SPSS User's Guide. New York: McGraw, 1986.

STEVENSON, WILLIAM J. *Business Statistics: Concepts and Applications.* 2nd ed. New York: Harper, 1985.

TAYLOR, STEVEN J., and ROBERT BOGDAN. *Introduction to Quantitative Research Methods: The Search for Meanings.* 2nd ed. New York: Wiley, 1984.

WONNACOTT, THOMAS H., and RONALD J. WONNACOTT. *Introductory Statistics for Business and Economics.* 3rd ed. New York: Wiley, 1984.

Appendix B

Sample Formal Report

A SURVEY OF PSYCHOACTIVE DRUG USE AMONG
PHYSICIANS AND MEDICAL STUDENTS IN MASSACHUSETTS

Submitted to

Dr. Mary C. Garcia
Director of Project Funding
National Research Foundation

Submitted by

Dr. Paul R. Feinberg
Chairperson of the Committee on Physician Impairment
University of Massachusetts Hospital

November 11, 1991

UNIVERSITY OF MASSACHUSETTS HOSPITAL
1618 Breckinridge Avenue
Boston, Massachusetts   38400
(617) 335-7531

November 11, 1991

Dr. Mary C. Garcia
Director of Project Funding
National Research Foundation
1020 Constitution Avenue
Washington, D.C. 20005

Dear Dr. Garcia:

During our discussion at the Atlanta American Medical
Association Conference in September 1990, you asked
to receive the results of a drug abuse survey that I was
conducting at the time. Enclosed is the report based on that
study—"A Survey of Psychoactive Drug Use Among Physicians
and Medical Students in Massachusetts."

The report presents data and information on psychoactive drug
use in a cross-section of practicing physicians and medical
students in Massachusetts. Its purpose is to provide directors
of impaired-physician programs, medical professionals, and
the general public with a clear picture of the extent to which
drugs are used by practicing physicians and future physicians.
The report examines the frequency, recency, and purpose
of drug use among the physicians and students, as well
as drug-related impairments suffered by those health care
professionals.

Results from the study suggest that the percentage of
practicing physicians using psychoactive drugs for recreation
is rising sharply. The incidence of addiction and impairment,
however, is highest among medical students. Principal drug
problems include students' recreational use of marijuana
and cocaine and physicians' self-treatment with opiates and
tranquilizers.

Clearly, the number of physicians who practice in a
drug-impaired state will steadily increase unless behavioral

Dr. Garcia   iii

patterns can be changed. Medical students and practitioners
need to become better educated about drug use, the harm it
can cause their ability to practice effectively, and the risks of
slipping beyond occasional use into addiction.

After examining this report, I'm sure that you will agree with
me that drug abuse among the state's physicians and medical
students is a serious problem. I am already designing studies
that will identify effective prevention strategies. Perhaps the
National Science Foundation, through its funding, would be
interested in collaborating with the project. I will contact you
within the next few weeks to discuss this matter further.

Sincerely,

Paul R. Feinberg

Paul R. Feinberg, M.D.

(Authors' note: This page was intentionally left blank.)

v

TABLE OF CONTENTS

page

vi

LIST OF ILLUSTRATIONS

vii

EXECUTIVE SUMMARY

This report presents data and information on psychoactive drug use in a cross-section of medical students and practicing physicians in Massachusetts. Its purpose is to provide directors of impaired-physician programs, medical professionals, and the general public with a clear picture of the extent to which drugs are used by practicing physicians as well as future physicians.

The analysis contained in the report focuses on the frequency, recency, and purpose of drug use among a sample of physicians and medical students randomly chosen from professional societies and professional schools in Massachusetts. Moreover, the report examines drug dependence and drug-related impairments among those two sample populations.

Conclusions

This study suggests that the extent of drug use by physicians and medical students in Massachusetts for instrumental use and self-treatment has not increased significantly in the past several years. However, the percentage of practicing physicians using psychoactive drugs for recreation has risen sharply. Nevertheless, recreational drug use among physicians was still lower than that among medical students in the state.

Understandably, the greater percentage of drug-using medical students resulted in higher incidence of addiction and impairment. The principal problem was recreational use of marijuana and cocaine by medical students and self-treatment with opiates and tranquilizers by physicians.

Escalating drug use by medical professionals is a reflection of trends toward increased casual drug use in society at large. As younger doctors with higher rates of drug use replace older physicians, the number of physicians who practice in a drug-impaired state will steadily increase unless behavioral patterns can be changed.

Confidential

viii

Recommendations

Medical students and practitioners need to become better educated about drug use, the harm it can cause their ability to practice effectively, and the risks of slipping beyond occasional use to addiction. Preventive programs for medical students and residents are the most practical and effective measures for reducing or preventing future drug use by these two groups. Medical schools and hospitals should offer educational programs that examine the adverse effects of recreational drug use (giving special emphasis to marijuana and cocaine) and self-treatment (emphasizing the abuse of opiates and tranquilizers specifically).

Confidential

1.0 INTRODUCTION

The purpose, scope, sources, limitations of the study, as well as working definitions for key technical terminology are presented in the following sections.

1.1 Purpose

This report presents data and information on psychoactive drug use in a cross-section of medical students and practicing physicians in Massachusetts. Its purpose is to provide directors of impaired-physician programs, medical professionals, and the general public with a clear picture of the extent to which drugs are used by practicing physicians as well as future physicians. In the context of this report, the term *impaired physicians* refers to medical doctors unable to practice or perform daily activities because of their abuse of psychoactive drugs.

1.2 Scope

This study focuses on the frequency, recency, and purpose of drug use among a sample of physicians and medical students randomly chosen from professional societies and professional schools in Massachusetts. Moreover, the report examines drug dependence and drug-related impairments among those two sample populations.

1.3 Sources

The report draws much of its primary data from responses given by 337 physicians and 381 medical students to a multiple-choice questionnaire that maintained the anonymity of the respondents. (A copy of the survey is provided in the appendix of this report.) As a means of comparison, 312 pharmacists and 278 pharmacy students were also surveyed. According to several similar studies, self-reported information on the use of licit and illicit drugs is normally reliable data (O'Malley, 1983, p. 805).

Confidential

There is, however, an overall tendency for respondents to underreport the frequency of drug use (O'Malley, 1983, p. 821). The data provided here, therefore, are unlikely to overstate the problem of drug use among these groups.

Secondary sources used in this report include journals containing information on drug dependence among medical professionals, most notably the *Journal of the American Medical Association*. "Psychoactive Drug Use Among Practicing Physicians and Medical Students" by W. E. McAuliffe et al. was particularly helpful.

1.4 Limitations

Though medical professionals abuse a range of drugs, such as alcohol and Valium, this report is limited to their abuse of marijuana, amphetamines, Ritalin® (methylphenidate), Preludin® (phenmetrazine), cocaine, barbiturates, Doriden® (glutethimide), Quaalude® (methaqualone), Darvon® (propoxyphene), Talwin® (pentazocine), tranquilizers, codeine, Percodan® or Percocet® (oxycodone), Demerol® (meperidine), morphine, fentanyl, heroin, and hallucinogens. In reporting the data, we grouped the drugs into the following categories:

- Marijuana
- Cocaine
- Hallucinogens
- Stimulants
- Sedatives
- Tranquilizers
- Opiates

1.5 Working Definitions

Hallucinogens: Drugs that distort perception, cause mood swings, disturb thought processes, and often are accompanied by optical or auditory hallucinations.

Confidential

An example of a hallucinogen is LSD, lysergic acid diethylamide (Katsung, 1982, p. 358; *Stedman's*, 1982, p. 618).

Instrumental drug use: The taking of drugs to perform better or longer in any activity, such as sports, work, or study (McAuliffe, 1984, p. 39).

Opiates: Chemical agents that are preparations or derivatives of opium. Such compounds, also known as *narcotic analgesics*, relieve pain without causing unconsciousness (Katsung, 1982, p. 339).

Psychoactive drugs: Drugs that alter mood, behavior, or thinking processes (*Stedman's*, 1982, p. 1164).

Recreational drug use: The taking of drugs for sensation-seeking (i.e., euphoria), for social acceptance (i.e., "going along with the crowd"), or for curiosity (McAuliffe, 1984, p. 39).

Sedatives: Medications that reduce anxiety, producing a calming effect with little or no impairment of mental or motor function (Katsung, 1982, p. 247).

Self-treatment: The taking of drugs under one's own supervision for a medical need, such as to relieve pain or anxiety or to facilitate weight loss (McAuliffe, 1984, p. 39).

Stimulants: Drugs that excite, imparting a sense of increased vitality and energy (Katsung, 1982, p. 247).

Tranquilizers: Medications that induce drowsiness and sleep (Katsung, 1982, p. 247).

2.0 RESULTS

The following discussion examines findings on the frequency and recency of drug use among surveyed medical professionals, their purpose in using the drugs, the degree of their drug dependence, and subsequent drug-related impairments.

Confidential

2.1 Frequency and Recency of Drug Use

The following discussion addresses, in separate subsections, the frequency and recency of drug use among physicians and medical students.

2.1.1 Physicians

Of the physicians surveyed, 59.2% have used psychoactive drugs for one reason or another (e.g., recreation, self-treatment, or instrumental use), as shown in Table 1. The total number of lifetime episodes of drug use ranges from zero

TABLE 1. Psychoactive Drug Use Among Physicians, Pharmacists, Medical Students, and Pharmacy Students (Reproduced from McAuliffe, 1986, p. 806)

Type of Use	Physicians (337)	Pharmacists (312)	Medical Students (381)	Pharmacy Students (278)
Recreational, self-treatment, or instrumental				
Use at any time				
Percent	59.2	46.4[a]	77.2[a]	62.4[b]
No. of episodes	43.7	43.7	65.7[a]	64.6
Current use				
Past 12 mo. (percent)	33.3	19.3[a]	43.6[a]	41.1
Regular (once per month or more often) (percent)	9.5	7.1	16.1[a]	22.7[b]
By another's prescription, at any time				
Daily for month or longer (percent)	5.7	5.5	2.5[a]	3.0
Drug dependence at any time (percent)	3.3	2.3	5.2	3.9

[a] As compared to physicians.
[b] As compared to medical students.

Confidential

to 1,845. The mean, however, is 43.7 episodes. One-third of the physicians surveyed have used mood-altering drugs within the past year, and about one in every four recent users has been doing so regularly (at least once a week). In addition, 5.7% of the physicians sampled have taken psychoactive drugs every day for a month or longer while under the care of another physician, opiates and tranquilizers being the most frequently prescribed. Moreover, 3.3% have claimed to be dependent on drugs (McAuliffe, 1986, p. 808).

Compared with findings from a similar study on Massachusetts pharmacists, a considerably larger number of physicians have taken psychoactive drugs and more are currently using them. This result is primarily due to physicians' higher rates of self-treatment at any time (42%) and current self-treatment (25%). The percentages of pharmacists in these categories were 29 and 12%, respectively. Consequently, physicians have a higher rate of drug dependence than do pharmacists, though the difference (3.3 vs. 2.3%) was not significant (McAuliffe, 1986, p. 806).

2.1.2 Medical Students

The percentage of medical students who have used drugs (77.2%) was greater than that of physicians (59.2%). Medical students, then, have a higher number of lifetime episodes, a greater rate of current use, and a higher percentage of drug addiction than do physicians. The same general pattern seen between physicians and pharmacists is applicable to medical and pharmacy students. A greater percentage of medical students than pharmacy students have taken drugs. However, a larger percentage of pharmacy students who are currently using drugs are doing so on a regular basis.

2.2 Purpose of Drug Use

The most common types of drug use are recreational, self-treatment, and instrumental.

2.2.1 Physicians

As shown in Table 2, physicians took psychoactive drugs, for the most part, as a means for treating a medical problem. Recreational and instrumental use were the second and third most commonly mentioned reasons for drug use. The drugs most often taken were opiates and tranquilizers. Marijuana and cocaine were the major recreational drugs for the physicians sampled. However, the percentage use of those drugs was relatively small. As for frequency of use, fewer than 2% of

TABLE 2. Current and Lifetime Use of Drugs Among Physicians and Medical Students (Reproduced from McAuliffe, 1986, p. 807)

Purpose of use	Physicians (337) percent of sample						Medical Students (381) percent of sample					
	Current Use[a]		Lifetime Episodes			Ever[b]	Current Use[a]		Lifetime Episodes			Ever[b]
	Occ.	Reg.	1–10	11–60	≥ 61		Occ.	Reg.	1–10	11–60	≥ 61	
Recreational												
Marijuana	6	2	16	7	9	34	22	12	24	19	25	72
Cocaine	3	0	6	2	1	9	16	4	22	13	2	39
Hallucinogens	0	0	4	0	0	5	2	0	14	3	1	19
Stimulants	0	0	5	1	1	7	2	0	10	5	1	17
Sedatives	0	0	2	0	1	3	0	0	8	1	1	11
Tranquilizers	0	0	1	1	1	3	1	0	6	0	0	7
Opiates	0	0	3	0	2	5	2	0	8	1	1	11
Any recreational use	8	2	16	7	10	35	25	14	24	19	29	73
Self-treatment												
Stimulants	1	0	4	2	1	7	0	0	3	0	1	4
Sedatives	2	1	4	1	2	8	1	1	2	1	1	3
Tranquilizers	9	5	11	6	4	23	5	2	9	4	1	14
Opiates	11	2	21	7	2	34	8	1	21	4	1	27
Any self-treatment	18	7	19	13	7	42	11	4	19	8	5	33
Instrumental	?	?	12	2	2	16	?	?	14	2	1	17

[a] *Occasional* refers to less than once per month, and *regular* use once per month or more often.

[b] Some values differ slightly from the sums of lifetime episodes because the number of episodes was unspecified in some cases.

?—Data not obtained.

the physicians used any one of the drug categories with the exception of marijuana and tranquilizers (McAuliffe, 1986, p. 807).

2.2.2 Medical Students

Recreational use among medical students was much greater than among physicians for all drug categories (Table 2). Moreover, students used psychoactive drugs twice as much for recreation as for self-treatment. A significant portion of current drug use by this group involved marijuana and cocaine (12 and 4%, respectively, of the students sampled). In terms of self-treatment, tranquilizers and opiates had the highest rates of current use and number of lifetime episodes, but these values were lower than those obtained for physicians (McAuliffe, 1986, p. 806).

2.3 Drug Dependence

2.3.1 Physicians

Eleven of the 337 physicians (3.3%) reported that they have been or are presently dependent on one or more drugs. Of the 11, six physicians used the drug for recreational purposes, which led to their dependence. Three other physicians became addicted while treating an ailment—two under their own supervision and the other physician while under the guidance of another doctor. The remaining two physicians did not specify the cause of their addiction. At the time of the survey, seven of the physicians were still using drugs. Four physicians were no longer taking their drug of addiction, in an attempt either to recover or to remain free of the dependence (McAuliffe, 1986, p. 806). Table 3 is a breakdown of the drugs and the frequency with which drug-dependent physicians used them.

2.3.2 Medical Students

Twenty of the 381 medical students (5.2%) reported being dependent on a drug at one time or another. Fourteen of the

TABLE 3. Drug Dependence Among Physicians Sampled

Drug of Dependence	No. of Drug-Dependent Physicians in the Sample
Amphetamines	4[a]
Marijuana	2
Opiates	1
Sedatives	2
Tranquilizers	2

[a] One physician reported multiple addiction.

20 became "hooked" on the drug by using it for recreational purposes—four as a means of self-treatment, two for multiple reasons. Fifteen of these future physicians reported taking the drug during the time of the survey. Five were abstaining (McAuliffe, 1986, p. 808). As illustrated in Table 4, the drug most often abused by drug-dependent medical students in this sample population was marijuana, followed by tranquilizers, cocaine, opiates, and amphetamines.

2.4 Drug-Related Impairments

Physicians reported fewer drug-induced impairments than did students (Table 5). However, a significant number (7.1%)

TABLE 4. Drug Dependence Among Medical Students Sampled

Drug of Dependence	No. of Drug-Dependent Medical Students in the Sample
Marijuana	12
Tranquilizers	3
Cocaine	2
Opiates	2
Amphetamines	1

Confidential

TABLE 5. Drug-Related Impairments Among Physicians and Medical Students

Type of Drug-Related Impairments	Physicians (337)	Medical Students (381)
	percent of sample	
Missing work/school	2.1	15.7
Falling seriously behind at work/school	1.3	10.5
Trouble getting along with others	2.7	6.4
Worrying about using drugs too much	7.1	17.1
Having an accident	0.9	2.6
Seriously considering suicide	0.9	0.8
Caring poorly for patients/ doing poorly in school	1.8	2.4
Seeking professional help	1.5	1.3

reported worrying excessively about their drug use, while 2.1% missed work due to their dependence.

The primary impairment for students, like physicians, was their anxiety over their drug use. A large percentage of students (15.7%) also reported that missing school was an important impairment to their work, while 10.5% noted that their drug dependence had resulted in their falling seriously behind in school work.

3.0 DISCUSSION

This section evaluates the significant findings in frequency and recency of drug use, purpose of drug use, drug dependence, and drug-related impairments.

3.1 Frequency and Recency of Drug Use

The greatest dissimilarity in drug use was not between groups in different fields (physicians and medical students vs. pharmacists and pharmacy students), but rather between the professionals and the students in each field. This result is not surprising. The relatively high rates of recreational use by students reflect increasing acceptance of casual drug use in society at large.

3.2 Purpose of Drug Use

The correlation of current and lifetime use among physicians and medical students was only moderate (McAuliffe, 1986, p. 807). The major drug problems were recreational use of marijuana and cocaine by medical students and self-prescription of opiates and tranquilizers by physicians.

3.3 Drug Dependence

The drug dependence among medical students was higher (5.2%) than that among physicians (3.3%). This is due, in part, to differing attitudes held by these groups toward drugs. The higher incidence of dependence among medical students is indicative of their higher recreational use. Notably, drug use by younger physicians (26–30 years old) was more comparable to that of medical students than to drug use by older physicians (McAuliffe, 1984, p. 38).

Accessibility seems to have played a role in the drug dependence of, as well as in the extent of drug use by, both physicians and medical students (Table 2). Amphetamines caused most of the dependence in the physicians sampled. In contrast, addicted medical students were, by far, more dependent on marijuana than were physicians.

Confidential

3.4 Drug-Related Impairments

Because medical students used drugs with greater regularity than did physicians, it is not unexpected that the percentage of medical students impaired by drug use was higher than that of physicians. What is surprising, however, is that both physicians and students agreed that anxiety surrounding their drug use and their missing work/school were the most problematic drug-related impairments that they suffered.

4.0 CONCLUSIONS

This study, as well as previous studies, suggests that the extent of drug use by physicians and medical students in Massachusetts for instrumental use and self-treatment has not increased significantly in the past several years. However, the percentage of practicing physicians using psychoactive drugs for recreation has increased markedly. Nevertheless, recreational drug use among physicians was still lower than that among medical students within the state.

Understandably, the greater percentage of drug-using medical students resulted in higher incidence of addiction and impairment. The principal problem was recreational use of marijuana and cocaine by medical students and self-treatment with opiates and tranquilizers by physicians. Recent surveys of Massachusetts pharmacists and pharmacy students show that these populations had the lowest rates of drug use, presumably due to more extensive education and greater knowledge of drugs and their effects.

Escalating drug use by medical professionals is a reflection of trends toward casual use in society at large. As younger doctors with higher rates of drug use replace older physicians, the number of physicians who practice in a drug-impaired state will steadily increase unless behavioral patterns can be changed.

Confidential

5.0 RECOMMENDATIONS

Medical students and practitioners need to become better educated about drug use, the harm it can cause their ability to practice effectively, and the risks of slipping beyond occasional use to addiction. Preventive programs for medical students and residents are the most practical and effective measures for reducing or preventing future drug use by these two groups. Medical schools and hospitals should offer drug education programs that examine the adverse effects of recreational drug use (giving special emphasis to marijuana and cocaine) and self-treatment (emphasizing the abuse of opiates and tranquilizers specifically).

REFERENCES

Katsung, B. G. (Ed.). (1982). *Basic and clinical pharmacology*. Los Altos, CA: Lange Medical.

McAuliffe, W. E., Rohman, M., Santangelo, S., Feldman, B., Magnusson, E., Sobol, A. and Weissman, P. (1986). Psychoactive drug use among practicing physicians and medical students. *The New England Journal of Medicine, 315*; 805–810.

McAuliffe, W. E., Wechsler, H., Rohman, M., Soboroth, S. H., Fishman, P., Toth, D., Friedman, R. (1984). Psychoactive drug use by young and future physicians. *The Journal of Health and Social Behavior, 25*; 34–54.

O'Malley, P. M. (1983). Reliability and consistency in self-reports of drug use. *The International Journal of the Addictions, 18*; 805–824.

Stedman's medical dictionary. (1982). (24th ed.). Baltimore: Williams & Wilkins.

ACKNOWLEDGMENTS

Applied Magnetics Corporation: for use of Figure 4.22 from the company's 1987 Annual Report.

Arch Petroleum, Inc.: for use of Figure 4.13 from *Investor Focus—March 1990* Factsheet.

Congressional Information Service, Inc.: for use of Figure 7.11 from *Checklist of State Publications*, Vol. 2, 1977.

Dow Jones & Company, Inc.: for use of Figure 7.12 from *The Wall Street Journal Index*, Vol. III, 1988.

H. W. Wilson: for use of Figure 7.5 from *Bibliographic Index: A Cumulative Bibliography of Bibliographies*, Vol. 28, 1988; Figure 7.13 from *Business Periodicals Index*, August 1983–July 1984; Figure 7.7 from *Cumulative Book Index*, 1989.

Little, Brown and Company: for use of a quotation from Richard Mitchell, *Less Than Words Can Say*, copyright 1979 (Boston, MA). Reprinted by permission of the publisher.

Marquis Who's Who: for use of Figure 7.6. Copyright © 1985–86, Marquis Who's Who, Inc. Reprinted by permission from *Who's Who in Finance and Industry*, 24th ed., 1985–86.

Moody's Investors Service: for use of Figure 7.9 from *Moody's Bank and Finance Manual*, Vol. I, 1979.

Nike, Inc.: for use of Figure 4.23 from Nike, Inc.'s Interim Report of February 28, 1989.

Oxford University Press: for use of material on the "Direct Writing Process" from Peter Elbow, *Writing With Power: Techniques for Mastering the Writing Process*, copyright 1981 (New York, NY). Reprinted (included) by permission of the publisher.

Prentice-Hall: for use of Figure 12.34 from *Principles of Marketing*, 4th ed., © 1989, by Philip Kotler and Gary Armstrong. Reprinted by permission of Prentice Hall, Englewood Cliffs, New Jersey.

R. R. Bowker: for use of Figure 7.8. Reprinted with permission of R. R. Bowker, a division of Reed Publishing (USA) Inc. from *Business and Economic Books 1876–1983*, © 1983, (p. 3187).

Standard & Poor's Corporation: for use of Figure 7.10 from *Standard & Poor's Register of Corporations, Directors, and Executives*. Vol. 1, 1991. Reprinted by permisison of the publisher Standard & Poor's/McGraw-Hill.

West Publishing Company: for use of Figure 12.25. Reprinted by permission from *Organizational Behavior*, 5th ed. by D. Hellreigel, J. W. Slocum, and R. W. Woodman, copyright © 1989 by West Publishing Company. All rights reserved.

Index